West's Law School Advisory Board

PROBLEMS AND MATERIALS ON BANKRUPTCY LAW AND PRACTICE

Second Edition

■ ■ ■

By

Stephen L. Sepinuck
Associate Dean for Administration
Professor of Law
Director, Commercial Law Center
Gonzaga University School of Law

Linda J. Rusch

Gregory M. Duhl
Professor of Law
Managing Director, Center for Negotiation and Justice
William Mitchell College of Law

AMERICAN CASEBOOK SERIES®

WEST®

Mat #41266660

610 Opperman Drive
St. Paul, MN 55123
1-800-313-9378

Printed in the United States of America

ISBN: 978–0–314–28103–6

To Doug, Kari, and Anna

LJR

To Sandra, Ben, and Jacob, who make life worth living.

SLS

To my parents Stuart and Elaine

GMD

Preface

This book is designed for an introductory, three-credit course on bankruptcy. In creating it, we have drawn on our three decades of collective experience in teaching this course, our experience teaching other commercial law and statutory courses, as well as our work in private practice and in various commercial law reform projects.

Our general approach to teaching code-based subjects is to focus on problems, rather than cases. However, because this course is typically populated by students who have already had one or more other commercial-law, statutory courses, we do not focus heavily on imparting the skills necessary for statutory construction. We expect students to come into this course having experience with reading statutory text in order to identify ambiguities and construct possible interpretations. Instead, we concentrate on the substance of bankruptcy law and its effect on bankruptcy and commercial practice. There is more than enough there to fill many books.

We love this area of law. Bankruptcy cases directly or indirectly affect tens of millions of Americans every year and employ thousands of attorneys. The law governing them is extraordinarily dynamic, as a result of both the thousands of judicial decisions issued each year and frequent legislative tinkering. Bankruptcy law also has a profoundly broad impact: affecting commercial activity at virtually every level, from structuring a transaction to collecting a debt. And it is filled with fascinating policy issues. We hope that our affection is evident, at least occasionally, in the pages that follow and that some of our affection for this area might even be infectious as you work your way through these materials.

We invite all who use this book – teachers and students alike – to send us their comments about this book. Only with them can we possibly improve it.

ACKNOWLEDGMENTS

A book such as this, which is intended not as a treatise but as a teaching tool, needs input from a variety of people with different levels of experience and different learning styles. We are therefore deeply grateful to all our students who provided suggestions and noted errors on earlier drafts and editions of this book. We also appreciate their willingness to be the test subjects of a work in progress.

SUMMARY OF CONTENTS

TABLE OF CONTENTS

TABLE OF CASES

Problem 2-1

A. Identify all of the things that the government *could* do with, to, and for individuals who lack the ability to repay their debts. Which of those things *should* the government do? More generally, should the legal system: (i) get involved in the debt collection and forgiveness process in a systematic way; (ii) leave the debtor and the debtor's creditors to whatever rights and remedies are available to them under contract and other law; or (iii) use the criminal laws to compel repayment?

B. If the legal system should get involved in a systematic way (*e.g.*, through federal bankruptcy law), what are the policies at stake? To effectuate those policies, should the legal system treat all debtors alike? All creditors? All of the debtor's financial obligations? If not, which debtors, creditors, or financial obligations should the legal system treat differently and why?

Most would probably agree that the law's general response to people with serious financial problems should depend on how and why those problems arose. Many would also agree that most bankruptcy debtors fall into at least one of three *nonexclusive* groups: the unlucky, the foolish, and the dishonest.[6] It is probably fair to say that the Bankruptcy Code, as enacted in 1978, was premised on the assumption that most bankruptcy debtors had simply been unlucky but that luck tends to even out over time. In other words, the Code regarded a debtor's massive debt not as a symptom of some other problem, but as the problem itself. Accordingly, simply relieving the debtor of most or all debts would solve the problem and enable the debtor to return to the economic community as a productive participant.

Since 1978, the almost endless stream of amendments to the Bankruptcy Code have been premised on the assumption that many debtors are or were dishonest or foolish; indeed, that the mere act of filing for bankruptcy protection and seeking to escape from their lawful debts was itself deceitful or improper. As a result, these amendments placed more and more obstacles to discharging a debtor's financial obligations and left those debtors who overcame those obstacles with more and more of their debts intact.

---

[6] For those familiar with Yiddish, the terms schlimazel, schlemiel, and gahniff can be substituted. A gahniff is a thief. Schlemiels and schlimazels are closely related terms. The classic distinction is that a schlemiel is someone who goes to a fancy dinner party and spills the soup. A schlimazel is the person the schlemiel spills it on. *See* LEO ROSTEN, THE JOYS OF YIDDISH 343–46 (1968).

Although there is a great deal of statistical information available about the individuals and businesses that seek bankruptcy protection, there is little reliable information about the percentage of them that are unlucky, foolish, or dishonest. This may be because a debtor's financial misfortunes are rarely attributable to a single event and, even when they are, that event may in turn be explained by bad luck, a poor choice or careless action, or dishonesty. For example, consider an individual who has been fired from a job and is unable to find another. The job loss may have resulted from: (i) the employer's decision to downsize (the debtor's bad luck); (ii) the debtor's poor job performance (foolishness or carelessness); or (iii) discovery of the debtor's embezzlement (dishonesty). Similarly, extensive medical bills for the debtor or a dependent of the debtor may have been caused by: (i) a sudden and unavoidable illness (bad luck); (ii) risky behavior, such as drunk driving (foolishness); or (iii) a beating after being caught cheating at poker (dishonesty). The same holds true for businesses. Their financial collapse could be caused by: (i) a general economic downturn (bad luck); (ii) operating in accordance with a poor business plan or with inadequate capitalization (foolishness); or (iii) using company assets in a scheme to defraud investors (dishonesty).

Added to all of this is the fact that it is probably too difficult and costly to ascertain the underlying causes in each individual case. A bankruptcy process that attempted to address the precise causes of each debtor's financial woes and then devise an individually tailored solution would be enormously expensive to administer, even if the causes could be identified and effectively addressed. As a result, bankruptcy policy must be premised on assumptions about the characteristics of bankruptcy debtors in the aggregate.

Another facet of bankruptcy policy is that the causes of the debtor's financial problems may be distinct from the event that impels the debtor (or the debtor's creditors, in the case of an involuntary bankruptcy) to file a bankruptcy petition. In other words, most debtors who experience financial distress try for extended periods of time to deal with that distress before seeking bankruptcy protection. Such efforts may include cutting expenses, borrowing from an available source, or negotiating for a reduction or deferral of debt payments. What usually triggers the decision to file a bankruptcy petition is not the debt itself but some creditor action to enforce the debt.

For example, one of us worked for a law firm that represented a regional airline that had serious cash-flow problems. The airline owed substantial amounts to the Internal Revenue Service for unpaid taxes that it withheld from its employees as required under tax law. The law firm negotiated a payment plan with an IRS official and the airline was making slow progress in reducing the debt. However, when the official went on vacation, someone else at the IRS examined the case file and decided to file a notice of federal tax lien against the airline, an act that cut off the airline's ability to finance its operations. The airline filed for bankruptcy the next day. Similar events trigger many individual bankruptcy filings. An individual may be in default on a home mortgage loan for many months before being impelled to file for bankruptcy protection by a foreclosure sale scheduled to occur in the next few days or hours.

B. THE COUNSELING SOLUTION

In the early 2000s, there was a growing call to deal with the increasing number of individuals in dire financial straits through consumer credit counseling. These calls were premised on the belief that consumers' misuse and abuse of credit cards is what caused many or most of their financial problems. In fact, a fairly recent statistical analysis of whether mandatory credit counseling helps Chapter 13 debtors showed a slight negative correlation: debtors who were counseled were less likely to complete their payment plans.[7] Beyond that, the consumer credit counseling industry has come under widespread attack. While some counseling agencies provide truly valuable guidance to debtors for little or no fee, others are profit-making or fee-generating enterprises that provide little assistance to debtors. Some are even financed by creditors and purposefully refrain from advising debtors about ways to reduce their obligations.[8]

Nevertheless, the recent bankruptcy reform legislation made credit counseling a prerequisite to filing a voluntary bankruptcy petition for most individuals. Read Bankruptcy Code § 109(h).[9] The legislation did, however, implicitly acknowledge some of the problems with credit counseling by placing substantial restrictions on the agencies

---

7 *See* Jean Braucher, *An Empirical Study of Debtor Education in Bankruptcy: Impact on Chapter 13 Completion Not Shown*, 9 AM. BANKR. INST. L. REV. 557, 578 (2001).

8 *See, e.g.*, David A. Lander, *Recent Developments in Consumer Debt Counseling Agencies: The Need for Reform*, AM. BANKR. INST. J., Feb. 2002, at 14. In May 2006, the Internal Revenue Service revoked the tax exempt status of the nation's largest educational credit counseling services, representing 41% of the $1 billion credit counseling industry, after IRS audits revealed that the credit counseling agencies "exist mainly to prey on debt-ridden customers." *I.R.S. Ends Tax Exempt Status for Some Credit Counselors*, N.Y. TIMES, May 16, 2006, at C6.

9 From here on, citations to section numbers refer to sections of the Bankruptcy Code, codified in Title 11 of the United States Code, unless otherwise indicated.

Because § 109(h)(1) refers to a petition filed "by such individual," the credit counseling requirement does not apply to involuntary cases.

that may provide it and permitting an individual debtor to forego credit counseling if the U.S. Trustee for the district in which the debtor resides determines that approved budget and credit counseling services are not reasonably available. *See* §§ 109(h)(2), 111.

Still, from a policy perspective, the decision to impose the credit counseling requirement is questionable. One bankruptcy court recently summed up the situation in this manner:

> Credit counseling was a significant aspect of the new bankruptcy legislation because the requirement was intended to provide debtors with education as to all of their options when experiencing financial difficulty, *before* a resort to bankruptcy protection was necessary. Congress envisioned that credit counseling would provide individuals with the skills necessary to lead financially responsible lives. This facially well-intentioned section of the BAPCPA has evolved into an expensive, draconian gate-keeping requirement that has prevented many deserving individuals from qualifying for bankruptcy relief. The credit counseling requirement has not proven to be of assistance to debtors in seeking relief outside of the bankruptcy context, as shown by a recent survey of credit counseling agencies performed by the National Association of Consumer Bankruptcy Attorneys. That study determined that of 66,335 consumers served by the participating credit counseling agencies, a paltry 3.3 percent qualified for alternative (*i.e.*, non-bankruptcy) debt management treatment. Additionally, many of these same credit-counseling agencies have come under fire for fraudulent practices; some have lost their not-for-profit status. The requirement that a debtor seek "credit counseling" before being eligible for bankruptcy relief is quickly becoming the most outrageous fleecing of consumer debtors in this Court's memory – a perfunctory exercise with little or no substance which leaves a putative debtor \$50–\$100 the poorer.[10]

Irrespective of its wisdom, the counseling requirement now exists and can present a significant impediment to obtaining immediate bankruptcy relief if, as is not uncommon, the debtor delays seeking assistance from bankruptcy counsel until a day or two before a scheduled foreclosure sale of the debtor's home.[11] The debtor might be

---

[10] *In re Elmendorf*, 345 B.R. 486, 490 (Bankr. S.D.N.Y.), *aff'd*, 2006 WL 3240522 (S.D.N.Y. 2006), *vacated and remanded*, 619 F.3d 156 (2d Cir. 2010).

[11] *See, e.g., In re Talib*, 335 B.R. 417 (Bankr. W.D. Mo.), *reconsideration denied*, 355 B.R. 424

unable to obtain credit counseling in time to file a petition and halt the foreclosure. In addition, note that § 109(h) requires that the debtor receive credit counseling "during the 180-day period *preceding the date* of filing." This phrasing suggests that the counseling must be completed not merely before the petition is filed, but before *the date* on which the petition is filed, and courts are divided on how to apply this rule if the debtor completes counseling on the same day as the petition but a few hours or minutes before filing it.[12]

C. THE BANKRUPTCY SOLUTION

1. The Governing Law

Virtually any source of law – constitution, statute, regulation, or rule – on virtually any subject – torts, contracts, property, taxation, antitrust, *etc.* – can be relevant to a bankruptcy proceeding. However, certain legal sources relate solely to bankruptcy, and these are what most lawyers mean when referring to "bankruptcy law." Most of this bankruptcy law is federal, and is codified in three places in the United States Code. Title 28 – the Judicial Code – contains the provisions on the bankruptcy court system and its jurisdiction, bankruptcy judges, and the structure of the United States trustee system. Title 18 – the Criminal Code – defines the criminal conduct relating to bankruptcy. Title 11 – the Bankruptcy Code – contains both the substantive and procedural law governing bankruptcy liquidation and reorganization cases. Learning bankruptcy law is a matter of learning both a set of substantive rules that alter the relationship between a bankruptcy debtor and its creditors and a set of procedural rules that dictate how that alteration will or may occur. Of course, a full understanding requires not merely knowledge of the rules themselves, but also an appreciation for how courts apply the rules and how the rules affect people's behavior and expectations.

(Bankr. W.D. Mo. 2005) (debtor who first sought credit counseling on the afternoon before the day of a scheduled foreclosure sale but could not obtain the required counseling for approximately two days was not eligible for an exigent circumstances waiver).

12 *See In re Gossett*, 369 B.R. 361 (Bankr. N.D. Ill. 2007) (discussing the split in authority).

(a) The Bankruptcy Code

The Bankruptcy Code is divided into nine main chapters (numbered 1, 3, 5, 7, 9, 11, 12, 13, and 15). The first three chapters cover general material applicable, for the most part, to all bankruptcy cases. More specifically:

> Chapter 1 contains, among other things, the definition section (§ 101), various rules of construction (§ 102), a general grant of power to bankruptcy courts (§ 105), and rules on the tolling of various time limits (§ 108). It also specifies who may be a debtor under each of the different kinds of bankruptcy cases (§ 109).
>
> Chapter 3, entitled "Case Administration," covers how a case is begun and deals with some of the players in a bankruptcy proceeding by detailing their powers and providing for their compensation. The chapter also contains various administrative provisions including the automatic stay (§ 362), limitations on the use, sale, and lease of property (§ 363), rules for obtaining credit (§ 364), and rules regarding the assumption or rejection of certain contracts and leases (§ 365).
>
> Chapter 5 contains much of the substantive law of bankruptcy, including rules regarding creditors' claims (§§ 502–507), the debtor's duties (§ 521), what property constitutes the bankruptcy estate and will thereby be available to pay creditors' claims (§ 541), and the trustee's important avoiding powers (§§ 544–549).

Each of the final six chapters governs a particular type of bankruptcy proceeding (commonly referred to by the number of the governing chapter, *i.e.*, "a Chapter 7 case") or by type (liquidation or reorganization). The availability of these six chapters depends on the debtor's eligibility, *see* § 109, and on what the debtor or other person filing the bankruptcy petition seeks to accomplish.

Students should always bear in mind that under § 103, the provisions of Chapters 1, 3, and 5 apply in any kind of case brought under the Bankruptcy Code, whether it be a liquidation under Chapter 7 or reorganization under Chapter 11, 12, or 13. In contrast, the provisions found in Chapters 7, 9, 11, 12, 13, and 15 are not generally applicable; they apply only to cases brought under their particular chapter.[13]

---

[13] Some sections in these Chapters are, however, incorporated into another Chapter by an express cross-reference. *See, e.g.*, § 1106 (incorporating certain portions of § 704).

(b) The Bankruptcy Rules

In bankruptcy, as in federal practice generally, matters of procedure are, for the most part, governed by rules promulgated by the Supreme Court rather than by provisions of the United States Code. The rule-making enabling statute for bankruptcy is 28 U.S.C. § 2075. It authorizes the Supreme Court to prescribe rules for practice and procedure in bankruptcy. If, within 90 days after such rules are submitted to Congress, Congress fails to pass a law amending the rules or preventing them from becoming effective, they take effect and have the force of law so long as they are not inconsistent with the Bankruptcy Code or with other statutes. There is relatively little of a procedural nature in the Bankruptcy Code or in Title 28; Congress purposely left a wide-open field for the Court to occupy by exercising its rule-making power. And, at present, there are 215 different Bankruptcy Rules (compared to only 192 sections in the six bankruptcy chapters covered in these materials – don't worry, we will not cover all 192 sections) and many Official Forms.

We will cover only a few of these Rules, but that does not mean that the remainder are unimportant. Rule 2004, for example, authorizes any interested party to conduct an examination of anyone else and to require the person examined to produce relevant documents, in an effort to learn information about the debtor's financial condition. This authorization can be a valuable and powerful tool for creditors. Most bankruptcy courts also have their own local rules and many have local forms, such as a model Chapter 13 plan, that debtors and their counsel are expected to use.

Practitioners need to be well versed in not only the provisions of the Bankruptcy Code, but also in the Bankruptcy Rules, the local court rules, and both the Official Forms and the local forms. Failure to comply with the applicable Code provisions and the applicable rules, or to use the required forms, might result in sanctions.

2. *The Leading Players*

To understand the drama of bankruptcy, one needs to know both who the players are and what they do. Unfortunately, it is all but impossible to separate these two issues; many of the players are identified by what they do. For lack of a better alternative, we will begin by identifying the leading members of the cast and describe their roles. From there, we will explore the drama itself: what happens in a typical bankruptcy case. Then we will return to the supporting cast and other actors who may make a cameo appearance. As you read this material, bear in mind that it is merely an overview of what will be covered in the remainder of the book.

(a) The Bankruptcy Court

All bankruptcy cases are filed in federal court and each is – at a fundamental level – a judicial process. Most of what occurs does so with either the bankruptcy court's express approval or under its direct or indirect supervision. Unfortunately, the existing bankruptcy court system, enacted by the Bankruptcy Amendments and Federal Judgeship Act of 1984 ("BAFJA"),[14] is a mixture of congressional compromises and is both confusing and possibly unconstitutional. To understand it, one must examine its tortuous history.

1978

The 1978 Bankruptcy Reform Act, which brought us the Bankruptcy Code, upgraded the status and powers of bankruptcy courts and bankruptcy judges. It did not, however, establish Article III bankruptcy courts with judges who enjoyed the full powers of a federal district court judge.[15] It created bankruptcy courts that were nominally referred to as adjuncts of the federal district courts but were in fact virtually independent of them. Judges were appointed by the President, with the advice and consent of the Senate, to serve 14-year terms. Bankruptcy judges were given broad powers to hear all Title 11 bankruptcy cases and all proceedings "arising under title 11 or arising in or related to cases under title 11."[16] They thus could decide matters involving either federal or state law, hold jury trials, and issue declaratory judgments.[17] The only limitation on their power was that bankruptcy judges could not punish criminal contempt committed outside the presence of the court and could not enjoin other courts.[18]

In 1982, the Supreme Court invalidated the entire grant of jurisdiction to bankruptcy courts in *Northern Pipeline Construction Co. v. Marathon Pipe Line Co.*[19] The Court's decision did not produce a majority opinion, and that has resulted in some

---

[14] Pub. L. No. 98-353, 98 Stat. 333 (1984).

[15] Article III of the Constitution requires judges exercising the judicial power of the United States to be appointed to serve during good behavior, sometimes referred to as life tenure, and to be protected against salary diminution. Because the 1978 Act provided for 14-year terms rather than life tenure, bankruptcy judges were not Article III judges. Presumably, Congress created and staffed the courts under its Article I powers to create uniform laws on bankruptcy and to regulate interstate commerce.

[16] 28 U.S.C. § 1471(b) (repealed).

[17] 28 U.S.C. §§ 1481, 2201, 2256 (repealed).

[18] 28 U.S.C. § 1481 (repealed).

[19] 458 U.S. 50 (1982).

uncertainty about the ruling's full import. Justice Brennan, writing for a plurality of four Justices, ruled broadly that the creation of non-Article III courts to handle the wide range of matters authorized by the jurisdictional grant of authority to them was unconstitutional. He concluded that the grant of authority went well beyond previously recognized exceptions to the requirement that judges be given life tenure and that, although labeled as adjuncts to the district courts, bankruptcy courts were quite independent.

Justice Rehnquist, writing for himself and Justice O'Connor, concurred on a narrower ground. They believed that non-Article III courts were prohibited from deciding only those traditional common-law issues having little direct relationship to the bankruptcy case, such as Marathon's state-law contract action against a defendant that had no other connection to the bankruptcy proceeding. Three Justices dissented, including Chief Justice Burger. He then took the unusual action of writing a separate opinion explaining the narrow limits of the *Marathon* holding and advising Congress that the best way to solve the problem (*i.e.*, the easiest way to get a majority of the Court to uphold a jurisdictional grant similar to the one made) was to address the concerns of Justices Rehnquist and O'Connor by rerouting traditional common-law matters to the federal district courts, leaving everything else within the jurisdiction of the bankruptcy courts. Justice Brennan's opinion sharply disagreed with Chief Justice Burger's suggestion, but Justice Rehnquist's opinion did not.

The Court twice stayed its decision in *Marathon* to give Congress time to act. When Congress failed to respond, the Court established emergency rules of action along the lines of the Chief Justice's suggestions. Finally, in July 1984, Congress passed the BAFJA, which created a court system closely modeled on the emergency rules and Chief Justice Burger's suggestions.

Under the current system, the federal district courts are vested with primary bankruptcy jurisdiction. 28 U.S.C. § 1334. Bankruptcy judges are appointed for each judicial district. They are appointed by the circuit courts of appeal for 14-year terms and may be removed only by the judicial council for the circuit and "only for incompetence, misconduct, neglect of duty, or physical or mental disability." 28 U.S.C. § 152. They "constitute a unit of the district court to be known as the bankruptcy court for that district." 28 U.S.C. § 151. The exact meaning of this statement and the exact nature of the relationship between district courts and bankruptcy courts remain somewhat unclear.

What is clear is that Congress has authorized district courts to "refer" to the bankruptcy judges all cases and proceedings within the district court's bankruptcy jurisdiction. 28 U.S.C. § 157(a). And, in fact, every district court in the country has adopted a policy of virtually always making such a complete reference. Thus, bankruptcy courts are now performing the trial court function except when the law specifically limits that role and reserves certain powers to the district courts.

The extent of the bankruptcy judges' power to act in referred matters depends largely on whether the matter is classified as a "core" proceeding. In core proceedings, bankruptcy judges may "hear and determine" the matter – that is they may conduct the entire proceeding and may enter a final judgment, subject only to timely appeal.[20] The district court's role in such matters is one of usually two[21] possible tribunals to hear an appeal of the bankruptcy court's rulings:

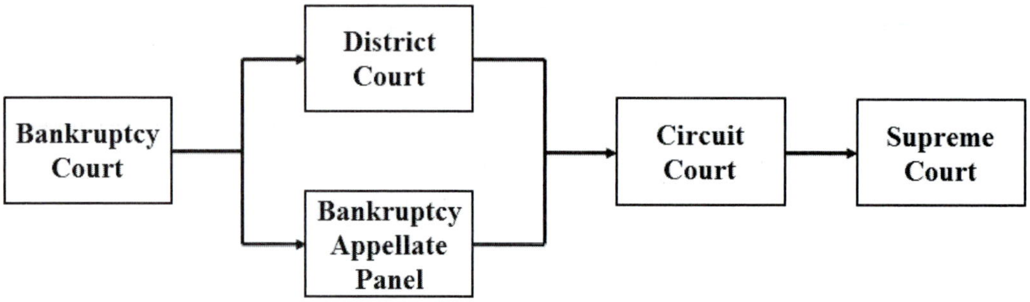

The district court's decisions on appeal from the bankruptcy court are of course binding on the bankruptcy court in that case. Whether they are binding precedent in future bankruptcy court cases is unclear, particularly if the district court has more than one judge who decides bankruptcy appeals and who might decide the same issue differently.[22]

Alternatively, the parties may – and frequently do – choose to litigate an appeal of a bankruptcy court decision before a Bankruptcy Appellate Panel ("BAP"), a group of three bankruptcy judges from the judicial circuit (if a BAP is established for that judicial

---

[20] 28 U.S.C. § 157(b)(1). Bankruptcy courts have civil contempt power based upon 11 U.S.C. § 105 and Bankruptcy Rule 9020, although some courts have found that bankruptcy courts do not have criminal contempt power for actions outside of the court's presence. *See In re Bradley*, 588 F.3d 254, 266 (5th Cir. 2009); *In re Hercules Enters., Inc.*, 387 F.3d 1024, 1027 (9th Cir. 2004); *In re Dyer*, 322 F.3d 1178, 1190 (9th Cir. 2003).

[21] The Bankruptcy Abuse Prevention and Consumer Protection Act of 2005, Pub. L. No. 109-8, § 1233(a)(2), 119 Stat. 23, 202 (2005), created a third avenue: a direct appeal from a bankruptcy court to a circuit court, if the bankruptcy court certifies the issue as needing immediate review at that level. *See* 28 U.S.C. § 158(d)(2).

[22] *See In re Romano*, 350 B.R. 276 (Bankr. E.D. La. 2005) (discussing the various approaches and rationales).

circuit).[23] Here, too, there is disagreement about whether bankruptcy courts are bound by decisions of the BAP in their circuit, in part because panel decisions do not bind the district courts (because the BAP occupies an equal place in the appellate hierarchy) and thus a bankruptcy court could face conflicting rulings from the panel and the district court in the district in which it sits.[24]

In noncore proceedings (which are "otherwise related" to cases under Title 11), bankruptcy judges may issue final orders only with the parties' consent. In noncore proceedings in which the parties do not consent, the function of bankruptcy court judges is similar to that of special masters or magistrates: they submit proposed findings of fact and conclusions of law to the district court, which reviews *de novo* any "matters to which any party has timely and specifically objected."[25]

Most important matters in a bankruptcy case constitute core proceedings. A nonexclusive list of fifteen core matters appears in 28 U.S.C. § 157(b)(2). These include: all matters concerning the administration of the bankruptcy estate or affecting the liquidation of the assets of the estate; the validity and amount of claims against the estate and of exemptions from the estate; proceedings to recover preferential and fraudulent transfers; motions for relief from the automatic stay; proceedings to determine the availability of a discharge or the dischargeability of certain debts; and determinations regarding the validity, extent, and priority of liens. Very few matters that arise in a typical bankruptcy case are noncore. Noncore claims expressly include only the liquidation of personal injury and wrongful death claims against the estate.[26] They apparently also include *Marathon*-type proceedings, involving a nonbankruptcy claim that the debtor possessed at the time the bankruptcy case began against someone who otherwise does not participate in the bankruptcy proceeding, and certain suits between

---

[23] *See* 28 U.S.C. § 158(b), (c)(1). Each of the First, Sixth, Eighth, Ninth, and Tenth Circuits has a BAP.

[24] *Compare In re Hunter*, 380 B.R. 753 (Bankr. S.D. Ohio 2008) (ruling that bankruptcy courts are bound), *with In re Boyd*, 414 B.R. 223 (Bankr. N.D. Ohio 2009) (ruling they are not). BAP decisions are apparently not binding on district courts. *See, e.g.*, *Bank of Maui v. Estate Analysis, Inc.*, 904 F.2d 470 (9th Cir. 1990).

[25] 28 U.S.C. § 157(c). Note that when acting as an appellate tribunal with respect to core matters, the district court reviews facts on a "clearly erroneous" standard. Rule 8013. When reviewing noncore matters, the district court uses a "*de novo*" standard. This does not mean that the district court must conduct a new trial or receive further evidence; it need only make an independent judgment and it may, if it chooses, rely on the record before the bankruptcy judge.

[26] *See* 28 U.S.C. § 157(b)(2)(O).

third parties, such as a suit by a creditor against a guarantor of the debtor's obligations, which might indirectly affect the bankruptcy estate.

Bankruptcy court proceedings are generally conducted without a jury. Normally this is not a problem. The Seventh Amendment guarantees a jury trial only in those types of traditional common-law actions in existence at the time the Amendment was ratified, and thus is inapplicable to most bankruptcy matters. However, in 1989, the Supreme Court ruled that a person who has not filed a claim in bankruptcy court – and thereby becomes involuntarily involved in a bankruptcy case – has a Seventh Amendment right to a jury trial when sued by the bankruptcy trustee to recover a fraudulent transfer.[27] The Court expressly refused to decide whether the United States Code permitted bankruptcy courts to conduct jury trials in fraudulent transfer actions and, more important, refused to decide whether the Seventh Amendment or Article III permits jury trials of such actions to be held before non-Article III bankruptcy judges.[28] Congress has since expressly authorized bankruptcy courts to conduct jury trials, but only "if specially designated to exercise such jurisdiction by the district court and with the express consent of all the parties."[29] The consensual nature of this authorization should insulate it from constitutional attack. Nevertheless, should the Court ever rule that one or more parties have a right to a jury trial in other core proceedings, and that non-Article III courts cannot conduct such trials, the bankruptcy court structure could come tumbling down.

Unfortunately, another wrinkle in the complex tapestry of bankruptcy court jurisdiction was added by the Supreme Court's 2011 decision in *Stern v. Marshall*.[30] After the debtor in that case – Anna Nicole Smith – filed for bankruptcy, her stepson filed a proof of claim seeking damages for defamation. He also filed a complaint to have the debt declared nondischargeable. The debtor then filed a counterclaim alleging tortious interference with a gift she expected to receive from her late husband. The bankruptcy court awarded her over $400 million in compensatory damages and $25 million in punitive damages. On appeal, the district court recognized that the debtor's counterclaim fell within the literal language of the statutory definition of a "core" proceeding but concluded that the counterclaim could not constitutionally be decided

---

27 *Granfinanciera, S.A. v. Nordberg*, 492 U.S. 33 (1989).

28 *Id.* at 64.

29 28 U.S.C. § 157(e) (added by § 112 of the Bankruptcy Reform Act of 1994, Pub. L. No. 103-394, 108 Stat. 4106, 4117).

30 131 S. Ct. 2594 (2011).

by a bankruptcy judge. The district court therefore treated that bankruptcy judge's ruling as a proposed finding and made an independent assessment of the counterclaim. It awarded the debtor compensatory and punitive damages in excess of $88 billion. However, because the district court's judgment was rendered after a contrary ruling by a Texas court in parallel proceedings, which itself came after the bankruptcy court's ruling, the Ninth Circuit ruled that the district court should have given preclusive effect to the state court judgment. Thus, on further appeal, the issue became whether the bankruptcy judge had authority to enter a final judgment on the counterclaim. If the judge was so authorized, the district court was not bound by the later Texas court decision. If, however, the bankruptcy judge lacked such authority, the Texas court decision was first in time and binding.

The U.S. Supreme Court, in a 5-4 decision, ruled that Anna Nicole Smith's counterclaim was a core proceeding. The bankruptcy judge was therefore authorized *by statute* to enter a judgment. However, the Court ruled that this statutory authorization was unconstitutional: even though the stepson had filed a claim in the bankruptcy proceeding, the bankruptcy court lacked constitutional authority to enter a final judgment on a state-law counterclaim that was not and need not be resolved in the process of ruling on the stepson's claim.

This ruling struck a lethal blow to the general view that the 1984 amendments had resolved the constitutional problem identified in *Marathon* and resurrected issues long thought settled about the scope of bankruptcy court authority and jurisdiction. Lawyers and judges are no longer certain what bankruptcy judges may decide and also disagree about how significant this uncertainty is.[31]

The intricacies of bankruptcy court jurisdiction and power are beyond the scope of this book. For our purposes, you should assume that the bankruptcy judge will decide all contested issues other than the debtor's state-law claims and noncompulsory counterclaims against someone else. Further, the bankruptcy judge will decide these issues just as any Article III judge would decide them, albeit without a jury. For the most part, this reflects the reality of how the bankruptcy process works.

There is one other important thing worth noting about bankruptcy courts: they produce a staggering, almost overwhelming, number of decisions, both published and unpublished. If you think about it, this should not be surprising for several reasons. First, a very large number of bankruptcy cases are filed each year. Second, by nature, bankruptcy proceedings are judicial and many of the disputes that arise in them must be

---

[31] *See* Tyson A. Crist, *Stern v. Marshall: Application of the Supreme Court's Landmark Decision in the Lower Courts*, 86 AM. BANKR. L.J. 627 (2012).

resolved by the court. Consequently, there is a tremendous amount of bankruptcy litigation and judicial decision making. That sometimes makes researching bankruptcy law issues an exhausting endeavor. On the other hand, it can also make for creative lawyering. There are so many decisions that, on almost every issue, you can find some authority for whatever position you want to argue. That means the lawyer who can argue the point most persuasively – whether based on the statutory text, policy, or the structure and operation of the Bankruptcy Code – will often win.

(b) The Trustee

The moment a bankruptcy petition is filed under Chapter 7, 13, or 11 of the Bankruptcy Code, an "estate" is created consisting of most of the debtor's prepetition assets. § 541(a). All Chapter 7 cases are administered by a "trustee." The trustee represents and administers the bankruptcy estate. § 323(a). In essence, this means that the Chapter 7 trustee represents the debtor's creditors, at least those with unsecured claims. The trustee protects their interests by: gathering, managing, and maintaining the debtor's property (which, of course, means insuring it too),[32] selling the property for as much as can reasonably be obtained, and distributing the proceeds to the claimants according to the priorities established by the Code. The trustee is also responsible for: (i) scrutinizing the claims filed, to make sure none is illegitimate or inflated; (ii) examining the exemptions claimed by the debtor, to make sure none is improper; and (iii) objecting to the debtor's discharge, if grounds to do so exist. In performing these tasks, the trustee is empowered to investigate the debtor's financial affairs. § 704(a).

In Chapter 7 cases, promptly after entry of the "order for relief," which is usually the filing of the bankruptcy petition,[33] the United States Trustee appoints an interim trustee from a panel of private trustees. At the first meeting of creditors (which typically occurs within 20 to 40 days after the order for relief), the unsecured creditors have the right to replace the interim trustee and elect a qualified trustee of their own choosing by a majority vote. To do this, creditors holding at least 20% of the total amount of the unsecured claims against the debtor must call for the election. § 702(c). An elected

[32] *See* § 704. This duty also includes recovering property that the debtor transferred before the bankruptcy case was filed but which the Bankruptcy Code nevertheless makes available to the debtor's creditors. *See* § 541(a)(3).

[33] *See* §§ 301, 303.

trustee need not be a member of the panel. However, trustees are rarely elected, primarily because of the substantial creditor effort needed to meet the statutory requirements for an election and because there is usually little reason to do so. If no election takes place, the interim trustee continues to serve as the trustee for the remainder of the case. § 702(d). The trustee is paid from the proceeds of the estate. §§ 330, 326.

Chapter 13 cases are also administered by a trustee, but a Chapter 13 trustee's duties are generally more limited than those of a Chapter 7 trustee. This is because usually there will be no liquidation of the debtor's assets or significant investigation of the debtor's financial affairs in a Chapter 13 case. Instead, the trustee reviews the debtor's payment plan to ensure that it complies with the Code's requirements and then acts as a conduit through which payments are made to creditors. For Chapter 13 cases, there is ordinarily at least one standing trustee in each district to whom all of the cases under that chapter are assigned as the petitions are filed. The creditors have no opportunity to elect someone else. § 1302.

In most Chapter 11 cases, there is no trustee. Although the court may order the appointment of a trustee for cause, § 1104(a), this rarely occurs. Instead, the debtor becomes a "debtor in possession" and is normally given most of the powers of a trustee. *See* §§ 1101(1), 1107(a).

(c) The Debtor

No cast roster would be complete without the debtor. Still, while the debtor can play an important role, it would be a mistake to assume that the debtor is the star of the show. Particularly in Chapter 7 cases, where the trustee takes charge of and liquidates the bankruptcy estate, reviews claims and exemptions, and makes distributions to creditors, the debtor's role may be fairly limited. A consumer debtor must file a statement indicating what the debtor intends to do with the collateral for any secured claim and must perform that stated intention within a fairly short time frame. § 521(a)(2). The debtor must also be prepared to respond to any objection to a claimed exemption or to any complaint attacking the debtor's discharge. In most cases, however, no such objection or complaint is ever filed. Business entities in Chapter 7 have even less of a role. Because they can receive no discharge and are generally entitled to no exemptions, and because the trustee is the one administering the estate, they have virtually no lines to speak at all.

In Chapter 13 cases, the debtor is a more central player, and proposes a plan to repay creditors using the debtor's postpetition earnings. Those earnings in turn are dependent on the debtor remaining gainfully employed or otherwise financially productive. A Chapter 13 debtor who suffers a postpetition job loss or income-reducing injury will often default on the repayment plan, which often leads to a dismissal of the Chapter 13 case.

In Chapter 11 cases, the debtor plays a starring role because, as the "debtor in possession," the debtor is in charge of operating its business, § 1108, proposing a reorganization plan, § 1121, and managing the bankruptcy estate. § 1107.

3. *The Processes*

As indicated above, there are six main types of bankruptcy proceedings, each governed by a different chapter of the Bankruptcy Code (Chapters 7, 9, 11, 12, 13, and 15). This book covers only three of them: Chapters 7, 11, and 13.[34]

(a) Chapter 7

liquidation

Chapter 7 governs "liquidations," sometimes colloquially referred to as "straight bankruptcies." Its purpose is to achieve a fair distribution to creditors of whatever nonexempt property the debtor has and to give the individual debtor a fresh start by discharging the debtor's obligations to pay the unpaid portion of most debts.

Chapter 7 liquidations are used both by individuals and businesses and in most routine cases take three to six months. The case is commenced when the debtor files a petition for bankruptcy relief and pays the appropriate filing fee, or when creditors take

---

[34] Chapter 9 governs the bankruptcies of municipalities. Chapter 15 deals with cross-border cases. Both are too specialized to be covered in this book designed for an introductory course. Chapter 12 was enacted to give special relief to a "family farmer with regular annual income," and a "family fisherman with regular income," both of which are defined terms. *See* § 101(18), (19), (19A), (19B), (20), (21). Individuals, partnerships, and corporations are potentially eligible debtors under Chapter 12 so long as the debtor's total indebtedness does not exceed specified limits: $3.79 million for family farmers, $1.75 million for family fishermen. These amounts are adjusted every three years to reflect inflation. § 104. Because of its specialized nature, and the fact that its provisions closely resemble those in Chapter 13, Chapter 12 is also not covered in this book.

TABLE OF FEDERAL STATUTES, RULES & FORMS

Bankruptcy Code
(Title 11)

Bankruptcy Rules

Official Bankruptcy Forms

Other Federal Statutes

TABLE OF UNIFORM STATUTES

Uniform Commercial Code

Uniform Fraudulent Transfer Act

Problems and Materials on Bankruptcy Law and Practice

Second Edition

PART I

AN INTRODUCTION TO BANKRUPTCY LAW AND PRACTICE

Chapter One
Background on State Law and Debt Collection

The bulk of this book focuses on how the federal Bankruptcy Code (codified in Title 11 of the United States Code) modifies the rights of creditors and debtors. However, it is important to remember that bankruptcy law is built on a large foundation of nonbankruptcy law. A working knowledge of what rights the parties have under nonbankruptcy law is a prerequisite to understanding bankruptcy. This is because, as a general matter, the Bankruptcy Code does not create creditors' rights; instead, it limits some of those rights, eliminates others, and provides a mechanism to enforce those that remain. For example, the Bankruptcy Code may temporarily enjoin a creditor's efforts to collect the debt owed to it, may discharge the debtor's obligation to the creditor entirely, or may alter a creditor's claim to specific assets of the debtor. Yet in all cases, the analysis begins with whatever nonbankruptcy rights exist.

Whether a person owes an obligation to another is usually not determined by bankruptcy law. For example, the Uniform Commercial Code (U.C.C.), which is enacted at the state level, and the general law of contract and tort, will have much to say about what obligations the debtor owes to another individual or entity. Other state and federal laws impose additional obligations on a debtor. These may include taxes, fines, or liability for failing to comply with any of a large variety of business, environmental, or other regulatory rules. Bankruptcy is a process for dealing with obligations created under other law.

Creditors also come to bankruptcy armed with a wide array of property rights in the debtor's assets. The local real property law (often codified in part in state statutes) and the rules governing the creation, perfection, and enforcement of security interests in personal property (governed in large part by U.C.C. Article 9) form a critical part of the edifice of property rights upon which bankruptcy is built. Both a mortgage and a U.C.C. Article 9 security interest are typically created as a matter of contract between the debtor and creditor. The debtor, in consideration for a loan or other value from the creditor, grants the creditor an interest in the property (a mortgage[1] if in real property, a security interest if in personal property) to secure the repayment of the loan or other debt to the creditor. These consensual arrangements give the creditor a property interest (called a

---

[1] In some states, the interest in real property is created by a "deed of trust." Mortgages and deeds of trust have the same function – to create an interest in real property to secure an obligation.

"lien") in the debtor's real property identified in the mortgage and the debtor's personal property identified in the Article 9 security agreement.

In addition to consensual liens – mortgages and U.C.C. Article 9 security interests – sometimes a state or federal statute or common-law rule will give a creditor a lien on property to secure an obligation. Common examples of such nonconsensual liens are a mechanic's lien to secure payment due for improvements to real estate, an artisan's lien to secure payment due for repairs of personal property, and a landlord's lien on personal property located on the leased premises to secure the payment of rent. Another example is a tax lien on a taxpayer's property in favor of the taxing authority (state or federal) to secure payment of the taxes due. While statutory liens created as a matter of federal law are uniform across the United States, the number and types of statutory and common-law liens created under state law vary widely from state to state.

A lien, whether consensual or nonconsensual, is important because it greatly enhances the lienholder's ability to collect the obligation owed to it under nonbankruptcy law. Although the enforcement mechanisms vary,[2] the lienholder is typically entitled to seize the property subject to the lien, sell it, and use the sale proceeds to pay the debt owed, returning any surplus to the debtor.

Critical to understanding bankruptcy law is understanding U.C.C. Article 9, which we briefly explain here and return to in chapter six.[3] A creditor and debtor create a security interest (a lien) in the debtor's personal property through a process called "attachment." In most cases,[4] attachment requires: (1) that value has been given (typically from the creditor to the debtor); (2) the debtor has rights in the collateral or the power to transfer rights in the collateral to the creditor; and (3) the debtor has authenticated a security agreement that describes the collateral. U.C.C. § 9-203(b). Upon attachment of the security interest, the creditor – referred to as a secured party – acquires rights in the collateral (*i.e.*, the personal property securing repayment of the

---

[2] If the debtor has granted a mortgage on real estate to secure a loan, the process the mortgagee (the creditor) uses to enforce the mortgage will be governed by the applicable foreclosure statute in the relevant state. If the creditor has a U.C.C. Article 9 security interest in the debtor's personal property, Article 9 details the processes available to the creditor to extract value from the collateral to satisfy the debt owed.

[3] A complete understanding of bankruptcy also requires an understanding of real property law and finance, including the laws governing recording of mortgages.

[4] U.C.C. Article 9 provides for some security interests to be created using other means. U.C.C. § 9-203(b)–(i). For purposes of learning bankruptcy law, these other means need not be explored in any depth.

loan or the performance of an obligation) and has remedies against the collateral that a creditor without a lien does not have. For example, if the debtor defaults in repaying the secured obligation, the secured party may take possession of the collateral and may sell the collateral in an effort to recover the amount owed. U.C.C. §§ 9-609(a), (b), 9-610.

For a security interest to have priority over the rights of others with an interest in the collateral – such as a buyer, another secured party, or a judicial lienholder – the secured party must generally "perfect" the security interest, a process that normally involves providing public notice of the security interest (a rough analog to recording a mortgage). The method used to perfect a security interest varies for different types of collateral. The most common methods used to perfect a security interest in the debtor's goods are: (i) by filing a financing statement – a brief notice that identifies the debtor, the secured party, and the collateral – in the applicable governmental office of the state in which the debtor is located; and (ii) if the collateral is a motor vehicle, by applying to the Department of Motor Vehicles that issued a certificate of title for the vehicle to have the security interest noted on the certificate. U.C.C. §§ 9-310, 9-311. The bankruptcy process is often the crucible in which perfection of a security interest is tested because, as we will see, the bankruptcy trustee has the power to avoid an unperfected security interest and relegate the creditor to the status of a creditor without a lien. 11 U.S.C. § 544.

Creditors that have a consensual or nonconsensual lien (secured creditors) in a debtor's collateral fare better under bankruptcy law, for the most part, than creditors without a lien (unsecured creditors). Secured creditors generally are entitled to receive – either in the bankruptcy process or outside it – the value of the debtor's property that is subject to the lien or the amount of the debtor's outstanding debt, whichever is less.

Unsecured creditors have far fewer rights and options for collecting – either inside or outside of the bankruptcy process – the debts rightfully due them. Various laws, such as the Fair Debt Collection Practices Act, may prevent the creditor from harassing the debtor for payment.[5] Unless the debtor is cooperative, an unsecured creditor's best option may be to bring a civil action in the hope of obtaining a judgment against the debtor.[6] Of course, entry of a judgment may not enhance the debtor's eagerness or

---

[5] 15 U.S.C. §§ 1692–1692o.

[6] A secured creditor (including an Article 9 secured party and a mortgagee of real property) usually also has the ability to obtain a judgment against the debtor for the obligation owed, in addition to its rights to seize and sell the property subject to the secured creditor's lien for application against the obligation owed. Of course, a secured creditor is not entitled to collect more than the total amount of the obligation owed. Enforcement of its lien in the property is thus an additional remedy that the

ability to pay. The debtor may continue to ignore the creditor's demands for payment and may even take steps to avoid the creditor's efforts to extract payment. However, a judgment does entitle the creditor to use various additional collection mechanisms.

Before discussing those mechanisms, a word of warning is in order. What follows is a broad outline of the judgment collection process. This summary is generic because the judgment collection process varies both in substance and in terminology from state to state.[7] This summary is offered merely to provide a foundation for the study of bankruptcy law and should not – must not – substitute for a thorough understanding of the relevant state or federal rules in the event you later represent either a creditor trying to collect on a judgment or a debtor trying to resist such efforts.

The process of collecting on a judgment involves seizing some of the debtor's assets, selling them, and then applying the proceeds of sale against the amount of the judgment debt owed. The first step in this process is, of course, to identify and locate the debtor's assets. Finding the judgment debtor's real estate is often not difficult because the debtor's ownership will likely be a matter of public record. In most states, the judgment creditor can then record the judgment and that act gives the judgment creditor a lien on whatever real estate the defendant owns in the county in which the lien is recorded.

Locating the judgment debtor's personal property is often more challenging. Fortunately, most states permit the judgment creditor to question the debtor under oath about what assets the debtor has and where they are located.[8] Such questions are posed during a postjudgment deposition or through postjudgment interrogatories. The problem with this discovery-like process is that it is expensive and, by the time the creditor learns what assets the debtor has and where they are located, and the creditor completes the paperwork and obtains the authorization necessary to seize the assets, the debtor may have moved the assets or otherwise put them beyond the creditor's reach.

If a judgment creditor does successfully identify and locate personal property of the debtor, or learns of the debtor's place of employment, the creditor typically has two options on how to proceed: execution and garnishment. A writ of execution is generally used against the debtor's tangible personal and real property. The creditor obtains a writ

---

secured creditor has that increases the likelihood of full satisfaction of the debtor's obligation.

7 If the creditor is a federal entity, federal law will often govern the debt collection process. *See, e.g.*, 28 U.S.C. §§ 3001–3308.

8 The postjudgment discovery process allows the creditor to ask questions about both personal property and real estate assets.

of execution from the court clerk (typically the court that entered the judgment) and delivers that writ to the sheriff (or other law enforcement officer). The writ directs the sheriff to seize and sell whatever assets of the debtor it specifies. The seizure process is called a "levy." A levy is ordinarily effected by the sheriff taking possession of the property. However, if the property is too large to move (such as factory equipment), state law may authorize a levy to occur by posting a notice on the property or by filing a notice in the applicable public record.

A writ of garnishment is typically used to collect on intangible assets, particularly obligations owed to the debtor by a third party. For example, if an employer or bank owes money to the debtor (such as wages or the funds from a deposit account), the creditor may obtain a writ of garnishment from the court clerk and serve that writ on the employer or bank (the garnishee). The writ directs the garnishee to pay the obligation either to the creditor or to the court, rather than to the debtor.

Generally, a levy pursuant to a writ of execution creates a judicial lien on the assets seized. Similarly, the service of a writ of garnishment creates a judicial lien on the obligation garnished. In other words, the judgment creditor can obtain an interest in the debtor's property through judicial process.[9]

Once personal property is levied on or real property becomes subject to a judgment lien, the property can be sold pursuant to a process prescribed by state statute. Sometimes the sale is conducted as an auction by the sheriff after public notice is given. The proceeds of the sale are used to satisfy the costs of execution (*i.e.*, the levy and the sale) and then applied to the judgment debt. Prices obtained at execution sales are usually quite low in comparison to the value of the asset. Most courts, however, will not invalidate an otherwise properly conducted execution sale on the basis of low price alone. However, if there was some irregularity in the sale process and a shockingly low price was obtained, the court may set aside the sale and require that the sale be conducted again. The judgment creditor may continue to levy on and garnish property of the debtor until the debtor runs out of assets or the judgment debt is paid. However, before incurring the cost of pursuing collection remedies, judgment creditors should evaluate whether the likelihood and amount of recovery justify the expense.

---

[9] This judicial lien, however, usually does not arise until after judgment has been entered against the debtor and the appropriate step in the postjudgment enforcement process has been taken (*e.g.*, levy) as described above.

Some judgment debtors have the ability to "exempt" – *i.e.*, to shield – some of their real and personal property from execution and garnishment.[10] Usually exemptions are available only to debtors who are human beings, not to other types of entities (such as partnerships, trusts, corporations, or limited liability companies). Exemptions are considered necessary for three reasons. First, exemptions prevent the debtor from becoming impoverished. After all, if a creditor could use judicial process to impoverish the debtor, the law would be elevating the creditor's interest over the public interest. As a result, most states exempt some basic "life necessities," such as food up to a certain value or a homestead. In addition, federal law restricts the amount of a debtor's wages that may be garnished.[11] Second, some of the debtor's exempt property may have no meaningful resale value even though it would be difficult or costly for the debtor to replace. Seizure of such assets – family photographs or used clothes, for example – would be counter-utilitarian. Third, some property is exempt for spiritual or humanitarian reasons. Thus, items such as family bibles and inexpensive wedding rings are often exempt.

Despite the various rationales for exemptions, some states are rather miserly in what they permit a debtor to protect from creditors. In contrast, some states have very generous exemptions (such as a homestead of unlimited value). Some states exempt odd things, such as a pew in the church, a burial plot, or ten chickens. The type of property, the value of the property, and the types of debtors that may use the exemptions vary widely from state to state. As we will see, debtors who file for bankruptcy are also entitled to exempt certain of their property from the bankruptcy estate.

On some occasions, a creditor may be able to go after the debtor's assets even prior to judgment. Most states permit issuance of a prejudgment writ of attachment (similar to a postjudgment writ of execution) or a prejudgment writ of garnishment in certain defined circumstances. Using these processes, a creditor may have the sheriff seize the debtor's asset or may require an obligor to pay to the court the amount the obligor owes to the debtor before judgment is rendered against the debtor. Such prejudgment processes are generally available only if the creditor can demonstrate to the court that the debtor is trying to hide assets in anticipation of an adverse judgment. In addition, state statutes may require that the debtor be provided notice and an opportunity for a hearing prior to issuance of the writ and may require that the creditor post a bond to

---

[10] Generally, debtors can exempt property subject to a U.C.C. Article 9 security interest or a mortgage only to the extent the property's value exceeds the amount of the secured obligation.

[11] *See* 15 U.S.C. §§ 1671–1677.

protect the debtor from damages in the event that judgment is not entered against the debtor. Like their postjudgment counterparts, though, these prejudgment processes create a lien on the assets of the debtor that are levied on or garnished. Because these processes can interfere with the debtor's property rights even though there has been no judgment of liability in favor of the creditor, they are subject to scrutiny as a potential violation of the debtor's constitutional protections against unlawful seizure or denial of due process.[12] In analyzing these issues, courts generally balance the fairness and efficacy of the procedures available to protect the debtor's property interest against the creditor's interest in eventually collecting on the judgment.

There are two other state-law processes that are occasionally available to creditors and which are worthy of note: an assignment for benefit of creditors and a receivership. In an assignment for benefit of creditors, a debtor voluntarily turns over all of its property to an assignee. The assignee invites creditors to submit claims against the debtor and uses the assigned property to pay those claims as well as the cost of administration. In many jurisdictions, such an assignee must post a bond and obtain court approval of any distribution to creditors, and the assignee has fiduciary duties in regard to the debtor's property. Unlike a bankruptcy proceeding, however, an assignment for benefit of creditors does not result in a discharge of the debtor's obligations to the extent those obligations are not satisfied through the assignment and distribution process. While some or all of the debtor's creditors may agree to regard their distribution as full satisfaction of the debtor's liability even if the distribution was not sufficient to pay all that was owed to that creditor,[13] such an agreement would be voluntary, and not, as in bankruptcy, be imposed by operation of law.

A receivership is an equitable device courts use to protect creditors with interests in the debtor's property. Prior to the availability of a federal bankruptcy process, receiverships were often used to keep the debtor's business operating. Receiverships allowed assets to be liquidated in an orderly fashion, rather than in a rushed sale. They also allowed for the business to be operated while it reorganized or facilitated a sale of the business as a going concern. Even today, creditors seek the appointment of

---

[12] *Connecticut v. Doehr*, 501 U.S. 1 (1991) (procedural due process); *Soldal v. Cook Cnty.*, 506 U.S. 56 (1992) (search and seizure).

[13] At common law, this process of multiple creditors' compromise of debts owed is called a composition agreement. Each creditor's agreement to compromise the debt it is owed provides consideration for the promises of the other creditors to compromise the debts they are owed. The assignment for benefit of creditors process may, but does not necessarily, employ this common-law method of getting agreement of creditors to accept less than full satisfaction of debts.

receivers, typically to take charge of real property that is subject to a mortgage. The main reason for using this process is to protect the value of the property from depreciation that may result from the debtor's misuse of the property. Indeed, many mortgages of commercial property expressly authorize the mortgagee to seek appointment of a receiver and mortgagees occasionally avail themselves of this right to preserve the value of their lien on the property. Not surprisingly, receivers are also subject to court supervision and bonding requirements, as well as to fiduciary duties regarding the debtor's property.

Although both of these processes are available as a matter of state law today, they have more limited utility given the wide availability of the bankruptcy process.[14] As you study the bankruptcy process, you will see similarities to the assignment for benefit of creditors process in the bankruptcy liquidation process and to the receivership process in the bankruptcy reorganization process.

---

[14] Indeed, as a matter of federal constitutional law, Congress has the exclusive power to enact bankruptcy laws. U.S. CONST. art. I, § 8.

CHAPTER TWO
BANKRUPTCY BASICS

Bankruptcy law has a tremendous impact on our society. Since 1996, more than one million individuals have filed for bankruptcy protection almost every year.[1] That figure does not include the corporations and partnerships that also filed or the millions of creditors of all of the bankruptcy debtors. In short, bankruptcy directly affects a large number of individuals and businesses each year.

From the lawyer's perspective, bankruptcy is even more important. It permeates almost all areas of legal practice, from family law and personal injury, to almost any type of commercial work. It is particularly significant in transactional work, where almost all commercial planning is done against the backdrop of a possible bankruptcy.

Bankruptcy law provides a process for dealing with a debtor whose financial obligations have become overly burdensome. Before getting into the specifics of how bankruptcy law attempts to solve debtors' financial problems, however, it is useful to have a better understanding of what those problems are.

A. DEBTORS AND THE PROBLEMS THEY FACE

We are all debtors. Almost all individuals owe utility bills and taxes. Most adults have obligations on a mortgage or for rent. Many also owe on student loans and for credit card charges. Businesses typically owe for many of the same things – utilities, taxes, and rent – but also for supplies and labor. Many businesses also borrow to obtain the finances necessary to start up, to fund their operations, or to expand.

If everyone is a debtor, what prompts only a small percentage – a large number but a small percentage – to seek relief from their debts? While the causes that impel debtors to seek protection from their creditors are legion, there are several recurring reasons. Individuals who get into financial trouble typically have faced a major calamity, such

---

[1] The two exceptions were the years 2006 and 2007, shortly after the 2005 amendments went into effect. Those amendments caused a rush to file in 2005 – more than two million individuals sought bankruptcy protection in 2005 alone – resulting in fewer individuals needing to file over the next two years. For statistics on filings organized by year, bankruptcy chapter, judicial district, and state, see http://www.uscourts.gov/Statistics/BankruptcyStatistics.aspx.

as a job loss,[2] a divorce,[3] a personal injury to – and resulting medical bills for – themselves or one of their dependents,[4] an unanticipated or chronic illness, or an uninsured casualty to their property. Indeed, even credit card companies, which lobbied strongly to make bankruptcy relief more difficult for individuals to obtain, at one point acknowledged that unemployment and divorce are major contributors to the large number of bankruptcy filings.[5]

Businesses also occasionally suffer a calamity, such as a strike (as with Eastern Airlines and Greyhound Bus Lines) or a product failure (as with asbestos for Johns Manville and the Dalkon Shield for A.H. Robins). More commonly, their financial problems are attributable to inadequate capitalization, poor business planning, an economic recession, negative cash flow, or some combination of these things.

While a few individuals and businesses who file for bankruptcy protection may be seeking relief from only minor or short-term financial difficulties, that is not the typical scenario. Most bankruptcy debtors are facing significant financial problems. Some of these problems may be of the debtor's own making. Other debtors bear no blame for the predicaments in which they find themselves. Whether any bankruptcy system can adequately account for the different causes of bankruptcy and provide an appropriate response for each is highly questionable. Whether our current system comes anywhere close to striking the proper balance will be a question we consider throughout this book.

---

[2] A study of individuals who filed no-asset Chapter 7 bankruptcy petitions in 2000 revealed that 19% were unemployed at the time of filing, compared with a general unemployment rate of about 4%. Perhaps more interesting was the job tenure of the 81% who were employed: 30% of them had been employed for only one year or less and their median job tenure – two years – was only 43% of the national median of 4.7 years. *See* Gordon Bermant & Ed Flynn, *Just Recently Hired: Job Tenure Among No-Asset Chapter 7 Debtors*, 21 AM. BANKR. INST. J., May 2002, at 22.

[3] While divorce affects all socio-economic classes – the rich as well as the poor – it almost invariably causes financial loss for at least one party to the marriage. This is because a divorced couple typically will try to maintain two separate households whereas before divorce they kept only one. Even for the affluent, the sudden rise in expenses is often unmanageable.

[4] *See* David U. Himmelstein, Elizabeth Warren, Deborah Thorne & Steffi Woolhandler, *Illness and Injury as Contributors to Bankruptcy*, 24 HEALTH AFFAIRS 63 (Web Supp. 2005) (concluding that medical problems – which generate bills and reduce the ability to earn income – contributed to almost half of the personal bankruptcies in 2001).

[5] *See* VISA U.S.A., INC., CONSUMER BANKRUPTCY: CAUSES AND IMPLICATIONS (July 1996).

the procedural initiative to file what is referred to as an "involuntary petition." §§ 301, 302, 303.

Filing the petition invokes one of the most important attributes of the bankruptcy process: the automatic stay. *See* § 362(a). The stay is an injunction against virtually all creditor collection activity, whether targeted at the debtor or at the debtor's property. The stay's prohibition on collection efforts frequently provides an immediate benefit to the debtor by preventing, among other things, the commencement or continuation of lawsuits, mortgage foreclosures, garnishments, executions, and repossessions. The stay also benefits creditors, at least in theory, by preserving the status quo. Each creditor is assured that all of the other creditors of the debtor are similarly enjoined and that an orderly and reasonably fair process will be used to identify, sell, and distribute the debtor's assets.

Despite its broad scope, the stay does not normally prohibit creditors from seeking payment from co-obligors or guarantors. Moreover, secured creditors may be able to have the stay lifted under certain circumstances in order to repossess and sell collateral, *see* § 362(d), and they may begin litigation immediately after the bankruptcy filing to have the stay lifted. Nevertheless, the stay gives the debtor at least a brief respite during which the debtor may be able to arrange for refinancing of secured obligations or a more orderly sale of the encumbered property with the expectation of realizing a better price.[35]

Shortly after the filing there will be a "first meeting of the creditors." *See* § 341. This meeting is likely to be attended by the debtor, the debtor's lawyer, and the trustee. In the typical consumer Chapter 7 case, however, no creditors will come to the meeting of the creditors. Knowing that the typical consumer debtor has no assets available for distribution, these creditors do not find it productive to attend the meeting, particularly given that the trustee essentially represents their interests. During this meeting, the trustee will ask the debtor questions in an effort to locate missing property or uncover fraudulent transfers.

Much of the activity in a typical Chapter 7 case will center around the trustee's primary responsibilities of collecting the debtor's property, turning it into cash, and distributing it to creditors. *See* §§ 704, 726. The property subject to the bankruptcy process in a Chapter 7 case – collectively known as the "bankruptcy estate" or simply as the "estate" – includes:

---

[35] As we will learn in chapter seven of this book, the stay would prohibit the debtor or creditors from actually consummating such a transaction.

1. All of the debtor's legal and equitable interests when the case begins. § 541(a)(1). For individual debtors, these typically include: the debtor's ownership interest or equity in a house, furniture, and other household goods; clothing; a car; and deposit accounts at a bank, savings & loan association, or credit union. The legal and equitable interests of corporate and other business debtors include the debtor's interest in its business equipment, inventory, fixtures, accounts receivable, any real estate, and bank accounts.

2. Property that the debtor transferred prior to the commencement of the case that the trustee is able to recover for the benefit of creditors. §§ 541(a)(3), 550(a). This includes: gifts to the friends and relatives of individual debtors; certain payments or grants of security interests to unsecured creditors that "prefer" them over other creditors; and fraudulent transfers.

3. Certain property that the debtor acquires after the commencement of the case. This includes bequests and inheritances that the debtor receives or becomes entitled to receive within 180 days after the commencement of the case. § 541(a)(5).

4. Most anything else acquired with property of the estate, including the earnings and sale proceeds of a business debtor. § 541(a)(6), (7).

Despite the broad scope of the forgoing, there are two main limits on its reach. First, the list of estate property in a Chapter 7 bankruptcy does not include an individual debtor's future wages or salary. Postpetition earnings from personal services are not part of the bankruptcy estate. § 541(a)(6). Second, when the debtor is an individual, the debtor may exempt certain property from the estate and thereby from distribution to unsecured creditors. § 522(b). The types and value of property that the debtor may exempt varies significantly from state to state. Typical examples of exemptible property are the debtor's clothes, household goods, and all or a portion of any equity that the debtor has in a principal residence. At the beginning of the case, a debtor entitled to exemptions files a list of all property claimed as exempt. The trustee or any creditor may object to any claimed exemption, § 522(*l*), Rule 4003, and if such an objection is timely filed, the bankruptcy court will decide whether the claimed exemption is valid.

After the exemptions are claimed and, if necessary, disputes about them resolved, the trustee sells the remaining assets to generate cash for distribution to creditors. Ordinarily, to share in the distribution of assets from the bankruptcy estate, a creditor must file what is known as a "proof of claim." *See* § 501; Rules 3002, 3003; Official Form 10. This essentially consists of whatever documentation is necessary for the creditor to demonstrate the validity, nature, and amount of its claim. At or about the time the petition is filed, a debtor provides the court with a list of creditor claims. The court then mails the creditors a notice of the bankruptcy case along with instructions on filing proofs of claim. In general, creditors must file their proof of claim within 90 days after the first date set for a meeting of creditors. Rule 3002. Once a proof of claim has been timely filed, the claim will be "allowed" (and thereby entitle the creditor to share in distributions from the estate) unless a party in interest objects. § 502. Objections to claims are resolved by the court. To avoid unnecessary paperwork, however, if the debtor's schedules indicate that there are no nonexempt assets available for distribution – so-called "no asset" cases – creditors are advised not to file a proof of claim unless subsequently instructed otherwise, and there is no need for the court to deal with any objections to claims.

Of course, having an allowed claim does not guarantee that the claimant will be paid in full or even in part. In a Chapter 7 case, the percentage of payment depends largely on how much, in money and other assets, the trustee is able to bring into the estate and the total amount of all of the allowed claims. However, other factors also affect the amount paid on a given claim. For example, the claims of secured creditors are generally ignored in a Chapter 7 proceeding. They are not paid by the trustee but the creditor retains its interest in the collateral. The secured creditor then extracts value from the collateral, such as by foreclosing on it, either after the case is closed or when the creditor is otherwise granted relief from the automatic stay. Moreover, while the Code itself, at least in a Chapter 7 case, is designed to distribute the bankruptcy estate to unsecured creditors on a pro rata basis, certain claims are accorded a priority position in the distribution scheme. *See* §§ 726, 507, 503. For example, unsecured claims for taxes and child support take precedence over most other claims. So too does an employee's claim for wages against a business debtor. Not surprisingly, the trustee's fees, along with the other costs of administering the estate, are also accorded priority treatment. All priority claims must be paid in full before general claimants receive any distribution. Throughout the case, the court may be called on to resolve a dispute about the priority of any given claim.

To the extent an individual debtor's debts remain unpaid after the trustee's distributions, the debts may be "discharged." That is, creditors are enjoined from seeking to extract repayment of the debt from the debtor. §§ 727(a), 524(b). However, not all claims are dischargeable and not all individual debtors are entitled to a discharge. Claims for taxes and child support, as well as for certain torts and educational loans, are nondischargeable. §§ 523(a), 727(b). That is, to the extent they are unpaid by the trustee, they will survive the bankruptcy process. Debtors who misbehave, such as by lying to the court, destroying records, or concealing assets, get no discharge of any of their debts. § 727(a)(2)–(6). Neither do corporations, § 727(a)(1), persons who received a discharge in a Chapter 7 or 11 proceeding commenced within the previous eight years, § 727(a)(8), or some debtors who received a Chapter 12 or 13 discharge in a case commenced within the previous six years, § 727(a)(9).

Objections to the debtor's overall discharge must be resolved during the bankruptcy case by the bankruptcy court. In contrast, disputes about the dischargeability of a specific debt may be litigated in bankruptcy court any time during the bankruptcy proceeding, or may be resolved by any other federal or state court after the case is over if the creditor seeks to enforce the debt despite the debtor's general discharge. *Cf.* § 523(c); Rule 4007.

With all of this said, it is important to note that not all debtors are permitted to be in Chapter 7. Beginning with the most recent amendments to the Bankruptcy Code in 2005, debtors whose monthly household income exceeds the median income in that state for a household of the same size are subject to a means test. Those who fail the test are presumptively ineligible for Chapter 7 relief.[36] § 707(b). They are relegated to the relief available under other chapters, typically Chapter 13 but also possibly Chapter 11.

(b) Chapter 13

A Chapter 13 case is similar in many respects to a Chapter 7 case. The case begins with the filing of a petition, which creates an estate, § 541, and invokes the automatic stay, § 362. The stay is broader in Chapter 13 cases because it also enjoins actions against co-debtors or guarantors, § 1301. The general provisions on claims allowance apply, §§ 501, 502, including the rules on priority, § 507, but some accommodation is made for postpetition claims, § 1305. A debtor also has exemptions in a Chapter 13 case, § 522.

---

36 Banks, railroads, and insurance companies are also ineligible for Chapter 7 relief. *See* § 109.

In other respects, however, a Chapter 13 case is markedly different from one under Chapter 7. The most significant difference is that a Chapter 13 case is not a liquidation proceeding but a rehabilitation process for an individual with regular income.[37] In addition to the property specified in § 541, the debtor's postpetition wages or salary are included in the bankruptcy estate, § 1306(a)(2), and the debtor is put on a budget. In essence, whatever postpetition income is left over after paying the debtor's reasonable living expenses is used to pay creditors' claims in whole or in part. In exchange for making future income available to creditors – something that does not happen in Chapter 7 – the debtor generally is permitted to retain his or her assets. Thus, in Chapter 13 the debtor keeps assets and gives up future income to creditors, whereas in Chapter 7 the debtor keeps future income but gives up existing, nonexempt assets. Approximately 30% of individuals who file for bankruptcy protection do so under Chapter 13; almost all of the rest do so under Chapter 7.[38]

Payments to creditors in Chapter 13 are funneled through the standing trustee. Typically, the payment plan lasts for three years, but it may extend to five years either for cause or if the debtor's monthly household income exceeds the median monthly income for the same size household in that state. § 1322(d). Unless creditors will be paid in full, the debtor must transfer all disposable income (income less reasonable and necessary living expenses) to the trustee. The trustee takes a statutorily prescribed percentage and distributes the rest to creditors according to the priority of their claims. At the end of the payment plan, the debtor receives a discharge of most unpaid debts. In fact, as originally enacted in 1978, the Code created incentives to debtors to use Chapter 13 by giving them a larger discharge; several debts that are nondischargeable in Chapter 7 were dischargeable in Chapter 13. Now, because of amendments to the Code over time, the differences between the scope of a Chapter 7 discharge and a Chapter 13 discharge are minor. *See* §§ 1328(a), 727(a). Chapter 13 remains attractive for debtors, however, because debtors can use its provisions to keep their homes and other nonexempt assets.

From a creditor's standpoint, payment may take a lot longer in Chapter 13 than in Chapter 7. However, creditors are theoretically compensated for this. Each creditor must receive – in present value terms – at least what that creditor would have received

---

[37] Chapter 13 is available only to individuals, and not to other entities such as corporations and partnerships. *See* §§ 101(30), 109(e).

[38] *See* U.S. Bankruptcy Courts – Business and Nonbusiness Cases Commenced by Chapter of the Bankruptcy Code During the 12-Month Period Ending September 30, 2012, *available at* http://www.uscourts.gov/Statistics/BankruptcyStatistics.aspx.

if the debtor had gone into Chapter 7. § 1325(a)(4). This rule provides little protection for most Chapter 13 creditors, though, because often individuals in Chapter 13 have no nonexempt assets, and thus the creditors would have received no distribution if the debtor had filed under Chapter 7.

To be eligible for relief under Chapter 13, the debtor must generally have unsecured debts totaling less than $383,175 and secured debts less than $1,149,525. § 109(e). These amounts are adjusted for inflation every three years. *See* § 104. A debtor whose debts exceed either or both of these limits may be limited to relief under Chapter 11.

(c) Chapter 11

Chapter 11 is a unified set of provisions for all kinds of "reorganizations." It is used most often by those engaged in business, whether doing so as an individual or through a partnership, limited liability company, or corporation. It applies to corporations whose shares are publicly traded as well as to those whose stock is closely held. However, it is also available to individuals without a business and may be desirable to those who have too much debt to be eligible for Chapter 13.

Congress favors reorganizations over liquidations for a variety of reasons. Reorganizations get debtors and creditors to work together, rather than merely operate under some arbitrarily imposed scheme. They presumably lead to a greater percentage of recovery for creditors, although this is by no means certain. And they allow a floundering business the chance to stay afloat and thus remain a contributing part of the economy and a source of employment.

debtor have control of finances

To make reorganization proceedings attractive to debtors, debtors in Chapter 11[39] are empowered to remain in control of their financial affairs as a "debtor in possession," rather than have a trustee come in and take over. §§ 1107, 1108. They also have the exclusive right to file a "plan of reorganization" – their blueprint for dealing with their financial affairs and for paying their creditors – for the first 120 days after the filing.[40] § 1121(b). They can even continue to incur new debts, albeit in many cases only with the consent of their creditors or the court. § 364.

---

[39] As with other types of bankruptcy cases, in a Chapter 11 case, an estate is created, §§ 541, 1115, the automatic stay applies, § 362, claims are allowed or disallowed, §§ 501, 502, some claims are classified as priority claims, § 507, and if the debtor is an individual, exemptions apply, § 522. As discussed earlier, the provisions of Bankruptcy Code Chapters 1, 3, and 5 apply to a Chapter 11 case.

[40] In large bankruptcy cases, courts routinely extend this exclusive period.

The rules governing plans of reorganization are few largely because Chapter 11 is fundamentally a consensual process. The plan will typically organize creditors into groups – called "classes" – and detail how each class will be treated. In other words, it will specify when and to what extent the creditors in each class will be paid. The creditors are then entitled to vote on the plan. Unless a majority of the voting claimants in each class, and two-thirds of the amount of the voted claims in each class, approve the plan, the plan will generally not be confirmed. *See* §§ 1126(c), 1129(a)(8). There is, however, a heavily regulated process a Chapter 11 debtor can use to confirm – "cram down" – a plan despite the existence of one or more dissenting classes. *See* § 1129(b). One other notable requirement is that each claimant must either accept the plan or be paid, in present value terms, at least the amount the creditor would have recovered in Chapter 7. § 1129(a)(7).

If the plan complies with the Code's requirements, and if the court determines that the plan is feasible, it is "confirmed" (*i.e.*, put into effect). Typically, plans provide for payment of only a small portion of nonpriority debts, and even that may be postponed for many months or several years. The remainder of the debtor's obligations are discharged. § 1141. In short, the debtor is given a fresh start through the binding effect on all concerned of a confirmed plan of reorganization.

As this brief explanation suggests, reorganization proceedings require a great deal of negotiation. Because of that, they can also generate a lot of animosity and litigation. Issues likely to be disputed include: what the debtor may do with available cash, particularly how much of it may be used to pay the salaries of officers, directors, and other upper-level management of corporate debtors; which employees should be laid off; which unperformed contracts and unexpired leases of the debtor should be assumed and which rejected, and by when such decisions must be made; and what protection the debtor must offer to secured creditors for its continuing use of the collateral. *See* §§ 361, 362(d), 363.

Throughout the potentially hostile exchanges over these issues, the debtor in possession will negotiate with its various creditors, and the creditors will negotiate among themselves, to determine whether they can agree to a plan that satisfies the requirements of the Code. Ultimately these negotiations may bear fruit in the form of a plan agreed to by all. More likely, they will produce a partial agreement, and the debtor will then ask the court to impose the plan on the remaining creditors. At that point the parties will argue about, and possibly litigate, whether the plan complies with the requirements of the Code and can be confirmed. *See* § 1129. Although statistics are surprisingly meager, most cases never make it to the confirmation stage.

For these reasons, the Chapter 11 process has been likened to bargaining over a dish of ice cream in a warm room. The debtor's business is frequently losing money – sometimes hemorrhaging it – during the bankruptcy process. If the parties fail to reach prompt agreement on a plan of reorganization, they may find themselves with little left to divvy up. When this happens, the debtor may simply dismiss the case or, more likely, convert the case to a Chapter 7 liquidation. *See* § 1112. Indeed, folklore has it that most business bankruptcies wind up in Chapter 7 even though many, and perhaps most, begin life as a Chapter 11.

4. The Supporting Cast

(a) The United States Trustee

To separate the judicial and administrative roles in bankruptcy proceedings, Congress created the United States Trustee system. Under this system, responsibility for supervising most of the administration of bankruptcy estates was given to the applicable United States Trustee. There are 21 United States Trustees, each overseeing a group of federal judicial districts. 28 U.S.C. § 581(a). The Attorney General appoints a United States Trustee for each region for a five-year term and has general supervisory power over the person appointed. 28 U.S.C. §§ 581, 586(c). The Attorney General may also appoint (and remove) Assistant United States Trustees. 28 U.S.C. § 582.

The United States Trustee appoints the members of a panel of trustees for each judicial district. 28 U.S.C. § 586(a)(1). Qualifications for membership on these panels are prescribed by the Attorney General. 28 U.S.C. § 586(d). In each Chapter 7 case, the United States Trustee appoints a person from the panel to serve as the trustee in that case (unless creditors elect someone else pursuant to § 702). § 701(a)(1).

In Chapter 11 cases, the United States Trustee also appoints a private trustee, but only if the court orders that there should be one in the case. The person appointed need not be a member of the standing panel. § 1104(d). In Chapter 13 cases, the United States Trustee may act as trustee but, more typically, appoints a standing trustee who oversees all of the Chapter 13 cases in a particular judicial district. §§ 1202(a), 1302(a); 28 U.S.C. § 586(b).

Most important, the United States Trustee is responsible for generally supervising all Chapter 7, 11, and 13 cases and for supervising the actions of the trustee who may be serving in those cases. *See* 28 U.S.C. § 586(a)(3), (b). To fulfill this responsibility, the United States Trustee is empowered: (i) to monitor applications for employment of professionals and applications for compensation and reimbursement of expenses; (ii) to monitor plans filed in reorganization cases and to monitor creditors' committees in Chapter 11 cases; and (iii) to ensure that all required schedules and other papers and reports are timely and properly filed and that required filing or similar fees are paid. The statute also authorizes the United States Trustee to report to and advise the court concerning all matters of administration and to take any necessary steps to ensure that cases under the Code progress expeditiously. 28 U.S.C. § 586(a)(3)(A)–(H).

It should be emphasized that the United States Trustee is not an official with enforcement powers and cannot make orders in the sense that a court or even an administrative agency makes orders that require compliance with prescribed regulations. Rather, the influence of the United States Trustee is exercised through his or her standing to file an appropriate motion, complaint, or objection that seeks a ruling by the bankruptcy court on a matter of administration as to which there has been no voluntary compliance. *See* § 307.

The United States Trustee system is funded out of filing fees and other assessments made in bankruptcy cases. *See* 28 U.S.C. §§ 1930, 589a.

(b) The Debtor's Attorney

While the trustee in a Chapter 7 case is concerned about gathering and liquidating all of the debtor's nonexempt assets and paying legitimate claims out of those proceeds, the debtor's attorney is concerned with helping the debtor through the bankruptcy process and with protecting the debtor's postbankruptcy life. The debtor's attorney therefore typically helps the debtor fill out and file the petition and accompanying forms (such as the schedules of assets and liabilities). The debtor's attorney may also be needed to assist the debtor if creditors object to any exemption the debtor has claimed, to the dischargeability of a particular debt, or to the debtor's discharge in general. The debtor's attorney is also involved in any negotiations concerning the debtor reaffirming a debt that would otherwise be discharged. While the debtor's attorney must disclose to the bankruptcy court any compensation received from the debtor in the year prior to the bankruptcy filing, so that the court can evaluate the reasonableness of that compensation, *see* § 329, the debtor's attorney in a Chapter 7 case is not compensated from the estate property. Instead, the debtor must either pay the attorney prior to filing the petition or use exempt assets or postpetition earnings to compensate his or her attorney.

how attorney paid

The debtor's attorney in both a Chapter 13 and a Chapter 11 case has a more integral role in the process. In a Chapter 13 case, the debtor's attorney generally drafts the repayment plan and assists the debtor in getting the plan approved. The debtor's attorney in a Chapter 13 case must also disclose compensation that she or he has received, § 329, and may be compensated from estate assets, § 330. In a Chapter 11 case, the debtor's attorney is critical to: (i) helping the debtor obtain the myriad of court orders that are needed for the debtor in possession to continue to operate its business; (ii) negotiating the reorganization plan; and (iii) obtaining confirmation of that plan. In general, the debtor's attorney in a Chapter 11 case is compensated out of estate assets, but the court must approve both the appointment of the attorney and the amount of compensation. §§ 1107, 327, 329, 330.

(c) Secured Creditors

To use a metaphor, secured creditors – those with a lien on some property of the debtor – are the brats of bankruptcy. They want what is theirs, they want it now, and they often threaten to throw a fit if they do not get it. This is of course an unflattering and probably unfair generalization, but it nevertheless reflects the general way the Bankruptcy Code treats them. Secured creditors generally retain their interest in the debtor's property. Beyond that, many provisions of the Code seek to ensure that the secured creditor's interest in the collateral does not diminish in value. In Chapter 7 cases, this typically means that the secured creditors will eventually foreclose on the collateral, even though the bankruptcy process may delay that eventual outcome. In Chapter 13 cases, secured creditors typically continue to receive payment on the secured obligation according to the original payment schedule. In Chapter 11 cases, secured creditors' consent to a plan of reorganization is often critical and the debtor must often agree to the secured creditors' terms in order to obtain that consent.

5. *Bit Players*

(a) Unsecured Creditors

Unsecured creditors are like young children during the era when tykes were to be seen and not heard. If you think about it, at least in the context of a Chapter 7 case, this makes some sense. After all, the trustee represents the interests of the unsecured creditors. Thus, there is little need for individual creditors to become involved and most of the other players regard any attempted involvement by unsecured creditors as a nuisance. In addition, many Chapter 7 consumer bankruptcies are "no asset" cases. That is, after accounting for the costs of administering the estate, the secured creditors' liens on the property, and the debtor's allowable exemptions, there are no assets remaining to liquidate and distribute to the unsecured creditors. In such cases, the unsecured creditors have very little at stake. Admittedly, though, they can raise some problems for the debtor by objecting to the debtor's discharge or seeking to have the debts due them declared nondischargeable. This is often the case in Chapter 13 cases as well.

In Chapter 11 cases, where the debtor is generally permitted to continue operating its business, things are a bit different. There, much of the oversight of the debtor is left to a committee comprised of the creditors with the largest unsecured claims. §§ 1102, 1103. Such creditors will have much to say in how the debtor in possession conducts its affairs and will often play a significant role in negotiating the plan of reorganization.

(b) Co-Owners

Sometimes a bankruptcy debtor will own only some of the "sticks" representing the ownership rights in a particular piece of property. For example, the debtor may own some real estate as tenants in common, joint tenants, or tenants by the entirety with someone else. Similarly, the debtor may lease real or personal property, leaving the reversionary interest with the lessor. In general, only the debtor's rights to property are dealt with in bankruptcy. However, it is often not possible to deal with the debtor's interests without having some effect on the rights of any co-owners. This is particularly true with respect to community property. We will encounter several of the many ways the Bankruptcy Code deals with issues that arise because of co-ownership.

(c) Co-Debtors

Sometimes two or more people will be responsible for a single debt but only one of them will file for bankruptcy protection. The nonfiling co-debtor may be someone jointly and severally liable for the whole debt, a guarantor who is secondarily liable, or the principal obligor whose debt was guaranteed by the bankruptcy filer. In general, bankruptcy has no effect on the liability of co-debtors. The principal exception is that, in Chapter 13 cases, efforts to collect from some co-debtors are stayed during the case. § 1301.

(d) Prepetition Transferees

For the most part, the bankruptcy process deals with the debtor's assets and liabilities as they exist on the date the bankruptcy petition is filed. In the weeks and months prior to that filing, the debtor is likely to have made payments to creditors and possibly even given some property away. These transfers can significantly deplete the debtor's assets and thus potentially disrupt the bankruptcy distribution scheme. To prevent that disruption, the Bankruptcy Code includes some important provisions for recovering these transfers. §§ 544–549. We will study these provisions in chapter three of this book.

(e) Equity Interest Holders

A corporation or other business entity that files for bankruptcy protection is usually insolvent. Its stockholders or other owners are therefore likely to receive little back on their initial investment. In other words, their ownership interest is no longer likely to have any value. Occasionally, however, the debtor has the prospect of earning enough money to pay off its creditors over time. When that prospect exists and the debtor is undergoing a Chapter 11 reorganization, the owners of the debtor – denominated as interest holders – have a limited role to play. They remain in control of the debtor in possession, at least indirectly, and typically try to negotiate a plan of reorganization that will allow them to retain all or a portion of their equitable stake in the debtor. Particularly in large bankruptcy cases, there is some evidence that they are able to do just that.[41]

(f) Employed Professionals

Trustees, debtors in possession, and certain creditors' committees may, with court authorization, employ attorneys, accountants, and other professionals at the expense of the estate. §§ 327(a), 1103(a), 1107(a). Indeed, the court may authorize a trustee to act as the estate's attorney or accountant and to be compensated for both types of services if this authorization is in the best interests of the estate. § 327(d).

---

[41] *See* Lynn M. LoPucki, *Patterns in the Bankruptcy Reorganization of Large, Publicly Held Companies*, 78 CORNELL L. REV. 597 (1993).

A court order authorizing the employment must be obtained before services are rendered for compensation to come from the estate, although occasionally some courts will enter such an order nunc pro tunc. In addition, professional persons employed by the trustee or debtor in possession must generally be "disinterested," as defined in § 101(14), and free from adverse interests. § 327(a), (e). An attorney or accountant employed by a creditors' committee also may not hold or represent any adverse interest. Although the statute does not expressly require disinterestedness for them, *see* § 1103(b), disinterestedness is a practical necessity because lack of it is a ground for denying all compensation to someone so employed. § 328(c). Courts enforce the requirement of disinterestedness with some rigor, even when it appears that the conflict of interest is disclosed and assented to by parties to the case,[42] and attorneys who fail to disclose conflicts of interest are regularly denied compensation for their services.

Employed professionals can have many and varied duties. Typically, though, accountants are used to reconstruct the debtor's books and records to ascertain what assets the debtor has, to whom assets may have been transferred or where assets may have been hidden away, and who has valid claims. Attorneys are employed to litigate actions filed by or against the trustee, most commonly actions to bring assets into the estate or to determine the validity or liquidate the amount of a creditor's claim against the estate.

D. THE POLICIES

There are two principal policies underlying current bankruptcy law: (1) the fresh start and (2) providing for a fair and orderly distribution to creditors. The fresh start is grounded in the notion that a debtor should not be forever indentured by debts. At some point, after repayment efforts have been made, debtors should be granted relief from their debts and be allowed to start their lives over. In a nation founded largely by debtors, the idea of a fresh start should not be surprising.

A fair and orderly distribution to creditors is the quid pro quo for the fresh start. Debtors are expected to make their nonexempt assets available to creditors through a process that treats the creditors fairly. This means that creditors generally stand on equal footing and share on a pro rata basis, unless some other policy intervenes and warrants

---

[42] *See In re Sunbum5 Enters., LLC*, 2011 WL 4529648 (M.D. Fla. 2011) (reversing bankruptcy court order approving employment of attorney for the trustee, finding that trustee cannot "waive" the conflict of interest for purpose of satisfying the disinterestedness requirement).

granting one creditor or type of creditor priority over others. It also means that the process should be quick, inexpensive, and require a minimum of effort by creditors.

The tension between these two policies underlies virtually all of bankruptcy law and practice. The National Bankruptcy Review Commission expressed it well when it wrote in 1997:

> This year, more than a million American families will declare themselves bankrupt. They are bookkeepers, truck drivers, computer programmers, managers, department store clerks, loggers, executives, secretaries, accountants, plumbers' assistants, consultants, postal workers, machinists, day care workers, flight attendants, dentists, steelworkers, teachers, and waitresses. They work for large companies, for small companies, for the government, for themselves, and for no one. They are single mothers, single fathers, married couples, big families, and small families. What they have in common is that each one of them has filled out forms under penalty of perjury about their finances, walked into a courthouse, been sworn in for examination by a trustee, and waited for questions from their creditors. For nearly 1.3 million American families, the most important event of 1997 will be the public declaration that they are bankrupt.
>
> Consumer bankruptcy has become part of America's economic landscape. Once regarded as an unlikely legal alternative chosen by only a few desperate families, bankruptcy had become a refuge for one in every 96 American families by the time the National Bankruptcy Review Commission filed its report. Journalists, academics, and lobbyists trained their sights on the bankruptcy system. Bankruptcy, a centuries-old phenomenon, has become a part of the changing world of consumer credit.
>
> As bankruptcy filings increase, creditors justifiably worry whether a promise to repay has any meaning, while consumer advocates express concern that the financial distress of more than a million American families each year foreshadows a larger economic problem. The inherent conflict between the twin goals of bankruptcy – appropriate relief for those in trouble and equitable treatment for their creditors – ensures that it always will be an area of contention. To deal with financial loss, the bankruptcy system necessarily embraces competing interests. Recommendations fully endorsed by either debtors or by creditors would not maintain the balance essential to any consumer bankruptcy system. Bankruptcy is a system born of conflict and

competing values. To function well, it must remain unpopular and controversial.[43]

Problem 2-2

Without digging into the specifics of the Bankruptcy Code, which of the following would be a good candidate for bankruptcy? What advice would you offer to the others?

A. Astute is a computer programmer who lives in Silicon Valley. Over the last several years, while the economy was booming, Astute ran up large bills to purchase various luxury items (a Porsche, a major home video system, etc.). A few months ago, with the economy lagging, Astute's employer laid Astute off. Astute found substitute employment, but now earns only $65,000 per year instead of $125,000. Astute's unsecured debts total $30,000 (mostly on credit cards) and Astute owes about $25,000 on the Porsche (which is worth about that amount). Astute pays $2,400 per month in rent on a very nice apartment.

B. Baker is a single parent whose child had a major medical ailment last year. The child is now cured but Baker's outstanding medical bills exceed $60,000. Baker is employed at a local pastry shop, which pays Baker $28,000 per year but provides no health insurance. Baker owns a home valued at about $100,000 but is two months in arrears on the $95,000 home mortgage. Baker also owes about $2,000 on credit cards and to utility companies.

C. Couch is an auto mechanic who was laid off three years ago and has been unable to find or keep steady employment. Couch's unemployment benefits expired some time ago. Couch owes $2,600 on various credit cards and has no more available credit. Couch also owes several hundred dollars for utility services, and both the phone company and the cable company have already discontinued service. Couch lives in an apartment that has one old and worn sofa, no bed, a small television, one lamp, one plate, one fork, one knife, no spoons, and several beers. Couch is behind on the $300/month rent and the landlord is threatening eviction.

D. Dennis and Deirdre were married six years ago, shortly after they completed college. Dennis is employed as an architect and Deidre has

---

[43] NAT'L BANKR. REVIEW COMM'N, BANKRUPTCY: THE NEXT TWENTY YEARS 77–78 (Oct. 20, 1997).

elected to stay home and care for Evangeline (the baby) who has had a series of minor but recurring illnesses. The couple has had a difficult time making ends meet. Dennis earns $6,300 per month. With their rent, car payments, student loans, medical co-pays, not to mention food, clothing, utilities, gasoline, insurance, and other living expenses, they find themselves falling further behind each month. To cover their expenses, they have done what so many do: taken cash advances on their various credit cards. As a result, they have built up substantial credit card debt and can no longer make even the minimum monthly payments.

E. Edgar Systems, Inc. is a small business in financial difficulty. The company's total liabilities are greater than the value of its inventory, equipment, and other assets if past depreciation of the assets (particularly the equipment) is taken into account. Much of Edgar's debt is unsecured and it cannot pay its debt when due. Unsecured creditors are threatening to sue and secured creditors are threatening to foreclose. However, Edgar has loyal customers (*i.e.*, goodwill) and carries a positive allocation for this on its balance sheet, so that the current depreciated value of Edgar's total assets exceeds its total liabilities.

E. STARTING THE CASE

1. The Petition and Schedules

A bankruptcy case begins with the filing of a petition, a relatively simple document that identifies the debtor's name, address, approximate number of creditors and the estimated amount due them, the total value of the debtor's assets, and the chapter of the Bankruptcy Code under which the petition is filed. *See* Official Form 1. The filing fee (and associated fees and surcharges) is currently $306 for a petition under Chapter 7, $281 for a petition under Chapter 13, and $1,213 for a petition under Chapter 11.[44] *See* 28 U.S.C. § 1930(a). An individual debtor (not corporations or partnerships) may pay the fee in up to four installments, with the final payment due no later than 180 days after the petition is filed. 28 U.S.C. § 1930(a); Rule 1006(b); Official Form 3A. Alternatively, an individual debtor may obtain a waiver of the fee entirely if the debtor's

[44] A schedule of fees for motions, complaints, and other matters applicable in bankruptcy cases is available at http://www.uscourts.gov/FormsAndFees.aspx.

income is less than 150% of the "income official poverty line," as determined annually by the Office of Management and Budget. 28 U.S.C. § 1930(f).

Venue may be in any U.S. district in which the debtor's domicile, residence, principal place of business, or principal assets have been located for the previous 180 days (or the longest part of such 180 days if more than one district). 28 U.S.C. § 1408(1). Thus, some debtors may have a choice of jurisdiction in which to file.

voluntary petition

The vast majority of bankruptcy cases are voluntary – that is, the debtor is the person who files the petition. A voluntary petition constitutes the "order for relief." §§ 301(b), 302(a). In other words, the petition qualifies as a sort of court order approving the exercise of jurisdiction to administer the case. A tiny fraction of bankruptcy cases – less than 1% – are begun not by the debtor but with a petition filed by one or more creditors. In such involuntary cases, the court enters an order for relief only if it determines that: (i) the debtor qualifies for relief under the chapter under which the case is commenced; (ii) the debtor is not paying debts as they become due; and (iii) the petitioning creditors qualify in number and in the amount and type of claims they hold. § 303(a)–(h). The distinction between the petition and the order for relief can be important. Some provisions of the Bankruptcy Code and the Bankruptcy Rules are based on, and some time periods commence when, the petition is filed,[45] while others are based on or commence when the order for relief is entered.[46] For example, in voluntary cases the debtor must file a list of creditors with the petition,[47] and must also file, either with the petition or within 14 days thereafter, detailed schedules of assets, liabilities, and exemptions.[48] In contrast, the debtor need file those schedules in an involuntary case only after the court enters an order for relief.[49]

order for relief

The requirements for filing an involuntary petition are fairly detailed. Read § 303(b). The dollar amounts in this section are adjusted every three years. § 104. Normally, at least three creditors holding claims that are both noncontingent and undisputed must join in the petition. We will return briefly to who qualifies as a

---

45 *See, e.g.*, § 362 (governing the automatic stay); § 547(b)(4) (providing for the avoidance of certain prepetition preferential transfers).

46 *See, e.g.*, § 108(a)(2), (b)(2) (extending certain nonbankruptcy statutes of limitation and time periods to file pleadings in pending nonbankruptcy litigation); § 546(a)(1)(A) (placing a time limit on when the debtor or trustee may exercise certain bankruptcy avoiding powers).

47 *See* Rule 1007(a).

48 *See* Rule 1007(a), (c); Official Form 6.

49 *See* Rule 1007(c).

petitioning creditor in chapter five, after we discuss various types of claims. The requirement that the debtor has completed credit counseling does not apply.[50]

After the involuntary petition is filed, but before an order for relief is entered, the debtor remains authorized to operate its business and to use, acquire, and dispose of property. § 303(f). However, the court may impose restrictions on that authority if necessary to preserve the estate. § 303(g). On the other hand, the court may require the petitioners to post a bond to compensate the debtor for any damages caused by the petition if the court declines to order relief. § 303(e), (i).

The standard for ordering relief in an involuntary case normally requires that the debtor is generally not paying debts as they become due. § 303(h). This is different from being insolvent, which is defined as having a negative net worth. § 101(32). Courts have developed a variety of tests for determining whether a debtor is generally not paying debts as they mature,[51] but perhaps the most important factors are: (i) the number of debts unpaid each month compared to those paid; and (ii) the amount of the debts unpaid compared to the amount paid. As a result, a small number of delinquencies will be more significant for a debtor with only a small number of debts than for a debtor with many.

2. *The Means Test*

Section 707(b) affects whether an individual debtor should file under Chapter 7 or, in the alternative, under Chapter 11 or Chapter 13 of the Bankruptcy Code. Generally, a consumer debtor who has enough income to repay his or her debts is prohibited from filing under Chapter 7. If the debtor is an individual whose debts are primarily consumer debts,[52] the court may dismiss a Chapter 7 case if granting relief would be an abuse of the bankruptcy process. *See* § 707(b). For this purpose, abuse is presumed if the debtor has too much disposable income. The main purpose of this provision is to

debtor has too much income

---

[50] Section 109(h)(1) refers to a petition filed "by such individual," suggesting that the credit counseling requirement does not apply to involuntary cases. The few court decisions on this issue are in accord. *See, e.g.*, *In re Sims*, 2009 WL 161343 (Bankr. D. Kan. 2009) (collecting cases).

[51] *See, e.g.*, *In re Harmsen*, 320 B.R. 188, 201–03 (10th Cir. BAP 2005) (identifying several tests).

[52] "Consumer debt" is a term defined in § 101(8). It includes the purchase-money mortgage debt on an individual's principal residence. However, the term excludes not only debts incurred for business reasons, but also unpaid personal income taxes. *See, e.g.*, *In re Wisher*, 222 B.R. 634 (Bankr. D. Colo. 1998); *In re Brashers*, 216 B.R. 59 (Bankr. N.D. Okla. 1998).

impel debtors with significant income who nevertheless need bankruptcy protection to seek it instead under Chapter 11 or 13, where postpetition income will be available to creditors.

How much disposable income is "too much"? That is the subject of an unusually long and cumbersome provision: § 707(b). Before reading § 707(b), note that its paragraphs are not logically arranged. We recommend that you tackle them in the following order:

Paragraph	Content
(b)(1)	General rule
(b)(3)	Relevant things to consider in applying the general rule
(b)(7)	Income-based portion of the means test
(b)(2)	Ability-to-pay portion of the means test
(b)(6)	Income-based restriction on who may raise the issue of abuse based on something other than the means test
(b)(4)	Rules about who can be made to pay the costs of litigating a successful § 707(b) motion
(b)(5)	Rules about who can be made to pay the costs of litigating an unsuccessful § 707(b) motion

There are two preliminary things to note about the general rule of paragraph (1). First, abuse is not limited to a failure to satisfy the means test. We will briefly explore what else may constitute abuse in chapter ten. Second, the presumption of abuse that results from having excessive income is rebuttable. Courts are instructed to consider the totality of the circumstances and whether the debtor filed the petition in good faith. § 707(b)(3). That said, the presumption of abuse resulting from a failure to satisfy the means test is difficult to rebut. *See* § 707(b)(2)(B).

The means test consists of two independent inquiries. The first inquiry asks if the combined income of the debtor and the debtor's spouse exceeds the medium income for a household of the same size in the debtor's state. If not – if the debtor's income is below the median – then the debtor has passed the means test and no further calculations are necessary. § 707(b)(7).

The second inquiry consists of a rather complicated mathematical formula intended to determine if the debtor's projected postpetition monthly income, reduced by specified expenses, will total more than a minimum amount over the next five years. § 707(b)(2).

More specifically, the formula works as follows. If the debtor's total disposable income for the next 60 months:

(1) < $7,475: no presumption of abuses arises;
(2) ≥ $12,475: there is a presumption of abuse; and
(3) ≥ $7,475 but < $12,475, then if it is sufficient to pay at least 25% of the debtor's nonpriority, unsecured claims, there is a presumption of abuse.[53]

The formula used to compute the debtor's disposable income for this purpose is (ramp up your tolerance for complexity here):

$$(CMI - ME - (1/60 \times SO) - (1/60 \times SP)) \times 60$$

For this purpose:

CMI equals the debtor's Current Monthly Income, a term defined in § 101(10A) to mean, roughly, the debtor's average gross monthly income for the last six months.

ME equals the debtor's Monthly Expenses, calculated in part pursuant to the National and Local Standards periodically set by the IRS.[54] The National Standards are intended to cover such things as food, clothing, housing supplies, and miscellaneous expenses and vary with family size. The Local Standards are intended to cover more variable costs, such as utility services, rent, and transportation. The transportation expenses for a debtor with a vehicle are further divided into operating costs (which are local figures) and ownership costs (which are national figures), but a debtor who owns a vehicle outright – *i.e.*, the vehicle is neither leased nor encumbered by a lien – is not entitled to the ownership expense.[55]

Monthly Expenses also include the debtor's actual expenses for Other Necessary Expenses, a term which, judging by the official form that debtors must use in computing the means test, includes income taxes, social security taxes,

---

53 These two dollar amounts are subject to adjustment under § 104.

54 The National and Monthly Standards are adjusted periodically and different numbers will apply depending upon when the bankruptcy petition is filed. These numbers must be used when filing a petition for relief and Official Form 22, which is the form that implements the means test. These Standards can be found at http://www.justice.gov/ust/eo/bapcpa/meanstesting.htm.

55 *Ransom v. FIA Card Servs.*, 131 S. Ct. 716 (2011).

mandatory retirement fund contributions, life insurance expenses, and health care costs (beyond the cost of insurance premiums).

In addition to all of this, the debtor's Monthly Expenses include:

(1) Reasonable expenses for health insurance;
(2) Expenses to protect against family violence;
(3) Up to 5% more for food and clothing;
(4) Costs of caring for an elderly, infirm, or disabled household or family member;
(5) The administrative expenses that would arise in a Chapter 13 case (if the debtor would be eligible);
(6) Actual expenses, up to $1,875[56] per minor child to attend school; and
(7) Actual home energy costs, in excess of the IRS allowance, if reasonable.

SO equals the total payments due on the debtor's Secured Obligations for the next 60 months.

SP equals the total Support Payments the debtor is obligated to make for the next 60 months.

The term "current monthly income" is defined in § 101(10A). It refers to income "that the debtor receives" and which is "derived" during the six-month period ending before the filing of the petition. This phrasing raises some difficult allocation questions, such as how to deal with: (i) income received during the six-month period but attributable to work performed outside of the six-month period; and, conversely, (ii) income earned during the six-month period but received afterward. One thoughtful decision has concluded that "receives" and "derived" are different concepts and that both must be satisfied for the income to be counted. Accordingly, pursuant to that decision, the debtor must both receive and earn the income during the relevant six-month period.[57]

Okay, now that you have all that, try the following problem, using the charts for the current time period available on the Department of Justice website.[58]

---

[56] This amount is subject to adjustment under § 104.

[57] *See In re Arnoux*, 442 B.R. 769 (Bankr. E.D. Wash. 2010).

[58] *See supra* note 54.

Problem 2-3

[The periodic revisions to the National and Local Standards may require revisions to this Problem; check the book's website, www.sepinuckruschbankruptcy.com, for updates to this Problem before attempting to solve it.]

Remember Dennis and Deirdre from Problem 2-2. They currently live in Spokane, Washington, where Dennis is employed as an architect. Deirdre was employed as a claims specialist with an insurance company until the birth of the couple's daughter Evangeline three years ago. Since then, she has elected to stay home. With the loss of Deirdre's income, the couple has had a difficult time making ends meet.

They left school with a combined $80,000 in student loan debt, which they elected to pay over 15 years at $630 per month. They pay monthly rent of $1,250 for a two-bedroom apartment. They each have a car. Dennis purchased his car three years ago. It is currently worth about $8,000 and he pays $340/month on what was originally a four-year, $15,000 loan. The seller of the car has a security interest in it. Two years ago, Deirdre entered into a four-year lease of a new car. The lease calls for $225 in monthly payments.

Dennis earns $6,000 per month. From that, the following deductions are taken:

Income Taxes	$520
Social Security	$430
401k Plan Contribution	$300
Health Insurance	$200
	$1,450

With all of their payments, they find themselves falling further behind each month. As noted in Problem 2-2, they have taken out cash advances on their credit cards. As a result, they have built up substantial credit card debt and can no longer make even the minimum monthly payments. They currently owe the following:

Student Loans	$65,000
Car Loan	$3,800
Credit Cards	$16,200
	$85,000

None of these obligations qualifies as a priority claim in bankruptcy.

A. If Dennis and Deirdre file a joint bankruptcy petition under Chapter 7, would granting them relief be an abuse of that chapter? Use Official Form 22 to help you make that determination.

B. How, if at all, would the result be different if Dennis earned $5,800 per month, with no change in the deductions identified above? *See* § 707(b)(7).

C. How, if at all, would the analysis in Part A be different if the debtors indicated on their Statement of Intention that they planned to surrender Deirdre's car to the lessor? What if they had in fact surrendered the car prior to the trustee's motion to dismiss the case? *See In re Rudler*, 576 F.3d 37 (1st Cir. 2009); *In re Singletary*, 354 B.R. 455 (Bankr. S.D. Tex. 2006).

D. How, if at all, would the analysis in Part A be different if instead of owing $16,200 on various credit cards, the debtors owed $4,200 on credit cards and $12,000 in past-due federal income taxes? For this purpose, assume that the income tax debt would be a priority claim.

E. In reviewing the formula in § 707(b)(2), what might debtors do to satisfy the means test? In other words, what, if any, prepetition transactions could debtors enter into to make it more likely they will satisfy the means test?

3. *Attorney Liability Issues*

The 2005 amendments to the Bankruptcy Code include several provisions that can subject attorneys to liability or sanctions.[59] While a detailed discussion of all of these provisions is beyond the scope of this book, four deserve some attention.

First, if an attorney signs the debtor's Chapter 7 petition, that signature constitutes a certification that the attorney has conducted a reasonable investigation and that the petition is well grounded in fact and existing law. § 707(b)(4)(C). If the debtor's petition is later dismissed because it constitutes an abuse of the Bankruptcy Code – as it would, for example, if the debtor failed to satisfy the Chapter 7 means test – the

---

[59] *See* Catherine E. Vance & Corinne Cooper, *Nine Traps and One Slap: Attorney Liability Under the New Bankruptcy Law*, *in* BANKRUPTCY ABUSE PREVENTION AND CONSUMER PROTECTION ACT OF 2005, at 137–87 (ALI-ABA 2005).

attorney can be liable to the trustee for costs and attorney's fees associated with obtaining that dismissal. § 707(b)(4)(A).

Second, if an attorney signs the debtor's Chapter 7 petition, that signature constitutes a certification that the attorney has no knowledge, after conducting an inquiry, that the information in the schedules is incorrect. § 707(b)(4)(D). If this certification later proves to be untrue, the court may assess a civil penalty against the attorney. § 707(b)(4)(B). It remains unclear what kind of investigation will insulate the attorney from liability. Not surprisingly, some debtors' attorneys now decline to sign the petition, choosing instead to end the representation before the filing is made. *Cf.* Rule 9011.

The remaining rules apply to "debt relief agencies," a term that apparently includes lawyers who provide bankruptcy assistance for a fee to anyone whose debts consist mostly of consumer debts and whose nonexempt assets are worth less than $186,825.[60] Such attorneys must include the following disclosure in all of their advertisements for bankruptcy and debt-relief services: "We are a debt relief agency. We help people file for bankruptcy relief under the Bankruptcy Code." § 528(b). They must also provide to their debtor clients certain written notifications about the various forms of bankruptcy relief. §§ 342(b), 527(a). More significant – and problematic – are two other requirements: (i) they must provide some advice that is slightly inconsistent with the law; and (ii) they must refrain from providing some advice that may be in their clients' best interests.

The required advice pertains to the process for exempting assets, a subject explored more fully in chapter four of this book. Section 527 seems to require that attorneys advise their debtor clients in writing that all assets must be valued at replacement value. § 527(a)(2)(B), (c)(1), (3). However, while replacement value is the standard to be used for valuing consumer goods subject to a lien, *see* § 506(a)(2), it is far from clear that replacement value is the appropriate standard for valuing unencumbered goods or other assets.[61]

---

60 *See* § 101(3), (12A). The dollar amount is subject to adjustment under § 104. Note, the assisted person need not be a debtor. The provision is intended to reach those who counsel debtors but is phrased broadly enough to reach those who counsel creditors who are individuals with mostly consumer debts. Thus, for example, an attorney assisting a person trying to collect support from a former spouse would seemingly qualify as a debt relief agency. Moreover, there is apparently no *de minimis* exception or time limit, so that an attorney who only rarely or once represents consumers on bankruptcy matters qualifies as a "debt relief agency" forever.

61 *See infra* chapter six, § D.2.

The advice that attorneys are prohibited from giving is even more of a problem. Section 526(a)(4) prohibits debt relief agencies from advising a person to incur more debt in contemplation of bankruptcy.[62] However, borrowing money on the eve of bankruptcy is not necessarily illegal or improper, and is often in the client's best interest. For example, it may be wise for the client to refinance a mortgage at lower interest rates. Perhaps the client needs to borrow funds to purchase needed medicines. Maybe the client needs money to pay the costs associated with the bankruptcy filing. None of these borrowings would be illegal, none would make a subsequent bankruptcy an abuse, and none would be grounds for denying the bankruptcy discharge or declaring the particular debt nondischargeable. Nevertheless, this rule arguably prohibits attorneys from advising their clients to acquire such debt, even if the debtor intends to reaffirm the obligation.

Not surprisingly, attorneys have challenged these restrictions on First Amendment grounds. In 2010, the Supreme Court upheld the constitutionality of § 526(a)(4), but only after limiting its scope.[63] The Court concluded that § 526(a)(4) "prohibits a debt relief agency only from advising a debtor to incur more debt because the debtor is filing for bankruptcy, rather than for a valid purpose." Although the precise reach of this narrowed scope remains unclear, the Court discussed a variety of concerns that underlie the prohibition: (i) that the newly incurred debt might be dischargeable, and therefore incurred without the intent to repay; (ii) that the new debt might dilute the bankruptcy estate; (iii) that the new debt might affect the debtor's eligibility under one or more chapters of the Code; or (iv) that the new debt, particularly if it is secured, might affect how the means test is applied. The Court treated § 526(a)(4) as responding to all of these concerns, and thus, the prohibition appears to remain fairly broad. However, § 526(a)(4) does not encompass advice unrelated to bankruptcy, such as a recommendation to incur debt to buy needed food, shelter, or medical care.

The Court did offer one bone to debtors and their attorneys. The Court expressly noted that the statute prohibits merely *advising* the debtor to incur debt, noting that "[c]overed professionals remain free to 'tal[k] fully and candidly about the incurrence of debt in contemplation of filing a bankruptcy case.'" Therefore, attorneys who simply explain options and their consequences will apparently not violate § 526(a)(4). For the moment, however, it is unclear whether bankruptcy attorneys will feel comfortable relying on the distinction between information and advice.

---

[62] The clause is rather cumbersome and there are at least four different ways to read its provisions. *See* Vance & Cooper, *supra* note 59, at 165–66.

[63] *Milavetz, Gallop & Milavetz, P.A. v. United States*, 559 U.S. 229 (2010).

F. CONVERTING TO ANOTHER CHAPTER

It is very common for a Chapter 11 or Chapter 13 case to be converted to a Chapter 7 proceeding. Typically this occurs when it becomes apparent that the reorganization effort will fail for some reason. Much less commonly, a Chapter 7 proceeding is converted to a case under Chapter 11 or Chapter 13. A debtor in good faith apparently has the right to such a conversion if the case was not previously converted from one of those chapters to Chapter 7 and the debtor qualifies for relief under the chapter to which the case will be converted. *See* § 706(a), (d).

By far the most common situation in which the debtor seeks to convert a case from Chapter 7 to Chapter 11 or 13 is when the court has ruled that the Chapter 7 proceeding should be dismissed for cause under § 707 because the debtor fails the means test. In such cases, the court usually gives the debtor the option of dismissing the case or agreeing to a conversion, but the court need not always do so. A debtor who has acted in bad faith, such as by purposefully omitting or undervaluing assets on the bankruptcy schedules, has no right to convert to Chapter 13.[64]

A less common reason for converting arises when the bankruptcy case was commenced by an involuntary petition. Creditors filing an involuntary petition usually do so under Chapter 7. If the court enters the order for relief, the debtor may well exercise its right to convert the case to a reorganization and thereby remain in control of the estate assets. In fact, the debtor may convert the case prior to entry of the order for relief, in which case all issues surrounding whether relief should be granted become moot.

A debtor may also seek to convert after the bankruptcy court determines that a particular debt is nondischargeable in Chapter 7 but the debt would be dischargeable under another chapter of the Code.[65] The debtor may even seek to convert after receiving the discharge,[66] although that is fairly rare.[67]

---

[64] *Marrama v. Citizens Bank of Mass.*, 549 U.S. 365 (2007).

[65] This was more common prior to the 2005 amendments. Now, there are few debts that are nondischargeable in Chapter 7 but dischargeable in Chapter 13.

[66] *See, e.g.*, *In re Young*, 237 F.3d 1168 (10th Cir. 2001).

[67] In such a case, eligibility for relief under Chapter 13 is apparently determined from the date of the petition, not the date of the conversion. *In re Stern*, 266 B.R. 322 (Bankr. D. Md. 2001). Thus, the debtor cannot discharge debts in Chapter 7 so as to fall under the debt limitations for Chapter 13 eligibility, *see* § 109(e), and then convert the case.

PART II

THE BANKRUPTCY PROCESS

CHAPTER THREE
THE BANKRUPTCY ESTATE

At the moment a bankruptcy petition is filed, an "estate" is created by operation of law. It is as if a new corporation or trust had been formed and the debtor's assets deposited into it. Perhaps the best analogy is to a decedent's estate, which is created by law upon someone's death. Bankruptcy is essentially a financial demise, and filing a bankruptcy petition creates an estate consisting of all of the debtor's interests in property at the time the petition was filed.

A. PREPETITION PROPERTY INCLUDED IN THE ESTATE

Property of the estate is a deliberately expansive concept. Review § 541(a). It includes in the estate:

> (1) . . . all legal or equitable interests of the debtor in property as of the commencement of the case.

If a visual metaphor helps, we like to think of the estate as a vat into which the debtor's prepetition assets are poured:

As the empty space in the vat suggests, we will add to the vat as we explore more about bankruptcy. For now, though, it is important not to take the metaphor of assets as a liquid too literally. Some assets that are poured into the estate are quite illiquid – interests in real estate, for example – and selling them may be difficult, expensive, and time consuming. One of us used to own an undivided, one-quarter share of a remainder interest in some residential property (in which a stepmother resided and held a life estate). Try liquidating that!

The point is that, even when looking only at this single provision, the scope of the estate is broad. In another sense, however, this provision is also restrictive. If the debtor has a limited interest in a piece of property, then only that limited interest comes into the estate. For example, if the debtor is a lessee of a piece of property, only the debtor's leasehold comes into the estate, not the whole property. This of course makes sense. Inclusion of more would make being a landlord a risky and unprofitable business. Similarly, if the debtor has a lien on some item of property owned by another, then only the lien comes into the estate.

What if the debtor owns property subject to a lien? Consider the following case. In doing so, think about what rights in the property the debtor had the moment before the bankruptcy petition was filed.

UNITED STATES V. WHITING POOLS, INC.
462 U.S. 198 (1983)

Justice Blackmun delivered the opinion of the Court.

Promptly after the Internal Revenue Service (IRS or Service) seized respondent's property to satisfy a tax lien, respondent filed a petition for reorganization under the Bankruptcy Reform Act of 1978, hereinafter referred to as the "Bankruptcy Code." The issue before us is whether § 542(a) of that Code authorized the Bankruptcy Court to subject the IRS to a turnover order with respect to the seized property.

I

Respondent Whiting Pools, Inc., a corporation, sells, installs, and services swimming pools and related equipment and supplies. As of January 1981, Whiting owed approximately $92,000 in Federal Insurance Contribution Act taxes and federal taxes withheld from its employees, but had failed to respond to assessments and demands for payment by the IRS. As a consequence, a tax lien in that amount attached to all of Whiting's property.

On January 14, 1981, the Service seized Whiting's tangible personal property – equipment, vehicles, inventory, and office supplies – pursuant to the levy and distraint provision of the Internal Revenue Code of 1954. According to uncontroverted findings, the estimated liquidation value of the property seized was, at most, $35,000, but its estimated going-concern value in Whiting's hands was $162,876. The very next day, January 15, Whiting filed a petition for reorganization, under the Bankruptcy Code's

Chapter 11 in the United States Bankruptcy Court for the Western District of New York. Whiting was continued as debtor-in-possession.[1]

The United States, intending to proceed with a tax sale of the property, moved in the Bankruptcy Court for a declaration that the automatic stay provision of the Bankruptcy Code, § 362(a), is inapplicable to the IRS or, in the alternative, for relief from the stay. Whiting counterclaimed for an order requiring the Service to turn the seized property over to the bankruptcy estate pursuant to § 542(a) of the Bankruptcy Code. Whiting intended to use the property in its reorganized business.

The Bankruptcy Court determined that the IRS was bound by the automatic stay provision. Because it found that the seized property was essential to Whiting's reorganization effort, it refused to lift the stay. * * * [T]he court directed the IRS to turn the property over to Whiting on the condition that Whiting provide the Service with specified protection for its interests.

The United States District Court reversed, holding that a turnover order against the Service was not authorized by either § 542(a) or § 543(b)(1). The United States Court of Appeals for the Second Circuit, in turn, reversed the District Court. It held that a turnover order could issue against the Service under § 542(a), and it remanded the case for reconsideration of the adequacy of the Bankruptcy Court's protection conditions. The Court of Appeals acknowledged that its ruling was contrary to that reached by the United States Court of Appeals for the Fourth Circuit in *Cross Electric Co. v. United States*, 664 F.2d 1218 (1981), and noted confusion on the issue among bankruptcy and district courts. We granted certiorari to resolve this conflict in an important area of the law under the new Bankruptcy Code.

II

By virtue of its tax lien, the Service holds a secured interest in Whiting's property. We first examine whether § 542(a) of the Bankruptcy Code generally authorizes the turnover of a debtor's property seized by a secured creditor prior to the commencement of reorganization proceedings. Section 542(a) requires an entity in possession of "property that the trustee may use, sell, or lease under § 363" to deliver that property to the trustee. Subsections (b) and (c) of § 363 authorize the trustee to use, sell, or lease any "property of the estate," subject to certain conditions for the protection of creditors with an interest in the property. Section 541(a)(1) defines the "estate" as "comprised of all the following property, wherever located: (1) . . . all legal or equitable interests of

---

[1] With certain exceptions not relevant here, a debtor-in-possession, such as Whiting, performs the same functions as a trustee in a reorganization. § 1107(a).

the debtor in property as of the commencement of the case." Although these statutes could be read to limit the estate to those "interests of the debtor in property" at the time of the filing of the petition, we view them as a definition of what is included in the estate, rather than as a limitation.

In proceedings under the reorganization provisions of the Bankruptcy Code, a troubled enterprise may be restructured to enable it to operate successfully in the future. Until the business can be reorganized pursuant to a plan under §§ 1121–1129, the trustee or debtor-in-possession is authorized to manage the property of the estate and to continue the operation of the business. *See* § 1108. By permitting reorganization, Congress anticipated that the business would continue to provide jobs, to satisfy creditors' claims, and to produce a return for its owners. Congress presumed that the assets of the debtor would be more valuable if used in a rehabilitated business than if "sold for scrap." The reorganization effort would have small chance of success, however, if property essential to running the business were excluded from the estate. Thus, to facilitate the rehabilitation of the debtor's business, all the debtor's property must be included in the reorganization estate.

This authorization extends even to property of the estate in which a creditor has a secured interest. § 363(b), (c). Although Congress might have safeguarded the interests of secured creditors outright by excluding from the estate any property subject to a secured interest, it chose instead to include such property in the estate and to provide secured creditors with "adequate protection" for their interests. § 363(e). At the secured creditor's insistence, the bankruptcy court must place such limits or conditions on the trustee's power to sell, use, or lease property as are necessary to protect the creditor. The creditor with a secured interest in property included in the estate must look to this provision for protection, rather than to the nonbankruptcy remedy of possession.

Both the congressional goal of encouraging reorganizations and Congress' choice of methods to protect secured creditors suggest that Congress intended a broad range of property to be included in the estate.

The statutory language reflects this view of the scope of the estate. As noted above, § 541(a) provides that the "estate is comprised of all the following property, wherever located: . . . all legal or equitable interests of the debtor in property as of the commencement of the case." § 541(a)(1).[2] The House and Senate Reports on the

---

[2] Section 541(a)(1) speaks in terms of the debtor's "interests . . . in property," rather than property in which the debtor has an interest, but this choice of language was not meant to limit the expansive scope of the section. The legislative history indicates that Congress intended to exclude from the estate property of others in which the debtor had some minor interest such as a lien or bare legal title.

Bankruptcy Code indicate that § 541(a)(1)'s scope is broad. Most important, in the context of this case, § 541(a)(1) is intended to include in the estate any property made available to the estate by other provisions of the Bankruptcy Code. Several of these provisions bring into the estate property in which the debtor did not have a possessory interest at the time the bankruptcy proceedings commenced.[3]

Section 542(a) is such a provision. It requires an entity (other than a custodian) holding any property of the debtor that the trustee can use under § 363 to turn that property over to the trustee.[4] Given the broad scope of the reorganization estate, property of the debtor repossessed by a secured creditor falls within this rule, and therefore may be drawn into the estate. While there are explicit limitations on the reach of § 542(a), none requires that the debtor hold a possessory interest in the property at the commencement of the reorganization proceedings.

As does all bankruptcy law, § 542(a) modifies the procedural rights available to creditors to protect and satisfy their liens. In effect, § 542(a) grants to the estate a possessory interest in certain property of the debtor that was not held by the debtor at the commencement of reorganization proceedings.[5] The Bankruptcy Code provides secured

---

Cf. § 541(d) (property in which debtor holds legal but not equitable title, such as a mortgage in which debtor retained legal title to service or to supervise servicing of mortgage, becomes part of estate only to extent of legal title); 124 Cong. Rec. 33999 (1978) (remarks of Sen. DeConcini) (§ 541(d) "reiterates the general principle that where the debtor holds bare legal title without any equitable interest, . . . the estate acquires bare legal title without any equitable interest in the property"). Similar statements to the effect that § 541(a)(1) does not expand the rights of the debtor in the hands of the estate were made in the context of describing the principle that the estate succeeds to no more or greater causes of action against third parties than those held by the debtor. These statements do not limit the ability of a trustee to regain possession of property in which the debtor had equitable as well as legal title.

[3] *See, e.g.*, §§ 543, 547, and 548. These sections permit the trustee to demand the turnover of property that is in the possession of others if that possession is due to a custodial arrangement, § 543, to a preferential transfer, § 547, or to a fraudulent transfer, § 548.

[4] The House Report expressly includes property of the debtor recovered under § 542(a) in the estate: the estate includes "property recovered by the trustee under section 542 . . . , if the property recovered was merely out of the possession of the debtor, yet remained 'property of the debtor.'"

[5] Indeed, if this were not the effect, § 542(a) would be largely superfluous in light of § 541(a)(1). * * * The fact that § 542(a) grants the trustee greater rights than those held by the debtor prior to the filing of the petition is consistent with other provisions of the Bankruptcy Code that address the scope of the estate. *See, e.g.*, § 544 (trustee has rights of lien creditor); § 545 (trustee has power to avoid statutory liens); § 549 (trustee has power to avoid certain postpetition transactions).

creditors various rights, including the right to adequate protection, and these rights replace the protection afforded by possession.

This interpretation of § 542(a) is supported by the section's legislative history. Although the legislative reports are silent on the precise issue before us, the House and Senate hearings from which § 542(a) emerged provide guidance. Several witnesses at those hearings noted, without contradiction, the need for a provision authorizing the turnover of property of the debtor in the possession of secured creditors. Section 542(a) first appeared in the proposed legislation shortly after these hearings. The section remained unchanged through subsequent versions of the legislation.

Moreover, this interpretation of § 542 in the reorganization context is consistent with judicial precedent predating the Bankruptcy Code. Under Chapter X, the reorganization chapter of the Bankruptcy Act of 1878, the bankruptcy court could order the turnover of collateral in the hands of a secured creditor. Nothing in the legislative history evinces a congressional intent to depart from that practice. Any other interpretation of § 542(a) would deprive thc bankruptcy estate of the assets and property essential to its rehabilitation effort and thereby would frustrate the congressional purpose behind the reorganization provisions.[6]

We conclude that the reorganization estate includes property of the debtor that has been seized by a creditor prior to the filing of a petition for reorganization.

III

We see no reason why a different result should obtain when the IRS is the creditor. The Service is bound by § 542(a) to the same extent as any other secured creditor. * * *

Of course, if a tax levy or seizure transfers to the IRS ownership of the property seized, § 542(a) may not apply. The enforcement provisions of the Internal Revenue Code of 1954, 26 U.S.C. §§ 6321–6326, do grant to the Service powers to enforce its tax liens that are greater than those possessed by private secured creditors under state law. But those provisions do not transfer ownership of the property to the IRS.

The Service's interest in seized property is its lien on that property. The Internal Revenue Code's levy and seizure provisions, 26 U.S.C. §§ 6331 and 6332, are special procedural devices available to the IRS to protect and satisfy its liens, and are analogous to the remedies available to private secured creditors. *See* Uniform Commercial Code

---

6 Section 542(a) also governs turnovers in liquidation and individual adjustment of debt proceedings under Chapters 7 and 13 of the Bankruptcy Code. Our analysis in this case depends in part on the reorganization context in which the turnover order is sought. We express no view on the issue whether § 542(a) has the same broad effect in liquidation or adjustment of debt proceedings.

[§ 9-609]. They are provisional remedies that do not determine the Service's rights to the seized property, but merely bring the property into the Service's legal custody. At no point does the Service's interest in the property exceed the value of the lien. The IRS is obligated to return to the debtor any surplus from a sale. 26 U.S.C. § 6342(b). Ownership of the property is transferred only when the property is sold to a bona fide purchaser at a tax sale. In fact, the tax sale provision itself refers to the debtor as the owner of the property after the seizure but prior to the sale. Until such a sale takes place, the property remains the debtor's and thus is subject to the turnover requirement of § 542(a).

IV

When property seized prior to the filing of a petition is drawn into the Chapter 11 reorganization estate, the Service's tax lien is not dissolved; nor is its status as a secured creditor destroyed. The IRS, under § 363(e), remains entitled to adequate protection for its interests, to other rights enjoyed by secured creditors, and to the specific privileges accorded tax collectors. Section 542(a) simply requires the Service to seek protection of its interest according to the congressionally established bankruptcy procedures, rather than by withholding the seized property from the debtor's efforts to reorganize.

The judgment of the Court of Appeals is affirmed.

NOTE

The phrase "and by whomever held" was added to the end of the introductory paragraph of § 541 in 1984, in an apparent effort to codify the result in *Whiting Pools*. The Bankruptcy Amendments and Federal Judgeship Act of 1984, Pub. L. No. 98-353, § 456, 98 Stat. 333, 376. For a provocative analysis of whether *Whiting Pools* is still (or ever was) good law as a matter of policy, see Thomas E. Plank, *The Creditor in Possession Under the Bankruptcy Code: History, Text, and Policy*, 59 MD. L. REV. 253 (2000).

Whiting Pools dealt with what qualifies as a "legal or equitable interest[] of the debtor in property" under § 541(a)(1). Although the Court interpreted that language quite broadly, the fact remains that for something to become property of the estate, it must first of all be "property." Not every expectancy a debtor has qualifies as a property right. Consider a debtor who has season tickets to a professional sports team's home games. Teams routinely allow season ticket holders to buy season tickets for the next year, even though there may be quite a lengthy list of others who want season tickets. Is this expectancy a property right includable in the bankruptcy estate?

As is common in the bankruptcy arena, courts are split. Some have taken the position that the debtor's renewal option is just the expectation of receiving an offer, and thus is not a property right included in the estate.[7] Others have concluded that the debtor's option is property.[8] As is often the case, though, the split in authorities may be less a reflection of disagreement and more attributable to differences in the underlying facts or the applicable state property law. Remember, bankruptcy is built upon an edifice of state property and debt-collection law. Thus, there necessarily will be significant variations in how debtors from different jurisdictions are treated.

Moreover distinguishing property from nonproperty is often difficult. Consider a debtor's driver's license. It represents a valuable legal right, but one that is of no value to anyone else. It does not become property of the estate.[9] On the other hand, a liquor license, taxicab license, or other business permit may be property and thus become part of the estate.[10]

Now consider whether a restriction on transfer of the debtor's interest in property should be respected when the debtor files for bankruptcy protection. For example, assume a court determines that the debtor's prior purchase of tickets for a local team's current season gives the debtor a contractual right – rather than merely a hope – to buy season tickets for next year, and that this contractual right constitutes a legal or equitable interest in that property. Indeed, assume that the right to purchase tickets is a valuable one, something for which people without tickets would gladly pay. However, the agreement between the debtor and the ticket issuing entity expressly declares that the debtor's right to purchase those tickets is not transferrable and this restriction is enforceable under nonbankruptcy law. If that contractual restriction were respected, the bankruptcy estate – and, therefore, the debtor's creditors – would not be able to benefit

---

7 *E.g.*, *In re Harrell*, 73 F.3d 218 (9th Cir. 1996) (interest in Phoenix Suns season tickets not property of the estate); *In re Liebman*, 208 B.R. 38 (Bankr. N.D. Ill. 1997) (option to renew Chicago Bulls season tickets was not an interest in property).

8 *E.g.*, *In re I.D. Craig Servs. Corp.*, 138 B.R. 490 (Bankr. W.D. Pa. 1992) (renewal right to Pittsburgh Steelers season tickets is property of the estate).

9 *See, e.g.*, *In re Geiger*, 143 B.R. 30 (E.D. Pa. 1992), *aff'd*, 993 F.2d 224 (3d Cir. 1993).

10 *See, e.g.*, *In re Wheeler*, 431 B.R. 158 (N.D. Tex. 2005).

from this property right of the debtor. Indeed, crafty debtors, through careful contract drafting, might be able to shield much of their property from their creditors.

Now read § 541(c)(1). This is a remarkable provision. It overrides contractual and legal rules that prohibit the debtor from transferring particular property, to ensure that the estate acquires the debtor's rights in that property. It also overrides certain contractual provisions and legal rules that treat the debtor's insolvency or a bankruptcy filing as triggering a forfeiture. For example, if the debtor had a fee determinable in real property subject to a possibility of reverter triggered by bankruptcy, the debtor's bankruptcy would not in fact cause the debtor's fee interest to revert and it would instead pass to the bankruptcy estate. Be careful, though. While § 541(c)(1) renders restrictions on transfer and forfeiture-on-bankruptcy clauses unenforceable, it does not transform nonproperty into property. Whether something constitutes an interest in property at all is a separate, predicate issue determined by nonbankruptcy law.[11]

One anti-alienation restriction remains effective. Read § 541(c)(2).[12] This provision effectively excludes "spendthrift trusts" from the bankruptcy estate. A spendthrift trust is a device typically used to redistribute wealth within a family. Its purpose is to assure that the beneficiary will be the exclusive recipient of distributions from the trust. It does this by providing that the beneficiary's right to receive distributions cannot be voluntarily assigned or involuntarily transferred by judicial process to the beneficiary's creditors. This legal invention allows the beneficiary to continue to enjoy the fruits of the trust while the beneficiary's creditors go unpaid.

Bear in mind, however, that there is one widespread limitation on the efficacy of spendthrift trusts: most states do not permit a person to create a valid spendthrift trust for himself or herself (also known as a self-settled trust).[13]

---

[11] In a very interesting opinion, one court ruled that a deposit account containing prepetition contributions to the debtor's campaign for reelection as a state representative was property of the estate. *In re Chambers*, 451 B.R. 621 (Bankr. N.D. Ga. 2011). The court concluded that a state statute restricting how the funds could be used did not determine ownership of the funds.

[12] The § 541(c)(2) exclusion applies only to a beneficial interest in a trust. Thus, if the debtor has an asset – such as an annuity – that does not qualify as a trust, the asset will be included in the bankruptcy estate even if it contains a restriction on transfer. *Compare In re Laher*, 496 F.3d 279 (3d Cir. 2007) (debtor's annuity established through employer-sponsored retirement plan was a trust and debtor's interest was excluded under § 541(c)(2)), *with Hill v. Dobin*, 358 B.R. 130 (D.N.J. 2006) (annuities that were neither ERISA-qualified plans nor pension plans created and controlled by an employer were not trusts and debtor's interest was not excluded under § 541(c)(2)).

[13] *See, e.g.*, *In re Brown*, 303 F.3d 1261, 1266–67 (11th Cir. 2002) (based on Florida law); *see also* RESTATEMENT (SECOND) OF TRUSTS § 156(1) (1959); *In re Cutter*, 398 B.R. 6 (9th Cir. BAP 2008)

retirement plan is excluded

Although the legislative history of § 541(c)(2) indicates that it was aimed at spendthrift trusts, it is not so limited. One of the principal uses of this provision now is to exclude the debtor's retirement plan benefits from the bankruptcy estate. If the retirement plan is "ERISA-qualified" it will include a restriction on alienation. *See* 29 U.S.C. § 1056(d)(1); 26 U.S.C. § 401(a)(13). As a result, the debtor's interest in the plan will be excluded from the estate.[14] Note, most individual retirement plans (usually called IRAs) do not contain a restriction on alienation and thus are not excluded from the bankruptcy estate under § 541(c)(2).[15]

The bottom line on all of this is that most restrictions on alienation will not prevent the debtor's interest in property from becoming part of the bankruptcy estate, subject to the exception for the debtor's beneficial interest in the types of trusts specified in § 541(c)(2).

B. POSTPETITION PROPERTY INCLUDED IN THE ESTATE

Ch. 7 - postpet not include

The estate is comprised mainly of property rights that the debtor owns when the petition is filed. Property that the *debtor* acquires postpetition is generally excluded from the estate in a Chapter 7 case. In particular, earnings from services performed by an individual debtor after the commencement of a Chapter 7 case are not included in the estate, § 541(a)(6), although property that an individual debtor acquires after the commencement of the case and the individual's postpetition earnings are included in

---

(property contributed to self-settled Californian spendthrift trust was property of the debtor's estate).

At least seven states appear to permit self-settled spendthrift trusts. *See* ALASKA STAT. § 34.40.110; DEL. CODE ANN. tit. 12, §§ 3570–3573; NEV. REV. STAT. §§ 166.040–166.050; R.I. GEN. LAWS §§ 18-9.2-1–18-9.2-7; S.D. CODIFIED LAWS § 55-1-36; TENN. CODE ANN. §§ 35-16-101–35-16-112; UTAH CODE ANN. § 25-6-14. Colorado also permits self-settled spendthrift trusts but such a trust is void as against existing creditors. *See* COLO. REV. STAT. § 38-10-111. Section 548(e) permits the trustee to avoid transfers to a self-settled spendthrift trust within ten years prior to the bankruptcy filing if made with intent to hinder, delay, or defraud a creditor.

[14] *Patterson v. Shumate*, 504 U.S. 753 (1992). If the retirement plan's restriction on alienation is unenforceable (in which case plan will not be ERISA-qualified), then § 541(c)(2) will not apply. Employer-created 401(k) and 403(b) plans generally are ERISA-qualified.

[15] The debtor's interest in an IRA that has such a restriction is excluded from the estate under § 541(c)(2). *See, e.g.*, *In re Yuhas*, 104 F.3d 612 (3d Cir. 1997) (based on NJ law). Moreover, even if the debtor's interest in an IRA is initially included in the bankruptcy estate under § 541, that interest is likely to be exemptible. *See infra* chapter four.

Chapter 11 and Chapter 13 cases. §§ 1115, 1306. The remainder of this discussion regarding postpetition property included in the estate applies to Chapter 7 cases; we will revisit the property of the estate question in chapters eleven and twelve of this book when we consider Chapter 13 and Chapter 11 cases, respectively.

It is useful to think of two vats: one containing property of the estate and one containing property that remains the debtor's and is not part of the estate:

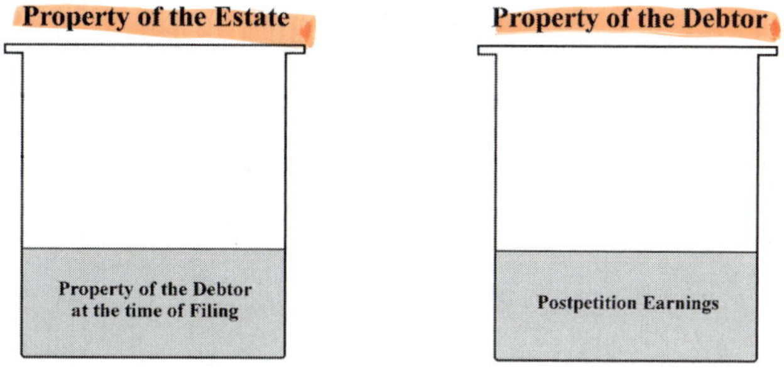

Certain rights arising postpetition are then added to the estate of all debtors. These include any interest in property that the *estate* acquires postpetition, § 541(a)(7), such as by the trustee avoiding certain prepetition transfers. *See* §§ 544, 548. They also include "[p]roceeds, products, offspring, rents, or profits of or from property of the estate." § 541(a)(6). Thus, if the estate includes some Microsoft stock, any stock dividends declared postpetition would be included in the estate. Similarly, if the trustee sells the stock, the sale proceeds are part of the estate.

There is one big exception to the distinction between what the *debtor* acquires postpetition and what the *estate* acquires postpetition. Read § 541(a)(5). This provision includes in the estate all property acquired by bequest, inheritance, settlement incident to divorce, or life insurance, to which the debtor becomes entitled within the 180 days after the petition date.[16] This provision prevents a debtor who expects to receive such an infusion of capital from strategically declaring bankruptcy and discharging debts shortly before acquiring the assets.[17]

---

[16] The debtor is required to disclose any receipt or entitlement to such property within 14 days of learning of it. Rule 1007(h).

[17] Note, however, the provision apparently does not reach property that a debtor may acquire by certain will substitutes, such as a right of survivorship. See *In re Hall*, 441 B.R. 680 (10th Cir. BAP 2009), in which the debtor's father passed away 18 days after the petition was filed. As a result, the debtor became entitled to receive: (a) certificates of deposit; (b) a one-fifth interest in certain real

Thus, at this point, our property of the estate vat looks like this:

Property of the Estate

C. PROPERTY EXCLUDED FROM THE ESTATE

1. *Property Held in Trust*

Read § 541(d). The application of § 541(c)(2) to spendthrift trusts is different from the application of § 541(d) to other trusts. Although both provisions effectively keep property out of the bankruptcy estate, they do so for different reasons and act on different types of property interests. A debtor whose interest in a spendthrift trust is kept out of the estate by § 541(c)(2) is the *beneficiary* of the trust. In contrast, § 541(d) keeps out of the estate any property in which the debtor has bare legal title but no equitable interest: in other words, trust property that the debtor administers as *trustee*. The underlying principle is fairly obvious: the trustee of a trust (if not also one of the beneficiaries) has legal title to the trust corpus merely to facilitate administration of the trust agreement. To nevertheless treat the trust corpus as property of the estate, thereby making it available to the debtor's creditors, would in essence require a defalcation and breach of the debtor's fiduciary duties. Moreover, it would do so when the creditors had no real expectation of going after trust assets and would seriously undermine the utility of trust arrangements by imposing a significant impediment to the use of individuals as

---

property; (c) United States bonds; and (d) an individual retirement account, all as a payable-on-death beneficiary or similar beneficiary designation. The court ruled that although "payable on death" designations for financial assets and transfer on death deeds are often used as will substitutes, the beneficiary does not acquire the property by "bequest, devise, or inheritance," the phrase used in § 541(a)(5). Accordingly, none of the property was included in the debtor's bankruptcy estate.

trustees. Accordingly, only the debtor's bare legal title, without any equitable interest, comes into the estate.

While the underlying principle is obvious, sometimes application of the rule is difficult. Consider, for example, a trustee who embezzles from the trust, say by using trust funds to buy assets for personal use. The trust certainly has a cause of action against the trustee for breach of a fiduciary duty. Less clear is whether the assets purchased with the embezzled funds will be included in the bankruptcy estate of the trustee. Nonbankruptcy law would likely impose a "constructive trust"[18] on all proceeds of the stolen funds to protect the victims of the theft. Should the proceeds therefore be excluded from the bankruptcy estate under § 541(d) and thus made available to the victims rather than to creditors? The intuitive answer to this question for most people is probably yes. However, what if the constructive trust arose in a different context? Consider an employee who embezzles money from an employer or a thief who steals money from people's homes, and who buys assets with the stolen loot. The law would likely impose a constructive trust in that situation too, but should the victim of the theft necessarily be preferred over other creditors of the criminal, bearing in mind that they may include other tort victims who cannot so readily trace down the proceeds of their property?[19] Put another way, how much should bankruptcy law respect this constructive trust remedy, given that it alters the bankruptcy priority and distribution scheme? Should it matter whether a court imposes the constructive trust prepetition or whether it is sought postpetition from the bankruptcy court?[20]

The use of constructive trusts in bankruptcy remains quite controversial.[21] Nevertheless, they continue to be recognized, even in favor of members of the debtor's

---

[18] In law, "constructive" is a euphemism for fictional.

[19] *See United States v. Andrews*, 530 F.3d 1232 (10th Cir. 2008) (analyzing the competing rights of fraud victims in request for constructive trust by some fraud victims); RESTATEMENT (THIRD) OF RESTITUTION AND UNJUST ENRICHMENT § 59(4) cmt. g (2011).

[20] *See In re Newpower*, 233 F.3d 922, 932 (6th Cir. 2000) (indicating that timing does matter); *In re Peregrine Fin. Grp., Inc.*, 487 B.R. 498 (Bankr. N.D. Ill. 2013) (no constructive trust exists under Illinois law until a court imposes it). *But cf.* RESTATEMENT (THIRD) OF RESTITUTION AND UNJUST ENRICHMENT § 55 cmt. e (2011) (a constructive trust exists from the moment of the transaction, not a judicial decree).

[21] *See* Andrew Kull, *Restitution in Bankruptcy: Reclamation and Constructive Trust*, 72 AM. BANKR. L.J. 265 (1998); Emily Sherwin, *Constructive Trusts in Bankruptcy*, 1989 U. ILL. L. REV. 297.

family.[22] Creditors seeking repayment – or defending against a preference action – are well advised to consider whether such an equitable remedy would be available outside of bankruptcy. If so, raising a trust argument may make the difference between no recovery and full recovery.

The same applies to statutory trusts. For example, in *In re Megafoods Stores, Inc.*,[23] the debtors operated a chain of grocery stores and, in the course of business, collected state and local sales taxes from their customers. The debtors then deposited the tax funds into their bank accounts, commingling those tax receipts with the proceeds from sales of merchandise. State law required the debtors to remit the collected taxes to the state monthly but, as of the petition date, the debtor had failed to do so for several months. The debtors claimed that their funds on deposit were estate property. The court concluded otherwise, based on a state statute that declared taxes so collected to be held in trust for the benefit of the state. It did not matter, the court ruled, that the debtor had commingled the collected taxes with other funds because the state had shown that, from the date of collection to the date of the petition, the debtors' deposit account balance never fell below the amount of the state's sales tax claims. In other words, the state traced the collected taxes to specific deposit accounts and then, using the "lowest intermediate balance rule" as a tracing principle, showed that the collected taxes remained in those deposit accounts. If, however, the state had been unable to trace the collected taxes to an extant deposit account or other asset, or had failed to timely raise the issue, it might have lost the benefit of the statutory trust.[24]

The rationale underlying the § 541(d) exclusion of assets that the debtor holds in trust for others also supports § 541(b)(7). That provision excludes from the estate wage deductions and employee contributions that are intended to be placed in employee benefit plans, deferred compensation plans, or other types of retirement plans. Once these funds are turned over to a plan administrator, they are likely to qualify as trust funds and therefore fall under the § 541(d) exclusion. Before then – that is, after they have been withheld from employees' pay but before they have been transferred to the plan administrator – they may not qualify as trust funds under nonbankruptcy law. This is particularly likely if the funds have not been segregated from the employer's other

---

22 *See, e.g., In re McDowell*, 258 B.R. 296 (Bankr. M.D. Ga. 2001).

23 163 F.3d 1063 (9th Cir. 1998).

24 *See, e.g., Ins. Co. of State of Penn. v. HSBC Bank of USA*, 882 N.E.2d 381 (N.Y. 2008). *But cf. Begier v. United States*, 496 U.S. 53 (1990) (by paying the IRS, the debtor identified the funds so remitted as the collected trust funds taxes, and no further tracing was required).

assets. Section 541(b)(7) apparently protects employees if either the employer or employee files for bankruptcy while such funds are in this state of limbo.[25]

2. *Certain Educational Savings*

In 2005, Congress decided to exclude from the bankruptcy estate funds contributed to educational IRAs and qualified state tuition programs (*e.g.*, 26 U.S.C. § 529 plans). *See* § 541(b)(5), (6). To qualify for the exclusion, the funds must have been contributed at least 365 days before the petition. Moreover, there is a $6,225[26] limit – calculated separately for each designated beneficiary – for funds contributed less than 720 days before the bankruptcy filing.

As a result of this exclusion, along with that for spendthrift trusts and interests in ERISA-qualified pension plans, the debtor's vat of assets is a bit larger than previously indicated. At this point, it can be depicted as follows:

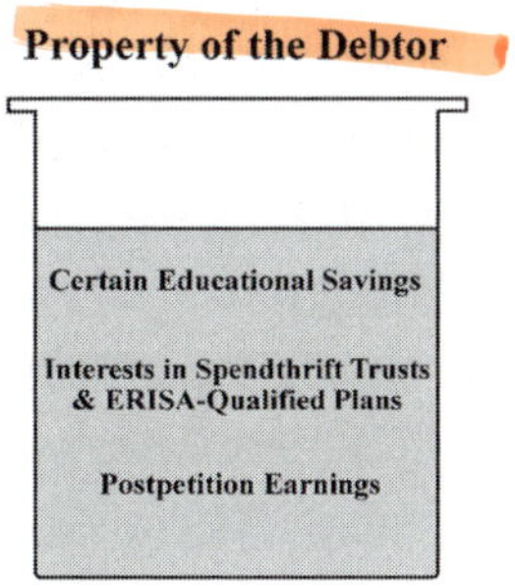

3. *Other Exclusions*

No single, coherent theory explains the other paragraphs of § 541(b). Instead, the various other exclusions from the bankruptcy estate for which § 541(b) provides appear

---

[25] This limbo could occur in a Chapter 7 if the employee filed after the funds are withheld, but before being transferred to the plan administrator. In a Chapter 13 proceeding, the debtor's postpetition earnings from personal services are included in the bankruptcy estate. § 1306(a)(2). On whether § 541(b)(7) excludes from the estate the amounts an employer withholds from the debtor's *postpetition* pay for contribution to an employee benefit plan or deferred compensation plan, see *In re Seafort*, 669 F.3d 662 (6th Cir. 2012) (discussing three approaches).

[26] This amount is subject to adjustment under § 104.

to represent successful lobbying efforts of various industries: real estate lessors, § 541(b)(2); the oil and gas industry, § 541(b)(4); pawnbrokers, § 541(b)(8); and money order sellers, § 541(b)(9). This is not the last time that we will see the intermixing of some statutory rules supported by a unifying rationale with others designed to benefit special interest groups.

D. Allocation Problems

Because the bankruptcy estate in a Chapter 7 case contains the property rights that the debtor had at the moment the bankruptcy petition was filed – but not most of the assets that the debtor acquires postpetition – it is occasionally necessary to determine when the debtor acquired certain rights. For most property rights this is not difficult. For example, it is easy to determine when the debtor bought a car or received a gift. For some property rights, particularly intangible rights, the determination is more difficult.

Consider, for example, a debtor who is employed at the minimum wage and paid weekly on Friday afternoons. The debtor files for bankruptcy protection at noon on Wednesday. At that time, the debtor had no immediate right to receive payment for the work already done that week. The debtor's right to payment for 2½ days had accrued but had not yet matured, given the nature of the employment relationship.

Nevertheless, it is fairly easy to see that when the debtor is paid on Friday, the payment is partially allocable to the prebankruptcy past and partially allocable to the postpetition period. Moreover, it is also easy to see that the allocation should be based on the proportion of the pay period that fell prepetition. Unfortunately, not all rights are so easily divisible into pre- and postbankruptcy periods. Nevertheless, because bankruptcy is by necessity a finite process that determines creditors' rights based upon the assets and rights that the debtor has at the time the bankruptcy petition is filed, allocations will have to be made.

1. Tax Refunds

Consider the following problem.

Debtor is employed at a salary of $2,000 per month. Debtor's employer withheld income tax at the rate of $400 per month. Debtor filed a Chapter 7 petition on August 1 and continued employment at the same salary and with

> the same withholding for the remainder of the year. Debtor filed a tax return in March of the following year. Debtor had no income other than the $24,000 in salary and therefore incurred income tax liability of $4,500. Since Debtor's employer has withheld $4,800, Debtor received a $300 tax refund in May. What part of the refund is property of the estate?

Some courts, perhaps most, simply allocate the refund based on the proportion of the taxable year that fell prepetition.[27] That may work adequately in a simple scenario, such as when income is earned, deductible expenditures are made, and taxes are withheld evenly over the tax year. However, in other cases it will be arbitrary. For this reason, some courts use a different approach when presented with evidence that an allocation based on the relative duration of the pre- and postpetition periods does not accurately reflect the portion of the refund attributable to those respective periods.

> "Pro rata by days" assumes that the value of a debtor taxpayer's legal or equitable interest in a tax refund increases more or less linearly over the course of the tax year. That assumption, in turn, rests on the further assumption that the debtor had a steady income during the tax year, had regular withholding of income taxes throughout the tax year, and had an interest in any refundable tax credits that grew regularly over the tax year. At least in the case of the Donnells, these assumptions are belied by the evidence presented by the Debtors. For example, Mr. Donnell's post-petition withholding was almost double the pre-petition amount, although he filed his bankruptcy petition in late May of his tax year. The record shows that all of Mrs. Donnell's "earned income" – an important figure in calculating the tax credits at issue in this case – occurred in the post-petition period. The inference that the value of these debtors' legal or equitable interest in their tax refunds grew linearly over the course of the year would thus, in this case, be error.[28]

---

[27] *See, e.g.*, *In re Meyers*, 616 F.3d 626 (7th Cir. 2010) (allocating a tax refund based on the portions of the taxable year falling pre- and postpetition is appropriate for debtors whose income and withholdings were fairly stable); *In re Montgomery*, 224 F.3d 1193 (10th Cir. 2000) (earned income tax credits are allocated proportionally over the tax year).

[28] *In re Donnell*, 357 B.R. 386, 396–97 (Bankr. W.D. Tex. 2006); *see also In re Christie*, 233 B.R. 110 (10th Cir. BAP 1999) (entire tax refund was property of the self-employed debtors who made no prepetition tax payments, only postpetition tax payments).

A different allocation problem may arise over the right to a tax refund if a married couple files a joint tax return but only one of them files for bankruptcy protection. In such a case, the court must ascertain the portion of the couple's total tax liability attributable to each and compare that to the tax payments that each of them made.[29]

2. *Contingent Rights*

Allocation becomes even more problematic when the debtor's rights are not only unmatured and unliquidated, but also contingent. When that is the case, there are often three interrelated issues for the court to confront. First is whether the contingency is so strong as to prevent the right from coming into the estate. A debtor may have a legal right as of the petition date to be recompensed for all future tort injuries the debtor suffers, but if no tort has yet occurred, there is nothing for the estate to administer. Put another way, is the contingency so strong that, as of the petition date, the debtor has merely an expectancy, rather than a property right?

In re Dittmar
618 F.3d 1199 (10th Cir. 2010)

Kelly, Circuit Judge.

[Debtors are employees of Spirit AeroSystems, Inc., which agreed to establish an equity participation program ("EPP") for employees and agreed to contribute stock appreciation rights ("SARs") to the program if certain "payment events" occurred. The SARs would expire in fifteen years if no payment event occurred. The collective bargaining agreement ("CBA") did not provide a detailed description of the EPP and did not define the term "participating employees." Prior to voting on the CBA, the union members attended a slide presentation discussing the EPP. The slides indicated that participants would be awarded options (approximately 1,000 options per employee); an option was a right to share in Payment Event profits on one share of stock. The value

---

[29] *See In re Palmer*, 449 B.R. 621 (Bankr. D. Mont. 2011) (collecting approaches); *In re Smith*, 2011 WL 345865 (Bankr. S.D. Ind. 2011) (spouses presumptively share equal ownership of a right to a tax refund, which may be rebutted only by evidence of a domestic relations court order or an enforceable, written, prepetition contract).

of the option would be determined upon a Payment Event with a participant ultimately receiving proceeds less the exercise price of the option.

Shortly after ratification of the CBA, Debtors filed their bankruptcy petition. More than a year later, Spirit memorialized the EPP in a document. The full plan document defined which employees were eligible to participate in the EPP, as well as the SARs each eligible employee would receive under the EPP. One month later, a payment event (an IPO) occurred. The SARs were worth $61,440 per employee. Participating employees received $34,556 in cash and 1,034 shares of Spirit Class A common stock.

The bankruptcy trustees filed motions to compel turnover of the distributions received from the SARs as property of the bankruptcy estate. The bankruptcy court denied turnover. A split panel of the BAP affirmed.]

Discussion

* * *

We first consider whether and to what extent Debtors have an interest in the SARs under Kansas law. We then consider whether that interest existed before Debtors filed their bankruptcy petitions. Finally, we turn to whether the SARs are property of the bankruptcy estate under § 541.

A. *Nature of Debtors' Interest*

Debtors' interest in the SARs is similar to an employee's interest in a stock option plan. Employees with stock options own contractual rights to purchase stock in the future that are subject to certain limitations of use and to the possibility of defeasance by later events. Such postponed enjoyment does not disqualify these interests as property. * * * That the EPP required a payment event as condition precedent does not alter this analysis.

Once Debtors satisfied the condition for being participating employees (completing ninety days of employment for the new company), they were eligible to participate in the EPP. These employees held contingent property rights. While the value of the SARs before any payment event occurred may have been de minimis, that does not mean that Debtors did not have a property interest in the SARs. The nature of that interest and whether it is legally recognizable is a different question than its valuation.

B. *Creation of the Property Right*

Trustees argue that the CBA, which was approved before Debtors filed for bankruptcy, created the SARs rights. Debtors counter that, if their interest is a property interest, it was not created until the EPP was memorialized – which did not occur until after the bankruptcy filings. The EPP provisions in the CBA indicate that the program applies to "participating employees," but "participating employees" was not defined within the CBA document. The bankruptcy court concluded that Debtors did not have an enforceable right until the EPP document defined which employees were "participating employees." Taking a different view, the BAP majority concluded that Debtors had a mere expectancy until the payment event occurred. We believe the key question is whether the EPP provisions in the CBA were merely "an agreement to agree" or whether they evidenced a binding agreement that would be formalized at a later date. If the latter is the case, Debtors' property rights were created at the time the CBA was ratified.

* * * While many of the EPP provisions are established in the CBA document, there are at least two ambiguities. First, the "agree to establish [an EPP]" language in the CBA is susceptible to two possible meanings: (1) it could indicate a present agreement with the understanding that formalization of the EPP will occur in the future; or (2) it could reflect an agreement not to be bound until the plan has been exccuted. In addition, the CBA does not define the term "participating employees."

The summary judgment record contains extrinsic evidence regarding the parties' intent. * * * This extrinsic evidence supports Trustees' position that the EPP terms were part of the CBA negotiations. Debtors have not offered evidence to the contrary. Accordingly, the evidence fully supports the contention that the CBA included a binding agreement about the EPP rather than "an agreement to agree" on the parameters of the EPP at some later point. * * *

C. *Property of the Bankruptcy Estate Under § 541*

Under federal law, the bankruptcy estate includes, with enumerated exceptions, "all legal or equitable interests of the debtor in property as of the commencement of the case." 11 U.S.C. § 541(a)(1). * * * Debtors argue that their interests were merely "the hope, anticipation, or expectation that in the event of a [payment] event, they would receive a share of the profits" because their interests were entirely dependent upon the economic decisions of Spirit. This suggests that a contingent interest cannot become property of the bankruptcy estate unless the contingency is entirely in the control of the interest holder. Such a rule amounts to nothing more than a statement that virtually no contingent interest can be property of the bankruptcy estate – a position that clearly conflicts with our precedent. As discussed above, Debtors' interest in the SARs is similar to an employee's interest in stock options. As long as the employee had a legal interest in the options prior to filing for bankruptcy, the options are sufficiently rooted in the pre-bankruptcy past to become part of the bankruptcy estate. That vesting of the options is contingent on a term of employment – a condition that is not exclusively within the employees' control – does not remove this pre-petition interest from the bankruptcy estate. *See, e.g., In re Wick*, 276 F.3d 412, 415 (8th Cir. 2002) (noting that unvested options contingent on continued employment are property of the estate because contingencies – even those that require additional post-petition services or those that may defeat the right to enjoyment of the property – do not bar a property interest from becoming part of the estate). Like stock options, the fact that the SARs are contingent on post-petition events does not mean that Debtors' interest in them is not rooted in the pre-bankruptcy past.

Neither the parties nor the courts below found any cases with similar facts. Instead they rely on contingent employee benefits cases where a program entitling the debtor to payment is in existence before the debtor files for bankruptcy and the eventual payment to the debtor is contingent on several factors, *e.g.*, employment for a certain amount of time or profitability of the company. These cases help illustrate when a contingent interest is rooted in the pre-bankruptcy past and when the interest is so speculative that it was a mere expectancy at the time the bankruptcy petition was filed.

One line of cases concludes that contingent interests are property of the bankruptcy estate even if the rights do not accrue or are uncertain until a date after the bankruptcy filing. [Under this line of cases,] contingencies like continued employment and company profit do not transform the employee's interest into a mere expectancy that is excluded from the bankruptcy estate when the interest is rooted in the pre-bankruptcy past.

The BAP majority cited a second line of cases where employee bonuses were excluded from the bankruptcy estate. * * * At bottom, this line of cases suggests that an employer's promise to pay a bonus is not enforceable where the employer reserves the right to withhold payment at its discretion. Thus, the employee had no right to the bonus at the time the bankruptcy petition was filed. Accordingly, the employee's interest in the bonus was a mere expectancy and should not be part of the bankruptcy estate.

We believe the SARs created by the CBA are more akin to the contingent pre-petition property rights described in the former line of cases than the mere expectancies based on discretionary bonuses described in the latter. Spirit had a contractual obligation to make payments if the IPO occurred. This obligation existed before Debtors filed for bankruptcy. Debtors' interest in the SARs are sufficiently rooted in the pre-bankruptcy past. The SARs are properly part of the bankruptcy estate under § 541.

Reversed.

HOLLOWAY, Circuit Judge, dissenting.

I respectfully dissent. I would affirm the judgment of the bankruptcy court. The Debtors' interests in the stock appreciation rights (SARs) were too uncertain to be included within their bankruptcy estates.

* * * The majority opinion outlines three steps for the analysis: first, whether the Debtors have a property interest in the SARs under Kansas law; second, whether the interest existed at the time the Debtors filed their petitions; and third, whether the property interests are property of the bankruptcy estate under 11 U.S.C. § 541. This seems to be correct, but applying the approach in this context presents a real challenge. * * * On the first question * * * I agree with the majority that the SARs at issue here are property rights under state law. * * * I [also] agree with the majority that the evidence showed that the property interests came into existence with the execution of the collective bargaining agreements and thus were in existence when the Debtors filed their petitions.

Were the Debtors' interests property of their bankruptcy estates?

The third and pivotal issue is whether the Debtors' property interests in the SARs became property of the bankruptcy estates. Analysis here must begin with the extremely broad language used by the Supreme Court and Congress to describe property of the estate. In a case under the Bankruptcy Act, the Court said that the bankruptcy estate includes "everything of value the bankrupt may possess . . . when he files his petition" and that an interest is not excluded "because it is novel or contingent or because enjoyment must be postponed." *Segal v. Rochelle*, 382 U.S. 375, 379 (1966). Our court and others have noted that Congress, in passing the Bankruptcy Code, specifically endorsed this language, so it remains valid.

As the majority opinion discusses, courts nevertheless have found that some property interests are too remote and speculative to be included in the bankruptcy estate. Significantly, the SARs in this case were subject to multiple contingencies and potentially to a very long period of uncertainty.

As the majority opinion notes, no cases have been cited or found that deal with facts closely analogous to those we deal with here. We are further hindered by the lack of analytical guidance offered by the cases. There does not appear to be even a framework to guide us as we contemplate the inherently inexact process of trying to determine what level of uncertainty must be present for a property interest to be outside the scope of section 541(a)(1), a scope that all agree is quite broad indeed.

* * *

One clear principle that should undergird our analysis is that the facts must be considered as of the date that the Debtors filed their petitions. The bankruptcy estate comprises "all legal or equitable interests of the debtor in property as of the commencement of the case." 11 U.S.C. § 541(a)(1). The trustee "succeeds only to the title and rights in property that the debtor had at the time she filed the bankruptcy petition." *In re Graves*, 609 F.3d 1153, 1156 (10th Cir. 2010). A second overriding policy is "that bankruptcy cases be handled in a speedy and expeditious manner." *Turney v. FDIC*, 18 F.3d 865, 869 (10th Cir. 1994).

The majority finds that cases involving annual employee bonuses have the most similar context and therefore provide some guidance for our task. As discussed in the majority opinion, a single factor appears to distinguish at least some of the cases holding that an employee bonus is property of the employee's bankruptcy estate from those holding the bonus is not property of the estate. That factor is whether the employer had discretion to withhold a bonus, even when all conditions attached to the bonus by that particular employer were satisfied.

The majority apparently accepts the reasoning of the courts which hold that employer discretion whether to grant an annual bonus or not may be decisive. The majority apparently concludes, however, that although discretion whether to award a benefit results in the benefit being outside the bankruptcy estate, discretion to control the conditions that activate the awarding of the benefit does not. I find the distinction unconvincing.

If employer discretion is to be the controlling factor, then I see no reason why the discretion vested in the employer here – which was absolute discretion to create or eschew creating the conditions that would lead to Debtors eventually receiving tangible benefits – should be an exception to such a rule. Moreover, this case can and should be decided without adopting the rule that employer discretion is controlling. * * *

In this case, the employer not only had discretion whether to initiate any "payment event" and thus activate its obligation to create the SARs, but its obligation was further conditioned on an arbitrary factor that the event first had to create at least fifteen percent annual profit for the initial investors. Further, and quite significant in my view, the employer here, unlike in the cases discussed by the majority and cited by the parties, retained the power to postpone its decision for up to fifteen years. Given the majority's apparent agreement with cases that hold that employer discretion either to pay or to withhold an annual bonus results in the benefit being outside the bankruptcy estate, one would expect that the benefit in this case, with its multiple contingencies and prolonged period of latency, would be an *a fortiori* case in which the SARs are outside the bankruptcy estates.

* * *

Viewing these Debtors' property rights in the SARs at the time of the commencement of their cases, and mindful of the policy mandating expeditious handling of the estates, I conclude that the SARs were properly held by both courts below to be outside the bankruptcy estates and so not subject to turnover to the Trustees.

Conclusion.

It is challenging to find the demarcation between contingent property interests that are properly included in the estate of a bankrupt and those that are so extremely novel or contingent that they are not so included. I conclude and would hold that the SARs at issue here were not part of the Debtors' estates because at the critical time that the petitions were filed by the Debtors, the interests were subject to multiple contingencies, including the likelihood that they would remain only contingent interests for some years post-petition. I therefore respectfully dissent.

NOTE

In *In re Klein-Swanson*, 488 B.R. 628 (8th Cir. BAP 2013), the debtor, a long-time employee of IBM, was eligible to receive bonuses under two IBM programs: (a) the Excellence Award and (b) the Growth Driven Profit ("GDP") program. The Excellence Award was a quarterly bonus program under which IBM was allocated funds for Excellence Awards to work teams. The team supervisor was then charged with deciding, based on each member's performance during the quarter, how much, if any, of the Excellence Award funds for the team would go to each member. The decision to make an award was entirely within IBM's discretion. GDP bonus payments were based on the "personal business commitment" of an employee and IBM's year-over-year profit and growth. The decision whether to make a GDP program payment was similarly in the complete discretion of IBM: the GDP program documents state that "[n]o employee earns or otherwise becomes entitled to payment, or any portion of a payment, under the GDP program prior to payment by IBM."

Shortly after the debtor filed her chapter 7 bankruptcy petition, the debtor received an Excellence Award in the amount of $8,000 and a GDP program payment of $16,072, both for work she had performed prepetition. The trustee sought to have those funds treated as property of the estate. The court ruled otherwise:

> As of the petition date, the Debtor had no interest (contingent or otherwise) in the payments from IBM because IBM had the absolute discretion to decide that it would not make an award to the Debtor under either of its programs. The Trustee asserts that the estate had a contingent interest in the bonuses because the Debtor's receipt of such bonuses came from the Debtor's prepetition services and IBM bonus programs that were in place prepetition. The Trustee also notes that the Debtor was eligible for the bonuses on the petition date. But IBM did not exercise its discretion to award the bonuses until postpetition and, as of the petition date, the Debtor had nothing more than a hope or expectation that she would receive the payments. The awards were made postpetition and they rightfully belong to the Debtor.
>
> According to the Trustee, the contingency that existed on the petition date was IBM's exercise of its discretion to make awards to the Debtor. But before IBM actually exercised its discretion postpetition, the Debtor had no interest in either bonus pool. Therefore, * * * on the petition date the Debtor * * * had a contingent interest in nothing.

Id. at *4.

The second issue relating to contingent rights arises if the debtor has a property right as of the petition date but the value of the right will be affected by the debtor's postpetition personal services. Recall that earnings from an individual debtor's postpetition services are expressly excluded from property of the estate in a Chapter 7 case. *See* § 541(a)(6). How is the right in such a case to be apportioned between the pre- and postpetition periods?

Consider the case of an employee whose employer routinely distributes significant bonuses at the end of each year. If the debtor truly has a right to the bonus – in other words, it is not a mere expectancy subject to the employer's discretion – most courts will include the prepetition portion in the estate. Making the allocation between the prepetition and postpetition periods is often simply a matter of calculating the percentage of the working year that fell before the petition and multiplying that number by the amount of the bonus. However, the allocation can sometimes be difficult, depending on how the amount of the bonus is calculated.

In *In re Ryerson*, 739 F.2d 1423 (9th Cir. 1984), for example, the debtor was a district manager at an insurance company. Pursuant to his employment agreement, the debtor was apparently entitled to a termination payment when his employment ended. The payment was to be in an amount equal to the service commission overwrite paid to Ryerson during the six months immediately preceding termination, times a factor determined by the number of years of service as district manager. Ryerson's employment terminated approximately ten months after his bankruptcy filing and he received a termination payment of $18,588.

The bulk of the court's opinion dealt with the contingent nature of Ryerson's right to a termination payment. No termination payment was due unless Ryerson had served at least one full year as district manager (he had served more than four as of the petition date), was in good standing on the date of his termination, and was not guilty of certain specified forms of misconduct. Ryerson argued that an unvested, contingent interest such as his is not includable within the bankruptcy estate if it cannot be transferred by the debtor or levied upon or otherwise reached by the debtor's creditors. The court rejected Ryerson's argument, noting that, in enacting the Bankruptcy Code, Congress expressly chose to alter prior law by including contingent rights in the estate.

Having concluded that Ryerson's right to the termination payment was property of the estate, the court then had no difficulty concluding that any payments paid upon termination were also property of the bankruptcy estate, "at least to the extent the payments are related to prebankruptcy services." *Id.* at 1425. However, that did not fully resolve the issue:

> Our ruling does not necessarily mean that all of the $18,588 is property of the bankruptcy estate. The Bankruptcy Appellate Panel determined that only the debtor's interest at the time of bankruptcy is property of the estate; any interest attributable to post-filing services was expressly excluded from the estate. We agree. Section 541(a)(6) excludes from the estate "earnings from services performed by an individual debtor after the commencement of the case." Thus any portion of the $18,588 related to services performed after [the petition date] are not includable within the bankruptcy estate.

Id. at 1426. The court remanded the case but offered no guidance on how the bankruptcy court should make the allocation.

QUESTION

How should the termination payment in *Ryerson* have been allocated between the pre- and postbankruptcy periods?

The third issue relating to contingent rights is a practical one: how is the trustee to extract value from that right? Consider the following case, which involved facts similar to those in *Ryerson*.

IN RE CLAY

241 B.R. 534 (Bankr. N.D. Tex. 1999)

Akard, Bankruptcy Judge.

Myrtle McDonald, the Trustee-in-Bankruptcy (Trustee) for Paul Clay and Mary Clay (Debtors), seeks to have Farmers Insurance Exchange, Truck Insurance Exchange, Fire Insurance Exchange, Mid-Century Insurance Company, Farmers New World Life Insurance Company, Texas Farmers Insurance, and Farmers Texas County Mutual (Companies) turn over to her the "Contract Value" of Mr. Clay's Agent Appointment Agreement (Agreement). She asserts that the Agreement is property of the bankruptcy estate under § 541 of the Bankruptcy Code and that the Contract Value should be turned over to her pursuant to § 542 of the Bankruptcy Code.

The court finds Contract Value to be part of an unassumable executory contract for personal services under § 365, and thus it is not property of the estate. The court further finds that although the Contract Value might have had value to the estate on the date of filing, any contingent interest the Trustee had in Contract Value expired twelve months following the Debtors' voluntary filing of their bankruptcy petition.

FACTS

Effective October 1, 1984, Mr. Clay entered into a Farmers Insurance Group of Companies Agent Appointment Agreement to serve as an insurance agent for the Companies in Pampa, Texas. On November 24, 1997, the Debtors filed for relief under Chapter 7 of the Bankruptcy Code. They scheduled $190,000 in Contract Value under the Agreement as an asset. The Debtors also scheduled an obligation to the Farmers Insurance Group Federal Credit Union (Credit Union) in the amount of $83,000 secured by a lien on the Contract Value. The schedules showed tax obligations of $137,523.40 and general unsecured debts of $15,024.57.

The Trustee did not assume the Agreement subsequent to the bankruptcy filing. Mr. Clay continued to operate as an agent for the Companies under the Agreement. Neither Mr. Clay nor the Companies terminated the Agreement.

AGREEMENT

The Agreement appointed Mr. Clay as an agent to sell policies issued by the Companies. The Companies agreed to pay him new business and service commissions in accordance with their established schedules, to give him training and advertising assistance, and to make group life and medical insurance available to him. Mr. Clay agreed to sell insurance for the Companies and to submit every request or application for insurance of the type provided by the Companies to them. Mr. Clay was to provide his own office as well as a fidelity bond. The Agreement could be terminated by the mutual consent of the parties or by either party on three months written notice.

Paragraph G of the Agreement provides that in the event of termination of the Agreement, the Companies will pay the Contract Value to Mr. Clay or his heirs, except in the case of embezzlement when there would be no payment. The Contract Value is based upon:

> (1) the amount of service commissions paid to the Agent on active policies during either the six month or twelve month period immediately preceding termination; (2) the number of policies in the Agent's active code number; (3) the number of years of continuous service as an Agent for the Companies immediately prior to termination.

The Agreement provides that if an agent has less than fifty policies in an active code number, there will be no Contract Value. Otherwise, the Contract Value will be computed for each company in accordance with a schedule contained in the Agreement.

* * *

POSITIONS OF THE PARTIES

The Trustee asserts that the Agreement is property of the estate under § 541 of the Bankruptcy Code and that the Contract Value (less the amounts owing to the Credit Union) should be paid to the Trustee under § 542 of the Bankruptcy Code. The Companies state that the Contract Value is neither a matured debt nor money owed to Mr. Clay. Thus, it is not subject to turnover under § 542 because it is neither property the Trustee may use, sell, or lease, nor is it property that the Debtor could exempt. The Companies filed a third party action against Mr. Clay asserting that the Trustee's action should be against Mr. Clay instead of against the Companies. Mr. Clay asserts that he has no entitlement to the Contract Value until the Agreement is terminated and that the Contract Value is in the nature of a trust for Mr. Clay's retirement.

ISSUE

The Agreement provides that the Contract Value is to be paid upon termination. The Trustee has no better rights under the Agreement than the Debtor. Consequently, the Trustee cannot force payment of the Contract Value as long as the Agreement remains in force. Therefore, the issue becomes whether the Trustee can terminate the Agreement in order to receive the Contract Value for the benefit of the creditors. The Debtor asserts that if the Agreement is terminated, he would not be given a new agent's appointment by the Companies because of his bankruptcy and the fact that he does not have a college degree. He asserts that the Companies are no longer appointing agents who do not have college degrees.

DISCUSSION

Property of the Estate

The court first determines whether the Agreement, and thus the Contract Value, is property of the estate. All legal and equitable interests of the debtor become property of the estate upon commencement of the case. § 541(a)(1). The Fifth Circuit, however, has stated that, "[u]nlike other assets of the debtor, the interest in an executory contract does not automatically vest in the bankruptcy estate at the time of filing." *In re Tonry*, 724 F.2d 467, 469 (5th Cir. 1984). An executory contract becomes part of the bankruptcy estate when the contract is assumed by the trustee. However, the executory contract is nonassumable if, under applicable law, any party other than the debtor may decline to accept performance by the trustee. § 365(c)(1)(A), (B). If an executory contract is nonassumable, and thus not part of the bankruptcy estate, it may still have value at the date of filing, measured on a quantum meruit basis of the services performed before the bankruptcy filing. *See In re Avery*, 947 F.2d 772, 774 (5th Cir. 1991).

The Agreement fits within the generally accepted definition of an executory contract which states "a contract under which the obligation of both the bankrupt and the other party to the contract are so far unperformed that the failure of either to complete performance would constitute a material breach excusing performance of the other." *In re Cajun Elec. Power Co-op., Inc.*, 230 B.R. 693, 702 (Bankr. M.D. La. 1999). In her trial brief, the Trustee also acknowledges that the Agreement is an executory contract for personal services and cannot be assumed. The Agreement, as an executory contract for personal services, is not part of the bankruptcy estate. However, the analysis does not stop there. Any amounts the Debtor earned under the contract prior to filing his petition are property of the estate. Therefore, the court must determine if Contract Value includes payment for any prepetition services rendered.

Contract Value Attributable to Fees Earned Prepetition

The personal service cases cited by the Trustee dealt with determinable amounts related to prepetition services. *See In re Kemp*, 52 F.3d 546, 554 (5th Cir. 1995) (prepetition earned income withheld by the employer is property of the estate); *In re Avery*, 947 F.2d at 774 (fees earned prepetition under an attorney's executory contracts are property of the estate); *In re Ryerson*, 739 F.2d 1423, 1425 (9th Cir. 1984) (fees related to prebankruptcy services paid through contact value received upon termination of position are property of the estate); *In re Tomer*, 128 B.R. 746, 762 (Bankr. S.D. Ill. 1991) (deferred commissions on prepetition policies are property of the estate). The most factually similar case cited by the Trustee, *Ryerson*, dealt with a trustee seeking turnover of the debtor's interest in "contract value." Ryerson was also an agent working under an agreement with Farmers Insurance. However, Ryerson terminated his agreement eight months after filing his Chapter 7 petition. The court held that any portion of the contract value relating to prepetition services was part of the bankruptcy estate and any postpetition services were not included in the estate. *Ryerson*, 739 F.2d at 1425–26.

Because Ryerson filed his bankruptcy petition within twelve months of termination, prepetition contract value could easily be determined. Contract value was calculated upon Ryerson's termination and Ryerson had a legal right to contract value at that point. The Agreement in this case has not been terminated.

The Agreement provides that the Contract Value is to be determined and paid upon termination and that no Contract Value exists if the agent either embezzles from the company or fails to have at least fifty policies in his active code number at the time of termination. The only way Contract Value can accurately be determined is through the calculation stated in the contract based on "either the six month or twelve month period *immediately preceding termination*" (emphasis added). Contract Value cannot be determined, and thus cannot come into quantifiable existence, until termination. Contract Value, therefore, cannot be apportioned between prepetition and postpetition services until the value is actually determined. If the Agreement were terminated within twelve months of the Clays' filing of their petition, Contract Value could be determined and a portion of that value would clearly be property of the estate. However, neither party to the contract has sought to do so. Both Mr. Clay and Farmers expressed their desire to continue, not terminate, the Agreement.

Forced Termination of the Contract

This court agrees with the conclusions of the *Groves* Court. *In re Groves*, 120 B.R. 956 (Bankr. N.D. Ill. 1990). Ms. Groves was required to make employee contributions to her retirement plan through mandatory wage deductions under her employment agreement with the state. Ms. Groves could only withdraw her contributions upon termination of employment or disability. After filing her Chapter 7 petition, the trustee filed an adversary proceeding to recover the contributions. *Id.* at 958. The court held that although the contributions were property of the estate, the court could not order turnover of the contributions while the debtor was still employed by the state. The court said:

> Nothing in the Bankruptcy Code or Rules gives the bankruptcy court the power to force the debtor to quit her job in order to mature her claim . . . for the benefit of the trustee. . . . It would be antithetical to the fresh start purpose of the Bankruptcy Code for this court to order the debtor to leave her employment. . . . By the same token, however, nothing in the Bankruptcy Code or Rules allows this court to rewrite the agreement between the debtor and [her employer].
>
> [T]he trustee has succeeded to exactly what the debtor had in terms of recovery . . . as of the date of the petition, *i.e.*, a contingent right to the return of the money in the event the debtor's employment by the state is terminated.

Id. at 965–66.

As discussed in *Groves*, a trustee has the same options as with any other property interest. The options are as follows: (1) keep the Chapter 7 case open and see if the contingent interest matures, *i.e.*, if the agreement is terminated within twelve months of filing, so that Contract Value could be determined; (2) sell the contingent right to Contract Value for whatever the market will bid; or, (3) if no buyer exists and it is unreasonably burdensome to keep the estate open, the trustee can seek an order authorizing her to abandon the contingent right.

The Clays filed their petition on November 24, 1997. Clearly, twelve months have passed without termination of the Agreement. Thus, the estimated value of $190,000 never matured into Contract Value that the Debtor could force Farmers to pay. Neither Mr. Clay nor the Trustee is entitled to payment of Contract Value at this time.

CONCLUSION

The court finds Contract Value is not property of the estate and any contingent interest the Trustee had in Contract Value expired twelve months following the Debtors' voluntary filing of their bankruptcy petition.

Problem 3-1

A. Two days after filing for bankruptcy protection, Diana wins $2,000,000 in the state lottery. She bought the ticket prepetition. Are the winnings property of the estate? What if she bought the ticket postpetition?

B. Danny, who is employed and paid $1,500 semi-monthly for the preceding half month, filed a Chapter 7 bankruptcy petition on May 8. On May 15, Danny received his regular paycheck from his employer. What portion, if any, of that amount is property of Danny's bankruptcy estate?

Problem 3-2

Pursuant to a prepetition divorce judgment, Dispirited was entitled to receive $1,500 in alimony and $1,000 in child support from Unreliable on the first of each month. When Dispirited filed for bankruptcy protection on May 28, Unreliable still owed Dispirited alimony and support for both April and May. Shortly after filing for bankruptcy, Unreliable sent Dispirited a check for $7,500, representing the alimony and support for April, May, and June. How much, if any, of the proceeds of that check constitutes property of the estate? Think about who benefits from receiving the past-due child support versus who benefits from receiving the past-due alimony.

Problem 3-3

For several years, Digitalis took a prescription drug for a chronic medical condition. The drug manufacturer removed the drug from the market two years ago. After filing a bankruptcy petition, Digitalis received notification of a class action against the drug manufacturer for concealment of risks associated with taking the drug. The notification also provided information about a proposed settlement of the action and indicated that, unless Digitalis opted out of the class, Digitalis would be entitled to $30,000 of the proposed settlement.

A. Is all or any portion of that settlement property of the estate? Consider whether the conduct giving rise to the cause of action is rooted in Digitalis's prepetition past or in his postpetition right to a recovery.

B. Does it matter if, under applicable state law, the statute of limitations does not begin to run until the debtor knows or should know about the cause of action? Think about whether the cause of action existed at the time of filing. *See In re Webb*, 482 B.R. 669 (Bankr. M.D. Ga.), *reconsidered*, 484 B.R. 501 (Bankr. M.D. Ga. 2012).

Problem 3-4

As part of her estate planning, Grandmother is contemplating putting $10 million in trust for her grandson, David. Because David is something of a spendthrift, Grandmother wants to limit David's current access to the funds. The most recent draft of the trust agreement provides that David will receive $10,000 each month from the trust's income but none of the remaining income and none of the corpus until David reaches the age of 50. The language she is contemplating does not create a spendthrift trust.

A. Before Grandmother signs the trust agreement, she wants to know what will happen if, after she signs it, David were eligible and filed for Chapter 7 bankruptcy protection. Specifically, what assets, if any, related to the trust would become part of the bankruptcy estate? In answering this, consider the different property in which David might have rights: (i) the trust corpus; (ii) future trust income; (iii) the remainder; and (iv) past distributions from the trust.
B. How would your answer to Part A change if Grandmother decides to create a spendthrift trust?
C. What bankruptcy implications would there be if the trust agreement provided that David was to get the corpus and remaining income upon Grandmother's death, rather than upon reaching the age of 50? *See* § 541(a)(5)(A).

Now consider this general counseling problem related to the debtor's assets that may be property of the estate:

Problem 3-5

You represent consumers who file for bankruptcy protection. For the most part, they do not come to you with a comprehensive list of their assets and liabilities. Because they file their bankruptcy schedules under penalty of perjury, you want to help them be sure to list all of their assets. Review the types of personal property listed on Form 6, Schedule B. What other types of personal property – particularly intangible property – will you specifically ask your clients if they own in an effort to jog their memories?

E. RECOVERED PROPERTY

Section 542(a) gives the trustee broad power to require any entity that possesses property of the estate to turn such property over to the trustee. Of course, as much of the reading so far illustrates, not all of the debtor's assets may be realty or tangible personal property. Some of it is likely to be intangible personal property not capable of possession, such as contract rights, bank deposits, or accounts receivable. Section 542(b) gives the trustee the power to require any entity that owes an obligation constituting property of the estate to make payment to the trustee.

Yet the trustee's powers extend well beyond these rights. Bankruptcy is an equitable proceeding. To do equity, it is occasionally necessary to reach back in time – to before the bankruptcy petition was filed – and recapture property that the debtor previously transferred away or which a creditor previously seized and make that recovered property available to creditors. Section 541 includes such recovered property in the estate. *See* §§ 541(a)(3), (4), 550, 551. In essence, these assets are poured into the vat comprising the estate:

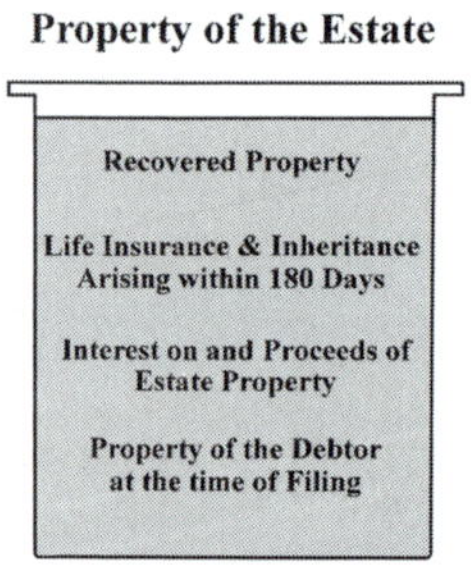

Two of the most important types of transfers that the bankruptcy trustee is empowered to avoid are preferences and fraudulent transfers. Both are discussed below. We will encounter other avoiding powers of the trustee and the debtor in chapter six.

1. Preferences

Outside of the bankruptcy process, debt collection from an insolvent debtor is a cross between a wedding banquet and a feeding frenzy. On the one hand, creditors whom the debtor favors – whether through familial affection or commercial need – are apt to receive a disproportionate share of the debtor's available assets. On the other hand, creditors who seek to compel payment through legal process or other means operate in a first-come, first-served world, where only those who diligently fight for a share of the debtor's wealth will get anything. In short, the ones who are fed from the debtor's wealth are those whom the debtor invites to the table and those pesky few who grab an uninvited chair. The patient creditors, those who try to accommodate the debtor but who do not become one of the debtor's favorites, are left hungry.

One of the principal tenets of bankruptcy is that the process should be fair to creditors. This normally means that, absent some policy warranting favored treatment for some claimants, creditors should share ratably in the debtor's available assets. Clearly, there is a tension between this tenet and prebankruptcy practice. If, shortly before bankruptcy, a debtor were permitted to pay a favored creditor or a shark-like creditor were able to extract payment, then the principle of creditor equality during bankruptcy would become meaningless. The bankruptcy estate might contain only the crumbs left after selected creditors had their fill.

Preference law is an attempt to deal with this problem. It is designed to undo certain prebankruptcy transactions that frustrate the bankruptcy distribution scheme. Thus, if the bankruptcy estate has only enough assets to pay unsecured creditors ten cents on the dollar, and shortly before bankruptcy the debtor paid one unsecured creditor in full, preference law would "avoid" the "transfer" and compel the creditor to return the money received. The formerly preferred creditor would then stand in line with the other unsecured creditors hoping for payment in the bankruptcy proceeding. In short, preference law is an effort to deal with the fact that the bankruptcy process occupies just a small part of the timeline of the debtor's financial affairs, and it allows the bankruptcy court to go back in time, to before the bankruptcy petition was filed, and unwind certain transactions that frustrate bankruptcy policy. The law puts the debtor and the unsecured creditor back in the relative positions they occupied before the avoidable transfer was made. Assets the debtor transferred are recovered, and the debt to the creditor that was paid is revived. In a few bankruptcy cases, the only significant assets in the estate are preference claims against certain creditors.

What has been written so far makes preference law seem reasonable and appropriate. That is because it was written from the bankruptcy lawyer's perspective (or perhaps from the unpaid creditor's perspective). From the preferred creditor's perspective, preferences are monstrous. The idea that, after a lawfully created debt has been properly paid, the creditor may have to disgorge the money seems to them preposterous. Why, they ask, should a diligent creditor who compelled payment have to return it so that slothful creditors may share in those assets?

A traditional response to this question notes that preference law encourages creditor restraint, which helps debtors with cash flow problems get through difficult times and thereby helps save businesses and jobs. You should question that response, however, for two reasons. First, it is far from clear that the economy truly benefits from creditor restraint. Perhaps the economy would benefit more if creditors diligently pursued their debtors and got money out of doomed enterprises and invested it in more productive uses. Unless and until empirical research can tell us which approach produces the most social utility, we should not jump to any conclusion. Second, it is not at all clear that preference law promotes creditor restraint. A diligent creditor who extracts a preferential payment may have to return the money, but otherwise suffers no penalty. In short, creditors have everything to gain by seeking payment (perhaps they will get it and get to keep it, either because the debtor never files for bankruptcy protection or does so after enough time has passed to insulate the payment from avoidance) and nothing to lose except the costs of enforcement, which may be fairly minimal.

Nevertheless, despite creditor criticism, preference law does further the bankruptcy policy of fair and equal treatment of creditors once the debtor files bankruptcy.

(a) The Six Elements

Section 547(b) outlines the elements of an avoidable preference. Each of the six elements listed below must be met in order for the trustee to recover the preference. They are:

(1) A transfer of an interest in the debtor's property – § 547(b)
(2) To or for the benefit of a creditor – § 547(b)(1)
(3) Made on account of an antecedent debt – § 547(b)(2)
(4) Made while the debtor was insolvent – § 547(b)(3)
(5) Made within the 90 days preceding the bankruptcy petition, or within one year if made to or for the benefit of an insider – § 547(b)(4)
(6) That enables the creditor to receive more than if the transfer had not been made and the debtor's assets were liquidated under Chapter 7 – § 547(b)(5).

The first thing to notice about these elements is that no particular state of mind is required for either the creditor or the debtor. In other words, there need be no intent to prefer or to be preferred. Because of this, there is no blame associated with making or receiving a transfer that later proves to be preferential. While that may seem strange, it is tempered, as we will see, by numerous affirmative defenses that insulate many ordinary transfers from avoidance.

Now for a closer look at each element.

(i) A Transfer of an Interest of the Debtor in Property

There are at least three things worth noting about this element. First, "transfer" is defined very broadly in § 101(54). It may be by any method, and may be direct or indirect, absolute or conditional, voluntary or involuntary. It does not matter, for example, whether the debtor pays the creditor by check or the creditor has the sheriff levy upon property pursuant to a writ of execution. Both are a type of transfer and are potentially avoidable as a preference.

Second, the transfer need not involve all of the rights to a particular piece of property; it need only concern "an interest . . . in property." Consequently, transferring an easement or life estate can be preferential. So too, as we will see in chapter six, can transferring a security interest.

Third, and most important, the interest in property transferred must have been the debtor's, not someone else's, interest in property. Consider the following hypothetical.

> To start up a new business, Debtor borrows money from Creditor. One of Debtor's relatives, Guarantor, guaranteed this obligation. The contract of guaranty allows Guarantor to seek reimbursement from Debtor for any payments Guarantor makes to Creditor on Debtor's behalf. Debtor later defaults on the obligation and Guarantor pays Creditor. Two weeks later, Debtor files for bankruptcy protection. May the bankruptcy trustee recover the payment from Creditor?

The answer is no. Because the payment was not made out of the debtor's property, the transfer is not avoidable. Does this make sense? Well, yes. Sure Creditor was preferred over Debtor's other creditors, but not out of assets that would have become part of the bankruptcy estate. All that happened when Guarantor paid Creditor, from the trustee's perspective, was that Guarantor was substituted for Creditor on Debtor's list of creditors, because normally a guarantor has a right to be reimbursed from the debtor for payments the guarantor makes to the debtor's creditors.[30] Debtor's total assets and total liabilities, however, remained unchanged. Put another way, none of Debtor's other creditors were affected. Perhaps this can best be illustrated by looking at Debtor's balance sheet.

---

30 *See* RESTATEMENT (THIRD) OF SURETYSHIP AND GUARANTY § 26 (1996).

Assume that before Guarantor's payment, Debtor had $20,000 in nonexempt assets and owed each of four entities, including Creditor, $10,000. Debtor's balance sheet might have looked like this:

Assets		**Liabilities**	
Various	$20,000	Creditor	$10,000
		Bank A	$10,000
		Bank B	$10,000
		Bank C	$10,000
Total	$20,000	Total	$40,000

Clearly, Debtor was insolvent because Debtor's liabilities exceeded assets and, if each claimant were entitled to the same priority (and assuming no costs of liquidation or distribution), each would expect to receive 50¢ on the dollar in bankruptcy.

After the payment by Guarantor, Creditor is no longer owed any money but, by virtue of the right of reimbursement, Guarantor is. Otherwise, everything else is the same. Debtor's balance sheet thus now looks like this:

Assets		**Liabilities**	
Various	$20,000	***Guarantor***	$10,000
		Bank A	$10,000
		Bank B	$10,000
		Bank C	$10,000
Total	$20,000	Total	$40,000

Debtor's other creditors – the three banks – were totally unaffected by Guarantor's payment to Creditor. Although Creditor received payment in full, the principle of creditor equality was not compromised because none of the other creditors was hurt. More significant, a contrary result would undermine the efficacy of guarantees and thus potentially have serious adverse consequences on the availability of credit in our economy. So, the transfer is not avoidable. Put another way: no harm, no foul.

One corollary to the requirement that the property transferred be the debtor's is the so-called "earmarking" doctrine. Suppose, shortly before bankruptcy, the debtor borrows money from A for the express purpose of paying a debt to B (perhaps because

A was willing to provide better credit terms). The debtor receives the funds from A and then transfers the funds to B. Certainly when the debtor receives the funds from A, they become the debtor's property. The "earmarking" doctrine[31] essentially treats the loan from A as never having been an asset of the debtor. It applies when: (1) there was an agreement between the new lender and the debtor that the funds would be used to pay a specified existing creditor; (2) that agreement was performed according to its terms; and (3) the transaction as a whole does not diminish the size of the estate.[32] Essentially, as long as the debtor's access to the funds is restricted, payment of the old creditor will not be avoidable.[33] Although criticized, the doctrine survives perhaps because an earmarked transaction is functionally the same as having the new lender deal directly with the old creditor, buying the old creditor's rights against the debtor. That certainly involves no asset of the debtor and is not an avoidable transfer.

(ii) To or for the Benefit of a Creditor

Only transfers that benefit creditors can be preferential. Giving assets away to friends, family, or charities cannot be preferential. Such transfers may be avoidable for other reasons – they may, for example, be fraudulent transfers, *see* § 548 – but only creditors can receive a preference. The term "creditor" is defined in § 101(10) and in critical part focuses on whether the person or entity has a claim against the debtor. "Claim" is defined in § 101(5) as a right to payment, regardless of whether payment is

---

[31] While no longer so limited, the doctrine arose out of cases in which the new creditor providing funds was itself obligated to pay the prior debt as a guarantor. In other words, the guarantor gave the debtor money with instructions to pay the creditor, which the debtor did. If the transfer to the creditor were avoided as preferential, the creditor would seek repayment from the guarantor, who would then have to pay a second time. This result was thought to be highly inequitable. *See In re Moses*, 256 B.R. 641, 645–47 (10th Cir. BAP 2000) (ruling that the doctrine should be limited to such co-debtor situations).

[32] *In re Winstar Commc'ns, Inc.*, 554 F.3d 382, 400 (3d Cir. 2009). Note, if the debt to the new creditor is secured and the debt paid off was not, then the estate has been diminished and the doctrine does not apply. *E.g.*, *In re Flanagan*, 503 F.3d 171 (2d Cir. 2007).

[33] *See, e.g.*, *In re Entringer Bakeries, Inc.*, 548 F.3d 344 (5th Cir. 2008) (earmarking doctrine did not insulate from avoidance as a preferential transfer a payoff of a bank with funds provided by a refinancing lender because the debtor had control of the funds before making the payment and because the debtor had never stipulated to the refinancing lender that it would use the funds to pay the bank).

currently due, the amount owed is liquidated or certain, or the creditor has a right to an equitable remedy.

Notice that this criteria provides that the transfer be "to" the creditor or "for the benefit of a creditor." Sometimes a transfer to one person may in fact benefit another person, as when a senior creditor's lien is paid off, allowing an undersecured junior creditor's lien to become fully secured. Such a transfer would be *to* the senior secured creditor but would preferentially *benefit* the junior undersecured creditor. Such a transfer would be an avoidable preference even if the senior creditor did not receive more than it would have in a Chapter 7, as long as the benefitted junior creditor stood to receive more on account of that transfer than it would have gotten in a Chapter 7 proceeding and the other elements of § 547(b) were satisfied. This aspect of preference law will be further discussed when we explore who has liability under § 550 for an avoidable preference.

(iii) On Account of an Antecedent Debt

The Code does not define what an "antecedent debt" is, but there is rarely any dispute over its meaning. All this requirement means is that the debt must have arisen prior to the preferential payment. For the most part, this element adds little to the previous requirement that the transfer be to or for the benefit of a creditor. If the transferee or the person benefitted qualified as a creditor, then there necessarily was a debt.

When does a debt arise? That is a question of nonbankruptcy law. Consider the following two examples:

1. A goes to a grocery store and selects an item for purchase. A brings it to the checkout counter and pays for it.
2. B contracts to buy goods. The contract calls for payment within 30 days after delivery. The goods are delivered and 28 days later B pays.

In the first example, there was no antecedent debt. Indeed, there was no contract at all until payment was made. Put another way, the debt was created and payment was made simultaneously. In contrast, the second example does involve an antecedent debt.

Although the obligation may not have matured, it did exist and predate the payment.[34] Indeed, in that fact pattern the creditor intended to extend credit.

This is not to say that there must have been a voluntary extension of credit for an antecedent debt to arise. Consider an accident between a driver and a bicyclist. Even if, immediately upon exiting the car, the driver hands the cyclist a check in settlement of any resulting injury claim, it would still be payment of an antecedent debt. An antecedent debt can also be contingent or disputed and still form the basis of an avoidable preference.

(iv) While Insolvent

The debtor is presumed to have been insolvent for the 90 days preceding the bankruptcy filing. § 547(f). Although the ultimate burden of proof on this point remains with the trustee, § 547(g), the preference defendant must produce some evidence to rebut the presumption before the trustee is required to address the issue.[35]

The Bankruptcy Code defines "insolvent" as a sum of all liabilities that exceeds the value of all nonexempt assets owned; in other words, as having a negative net worth after excluding any assets that the debtor, if an individual, may exempt.[36] § 101(32). This is an easy test to state, but often challenging to apply. Valuing assets is frequently difficult and subject to much speculation. Beyond that, there is not complete agreement on what the proper valuation standard should be. The Code requires a "fair" valuation, *see* § 101(32), but that vague standard leaves open the question of whether the assets should be valued at liquidation value, at replacement cost, as a going concern, or in some other manner. As we will see, such valuation problems permeate much of bankruptcy practice. They arise in many different contexts and often require different

---

[34] Unmatured debts are still debts and can create a valid claim. *See* § 101(5), (12).

[35] *See* S. REP. NO. 95-595, at 178–79; *In re Sierra Steel, Inc.*, 96 B.R. 275, 277 (9th Cir. BAP 1989).

[36] Note, this is different from the definition in the Uniform Commercial Code, under which either having a negative net worth (while still counting exempt assets) *or* not being able to pay debts as they become due makes a person insolvent. *See* U.C.C. § 1-201(b)(23). Under the Uniform Fraudulent Transfer Act, insolvency is defined as having liabilities that exceed assets, but a person not able to pay debts as they become due is presumed to be insolvent. UFTA § 2(a), (b).

answers. For preference purposes, however, the prevailing approach is aptly described in the following excerpt from *In re Dak Industries, Inc.*[37]

> To succeed in a preference action, a trustee must show, inter alia, that the debtor was insolvent at the time of the contested transaction.[38] § 547(b). The Bankruptcy Code defines insolvency, for a corporation, as a "financial condition such that the sum of such entity's debts is greater than all of such entity's property, at fair valuation." § 101(32). Although the Code does not define "fair valuation," courts have generally engaged in a two-step process of analysis. First, the court must determine whether a debtor was a "going concern" or was "on its deathbed." Second, the court must value the debtor's assets, depending on the status determined in the first part of the inquiry, and apply a simple balance sheet test to determine whether the debtor was solvent.[39] We agree that a "fair valuation" of a debtor's assets must begin with a determination of whether a debtor is "a going concern" and end with the application of a balance sheet test to determine solvency.

2 step process

Problem 3-6

Refer back to Edgar Systems, Inc. in Problem 2-2. Is Edgar Systems insolvent within the meaning of § 547(b)(3)? How should assets be valued for the purposes of analyzing preference actions? Does it matter under which chapter of the Bankruptcy Code the debtor is filing? *See In re Taxman Clothing Co.*, 905 F.2d 166 (7th Cir. 1990).

---

[37] 170 F.3d 1197, 1199–1200 (9th Cir. 1999).

[38] In general, the trustee in a preference action is entitled to rely on a presumption that the debtor was insolvent during the preference period. However, if a creditor produces some evidence that the debtor was solvent, as in this case, the trustee bears the burden of proof with respect to the debtor's insolvency.

[39] If the debtor was a going concern, the court will determine the fair market price of the debtor's assets as if they had been sold as a unit, in a prudent manner, and within a reasonable time. If the company was on its deathbed, *i.e.*, only nominally extant, then the court will determine the liquidation value of the assets, such as a price expected at a foreclosure sale.

(v) Made Within 90 Days (or One Year to an Insider)

One might think that this element is clear enough that there could be no issue about how it applies to any particular situation. Nevertheless, while this element is rarely contested, it has raised two interesting questions.

First, is the preference period to be calculated by counting forward from the date of the transfer or backward from the date of the petition? This actually can make a difference. Bankruptcy Rule 9006(a), which is based on Federal Rule of Civil Procedure 6(a), provides that the last day in any statutory period is not to be counted if it is a Saturday, Sunday, or legal holiday. Thus, if a petition were filed on a Friday, the 90th day before the petition was filed would be a Saturday. If the period is to be calculated by counting backward, the preference period would be extended to the previous Friday. If the period is to be calculated by counting forward from the date of the transfer, any petition filed on a Friday generates a preference period of 90 days. The majority of courts that have looked at the issue, including one circuit court, have ruled that the period is to be calculated by counting backward.[40]

Second, if the debtor pays an obligation by check, when does the transfer occur for the purpose of § 547(b)? Is it when the check is mailed, received, deposited, or paid by the drawee bank? This issue arises frequently and has made it all of the way to the Supreme Court, which ruled that the transfer occurs on the date the check is honored.[41] This probably makes sense because this date is (a) consistent with Article 3 of the Uniform Commercial Code; (b) easiest to prove; and (c) less subject to manipulation.[42] Note, however, this rule applies to regular checks. If the check is a cashier's check, the transfer occurs upon delivery.[43]

---

[40] *See In re Nelson Co.*, 959 F.2d 1260, 1266–67 (3d Cir. 1992). *But see In re Greene*, 223 F.3d 1064 (9th Cir. 2000) (ruling that § 547(b) is a substantive rule, not a procedural one, so that Rule 9006 is wholly inapplicable).

[41] *Barnhill v. Johnson*, 503 U.S. 393 (1992).

[42] Note, a different rule apparently applies for the purposes of § 547(c)(2) and (4). Courts have generally adopted a date-of-delivery rule for those preference defenses. *See, e.g., In re Wildwood Indus., Inc.*, 2012 WL 5246507 (Bankr. C.D. Ill. 2012) (collecting cases). On the other hand, courts have adopted the date-of-honor rule for § 549 purposes, dealing with postpetition transfers. *See, e.g., In re Oakwood Mkts., Inc.*, 203 F.3d 406 (6th Cir. 2000).

[43] *In re Lee*, 179 B.R. 149 (9th Cir. BAP 1995), *aff'd*, 108 F.3d 239 (9th Cir. 1997) (concluding delivery, not purchase, is the relevant time); *see also* U.C.C. § 3-310(a).

One other thing to note about this element is its interaction with the presumption of insolvency. Even if the preferred creditor is an insider, *see* § 101(31) (defining "insider"), so that a one-year preference period applies instead of the normal 90-day period, the presumption of insolvency created by § 547(f) extends only to the 90 days preceding the filing. Thus, if the trustee goes after an insider creditor for a transfer made more than 90 days but less than one year before the filing of the petition, no presumption of insolvency will apply.

(vi) That Enables a Creditor to Receive More

This element is the heart of preference actions. It requires proof that a creditor did in fact benefit by the transfer by receiving more than it otherwise would have if the debtor had not made the transfer and the debtor had filed Chapter 7. In most Chapter 7 liquidations, this is easy to determine, once the size of the estate and the priority of the various claimants is determined. In Chapter 11 or 13 cases, however, the court must determine what the creditor would have received had the allegedly preferential transfer not been made and the debtor had liquidated under Chapter 7. As should be apparent, that may be difficult to determine with any accuracy, because it presupposes a liquidation of the debtor's assets that is in fact not occurring. As a general rule of thumb, however, and regardless of what chapter a debtor has filed under, any payment by an insolvent debtor to a nonpriority, unsecured creditor will have preferential effect.

Problem 3-7

At the beginning of June, Dickinson had $6,000 in nonexempt assets and $10,000 in liabilities (none of which are priority claims in bankruptcy), of which $4,000 was owed to Cummings. During that month, Dickinson paid Cummings $2,000 in cash, with the understanding that the balance would be paid later. In July, before any additional payments were made, Dickinson filed for bankruptcy protection under Chapter 7, and at that time had $4,000 in nonexempt assets and $8,000 in liabilities.

A. May the trustee avoid the June payment to Cummings?

B. How, if at all, would the analysis in Part A change if Dickinson's debt to Cummings was guaranteed by Granger, who has ample assets?

(b) The Nine Defenses

Congress has given creditors nine affirmative defenses to preference actions. *See* § 547(c). For all such defenses, the creditor has the burden of proving their applicability. § 547(g). Three of these defenses, § 547(c)(3), (5) and (6), expressly relate to secured claims, and a fourth, § 547(c)(1), while not referencing secured claims, is in fact used almost exclusively by secured creditors. These four defenses will be covered in chapter six. The remaining five defenses are discussed below in increasing order of importance.

(i) De Minimis Transfers – § 547(c)(8) and (c)(9)

Section 547(c)(8) provides a defense for reasonably small consumer payments. Only if the aggregate value of all of the property transferred is worth $600 or more is the transfer avoidable.[44] Unfortunately, its wording is a bit ambiguous. Consider the following problem.

> Retailer obtained a $3,000 judgment against DeMinimis for failure to pay for several items DeMinimis purchased on credit. Retailer then obtained a writ of garnishment against DeMinimis's employer, who, over the next two months, made four $400 payments to Retailer pursuant to the writ (out of DeMinimis's wages). DeMinimis then filed for Chapter 7 bankruptcy protection and the trustee now seeks to recover the payments from Retailer. Are the payments avoidable?

The issue is whether the trustee is permitted to aggregate the separate transfers to the single creditor. The word "aggregate" strongly suggests yes but the use of the singular "transfer" suggests not. If aggregation is not permitted, a consumer debtor desirous of preferring a creditor could get around § 547(b) simply by making a series of transfers each of less than $600. Moreover, the terms "aggregate" and "all" in § 547(c)(8) would appear to be meaningless. Fortunately, the ambiguity is resolved by § 102(7), which provides that singular terms include the plural. As a result, courts have

---

[44] Note, this is *not* one of the Code's dollar amounts that adjusts with inflation. *See* § 104(b).

ruled that aggregation is permitted and, on the facts of the illustration, the payments to Retailer should be avoidable.[45]

The 2005 amendments to the Bankruptcy Code added a similar defense for nonconsumer transfers, albeit with a much higher dollar amount: $6,225.[46] While it suffers from the same ambiguity that § 547(c)(8) does, it protects a large number of business transfers from avoidance.

(ii) Spousal and Child Support Payments – § 547(c)(7)

This defense is one of many provisions of the Bankruptcy Code designed to protect domestic support claimants. The other protections for such claimants include: an exception from the discharge, § 523(a)(5); immunity from exemptions, § 522(c); and priority over other claimants, § 507(a)(1). The combined effect of these provisions is to encourage the debtor to make preferential payments of support obligations.

(iii) The Net Result Rule – § 547(c)(4)

Some businesses and even a few individuals have a revolving line of credit under which they are constantly making payments to and then borrowing more from the same creditor (often by repeatedly purchasing goods on credit). If there were no preference protection at all for such relationships, the creditor would run a severe risk if the debtor filed for bankruptcy: not only would the creditor stand to lose whatever amount the debtor owed on the date the bankruptcy petition was filed, but might also have to disgorge prior payments that had been followed by extensions of additional credit.

Consider the following example of a debtor who files for bankruptcy on July 21. At the end of April, the debtor owed a supplier $10,000 and then made the following

---

[45] *See In re Bay Area Glass, Inc.*, 454 B.R. 86 (9th Cir. BAP 2011); *In re Transcon. Refrigerated Lines, Inc.*, 438 B.R. 520 (Bankr. M.D. Pa. 2010) (both collecting cases).

[46] Originally $5,000 but adjusted periodically, *see* § 104. This defense was one of three recommendations made in 1997 by the National Bankruptcy Review Commission relating to preference actions that Congress adopted in 2005. The others were to expand the scope of the defense in § 547(c)(2) for transfers in the ordinary course of business and to amend 28 U.S.C. § 1409 to make the district of the preference defendant's residence the proper venue for any action against a noninsider to avoid a transfer of less than $10,000 on a nonconsumer debt. That amount has since been adjusted for inflation to $12,475. *See* § 104.

payments, followed by additional extensions of credit (noted in the column labeled "new value"):

Date	Payment	New Value
May 1	$10,000	
May 15		$11,000
June 1	$11,000	
June 15		$12,000
July 1	$12,000	
July 15		$13,000

Without the § 547(c)(4) defense, each of the three listed payments would be an avoidable preference. In addition, the supplier would potentially lose all or most of the $13,000 debt outstanding on the date the petition was filed. In sum, the supplier would stand to lose $46,000. In reality, however, the supplier may not have provided goods or services in May, June, or July had not the debtor made the payment listed two weeks before each new extension of credit. In other words, each payment the debtor made allowed the debtor to borrow again.

Section 547(c)(4) partially protects the supplier in this example by insulating from preference avoidance each payment *to the extent* it is followed by a subsequent grant of new value. The defense therefore "encourages creditors to continue their revolving credit arrangements with financially troubled debtors, potentially helping the debtor to avoid bankruptcy altogether."[47] Protecting such creditors is thought to be fair to other creditors of the debtor because the preferential payments are replenished by the preferred creditor's extension of new value.

Now try the following problem.

Problem 3-8

Which transfers are avoidable and to what extent if, within the preference period, the prepetition transactions were as follows, again assuming the debtor owed the creditor $10,000 at the end of April:

---

[47] *In re Toyota of Jefferson, Inc.*, 14 F.3d 1088 (5th Cir. 1994).

Date	Payment	New Value
May 1	$10,000	
May 15		$41,000
June 1	$20,000	
June 15	$10,000	
July 1		$5,000
July 15		$18,000

(iv) Payments in the Ordinary Course – § 547(c)(2)

The classic preference involves a privileged creditor – perhaps an insider – with knowledge of and influence over the affairs of the debtor who, seeing that the debtor is sinking into insolvency, obtains payment from the debtor before the debtor's financial problems become manifest. Indeed, § 60b of the old Bankruptcy Act made avoidable only those preferences received when the creditor had "reasonable cause to believe that the debtor [was] insolvent." Thus, only if the creditor was on notice that receipt of property from the debtor might prejudice the rights of other creditors could the transfer be avoided.

This notice requirement was excluded from the Bankruptcy Code because it was too difficult for trustees to prove. On the other hand, many, if not most, creditors paid shortly before a bankruptcy filing have not taken advantage of any special status that they have and indeed may not be aware that the debtor is in financial trouble. After all, most debtors in financial trouble try to hide their insolvency and often succeed for an extended period of time. Accordingly, some protection was thought necessary for creditors that did nothing out of the ordinary. This protection is codified in § 547(c)(2). ***Do not read this provision yet.*** It excepts from preference avoidance payments made in the ordinary course of business and it is by far the most important of the preference defenses.

Does this protection undermine the principle of creditor equality? Sure it does. Yet consider this. Normally, in the 90 days preceding bankruptcy, the debtor pays many unsecured debts of a recurring nature as they become due. An individual debtor, for example, pays utility bills and usually at least minimum payments on credit card balances. A business debtor normally purchases both inventory and the services of employees on terms that call for payment within reasonably short time frames, from seven days to as long as six months, and even an insolvent debtor may pay many of these obligations as they become due. Without the § 547(c)(2) defense, such payments would become avoidable preferences if the debtor were to go into bankruptcy less than three months later. Such a result may not be appropriate. After all, there are policy considerations in play in addition to creditor equality. One important goal of commercial law is certainty and finality in transactions. If large numbers of ordinary commercial transactions can be unwound in later legal proceedings, all transactions of that type might become more expensive as creditors charge for the increased risk or incur expense to minimize the risk. To put it simply, bankruptcy law should not impel the typical creditor—such as a utility company, supplier, or employee—to run a credit check every week or month, or to go through the hassle and expense of taking a security interest. Section 547(c)(2), by immunizing transfers made in the ordinary course of business, makes sure that most creditors do not need to take such precautions.

As currently phrased, the § 547(c)(2) defense requires proof of two elements, the second of which can be satisfied in either of two ways:

(1) The debt was incurred in the ordinary course of business or financial affairs of the debtor and the transferee; *and*

(2)(a) The payment was made in the ordinary course of business or financial affairs of the debtor and the transferee; *or*

(b) The payment was made according to ordinary business terms.[48]

Debt incurred in the ordinary course of the parties' business or financial affairs. Although there is some evidence that the § 547(c)(2) defense was designed, at least initially, to protect payments only on short-term trade debt,[49] the Supreme Court ruled

---

[48] The 2005 Amendments made the last two elements alternatives. Prior to that time, the creditor had to prove all three requirements to use this defense.

[49] As originally enacted, the provision created a defense to preference avoidance only for transfers "made not later than 45 days after such debt was incurred." This 45-day rule caused some problems because much short-term trade debt calls for payment beyond 45 days and because it is not always easy to determine when the debt was incurred. For example, suppose a debtor receives an invoice that covers a series of purchases of goods or services, as in the case of a telephone bill covering a series of long distance calls or a credit card bill covering a month of purchases. The debtor sends the creditor a check 25 days later. Some of the underlying charges covered by the bill were likely made more than 45 days before payment. If the debtor paid only a portion of the bill, which of the charges should the payment be deemed to have covered? In 1984, Congress addressed this problem by repealing the 45-day rule.

in 1991 that even long-term capital financing can be incurred in the ordinary course of the business or financial affairs of the lender and borrower.[50] In doing so, the Court gave short shrift to the argument that long-term capital financiers do not need the protection of § 547(c)(2) because their loans tend to be individually negotiated and documented – as well as secured – and thus any concern about adding to the cost of such transactions would not be applicable. As a result of the Court's decision, there is now rarely a dispute about this element of the defense.[51]

Payment made in the ordinary course of the parties' business or financial affairs. In a widely respected decision, *In re Craig Oil Co.*,[52] the Eleventh Circuit greatly restricted the § 547(c)(2) defense through its interpretation of the second element. In that case, one of the debtor's suppliers essentially threatened to join in filing an involuntary bankruptcy petition against the debtor after learning of the debtor's financial difficulties. The supplier requested financial statements and assurance of the debtor's "good faith," mentioning that some of the supplier's customers paid their bills by wire transfer. As a result of the supplier's conduct, the debtor began paying its bills to the supplier by cashier's check. The debtor continued to make payments even after it stopped making purchases from the supplier. When bankruptcy ensued, the trustee sued to recover the amount of 14 checks, alleging that they were avoidable preferences. The supplier asserted a § 547(c)(2) defense to this action. The bankruptcy court held that neither prong of what is now the second element of § 547(c)(2) was satisfied and the Eleventh Circuit affirmed.

The court quoted legislative history indicating that the purpose of § 547(c)(2) was to "leave undisturbed normal financial relations, because [it] does not detract from the general policy of the preference section to discourage unusual action by either the debtor or his creditor during the debtor's slide into bankruptcy."[53] The court then drew a distinction between "normal" debt collection and payment practices, which are protected

---

[50] *Union Bank v. Wolas*, 502 U.S. 151 (1991).

[51] Because long-term capital financing is something debtors may do only once, implicit in the Court's decision was the suggestion that a debt may be incurred in the ordinary course of business of both the debtor and the creditor even though the transaction giving rise to it was their first with each other. Lower courts have now expressly so ruled. *See, e.g.*, *In re Ahaza Sys., Inc.*, 482 F.3d 1118 (9th Cir. 2007).

[52] 785 F.2d 1563 (11th Cir. 1986).

[53] *Id.* at 1566.

by § 547(c)(2), and "unusual" practices, which are not. In this case, unusual collection efforts prompted the debtor's payments. The court also found that the payments were not made under normal conditions: the debtor made payment by cashier's check even though it had never done so before. Furthermore, it continued to make payments after it no longer needed the creditor's supplies and even though it had cash flow problems and was having difficulty paying other creditors. The court concluded that the debtor was favoring the supplier in order to ensure that the supplier would not join in an involuntary petition. This, the court reasoned, is precisely the type of preferential treatment at which § 547 is targeted.

Although the court in *Craig Oil* ruled that neither of the standards now codified in subparagraphs (A) and (B) of § 547(c)(2) was satisfied, it appeared to focus principally on (A): that the transfer be in the ordinary course of business or financial affairs of the two parties. It ruled that such a transfer must be consistent with the parties' long-standing relationship and not significantly deviate from the manner in which they have conducted business *with each other.*

Payment made according to ordinary business terms. Subparagraph (B) requires that the transfer be made according to ordinary business terms and thus be consistent with how the parties – and their competitors – deal with others. For many years, creditors feared that subparagraph (B) would be interpreted as requiring an expensive – perhaps unattainable – showing that there is some single, uniform set of industry-wide credit terms. Judge Posner alleviated those fears somewhat in 1993 in *In re Tolona Pizza Products Corp.*,[54] in which he wrote the following:

> the creditor must show that the payment he received was made in accordance with the ordinary business terms in the industry. But this does not mean that the creditor must establish the existence of some single, uniform set of business terms * * * . Not only is it difficult to identify the industry whose norm shall govern (is it, here, the sale of sausages to makers of pizza? The sale of sausages to anyone? The sale of anything to makers of pizza?), but there can be great variance in billing practices within an industry. Apparently there is in this industry, whatever exactly "this industry" is * * * . The law should not push businessmen to agree upon a single set of billing practices; antitrust objections to one side, the relevant business and financial

---

[54] 3 F.3d 1029 (7th Cir. 1993).

> considerations vary widely among firms on both the buying and the selling side of the market.
>
> We conclude that "ordinary business terms" refers to the *range* of terms that encompasses the practices in which firms similar in some general way to the creditor in question engage, and that only dealings so idiosyncratic as to fall outside that broad range should be deemed extraordinary and therefore outside the scope of [subparagraph (B)].[55]

Range of terms

This formulation, which has been adopted in almost every other circuit, gives § 547(c)(2)(B) some independent function without imposing an impossible burden on creditors. Moreover, several courts allow unusual practices to satisfy the standard if the practices were long-standing and predate the debtor's slide into bankruptcy.[56]

Nevertheless, even under this standard, creditors frequently have difficulty providing the requisite proof. This is often because evidence of industry practices – not merely of the debtor's practices with other creditors – is necessary to prove that payments were in the ordinary course of business, and sometimes competitors regard their credit practices as proprietary or, due to antitrust concerns, are unwilling to disclose them. Other times it is because the creditor's evidence is not directed at what the court determines to be the appropriate industry, or because the defendant's own personnel are the only ones testifying about what the industry standard is.

Problem 3-9

> Dependable Delivery entered into a written transportation agreement with Careful Carriers under which Careful agreed to pick up and deliver freight for Dependable in the geographical area Careful served. In exchange, Dependable was to pay Careful a percentage of the amounts it billed to shippers. The agreement provided that Dependable would make payment "on or before the 30th day after the shipment" had been delivered. The parties had operated under this agreement for two years, when Dependable filed a bankruptcy petition. In the 12 months preceding the 90 days before the filing of the

---

55 *Id.* at 1033.

56 *See, e.g., In re Molded Acoustical Prods., Inc.*, 18 F.3d 217, 225 (3d Cir. 1994) (suggesting that the longer the pre-insolvency relationship between the debtor and the creditor, the more the creditor will be allowed to vary its credit terms from the industry norm yet remain within the safe harbor of § 547(c)(2)(B)).

bankruptcy petition (the "preference period"), Careful received 259 checks from Dependable covering 720 invoices. Despite the 30-day payment requirement, Careful received these payments, on average, 62 days after the date of invoice. During the 90-day period, Dependable paid Careful $245,000 for services rendered under the agreement.

A. If the payments during the preference period were, like the ones prior to the period, generally made about 60 days after the invoice date, and thus after the 30-day contractual due date, do they nevertheless qualify for the § 547(c)(2) defense?

B. If the payments during the preference period were generally made about 28 days after the invoice date, and thus by the contractual due date, do they qualify for the § 547(c)(2) defense? *See Lovett v. St. Johnsbury Trucking*, 931 F.2d 494 (8th Cir. 1991).

C. If the payments during the preference period were generally made about 90 days after the invoice date, do they qualify for the § 547(c)(2) defense? *See In re Circuit City Stores, Inc.*, 479 B.R. 703 (Bankr. E.D. Va. 2012).

(c) Persons Liable

Section 547 by itself merely "avoids" a transfer. Another provision, § 550, imposes liability on the preferred creditor to return the property transferred or its value. Note, however, that the preferred creditor need not be the transferee. Recall that § 547(b) covers transfers "to *or for the benefit of* a creditor." Consider the following hypothetical:

> After passing the applicable examinations, Dentist wishes to begin a solo dental practice. To get the funds necessary to open an office, acquire the necessary tools and equipment, and advertise, Dentist wants to borrow $75,000 from Bank. Bank is willing, but only if Parents guaranty the debt. Parents do so and the loan is made. Dentist's practice flounders for a while. On May 1, while Dentist is insolvent, Dentist pays Bank $20,000, which is all of Dentist's available cash. Dentist then keeps other creditors at bay for a while, and files for bankruptcy on September 15th.

Although the Bank in this hypothetical received a transfer of the debtor's interest in property that enabled it to obtain more than it would have in a Chapter 7 proceeding, the transfer it received was outside the 90-day preference period and thus not normally avoidable. However, the payment also benefitted Parents by reducing their liability on the guaranty. Parents are creditors of Dentist because they have a common-law right to be reimbursed by Dentist for any payment they make to Bank on Dentist's behalf.[57] Because Parents are insiders of Dentist, *see* § 101(31)(A), a one-year preference period applies to any transfer to them or for their benefit. Thus, even though they did not receive the transfer, the transfer to Bank is nevertheless avoidable under § 547.

The interesting question is who is liable. Certainly Parents should be liable because they are the preferred creditors. And, in fact, § 550(a)(1) makes them liable; it expressly imposes liability on "the entity for whose benefit the transfer was made." Is Bank also liable? As originally enacted, § 550 seemed to say yes. That transfer is avoidable under § 547, and § 550(a)(1) makes the transferee of an avoidable transfer – in this case, Bank – liable. The Seventh Circuit confirmed this result in *Levit v. Ingersoll Rand Financial Corp.*[58]

The decision sent commercial lenders into a tizzy. They argued that it made lenders who received guarantees from an insider of the debtor worse off because it subjected them to the longer, one-year preference period. Congress addressed their concerns in the Bankruptcy Reform Act of 1994, which added § 550(c) to the Code to overrule *Levit*.[59] That amendment prevents the noninsider lender from being liable for a transfer to an insider made more than 90 days before the bankruptcy filing.[60]

It is important to understand what this amendment did not do, however. First, although the amendment overruled the result of *Levit* (with respect to transfers made more than 90 days before the filing), it did not overrule the decision's more basic observation that a transfer avoidable under § 547(b) because it benefitted one creditor could be recovered from a transferee, regardless of whether the transfer resulted in a preference as to that transferee. Thus, transfers within the 90-day period to a creditor

---

57 *See, e.g.*, RESTATEMENT (THIRD) OF SURETYSHIP AND GUARANTY § 22 (1996).

58 874 F.2d 1186 (7th Cir. 1989).

59 *See* Pub. L. No. 103-394, § 202, 108 Stat. 4106, 4121 (1994).

60 A more recent amendment further solidified this result by adding to the Code § 547(i), which makes the transfer avoidable only with respect to the insider. *See* Bankruptcy Abuse Prevention and Consumer Protection Act of 2005, Pub. L. No. 109-8, § 1213(a)(2), 119 Stat. 23, 194–95 (2005). This change was not necessary to insulate the noninsider from liability for prepetition payments but was necessary to insulate it from avoidance of other types of transfers, notably the grant of a lien on property of the debtor. How preference law affects security interests and secured claims is covered in chapter six.

that benefitted another creditor, either an insider or noninsider, are recoverable from the transferee.

Second, the amendment did not in any way lessen the preference liability of the insider guarantor. In short, nothing in the amendment altered the liability of Parents. Because of that, the amendment did not fully satisfy lenders who obtain guarantees. While it did insulate the transferees from preference attack for all transfers made to them more than 90 days before the filing (as long as the transferee was not an insider), it left their guarantors vulnerable to such attack, which could weaken the financial position of the guarantors. In other words, if prepetition transfers from Dentist to Bank preferred Parents yet, because Bank was not fully paid off, Parents still owed more money on the guaranty, Bank is effectively left competing with the bankruptcy estate for Parents' assets. To resolve this problem, some lenders require their guarantors to waive all rights to indemnification, contribution, and subrogation from the debtor. This prevents the guarantors from qualifying as "creditors" of the debtor, *see* § 101(10), and therefore any transfers either to them or for their benefit cannot be avoidable preferences.[61]

2. *Fraudulent Transfers*

An oft-quoted maxim of the law is that "a debtor must be just before being generous." The idea behind this maxim is that before the debtor gives property away, the debtor should provide for payment to the debtor's creditors. Since an insolvent debtor by definition cannot pay all creditors, insolvent debtors should not be permitted to make gifts while leaving their creditors without recourse. An insolvent debtor who does transfer property without getting reasonably equivalent value in exchange has made what the law refers to as a fraudulent transfer.

Fraudulent transfers are not limited to gifts or unequal exchanges. A debtor who makes a transfer in order to conceal assets or remove them from the jurisdiction in an effort to delay, hinder, or defraud one or more creditors has also made a fraudulent transfer. This is true even if the debtor received fair value for the property transferred.

In 1918, the National Conference of Commissioners on Uniform State Laws ("NCCUSL") promulgated the Uniform Fraudulent Conveyance Act ("UFCA"), later adopted by more than half of the states, to provide uniform rules on what constitutes a

---

[61] *Compare In re Valley Food Servs., LLC*, 2008 WL 5423495 (Bankr. W.D. Mo. 2008), *with In re Ne. Contracting Co.*, 187 B.R. 420 (Bankr. D. Conn. 1995). *But see In re USA Detergents, Inc.*, 418 B.R. 533 (Bankr. D. Del. 2009) (ruling that such a waiver is ineffective).

fraudulent transaction. The UFCA allows an aggrieved creditor to sue the recipient of a fraudulent transfer to rescind the transaction. In 1984, NCCUSL approved a new Uniform Fraudulent Transfer Act ("UFTA") to replace the UFCA. At present, 37 states and the District of Columbia have enacted the UFTA. Five others still have the UFCA and the remainder have nonuniform state statutes or common law that govern fraudulent transfers.

The most important provisions of the UFTA are § 4(a)(1), which covers transactions done with "actual intent to hinder, delay, or defraud" any creditor (sometimes called true fraudulent transfers), and § 5(a), which covers transfers for which an insolvent debtor received less than reasonably equivalent value (sometimes referred to as constructively fraudulent transfers). The former are avoidable by any creditor of the debtor, the latter only by those creditors whose claims arose before the transfer was made. A few more constructively fraudulent transfers are made avoidable by § 4(a)(2) by any creditor of the debtor. It covers transfers for which the debtor received less than reasonably equivalent value and, although not insolvent at the time, the debtor either: (i) was engaged in a business or transaction for which the debtor's remaining assets were unreasonably small or (ii) intended or should have reasonably believed that its debts were beyond its ability to pay as they came due.

These rules, or whatever analogous rules are in effect in a particular jurisdiction, are given effect in bankruptcy through § 544(b). However, when the bankruptcy trustee uses § 544(b) and state fraudulent transfer law to avoid a transfer, the trustee does so not merely for the benefit of the creditors who could have attacked the transfer, but for all creditors with allowable claims against the debtor. The import of this difference is that if a creditor was seeking to avoid a transfer under state law (outside the bankruptcy context), the creditor would not be able to avoid the transfer for more than the amount the debtor owes that creditor. For example, if the creditor was owed $100 and was seeking to avoid a transfer worth $500, the creditor could only do so to the extent of $100. *See* UFTA § 7(a). The bankruptcy trustee, however, is able to avoid the transfer to the full amount of the unsecured allowed claims of all of the debtor's creditors.

Aside from § 544(b), which authorizes the trustee to use state law to avoid certain transfers, § 548 of the Bankruptcy Code gives the trustee the express power to avoid certain fraudulent transfers made by the debtor. In fact, as the table after this paragraph shows, § 548 contains two sources of power for the trustee: § 548(a)(1)(A), an analog to UFTA § 4(a)(1), to avoid transfers made with the requisite fraudulent intent; and § 548(a)(1)(B), an analog to UFTA § 4(a)(2) and § 5(a), which covers constructively fraudulent transfers.[62] Perhaps the most critical difference between § 544(b) and § 548 is that § 548 covers only those transfers made within two years before the filing of the bankruptcy petition. In contrast, § 544(b), by implicitly referencing the UFTA, generally has a longer statute of limitations. Note, however, that these two restrictions measure different time frames. Section 548 deals with transfers made within two years before the filing of the bankruptcy petition,[63] while § 544(b) and the UFTA generally cover transfers made within the applicable time period prior to when suit is brought to rescind them.[64]

Avoidable Transfer	**UFTA** combined with § 544(b)	**Bankruptcy Code**
Made with actual intent to hinder, delay, or defraud	§§ 4(a)(1), 9(a)	§ 548(a)(1)(A)
Received less than reasonably equivalent value and engaged in business when undercapitalized	§§ 4(a)(2), 9(b)	§ 548(a)(1)(B)(i), (ii)(II)
Received less than reasonably equivalent value and incurred debts beyond ability to pay as they became due		§ 548(a)(1)(B)(i), (ii)(III)
Received less than reasonably equivalent value and was insolvent	§§ 5(a), 9(c)	§ 548(a)(1)(B)(i), (ii)(I)[65]

[62] Prior to June 1998, the bankruptcy provisions were numbered § 548(a)(1) and (2), respectively. They were renumbered as part of the Religious Liberty and Charitable Donation Protection Act of 1998. Pub. L. No. 105-183, 112 Stat. 517. Awareness of this renumbering is particularly important when reviewing cases that predate the change.

[63] Certain transfers to a self-settled trust are avoidable if made within ten years before the petition regardless of the fraudulent transfer criteria set forth in § 548(a). § 548(e)(1).

[64] UFTA § 9(a), (b) (four-year limitations period). States, however, may have enacted longer or shorter time periods.

[65] Under § 548, unsecured creditor's claim may arise before or after the fraudulent transfer.

Other than the different statutes of limitations, perhaps the most significant distinctions between § 548 and the combination of § 544(b) and the UFTA are in the defenses available to the transferee, as the following chart demonstrates.

<table>
<tr><th>Defenses</th><th>UFTA
combined with § 544(b)</th><th>Bankruptcy Code</th></tr>
<tr><td>Defense for good faith transferee of intentionally fraudulent transfer</td><td>Transfer unavoidable if reasonably equivalent value given, § 8(a)</td><td rowspan="2">Transferee protected to extent of value given, § 548(c), and for the lesser of the cost or value of any improvement, § 550(e)</td></tr>
<tr><td>Defense for good faith transferee of either intentionally or constructively fraudulent transfer</td><td>Liability adjusted as equities require, § 8(c), and transferee protected to extent of value given, § 8(d)</td></tr>
</table>

It is worth noting that the Federal Debt Collection Procedure Act is yet another source of law for avoiding fraudulent transfers, and it has in general a six-year limitations period, but applies only if the transferor is indebted to the federal government.[66]

(a) Actually Fraudulent Transfers

Proving intent to hinder, delay, or defraud can be difficult. After all, most debtors will not admit that they made the transfer with such intent. Typically, courts rely on objective but indirect evidence, usually referred to as "badges of fraud." These may include:

1. Transfers to a relative, close friend, or other insider.
2. Suspicious timing, such as immediately after a large adverse judgment.
3. Transfers on paper unaccompanied by an actual change of possession.
4. Transfers that put the debtor's assets in a foreign jurisdiction, particularly a jurisdiction that will make seizure through domestic judicial process difficult.
5. Secrecy.

Indeed, UFTA § 4(b) codifies these, as well as a few others, as badges of fraud.

---

66 *See* 28 U.S.C. §§ 3301–3308.

Problem 3-10

Deceitful, the defendant in a pending lawsuit, sold a parcel of real property to Buyer, who paid full market value of $100,000. Deceitful took the proceeds of the sale and deposited them in an out-of-state bank account under an assumed name. Shortly thereafter, the plaintiff obtained a judgment against Deceitful. Deceitful promptly filed a bankruptcy petition, before the plaintiff could take any action with respect to the real estate sale.

A. Assume Buyer had no knowledge of Deceitful's intentions at the time of the sale. The real estate is now worth $110,000.
   1. Can the trustee avoid the sale to Buyer under § 548 and, if so, what are Buyer's rights? *See* § 548(c).
   2. What would the result be under § 544(b) and the UFTA? *See* UFTA § 8.

B. How, if at all, would the answer to Part A differ if, during the sale negotiations, Deceitful had said to Buyer, "I hate to sell this property because I think it will go up in value, but I'm about to lose a lawsuit and I'd rather sell it now than lose it later"?

Problem 3-11

For several years, Devious operated a Ponzi scheme: an illegal pyramid investment scheme in which investors are promised a significant return on their investments, early investors are paid off with the funds provided by later investors, and much of the funds are syphoned off by the operator of the scheme. Ponzi schemes can appear to be legitimate and successful investment structures – in part because the early investors make money – but typically are insolvent from the outset and become more insolvent with every new investment because the promised return cannot be achieved.

On April 1, 2010, when Devious was just beginning his scheme, Investor transferred $100,000 to Devious in return for Devious's promise to pay back $200,000 two years later. On April 1, 2012, Devious dutifully paid Investor $200,000. Devious filed for bankruptcy protection on June 1, 2013. If Investor acted in good faith, what portion, if any, of the $200,000 payment to Investor can the trustee recover? *See* § 548(c); *Perkins v. Haines*, 661 F.3d 623 (11th Cir. 2011); *In re AFI Holding, Inc.*, 525 F.3d 700 (9th Cir. 2008).

One interesting problem involving what could be perceived to be a fraudulent transfer arises when an insolvent person disclaims a bequest or inheritance so that the property can go to a secondary legatee or heir – often a family member of the debtor – rather than to the debtor's creditors. Even though a disclaimer in this situation seems to fit easily into the type of transaction that fraudulent transfer law is intended to address, because state law typically requires that the property be distributed as if the debtor predeceased the decedent, most courts addressing the issue have concluded that the debtor never had rights in the property involved, merely an expectancy, and thus there is no transfer that can be avoided.[67]

(b) Constructively Fraudulent Transfers

Proving that a transfer is constructively fraudulent – that is, that the debtor was insolvent and received less than reasonably equivalent value – is typically much easier than proving a fraudulent transfer based upon an actual intent to hinder or delay creditors. If, as is often the case, no one disputes that the debtor was insolvent at the time of the transfer, even a very ordinary transfer can become avoidable.

Problem 3-12

A. Descendant recently completed schooling and has substantial debts for educational loans. As a result, Descendant is insolvent.
   1. In December, Descendant spent $25 to purchase and send to Grandmother a holiday gift. Is the purchase of the gift from the store an avoidable fraudulent transfer? Is the gift to Grandmother an avoidable fraudulent transfer?
   2. In January, Descendant purchased and gave to Child a new $115 parka. Child is a dependant of Descendant. Is the purchase of the parka from the store an avoidable fraudulent transfer? Is the gift to Child an avoidable fraudulent transfer?

---

[67] *See, e.g.*, *In re Laughlin*, 602 F.3d 417 (5th Cir. 2010) (discussing the cases). The analysis and result are different if the disclaimer is made postpetition because once the petition is filed, the trustee, not the debtor, is the party in interest in the probate proceeding and therefore the debtor lacks the authority to make the disclaimer. *See, e.g.*, *In re Schmidt*, 362 B.R. 318 (Bankr. W.D. Tex. 2007).

B. Stockholder owns all of the stock of Corporation, which operates a small construction company. Every year for the last two decades, Corporation has paid Stockholder a dividend of $1 per share.
   1. If Corporation is insolvent, would it be a fraudulent transfer for it to pay dividends this year?
   2. Stockholder wants to start a second business (not to be affiliated with Corporation) that will do landscaping work, and needs a loan from Bank to get that new business running. Bank demands collateral, so Stockholder has Corporation grant Bank a security interest in its construction equipment to secure Bank's loan to Stockholder. If that transaction leaves Corporation with inadequate capital to conduct its operations, would it be a fraudulent transfer?

C. Desperate's new business is undercapitalized and insolvent. Beyond that, there is insufficient cash on hand to make next week's payroll. Desperate takes the $2,000 in cash that is available and uses it to play blackjack at the nearest casino. Unfortunately, Desperate loses the whole $2,000. Can the trustee recover the money from the casino? *See In re Chomakos*, 69 F.3d 769 (6th Cir. 1995), *cert. denied*, 517 U.S. 1168 (1996).

Determining whether the debtor is insolvent for the purposes of fraudulent transfer law is much the same as for the purposes of preferential transfers. Accordingly, all of the issues about how to value the debtor's assets can arise in this context as well. Note, however, that unlike with preferences, there is no presumption of insolvency during the 90 days preceding the bankruptcy filing.

Often, the parties dispute whether what the debtor received was reasonably equivalent in value to what the debtor transferred away. Unfortunately, cases provide no set rule or clear guidance on how much or what percentage is reasonably equivalent. About the only predictions that can be made safely are that a gross disparity between the value of the item transferred and the value the debtor received helps support avoidance,[68] and that courts apply a totality of the circumstances approach.[69]

Reasonable equivalence is, of course, a fact to be determined at the time of the allegedly fraudulent transfer. However, courts and parties examining the issue often

---

[68] *See In re Lindell*, 334 B.R. 249 (Bankr. D. Minn. 2005) (payment of $50,000 for notes worth $130,000 was not reasonably equivalent value).

[69] *See, e.g.*, *ASARCO LLC v. Ams. Mining Corp.*, 396 B.R. 278 (S.D. Tex. 2008).

have the benefit of 20-20 hindsight. What may have looked like a fair deal at the time may, in retrospect, look unequal. Some courts do not hesitate to allow the use of subsequent events to demonstrate the gross nonequivalence of the bargain. In addition, some types of transactions routinely fail to yield fair market value and thus raise the specter of fraudulent transfer. Consider the Supreme Court's response to one of those typical transactions in the following case.

BFP v. RESOLUTION TRUST CORP.
511 U.S. 531 (1994)

Justice Scalia delivered the opinion of the Court.

This case presents the question whether the consideration received from a noncollusive, real estate mortgage foreclosure sale conducted in conformance with applicable state law conclusively satisfies the Bankruptcy Code's requirement that transfers of property by insolvent debtors within one year prior to the filing of a bankruptcy petition be in exchange for "a reasonably equivalent value." § 548(a)(2).

I

Petitioner BFP is a partnership, formed by Wayne and Marlene Pedersen and Russell Barton in 1987, for the purpose of buying a home in Newport Beach, California, from Sheldon and Ann Foreman. Petitioner took title subject to a first deed of trust in favor of Imperial Savings Association (Imperial)[70] to secure payment of a loan of $356,250 made to the Pedersens in connection with petitioner's acquisition of the home. Petitioner granted a second deed of trust to the Foremans as security for a $200,000 promissory note. Subsequently, Imperial, whose loan was not being serviced, entered a notice of default under the first deed of trust and scheduled a properly noticed foreclosure sale. The foreclosure proceedings were temporarily delayed by the filing of an involuntary bankruptcy petition on behalf of petitioner. After the dismissal of that petition in June 1989, Imperial's foreclosure proceeding was completed at a foreclosure sale on July 12, 1989. The home was purchased by respondent Paul Osborne for $433,000.

In October 1989, petitioner filed for bankruptcy under Chapter 11 of the Bankruptcy Code. Acting as a debtor in possession, petitioner filed a complaint in Bankruptcy Court seeking to set aside the conveyance of the home to respondent Osborne on the grounds

---

[70] Respondent Resolution Trust Corporation (RTC) acts in this case as receiver of Imperial. For convenience we refer to all respondents other than RTC and Imperial as the private respondents.

that the foreclosure sale constituted a fraudulent transfer under § 548 of the Code. Petitioner alleged that the home was actually worth over $725,000 at the time of the sale to Osborne. Acting on separate motions, the Bankruptcy Court dismissed the complaint as to the private respondents and granted summary judgment in favor of Imperial. The Bankruptcy Court found, inter alia, that the foreclosure sale had been conducted in compliance with California law and was neither collusive nor fraudulent. In an unpublished opinion, the District Court affirmed the Bankruptcy Court's granting of the private respondents' motion to dismiss. A divided bankruptcy appellate panel affirmed the Bankruptcy Court's entry of summary judgment for Imperial.

Applying the analysis set forth in *In re Madrid*, 21 B.R. 424 (9th Cir. BAP 1982), *affirmed on other grounds*, 725 F.2d 1197 (9th Cir.), *cert. denied*, 469 U.S. 833 (1984), the panel majority held that a "non-collusive and regularly conducted nonjudicial foreclosure sale . . . cannot be challenged as a fraudulent conveyance because the consideration received in such a sale establishes 'reasonably equivalent value' as a matter of law."

Petitioner sought review of both decisions in the Court of Appeals for the Ninth Circuit, which consolidated the appeals. The Court of Appeals affirmed. BFP filed a petition for certiorari, which we granted.

II

Section 548 of the Bankruptcy Code sets forth the powers of a trustee in bankruptcy (or, in a Chapter 11 case, a debtor in possession) to avoid fraudulent transfers. It permits to be set aside not only transfers infected by actual fraud but certain other transfers as well – so-called constructively fraudulent transfers. The constructive fraud provision at issue in this case applies to transfers by insolvent debtors. It permits avoidance if the trustee can establish (1) that the debtor had an interest in property; (2) that a transfer of that interest occurred within one year of the filing of the bankruptcy petition; (3) that the debtor was insolvent at the time of the transfer or became insolvent as a result thereof; and (4) that the debtor received "less than a reasonably equivalent value in exchange for such transfer." § 548(a)(2)(A). It is the last of these four elements that presents the issue in the case before us.

Section 548 applies to any "transfer," which includes "foreclosure of the debtor's equity of redemption." § 101(54). Of the three critical terms "reasonably equivalent value," only the last is defined: "value" means, for purposes of § 548, "property, or satisfaction or securing of a . . . debt of the debtor," § 548(d)(2)(A). The question presented here, therefore, is whether the amount of debt (to the first and second lienholders) satisfied at the foreclosure sale (a total of $433,000) is "reasonably equivalent" to the worth of the real estate conveyed. The Courts of Appeals have divided on the meaning of those undefined terms. In *Durrett v. Washington National Insurance Co.*, 621 F.2d 201 (1980), the Fifth Circuit, interpreting a provision of the old Bankruptcy Act analogous to § 548(a)(2), held that a foreclosure sale that yielded 57% of the property's fair market value could be set aside, and indicated in dicta that any such sale for less than 70% of fair market value should be invalidated. This "*Durrett* rule" has continued to be applied by some courts under § 548 of the new Bankruptcy Code. *See In re Littleton*, 888 F.2d 90, 92 n.5 (11th Cir. 1989). In *In re Bundles*, 856 F.2d 815, 820 (1988), the Seventh Circuit rejected the *Durrett* rule in favor of a case-by-case, "all facts and circumstances" approach to the question of reasonably equivalent value, with a *rebuttable* presumption that the foreclosure sale price is sufficient to withstand attack under § 548(a)(2). In this case the Ninth Circuit, agreeing with the Sixth Circuit, *see In re Winshall Settlor's Trust*, 758 F.2d 1136, 1139 (6th Cir. 1985), adopted the position first put forward in *Madrid* that the consideration received at a noncollusive, regularly conducted real estate foreclosure sale constitutes a reasonably equivalent value under § 548(a)(2)(A). The Court of Appeals acknowledged that it "necessarily part[ed] from the positions taken by the Fifth Circuit in *Durrett* . . . and the Seventh Circuit in *Bundles*."

In contrast to the approach adopted by the Ninth Circuit in the present case, both *Durrett* and *Bundles* refer to fair market value as the benchmark against which determination of reasonably equivalent value is to be measured. In the context of an otherwise lawful mortgage foreclosure sale of real estate,[71] such reference is in our opinion not consistent with the text of the Bankruptcy Code. The term "fair market value," though it is a well-established concept, does not appear in § 548. In contrast, § 522, dealing with a debtor's exemptions, specifically provides that, for purposes of that section, "'value' means fair market value as of the date of the filing of the petition." § 522(a)(2). * * * Section 548, on the other hand, seemingly goes out of its way to avoid that standard term. It might readily have said "received less than fair market value in exchange for such transfer or obligation," or perhaps "less than a reasonable equivalent of fair market value." Instead, it used the (as far as we are aware) entirely novel phrase "reasonably equivalent value." "[I]t is generally presumed that Congress acts intentionally and purposely when it includes particular language in one section of a statute but omits it in another," *Chicago v. Environmental Defense Fund*, 511 U.S. 328,

---

[71] We emphasize that our opinion today covers only mortgage foreclosures of real estate. The considerations bearing upon other foreclosures and forced sales (to satisfy tax liens, for example) may be different.

338 (1994), and that presumption is even stronger when the omission entails the replacement of standard legal terminology with a neologism. One must suspect the language means that fair market value cannot – or at least cannot *always* – be the benchmark.

That suspicion becomes a certitude when one considers that market value, as it is commonly understood, has no applicability in the forced-sale context; indeed, it is the very *antithesis* of forced-sale value. "The market value of . . . a piece of property is the price which it might be expected to bring if offered for sale in a fair market; not the price which might be obtained on a sale at public auction or a sale forced by the necessities of the owner, but such a price as would be fixed by negotiation and mutual agreement, after ample time to find a purchaser, as between a vendor who is willing (but not compelled) to sell and a purchaser who desires to buy but is not compelled to take the particular . . . piece of property." Black's Law Dictionary 971 (6th ed. 1990). In short, "fair market value" presumes market conditions that, by definition, simply do not obtain in the context of a forced sale.

Neither petitioner, petitioner's amici, nor any federal court adopting the *Durrett* or the *Bundles* analysis has come to grips with this glaring discrepancy between the factors relevant to an appraisal of a property's market value, on the one hand, and the strictures of the foreclosure process on the other. Market value cannot be the criterion of equivalence in the foreclosure-sale context. The language of § 548(a)(2)(A) ("received less than a reasonably equivalent value in exchange") requires judicial inquiry into whether the foreclosed property was sold for a price that approximated its worth at the time of sale. An appraiser's reconstruction of "fair market value" could show what similar property would be worth if it did not have to be sold within the time and manner strictures of state-prescribed foreclosure. But property that *must* be sold within those strictures is simply *worth less*. No one would pay as much to own such property as he would pay to own real estate that could be sold at leisure and pursuant to normal marketing techniques. And it is no more realistic to ignore that characteristic of the property (the fact that state foreclosure law permits the mortgagee to sell it at forced sale) than it is to ignore other price-affecting characteristics (such as the fact that state zoning law permits the owner of the neighboring lot to open a gas station). Absent a clear statutory requirement to the contrary, we must assume the validity of this state-law regulatory background and take due account of its effect. * * *

There is another artificially constructed criterion we might look to instead of "fair market price." One might judge there to be such a thing as a "reasonable" or "fair" forced-sale price. Such a conviction must lie behind the *Bundles* inquiry into whether the state foreclosure proceedings "were calculated . . . to return to the debtor-mortgagor his equity in the property." 856 F.2d at 824. And perhaps that is what the courts that follow the *Durrett* rule have in mind when they select 70% of fair market value as the outer limit of "reasonably equivalent value" for foreclosable property (we have no idea where else such an arbitrary percentage could have come from). The problem is that such judgments represent policy determinations that the Bankruptcy Code gives us no apparent authority to make. How closely the price received in a forced sale is likely to approximate fair market value depends upon the terms of the forced sale – how quickly it may be made, what sort of public notice must be given, etc. But the terms for foreclosure sale are not *standard*. They vary considerably from State to State, depending upon, among other things, how the particular State values the divergent interests of debtor and creditor. To specify a federal "reasonable" foreclosure-sale price is to extend federal bankruptcy law well beyond the traditional field of fraudulent transfers, into realms of policy where it has not ventured before. * * *

For the reasons described, we decline to read the phrase "reasonably equivalent value" in § 548(a)(2) to mean, in its application to mortgage foreclosure sales, either "fair market value" or "fair foreclosure price" (whether calculated as a percentage of fair market value or otherwise). We deem, as the law has always deemed, that a fair and proper price, or a "reasonably equivalent value," for foreclosed property, is the price in fact received at the foreclosure sale, so long as all the requirements of the State's foreclosure law have been complied with.

This conclusion does not render § 548(a)(2) superfluous, since the "reasonably equivalent value" criterion will continue to have independent meaning (ordinarily a meaning similar to fair market value) outside the foreclosure context. Indeed, § 548(a)(2) will even continue to be an exclusive means of invalidating some foreclosure sales. Although collusive foreclosure sales are likely subject to attack under § 548(a)(1), which authorizes the trustee to avoid transfers "made . . . with actual intent to hinder, delay, or defraud" creditors, that provision may not reach foreclosure sales that, while not intentionally fraudulent, nevertheless fail to comply with all governing state laws. Any irregularity in the conduct of the sale that would permit judicial invalidation of the sale under applicable state law deprives the sale price of its conclusive force under § 548(a)(2)(A), and the transfer may be avoided if the price received was not reasonably equivalent to the property's actual value at the time of the sale (which we think would be the price that would have been received if the foreclosure sale had proceeded according to law).

* * *

For the foregoing reasons, the judgment of the Court of Appeals for the Ninth Circuit is affirmed.

Justices Souter, Blackmun, Stevens, and Ginsburg dissented.

NOTES

1. *BFP v. Resolution Trust Corp.* applies only to § 548 actions, not to those brought under § 544(b) and the Uniform Fraudulent Transfer Act. However, UFTA § 3(b) expressly provides that a person who buys property at a "regularly conducted, noncollusive foreclosure sale or execution" gives reasonably equivalent value.

2. In a very interesting and somewhat controversial development, some bankruptcy courts have ruled that *BFP* does not apply to preference actions under § 547.[72] In one of those cases, a creditor with a lien securing a $70,000 debt foreclosed prepetition bought the property at the foreclosure sale for the amount of the debt. The property was worth in excess of $3 million. The court ruled that the foreclosure sale was an avoidable preference, noting that the issue in § 547(b)(5) is not whether the creditor provided reasonably equivalent value, merely whether it received "more" than what it would have received in a Chapter 7 liquidation. The decision raises the specter of using § 547 to unwind properly conducted foreclosure sales, provided the sale occurs in the preference period and the creditor is the buyer. If the buyer is not a creditor of the debtor, the benefit of the low price would not inure to or for the benefit of the creditor and § 547 would not apply.

Problem 3-13

Demonstrative is a motivational speaker who offers seminars to businesses and individuals. In prior years, Demonstrative's services were popular and generated a lot of income, most of which Demonstrative spent on a lavish lifestyle. More recently, the market for motivational speakers has dried up and Demonstrative has experienced a sharp drop in income. To make matters worse, a recent IRS audit revealed that Demonstrative had significantly

---

[72] *E.g.*, *In re Whittle Dev., Inc.*, 463 B.R. 796 (Bankr. N.D. Tex. 2011); *In re Villarreal*, 413 B.R. 633 (Bankr. S.D. Tex.), *appeal certified*, 2009 WL 2601298 (Bankr. S.D. Tex. 2009).

understated income for several years and, as a result, owed some $123,000 in back taxes and penalties. The IRS auditor informed Demonstrative that unless the tax liability were paid immediately, the auditor would recommend criminal prosecution.

Desperate for funds, Demonstrative sought to sell an impressionist painting for which Demonstrative had paid $70,000 two years ago and which an appraiser had recently valued at $80,000–$100,000. Demonstrative advertised the property for immediate sale and contacted some art dealers. Only two people responded. One expressed a willingness to pay $90,000 for it in about six weeks but was not willing to purchase at the current time. The other, Broker, offered to buy it immediately for $65,000 in cash. Demonstrative pleaded for more, but Broker said, "Your desperation is showing. Take it or leave it." Demonstrative reluctantly agreed and used the sale proceeds to pay the IRS.

Two months later, Broker resold the painting for $95,000 to Collector, who purchased in good faith. Three months after that, Demonstrative filed a Chapter 7 bankruptcy petition.

A. Can the bankruptcy trustee avoid the sale to Broker under § 548? If so, what rights does the trustee have against Broker and what rights against Collector? *See* § 550.
B. How, if at all, would the answer to these questions differ if the trustee used § 544(b) and the UFTA?
C. How, if at all, would the analysis in Part A change if, instead of filing for bankruptcy three months after Broker resold the painting, Demonstrative filed 18 months later. In the interim, the artist died, causing the painting to appreciate to $300,000?

Problem 3-14

Same facts as in Problem 3-13 except that Broker still owns the painting. In addition, Broker has spent $20,000 for restoration work on the painting, which at the time of Demonstrative's bankruptcy filing was worth $110,000. Assume that Broker purchased the property in good faith but that the transfer is nevertheless avoidable.

A. What may the trustee recover under § 548?
B. What may the trustee recover under § 544(b)?

Contributions to Religious and Charitable Organizations. In 1998, Congress somewhat curbed the scope of fraudulent transfer avoidance in bankruptcy. Consider the following hypothetical:

> Mr. & Mrs. Devout, while insolvent, contributed $12,000 (one-tenth of their annual income) to Church in the year preceding their Chapter 7 filing. The bankruptcy trustee sued Church to recover the money on the ground that it was fraudulent under § 548(a)(1)(B) because the Devouts did not receive reasonably equivalent value for their contributions. At no time did Church require the Devouts to pay a membership or attendance fee, or tie Church counseling services to donations. However, Church doctrine teaches that its members should tithe, that is, give one-tenth of their incomes annually.

Under classical fraudulent transfer principles, the transfers to Church were avoidable. Indeed, even though such tithing might be an expression of the Devouts' faith, the general maxim – that debtors must be just before they are generous – applies.

Throughout the 1990s, as the number of bankruptcy cases rose, fraudulent transfer actions against religious and charitable organizations significantly increased. Some of these organizations tried to defend against such claims by arguing that the donors did receive reasonably equivalent value: some tried to characterize the donor's tax deduction as value, others claimed that the spiritual counseling they provided constituted value, and some argued that the donations allowed the recipient to pay utilities and other expenses of operation, and the donors received the benefit of these while attending services. In general, though, none of these benefits to the donors, even if qualifying as "value," were really "in exchange for" the donation. Accordingly, most courts avoided these types of transfers.

Unhappy with this result, Congress passed, by a large bipartisan margin, the Religious Liberty and Charitable Donation Protection Act of 1998.[73] This Act amended both §§ 544 and 548 to define most charitable and religious donations as not being for less than reasonably equivalent value. It was a stunning reversal of hundreds of years of law. Under the new rules, debtors may contribute, without fear of later avoidance, up to 15% of their gross annual income – or more, if their practice has been to contribute more – to a religious or charitable organization. *See* §§ 548(a)(2), 544(b)(2); *see also* § 1325(b)(2) (permitting Chapter 13 debtors to continue to make such contributions).

---

[73] Pub. L. No. 105-183, 112 Stat. 517 (1998).

If these rules seem to give the debtor license to prefer religious and charitable organizations over the debtor's creditors, be aware that they are a defense only to avoidance of a constructively fraudulent transfer. That is, they exempt transfers to these organizations from avoidance for lack of reasonably equivalent value. If the debtor makes a donation with the intent to hinder, delay, or defraud a creditor, the donation is still avoidable.

Leveraged Buyouts. One common but nevertheless controversial use of fraudulent transfer law is to unwind a leveraged buyout. A typical leveraged buyout uses the assets of an acquired company (the "target") to secure the loans used by the acquiring company (usually a newly formed entity) to pay the purchase price to the shareholders of the target. This payment is immediately followed by a subsequent merger of the target into the acquiring company. The transaction often creates a burden on the resulting merged company that sends it into bankruptcy, leaving nothing for the unsecured creditors.

The potentially avoidable fraudulent transfers in such a transaction are: (i) the target's grant of a security interest in its assets, for which it received nothing in return; and (ii) the payments to the target's shareholders, who in effect used corporate assets to pay themselves ahead of the target's unsecured creditors. The payments to the shareholders – but not the target's grant of a security interest – may be insulated from avoidance by § 546(e), but whether it is or not remains controversial, especially if the target's stock was not publicly traded.[74]

3. *Preferences Redux*

Although § 544(b) is used most commonly to avoid fraudulent transfers, it is not in fact so limited. Indeed, its text does not expressly reference fraudulent transfers at all. Instead, it allows the trustee to avoid any transfer that a creditor with an unsecured claim could avoid. If applicable state law provides such creditors with an avoidance action different from a traditional fraudulent transfer action, then the trustee will have such additional rights.

In fact, several states have their own version of a preference avoidance action, such as UFTA § 5(b). Some of these have elements that are slightly different than those in § 547. For example, they may have a longer preference period, a longer statute of

---

[74] *See* Stephen E. Schilling, *Ambiguity and Bad Policy: Should § 546(e) of the Bankruptcy Code Be Applied to Leveraged Buyouts of Private Companies*?, 9 DEPAUL BUS. & COM. L.J. 471 (2011).

limitations, or fewer affirmative defenses. For that reason, trustees are well advised to consider whether state preference law may provide a remedy when § 547 would not.[75]

[75] *See, e.g.*, WASH. REV. CODE §§ 23.72.010–23.72.060 (providing that corporate transfers made any time within four months of the appointment of a receiver that enable the transferee to receive more than it otherwise would have can be avoided if the corporation was insolvent at the time of the transfer and if the transferee knew or had reasonable cause to know that the corporation was insolvent). *But cf. Sherwood Partners, Inc. v. Lycos, Inc.*, 394 F.3d 1198 (9th Cir.), *cert. denied*, 546 U.S. 927 (2005) (Bankruptcy Code preempts state law that gives the power to avoid preferences to an assignee for the benefit of creditors).

CHAPTER FOUR
EXEMPTIONS

The concept that certain property of individual debtors will be immune from attachment or execution through judicial process – *i.e.*, that it will be exempt from the reach of certain creditors – is not unique to American law and, in fact, has deep roots. The policy reasons underlying it are basic and threefold. One main purpose of exemptions is to make sure that people are able – and have the incentive – to be contributing members of society. Individual debtors may not be able to perform their jobs without the tools of their trades. Exempting such property helps to preserve their ability to earn a living. Protecting future wages ensures that individuals retain their incentive to continue working and to be productive members of society. Protecting retirement funds and disability payments helps prevent people from becoming public charges when their ability to maintain employment ceases. If the law permitted creditors to make their debtors destitute, and thereby a drain on the public purse, the law would effectively be creating a system that indirectly used public funds (assuming some level of a social safety net) to pay private debts.

Second, some property exemptions protect items of minimal or no value that would do little to satisfy obligations to creditors but may be costly or impossible for the debtor to replace. For example, used clothes, household goods, and family photographs may provide little recovery to a creditor that levies upon and sells them, far less than it would cost the debtor to replace them if the assets were, in fact, replaceable. Thus, protecting such assets serves a kind of utilitarian principle. Moreover, a creditor's threat to seize this type of property can lead a family to liquidate other assets, borrow from other people, or use other means to protect these items from creditors, even if that decision is not economically rational. To curb this leverage, most jurisdictions protect such personal property.

Finally, and for similar reasons, the law protects some property that may have value to creditors but to which the debtor has significant sentimental attachment. Creditor seizure of wedding bands, engagement rings, a household pet, and family heirlooms might leave the debtor emotionally destitute or lead to economically irrational decisions to protect such items from creditors. Accordingly, the exemption laws in most jurisdictions allow debtors to protect some such property, although particularly valuable items are often not exemptible.

Of course, none of these policies applies to corporations, partnerships, limited liability companies, or any other type of business entity. Accordingly, outside of bankruptcy, business entities generally cannot exempt property from their creditors. Inside the bankruptcy process, the law is the same: only individuals – human beings – are entitled to exemptions. *See* § 522(b)(1).

Outside of bankruptcy, exemptions protect the property from the debt collection processes described in chapter one. In other words, exempt property is immune from execution and garnishment, and from the judicial liens they create. Exemptions do not, however, shield property from statutory liens or consensual liens. Property that is otherwise exempt can still be encumbered by a statutory or consensual lien and any such lien properly created can be enforced. Thus, for example, if a debtor's homestead is otherwise exempt from execution process under the applicable state's law, that exemption does not protect the homestead from the lien created by a mortgage. The mortgagee may still foreclose on the mortgage and sell the homestead pursuant to the foreclosure process. Similarly, in most states a builder is entitled, by statute, to a mechanic's lien on any real property that the builder has improved to cover the unpaid price of the builder's services. This is true even if the property would otherwise be exempt from judicial process.

Inside of bankruptcy, exemptions operate a bit differently but with largely the same effect. In bankruptcy, exemptions operate to remove the exempt property from the bankruptcy estate. § 522(b)(1). Because the estate is used to pay unsecured creditors in Chapter 7 cases – and used to determine the minimum amount unsecured creditors must receive in Chapter 11 and 13 cases[1] – exempt property will not inure to the benefit of unsecured creditors in the bankruptcy process. Bear in mind, however, the act of exempting property in bankruptcy does not, by itself, affect any otherwise valid lien that has attached to the exempted property. As we will learn in chapter six, there are several bankruptcy provisions that a debtor or trustee may sometimes use to invalidate a lien. Some of these rules operate on exempt property, some on nonexempt property, and some on both. For now, though, you should assume that exempt property will be taken out of the estate, but that any otherwise valid lien on the exempt property will remain.

1 *See* §§ 1129(a)(7), 1325(a)(4).

A. STATE V. FEDERAL

It is important to remember that exemption laws exist outside of bankruptcy. Every state has exempted some property from attachment and execution by creditors. However, the type and value of property that each state has exempted varies significantly. In exercising its constitutional authority to establish "uniform laws on the subject of bankruptcy,"[2] Congress was presented with the difficult question of whether to create its own uniform list of exemptions to be used in bankruptcy proceedings or to allow debtors simply to avail themselves of their state's exemptions. It chose instead a third approach.

The Bankruptcy Code offers debtors a slate of federal exemptions, *see* § 522(d), but also allows *states* to "opt out" of that slate. *See* § 522(b). Through the opt-out mechanism, a state may preclude its own residents from using the federal exemptions when they file for bankruptcy.[3] Approximately two-thirds of the states have opted out of the federal slate of exemptions and therefore permit their citizens to claim only state exemptions. Residents of the remaining states may elect either the federal or state exemptions.

The result of this arrangement is that the exemptions available to individual debtors depend significantly on the state in which the debtor resides. Consider the chart of the various homestead exemptions, which is available on the book's web site, www.sepinuckruschbankruptcy.com. Although it deals with only one type of property – homes – it nevertheless illustrates the extreme variation in what states provide by way of exemptions. There is also great disparity in the types of other property that states permit a debtor to claim as exempt, as well as in the maximum amount of such exemptions. Query whether this level of variation is justifiable:

---

[2] U.S. CONST. art. I, § 8.

[3] Litigants have attacked this scheme as lacking the constitutionally mandated uniformity, as providing an impermissibly broad power delegation to state legislatures, and as a violation of the Supremacy Clause. However, the opt-out clause has survived such challenges. *See, e.g.*, *In re Storer*, 58 F.3d 1125 (6th Cir.) (the opt-out system does not violate Fifth Amendment due process or equal protection rights), *cert. denied*, 516 U.S. 990 (1995); *In re Sullivan*, 680 F.2d 1131 (7th Cir.) (rejecting impermissible delegation argument), *cert. denied*, 459 U.S. 992 (1982).

Several states have enacted bankruptcy-only exemptions statutes: statutes that provide exemptions only to debtors in bankruptcy that are different from the exemptions available to judgment debtors generally. Most courts to address the issue have held that these statutes survive constitutional attack. *See, e.g.*, *In re Schafer*, 689 F.3d 601 (6th Cir.), *cert. denied*, 133 S. Ct. 1244 (2012).

> It arguably would be reasonable to use state law exemptions if they reflected regional variations in cost of living or property use, but they do not. A comparison of state homestead exemptions and the relative cost of living reveals that state homestead exemptions do not reflect a relative cost of living assessment. For example, in 1991, Rhode Island had the fifth highest median home value in the country and yet had a homestead exemption of zero; conversely, Iowa had the third lowest home value in the nation and had an unlimited homestead exemption. No regional cost variation explains why California has very generous exemption laws while New York does not. The lack of rationale extends to personal property as well. For example, compare three states in which a reasonable car might be equally necessary to commute to work: Kansas permits its citizens to exempt up to $20,000 in a vehicle while Missouri exempts only $1,000, and, until recently, Nebraska had no automobile exemption at all.
>
> * * * Debtors with roughly equivalent economic profiles and similar property are receiving vastly dissimilar treatment through the federal bankruptcy system, and correspondingly their creditors do as well. A debtor who cannot save a car, a home, and household furniture under one state's exemption laws may look across the state line to see a similar debtor saving all of those items and more. In addition, although there has been significant revision in state exemption statutes since 1978, state exemption laws are sometimes a collection of archaic remains. Moreover, some states require a debtor to file a deed of exemption in advance of a bankruptcy filing in order to exempt certain property, a requirement that can become a trap for the poorly informed debtor.[4]

Regardless of whether this variation in available exemptions is good or not, it remains the law. Moreover, debtors residing in a state that provides the option of either the state or federal exemptions often need to choose carefully between the different sets of exemptions. A debtor cannot choose some state exemptions and some federal exemptions. *See* § 522(b). The debtor's choice of which exemptions to use will often depend on the specific types of property the debtor owns and the value of such property.

---

[4] NAT'L BANKR. REVIEW COMM'N, BANKRUPTCY: THE NEXT TWENTY YEARS 122–23 (Oct. 20, 1997).

Problem 4-1

Find the exemption statutes for the state in which you attend law school and use them to complete the chart below, so that you can compare that state's exemptions to the federal exemptions available under § 522(d).

	Your State's Exemption Amount	**Federal Exemption Amount**
Homestead		$22,975
Motor Vehicle		$3,675
Clothing		$12,250 aggregate limit; $575 per item limit
Books & Mementoes		
Household Goods		
Jewelry		$1,550
Tools of Trade		$2,300
Life Insurance Contract		$12,250
Prescribed Health Aids		No limit
Other Property		$1,225 + up to $11,500 (of unused homestead)

B. DETERMINING WHICH STATE'S EXEMPTION LAWS APPLY

Because all individual bankruptcy debtors may avail themselves of the exemptions provided by state law and state law determines whether debtors have the option to use the federal exemptions, it is necessary to know which state's exemption laws apply.[5] If

[5] Because the Bankruptcy Code looks to the "State or local law" of the debtor's residence for the applicable exemptions, an enrolled member of a Native American tribe who lives off of the reservation cannot rely on tribal law to exempt the right to receive a per capita distribution. *See, e.g., In re*

the debtor has not moved recently, this will not be much of an issue; the law of the jurisdiction in which the debtor resides is the law that governs. If, however, the debtor has moved within the two years preceding the bankruptcy filing, then a computation based on length of residency in each state during the 180 days prior to the two-year period determines the governing law. Read § 522(b)(1)–(3). In other words, if the debtor moved during the time represented by the lightly shaded area in the timeline below, then the jurisdiction in which the debtor lived for the greatest amount of time during the period represented by the darkly shaded area is the jurisdiction whose law applies.

Problem 4-2

Dunkirk filed for Chapter 7 bankruptcy protection on April 15, 2013. At that time, Dunkirk owned and lived in a house in Florida. Before moving to Florida, Dunkirk owned and resided in a house in St. Louis, Missouri. Which state's homestead exemption may Dunkirk use:

A. If Dunkirk moved to Florida on February 1, 2011?

B. If Dunkirk moved to Florida on June 1, 2011, and he had lived in Missouri for 15 years prior to the move?

C. If Dunkirk grew up in Wisconsin, moved from Wisconsin to Missouri on February 1, 2011, and then moved from Missouri to Florida on November 1, 2012?

D. What problems for Dunkirk, if any, might the answers to Parts B and C pose? *See* § 522(b)(3).

Howley, 439 B.R. 535 (Bankr. D. Kan. 2010), *on motion to amend*, 446 B.R. 506 (Bankr. D. Kan.), *appeal dismissed*, 2011 WL 440070 (D. Kan. 2011). It remains unclear whether a member of a tribe who resides on the reservation can use tribal law to supplement an exemption provided by state law.

C. EXEMPTIONS AVAILABLE TO ALL INDIVIDUAL DEBTORS

In 2005, Congress added a generous exemption for all debtors, whether they use the state or federal exemptions. *See* § 522(b)(3)(C), (d)(12). It covers retirement funds held in IRAs, Roth IRAs, and almost all types of employer-sponsored retirement plans, provided the funds are exempt from federal income tax. Unlike § 522(d)(10), which also exempts IRAs,[6] this new exemption is not limited to the amount "reasonably necessary for the support of the debtor" and the debtor's dependents. The only limitation is an inflation-adjusted cap of $1,245,475 on IRAs and Roth IRAs (not on other types of exempt funds). *See* §§ 522(n), 104. However, this cap can be increased "if the interests of justice so require" and in any event does not apply to amounts rolled over from other exempt plans. In short, virtually all of most individual debtors' retirement savings are likely to be exemptible.

All retirement

D. THE PROCESS OF CLAIMING EXEMPTIONS

1. In General

The process of claiming exemptions is fraught with issues about classification, valuation, timing, and competing claims to the debtor's property. Some of these issues are fairly simple and easy to resolve; others are more complicated and may lack a clear answer.

The first thing to note is that whether a specific item of property qualifies for a particular exemption depends first and foremost on what law applies. If the debtor is claiming the benefit of the federal exemptions, the issue is a matter of federal law. If, as is more likely, the debtor is seeking to use a state exemption, the issue is one of state law. Thus, for example, for debtors choosing state exemptions, what qualifies as "household goods" or "tools of trade" may vary from state to state.

1) Which law applies

The second thing to note about exemptions is that, as exemptible property transmutes from one thing to another, the exemption may or may not be lost. For example, a state law exempting a certain amount or percentage of an individual's wages is likely to cover the funds upon receipt, but may or may not still exempt them when deposited into a bank account containing nonexempt funds and is unlikely to cover any

2) transmuted?

---

6 *See Rousey v. Jacoway*, 544 U.S. 320 (2005).

nonexempt assets purchased with those funds.[7] Similarly, while most states allow an individual to exempt an interest in a motor vehicle, some may not allow the debtor to apply the motor vehicle exemption to insurance proceeds due for the destruction of a vehicle.[8]

The third thing to bear in mind about exemptions is that they are usually limited in amount. Thus, a debtor is often permitted to claim a car as exempt, but typically only up to a maximum value. This is necessary to prevent debtors from abusing their exemptions (putting $2 million into a custom-made car plated with gold).

What happens to a debtor whose exemptible property has a value in excess of the maximum exemption amount? The short answer is that the debtor would probably not be able to prevent execution, levy, and sale of the property outside of bankruptcy. The same result usually occurs in bankruptcy, at least in Chapter 7 cases. Consider a debtor whose car is worth $6,000 and whose state exemption for automobiles is limited to $2,500. That car is worth $3,500 to the bankruptcy estate:

Property Value		$6,000
Exemption Limit	(goes to debtor)	– $2,500
Residual Value	(goes to estate)	$3,500

In a Chapter 7 case, the trustee will sell the car, presumably for something close to its fair market value, give the debtor the $2,500 exemption amount, and distribute the remaining proceeds to creditors. Thus, unless property is worth less than the maximum exemption amount, the debtor will typically lose the property. Of course, the debtor can use the $2,500 received from the sale to buy a less expensive car, one that will remain exempt. Alternatively, a Chapter 7 debtor may be able to keep the car if the debtor has sufficient other assets – that is, other prepetition assets that are exempt or postpetition assets acquired from earnings, by gift, or through borrowing – to "purchase" the estate's interest from the trustee. In a Chapter 11 or 13 case, the debtor will often be able to

---

7 *See, e.g., In re Christensen*, 149 P.3d 40 (Nev. 2006) (exemptible wages retain their exempt character after payment and commingling in a deposit account, provided they remain traceable under a first-in, first-out approach; assets purchased with those funds are exempt only if they so qualify without regard to the exempt nature of the funds used to acquire them). As to what tracing formula to use – lowest intermediate balance rule; first-in, first-out; or a ratio based on the percentage of exempt to nonexempt funds deposited – see *In re Marve*, 484 B.R. 735 (Bankr. N.D. Ind. 2013).

8 *See In re Simpson*, 238 B.R. 776 (Bankr. S.D. Ill. 1999).

keep the car, but only if the debtor has enough other resources – such as postpetition income – to pay creditors the $3,500 excess over the exemption cap.

The fourth thing to note about exemptions is that more than one exemption may be available for a single piece of property. For example, a truck driver may be able to combine an exemption for motor vehicles with an exemption for tools of trade and apply both to a single truck. Such "stacking" of exemptions is common but whether it is available depends on two, independent things: (i) whether the property involved qualifies for each exemption under the applicable law; and (ii) whether the applicable law permits the two (or more) exemptions to be applied to the same piece of property. Many states do permit exemptions to be stacked.

The fifth thing to remember about exemptions is that they typically apply only to the debtor's equity in a piece of property. While our discussion of secured claims is generally put off until chapter six, it is important to understand that if property is subject to a valid and unavoidable lien, then the debtor may exempt only the equity in the property, if any, and in fact need exempt only the equity to prevent the trustee from selling the property.

For example, consider the same debtor with a $6,000 car, but this time the car is subject to a properly perfected security interest securing a $4,000 debt. Assume that the trustee in bankruptcy cannot avoid the debtor's lien. Such a debtor has only $2,000 of equity. The only portion of the car that the debtor may claim as exempt is this equity. Because the maximum exemption amount, $2,500, exceeds the debtor's equity, the debtor can exempt all of the equity in the car. If the debtor does so, a Chapter 7 trustee would have no incentive to sell the car ($4,000 in value being allocated to the secured creditor and the remaining $2,000 to the debtor):

Property Value		$6,000
Lien Debt	(value allocated to lienor)	– $4,000
		$2,000
Exemption ($2,500 limit)	(goes to debtor)	– $2,000
Residual Value	(goes to estate)	$0

Indeed, the debtor can probably prevent the trustee from attempting to sell the car. *See* § 554(b). Whether the debtor can prevent the *secured party* from repossessing and selling the car is another matter, one which will be discussed in chapter six. In a Chapter 11 or 13 case, the exemption again makes the car valueless to the estate and therefore irrelevant in determining how much unsecured claimants must be paid under the plan.

Given all this, debtors must often engage in a fair amount of planning when deciding how to allocate their exemptions. Try the following problem.

Problem 4-3

Diane and Duncan, a married couple, are long-time residents of the state in which you attend law school. Diane is a freelance photojournalist and Duncan is a personal trainer and scuba instructor. Because their income is irregular, they have struggled to make ends meet and have amassed significant credit card debt. Collectively, they own the following property:

Home	$125,000
Motor Vehicle	$5,000
Clothing	$300
Household Furniture	$2,000
Other Goods	$3,500
Wedding Ring	$2,000
Scuba Gear (used for work)	$6,000
Duncan's IRA Account	$7,800
Deposit Account	$800

The home is encumbered by a mortgage that secures a $75,000 debt. Diane and Duncan have approached you for advice about what property they could exempt if they filed a Chapter 7 bankruptcy petition.

A. 1. To what exemptions will they be entitled under state law and how should they allocate those exemptions? *See* § 522(m). Is there any vital information that you lack but which might significantly affect their decision? *See In re Miller*, 427 B.R. 616 (Bankr. N.D. Ohio 2009).

2. To what exemptions would they be entitled under federal law and how should they allocate those exemptions? For this purpose, assume their home state has not opted out of the federal exemptions.

3. Which exemption regime – state or federal – is better for Diane and Duncan and why?

B. How would your response to Part A change if Diane and Duncan did not own a home and instead rented an apartment?

The sixth thing to remember is that the costs of sale and the trustee's commissions must be factored in before determining what will happen to property in bankruptcy. For example, in *In re Thornton*,[9] the debtors had a home worth $27,000 that was encumbered by a mortgage securing a $14,250 debt. Thus the debtors had $12,750 of equity in their home. The court determined that the trustee would incur $600 in advertising costs and $1,350 in a 5% real estate commission to sell the house, and thus would be able to collect only $10,800 from selling the property. Of this amount, the debtors could exempt $9,275, leaving only $1,525 for the estate. The trustee would then be entitled to a $375 commission on this, *see* § 326, further reducing the amount available to creditors to only $1,150. This amounted to a 1.7% distribution on unsecured claims, which the court characterized as "*de minimis*." It therefore ordered the trustee to abandon the property. The end result was that the debtors got to keep their home (assuming they continued to pay the mortgagee). In short, property has to be worth something more than inconsequential value to the estate before Chapter 7 trustees and courts will require debtors to relinquish it.

To claim property as exempt, the debtor needs to list it as exempt on the debtor's schedules, which the debtor must file with the petition or shortly thereafter. *See* Official Bankruptcy Form 6, Schedule C; *see also* Rules 1007, 4003. The trustee or a creditor may object to a claimed exemption, but must generally do so within 30 days of the conclusion of the § 341 meeting of creditors, which in a Chapter 7 case must be held not less than 21, nor more than 40, days after the petition is filed. Rule 2003(a). The objecting party has the burden of proving that the claimed exemption is improper. Rule 4003(c).

In essence, then, exempt assets begin in the estate but are poured back into the debtor's vat if either no one objects or any objections are overruled. Thus, the debtor's vat of assets in a Chapter 7 case more accurately looks as follows:

Property of the Debtor

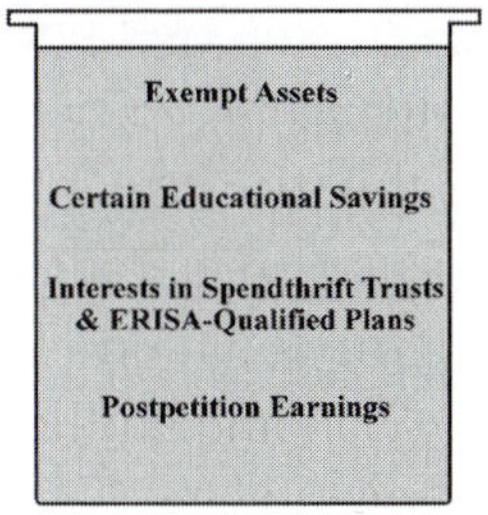

Suppose a debtor lists property as exempt even though there is not a colorable basis for doing so. An objection is made, but only after expiration of the 30-day period.

---

9 269 B.R. 682 (Bankr. W.D. Mo. 2001).

Should the exemption be allowed? In *Taylor v. Freeland & Kronz*,[10] the debtor claimed an employment discrimination lawsuit and its proceeds as exempt even though there was no basis for the exemption. The Chapter 7 trustee did not timely object. When the debtor ended up recovering $110,000 based on the lawsuit, the trustee sought turnover of the funds, arguing that they remained property of the estate. The Supreme Court ruled otherwise, holding that the debtor's cause of action was exempt once the time for objecting to the claimed exemption had expired. In doing so, the Court rejected the trustee's argument that this would create incentives for a debtor to claim baseless exemptions:

> Deadlines may lead to unwelcome results, but they prompt parties to act and they produce finality. In this case, despite what respondents repeatedly told him, [the trustee] did not object to the claimed exemption. If [the trustee] did not know the value of the potential proceeds of the lawsuit, he could have sought a hearing on the issue, *see* Rule 4003(c), or he could have asked the Bankruptcy Court for an extension of time to object, *see* Rule 4003(b). Having done neither, [the trustee] cannot now seek to deprive Davis and respondents of the exemption.
>
> [The trustee] suggests that our holding will create improper incentives. He asserts that it will lead debtors to claim property exempt on the chance that the trustee and creditors, for whatever reason, will fail to object to the claimed exemption on time. He asserts that only a requirement of good faith can prevent what the Eighth Circuit has termed "exemption by declaration." This concern, however, does not cause us to alter our interpretation of § 522(*l*).
>
> Debtors and their attorneys face penalties under various provisions for engaging in improper conduct in bankruptcy proceedings. *See, e.g.*, § 727(a)(4)(B) (authorizing denial of discharge for presenting fraudulent claims); Rule 1008 (requiring filings to "be verified or contain an unsworn declaration" of truthfulness under penalty of perjury); Rule 9011 (authorizing sanctions for signing certain documents not "well grounded in fact and . . . warranted by existing law or a good faith argument for the extension, modification, or reversal of existing law"); 18 U.S.C. § 152 (imposing criminal penalties for fraud in bankruptcy cases). These provisions may limit bad-faith claims of exemptions by debtors. To the extent that they do not, Congress may enact comparable provisions to address the difficulties that *Taylor* predicts will

[10] 503 U.S. 638 (1992).

follow our decision. We have no authority to limit the application of § 522(*l*) to exemptions claimed in good faith.[11]

Justice Stevens in dissent had the following to say about the majority's approach:

> The Court states that it has "no authority to limit the application of § 522(*l*) to exemptions claimed in good faith." It does not deny, however, that it has ample authority to hold that the doctrine of equitable tolling applies to the 30-day limitations period in Federal Rule of Bankruptcy Procedure 4003(b). In my view, such a result is supported not only by strong equitable considerations, but also by the common law, the widespread practice of the bankruptcy courts, and the text of § 522(b).
>
> * * * In this case, even if there was no fraud, and even if it is assumed that the trustee failed to exercise due diligence, it remains true that the parties injured by the trustee's failure to object within the 30-day period are innocent creditors. Moreover, it is apparently undisputed that there was no legitimate basis for the claim of an exemption for the entire award. Under these circumstances, unless the debtor could establish some prejudice caused by the trustee's failure to object promptly, I would hold that the filing of a frivolous claim for an exemption is tantamount to fraud for purposes of deciding when the 30-day period begins to run.[12]

Although *Taylor* gives debtors a broad license to exempt property, debtors who try to be too clever are apt to be sorry. For example, in one post-*Taylor* case, the debtor claimed two partnership interests as exempt, and valued each at $1.00. The trustee did not object, but simply found a purchaser more than happy to purchase the partnership interests for their market value, which was apparently far in excess of $1.00. The court ruled that while the trustee was barred from objecting to the claimed exemption, the exemption was limited to the amount claimed. Thus, the court allowed the trustee to sell the partnership interests, provided the trustee protected the debtor's $1.00 interest in each (presumably by giving the debtor $2.00).[13] In *Schwab v. Reilly*,[14] the Supreme

---

[11] *Id.* at 644–45.

[12] *Id.* at 646, 648.

[13] *Addison v. Reavis*, 158 B.R. 53 (E.D. Va. 1993), *aff'd without opinion*, 32 F.3d 562 (4th Cir. 1994).

[14] 130 S. Ct. 2652 (2010).

Court affirmed this approach and held that if the debtor claims an exemption in a specified amount (*e.g.*, "$200"), the exemption is limited to that amount, even if the debtor's bankruptcy schedules list the same amount for the value of the property. Thus, interested parties need not object to the exemption to preserve the trustee's ability to recover value in the asset beyond the dollar amount claimed as exempt.[15]

2. *Valuing Property and Calculating Exemptions*

There is no doubt that the bankruptcy estate is entitled to all postpetition appreciation in estate property. Therefore, all appreciation of items *partially* claimed as exempt belongs to the estate. Thus, for example, in the situation depicted below, the estate should get all of the value above the exemption limit: $1,500.

	Petition Date	Later
Value	$3,000	$3,500
Exemption Limit	$2,000	$2,000
Estate's Equity	$1,000	$1,500

However, if property appreciates postpetition but is still worth less than the total amount that the debtor may or did claim as exempt, the debtor is entitled to that appreciation.

	Petition Date	Later
Value	$3,000	$3,500
Exemption Limit	$4,000	$4,000
Estate's Equity	$0	$0

It remains somewhat unclear how to deal with postpetition appreciation of assets claimed to be wholly exempt if the postpetition appreciation takes the property's value above the amount claimed or available as exempt:

[15] In response to the Supreme Court's decision in *Schwab*, some debtors have declared as exempt "100% of the fair market value of" some identified property. Several trustees have objected that such a claim is improper under the applicable state exemption law and generally the trustees have been successful. *See, e.g.*, *In re Massey*, 465 B.R. 720 (1st Cir. BAP 2012). *But cf. In re Moore*, 442 B.R. 865 (Bankr. N.D. Tex. 2010) (indicating such a claimed exemption is proper but that, upon the trustee's objection, an evidentiary hearing will be held on whether the value of the property exceeds the available exemption amount).

	Petition Date	Later
Value	$3,000	$5,000
Exemption Limit	$4,000	?
Estate's Equity	$0	?

Some courts have held that the debtor's interest is limited to the amount that may be or is claimed as exempt, and postpetition appreciation above that amount inures to the benefit of the estate.[16] Indeed, although the Supreme Court's decision in *Schwab v. Reilly* did not expressly deal with postpetition appreciation, the Court nevertheless implied that such appreciation belongs to the estate when the exemption amount is limited. To conclude otherwise – *i.e.*, that appreciation belongs to the debtor – would impose on courts the formidable task of determining whether and to what extent the property truly appreciated, in which case the excess value belongs to the debtor, or was merely listed with an incorrectly low valuation on the debtor's schedules, in which case the excess belongs to the estate.

Nevertheless, given the lack of a definitive answer, trustees need to be somewhat vigilant in protecting the estate by objecting to unwarranted claims of exemptions or, when appropriate, by asking that the debtor clarify the exemption claim by stating an exact numerical value.

Problem 4-4

Determined is filing for Chapter 7 bankruptcy protection in a state that has a $40,000 homestead exemption. Determined's home is worth $100,000 and is subject to a mortgage of $60,000, and thus Determined's equity is fully exempt. Despite being insolvent, Determined has managed to make all mortgage payments on time. The mortgage lender is willing to ignore whatever technical defaults may have occurred and allow Determined to remain in the home, provided Determined continues to make the required monthly payments (presumably out of postpetition income). Determined's attorney is concerned, however, that each postpetition mortgage payment that Determined makes will reduce the mortgage debt and thereby increase Determined's equity above the exemption limit. What should the attorney do to protect Determined's home? *See* § 554.

---

16 *E.g.*, *In re Orton*, 687 F.3d 612 (3d Cir. 2012).

how's prop valued?

The discussion so far raises the question of how property is to be valued for the purpose of applying exemptions. There are two answers to this, the legal and the practical.

The legal answer relates to a recurring issue in bankruptcy: how is property to be valued? Is fair market value the appropriate standard? How about liquidation value? Replacement cost? Retail value? Wholesale value? Does it matter what will happen to the property? Are the costs of any sale to be deducted from the amount assigned? Put another way, is the assessment of value for the purpose of determining what and how much the debtor gets to keep – for which fair market value would seem appropriate – or is it to determine how much would come into the estate if the trustee were to sell it – for which liquidation value might be more appropriate?

If the debtor is using the federal exemptions under § 522(d), subsection (a) would appear to resolve the valuation question. It defines value for the purpose of § 522 as "fair market value." If, however, the debtor is using state exemptions, the answer is not so clear. Any limitations on the "value" of the property that the debtor may exempt would not necessarily be imbued with the Bankruptcy Code's definition of value. Thus, the result could conceivably vary depending on which state's exemptions the debtor was using. Nevertheless, the few courts to explore this question do not seem to rely on state law and generally agree that fair market value should be used without taking into account the debtor's financial exigencies or any costs of sale.[17]

The practical answer to the question, though, is that it rarely matters. For most types of used personal property – clothes, furniture, small appliances, and even jewelry – the debtor will simply assign a value. Rarely will it be worth anyone's time and effort to challenge the valuations of such items.[18] Although the trustee has the duty to investigate and sell any property that would generate value in excess of the claimed exemption amount, *see* § 704(a)(1), (3), (4), the costs of pursuing such an investigation

---

[17] *See, e.g.*, *In re West*, 328 B.R. 736, 750 n.8 (Bankr. S.D. Ohio 2004).

[18] See *West*, 328 B.R. 736, in which the debtor had purchased ten items of jewelry for $30,000 but later valued them at only $2,000 on her bankruptcy schedules. The trustee objected to the discharge under § 727(a)(4)(A), arguing that the debtor had made a false statement on the schedules, and submitted an expert appraisal of the jewelry for $8,900. The court overruled the trustee's objection because, following her attorney's advice, the debtor had estimated the jewelry's value as what a pawn shop would pay for it, she had no way of knowing that fair market value was the appropriate standard, and the trustee's expert testified that a pawn shop would pay only $3,860.

will often exceed any value the trustee may hope to reap from it.[19] For more valuable property, such as cars and investments, trustees are likely to be more thorough.

Perhaps more to the point, if the trustee can find a buyer willing to pay more for property than the costs of sale plus the exemption amount to which the debtor is entitled, then it really does not matter what the valuation standard is. The trustee will sell the property. If the trustee cannot find a buyer willing to pay more than that total, the trustee will abandon the property. § 554.

3. *Exemptions in Recovered Property*

What if, shortly before filing for bankruptcy protection and while insolvent, the debtor transfers exempt property to a favored creditor in payment of a debt or to a family member as a gift? In one sense that transfer is preferential or fraudulent. After all, the payment to the creditor had the effect of preferring that creditor. The gift was fraudulent because no reasonably equivalent value was received. In another sense, though, the transfer in no way impacted the debtor's creditors: if the transfer had not been made and the property retained, the debtor could have exempted it and creditors would not have had access to it.

Section 522 addresses this situation. If the prepetition transfer was voluntary, and the trustee recovers the property, the debtor will not be permitted to claim an exemption in it. *See* § 522(g)(1)(A). The property will come back into the estate and be available for all general creditors. In effect, the debtor is deemed to have waived the exemption, but that waiver is made to operate for the benefit of all creditors, not merely the prepetition transferee.[20]

debtor waived exemption

If, on the other hand, the prepetition transfer had been involuntary, say perhaps that a creditor had seized property pursuant to a writ of execution and levy,[21] the debtor may

---

[19] On the other hand, some experienced trustees have become quite expert at estimating the value of jewelry, and with loupe in hand have asked to examine the debtor's rings and watches during the debtor's examination at the meeting of creditors.

[20] The 30-day limit for objecting to a debtor's claimed exemption, *see* Rule 4003(b), might not apply to property the trustee recovers using its avoiding powers. Thus, for example, if the debtor voluntarily transferred property prepetition but nevertheless claims it as exempt on his or her schedules, the trustee need not object to the exemption within the 30-day period in order to object to the debtor's attempt to reap the benefit of avoidance under § 522(g). *In re Kuhnel*, 495 F.3d 1177 (10th Cir. 2007).

[21] While creditors cannot normally levy upon exempt property, if the debtor claims the federal

claim an exemption in any property the trustee recovers. § 522(g). If the trustee refuses to go after the property, as the trustee might if any recovery would be wholly exemptible, then the debtor may exercise the trustee's avoiding powers and seek to recover the property. § 522(h).

These rules on prepetition transfers of exemptible property do not apply postpetition. The debtor may, without restriction, voluntarily transfer assets determined to be exempt to any creditor or donee the debtor chooses. Why is a debtor permitted to voluntarily transfer exempt assets postpetition but not claim as exempt recovered assets that were transferred away prepetition? Perhaps due to concerns about the process of determining what property is exempt and what property is not, property is not determined to be exempt until after the bankruptcy petition is filed. Moreover, some creditors –*i.e.*, taxing authorities and support claimants – may be permitted to go after exempt assets. *See* §§ 522(c), 523(a)(1), (5). If the debtor transfers exempt assets away postpetition, those priority creditors had a crack at them. If the debtor transfers assets away prepetition, the priority creditors never had a crack at them and, maybe, the debtor should thus not be allowed to exempt them.

4. *Post-Bankruptcy Effect of Exemptions*

Section 522(c) provides that exempt property generally retains its status as exempt after bankruptcy. That is, with some exceptions, if the debtor remains liable for prepetition debts, the creditors on those debts cannot, after the bankruptcy case is closed, go after the property claimed as exempt during the bankruptcy process. Of course, to the extent that a debtor is claiming exemptions provided by state law, this provision is largely unnecessary. After all, a debtor who uses state exemptions would of course be able to continue to assert those exemptions postbankruptcy and to do so against both postpetition debts as well as whatever prepetition debts were not discharged.

However, because the federal exemptions provided for in § 522(d) apply only in bankruptcy, a debtor who uses the federal exemptions would not be able to assert them against nondischarged claims absent § 522(c). Thus, this provision gives lasting effect

---

exemptions in bankruptcy, some of the exempt property may not have been covered by state exemption laws prepetition. In this sense, § 522(g) and (h) are needed to help give effect to the federal exemptions in those jurisdictions that have not opted out.

to the federal exemptions.[22] The provision is also useful if: (i) the debtor moves post-discharge to a new state whose law does not exempt property that the debtor was able to exempt in bankruptcy; or (ii) the debtor moved prepetition but a former state's law governed exemptions in bankruptcy and permitted the debtor to exempt property that the debtor cannot exempt under the law of the debtor's current residence.

Two types of nondischarged claims are excepted from § 522(c): support claims and tax claims. This may not matter much with respect to tax claims because other federal law provides for exemptions from a levy to collect federal taxes.[23] The point, though, is that the exemptions applicable to such tax claims will be governed by that federal law, not by the Bankruptcy Code and certainly not by state exemption law. With respect to support claims, § 522(c) arguably does something much more significant: it seems to make such claims immune from exemptions and thereby allows the claimant to go after all of the debtor's exempt property. If so, the provision might significantly enhance the support claimant's rights by trumping the state exemption laws that applied prepetition, and thus provide some disincentive for filing for bankruptcy protection. However, what little case law there is under § 522(c) suggests that it does not have this effect.[24]

E. ABUSING EXEMPTIONS

There is an old maxim that applies in bankruptcy, as in other contexts: pigs get fat; hogs get slaughtered.[25] The sentiment behind this maxim is that being a little greedy is to be expected and will be winked at. It thus may pay off. Being very greedy, however, is repulsive, will be cause for sanction, and thus may lead to dire consequences.

---

[22] This is similar to the point made above that subsections (g) and (h) of § 522 allow the debtor to claim an exemption in property involuntarily seized prepetition. Those rules are most likely to be relevant to property protected by the federal bankruptcy exemptions but capable of being levied upon prepetition, before those exemptions apply.

[23] *See* 26 C.F.R. § 301.6334-1.

[24] *See In re Davis*, 170 F.3d 475 (5th Cir.) (ruling – in part because of this disincentive – that § 522(c) operates on federal exemptions only and does not preempt state law; in other words, § 522(c) "leave[s] exempt property exposed to post-bankruptcy liability only to the extent it would have been exposed if the bankruptcy had not occurred"), *cert. denied*, 528 U.S. 822 (1999).

[25] *See* Juliet M. Moringiello, *Distinguishing Hogs from Pigs: A Proposal for a Preference Approach to Pre-bankruptcy Planning*, 6 AM. BANKR. INST. L. REV. 103 (1998).

In the context of exemptions this comes up all of the time. Debtors frequently want to preserve whatever assets they have and take them beyond the reach of creditors. To do this, they frequently convert nonexempt assets into exempt assets shortly before filing for bankruptcy protection. In other words, they sell their nonexempt property to get cash and then use the cash to buy property that is exempt.

This practice smells a lot like a fraudulent transfer: transferring assets in an effort to delay, hinder, or defraud creditors. However, in at least one sense the practice is not only acceptable, but actually encouraged. After all, one of the main purposes of exemptions is to prevent the debtor from becoming a public charge. We therefore want debtors to take advantage of their exemptions.

Nevertheless, excessive conversion of nonexempt assets into exempt assets is just greedy. The pig begins to look a lot like a hog. Drawing the line between acceptable and unacceptable prepetition conversions is difficult. Consider the following two cases decided the same day by the same court. In doing so, pay close attention to the relief requested in each.

HANSON v. FIRST NATIONAL BANK
848 F.2d 866 (8th Cir. 1988)

Timbers, Circuit Judge.

A creditor bank appeals from a district court order * * * affirming the bankruptcy court's order which rejected the creditor's challenge to the debtors' claimed exemptions. On appeal, the creditor asserts that there was extrinsic evidence establishing the debtors' intent to defraud their creditors. We disagree. We hold that the bankruptcy court was not clearly erroneous in finding no fraudulent intent. We affirm.

I

* * * On November 30, 1983, appellees Kenneth Hanson and his wife Lucille Hanson (the "Hansons" or "debtors"), residents of South Dakota, filed a voluntary joint bankruptcy petition pursuant to Chapter 7 of the Bankruptcy Code. Appellant First National Bank in Brookings ("First National") is the principal creditor of appellees. The instant appeal arises out of First National's objections to the exemptions claimed by the Hansons.

First National loaned money to the Hansons who were farmers. The Hansons sustained financial problems which led to their default on the loans. Before filing for bankruptcy, the Hansons consulted an attorney. On the advice of counsel, the Hansons had appraised and sold certain of their property which would not be exempt under South

Dakota law. They sold to their son, Ronald Hanson, a car, two vans, and a motor home for a total of $27,115, the amount for which the property was appraised. Ronald had purchased the property with money he obtained from a bank loan. The debtors also sold some of their household goods and furnishings to Kenneth's brother, Allen Hanson, for $7,300, the appraised value.

A couple weeks prior to filing their bankruptcy petition, the Hansons used these proceeds to purchase life insurance policies with cash surrender values of $9,977 and $9,978 and, two days before filing their petition, had prepaid $11,033 on their homestead real estate mortgage which was held by First National. This property was exempt from their creditors' reach. Under South Dakota law, a debtor may exempt the proceeds of life insurance policies up to a total of $20,000 and he also may exempt his homestead.

First National objected to these exemptions, claiming that the debtors had converted non-exempt property to exempt property on the eve of bankruptcy with intent to defraud their creditors. At the hearing before the bankruptcy court on September 10, 1984, First National asserted that none of the property allegedly sold ever was transferred to the buyers. The debtors testified that the vehicles sold to their son, Ronald, were stored at their home because Ronald still lived with them while he was working part time and attending school part time. Part of the agreement, the debtors testified, included their permission to store the vehicles on their property. While the debtors said they occasionally used the vehicles, they did so only with express permission of their son. Ronald subsequently sold the motor home to a third party. The household goods and furnishings were stored in the Hansons' home, they said, because Allen Hanson, Kenneth's brother, was then living in Anchorage, Alaska, and could not retrieve the property immediately after the sale. First National did not assert, nor does it assert on appeal before us, that the transfers were for less than fair market value. The bankruptcy court from the bench denied First National's motion which objected to the exemptions. The court found that the Hansons had done what was permissible under the law and that their actions did not constitute extrinsic evidence of fraud.

First National appealed to the federal district court. * * * [T]he district court affirmed the bankruptcy court's order, concluding that it was not clearly erroneous. The instant appeal followed. The sole issue on appeal is whether the Hansons should not be allowed to claim their life insurance and homestead exemption as a product of fraudulent conveyances. We affirm.

II

* * * Under the Bankruptcy Code (the "Code"), a debtor is entitled to exempt certain property from the claims of his creditors. The Code permits a debtor to exempt either under the provisions of the Code itself if not forbidden by state law, § 522(b) & (d), or under the provisions of state law and federal law other than the minimum allowances in the Code. § 522(b)(2). When the debtor claims a state-created exemption, the scope of the claim is determined by state law.

It is well established that under the Code, a debtor's conversion of non-exempt property to exempt property on the eve of bankruptcy for the express purpose of placing that property beyond the reach of creditors, without more, will not deprive the debtor of the exemption to which he otherwise would be entitled. A leading bankruptcy commentator explains that this rule is just because "The result which would obtain if debtors were not allowed to convert property into allowable exempt property would be extremely harsh, especially in those jurisdictions where the exemption allowance is minimal." 3 Collier on Bankruptcy ¶ 522.08[4], at 40 (15th ed. 1984). Nevertheless, this rule is not absolute. Where the debtor acts with actual intent to defraud creditors, his exemptions will be denied. Since fraudulent intent rarely is susceptible of direct proof, courts long have accepted extrinsic evidence of fraud. Absent extrinsic evidence of fraud, however, the debtor's mere conversion of non-exempt property to exempt property, even while insolvent, is not evidence of fraudulent intent as to creditors.

The crux of the issue on the instant appeal is whether there was extrinsic evidence to establish that the Hansons transferred the property with intent to defraud their creditors. We may reverse the bankruptcy court's finding as to the debtors' actual intent only if it is clearly erroneous.

In *In re Olson*, 45 B.R. 501 (1984), debtors with a defunct business had placed non-exempt funds into their homestead asset, which was exempt property, just prior to filing their bankruptcy petition. The debtors, 55 and 56 years old, testified, on the advice of their attorney, that the reason they paid off the mortgages was to protect their homestead and to reduce their monthly living expenses, since they believed they would have difficulty finding employment after terminating their business. The bankruptcy court found that the debtors did not commit a fraudulent conveyance. The court permitted the debtors to exempt their entire homestead after finding that the debtors prior to bankruptcy used their savings to satisfy their mortgages, no business assets having been used and no debts having been incurred.

First National asserts here that the Hansons while insolvent committed a "classic badge of fraud" by transferring their property to family members and at the same time retaining the use and enjoyment of that property. First National asserts that the controlling case is *In re Cadarette*, 601 F.2d 648 (2d Cir. 1979). We disagree.

In *Cadarette*, the debtor, whose business was on the brink of financial collapse, transferred title to his expensive automobile, boat and trailer to his fiancee without consideration three weeks before filing his bankruptcy petition. The district court, reversing the decision of the bankruptcy court, held that the debtor's discharge was denied because of his fraudulent intent to shield his assets from his creditors. The Second Circuit, in affirming the district court, found a number of factors clearly evidencing the debtor's fraudulent intent. The court found significant, among other things, that "someone facing dire financial straits would choose to make a gift of a valuable and highly marketable automobile"; that eight days after the alleged transfer of the car a service charge of $399 was paid not by the alleged new owner but by the debtor, who further depleted his business assets by paying with a company check; that the debtor's fiancee lived only two houses away from him; and that he retained a key to the car and continued to use the car to the same extent as he previously had used it.

We find the instant case quite different from the situation in *Cadarette*. First National does not dispute the fact that the purchasers paid fair market value. The vehicles and household goods were not gifts. Title appears to have been transferred correctly. In the instant case, the debtors had reasonable explanations as to why the property they sold remained on their premises. Of particular significance, their son purchased the vehicles with a bank loan taken in his name and he subsequently resold the motor home to a third party, keeping all of the proceeds himself. The sale to family members, standing on its own, does not establish extrinsic evidence of fraud. * * *

The bankruptcy court found that First National did not establish any indicia of fraud: the Hansons did not borrow money to place into exempt properties; they accounted for the cash they received from the sales; they had a preexisting homestead; and they did not obtain goods on credit, sell them, and then place the money into exempt property. They sold the property for its fair market value and then used this money to take advantage of some of the limited exemptions available under South Dakota law on the advice of counsel.

To summarize: [w]e hold that the bankruptcy court was not clearly erroneous in finding no fraudulent intent by the Hansons and permitting them to claim their full exemptions. We believe that the instant case falls within the myriad of cases which have permitted such a conversion.

Arnold, Circuit Judge, concurring.

I agree with the result reached by the Court and with almost all of its opinion. I write separately to indicate some variation in reasoning and also to compare this case with the companion case of *Norwest Bank Nebraska v. Tveten*, 848 F.2d 871, also decided today by this panel.

* * * The Court is entirely correct in holding that there is no extrinsic fraud here. The money placed into exempt property was not borrowed, the cash received from the sales was accounted for, and the property was sold for fair market value. The fact that the sale was to family members, "standing on its own, does not establish extrinsic evidence of fraud."

With all of this I agree completely, but exactly the same statements can be made, just as accurately, with respect to Dr. Tveten's case. So far as I can tell, there are only three differences between Dr. Tveten and the Hansons, and all of them are legally irrelevant: (1) Dr. Tveten is a physician, and the Hansons are farmers; (2) Dr. Tveten attempted to claim exempt status for about $700,000 worth of property, while the Hansons are claiming it for about $31,000 worth of property; and (3) the Minnesota exemption statute whose shelter Dr. Tveten sought had no dollar limit, while the South Dakota statute exempting the proceeds of life-insurance policies is limited to $20,000. The first of these three differences – the occupation of the parties – is plainly immaterial, and no one contends otherwise. The second – the amounts of money involved – is also irrelevant, in my view, because the relevant statute contains no dollar limit, and for judges to set one involves essentially a legislative decision not suitable for the judicial branch. The relevant statute for present purposes is § 522(b)(2)(A), which authorizes debtors to claim exemptions available under "State or local law," and says nothing about any dollar limitations, by contrast to § 522(d), the federal schedule of exemptions, which contains a number of dollar limitations. The third difference – that between the Minnesota and South Dakota statutes – is also legally immaterial, and for a closely related reason. The federal exemption statute, just referred to, simply incorporates state and local exemption laws without regard to whether those laws contain dollar limitations of their own.

The Court attempts to reconcile the results in the two cases by characterizing the question presented as one of fact – whether the conversion was undertaken with fraudulent intent, or with an intent to delay or hinder creditors. In *Tveten*, the Bankruptcy Court found fraudulent intent, whereas in *Hanson* it did not. Neither finding is clearly erroneous, the Court says, so both judgments are affirmed. This analysis collapses upon examination. For in *Tveten* the major indicium of fraudulent intent relied on by the Bankruptcy Court was Dr. Tveten's avowed purpose to place the assets in question out of the reach of his creditors, a purpose that, as a matter of law, cannot amount to fraudulent intent, as the Court's opinion in *Hanson* explicitly states. The result, in practice, appears to be this: a debtor will be allowed to convert property into exempt form, or not, depending on findings of fact made in the court of first instance, the Bankruptcy Court, and these findings will turn on whether the Bankruptcy Court regards the amount of money involved as too much. With all deference, that is not a rule of law. It is simply a license to make distinctions among debtors based on subjective considerations that will vary more widely than the length of the chancellor's foot.

NORWEST BANK NEBRASKA V. TVETEN
848 F.2d 871 (8th Cir. 1988)

Timbers, Circuit Judge.

Appellant Omar A. Tveten, a physician who owed creditors almost $19,000,000, mostly in the form of personal guaranties on a number of investments whose value had deteriorated greatly, petitioned for Chapter 11 bankruptcy. He had converted almost all of his non-exempt property, with a value of about $700,000, into exempt property that could not be reached by his creditors. The bankruptcy court, on the basis of its findings of fact and conclusions of law, entered an order on February 27, 1987, denying a discharge in view of its finding that Tveten intended to defraud, delay, and hinder his creditors. The district court * * * affirmed the bankruptcy court's order. On appeal, Tveten asserts that his transfers merely constituted astute pre-bankruptcy planning. We hold that the bankruptcy court was not clearly erroneous in inferring fraudulent intent on the part of Tveten. We affirm.

I

* * * Tveten is a 59 year old physician in general practice. He is the sole shareholder of Omar A. Tveten, P.A., a professional corporation. He has no dependents. He began investing in various real estate developments. These investments initially were quite successful. Various physician friends of Tveten joined him in organizing a corporation to invest in these ventures. These investments were highly leveraged. The physicians, including Tveten, personally had guaranteed the debt arising out of these investments. In mid-1985, Tveten's investments began to sour. He became personally liable for an amount close to $19,000,000 – well beyond his ability to pay. Appellees Norwest Bank Nebraska ("Norwest Bank"), Business Development Corporation of

Nebraska ("Business Development"), and Harold J. Panuska ("Panuska") as trustee of the Harold J. Panuska Profit Sharing Trust and the Harold J. Panuska Employee Trust Fund, became creditors of Tveten as a result of his various investment ventures.

Tveten filed a Chapter 11 petition on January 7, 1986. Meanwhile, several creditors already had commenced lawsuits against him. Panuska had obtained a $139,657 judgment against him on October 9, 1985. Norwest Bank and Business Development had commenced an action against him but had not obtained judgment when Tveten filed for bankruptcy. On the date the Chapter 11 petition was filed, Tveten owed his creditors close to $19,000,000.

Before filing for bankruptcy, Tveten consulted counsel. As part of his pre-bankruptcy planning, he liquidated almost all of his non-exempt property, converting it into exempt property worth approximately $700,000. This was accomplished through some seventeen separate transfers. The non-exempt property he liquidated included land sold to his parents and his brother, respectively, for $70,000 and $75,732 in cash; life insurance policies and annuities with a for-profit company with cash values totaling $96,307.58; his net salary and bonuses of $27,820.91; his KEOGH plan and individual retirement fund of $20,487.35; his corporation's profit-sharing plan worth $325,774.5; and a home sold for $50,000.[26] All of the liquidated property was converted into life insurance or annuity contracts with the Lutheran Brotherhood, a fraternal benefit association, which, under Minnesota law, cannot be attached by creditors. Tveten concedes that the purpose of these transfers was to shield his assets from creditors. Minnesota law provides that creditors cannot attach *any* money or other benefits payable by a fraternal benefit association. Unlike most exemption provisions in other states, the Minnesota exemption has no monetary limit. Indeed, under this exemption, Tveten attempted to place $700,000 worth of his property out of his creditors' reach.

Tveten sought a discharge with respect to $18,920,000 of his debts. Appellees objected to Tveten's discharge. In its order of February 27, 1987, the bankruptcy court concluded that, although Tveten's conversion of non-exempt property to exempt property just before petitioning for bankruptcy, standing alone, would not justify denial of a discharge, his inferred intent to defraud would. The bankruptcy court held that, even if the exemptions were permissible, Tveten had abused the protections permitted a debtor under the Bankruptcy Code (the "Code"). His awareness of Panuska's judgment against him and of several pending lawsuits, his rapidly deteriorating business investments, and his exposure to extensive liability well beyond his ability to pay, all

---

[26] There were no claims that these transfers were for less than market value.

were cited by the court in its description of the circumstances under which Tveten converted his property. Moreover, the court concluded that Tveten intended to hinder and delay his creditors. Accordingly, the bankruptcy court denied Tveten a discharge.

Tveten appealed from the bankruptcy court order to the federal district court. In a memorandum opinion and order entered July 10, 1987, the district court affirmed the denial of a discharge, concluding that the bankruptcy court's finding as to Tveten's intent was not clearly erroneous.[27]

The instant appeal followed. Basically, Tveten asserts on appeal that as a matter of law we should reject the factors relied on by the bankruptcy court to infer that Tveten intended to delay, hinder and defraud creditors. We disagree. We affirm.

II

The sole issue on appeal is whether Tveten properly was denied a discharge in view of the transfers alleged to have been in fraud of creditors.

At the outset, it is necessary to distinguish between (1) a debtor's right to exempt certain property from the claims of his creditors and (2) his right to a discharge of his debts. * * * When the debtor claims a state-created exemption, the scope of the claim is determined by state law. * * *

A debtor's right to a discharge, however, unlike his right to an exemption, is determined by *federal*, not state, law. The Code provides that a debtor may be denied a discharge under Chapter 7 if, among other things, he has transferred property "with intent to hinder, delay, or defraud a creditor" within one year before the date of the filing of the petition. § 727(a)(2). Although Tveten filed for bankruptcy under Chapter 11, the proscription against discharging a debtor with fraudulent intent in a Chapter 7 proceeding is equally applicable against a debtor applying for a Chapter 11 discharge. The reason for this is that the Code provides that confirmation of a plan does not discharge a Chapter 11 debtor if "the debtor would be denied a discharge under section 727(a) of this title if the case were a case under chapter 7 of this title." § 1141(d)(3)(C).

Although the determination as to whether a discharge should be granted or denied is governed by federal law, the standard applied consistently by the courts is the same

[27] Before the district court entered its order, the Supreme Court of Minnesota held in a decision entered March 27, 1987, that annuities and life insurance contracts issued by a fraternal benefit society were exempt under Minnesota law, but that these statutory provisions violated the Minnesota Constitution. Accordingly, Tveten no longer will be able to claim these exemptions. Following the opinion of the Supreme Court of Minnesota, Tveten claimed an exemption for his pension in the amount of approximately $200,000. He and his creditors settled this issue before the bankruptcy court. He will retain this property as exempt.

as that used to determine whether an exemption is permissible, *i.e.*, absent extrinsic evidence of fraud, mere conversion of non-exempt property to exempt property is not fraudulent as to creditors even if the motivation behind the conversion is to place those assets beyond the reach of creditors.

As the bankruptcy court correctly found here, therefore, the issue in the instant case revolves around whether there was extrinsic evidence to demonstrate that Tveten transferred his property on the eve of bankruptcy with intent to defraud his creditors.

* * *

There are a number of cases in which the debtor converted non-exempt property to exempt property on the eve of bankruptcy and was granted a discharge because there was no extrinsic evidence of the debtor's intent to defraud. In *Forsberg v. Security State Bank*, 15 F.2d 499 (8th Cir. 1926), an old decision of our Court, a debtor was granted a discharge despite his trade of non-exempt cattle for exempt hogs while insolvent and in contemplation of bankruptcy. Although we found that the trade was effected so that the debtor could increase his exemptions, the debtor "should [not] be penalized for merely doing what the law allows him to do." We concluded that "before the existence of such fraudulent purpose can be properly found, there must appear in evidence some facts or circumstances which are extrinsic to the mere facts of conversion of nonexempt assets into exempt and which are indicative of such fraudulent purpose."

There also are a number of cases, however, in which the courts have denied discharges after concluding that there was extrinsic evidence of the debtor's fraudulent intent. In *Ford v. Poston*, 773 F.2d 52 (4th Cir. 1985), the debtor had executed a deed of correction transferring a tract of land to himself and his wife as tenants by the entirety. The debtor had testified that his parents originally had conveyed the land to the debtor alone, and that this was a mistake that he corrected by executing a deed of correction. Under relevant state law, the debtor's action removed the property from the reach of his creditors who were not also creditors of his wife. The Fourth Circuit, in upholding the denial of a discharge, found significant the fact that this "mistake" in the original transfer of the property was "corrected" the day after an unsecured creditor obtained judgment against the debtor. The Fourth Circuit held that the bankruptcy court, in denying a discharge, was not clearly erroneous in finding the requisite intent to defraud, after "[h]aving heard . . . [the debtor's] testimony at trial and having considered the circumstances surrounding the transfer." In *In re Reed*, 700 F.2d 986 (5th Cir. 1983), shortly after the debtor had arranged with his creditors to be free from the payment obligations until the following year, he rapidly had converted non-exempt assets to extinguish one home mortgage and to reduce another four months before bankruptcy, and had diverted receipts from his business into an account not divulged to his creditors.

The Fifth Circuit concluded that the debtor's "whole pattern of conduct evinces that intent." The court went further and stated:

> It would constitute a perversion of the purposes of the Bankruptcy Code to permit a debtor earning $180,000 a year to convert every one of his major nonexempt assets into sheltered property on the eve of bankruptcy with actual intent to defraud his creditors and then emerge washed clean of future obligation by carefully concocted immersion in bankruptcy waters.

In most, if not all, cases determining whether discharge was properly granted or denied to a debtor who practiced "pre-bankruptcy planning," the point of reference has been the state exemptions if the debtor was claiming under them. Although discharge was not denied if the debtor merely converted his non-exempt property into exempt property as permitted under state law, the exemptions involved in these cases comported with federal policy to give the debtor a "fresh start" – by limiting the monetary value of the exemptions. This policy has been explicit, or at least implicit, in these cases. In *Forsberg*, for example, we stated that it is not fraudulent for an individual who knows he is insolvent to convert non-exempt property into exempt property, thereby placing the property out of the reach of creditors

> because the statutes granting exemptions have made no such exceptions, and because the policy of such statutes is to favor the debtors, at the expense of the creditors, *in the limited amounts allowed to them, by preventing the forced loss of the home and of the necessities of subsistence*, and because such statutes are construed liberally in favor of the exemption. (emphasis added).

Similarly, in *In re Ellingson*, 63 B.R. 271 (N.D. Iowa 1986), in holding that the debtors' conversion of non-exempt cash and farm machinery did not provide grounds for denial of a discharge, the court relied on the social policies behind the exemptions. The court found that the debtors' improvement of their homestead was consistent with several of these policies, such as protecting the family unit from impoverishment, relieving society from the burden of supplying subsidized housing, and providing the debtors with a means to survive during the period following their bankruptcy filing when they might have little or no income. The court held that exemptions should further one or more of the following social policies:

> (1) To provide the debtor with property necessary for his physical survival; (2) To protect the dignity and the cultural and religious identity of the debtor; (3) To enable the debtor to rehabilitate himself financially and earn income in the future; (4) To protect the debtor's family from the adverse consequences of impoverishment; (5) To shift the burden of providing the debtor and his family with minimal financial support from society to the debtor's creditors.

In the instant case, however, the state exemption relied on by Tveten was unlimited, with the potential for unlimited abuse. Indeed, this case presents a situation in which the debtor liquidated almost his entire net worth of $700,000 and converted it to non-exempt property in seventeen transfers on the eve of bankruptcy while his creditors, to whom he owed close to $19,000,000, would be left to divide the little that remained in his estate. Borrowing the phrase used by another court, Tveten "did not want a mere *fresh* start, he wanted a *head* start." *In re Zouhar*, 10 B.R. 154, 156 (Bankr. D.N.M. 1981) (emphasis in original). His attempt to shield property worth approximately $700,000 goes well beyond the purpose for which exemptions are permitted. Tveten's reliance on his attorney's advice does not protect him here, since that protection applies only to the extent that the reliance was reasonable.

The bankruptcy court, as affirmed by the district court, examined Tveten's entire pattern of conduct and found that he had demonstrated fraudulent intent. We agree. While state law governs the legitimacy of Tveten's exemptions, it is federal law that governs his discharge. Permitting Tveten, who earns over $60,000 annually, to convert all of his major non-exempt assets into sheltered property on the eve of bankruptcy with actual intent to defraud his creditors "would constitute a perversion of the purposes of the Bankruptcy Code." *In re Reed*, 700 F.2d at 992. Tveten still is entitled to retain, free from creditors' claims, property rightfully exempt under relevant state law.

We distinguish our decision in *Hanson v. First National Bank*, decided today. *Hanson* involves a creditor's objection to two of the debtors' claimed exemptions under South Dakota law, a matter governed by state law. The complaint centered on the Hansons' sale, while insolvent, of non-exempt property to family members for fair market value and their use of the proceeds to prepay their preexisting mortgage and to purchase life insurance policies in the limited amounts permissible under relevant state law. The bankruptcy court found no extrinsic evidence of fraud. The district court * * * affirmed. We also affirmed, concluding that the case fell within the myriad of cases which have permitted such a conversion on the eve of bankruptcy.

III

To summarize: [w]e hold that the bankruptcy court was not clearly erroneous in inferring fraudulent intent on the part of the debtor, rather than astute pre-bankruptcy planning, with respect to his transfers on the eve of bankruptcy which were intended to defraud, delay and hinder his creditors.

Arnold, Circuit Judge, dissenting.

The Court reaches a result that appeals to one's general sense of righteousness. I believe, however, that it is contrary to clearly established law, and I therefore respectfully dissent.

Dr. Tveten has never made any bones about what he is doing, or trying to do, in this case. He deliberately set out to convert as much property as possible into a form exempt from attachment by creditors under Minnesota law. Such a design necessarily involves an attempt to delay or hinder creditors, in the ordinary, non-legal sense of those words, but, under long-standing principles embodied both in judicial decisions and in statute, such a purpose is not unlawful. * * *

A debtor's right to make full use of statutory exemptions is fundamental to bankruptcy law. To unsecured creditors, a debtor's conversion of his assets into exempt categories of property will always appear unfair, but this apparent unfairness is simply a consequence of the existence of exemptions under the jurisdiction's bankruptcy law.

* * *

To be sure, if there is extrinsic evidence of fraud, or of a purpose to hinder or delay creditors, discharge may and should be denied, but "extrinsic," in this context, must mean something beyond the mere conversion of assets into exempt form for the purpose of putting them out of the reach of one's creditors. If Tveten had lied to his creditors, like the debtor in *McCormick v. Security State Bank*, 822 F.2d 806 (8th Cir. 1987), or misled them in some way, like the debtor in *In re Reed*, 700 F.2d 986 (5th Cir. 1983), or transferred property for less than fair value to a third party, like the debtor in *Ford v. Poston*, 773 F.2d 52 (4th Cir. 1985), we would have a very different case. There is absolutely no evidence of that sort of misconduct in this record, and the Court's opinion filed today cites none.

One is tempted to speculate what the result would have been in this case if the amount of assets converted had been $7,000, instead of $700,000. Indeed, the large amount of money involved is the only difference I can see between this case and *Forsberg v. Security State Bank*, 15 F.2d 499 (8th Cir. 1926). It is true that the *Forsberg* opinion referred to "the limited amounts allowed to" debtors by exemptions, but whether exemptions are limited in amount is a legislative question ordinarily to be decided by the people's elected representatives, in this case the Minnesota Legislature. Where courts punish debtors simply for claiming exemptions within statutory limits, troubling problems arise in separating judicial from legislative power. * * *

If there ought to be a dollar limit, and I am inclined to think that there should be, and if practices such as those engaged in by the debtor here can become abusive, and I admit that they can, the problem is simply not one susceptible of a judicial solution according to manageable objective standards. A good statement of the kind of judicial reasoning that must underlie the result the Court reaches today appears in *In re Zouhar*, 10 B.R. 154 (Bankr. D.N.M. 1981), where the amount of assets converted was $130,000. The Bankruptcy Court denied discharge, stating, among other things, that "there is a principle of too much; phrased colloquially, when a pig becomes a hog it is slaughtered." If I were a member of the Minnesota Legislature, I might well vote in favor of a bill to place an over-all dollar maximum on any exemption.[28] But sitting as a judge, by what criteria do I determine when this pig becomes a hog? If $700,000 is too much, what about $70,000? Would it matter if the debtor were a farmer, as in *Forsberg*, rather than a physician? (I ask the question because the appellee creditor's brief mentions the debtor's profession, which ought to be legally irrelevant, several times.)

Debtors deserve more definite answers to these questions than the Court's opinion provides. In effect, the Court today leaves the distinction between permissible and impermissible claims of exemption to each bankruptcy judge's own sense of proportion. As a result, debtors will be unable to know in advance how far the federal courts will allow them to exercise their rights under state law.

Where state law creates an unlimited exemption, the result may be that wealthy debtors like Tveten enjoy a windfall that appears unconscionable, and contrary to the policy of the bankruptcy law. I fully agree with Judge Kishel, however, that

> [this] result . . . cannot be laid at [the] Debtor's feet; it must be laid at the feet of the state legislature. Debtor did nothing more than exercise a prerogative that was fully his under law. It cannot be said that his actions have so tainted him or his bankruptcy petition as to merit denial of discharge.

I submit that Tveten did nothing more fraudulent than seek to take advantage of a state law of which the federal courts disapprove.

I would reverse this judgment and hold that the debtor's actions in converting property into exempt form do not bar a discharge in bankruptcy.

---

[28] There is some irony in the fact that the exemption sought by the debtor in this case, that for benefits under annuities or life-insurance policies issued by fraternal associations, has been held unconstitutional under two provisions of the Minnesota Constitution. One such provision, Article 1, Section 12, provides that "[a] reasonable amount of property shall be exempt." The Supreme Court of Minnesota has held that the exemption statute involved in the present case is unconstitutional precisely because it contains no dollar limit. So the principle of limitation has been upheld, the debtor has in any event lost the exemption he sought, but he also loses his discharge under today's decision.

NOTES

1. A year after these two decisions were reported, the same court tried to reconcile them in a case involving a physician who converted approximately $400,000 in assets into exempt property on the eve of bankruptcy:

> We read *Tveten* and *Hanson* to reaffirm the rule that conduct sufficient to defeat discharge requires indicia of fraud beyond mere use of the exemptions. Under *Tveten, Hanson*, and the cases they discuss, extrinsic evidence can be composed of: further conduct intentionally designed to materially mislead or deceive creditors about the debtor's position; conveyances for less than fair value; or the continued retention, benefit or use of property allegedly conveyed together with evidence that the conveyance was for inadequate consideration. In addition, *Tveten* establishes that where an exemption, other than a homestead exemption, is not limited in amount, the amount of property converted into exempt forms and the form taken may be considered in determining whether fraudulent intent exists.
>
> * * * No exemption is more central to the legitimate aims of state lawmakers than a homestead exemption. * * * We hold that *Tveten* does not apply to homestead exemptions absent traditional extrinsic evidence of fraud unrelated to the amount of money involved. In addition, we remind the lower courts that there is nothing fraudulent per se about making even significant use of other legal exemptions. Ultimately, fixed dollar limits on the use of exemptions must be set by state legislatures. *Tveten* and *Hanson* sanction an exceptional use of judicial discretion. In light of the danger that judges will inadvertently fix inconsistent or arbitrary limits on statutory exemptions, we must err in favor of the debtor. The power sanctioned in *Tveten* should be reserved for exceptional cases and has no application to homestead exemptions.

In re Johnson, 880 F.2d 78, 82, 83–84 (8th Cir. 1989). On remand, Dr. Johnson still lost his discharge. *In re Johnson*, 124 B.R. 290 (Bankr. D. Minn. 1991). The court found extrinsic evidence of fraud in his acquisition of a whole life insurance policy with a cash surrender value just under the $4,000 exemption limit (Dr. Johnson had no dependents and therefore needed no insurance) and in his acquisition of a baby grand piano and harpsichord for about $8,000, both exempt under state law (Dr. Johnson played neither and actually kept the piano in storage).

2. Several state laws that exempt a debtor's property make express exception for property acquired with nonexempt assets in an effort to defraud creditors.[29] Others make exception for property acquired within a brief, specified period before bankruptcy. To the extent a debtor is relying on state law as the source for the exemption, these limitations may be important.

In another, more recent venture into fraudulent use of exemptions, the Eighth Circuit again confronted a debtor who sold everything to buy an exempt asset. This time, however, the only asset was a homestead. Nevertheless, the debtor lost the exemption. Can you reconcile this decision with *Hanson*, *Tveten*, and *Johnson*?

IN RE SHOLDAN
217 F.3d 1006 (8th Cir. 2000)

Beam, Circuit Judge.

Earl Jensen, the personal representative of the probate estate of debtor, Arthur Sholdan, appeals the district court's affirmance of a bankruptcy court order that sustained the bankruptcy trustee's objection to Sholdan's homestead exemption. We affirm.

Prior to filing for Chapter 7 bankruptcy, Sholdan liquidated almost all of his non-exempt property consisting of bank accounts, certificates of deposit and a mortgage against his former farmstead, and converted it into exempt property in the form of a house worth approximately $135,000. In his Chapter 7 bankruptcy petition, Sholdan listed his new house as an exempt homestead pursuant to Minnesota law. A short while thereafter, Sholdan died. The trustee of his bankruptcy estate (trustee) objects to Sholdan's homestead exemption claim on the grounds that Sholdan acquired title to the property in specific contemplation of filing bankruptcy and with the "intent to defraud" his creditors. Therefore, the trustee maintains that Sholdan and his successors in interest should be denied the benefit of the statutory exemption.

---

[29] *See, e.g.*, 735 ILL. COMP. STAT. 5/12-1001; *see also* FLA. STAT. §§ 222.29, 222.30 (which make an exemption unavailable "if it results from a fraudulent transfer or conveyance").

The Bankruptcy Code permits debtors to exempt property from the bankruptcy estate pursuant to provisions of state law. *See* § 522(b)(2)(A). The scope of a state-created exemption is determined by state law. Minnesota law provides an exemption for an individual's homestead. *See* Minn. Stat. Ann. §§ 510.01–.02 (West 1990). However, under section 513.44 of Minnesota's enactment of the Uniform Fraudulent Transfer Act (UFTA), a debtor may not claim a homestead exemption when he or she transfers the property "with actual intent to hinder, delay, or defraud" creditors. This same section contains a lengthy list of factors or "badges of fraud" which a court may look to for help in determining actual intent.

* * * [T]he bankruptcy court found that Sholdan had converted non-exempt property to exempt property with the "intent to defraud." Noting that direct evidence of fraudulent intent is rare, the bankruptcy court inferred such intent from applying the "badges of fraud" listed in section 513.44(b). The district court affirmed the bankruptcy court's decision. On appeal, Jensen argues that: (1) the bankruptcy court erred in applying the "badges of fraud" to determine whether Sholdan acted with an "intent to defraud"; and (2) the record does not support a finding of such intent.

* * *

First, we reject the argument that the bankruptcy court erred in applying the badges of fraud set forth in section 513.44(b) of the UFTA. Under Minnesota law, whether fraud exists in a situation involving the conversion of non-exempt to exempt assets is determined by reference to the UFTA. Although Jensen does not dispute that under *Tveten*, an exemption may be denied under section 513.44 of the UFTA if a debtor had the actual intent to defraud, he nevertheless argues that it was inappropriate for the bankruptcy court to use the "badges of fraud" listed in that section to infer such intent. Specifically, he claims that *Tveten* never took the additional step of sanctioning the use of a "badges of fraud" approach and that such an approach is inappropriate for exemption cases. We find this argument to be without merit.

We find the bankruptcy court's "badges of fraud" approach was appropriate. Although, not specifically referenced by the Minnesota Supreme Court in *Tveten*, we find such an approach to be implicit in *Tveten*'s holding that a court look to the standards governing fraudulent transfers for purposes of determining fraud in the exemption context. Use of the "badges of fraud" to infer fraudulent intent in conveyances and transfers is well settled under Minnesota law. We think the *Tveten* court's omission of a "badges of fraud" reference results from the fact that at the time of the *Tveten* decision there was no codification of specific badges of fraud, as exists currently under the UFTA, rather than from any desire to preclude the use of such badges. Compare UFCA, Minn. Stat. Ann. §§ 513.20–513.32 (West 1986) with UFTA, Minn. Stat. Ann. §§ 513.41–513.51 (West 1990).

That use of the badges of fraud is appropriate for inferring intent in an exemption case is also dictated by common sense. Badges of fraud represent nothing more than a list of circumstantial factors that a court may use to infer fraudulent intent. Given the fact that direct evidence of fraud is rare, a court in most instances can only infer fraud by considering circumstantial evidence. Furthermore, we note that under section 513.44(b), a court is not limited to only those factors or "badges" enumerated, but is free to consider any other factors bearing upon the issue of fraudulent intent. In sum, we find no error in the bankruptcy court's application of a traditional and well settled approach for determining fraud to a situation involving the conversion of assets from non-exempt to exempt status.[30]

Having decided that the bankruptcy court applied the correct legal standard for inferring whether there was evidence showing an "intent to defraud," we next turn to Jensen's argument that the evidence does not support such a finding. The question of whether an individual acted with intent to defraud in converting non-exempt property into exempt property is a question of fact, on which the bankruptcy court's finding will not be reversed unless clearly erroneous. *See Hanson v. First Nat'l Bank*, 848 F.2d 866, 868 (8th Cir. 1988). It is well settled that the mere conversion of non-exempt assets to exempt assets is not in itself fraudulent. *See id.* Before actual fraudulent intent can be found "'there must appear in evidence some facts or circumstances which are extrinsic to the mere facts of conversion of non-exempt assets into exempt and which are indicative of such fraudulent purpose.'" *Norwest Bank Nebraska v. Tveten*, 848 F.2d 871, 875 (8th Cir. 1988) (quoting *Forsberg v. Security State Bank*, 15 F.2d 499, 502 (8th Cir. 1926)). Our review of the record convinces us the bankruptcy court was not clearly erroneous in finding there was sufficient extrinsic evidence surrounding Sholdan's conversion of assets from which it could infer that he acted with the "intent to defraud."

The debtor was a retired farmer, ninety years of age and afflicted with serious medical problems. He had been recently named a defendant in a personal injury suit with claimed damages well in excess of his liability insurance coverage. He had no children. He had one nephew, Earl Jensen. Earl had a step-brother, Roger Jensen. In his will, the debtor bequeathed his entire estate to his sister, Earl Jensen's mother. If she predeceased the debtor, Roger Jensen's children were his beneficiaries. At the time of the purchase of the new house, the debtor had been living in an assisted-care facility.

---

30 We also reject Jensen's argument that the bankruptcy court impermissibly relied on Sholdan's age and the value of his house to infer fraudulent intent.

Prior to living in the assisted-care facility, he had resided in an apartment for thirteen years.

Then, in what was, as the bankruptcy court noted, a radical departure from his previous lifestyle, the debtor acquired approximately $162,000 by liquidating his bank account and certificates of deposit, and selling his mortgage rights in the farm to Roger Jensen. With the assistance of the Jensens and their attorneys, Sholdan then moved out of the assisted-care facility and purchased with cash a newly-built house worth approximately $135,000. As part of the purchase agreement, the debtor and Jensens asked the builder to add various finishes to the house, such as a deck and landscaping, and specifically inquired as to the amount by which the purchase price of the house would increase. Following the purchase, the debtor's sole source of income was a social security payment of $486 per month, which after covering the costs of his basic living expenses of $435 per month, would leave him with a yearly surplus of approximately $600. The property taxes on the new house amounted to $2,000 per year. Following immediately upon the heels of the purchase of the house, the debtor filed for Chapter 7 bankruptcy, listing the house as exempt under Minnesota's homestead exemption.

On these facts, we find the bankruptcy court correctly concluded there was ample evidence extrinsic to the mere conversion of assets that showed fraudulent intent on the part of the debtor. It is one thing to convert non-exempt assets into exempt property for the express purpose of holding it as a homestead and thereby putting the property beyond the reach of creditors. However, it is quite another thing to acquire title to a house for no other reason than to defraud creditors. "'While the homestead right is a valuable one . . . it was never intended, and it should never be permitted, to operate as a vehicle for fraud and rank injustice.'" *Kangas v. Robie*, 264 F. 92, 94 (8th Cir. 1920) (quoting *Esty v. Cummings*, 78 N.W. 242, 244 (Minn. 1899)).

For the foregoing reasons, the decision of the district court is affirmed.

Arnold, Circuit Judge, dissenting.

I respectfully dissent from the Court's opinion. The Court fails to identify any evidence of fraud extrinsic to Mr. Sholdan's conversion of non-exempt property for the purpose of protecting his assets from creditors. The controlling law in this Circuit is clear:

> [I]t is not a fraudulent act by an individual who knows he is insolvent to convert a part of his property which is not exempt into property which is exempt, for the purpose of claiming his exemptions therein, and of thereby placing it out of the reach of his creditors.

Forsberg v. Security State Bank, 15 F.2d 499, 501 (8th Cir. 1926).

Consistently with our precedent, the Court today acknowledges that "there must appear in evidence some facts or circumstances which are extrinsic to the mere facts of conversion of non-exempt assets into exempt." *Ante* (quoting *Norwest Bank Nebraska v. Tveten*, 848 F.2d 871, 875 (8th Cir. 1988)). But our rule is broader, including not only the fact of conversion but also the fact that the debtor's purpose in conversion is to evade his creditors. *See, e.g.*, *Tveten*, 848 F.2d at 874 (conversion not fraudulent "even if the motivation behind the conversion is to place those assets beyond the reach of creditors").[31] I believe that the Court's analysis of this case is flawed because it fails to recognize this principle.

The facts upon which the Court bases its holding show only that Mr. Sholdan, as allowed by law, purchased his home with the purpose of putting his assets beyond the reach of his creditors. The Court notes that the purchase was "a radical departure" from his previous lifestyle, initiated only in the face of his imminent liability and on the advice of an attorney. A debtor will always make some sort of departure when he converts property to protect his assets, and it is not normally the business of judges to decide what "lifestyle" a citizen should choose. The Court notes that Mr. Sholdan purchased a more expensive home than he needed or could afford; Mr. Sholdan also required the seller to make additions to the home so that its sale price would precisely equal the amount of assets which he sought to protect with his purchase. This simply shows that Mr. Sholdan sought to protect as much of his assets as the law allowed, a practice that we have found is not evidence of fraud. *Forsberg*, 15 F.2d at 502 (no evidence of fraud in converting assets to take maximum advantage of exemptions). None of this is extrinsic to Mr. Sholdan's act of conversion or his motivation to avoid creditors; it is therefore not evidence of fraud.

This Court has in the context of other exemptions considered whether the value of an exemption was so large that it went beyond the social policies justifying the exemption. *See Tveten*, 848 F.2d at 875–76 (8th Cir. 1988) ($700,000 exemption in annuities went beyond the goal of providing debtors with a fresh start). But we have explicitly rejected this practice for homestead exemptions, deferring to the state legislatures to cap the size of these exemptions. *In re Johnson*, 880 F.2d 78, 82 (8th Cir.

---

[31] Although neither the motive to evade creditors nor the act of conversion itself is extrinsic evidence of fraud, "[e]xtrinsic evidence can be composed [of] further conduct intentionally designed to materially mislead or deceive creditors about the debtor's position; conveyances for less than fair value; or, the continued retention, benefit or use of property allegedly conveyed . . . for inadequate consideration." *In re Johnson*, 880 F.2d 78, 82 (8th Cir. 1989). *See, e.g.*, *McCormick v. Security State Bank*, 822 F.2d 806 (8th Cir. 1987) (extrinsic evidence of fraud where debtor lied to loan officer about the state of his finances to gain time to liquidate nonexempt assets and purchase exempt home).

1989). Accordingly, the fact that Mr. Sholdan purchased a more expensive house than the Court thinks he needed is legally irrelevant, except to demonstrate that he was seeking to protect all the assets allowed under the exemption.

The Court characterizes Mr. Sholdan's use of the homestead exemption as a "rank injustice." The Supreme Court of Minnesota has itself "deplored the injustices which have arisen from the application of [the homestead exemption]." *O'Brien v. Johnson*, 148 N.W.2d 357, 361 (Minn. 1967). Nevertheless, in the same case, the Court found no fraud where tortfeasors, before judgment could be entered against them, sold their old home and transferred their residence to a much more expensive property. As in this case, the court found that the tortfeasors' purpose was to evade their creditors. As in this case, the new residence, a large commercial property of which living quarters were only a small part, far exceeded the tortfeasors' practical needs for a residence. The Court found no fraud because the tortfeasors' purpose of evading their creditors was not extrinsic to their use of the homestead exemption. *Id.* at 360. As to the injustice of allowing a debtor to escape his creditor so openly, the Court found that it was bound by well settled law to find no fraud without some extrinsic evidence of fraudulent intent. While Mr. Sholdan's case may not be a sympathetic one, his exemption is allowed under Minnesota law, and, like the Supreme Court of Minnesota, we are bound to allow it to him regardless of our sense of its impropriety.

Problem 4-5

Dickens is a resident of Arizona who, until recently, had been a partner in an accounting firm with many large, publicly traded corporate clients. Six months ago, Dickens's firm received several substantial fines from the SEC for improprieties in its accounting practices. At about the same time, it became a defendant in several class-action lawsuits in which the plaintiffs are seeking hundreds of millions of dollars in compensation for alleged malpractice and fraud. In the last few weeks, it has become evident that the accounting firm's liability insurance is not adequate to cover all of these claims and Dickens therefore has substantial personal financial exposure. Because of that, Dickens went to see Friend, an old college buddy who now practices bankruptcy law, for advice.

During their discussions, Friend learned that Dickens owns the following: a $450,000 home in suburban Phoenix subject to a $410,000 mortgage, a $21,000 Acura subject to an $18,000 security interest, $90,000 in mutual funds, and $15,000 in a deposit account. In accordance with Friend's advice, Dickens sold the mutual funds, deposited the proceeds into the deposit account, and then entered into the following transactions:

(1) Used $20,000 to remodel the kitchen, thereby raising the home's property value to $465,000, and used $45,000 to pay down the home mortgage to $365,000. The Arizona homestead exemption limit is $150,000. ARIZ. REV. STAT. ANN. § 33-1101; *see also* § 522(o); *In re Maronde*, 332 B.R. 593 (Bankr. D. Minn. 2005).

(2) Used $2,000 to pay down the car loan. The motor vehicle exemption is limited to $5,000. ARIZ. REV. STAT. ANN. § 33-1125(8).

(3) Used $300 to buy a new flute. In Dickens's hands, the flute is worth about $250. Neither Dickens nor any of Dickens's dependents plays the flute. Musical instruments are exempt up to $250. ARIZ. REV. STAT. ANN. § 33-1125(2).

(4) Used $500 to buy a dairy cow from Cousin who owns a farm about 100 miles away. Pursuant to the agreement, Cousin will board and care for the cow for $35/month. However, Cousin will pay Dickens $35/month for the right to the cow's milk. These two obligations are expressly to be set off against each other. Pets, horses, milk cows, and poultry are exempt up to a maximum value of $500. ARIZ. REV. STAT. ANN. § 33-1125(3).

(5) Used $12,200 to buy enough food to last six months. The food consists largely of frozen meat, fish, and poultry, but also includes a wide selection of canned foods and drinks. It includes some alcohol and some frozen lobster tails. A six-month supply of food and fuel is exempt without regard to dollar limitation. ARIZ. REV. STAT. ANN. § 33-1124.

(6) Used $25,000 to buy a whole life insurance policy with a cash surrender value equal to the purchase price. Such policies are exempt up to a value of $25,000, provided the debtor has owned them for two years. ARIZ. REV. STAT. ANN. § 33-1126(6).

Shortly after engaging in these transactions, Dickens files for Chapter 7 bankruptcy protection and claims all the property described above as exempt under Arizona law (Arizona has opted out of the federal exemptions). Some creditors object to the debtor's exemptions. Others object to the debtor's discharge. How should the court rule on those objections? What difference would it make, if any, if Dickens had engaged in some, but not all, of the transactions described?

Problem 4-6

> Darryl and Darcy are married. Three years ago, before their marriage, Darryl purchased a car that is now unencumbered and worth $5,000. The state in which they reside allows individuals to exempt an interest, up to $3,000 in value, in a motor vehicle. Shortly before Darryl and Darcy filed a joint bankruptcy petition, Darryl had record title to the car transferred from himself to he and Darcy jointly. To what extent, if any, may Darryl and Darcy claim an exemption in the car?

In the years leading up to the 2005 amendments to the Bankruptcy Code, there was much discussion of one particular perceived abuse of exemption laws: debtors who take advantage of a very high, often unlimited, homestead exemption.

In 1999, the General Accounting Office released a study on the use of unlimited homestead exemptions in the Southern District of Florida and the Northern District of Texas.[32] The study estimated that, of the 34,374 cases closed in 1998 in those districts, 16,531 involved a homestead exemption. It further estimated the average amount of the homestead exemption in those cases to be $15,525. However, it also estimated that in 156 cases the debtor claimed a homestead exemption greater than $100,000.

The study found that in some of these cases people were able to keep homes while writing off over a million dollars in debt. One example cited was a doctor in Texas who wrote off over $7 million in debt he owed when he lost a multimillion dollar lawsuit but was able to keep his $235,000 home. Another example cited was a Texas bankruptcy attorney who wrote off $1.2 million in debt while she continued to own her $400,000 home.

Congress could have limited the homestead exemption for everyone, as many argued it should. Instead, it changed the rules for which state's exemption laws apply, in an effort to crack down on debtors moving from states with little or no homestead exemption to states such as Florida or Texas, with unlimited homestead exemptions. *See* § 522(b)(3) (explored in Problem 4-2). In addition, Congress enacted § 522(o) and (p). Read those provisions. Subsection (o) is aimed at debtors who convert nonexempt assets into an exempt homestead with an intent to hinder, delay, or defraud creditors. It applies to transfers as long as ten years before the petition. Subsection (p) denies any

---

[32] U.S. GEN. ACCOUNTING OFFICE, USE OF HOMESTEAD EXEMPTIONS BY CHAPTER 7 BANKRUPTCY DEBTORS IN THE NORTHERN DISTRICT OF TEXAS AND THE SOUTHERN DISTRICT OF FLORIDA IN 1998 (1999), *available at* www.gao.gov/archive/1999/gg99118r.pdf.

exemption amount in a homestead above $155,675 attributable to an interest acquired within 1,215 days – 3⅓ years – before the petition.[33]

Problem 4-7

For the last 18 years, Dixon has lived in a suburb of Sarasota, Florida. Seven years ago, Dixon purchased a home for $350,000. Bank provided $300,000 of financing and secured that loan with a mortgage. Last week, Dixon filed for bankruptcy protection. The schedules filed with the bankruptcy petition list the house as worth $600,000 and the mortgage debt as $100,000. Previously, 1,215 days before the petition, the house was worth $400,000 and the mortgage debt was $250,000. Florida has opted out of the federal exemptions.

A. How much of a homestead exemption may Dixon claim? *See* § 522(p); *see also In re Willcut*, 472 B.R. 88 (10th Cir. BAP 2012).

B. How, if at all, would the analysis change if, two years before the petition, Dixon had borrowed $50,000 from Bank and used the loan proceeds to build a backyard pool, with the result that the property was worth $650,000 on the date of the petition and the mortgage debt was $150,000?

Problem 4-8

For 15 years, Dillman owned a home in Pawtucket, Rhode Island. To pursue a new job opportunity, Dillman sold the home for $400,000 and used all of the proceeds to purchase a new home in Newport, Rhode Island. The new job did not work out and Dillman eventually had to file for bankruptcy protection.

A. If Dillman files for bankruptcy protection 700 days after the move, how much of a homestead exemption will Dillman be entitled to claim? *See* § 522(p).

---

[33] *Cf.* § 522(p)(2)(B) (protecting some interests acquired as a result of an intrastate move). The amount listed in § 522(p) is subject to periodic adjustment. § 104.

Whether the BAPCPA provisions adequately deal with the "abuse" issue is a matter of debate. *See* Juliet M. Moringiello, *Has Congress Slimmed Down the Hogs?: A Look at the BAPCPA Approach to Pre-bankruptcy Planning*, 15 WIDENER L.J. 615 (2006).

B. How, if at all, would the answer to Part A change if 700 days before filing Dillman had moved from Pawtucket, Rhode Island to Minneapolis, Minnesota?

C. How, if at all, would the answer to Part B change if Dillman filed 800 days after the move?

Do the results in these three scenarios make sense? How would you have dealt with the problem that § 522(b)(3), (o), and (p) all address?

CHAPTER FIVE
CLAIMS

In a Chapter 7 case, once the trustee or the court has determined what property is within the bankruptcy estate and what property the debtor may exempt, the trustee begins assembling the nonexempt property for sale. The sale proceeds will eventually be distributed to creditors in the order and to the extent provided for in the Bankruptcy Code. In order to give each creditor the appropriate share, the trustee's attention now turns from the debtor to the creditors. In other words, the trustee determines which creditors have a claim that qualifies for a distribution and how much is owed to each. A debtor in a Chapter 13 case and a debtor in possession in a Chapter 11 case must do the same. That is because any repayment or reorganization plan must, to be confirmed, specify the extent to which claims against the estate will be paid and provide claimants with at least as much as they would realize if the bankruptcy case had been filed under Chapter 7. §§ 1129(a)(7), 1325(a)(4).

In connection with this, it is important to understand some basic terminology – in particular, the distinction between debts and claims. In general, "claims" are the rights of a creditor while "debts" are the obligations of a debtor. Thus, distributions from a bankruptcy estate are used to pay those things qualifying as "claims." *See* §§ 726(a), 1123, 1129, 1322, 1325. "Debts," in turn, are potentially subject to the discharge. *See* §§ 727(b), 1141, 1328. Not surprisingly, the terms "debt" and "claim" are correlative. Debt is defined in § 101(12) as "liability on a claim." Thus, the debtor cannot be discharged from an obligation unless the obligation constitutes a claim, as defined in the Bankruptcy Code. Because of this, the definition of "claim" serves the double function of identifying the obligations that will potentially be paid in bankruptcy as well as the obligations that may be discharged.

Section 101(5) defines "claim" broadly. Read it and then consider the following problem.

Problem 5-1

Section 101(5)(A) uses at least twelve adjectives for different types of claims. The significance of two of these adjectives – "secured" and "unsecured" – will be discussed in chapter six of this book. The remaining ten adjectives represent five dichotomies:

liquidated v. unliquidated	fixed v. contingent
matured v. unmatured	disputed v. undisputed
legal v. equitable	

A. Consult a legal dictionary to determine how each adjective is different. For each adjective, describe a debt of that type. Determine what relationship, if any, exists between these five dichotomies.

B. Determine which five adjectives apply to each of the following claims against Debtor:

   1. Supplier has sued Debtor for $50,000 for failure to pay for goods sold. Debtor has filed an answer admitting to the transaction and to receipt of the goods but alleging that the goods were defective, resulting in no liability.
   2. Pedestrian has sued Debtor for injuries sustained when Debtor ran over Pedestrian in Debtor's car. The claim is for $25,000 in medical bills, $5,000 in lost wages, and $170,000 for pain and suffering.
   3. Debtor owes Seller $5,000 for goods ordered last week. Pursuant to the parties' agreement, payment is due 30 days after delivery. Seller has not yet delivered the goods.
   4. Spouse has filed for divorce. In connection with that, Spouse is seeking an order requiring Debtor to pay Spouse $2,000 per month in support for the next five years. Debtor has not agreed to this and the court has not yet ruled on the request.

Understanding these adjectives can be important in several bankruptcy contexts. For example, we will see in chapter eleven of this book that, in applying the debt limits for Chapter 13 eligibility, only noncontingent and liquidated debts are counted. *See* § 109(e). Similarly, creditors with only certain types of claims are proper petitioners in an involuntary case. Review § 303(b) and the material in chapter two on filing an involuntary petition; then try the following problem.

Problem 5-2

Dougherty owns and operates a house painting business. The business, which is unincorporated, has for years been late paying its bills. Several of Dougherty's creditors, who happened to be lunching together yesterday, discussed their frustration with Dougherty's business practices. They are considering filing an involuntary Chapter 7 bankruptcy petition against Dougherty and have asked you to ascertain whether they may. Given the description of Dougherty's debts below, is there a group of Dougherty's creditors who collectively satisfy the § 303(b) requirements? If so, which of them must join the petition?

1. $8,000 on a guaranty of Daughter's college loan from Banker. Payment is not yet due from Daughter.
2. $7,000 to Supplier for paint delivered.
3. $40,000 to Mortgagee whose debt is secured by Dougherty's $50,000 home.
4. $10,000 to Brother-in-Law for a loan made seven months ago. No payment is currently due.
5. $5,000 to Former Employee for back pay that is the subject of a currently pending wrongful discharge action in state court.
6. Various amounts to more than 20 other institutional creditors (*e.g.*, utility providers, credit card issuers), none of whom is likely to join the petition.

Not all claims are entitled to a share of the bankruptcy estate. Only the claims that are "allowed" are eligible for a distribution from the estate. While the debtor's financial difficulties may encompass an extended period of time, both before and after the bankruptcy petition, the bankruptcy process itself is, and must be, relatively short. Accordingly, that process is concerned primarily with the debtor's prepetition affairs. Just as the bankruptcy estate is comprised principally of the debtor's prepetition assets, the claims that are allowed, and thereby entitled to share in the estate, are generally restricted to those that arose prepetition. Allowed claims are also generally restricted to the amount due as of the petition date. *See* § 502(b). However, if liability is established prepetition, postpetition events can affect the amount of the allowed claim. Thus, for example, if a prepetition contract makes the debtor responsible for the attorney's fees incurred by a claimant, the claimant's allowed claim can include amounts incurred in postpetition attorney's fees, including fees incurred in connection with the bankruptcy proceeding itself.[1] However, an unsecured creditor's allowed claim cannot include postpetition interest on the claim. The claims allowance process will be considered more fully in the material that follows.

---

1 *See, e.g.*, *Ogle v. Fid. & Deposit Co. of Md.*, 586 F.3d 143 (2d Cir. 2009), *cert. denied*, 130 S. Ct. 2373 (2010); *see also Travelers Cas. & Sur. Co. of Am. v. Pac. Gas & Elec. Co.*, 549 U.S. 443 (2007).

What about the costs of administering the bankruptcy estate? In a Chapter 7 proceeding, these typically include the costs of maintaining and selling the property of the estate. In a Chapter 11 proceeding, they may include the costs of running the debtor's business and paying its employees while the reorganization plan is formulated. In both Chapter 7 and Chapter 13 cases, these costs include the trustee's fees. All of these postpetition costs are obligations of the *estate*, not of the *debtor*. Because of the correlative nature of the terms "debt" and "claim," the Bankruptcy Code does not classify these costs as "claims." Instead, they are labeled as "administrative expenses." They are, however, paid out of the bankruptcy estate. Indeed, as we will see in chapter nine, administrative expenses are entitled to priority in the distribution scheme. §§ 503(b), 507(a)(2).

This last point deserves some emphasis. In this chapter, we consider what obligations qualify as claims and which claims are "allowed" and therefore eligible for a distribution from the bankruptcy estate. However, some non-claims – *i.e.*, administrative expenses – are also entitled to share in the assets of the estate. Moreover, not all allowed claims are treated equally. As we will see in chapter six, secured claims fare much better in bankruptcy than do unsecured claims. As we will see in chapter nine, unsecured priority claims fare better than unsecured nonpriority claims. Thus, many rules we will encounter later have a significant impact on what a creditor's rights are or how much the creditor will ultimately recover. Nevertheless, the allowance process we discuss in this chapter is important because it serves as the foundation for a prepetition creditor's rights in the bankruptcy case.

A. THE FILING AND ALLOWANCE PROCESS

A debtor who petitions for bankruptcy protection is required to list all creditors on the schedules filed with or shortly after the petition. *See* Rule 1007(b), (c); Official Form 6, Schedules D, E, F. Ordinarily, a creditor will receive a proof of claim form – Official Form 10 – with the notice of bankruptcy that the court sends. In general, to share in the distribution of assets from the bankruptcy estate, a creditor must file a "proof of claim." *See* § 501; Rules 3002, 3002.1, 3003. This essentially consists of whatever documentation is necessary for the creditor to demonstrate the validity, nature, and amount of its claim. It is important to note, though, that because a proof of claim is a public document, a creditor must redact confidential information in the documentation of its claim. For example, a provider of medical or psychiatric services should not indicate the precise pharmaceuticals or services provided to the debtor. Failure to redact such confidential information may subject the creditor to liability.[2]

In Chapter 7 or 13 cases, the creditor must file a proof of claim within 90 days after the first date set for a meeting of creditors. Rule 3002(c). However, in Chapter 7 "no-asset" cases – those in which there do not appear to be any nonexempt assets for distribution – the court will inform the creditors not to file any proof of claim unless and until otherwise notified. Rule 2002(e). Chapter 7 no-asset cases are so common that many creditors get into the habit of not filing proofs of claim and, inevitably, some creditors neglect to do so even when there are assets available for distribution.

In Chapter 11 cases, the court fixes a date by which proofs of claim must be filed. However, the creditor need not file a proof of claim if the creditor agrees with the amount and nature of the claim as listed on the debtor's schedules and if the claim is not identified as disputed, contingent, or unliquidated on those schedules. Rule 3003(b)(1). In such circumstances, the proof of claim is "deemed filed." § 1111(a).

Once a proof of claim has been timely filed, the claim will be "allowed" unless a party in interest objects. § 502. Only those claims that are allowed entitle the creditor to share in the assets of the estate. §§ 726(a), 1123, 1322. Objections to claims are resolved by the court. Rule 3007. They are also infrequent. Most claims in a consumer bankruptcy are allowed and share in available estate assets without any objection from the trustee or any other party. Consider how remarkable this is: a number of claims are satisfied, at least in part, without any judicial determination that money was in fact owed. The parties simply agree, either expressly or implicitly through inaction.

In some instances, however, the trustee or some other party may object to one or more claims. When this occurs, the objecting party may argue that there was no valid debt under the applicable nonbankruptcy law or that the amount of the debt is lower than the amount claimed. These circumstances are rare,[3] but when they do occur resolution of the dispute requires a sort of evidentiary hearing before the court, much like the trial of a lawsuit. In general, the bankruptcy court will resolve these disputes in a summary hearing and without a jury. Claims for personal injury torts or wrongful death, however, must be tried in federal district court, rather than in the bankruptcy court, and the right

---

2 *See, e.g.*, *In re Ortiz*, 477 B.R. 714 (E.D. Wis. 2012).

3 Because the trustee's compensation is based on the value of the assets distributed, but is unaffected by the number and amount of claims, the trustee has no financial incentive to scrutinize closely all claims.

to a jury is preserved.[4] In addition, if the claim arises from a contract that includes an arbitration clause, the validity of the claim may have to be resolved by arbitration.[5]

1. Calculating Claims

Here is an example of how a claim is calculated. Assume that Debtor has a charge account with Retailer. The credit terms require payment within 30 days and charge interest at 12% per year on any amounts remaining unpaid after 30 days. Retailer is also entitled to attorney's fees and collection costs up to 10% of the amount of the debt if it has to take any legal action to collect.

Three months before filing the bankruptcy petition, Debtor made a $100 charge, for which the debtor has since paid nothing. Two weeks before bankruptcy, the debtor made another $50 charge. Retailer would file a proof of claim for the first $100 charge, plus $2 in interest on that charge over the last two months (this assumes simple interest, without compounding), plus $50 for the second charge. The fact that payment is not yet due for the second charge is immaterial. *See* § 101(5) (defining "claim"). If Retailer had incurred prepetition collection expenses it could add those too, but let's assume there were as of yet no collection costs (the costs of completing the proof of claim do not count because they arose postpetition). Thus, retailer has a claim for $152, all of which is allowable under § 502 because it all arose prepetition.

If, after all of the estate assets are sold, the trustee has enough to pay unsecured claimants 10% of their claims (10 cents on the dollar), the trustee will send Retailer a check for $15.20. Absent unusual circumstances, the portion of the debt remaining unpaid will be discharged at the conclusion of the case.

If Retailer had made a clerical mistake and filed a claim for $162, it would have been allowed unless someone objected. § 502(a). It would, therefore, have received a slightly higher distribution than appropriate. Of course, a creditor who intentionally files an incorrect claim could be sanctioned because the proof of claim form requires a signature of the creditor, or the creditor's authorized agent, under penalty of perjury. Official Form 10. And an attorney that allows its creditor client to file an incorrect claim may also be sanctioned. *See* Rule 9011.

---

4 28 U.S.C. §§ 157(b)(2)(B), (b)(5), 1411.

5 *See, e.g.*, *In re Thorpe Insulation Co.*, 671 F.3d 1011 (9th Cir. 2012).

2. *Disallowed and Revived Claims*

Not all claims are allowed. Some are disallowed because a dispute is resolved in favor of the debtor. Using the example above, let's assume the $100 charge was for the purchase of a small appliance that did not work. If the Chapter 7 trustee objected, the claim would be disallowed because the trustee may assert all defenses to payment that the debtor has including, as in this case, a breach of warranty. § 502(b)(1).

Other claims are disallowed for policy reasons. Read § 502(b)(2)–(9). Again using the example above, assume that it will take five months for the trustee to liquidate Debtor's assets and distribute the proceeds to creditors. Pursuant to its contract, Retailer is entitled to interest on its claim for that period. However, any claim for "unmatured interest," *i.e.*, interest that had not yet accrued by the date the petition was filed, is disallowed. § 502(b)(2). Unsecured creditors generally get no postpetition interest.[6]

no post petition interest

Examine the other grounds for disallowance in § 502(b). Paragraph (5), which disallows unmatured support obligations, is a bit like paragraph (2). Most of the remaining paragraphs are all designed to protect the estate from claims deemed excessive for one reason or another.[7]

While some prepetition claims are disallowed, a very small number of postpetition claims are treated as prepetition, and then allowed or disallowed on that basis. § 502(h). The most common type of claim in this category is one arising from repayment of a preference. Consider the following scenario:

---

[6] If the debtor is actually solvent it may be required to pay postpetition interest on all claims (not merely those based on a contract that provides for interest). *See* §§ 726(a)(5), 1129(a)(7), 1325(a)(4); *see also* § 1322(b)(10) (postpetition interest on nondischargable claims).

[7] Subsection (k), which was added to the Code in 2005, allows – but does not require – the bankruptcy court to disallow up to 20% of a claim on an unsecured consumer debt if the creditor "unreasonably refused to negotiate" a reasonable alternative payment schedule proposed by a nonprofit credit counseling service on behalf of the debtor. This rule presumably is intended to apply some pressure on creditors to cooperate with debtors and agree to nonbankruptcy settlements. Whether it will have much effect is highly questionable. After all, most consumers who file for Chapter 7 bankruptcy relief have no nonexempt assets. Consequently, allowance or disallowance of a creditor's claim is immaterial. Furthermore, while the provision allows the debtor to move for this partial disallowance, the debtor usually has little incentive to do so because, to the extent the claim is not paid, it is likely to be discharged. A debtor in a Chapter 13 or 11 case, however, has an incentive to use this provision because to the extent the claim is allowed, it will have to be dealt with in the reorganization plan.

Before the petition is filed, Debtor owes a debt to Creditor. Shortly before the petition, Debtor pays that obligation in a manner that prefers Creditor. During the bankruptcy case, the trustee sues Creditor for the preference and recovers the payment. At this point, Creditor is still out money. Creditor extended credit, got paid, and then disgorged the payment. However, Debtor's obligation arose, in at least one sense, postpetition, when the preferential transfer was recovered. And postpetition claims are normally disallowed. However, the whole point of preference law is to unwind the preferential transfer and treat Creditor as if the transfer had not been made. To do that, the revived obligation needs to be treated as having arisen prepetition, and then allowed or disallowed on that basis. Section 502(h) does that. Section 501(d) then permits Creditor to file a proof of claim with respect to the revived claim. If the deadline for filing proofs of claims has passed before a final judgment is rendered against a creditor in an avoidance action, the creditor will have 30 days from entry of the judgment to file a proof of claim with respect to the revived claim. Rule 3002(c)(3).

On the subject of preferences, § 502(d) is another interesting provision. It is a sort of penalty provision: it disallows the claims of a creditor who fails to repay a preferential transfer. Thus, even if the preferential transfer were of minor consequence, say only $8,000, and the creditor's other claims exceeded $1,000,000, that entire large sum would be disallowed until the creditor returned the $8,000.[8]

Although courts are not in total agreement about this, there may be another crafty use of § 502(d). Pursuant to § 546(a), an avoidance action under § 547 may not be brought more than two years after commencement of the case. In other words, there is a two-year statute of limitations. However, even if a preference action is time-barred, the trustee may still be permitted to use § 502(d) to avoid the preferred creditor's claim unless that creditor voluntarily returns the preferential transfer.

Another postpetition claim treated as prepetition is a claim that arises in the "gap period" after the filing of an involuntary petition. As you may recall from chapter two, an involuntary petition does not constitute the order for relief. Instead, the court enters an order for relief some time later, only if it first determines that the petition was proper and the applicable conditions were satisfied. § 303. Although the automatic stay goes into effect immediately upon the filing of the petition and enjoins all creditor collection

---

[8] While § 502(d) can be used to disallow a claim of a creditor who fails to repay an avoidable preference, it apparently cannot be used to disallow payment of a postpetition administrative expense to such a creditor. *In re Ames Dep't Stores, Inc.*, 582 F.3d 422 (2d Cir. 2009), *cert. denied*, 130 S. Ct. 1527 (2010). *Contra In re MicroAge, Inc.*, 291 B.R. 503 (9th Cir. BAP 2002).

activity, § 362, it does not necessarily stop the debtor from incurring new debts. As a result, claims may arise after the petition is filed but before the order for relief is entered. Section 502(f) treats such "gap" claims as prepetition claims.

3. *Tardy Claims*

What happens if a creditor attempts to file a proof of claim after the time for doing so expires? The answer depends on the type of case. In Chapter 7, late-filed, nonpriority unsecured claims are effectively allowable, but subordinated to timely filed claims (unless the creditor had no knowledge of the bankruptcy in time to file on a timely basis but still managed to file before distributions were made). § 726(a)(2), (3). Tardy priority claims are allowed and retain their priority as long as the proof of claim is filed before the trustee makes distribution to claims of that priority.[9] § 726(a)(1).

In Chapter 13 cases, tardy claims are disallowed if objected to. *See* § 502(b)(9). The subordination provisions of § 726(a) do not apply,[10] and the rules do not permit an extension to be granted to most creditors.[11] If no one objects to the claim, however, the claim will be allowed. Whether it will be paid depends on what the plan provides.

In Chapter 11 cases, late filing is governed by Rule 9006(b)(1), which provides that a bankruptcy court may, for cause, on motion made after the bar date, permit a proof of claim to be filed late if the tardiness resulted from "excusable neglect." In *Pioneer Investment Services Co. v. Brunswick Associates Limited Partnership*,[12] the Supreme Court ruled that "excusable neglect" is not limited to things beyond the claimant's control. The Court explained that the rule on late filing in Chapter 7 is strict because of the need to distribute the estate promptly and close the case. In Chapter 11, on the other hand, the goals are to rehabilitate the debtor through a largely consensual process. Hence, an equitable balancing of the interests at stake is more appropriate. The Court indicated that all relevant circumstances should be taken into account in striking this balance but also agreed with several specific factors identified by the lower court: "the danger of prejudice to the debtor, the length of the delay and its potential impact on

---

9 It remains unclear what happens if a proof of claim is filed after distribution has been made on priority claims.

10 *See* § 103(b).

11 *See* Rules 3002, 9006(b)(3).

12 507 U.S. 380 (1993).

judicial proceedings, the reason for the delay, including whether it was within the reasonable control of the [claimant], and whether the [claimant] acted in good faith."[13] It expressly rejected the lower court's conclusion, however, that a claimant should not be responsible for the negligence of its attorney. Thus, the proper question in the case before it was whether the neglect of the claimants and their counsel was excusable.

The Court concluded that the claimants and their lawyer were acting in good faith and that there was no prejudice to the debtor or to the interests of efficient judicial administration. While the Court refused to treat as relevant any upheaval in the attorney's office, it did regard as significant the fact that notice of the bar date was provided in an unusual manner. Hence, although there was neglect in the sense that the lawyer was remiss in failing to apprehend the notice, the neglect was excusable.

B. CONTINGENT CLAIMS

Not only must the bankruptcy court resolve disputed claims and determine the amount of unliquidated claims, it must also estimate the amount of contingent claims. § 502(c). This can be a difficult task. By definition, a contingent claim requires that a certain event occur before liability accrues. That means the court must determine the probability that a specified event will happen. This represents a significant change from the law under the old Bankruptcy Act, but is necessary to deal with the fact that bankruptcy proceedings are intended to be of fairly short duration yet affect the rights of creditors permanently, whether they voluntarily participate in them or not. For example, a corporation liquidated in Chapter 7 will be left without any assets after the case is over and, in all likelihood, will be dissolved. A creditor will therefore have no chance to recover postbankruptcy. The only way the creditor can receive anything is if the creditor's rights qualify as a claim in the bankruptcy proceeding.

Fortunately, the problem of estimating contingent claims does not arise often. When it does, though, the bankruptcy court may be confronted with the problem of deciding whether the claim is sufficiently definite on the date of the petition to merit treatment in the bankruptcy process. This is much like the problem we saw in chapter three of determining whether the debtor's contingent rights should be included among the assets of the bankruptcy estate. Here, however, we are focusing on the other side of

---

[13] *Id.* at 393.

the bankruptcy balance sheet: whether the debtor's contingent obligations qualify as allowable claims.

Let us begin discussion of this issue with an easy case. Dastardly files for bankruptcy protection. Does Benevolent, Dastardly's mortal foe, have an allowable – *i.e.*, prepetition – claim for a battery that Dastardly might commit in the future? The obvious answer to this must be "no." The damages that Benevolent might suffer from a potential act of future violence is just too fanciful to treat as a claim.

This simple illustration shows that a bit of a tension exists between the congressional decision to allow claims regardless of whether they are contingent and the rule calling for disallowance of claims that are not prepetition. Presumably, to be allowable, the debtor must have engaged in some prepetition conduct that could give rise to the right to payment.

Now consider the following two more difficult scenarios:

1. Debtor A manufactures building insulation made with asbestos. Many of its employees have begun to suffer the severe effects of asbestosis, resulting from exposure to asbestos. Some of its customers and some end consumers have also become gravely ill. Many of the employees, customers, and consumers have already won products liability actions against Debtor A and the litigation costs for the pending and expected future claims are so substantial that Debtor A files for bankruptcy protection. Do the employees, customers, and consumers who have already been exposed but who have not yet manifested symptoms have claims? What about the consumers who have not yet been exposed as of the date of the petition but who will later be exposed and who, sometime after that, will become ill?

2. Debtor B manufactures and sells aircraft. Several aircraft have crashed, resulting in claims against Debtor B. In response, Debtor B filed for bankruptcy protection. Several months before the petition, Baker purchased an aircraft from Debtor B. That aircraft crashes postpetition because of a design or manufacturing defect. Does Baker have a claim on the petition date? What about the people who were passengers on Baker's plane when it crashed?

To deal with these issues, courts have developed two primary tests: (1) The Conduct Test; and (2) The Prepetition Relationship Test. As the following case indicates, in overruling a previously used third alternative, the tests are similar yet each has a slightly different focus, which can lead to different results in some instances.

IN RE GROSSMAN'S INC.
607 F.3d 114 (3d Cir. 2010)

SLOVITER, Circuit Judge.

This Court's Internal Operating Procedure provides:

> It is the tradition of this court that the holding of a panel in a precedential opinion is binding on subsequent panels. Thus, no subsequent panel overrules the holding in a precedential opinion of a previous panel. Court en banc consideration is required to do so.

We adhere strictly to that tradition. It is only on a rare occasion that we overrule a prior precedential opinion. We assemble en banc to consider whether this is such an occasion.

In the appeal before us, the Bankruptcy Court, affirmed by the District Court, followed our precedent in *Matter of M. Frenville Co.*, 744 F.2d 332 (3d Cir. 1984) ("*Frenville*"), to hold that a plan of reorganization did not discharge asbestos-related tort claims filed by Mary Van Brunt and her husband Gordon (the "Van Brunts") against Grossman's Inc. The underlying asbestos exposure occurred pre-petition but the injury manifested itself post-petition. The Appellant, JELD-WEN, Inc., successor to defendant Grossman's Inc. and its affiliates (hereafter "Grossman's"), asks us to overrule the holding of *Frenville.*

I.

Background

In 1977, Appellee Mary Van Brunt, who was remodeling her home, purchased products that allegedly contained asbestos. She purchased those products in upstate New York from Grossman's, a home improvement and lumber retailer. In April 1997, Grossman's filed petitions under Chapter 11 of the Bankruptcy Code.

The following are among the undisputed facts set forth in the Bankruptcy Court's Findings of Fact: "[a]t the time of the [bankruptcy], Grossman's had actual knowledge that it had previously sold asbestos containing products such as gypsum board and joint compound"; "Grossman's knew of the adverse health risks associated with exposure to asbestos"; it "was aware that asbestos manufacturers had been or were being sued by asbestos personal-injury claimants"; it "was aware that producers of both gypsum board and joint compound were being sued for asbestos-related injuries"; and it "was not aware of any product liability lawsuits based upon alleged exposure to asbestos-containing products that had been filed against [it]."

Grossman's proceeded to provide notice by publication of the deadline for filing proofs of claim. There was no suggestion in the publication notice that Grossman's might have future asbestos liability. Grossman's Chapter 11 Plan of Reorganization purported to discharge all claims that arose before the Plan's effective date. The Bankruptcy Court confirmed the Plan of Reorganization in December 1997.

Ms. Van Brunt did not file a proof of claim before confirmation of the Plan of Reorganization because, at the time, she was unaware of any "claim" as she manifested no symptoms related to asbestos exposure. It was only in 2006, almost ten years later, that Ms. Van Brunt began to manifest symptoms of mesothelioma, a cancer linked to asbestos exposure. She was diagnosed with the disease in March 2007.

Shortly after her diagnosis, the Van Brunts filed an action for tort and breach of warranty in a New York state court against JELD-WEN, the successor-in-interest to Grossman's, and fifty-seven other companies who allegedly manufactured the products that Ms. Van Brunt purchased from Grossman's in 1977. * * * After the Van Brunts filed their suit, JELD-WEN moved to reopen the Chapter 11 case, seeking a determination that their claims were discharged by the Plan. Ms. Van Brunt died in 2008 while the case was pending. Gordon Van Brunt has been substituted in her stead as the representative of her estate.

The Bankruptcy Court concluded that the 1997 Plan of Reorganization did not discharge the Van Brunts' asbestos-related claims because they arose after the effective date of the Plan. In so holding, the Bankruptcy Court relied on our decisions in *Frenville* and its progeny. *Frenville* held that a "claim," as that term is defined by the Bankruptcy Code, arises when the underlying state law cause of action accrues. The applicable New York law provides that a cause of action for asbestos-related injury does not accrue until the injury manifests itself. The Bankruptcy Court therefore reasoned that the Van Brunts had no "claim" subject to discharge in 1997 because Ms. Van Brunt did not manifest symptoms of mesothelioma – and thus the New York cause of action did not accrue – until 2006. The Bankruptcy Court entered judgment for the Van Brunts and against JELD-WEN, effectively allowing the Van Brunts to proceed with their claims in the New York state court.

The District Court affirmed the Bankruptcy Court's decision in every respect but one. The District Court reversed the Bankruptcy Court's conclusion that the breach of warranty claim arose post-petition, reasoning that the claim accrued under New York law at the time of delivery of the product and was discharged in the Grossman's bankruptcy. The Van Brunts have not appealed that determination. Instead,

JELD-WEN appeals the District Court's affirmance of the Bankruptcy Court's holding that the Van Brunts' tort claims were not "claims" under 11 U.S.C. § 101(5). * * *

III.
Discussion

A. The *Frenville* Accrual Test

In 1980, M. Frenville Co. was the subject of an involuntary petition for bankruptcy filed in New Jersey under Chapter 7 of the Bankruptcy Reform Act of 1978. Thereafter, involuntary petitions under Chapter 7 of the Code were filed against two principals of the company.

Later that year, four banks filed a lawsuit in a New York state court against the company's former accountants, Avellino & Bienes ("A & B"), alleging that A & B negligently and recklessly prepared the company's pre-petition financial statements and seeking damages for their alleged losses exceeding five million dollars. A & B filed a complaint in the bankruptcy court in New Jersey seeking relief from the automatic stay in order to implead Frenville as a third-party defendant in order to obtain indemnification or contribution under New York law. The bankruptcy court, affirmed by the district court, held that the automatic stay barred A & B's action. A & B appealed.

We reversed, holding that because the automatic stay applied only to claims that arose pre-petition, under New York law A & B did not have a right to payment for its claim for indemnification or contribution from Frenville until after the banks filed their suit against A & B. It followed that A & B's claim against Frenville arose post-petition even though the conduct upon which A & B's liability was predicated (negligent preparation of Frenville's financial statements) occurred pre-petition. It followed that the automatic stay was inapplicable. We emphasized that the "crucial issue" was when the "right to payment" arose as determined by reference to the New York law that governed the indemnification claim.

This court subsequently summarized *Frenville* as holding that "the existence of a valid claim depends on: (1) whether the claimant possessed a right to payment; and (2) when that right arose" as determined by reference to the relevant non-bankruptcy law. *In re Remington Rand Corp.*, 836 F.2d 825, 830 (3d Cir. 1988). The *Frenville* test for determining when a claim arises has been referred to as the "accrual test."

In the case before us, the District Court and Bankruptcy Court correctly applied the accrual test in holding that the Van Brunts' tort claims were not discharged by the Plan of Reorganization. According to *Frenville,* the claims arose for bankruptcy purposes when the underlying state law cause of action accrued. The New York tort cause of action accrued in 2006 when Ms. Van Brunt manifested symptoms of mesothelioma. The claims were therefore post-petition under *Frenville.*

The question remains, however, whether we should continue to follow *Frenville* and its accrual test. We have recognized that "[s]ignificant authority [contrary to *Frenville*] exists in other circuits." *Jones v. Chemetron Corp.*, 212 F.3d 199, 205–06 (3d Cir. 2000). A sister circuit has described our approach in *Frenville* as "universally rejected." *In re Andrews*, 239 F.3d 708, 710 n.7 (5th Cir. 2001). The courts of appeals that have considered *Frenville* have uniformly declined to follow it. At least one bankruptcy court has stated that *Frenville* "may be fairly characterized as one of the most criticized and least followed precedents decided under the current Bankruptcy Code." *In re Firearms Imp. & Exp. Corp.*, 131 B.R. 1009, 1015 (Bankr. S.D. Fla. 1991). * * * The criticism has been echoed by commentators.

Notwithstanding what appears to be universal disapproval, we decide cases before us based on our own examination of the issue, not on the views of other jurisdictions. Nevertheless, those widely held views impel us to consider whether the reasoning applied by our colleagues elsewhere is persuasive.

Courts have declined to follow *Frenville* because of its apparent conflict with the Bankruptcy Code's expansive treatment of the term "claim." The Bankruptcy Code, which was adopted by the Bankruptcy Reform Act of 1978, defines a "claim" as

> [a] right to payment, whether or not such right is reduced to judgment, liquidated, *unliquidated,* fixed, *contingent,* matured, *unmatured,* disputed, undisputed, legal, equitable, secured, or unsecured.

11 U.S.C. § 101(5) (emphasis added). The House and Senate Reports * * * state that "[b]y this *broadest possible definition* [of the term 'claim'] . . . the bill contemplates that all legal obligations of the debtor, no matter how remote or contingent, will be able to be dealt with in the bankruptcy case . . . [and] permits the broadest possible relief in the bankruptcy court." H.R. Rep. No. 95-595, at 309 (1977).

The Supreme Court has likewise noted that "claim" has "the broadest available definition." *FCC v. NextWave Personal Communications, Inc.*, 537 U.S. 293, 302 (2003). * * *

The *Frenville* court focused on the "right to payment" language in § 101(5) and, according to some courts, "impos[ed] too narrow an interpretation on the term claim," *In re Piper Aircraft, Corp.*, 58 F.3d 1573, 1576 n.2 (11th Cir. 1995), by failing to give sufficient weight to the words modifying it: "contingent," "unmatured," and "unliquidated." The accrual test in *Frenville* does not account for the fact that a "claim" can exist under the Code before a right to payment exists under state law.

We are persuaded that the widespread criticism of *Frenville*'s accrual test is justified, as it imposes too narrow an interpretation of a "claim" under the Bankruptcy Code. Accordingly, the *Frenville* accrual test should be and now is overruled.

B. When a Claim Arises

Our decision to overrule *Frenville* leaves a void in our jurisprudence as to when a claim arises. That decision has various implications. One such implication involves the application of the automatic stay provided in § 362 of the Bankruptcy Code which operates to stay the commencement or continuation of any "action or proceeding" that was or could have been commenced against the debtor. *See* 11 U.S.C. § 362(a)(1). * * *

Principal among the effects of the determination when a claim arises is the effect on the dischargeability of a claim. Under 11 U.S.C. § 1141(d)(1)(A) of the Code, the confirmation of a plan of reorganization "discharges the debtor from any debt that arose before the date of such confirmation." A "debt" is defined as liability on a "claim," *id.* § 101(12), which in turn is defined as a "right to payment," *id.* § 101(5). This is consistent with Congress' intent to provide debtors with a fresh start, an objective, noted the Second Circuit, "made more feasible by maximizing the scope of a discharge." *In re Chateaugay*, 944 F.2d 997, 1002 (2d Cir. 1991). On the other hand, a broad discharge may disadvantage potential claimants, such as tort claimants, whose injuries were allegedly caused by the debtor but which have not yet manifested and who therefore had no reason to file claims in the bankruptcy. These competing considerations have not been resolved consistently by the cases decided to date.

Moreover, the determination when a claim arises has significant due process implications. If potential future tort claimants have not filed claims because they are unaware of their injuries, they might challenge the effectiveness of any purported notice of the claims bar date. Discharge of such claims without providing adequate notice raises questions under the Fourteenth Amendment.

The courts have generally divided into two groups on the decision as to when a claim arises for purposes of the Code, with numerous variations. One group has applied the conduct test and the other has applied what has been termed the pre-petition relationship test. Illustrative of the cases that have adopted the conduct test is the decision of the Fourth Circuit in *Grady v. A.H. Robins Co.*, 839 F.2d 198 (4th Cir. 1988).

In *Grady*, the plaintiff had inserted a Dalkon Shield intrauterine contraceptive device several years before the manufacturer filed a petition for Chapter 11 bankruptcy. The plaintiff alleged that she experienced injuries from the Dalkon Shield, including the need for a hysterectomy. The district court, which did not refer the case to the bankruptcy court, determined that the plaintiff's claim arose "when the acts giving rise to [the defendant's] liability were performed, not when the harm caused by those acts was manifested." The court of appeals affirmed, finding that the plaintiff held a contingent claim that arose before the commencement of the bankruptcy case. The court cautioned that it was not deciding whether Grady's claim "or those of [future tort claimants] are dischargeable in this case." *Id.* at 203. It held only that because the Dalkon Shield was inserted in the claimant before the filing of the bankruptcy petition, it constituted a claim within the meaning of the automatic stay, i.e., a pre-petition claim.

In contrast, the Eleventh Circuit criticized a conduct test that would enable individuals to hold a claim against a debtor by virtue of their potential future exposure to "the debtor's product," regardless of whether the claimant had any relationship or contact with the debtor. *In re Piper*, 58 F.3d at 1577. It stated that approach would define a "claim" too broadly in certain circumstances and would "stretch the scope of § 101(5)" too far. * * *

Some of the courts concerned that the conduct test may be too broad have adopted what has been referred to as a pre-petition relationship test. Under this test, a claim arises from a debtor's pre-petition tortious conduct where there is also some pre-petition relationship between the debtor and the claimant, such as a purchase, use, operation of, or exposure to the debtor's product. One commentator opined that "[t]he 'pre-petition relationship test' ameliorates the problem often attributed to the 'conduct test' – that a bankruptcy proceeding cannot identify and afford due process to claimants." Barbara J. Houser, *Chapter 11 as a Mass Tort Solution,* 31 Loy. L.A. L. Rev. 451, 465 (1998).

In *Lemelle v. Universal Mfg. Corp.*, 18 F.3d 1268 (5th Cir. 1994), the plaintiff brought a wrongful death action against the successor corporation of a mobile home manufacturer that had emerged from Chapter 11 proceedings. The plaintiff alleged that the decedent's death was caused by the manufacturer's defective mobile home design and construction. The decedent died in a fire allegedly caused by the manufacturing defect about two years after the debtor's plan of reorganization was confirmed and approximately fifteen years after the design and manufacture of the mobile home. The district court determined that the plan of reorganization discharged all of the debtor's obligations, including the liability on the tort claim.

The Fifth Circuit reversed, noting that in order for the plaintiff's wrongful death claim to have been discharged in the debtor's bankruptcy, "at a minimum, there must be evidence that would permit the debtor to identify, during the course of the bankruptcy proceedings, potential victims and thereby permit notice to these potential victims of the pendency of the proceedings." *Id.* at 1277. The court found that the record was "devoid of any evidence of any pre-petition contact, privity, or other relationship between [the debtor], on the one hand, and [the plaintiff] or the decedents, on the other." *Id.* The court concluded that absent any such evidence, the district court could not find "that the claims asserted by [the plaintiff] were discharged in [the debtor's] bankruptcy proceedings." *Id.* The court reasoned that "even the broad definition of 'claim' cannot be extended to include . . . claimants whom the record indicates were completely unknown and unidentified at the time [the debtor] filed its petition and whose rights depended entirely on the fortuity of future occurrences." *Id.*

The Second Circuit followed a similar approach in an environmental regulatory context. In *In re Chateaugay*, 944 F.2d at 1004–05, the court held that the EPA's post-confirmation costs of responding to a release of hazardous waste, even if not yet incurred at the time of bankruptcy, involved "claims" under § 101(5). The court reasoned that "[t]he relationship between environmental regulating agencies and those subject to regulation provides sufficient 'contemplation' of contingencies to bring most ultimately maturing payment obligations based on pre-petition conduct within the definition of 'claims' [under the Bankruptcy Code]." *Id.* at 1005.

A somewhat modified approach was taken by the Eleventh Circuit in a case involving the bankruptcy of Piper Aircraft, Inc., a manufacturer of general aviation aircraft and spare aircraft parts. The bankruptcy court, affirmed by the district court, held that a class of future claimants who might assert, after confirmation of the debtor's plan of reorganization, personal injury or property damage claims against Piper based on its aircraft products that were manufactured or sold before the confirmation date, did not have claims under § 101(5). 58 F.3d at 1575–76. The bankruptcy and district courts had adopted the pre-petition relationship test which, according to the court of appeals, requires "some prepetition relationship, such as contact, exposure, impact, or privity, between the debtor's pre-petition conduct and the claimant in order for the claimant to have a § 101(5) claim." *Id.* at 1576.

The court of appeals agreed that the pre-petition relationship test was generally superior to either our test in *Frenville* or the "conduct test" adopted by other courts of appeals. It also held that claimants having contact with the debtor's product post-petition, but prior to confirmation, also could be identified during the course of the bankruptcy procedure. It thus framed what it chose to denominate as the "*Piper*" test as follows:

> [A]n individual has a § 101(5) claim against a debtor manufacturer if (i) events occurring before confirmation create a relationship, such as contact, exposure, impact, or privity, between the claimant and the debtor's product; and (ii) the basis for liability is the debtor's prepetition conduct in designing, manufacturing and selling the allegedly defective or dangerous product.

Id. at 1577. The court stated that "[t]he debtor's prepetition conduct gives rise to a claim to be administered in a case only if there is a relationship established before confirmation between an identifiable claimant or group of claimants and that prepetition conduct." *Id.* * * *

The pre-petition relationship test in *Piper* has been criticized for narrowing the definition of "claim" under 11 U.S.C. § 101(5). In a final report issued in 1997, the National Bankruptcy Review Commission proposed a definition of "claim" that incorporated the conduct test, albeit with some limitations, rather than the pre-petition relationship test. * * *

Irrespective of the title used, there seems to be something approaching a consensus among the courts that a prerequisite for recognizing a "claim" is that the claimant's exposure to a product giving rise to the "claim" occurred pre-petition, even though the injury manifested after the reorganization. We agree and hold that a "claim" arises when an individual is exposed pre-petition to a product or other conduct giving rise to an injury, which underlies a "right to payment" under the Bankruptcy Code. Applied to the Van Brunts, it means that their claims arose sometime in 1977, the date Mary Van Brunt alleged that Grossman's product exposed her to asbestos.

That does not necessarily mean that the Van Brunts' claims were discharged by the Plan of Reorganization. Any application of the test to be applied cannot be divorced from fundamental principles of due process. Notice is "[a]n elementary and fundamental requirement of due process in any proceeding which is to be accorded finality. *Mullane v. Central Hanover Bank & Trust Co.*, 339 U.S. 306, 314 (1950). * * *

Whether a particular claim has been discharged by a plan of reorganization depends on factors applicable to the particular case and is best determined by the appropriate bankruptcy court or the district court. In determining whether an asbestos claim has been discharged, the court may wish to consider, inter alia, the circumstances of the initial exposure to asbestos, whether and/or when the claimants were aware of their vulnerability to asbestos, whether the notice of the claims bar date came to their attention, whether the claimants were known or unknown creditors, whether the claimants had a colorable claim at the time of the bar date, and other circumstances specific to the parties, including whether it was reasonable or possible for the debtor to establish a trust for future claimants as provided by § 524(g). * * *

NOTE

As the *Grossman's* opinion indicates, one issue often closely related to claim status, particularly when mass torts are involved, is due process. To treat a future injury as a claim and to discharge it without notice to the person who will be injured presents significant constitutional problems. The same types of notice and due process problems arise in class action litigation. For a thoughtful discussion of this, see *Fogel v. Zell*, 221 F.3d 955 (7th Cir. 2000), in which Judge Posner invalidated a settlement between the bankruptcy trustee and the entities that had acquired the debtor's assets. The settlement, which had been approved by the bankruptcy court, barred recovery to anyone whose prepetition purchase of the debtor's defective products resulted in injury (prepetition or postpetition) if they did not file a proof of claim by the bar date, even though some of these potential claimants had no notice or knowledge of the bar date.

Problem 5-3

Review the contingent obligations of Debtor A and Debtor B described in the illustrations on page 183.

A. Do the creditors in each of these illustrations want their contingent rights to be treated as claims? Do the debtors? Does it matter whether the bankruptcy proceeding is under Chapter 7 or Chapter 11?

B. For each contingent obligation of Debtor A and Debtor B, determine whether it qualifies as a claim under the Prepetition Relationship Test.

One common type of contingent claim is the fee claim of the debtor's attorney for legal services contracted for prepetition but rendered postpetition. If the prepetition fee agreement requires payment of a flat fee for all services – both prepetition and postpetition – a majority of courts treat the entire debt as a prepetition claim.[14] The result may be different, however, with respect to postpetition services if the fee

---

[14] *See, e.g., Bethea v. Robert J. Adams & Assocs.*, 352 F.3d 1125 (7th Cir. 2003); *In re Waldo*, 417 B.R. 854 (Bankr. E.D. Tenn. 2009). *See also Walton v. Clark & Washington, P.C.*, 454 B.R. 537 (Bankr. M.D. Fla. 2011) (by accepting prepetition a post-dated check for postpetition services, debtor's attorneys had a prepetition claim). *Contra In re Hines*, 147 F.3d 1185 (9th Cir. 1998).

agreement provides for compensation on an hourly basis.[15] In a Chapter 13 case, the debtor's attorney may be entitled to compensation from the estate under § 330(a)(4), which requires consideration of the "benefit and necessity of such services to the debtor," among other considerations. In addition to this, other professional compensation may be allowed as administrative expense in a Chapter 13 case. In Chapter 11 cases, the fees of an attorney employed by the debtor in possession may qualify as an administrative expense and be payable out of the estate, subject to the general requirement that they benefit the estate. §§ 327, 330, 503, 1107.

Another common type of contingent claim is that of a person who has guaranteed one of the debtor's obligations. Most guarantors are entitled to reimbursement from the debtor once they pay the guaranteed obligation.[16] Thus, a guarantor has a contingent claim: a claim contingent on the guarantor paying the creditor. Section 502(e) has special – and important – rules to deal with such claims. After reading that subsection, answer the problem below.

Problem 5-4

Bank made an unsecured loan to Davenport, and Surety guaranteed payment. When Davenport filed for Chapter 7 bankruptcy protection, the unpaid balance of the loan was $10,000. Assume that distributions in the bankruptcy will pay unsecured creditors 40% of their claims.

A. If Bank files a proof of claim in bankruptcy for $10,000 on the loan and Surety files a proof of claim for $6,000 for reimbursement, how much will each receive from the bankruptcy estate? *See* § 502(e)(1)(B). What rights does Bank have against Surety?

B. How, if at all, would the analysis of Part A change if Surety had paid Bank $10,000 on the guaranty before Davenport filed for bankruptcy?

C. If Bank does not file a proof of claim, does Surety have a claim in bankruptcy? Is it allowable? What should Surety do to protect itself? *See* §§ 501(b), 502(e)(2).

D. Assume that before the bankruptcy petition was filed Surety paid Bank $4,000 and that on the date of bankruptcy $6,000 remained unpaid. Both Bank and Surety file proofs of claim in bankruptcy. How much will each receive? *See* § 502(e)(1)(B). What rights does Bank have against Surety?

---

[15] *See, e.g., In re Chase*, 372 B.R. 133 (Bankr. S.D.N.Y. 2007).

[16] *See* RESTATEMENT (THIRD) OF SURETYSHIP AND GUARANTY § 22 (1996).

C. EQUITABLE RIGHTS

A "claim" is defined in § 101(5)(B) to include a "right to an equitable remedy for breach of performance if such breach gives rise to a right to payment." What this means is not entirely clear. The structure of this clause – an equitable right is a claim if – strongly suggests that some equitable rights are claims, but not all of them. Equitable rights are claims only if their breach gives rise to a right to payment. However, given that many equitable rights, including the right to an injunction, apply only when the right to money damages is inadequate, when does a breach of performance give rise to a right to payment? Consider the following three scenarios:

1. Dirtycorp has for years been dumping toxic waste onto several acres of land. The EPA recently secured a court order directing Dirtycorp to clean up the site and to stop all further dumping. If Dirtycorp files bankruptcy, is that order a claim?

2. When Dentist turned 60, Dentist decided to retire. Dentist sold her small-town, rural practice to Purchaser and, as part of the sales agreement, promised not to compete against Purchaser in the town for three years. Dentist entrusted the sales proceeds to Broker, who invested them in high-risk, start-up companies. All of the money was lost and Dentist was left with no income or retirement savings. Dentist, who has never had another trade, opened a new dental practice in town in order to generate income. If Dentist files for bankruptcy, does Purchaser have a claim against Dentist for damages for prepetition competition? Does Purchaser have a claim against Dentist for postpetition competition?

3. Despicable physically abused Spouse during their marriage and stalked Spouse after their divorce. Several months ago, Spouse obtained a court order enjoining Despicable from coming within 100 yards of Spouse's residence or place of employment. If Despicable files bankruptcy, does Spouse have a claim against Despicable?

Note the implications of these questions. If the equitable right gives rise to a claim, then the holder of the equitable right can potentially share in any distribution from the bankruptcy estate. More significantly, because "debt" is defined as "liability on a claim," § 101(12), if any of these rights qualifies as a claim, the debtor's correlative obligation can potentially be discharged in bankruptcy. Are any of these obligations of a type that a debtor should be able to escape?

The Supreme Court dealt with the first scenario in *Ohio v. Kovacs*.[17] In that case, a state court had issued an injunction ordering the debtor to clean up an environmentally contaminated site. The state court later appointed a receiver to take possession of the property. Cleanup was underway when the debtor filed bankruptcy. After accepting a finding below that all the receiver wanted was money to defray the cleanup costs, the Supreme Court concluded that the cleanup order had essentially been converted into an obligation to pay money. Accordingly, it qualified as a claim and was dischargeable. The Court emphasized, however, that it was not deciding whether the injunction against further pollution was also a claim.[18]

The third scenario is not the subject of much litigation, probably because most everyone agrees it is not a claim. That is because violation of the court's no-stalking order will not give rise to right to payment *to the victim*; it will instead subject the debtor to sanctions for contempt of court.

The second scenario has been the source of some controversy. There is no doubt that the right to damages for a prepetition violation of the covenant not to compete is a claim, but what about the right to an injunction against postpetition competition? A few courts have ruled that such a right is, or at least can be, a claim.[19] However, the bulk of authority is to the contrary.[20] As a result, in most jurisdictions the debtor cannot discharge the duty not to compete.

The policy implications of this conclusion may be troubling, especially if – as with Dentist in the hypothetical above – the debtor has no other viable source of income. In such a case, bankruptcy may fail to achieve one of its principal goals: giving the debtor a fresh start. This concern may be exacerbated by the fact that postpetition payments to the debtor pursuant to a prepetition noncompetition agreement are generally regarded as an asset of the estate. As a result, there is some lack of symmetry: payments to the debtor for not competing postpetition are sufficiently rooted in the prebankruptcy past

---

[17] 469 U.S. 274 (1985).

[18] *Id.* at 284.

[19] *See, e.g.*, *In re Brown*, 1997 WL 786994 (E.D. Pa. 1997); *In re Ward*, 194 B.R. 703 (Bankr. D. Mass. 1996); *In re Kilpatrick*, 160 B.R. 560 (Bankr. E.D. Mich. 1993).

[20] *See Kennedy v. Medicap Pharmacies, Inc.*, 267 F.3d 493 (6th Cir. 2001); *In re Udell*, 18 F.3d 403 (7th Cir. 1994); *In re Stone Res., Inc.*, 458 B.R. 823 (E.D. Pa. 2011), *rev'd on other grounds*, 482 F. App'x 719 (3d Cir. 2012); *In re Quattrin*, 2011 WL 2112415 (Bankr. N.D. Cal. 2011).

to be an asset of the estate but the debtor's obligation not to compete is not a debt that gives rise to a claim. Thus, the debtor can neither keep the postpetition money nor discharge the postpetition duty.

Problem 5-5

> Duplex owns an unimproved parcel of real estate that is part of a development. All of the lots within the development are subject to restrictions on the size and style of any structure that may be erected. Can Duplex get around those restrictions by declaring bankruptcy and treating the restrictions as equitable rights giving rise to dischargeable claims?

One type of equitable right that is not a "claim" is an ownership interest in the debtor. Thus, the holder of common stock in a corporation that has petitioned for bankruptcy normally has no claim against the estate by virtue of owning the stock.[21] The same is true for those who have invested in a partnership, limited liability company, or other type of entity. These are not claims because the equitable right is not a remedy that arises out of a breach of performance, as required by the definition of claim. § 101(5). Of course, the owners of a business entity may, in addition to contributing assets in exchange for their ownership interest, have also loaned money to the entity. In the normal course of affairs, such owners will have a claim for the unpaid balance of the loan but no claim attributable to their ownership interest.

Unfortunately, it is not always easy to distinguish an equity investment from a loan. Several investment structures, such as preferred stock, have elements of both. Beyond that, the parties' behavior may belie whatever the relevant documents would otherwise suggest. In other words, even though an influx of cash or extension of credit to a business entity from its owner is documented as a loan, if the entity never makes payments when they are due and the understanding is that the entity will pay only once it is profitable, the arrangement may be recharacterized by the bankruptcy court as an equity interest rather than a claim.[22]

---

[21] The stockholder may have a claim if the corporation has declared but not paid a dividend.

[22] *See, e.g.*, *In re Official Comm. of Unsecured Creditors for Dornier Aviation (N. Am.), Inc.*, 453 F.3d 225 (4th Cir. 2006).

D. EXECUTORY CONTRACTS AND UNEXPIRED LEASES

Most commercial enterprises and even many consumers enter into various contracts. These include agreements to buy and sell goods, rent real estate, and participate in franchise agreements. It is not uncommon, therefore, for a debtor to have several unperformed contracts when a bankruptcy petition is filed.

If the debtor has fully performed its contractual duties prior to the bankruptcy petition, and thus the other contracting party is the only one whose performance remains due, then the debtor's contractual rights against the other party are simply an asset of the bankruptcy estate. Conversely, if the other party has fully performed and only the debtor's performance is due, then the debtor's duties to the other party represent a claim against the estate. When neither party has fully performed and some substantial aspect of performance (other than merely the payment of money) remains due from both of them, the contract is labeled "executory" and constitutes both an asset and a liability of the estate.[23]

executory contracts

In such instances, the other party to the contract has a claim against the estate for the value of the debtor's performance. Yet to value that claim reliably, it is necessary to know whether the trustee (or the debtor in possession in a Chapter 11 case or the debtor in a Chapter 13 case) plans to perform the contractual duties that remain to the other party. If the trustee does perform, and does so properly, then nothing else should be owed to the other party. If the trustee instead chooses to breach the contract, then the other party should have a claim that entitles it to share in the assets of the estate.

Section 365 deals with this dilemma by requiring the trustee to assume or reject executory contracts and unexpired leases. § 365(a), (d). If the trustee rejects the contract or lease, it is treated as a prepetition breach, producing a prepetition claim.

---

[23] *See In re Interstate Bakeries Corp.*, 690 F.3d 1069 (8th Cir. 2012). This analysis of what constitutes an executory contract is called the "Countryman" test and is based upon a famous law review article written by law professor Vern Countryman in 1973. Application of the test is often anything but clear. *See* Jay Lawrence Westbrook, *A Functional Analysis of Executory Contracts*, 74 MINN. L. REV. 227 (1989); Michael T. Andrew, *Executory Contracts Revisited: A Reply to Professor Westbrook*, 62 U. COLO. L. REV. 1 (1991). Moreover, in some settings, the result suggested by the Countryman test is generally disregarded because the result is not considered desirable. For example, consider whether a typical security agreement or mortgage is an executory contract. Many times, both the secured party and the debtor have substantial unperformed obligations beyond the payment of money. For example, the debtor often has obligations to maintain the collateral and the secured party may have obligations to take reasonable care of collateral in its possession. However, these types of obligations are not considered sufficient to make the mortgage or security agreement an executory contract.

§§ 365(g), 502(g). If, on the other hand, the trustee assumes the contract or lease, its obligations generally become binding on the bankruptcy estate. However, the trustee is often authorized to assign to another entity the rights and duties of an assumed contract or lease, § 365(f)(1), and if the trustee does so, the bankruptcy estate will have no liability for a future breach by the assignee. § 365(k). A decision to assume, reject, or assign must be approved by the bankruptcy court. § 365(a); Rule 6006.

There are numerous other rules regarding executory contracts and unexpired leases. Before looking at them, however, it is useful to understand the economic incentives applicable to the decision whether to assume or reject. Consider the following hypothetical:

> Driller, Inc. is an independent oil refinery. Bad market conditions and excessive overhead have caused the company to lose money for the past five consecutive quarters. It has now filed for bankruptcy under Chapter 11. Driller has an outstanding contract with Power Company that requires Driller to furnish 100,000 barrels of oil, a substantial portion of Driller's annual output, to Power Company for $55/barrel. This price seemed lucrative eleven months ago when the contract was negotiated, but now appears to be a disaster. Turmoil in the Middle East has caused the price of oil to rise to $65/barrel. Driller has enough assets to pay unsecured creditors 30 cents on the dollar. What should Driller do?

If Driller assumes the contract, it will have to provide the oil to Power Company at $55/barrel. If Driller rejects the contract, it can sell the oil elsewhere for $65/barrel and Power Company will have a claim for breach of contract. Under general contract principles, Power Company's claim would be for the $10/barrel difference between the contract price and the prevailing market price.[24] However, as a general, unsecured creditor, Power Company will get only 30 cents on the dollar for that claim.[25] In short, if Driller rejects the contract, it will pay damages to Power Company in "bankruptcy dollars," which are worth far less than real dollars. On these facts, there is an economic incentive to reject (*i.e.*, to breach) the contract. This economic incentive to reject is in some situations enhanced by the rules in § 502(b)(6) and (7), which limit the amount of an allowed claim for breach of a lease of real property or an employment contract.

Incentive to breach contract

---

[24] *See* U.C.C. § 2-713(1).

[25] This is no different than if the breach occurred before the bankruptcy petition was filed.

Nevertheless, rejection is not always the better financial option for the debtor. If, continuing with the hypothetical illustration above, the market price had fallen rather than risen, it would be in Driller's best interest to assume the contract.

Let us now turn to the rules regarding assumption, assignment, and rejection. The rules are exceptionally complex and therefore it is useful first to understand the basic structure of the section's subsections:

Assumption (by trustee)	Rejection (by trustee)	Termination (by other party)	Assignment (by trustee)
Authority: (a)	Authority: (a)	(e)	Authority: (f)
Requirements: (b)	Timing: (d)		Consequence: (k), (*l*)
Limitations: (c)	Consequence:		
Timing: (d)	(g), (h), (i), (j), (n), (p)		
Required: (o)			

There are three requirements to assume a contract or lease under Chapter 7 if the debtor was already in default: the trustee must promptly cure the default (*e.g.*, pay the arrearages), compensate the other party for any resulting loss, and provide adequate assurance of future performance. § 365(b)(1). For this purpose, a contract clause that makes filing bankruptcy or insolvency a default is ineffective. § 365(b)(2); *see also* § 541(c). The trustee is permitted to ignore such defaults to effectuate the principal policy underlying § 365: to preserve contracts and leases that are of potential value to the estate. Subsection (e) further effectuates this policy by preventing the counterparty from terminating the lease or contract for the same types of defaults.

There are three limitations on the types of contracts and leases that can be assumed. Chief among these limitations is any applicable nonbankruptcy law that excuses the other party from accepting performance from or rendering performance to an entity other than the debtor or debtor in possession. § 365(c)(1). The classic example of this is a personal services contract, such as a contract with an artist to paint a painting.[26] In such a case, the counterparty may terminate the contract or lease. § 365(e)(2). The other two types of agreements that cannot be assumed are contracts to make a loan and nonresidential real property leases that were terminated prepetition. § 365(c)(2), (3).

With regard to timing, § 365 contains a variety of rules governing the deadline for the trustee's decision on whether to assume or reject the unexpired lease or executory contract. It also contains rules on whether, before that decision is made, the estate is obligated to perform those duties that become due under the contract or lease. § 365(d).

---

26 *See* RESTATEMENT (SECOND) OF CONTRACTS § 318 cmt. c (1981).

Subsection (f) allows the trustee to assign an assumed contract or lease despite most contractual and legal restrictions on assignment. This rule is designed to help the estate realize upon the value of the contract or lease. However, because assignment is conditioned on assumption, the trustee's power to assign does not apply if nonbankruptcy law would excuse the other party from accepting substituted performance.

One of the most controversial questions regarding executory contracts and unexpired leases is "what are the consequences of rejection?" We know that rejection results in a claim for breach and that this claim is treated as a prepetition claim. But are there additional consequences? For example, if the debtor was a lessee of real or personal property, must the leased property be surrendered to the lessor? If the debtor was the lessor, must the lessee return the property to the estate? If the debtor was a licensor of intellectual property, such as a trademark or copyright, must the licensee immediately cease using the intellectual property, even though such a requirement might destroy the licensee's business? The Bankruptcy Code provides answers to only some of the questions for only some types of contracts and leases. *See* § 365(d)(4), (h), (i), (j), (n), (p).

In thinking about these subsections and the consequences of rejection generally, consider what rights the aggrieved party would have outside of bankruptcy if the debtor breached the relevant contract. Should the aggrieved party have those same rights against the debtor in bankruptcy if the executory contract or unexpired lease is rejected? We will return to some of these issues in chapter twelve.

It is now time for you to read § 365 and then apply it to the following problems.

Problem 5-6

For each of the contractual arrangements described below, determine: (i) whether it is an executory contract; (ii) whether the trustee or debtor in possession may assume it; and (iii) whether the trustee or debtor in possession may assign it.

A. Dirt Removal, LLC is a franchisee of Cleaning Solutions, Inc. Under the terms of the franchise agreement, Dirt Removal is entitled to operate a carpet cleaning business in a specified geographic area under the Cleaning Solutions name. Dirt Removal is required to maintain specified professional standards, purchase a specified minimum of goods each month, and pay a monthly franchise fee. Cleaning Solutions is required to defend and maintain the integrity of the Cleaning Solutions brand and trademarks, sell cleaning products to Dirt Removal at set prices, and not authorize any competing use of its trademarks in the specified geographic area. The agreement expressly prohibits Dirt Removal from assigning any of its rights under the agreement to anyone without Cleaning Solutions' prior, written consent. Dirt Removal filed a Chapter 11 bankruptcy petition three weeks ago.

B. DeSyn Services, LLC has a three-year agreement to provide landscaping services to Commercial Office Park. Under the terms of the agreement, DeSyn Services is regularly to mow the grass, remove debris, and plant, prune, and fertilize the shrubbery throughout the four-acre office park. In return, Commercial Office Park is to pay a monthly fee. The agreement prohibits DeSyn Services from assigning any of its rights or delegating any of its duties under the agreement to anyone without Commercial Office Park's prior, written consent. DeSyn Services filed for Chapter 11 bankruptcy protection last week.

Problem 5-7

Three years ago, Design Industries ("DI") leased retail space in a building on Main Street in Streeterville. The lease has a 10-year term and calls for rent of $30,000 per year. The lease also provides that each of the following is an event of default: (i) failing to pay rent when due; (ii) the filing of a bankruptcy petition by or against DI; (iii) any assignment by DI of its rights under the lease without the prior consent of Landlord; (iv) DI's failure any time during the term of the lease to provide tax returns and financial statements to Landlord within 30 days after the end of DI's tax year; and (v) DI's failure to maintain an asset-to-liability ratio of at least 1:2 at any time during the term of the lease.

Sixty days ago, DI's tax year ended. Fifteen days ago, because DI had failed to provide Landlord with DI's most current tax return, Landlord sent DI a notice of lease termination. The notice instructed DI to vacate the premises in 20 days.

A. Which of the events of default in the lease are enforceable in bankruptcy? *See* § 365(e)(1), (f)(1), (3).

B. DI has come to you for advice on what, if anything it can do to prevent the Landlord from evicting it. Specifically, DI wants to know if filing for bankruptcy would somehow prevent Landlord from terminating the lease.

C. DI also informs you that it has found a sporting goods store that is willing to sublease the space for $40,000 per year. Would entering into a sublease with the sporting goods store and then filing bankruptcy allow DI to capture the $10,000 profit from the sublease? *See* § 365(b)(2), (f).

Problem 5-8

Deanna has a year-to-year lease of an apartment. Two years ago, she entered into a four-year lease of a new car. Both the apartment lease and the car lease make filing for bankruptcy protection a default. Deanna filed for Chapter 7 bankruptcy relief on June 15. On that date, Deanna was current on the apartment rent but six weeks behind on the car lease payments.

A. Is the trustee obligated to make payments to the landlord or the car lessor? *See* § 365(d)(3), (4)?

B. If the trustee fails to act with respect to either lease, what is deemed to happen to them? *See* § 365(d)(1).

C. If the trustee rejects the apartment lease, may Deanna assume it? If the trustee rejects the car lease, may Deanna assume it? *See* § 365(p). If not, is the default-on-bankruptcy clause enforceable? *See* §§ 365(e), 541(c). Upon rejection, must Deanna give up the apartment and the car?

D. If neither the trustee nor Deanna assumes either lease, are the postpetition rent on the apartment and the postpetition payments due on the car lease allowable claims? *See* §§ 502, 365(g).

CHAPTER SIX
SECURED CLAIMS

A. IN GENERAL

The Bankruptcy Code tries to treat claimants equitably, not equally. As a result, and as we will see, the Code distinguishes among claims, such as by giving a select few priority in the bankruptcy distribution scheme and making others exempt from the discharge. By far the most significant distinction the Code makes is the one between secured and unsecured claims. This distinction affects almost every way in which a claim is handled in bankruptcy and greatly impacts a claimant's recovery. To illustrate this, take a quick look ahead at the bankruptcy distribution scheme in a Chapter 7 case under §§ 503(b), 507(a), and 726(a) (see the chart on page 311). Notice what is conspicuously absent from the list: secured claims. This is because *unsecured* claims are treated as general claims against the bankruptcy estate, for which they are generally entitled to their pro rata share. In contrast, *secured* claims are treated as claims to specific property – the collateral – and they extract value directly from that property. Put another way, even though property of the debtor that is subject to a lien will come into the estate – recall the Supreme Court's decision in *Whiting Pools*, excerpted in chapter three – it is only the debtor's equity in that property that is available for distribution to unsecured claimants. The value of the property encumbered by the lien is reserved for the secured claimant.

Returning to our visual metaphor, unsecured claimants line up for a distribution (administered by the trustee) from the spigot on the right side of the estate vat depicted below. In contrast, secured claimants syphon off their collateral from the left spigot.

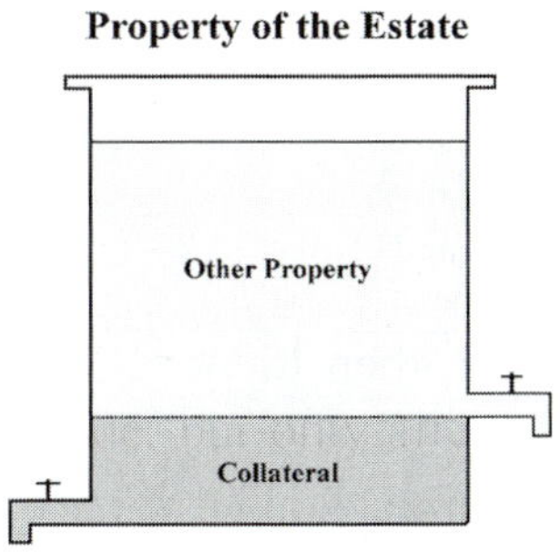

Note, however, that despite the metaphor of assets mixed as a liquid, each secured claimant extracts value from its own collateral, not out of some cocktail formed from all of the estate property collateralizing obligations owed to claimants.

Two things follow from this approach to the treatment of secured claims. First, because the Chapter 7 trustee makes distributions only to unsecured claimants, no proof of claim need be filed in Chapter 7 cases for a secured claim. *See* Rule 3002. Second, to obtain payment of a secured claim, the creditor will extract value from the collateral, usually outside of the bankruptcy process, either upon expiration or lifting of the automatic stay as to that creditor and that collateral. This is so regardless of how the lien was created and even though – as is often the case – little or nothing is paid on nonpriority, unsecured claims through the Chapter 7 process.

A corollary to this second point is that a claim is *not* classified as a "secured claim" merely because the creditor has a lien on some of the debtor's property. Instead, it is a secured claim only if and *to the extent* the claimant has an interest in the estate's property. The authority for this proposition is in § 506(a), which provides that "[a]n allowed claim of a creditor secured by a lien on property in which the estate has an interest . . . is a secured claim to the extent of the value of such creditor's interest in the estate's interest in such property." This rather cryptic language is fairly simple to understand: the amount of a secured claim is limited by the value of the collateral. For example, a creditor owed $1,000 who has the only lien on property worth $1,000 or more has a $1,000 claim that is fully secured. However, if the collateral were worth only $800, then the secured claim would be limited to $800, and the creditor would have an unsecured claim for the $200 balance due. In short, a creditor with an *undersecured* claim has both a secured claim and an unsecured claim.

The arithmetic gets a bit more complicated – but not much more – if there are multiple liens on the same property. Now, in addition to knowing the amount due to each lienor and the value of the collateral, we also need to know the relative priorities of the liens. Consider the following:

Property Value	$1,000
Debt to Lienor A	$800
Debt to Lienor B	$3,000

If Lien A has priority over Lien B, then Lienor A has an $800 secured claim. That leaves only $200 of value in the collateral left for Lienor B, who therefore has a $200 secured claim and a $2,800 unsecured claim:

Property Value	$1,000
Debt to Lienor A	– $800
Residual Property Value	$200
Debt to Lienor B	$3,000

If Lien B had priority, the result would be substantially different: Lienor B would have a $1,000 secured claim and a $2,000 unsecured claim; Lienor A would have an $800 unsecured claim.

Because secured claims are satisfied out of the collateral, they are partially unaffected by the debtor's discharge. This is because a discharge affects only the personal liability of the debtor. It does not affect or cancel the debt itself.[1] If third parties are liable on the debt, they remain liable. For example, a guarantor or other surety remains liable even though the debtor's obligation is released as a result of the discharge. A contrary rule would, of course, significantly impair the usefulness of a guaranty. Similarly, if the debt is secured by property of a third party, that property can be reached to the full extent permitted outside of bankruptcy. § 524(e).

The same rule applies if the discharged obligation is secured by a lien on the debtor's property. The debt and the lien continue to exist even after the bankruptcy court has discharged the debtor from personal liability. The Supreme Court recognized this rule more than a century ago in *Long v. Bullard*,[2] and even though the rule is not expressly codified in the current Bankruptcy Code, it is understood to survive and several Code provisions imply its continuing vitality. *See, e.g.*, § 506(d). Indeed, a contrary rule would completely undermine the benefit of security agreements and mortgages.

So, to put it succinctly, although the debtor's personal liability for a debt is discharged, the debt itself and the *in rem* liability of any collateral for that debt remain unaffected by the bankruptcy discharge.[3]

From the brief discussion above, we know that the court must ascertain the value of the collateral to determine whether and to what extent a creditor has a secured claim.

---

1 *See* § 524(a)(2) (providing that a discharge operates as an injunction against efforts to collect a debt "as a personal liability of the debtor").

2 117 U.S. 617 (1886).

3 Charges against the debtor's property for which the debtor has no personal liability are still cognizable in bankruptcy as "claims" as they affect property of the estate or of the debtor. *Johnson v. Home State Bank*, 501 U.S. 78 (1991) (dealing with an obligation discharged in a previous bankruptcy but secured by a lien on the debtor's home).

Valuation is a recurring issue in bankruptcy. We encountered some of the different standards for valuation in chapter four when we talked about exemptions. The same issue arises in this context of determining the amount of secured claims, but here there is some statutory guidance, in § 506(a)(1), which instructs that value "be determined in light of the purpose of the valuation and of the proposed disposition or use of such property." Would this mean in a Chapter 7 that the focus should be on liquidation value and in a Chapter 11 or 13 the focus should depend on what use the reorganized debtor has for the property?[4]

B. LIEN STRIPPING

Assuming there is no valuation problem, are there limitations on the basic concept regarding calculation of the secured claim? Consider the following scenario:

> *Scenario 1:* Shortly before filing for Chapter 7 bankruptcy protection, Despondent inherits the family homestead, which is subject to a mortgage securing a $120,000 debt to Mortgagee. The property, which is not in very good condition, is worth only $39,000 but has great sentimental value to Despondent and Despondent's family. Despondent, with the financial assistance of several family members, very much wishes to retain the property.

Now read § 506(d), which seemingly covers such situations.[5] It is the first of several provisions of the Bankruptcy Code that can be used to avoid a lien, either in whole or in part.

Subject to two minor exceptions, § 506(d) treats a lien as void to the extent that it secures a claim that is not an allowed secured claim. As we have already seen, § 506(a) treats an allowed claim as a secured claim only up to the value of the collateral. The

---

4 More specific guidance is provided in § 506(a)(2) if the debtor is an individual in Chapter 7 or Chapter 13 and the collateral is personal property. In such cases, the collateral is to be valued at its "replacement value" on the petition date.

5 Because the property is real estate, it is not covered by § 722 and thus Despondent has no right to redeem it. Reaffirmation pursuant to § 524 would not seem to make much sense because the property is worth so much less than the debt. Nevertheless, if the valuation is correct, the mortgagee's economic interest in the property is limited to its $39,000 value and it would arguably be unfair to require payment of any more than that for the debtor to retain it. We will consider redemption and reaffirmation in chapter eight.

implication of this is that § 506(d) invalidates a lien to the extent that a creditor is undersecured. Consider how this might work in the hypothetical illustration above.

> *Scenario 1 (continued):* Despondent files a complaint to "strip down" Mortgagee's lien to the $39,000 value of the property, on the ground that under § 506(d) Mortgagee's lien is void to the extent it is not an allowed secured claim. Read literally, the provision allows Despondent and the court to do this. If Despondent can borrow enough money to redeem the property by paying off the remaining amount of the lien ($39,000), Despondent can not only keep the property and its sentimental value, but Despondent would also realize any subsequent increase in value of the land. Conversely, Mortgagee would lose that appreciation, something Mortgagee might have been able to realize under nonbankruptcy law, which would normally permit Despondent to free the property from the lien only by paying the full amount of the debt: $120,000.[6]

Now consider this variation.

> *Scenario 2:* Distressed owns a home worth $95,000 but subject to a first mortgage in favor of Bank and a second mortgage in favor of Finance Company. Distressed owes Bank $100,000 but is current on all payments. Distressed owes Finance Company $40,000 and is a few months in arrears. Distressed files for Chapter 7 bankruptcy protection and wishes to retain the home. Bank is willing, even in the absence of a reaffirmation agreement, to allow Distressed to remain in possession as long as Distressed makes the required monthly payments. Distressed is keen to do this, in part because Distressed has no source of credit to finance the acquisition of another home and in part because Distressed hopes to build up equity in the property by making the monthly payments. However, for Distressed to retain any equity resulting from postpetition payments to Bank (or from any appreciation in the value of the home), Distressed must avoid – "strip off" – the second mortgage. Otherwise, Finance Company stands to capture much of that equity. If read literally, § 506(d) allows Distressed to avoid the second mortgage completely because it does not secure an "allowed secured claim" at all.

---

6 If Mortgagee had foreclosed on the real property, in those states that allow post-sale redemption, Despondent would be able to redeem by paying the foreclosure sale price to the purchaser at the foreclosure sale.

Prior to 1992, many courts adopted this literal interpretation of § 506(d). However, in *Dewsnup v. Timm*,[7] a Chapter 7 case, the Supreme Court rejected this reading of § 506(d) in a strip down case similar to Scenario 1. Justice Blackmun, writing for the Court, noted that, prior to enactment of the Bankruptcy Code, liens passed through bankruptcy unaffected. Under this rule, debtors could not redeem property from a mortgagee unless they paid the debt in full. He then concluded that the new Code did not unambiguously repeal this rule and decided not to assume that Congress wished to grant debtors a broad new remedy to strip down liens. Blackmun therefore interpreted "allowed secured claim" in § 506(d) as not necessarily referencing the definition of that phrase in § 506(a). In his view, all § 506(d) does is avoid liens that secure disallowed claims; that is, claims the debtor does not legally owe. Consequently, if an obligation is not truly owing, any lien securing the obligation is void. In essence, the majority read § 506(d) as though the word "secured" in the phrase "allowed secured claim" were deleted. Thus, after *Dewsnup*, a debtor's attempt to strip down a lien in a situation like that involving Despondent would fail. Future appreciation belongs to the secured creditor.

The Court's decision left most commentators astonished. The Court seized on a nonliteral interpretation of the Code that no lower court had adopted and which none of the litigants had even advocated. Justice Scalia was almost apoplectic in dissent. Although he readily conceded that allowing the secured creditor to retain the benefit of subsequent appreciation was quite defensible on policy grounds, the Court's almost anti-textual statutory interpretation was both highly dubious and inconsistent with the Court's prior bankruptcy jurisprudence. On its face, § 506(d) voids a lien to the extent the claim it secures is not both an "allowed claim" and a "secured claim" under § 506(a). Scalia derided the premise of the majority: that somehow "allowed secured claim" in § 506(d) meant something different from the definition of that phrase in § 506(a), another subsection of the very same section.

Some lower courts, concerned about the policy ramifications of retaining completely underwater liens, have refused to extend *Dewsnup* to strip off situations akin to that involving Distressed (Scenario 2 above).[8] However, such situations seem on their face to be controlled by the Supreme Court's analysis and a greater number of courts,

---

7 502 U.S. 410 (1992).

8 *E.g.*, *In re McNeal*, 477 F. App'x 562 (11th Cir. 2012). If the collateral is consumer goods and is exempt or has been abandoned by the trustee, then the debtor does not need § 506(d) to avoid the underwater lien: the debtor may redeem the property from the lien using § 722 while paying nothing to the lien creditor. We will discuss redemption in chapter eight.

including three circuit courts, have concluded that liens securing wholly unsecured claims survive.[9] As we shall see, though, something similar to lien stripping may be available through a plan under Chapter 11 or 13, even for partially secured claims, if the collateral is not the debtor's home.

One important impact of *Dewsnup* has little to do directly with lien stripping. Prior to the decision, secured claimants in Chapter 7 cases often had to choose between competing strategies. If, in an effort to speed their recovery, they moved for relief from the stay, arguing that the debtor had no equity in the property, they submitted evidence tending to minimize value of the collateral. This set the debtor up to strip down the lien and effectively redeem the property for potentially far less than the debt. After *Dewsnup*, with lien stripping unavailable, there is no longer such a disincentive to seeking relief from the stay under § 362(d)(2) in a Chapter 7 case.[10] Relief from the automatic stay is discussed in chapter seven of this book.

C. LIENS ON COLLATERAL ACQUIRED POSTPETITION

The postpetition effect of prepetition security interests is an important issue in reorganization cases and, in particular, reorganization of businesses. Section 9-204(a) of the Uniform Commercial Code allows a security interest to attach to personal property acquired by the debtor after the security agreement is signed, if the security agreement so provides. Secured creditors that lend against inventory or accounts commonly take advantage of this by drafting the security agreement to grant them a "floating lien" on all of the debtor's inventory or accounts, whether then owned or subsequently acquired. In such a transaction, after the debtor signs the security agreement, the security interest will attach automatically to any new property (of the type described in the agreement) that the debtor acquires. Similarly, in commercial real estate financing, the mortgagee typically takes an interest in future rents and profits, as

---

9 *See, e.g.*, *In re Woolsey*, 696 F.3d 1266 (10th Cir. 2012); *In re Talbert*, 344 F.3d 555 (6th Cir. 2003); *Ryan v. Homecomings Fin. Network*, 253 F.3d 778 (4th Cir. 2001); *In re Laskin*, 222 B.R. 872, 875–76 (9th Cir. BAP 1998) (also ruling that the debtor had no standing to raise the issue).

10 In Chapter 11 and 13 cases, however, the creditor still faces a dilemma. To obtain relief from the stay under § 362(d)(2), the creditor needs to show that the debt exceeds the value of the collateral, and thus the creditor normally tries to prove that the collateral has a low value. If relief is nevertheless denied, perhaps because the property is necessary to a successful reorganization, that low valuation may be used to calculate the creditor's secured claim, thereby reducing the creditor's recovery under a plan of reorganization.

well as in the real estate itself, and the mortgagee's lien in the future rents and profits arises automatically when the mortgagor acquires them.

The Bankruptcy Code is somewhat hostile to these arrangements. Section 552(a) invalidates prepetition security interests in property acquired postpetition. Because inventory and accounts constantly turn over and newly acquired property is not covered by the security interest, a secured creditor's floating lien could well lose its buoyancy, sinking to insignificance within weeks after the debtor files.

However, § 552(b) significantly limits the effect of § 552(a). Section 552(b)(1) allows secured claimants to retain their liens on postpetition *proceeds* of prepetition collateral. "Proceeds" is not defined in the Bankruptcy Code but is generally understood to be a sort of value-tracing concept: what one gets when one sells or otherwise disposes of the original collateral. "After-acquired property" is not generally a value-tracing concept. Thus, the general policy underlying these two provisions seems to be that the creditor's position should not be enhanced by postpetition transactions, but it should not be wholly destroyed by them either. To illustrate how this works consider the following example:

> Pursuant to an agreement with Debtor, Secured Party has a prepetition perfected security interest in inventory and the security agreement provides that the security interest attaches to all after-acquired inventory. Under Article 9, a security interest also automatically attaches to all identifiable proceeds of inventory. U.C.C. § 9-315. At the time Debtor filed for bankruptcy, the value of the inventory was $100,000 and the debt owed to Secured Party was $90,000. After the bankruptcy petition was filed, Debtor purchased inventory on credit from Supplier. Secured Party's security interest is prevented from attaching to that new inventory by § 552(a). During the bankruptcy, Debtor sold $20,000 worth of inventory for $20,000 in cash. Secured Party's security interest in the $20,000 cash is protected by § 552(b)(1) as proceeds of the prepetition inventory. If the debtor then used the cash to buy new inventory, Secured Party's security interest in that new inventory would also be protected by § 552(b)(1) as proceeds of the cash.

In applying § 552 and the policy underlying the section, the Court of Appeals for the Fourth Circuit suggested the following analytical approach:

> In order to determine the applicability of the exception in Section 552(b), we must undertake a [three]-part inquiry. First, is there a prepetition security agreement that by its terms extends to [the debtor's] prepetition inventory,

> accounts and proceeds? Second, did [the debtor] receive the proceeds of the prepetition inventory and accounts after the filing of the petition? Third, is [the debtor's] postpetition inventory second generation proceeds of prepetition inventory and accounts, and are [the debtor's] postpetition accounts proceeds of postpetition inventory?[11]

In analyzing these questions, the court cited, quoted, and relied on the definition of "proceeds" under Article 9 of the Uniform Commercial Code as it existed prior to the amendments to Article 9 that went into effect in 2001. That raises two questions. First, why should the term "proceeds" in § 552(b) carry the meaning ascribed to it by state law? Second, assuming that the state-law definition is relevant, did the 2001 amendments to Article 9, which significantly expanded the definition of "proceeds," *see* U.C.C. § 9-102(a)(64), alter the meaning of § 552(b) and expand the postpetition reach of security interests?[12]

A related problem concerns the extent to which postpetition rents are covered by a prepetition mortgage. Invariably, mortgagees of commercial real estate include an assignment of rents with their mortgages, and the postpetition treatment of these rents is often a critical aspect of any subsequent bankruptcy proceeding. Section 552(b)(2) provides that postpetition rents are encumbered by a prepetition mortgage or security agreement and, just in case state law would not regard room charges at a hotel or motel as "rents," expressly extends this rule to such charges as well. However, when something other than lodging, yet related to real estate, is involved, some question remains whether the postpetition receipts qualify as "rents" and are therefore subject to a prepetition lien. This issue can be critical to a bankruptcy case. Consider the amounts charged by a hotel for food and drink or by a nursing home for lodging and care of a resident, for example.

Another related issue derives from the fact that, by its terms, § 552(a) applies only to consensual security interests and mortgages: "lien[s] resulting from any security agreement." *See* § 101(50), (51). Nowhere does it or any comparable provision of the

---

11 *In re Bumper Sales, Inc.*, 907 F.2d 1430, 1436–37 (4th Cir. 1990).

12 In other words, did Congress mean to cede the underlying bankruptcy policy behind § 552 to the states by acquiescing in whatever definition of proceeds the states may care to adopt? *See, e.g.*, *In re Las Vegas Monorail Co.*, 429 B.R. 317, 343 (Bankr. D. Nev. 2010) (choosing to apply the expanded definition of "proceeds" in revised Article 9 but nevertheless concluding that income generated by the operation of a monorail was not proceeds of the franchise agreement permitting the debtor to operate the monorail); *see also In re Tracy Broadcasting*, 469 B.R. 55 (D. Colo. 2011) (applying the expanded definition without discussion), *rev'd on other grounds*, 696 F.3d 1051 (10th Cir. 2012).

Bankruptcy Code apply to nonconsensual liens. Some state statutes governing attachment and execution allow a creditor to obtain a lien not only on existing property of the debtor, but also on property acquired by the debtor in the future. Garnishment statutes are a common example. While the Supreme Court has ruled that the fresh start policy of bankruptcy prevents a prebankruptcy assignment of wages from applying to postbankruptcy wages,[13] it was never settled under the Bankruptcy Act whether that policy applied to the assignment of other types of future property. With respect to consensual liens, § 552(a) now decides that question against the secured creditor. The ability of nonconsensual liens to encumber postpetition property is an issue that remains open.[14]

Problem 6-1

A. Dragster Auto Mechanics, Inc. runs an automobile repair service. Three years ago, Dragster obtained an operating loan from First Finance and to secure that loan granted First Finance a security interest in all its "inventory and accounts now owned or hereafter acquired." First Finance properly perfected its security interest. Dragster's business has not done well and the corporation recently filed for bankruptcy protection under Chapter 11. After the filing, Dragster purchased $4,000 in new inventory, paying $3,000 in cash and promising to pay the balance in 45 days. After that, Dragster generated $2,000 in accounts receivable based on services rendered to customers after the bankruptcy filing. To what extent, if any, do the inventory and accounts acquired postpetition serve as collateral for Dragster's debt to First Finance? *See* § 552; U.C.C. § 9-102(a)(64).

B. Dillon owns and runs Rumble Fish Co., a small, incorporated business. Dillon guaranteed a loan from Lender to Rumble Fish and secured that

---

[13] *Local Loan Co. v. Hunt*, 292 U.S. 234 (1934).

[14] Yet another related issue involves future advances. In many lending arrangements, the debtor gives the creditor not merely an interest in after-acquired collateral and proceeds to secure existing debt, but also an interest in collateral (both that existing at the time the agreement was entered into and acquired thereafter) to secure any additional loans or credit that the lender may extend to the debtor in the future. These "future advances" clauses are not dealt with in § 552. Instead, the creditor's ability to secure obligations that the bankruptcy estate incurs subsequent to the filing of the petition with property of the estate is governed by § 364. In brief, the future advances clause is not operative to secure postpetition lending to the debtor in either prepetition or postpetition property. That provision is covered in more detail in chapter twelve.

> guaranty with a mortgage on Dillon's house. The guaranty agreement covers all existing and future indebtedness of Rumble Fish to Lender. After Dillon files for Chapter 7 bankruptcy protection, Lender makes an additional advance to Rumble Fish. Does Lender's claim against Dillon include the postpetition advance? *See* §§ 502, 506. Is the postpetition advance secured by Dillon's house? *See In re Stanton*, 303 F.3d 939 (9th Cir. 2002).

D. POSTPETITION INTEREST AND EXPENSES

Pursuant to § 502(b), the amount of a claim is determined as of the petition date. Claims for postpetition interest are normally disallowed. § 502(b)(2). Thus, creditors are generally not entitled to compensation for any delay in payment that results from the bankruptcy process.[15] A big exception to this rule exists with respect to secured claims. Section 506(b) allows an oversecured creditor – that is, a creditor whose interest in the collateral exceeds the amount of the debt owed – to recover from the collateral "interest on such claim, and any reasonable fees, costs, or charges provided for under the agreement or State statute under which such claim arose." There are two important points to note about this rule.

First, the introductory clause of the subsection limits the amount of interest, fees, costs, and charges the creditor may recover; such amounts are allowable only to the extent the creditor is oversecured. Thus, for example, a creditor with an allowed claim for $999 and a lien on property worth $1,000 is entitled to only $1 in postpetition interest.

Second, nothing in § 506(b) dictates what interest rate is to be used. In general, courts have used the contract rate of interest in cases involving consensual liens while resorting to the legal rate of interest with respect to judicial or statutory liens. Query what is most appropriate. Consider this illustration and the analysis that follows.

> Creditor has a mortgage on Duplex's apartment building. The mortgage debt is $1,000,000 and the value of the building is at least $1,300,000. The mortgage note calls for interest at the rate of 9% up until default and at 18% after default. The legal rate of interest is 12%, the prime lending rate is 5%, and the market rate for similar apartment mortgage loans is currently about

---

[15] An exception exists if the estate is solvent. *See* §§ 726(a)(5), 1129(a)(7), 1325(a)(4).

8%. The mortgage note provides that filing for bankruptcy protection is an event of default. What interest rate should apply postpetition to Creditor's claim?

If bankruptcy law is seen as essentially a specialized federal procedure for honoring substantive rights created by state law, a procedure that is perhaps more efficient than the race-to-the-courthouse collection system applicable under state law, it is appropriate that state substantive rights be left unaltered to the greatest extent possible. Under this view, oversecured creditors should earn interest at the rates they enjoyed under nonbankruptcy law. If, on the other hand, bankruptcy law is seen as imposing its own redistributive and rehabilitative policies, state created nonbankruptcy rights may have to yield.

Of course, both visions of bankruptcy law are partly true and both find some support in various provisions of the Bankruptcy Code. The tension between these different visions of bankruptcy was manifested in the Fifth Circuit's decision in *In re Laymon*.[16] The court reviewed a bankruptcy court decision awarding an oversecured consensual creditor interest at the federal judgment rate. It reversed in favor of the contract rate because that was the prevailing pre-Code rule and Congress did nothing to alter it. However, the court waffled on whether to apply the pre-default rate of 10% or the post-default rate of 18%. While respect for state law would call for awarding the 18% rate, the court noted that pre-Code law gave courts some flexibility – permitting them not to apply an inequitable or unconscionable contract rate – and it then remanded the issue to the bankruptcy court with a vague mandate to do equity. Courts continue to struggle with this issue but the prevailing approach is to presume that an oversecured creditor is entitled to postpetition interest at the contractual default rate but to permit equitable considerations to rebut that presumption.[17]

---

16 958 F.2d 72 (5th Cir. 1992).

17 *See, e.g.*, *In re SW Bos. Hotel Venture, LLC*, 479 B.R. 210, 227 (1st Cir. BAP 2012); *In re Gen. Growth Props., Inc.*, 451 B.R. 323, 326–28 (Bankr. S.D.N.Y. 2011) (contractual default rate should apply unless there is creditor misconduct or the rate would harm unsecured creditors, impair the debtor's fresh start, or constitute a penalty).

E. AVOIDING LIENS

All of the information about secured claims in this chapter assumes that the claimant's lien will not be avoided – that is, invalidated – in bankruptcy. However, several different Code provisions allow the trustee or debtor to avoid a creditor's lien.[18] These provisions serve a variety of different policies, yet each is important. If some provision of the Bankruptcy Code allows the debtor or the trustee to avoid a lien, then to the extent the lien is avoided the creditor is left with an unsecured claim. In this context, recall that secured claims are generally paid in full whereas unsecured claims rarely fare so well. In addition, avoiding a lien frees up more of the collateral's value for the estate, § 551, or, if the debtor can exempt that value, for the debtor. *See* § 522(g), (h), (i). In short, the trustee's or debtor's recovery in a successful action to avoid a lien is normally the property transferred: the lien itself.[19] Thus, lien avoidance is one of the most critical moves that the players may make in the game of bankruptcy. The stakes are often very high.

1. Strong-Arm Powers – § 544

In chapter three we examined the power of the bankruptcy trustee under § 544(b) to avoid certain fraudulent prepetition transfers of the debtor. That power is derived from the nonbankruptcy rights – typically under state law – of an unsecured creditor to avoid certain transfers. An additional power is granted to the trustee under § 544(a), commonly referred to as the strong-arm clause. This clause grants to the trustee whatever power – again arising under nonbankruptcy law – a creditor or purchaser has to avoid certain liens and other transfers of an ownership interest in property.

There are two principal parts to § 544(a). First, the trustee is granted, as of the date of the bankruptcy petition, the status of a creditor with a judicial lien on all of the

---

[18] In Chapter 11 cases, the debtor in possession has most of the rights and powers of the trustee, including the right to pursue lien avoidance actions. § 1107(a).

[19] Section 550(a) expressly indicates that the trustee may recover "the property transferred, or, if the court so orders, the value of such property." Recall the discussion of § 550 in chapter three. So, under what circumstances would the trustee (or debtor) want – and be entitled – to recover a judgment for the value of the avoided lien rather than the lien itself? The most common answers are when the collateral has since depreciated or been sold or destroyed or the secured obligation has been fully or partially paid off. *See, e.g.*, *In re Trout*, 609 F.3d 1106 (10th Cir. 2010); *In re Taylor*, 599 F.3d 880 (9th Cir. 2010); *In re Patterson*, 2012 WL 1292642 (Bankr. N.D. Ga. 2012).

debtor's property. § 544(a)(1). If, under nonbankruptcy law, that status gives the trustee priority over some other entity's interest in property of the debtor or property transferred by the debtor, then the trustee may use § 544(a)(1) to take priority over – and thus effectively invalidate – such entity's property rights.

The primary effect of § 544(a)(1) is to invalidate security interests that were unperfected when the bankruptcy petition was filed.[20] Under § 9-317(a)(2) of the Uniform Commercial Code, a lien creditor has priority over a creditor with an unperfected security interest. By granting the bankruptcy trustee the status of a lien creditor, § 544(a)(1) allows the trustee to use § 9-317(a)(2) to invalidate any unperfected security interest in the debtor's property. To illustrate, consider the following example:

> In January 2012, Debtor granted Lender a security interest in Debtor's manufacturing equipment to secure a loan. Lender neither filed a financing statement nor took possession of the equipment and thus it failed to perfect the security interest. In June 2013, Debtor filed a Chapter 7 bankruptcy petition. Under § 544(a), the bankruptcy trustee has the status of a lien creditor that has obtained its lien on the bankruptcy petition date. Under U.C.C. § 9-317(a)(2), Lender's security interest in the equipment would be subordinate to a lien creditor who had levied on that date. Thus, under § 544(a), the bankruptcy trustee can avoid Lender's security interest in Debtor's equipment.[21]

The trustee's power to avoid a lien under § 544 is limited by § 546(b)(1)(A). To illustrate the application of this section, consider a secured party who has a purchase-money security interest ("PMSI") in the debtor's property. A PMSI is a security interest: (i) retained by the seller of collateral to secure all or part of the collateral's price; or (ii) granted to a lender who provides the debtor with the value the debtor uses to purchase all or part of the collateral. U.C.C. § 9-103. For example, if Jeweler sells Debtor a ring on credit and retains a security interest in the ring to secure Debtor's

---

[20] Refer back to Chapter 1 for a discussion of perfection.

[21] Technically, U.C.C. § 9-317(a)(2) does not allow a judicial lien creditor to *avoid* an unperfected security interest; it merely gives the judicial lien *priority* over the unperfected security interest. The collateral continues to be encumbered by the security interest and the secured party is entitled to the value of the collateral in excess of the amount owing to the judicial lien creditor (up to the amount of the secured obligation). The same is true with respect to unrecorded mortgages under every state's real property recording statutes: a judicial lien has priority but is not entitled to avoid the unrecorded mortgage. In spite of this, bankruptcy courts regularly and almost uniformly interpret § 544(a) as empowering the trustee to *avoid* unperfected liens.

obligation to pay the remainder of the purchase price, Jeweler has a PMSI in the ring. Similarly, if Bank loans Debtor money to enable Debtor to purchase a ring from Jeweler, that money is used to pay Jeweler (likely by Bank directly paying Jeweler all or part of the purchase price), and Bank acquires a security interest in the ring to secure repayment of the loan, Bank has a PMSI.[22]

Under Article 9, if a secured party with a PMSI perfects by filing a financing statement within 20 days after the debtor takes possession of the collateral, the PMSI secured party has priority over a lien creditor whose lien arose between the time the security interest attached and the time it was perfected. U.C.C. § 9-317(e). Section 546(b)(1)(A) gives U.C.C. § 9-317(e) effect in bankruptcy by making the bankruptcy trustee's avoidance powers subject to that rule. Thus, the trustee cannot avoid the lien if the debtor files bankruptcy after the security interest has attached, but before the PMSI is perfected, provided the PMSI secured party perfects by filing a financing statement during that 20-day period.[23] Note, the secured party is permitted to perfect its security interest in this situation without violating the automatic stay. *See* § 362(b)(3).

The following diagram depicts the interaction of § 544(a), § 546(b)(1)(A), and U.C.C. § 9-317(e).

If the security interest is perfected before the bankruptcy petition is filed (whether in the shaded area or before it), then perfection would precede the bankruptcy trustee's status as lien creditor, the trustee would not be entitled to priority under U.C.C. § 9-317, and the trustee could not avoid the security interest under § 544(a). If the security interest is perfected postpetition by the filing of a financing statement in the shaded area – *i.e.*, within the 20 days after the debtor receives possession of the collateral – then § 546(b)(1)(A) and U.C.C. § 9-317(e) operate to prevent the bankruptcy trustee from avoiding the security interest under § 544(a). If the secured party attempts to perfect

---

[22] Note that the PMSI is not created automatically. The creditor must obtain the debtor's agreement, typically in a record, that the property secures the purchase price or value extended to enable the debtor to purchase the property. U.C.C. § 9-203.

[23] If the secured party perfects by complying with a certificate of title statute, the same rule applies. *See* U.C.C. § 9-311(b) (treating compliance with such a statute as the equivalent of filing a financing statement).

postpetition but outside of the shaded area – *i.e.*, more than 20 days after the debtor received possession of the collateral – § 546(b)(1)(A) would not apply and the trustee could avoid the security interest under § 544(a). Not only that, but the secured party's attempt to perfect would likely violate the automatic stay.[24]

The second major part of § 544(a) is § 544(a)(3). This gives the trustee the status of a bona fide purchaser of all of the debtor's real property. Combining this authority with state real property law, the trustee may invalidate unrecorded mortgages on and unrecorded deeds of real property of the debtor.[25]

One major point to note about § 544(a) is that any knowledge the trustee may have of an unperfected or unrecorded interest is irrelevant. Even if state law limits avoidance to those without knowledge of the unrecorded interest (something more likely under the applicable real estate recording statutes than under Article 9), for the purpose of § 544(a), the trustee is conclusively presumed to lack that knowledge.[26] More than that, even if every creditor of the debtor had advance knowledge of the unrecorded lien, and thus could not avoid it under state law, the trustee can nevertheless still avoid it. This is in contrast to § 544(b) (discussed in chapter three), which permits the trustee to invoke state fraudulent transfer law. Under that provision, there must be an actual creditor who has the power to avoid the fraudulent transaction into whose shoes the trustee may step.

One minor point to note about § 544(a)(3) is its potential interaction with § 541(d). Recall that § 541(d) keeps out of the estate the equitable rights to property in which the debtor has merely legal title. For example, if state law creates a constructive trust in favor of some creditors, those creditors may be able to recover the assets imbued with that trust and prevent the assets from being administered by the trustee for the benefit of other claimants.[27] However, if § 544(a)(3) allows the trustee, as a bona fide purchaser

---

[24] *But cf.* § 362(b)(3) (creating an exception to the stay which, depending on the facts, may permit action to perfect a bit beyond expiration of the 20-day period).

[25] There is occasionally overlap between § 544(a)(1) and (a)(3). In some states, both a judicial lienor and a bona fide purchaser have priority over an unrecorded mortgage. In others, a bona fide purchaser has priority over an unrecorded mortgage, but an unrecorded mortgage has priority over a judicial lien. In instances when both a judicial lienor and a purchaser would have priority, the trustee may use the authority under either paragraph to avoid the mortgage lien.

[26] Although the matter is in some dispute, apparently a debtor in possession in Chapter 11, exercising the powers of the trustee, *see* § 1107, is also conclusively deemed to be without knowledge. *See In re Kim*, 161 B.R. 831 (9th Cir. BAP 1993).

[27] *See supra* pages 69–70.

of real estate, to take priority over the beneficiary of a constructive trust, then the trustee will be able to keep the property in the estate.

Read § 551, which provides that an avoided lien is preserved for the benefit of the estate. The following problem explores the relevance of that rule.

Problem 6-2

On February 1, in return for a $3,000 loan, Diner gave Bank One a security interest in certain ovens worth $10,000 and used as equipment. Bank One never filed a financing statement and thus its security interest is unperfected. On July 1, Diner gave a security interest in the same equipment to Bank Two in return for a $6,000 loan. Bank Two perfected its security interest by filing a proper financing statement the day it advanced the funds. In December, Diner files for Chapter 7 bankruptcy protection. Under Article 9, Bank Two's perfected security interest has priority over Bank One's unperfected security interest. U.C.C. § 9-322(a). What happens to the two security interests and who among Bank One, Bank Two, and the trustee has priority? *See* §§ 544, 551; *see also* U.C.C. § 9-317(a).

2. *Preferences Revisited – § 547*

There are two main intersections of preference law and secured claims. The first involves whether a prepetition *payment* to a secured creditor is an avoidable preference. The second, and far more important, concerns whether the *creation of the lien* itself – either involuntarily through the creation of a judicial lien or voluntarily through the grant of a security interest or mortgage – is a preferential transfer of property rights.

(a) Prepetition Payments

Recall that an avoidable preference is a transfer that enables the creditor to receive more than such creditor would have received had the transfer not been made and the debtor's estate liquidated under Chapter 7. § 547(b)(5). If a creditor is fully secured – in other words, if the collateral is worth as much or more than the amount of the debt it secures – then the creditor would receive full payment upon liquidation of the debtor's assets.[28] Accordingly, any prepetition payment to such a creditor could not have increased such creditor's recovery. In short, it could not be preferential as to that creditor. Looking at it from the trustee's perspective, the estate was not depleted by the transfer of a prepetition payment to the fully secured creditor. Although the estate lost cash equal to the amount of the payment, it gained an equal amount of equity in the collateral.[29]

If the creditor were undersecured, however, the result would be different. For example, consider a creditor who is owed $1,000 and has a valid and unavoidable lien on property worth $800. If the debtor were to pay the entire debt within the preference period and while insolvent, the creditor would be preferred and the transfer would be avoidable (barring the availability of one of the preference defenses). In essence, the creditor would get the $1,000 payment instead of $800 on the secured claim and something less than $200 on the unsecured claim. In fact, if the debtor made only a partial payment to the secured creditor, that too would be preferential. Because the collateral would still remain, any payment necessarily reduces first the unsecured portion of the creditor's claim.[30] If the debtor is truly insolvent and cannot pay creditors in full, the prepetition payment will be preferential and avoidable (again, barring the availability of a preference defense).

So, in sum, prepetition payments to undersecured creditors have preferential effect and will be avoidable unless some preference defense exists. Prepetition payments to fully secured creditors have no preferential effect as to the secured creditor. The one exception to this is when the creditor's lien is itself avoidable, either as a preference or

---

[28] This is a hypothetical inquiry and does not imply that the collateral will in fact be sold and the secured party paid in bankruptcy. As we have already seen, the trustee does not make distributions on secured claims. *See* § 726. If the collateral has value to the estate, the trustee may sell the collateral, but will typically do so subject to the secured creditor's lien. *See* § 363(b), (e), (k). To obtain payment, the creditor will then either have to foreclose or persuade the buyer to pay to avoid foreclosure. If the collateral does not have value to the estate, then the creditor will usually foreclose on the collateral after the stay has been lifted, § 362, or the trustee has abandoned the property, § 554. The options and processes available to the secured creditor are discussed more fully in chapter eight.

[29] *See, e.g.*, *In re Stinson Petroleum Co.*, 506 F. App'x 305, 310 (5th Cir. 2013). Even if the estate were depleted by the payment – as might be true if the debtor could exempt the increased equity in the collateral – the main point would remain that there has been no preferential benefit to the creditor who received the payment.

[30] If, however, the payment were made with the collateral itself, there would be no preferential effect and hence the transfer would not be avoidable as a preference. *In re El Paso Refinery, L.P.*, 171 F.3d 249, 254–55 (5th Cir. 1999).

for some other reason. If the creditor's lien can be eliminated in bankruptcy, then any prepetition payment to such a creditor is essentially a payment to an unsecured creditor.

In some circumstances, however, payments to a fully secured creditor may be recovered because they have the effect of benefitting a different creditor. This issue was discussed in chapter three. Consider the following problem.

Problem 6-3

Several years ago, Doubletime gave First National Bank a security interest in certain equipment to secure a loan. First National properly perfected that interest. In January of this year, in desperate need of cash, Doubletime borrowed money from Second Place Finance Company, granting Second Place a security interest in the same property. Second Place perfected its interest that same day. Under U.C.C. Article 9, First National Bank's security interest in the equipment has priority over Second Place's security interest in that equipment. In mid-February, Doubletime made a $8,000 payment to First National Bank, reducing its debt from $50,000 to $42,000. On March 1, Doubletime filed for bankruptcy protection. At that time, the debt to First National was $42,000, the debt to Second Place was $20,000, and the collateral was worth $65,000. Is the February payment avoidable as a preference? *See* § 547(b). If so, who is liable for it? *See* § 550.

(b) Creation of the Lien

Generally speaking, if a debtor pays an unsecured, nonpriority creditor within the preference period, that payment will be an avoidable preference (assuming no preference defense exists). § 547(b). The same is true with respect to transfers of property other than cash to such a creditor: § 547(b) applies to transfers of any "interest of the debtor in property" and payments in kind deplete the estate just as much as do payments in cash.

Applying this principle further, if the debtor transfers a limited property right, such as a lien, rather than complete ownership of a piece of property, the same result follows. If value was transferred, then the creditor was preferred. Remember too that an avoidable transfer need not be a voluntary one. *See* § 101(54) (defining "transfer"). If a creditor acquires a lien without the consent of the debtor, which is how most judicial liens are created, that too can be a preferential transfer.

Problem 6-4

Demobilized owns a car worth $8,000. Last week, Chiropractor, who had an outstanding $6,000 judgment against Demobilized, had the sheriff levy on the car. The levy gave Chiropractor a judicial lien on the car. This week, Demobilized filed for bankruptcy protection. May the trustee avoid Chiropractor's lien as a preference?

Before you jump to the conclusion that all security interests obtained in the preference period are avoidable, remember that an avoidable preference must be a transfer on account of an antecedent debt. § 547(b)(2). Consider the following problem.

Problem 6-5

On February 1, Diner gave a security interest in certain equipment to Bank One to secure a long overdue $8,000 debt. Bank One perfected its lien that day. On February 3, Diner gave a security interest in the same equipment to Bank Two in return for a $9,000 loan. Bank Two advanced the funds and perfected its security interest on that day. On March 1, Diner filed for Chapter 7 bankruptcy protection. As between Bank One and Bank Two, Bank One would have priority under Article 9. U.C.C. §§ 9-317(a), 9-322(a). Assuming the collateral is worth $15,000, has either Bank One or Bank Two received an avoidable preference? If so, what is the effect of the trustee avoiding that preference? *See* §§ 547, 551.

Even if a lien is granted to secure an antecedent debt, any of several preference defenses may come to the aid of the secured party. Their collective reach protects the vast majority of consensual liens from preference attack. Before examining those defenses, however, one more point must be made. Occasionally, what appears to be one transaction may involve two or more transfers of the debtor's property. When that is the case, it is important to analyze each transfer separately to determine whether it is an avoidable preference. Consider the following problem. In doing so, begin by identifying the different transfers. Then analyze the transfers in chronological order.

Problem 6-6

Digger is a gardener with a number of residential clients. While insolvent and less than three months before filing for Chapter 7 bankruptcy protection,

> Digger traded a back hoe for a riding mower. The back hoe was subject to a perfected security interest in favor of Seller, who neither knew of nor consented to the trade. At the time, the debt to Seller was $9,000 and the back hoe was worth $8,000. The riding mower was also worth $8,000. Assume that, under U.C.C. Article 9, Seller's security interest: (i) continues in the back hoe; and (ii) attaches to and is perfected in the riding mower, as proceeds of the back hoe. *See* U.C.C. § 9-315. Is there an avoidable preference here? *See* § 547(b)(5); U.C.C. § 2-312. In answering this, consider how, if at all, Digger's other creditors were affected by the trade.

(i) Contemporaneous Exchanges – § 547(c)(1)

One element of an avoidable preference is that the transfer be "for or on account of an antecedent debt." § 547(b)(2). Thus, if an insolvent buyer purchases goods and pays for them at the time of sale by transferring money or other property to the seller, there is no preference because the buyer's payment is contemporaneous with the buyer's acquisition of the goods: that is, there is no antecedent debt. Put another way, the buyer's assets change form but their overall value remains relatively stable, and thus the buyer's creditors are not injured.

However, suppose there is a short delay between the time the obligation is incurred and the time when property in payment of the obligation is transferred. Does the short delay make the debt antecedent? Yes. But should the transfer of property be an avoidable preference? The Supreme Court considered this issue in *Dean v. Davis*.[31] On September 3, the debtor obtained a loan from Dean on the debtor's promise to secure the loan by a mortgage on all of his property. The proceeds of the loan were used by the debtor to pay a debt owed to a bank. The mortgage was executed on September 10 and recorded the next day. Within a few days, a petition for involuntary bankruptcy was filed against the debtor. The trustee in bankruptcy brought an action under the old Bankruptcy Act to set aside the mortgage. The Supreme Court, in reversing the court of appeals' conclusion that the mortgage could be set aside as a preference, stated:

> Preference implies paying or securing a pre-existing debt of the person preferred. The mortgage was given to secure Dean for a substantially contemporaneous advance. The bank, not Dean, was preferred. The use of

---

[31] 242 U.S. 438 (1917).

Dean's money to accomplish this purpose could not convert the transaction into a preferring of Dean, although he knew of the debtor's insolvency.[32]

Section 547(c)(1) codifies this holding of the Supreme Court. If the parties intend a contemporaneous exchange of a loan for a security interest or mortgage and the transfer of the lien is delayed for a short time but is nevertheless substantially contemporaneous, then the security interest or mortgage cannot be avoided.

A superficially similar but nevertheless distinct problem arises when the making of the loan and the creation of the security interest are contemporaneous, but there is a delay between the creation of the security interest – *i.e.*, attachment – and perfection of that security interest. There is no true preference in these cases because the transfer (*i.e.*, attachment) of the security interest to the creditor was not on account of an antecedent debt. *Cf.* § 547(b)(2). Rather, the problem of delayed perfection is the perceived evil of the secret lien. The classic case is that of a debtor in financial difficulty who wants to conceal from general creditors the true state of its financial condition. The debtor obtains an emergency loan from a creditor and grants that creditor a mortgage on real property or a security interest in personal property to secure the loan. The property involved might well be most of the debtor's previously unencumbered assets. If public notice of the transaction were given by recording the mortgage or filing a financing statement with respect to the security interest, the result might be that other creditors would be deterred from giving the debtor further unsecured credit because of the absence of unencumbered assets. To avoid this result, the creditor might be induced not to record the mortgage or file the financing statement.

Essentially, the issue is one of fraud on creditors, not preference. Under many states' real property recording statutes, an unrecorded real property mortgage has priority over a subsequent judgment lien. The holder of an unperfected security interest in personal property takes a greater risk by not promptly perfecting because an unperfected Article 9 security interest does not have priority over a subsequent judicial lien. *See* U.C.C. § 9-317(a)(2). However, as we have seen, both an unrecorded mortgage and an unperfected security interest are avoidable by a bankruptcy trustee. § 544(a). In either case, however, the creditor could protect its lien by promptly perfecting at the first sign that other creditors may levy on assets of the debtor or that a petition for bankruptcy relief is forthcoming. In the classic case, the creditor is an insider with access to information that provides some assurance that the creditor will

---

32 *Id.* at 443.

have sufficient advance notice of facts that will allow the creditor to perfect before the bankruptcy petition is filed.

It is understandable that there should be a policy against secret liens, and such a policy is expressed in the Bankruptcy Code. However, instead of dealing with the problem directly as a case of fraud on creditors, Congress discouraged the secret lien by a provision in the preference section. In other words, Congress dealt with the evil of secret liens by turning them into constructive preferences. This is accomplished through a conclusive presumption that a consensual lien becomes effective at the time it is perfected, rather than at the time it is created. Certain grace periods are allowed for the creditor to perfect. If the creditor does not perfect within these periods, the lien is treated as having been given at the time of perfection, rather than attachment, thus creating a time gap between the incurring of the obligation and the transfer of the debtor's interest in property. The transfer would then be on account of an antecedent debt. The relevant provision is § 547(e)(2). Consider the following hypothetical.

> On July 1, Bank (a noninsider) lends money to Debtor and receives in return a security interest in some of Debtor's assets. Some time later, Bank perfects its security interest. Unfortunately, a few months later, Debtor defaults and files for bankruptcy protection. Is the transfer of the security interest an avoidable preference?

Under § 547(e)(2), the transfer of a security interest will be deemed to have occurred when the interest attached, if perfection occurred within the following 30 days. Thus, for example, if Bank perfected on July 12, the transfer of the security interest is deemed to have occurred on July 1:

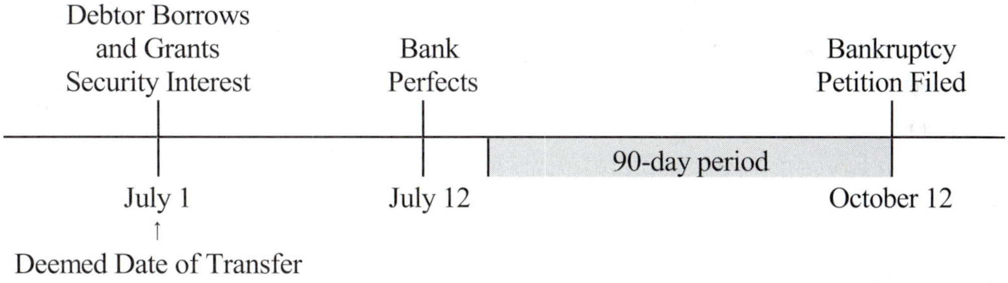

Because of this, the transfer of the security interest is simultaneous with the loan, and thus is neither on account of an antecedent debt nor within the 90-day preference period for transfers to noninsiders. The transfer of the security interest therefore cannot be avoidable as a preference. *See* § 547(b)(2), (4).

If, however, perfection occurred more than 30 days after the security interest attached, the transfer of the security interest would be deemed to have occurred when the security interest became perfected. § 547(e)(2). Thus, if Bank perfected on August 10, the security interest would be deemed to have been transferred on August 10:

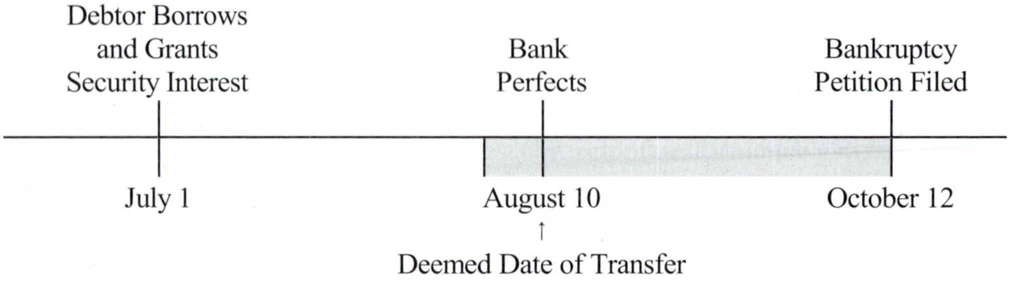

Two consequences flow from this deemed delay in the date of transfer. First, the transfer of the security interest is no longer simultaneous with the loan. Instead, it is substantially after the loan was made and thus on account of an antecedent debt. Second, the transfer of the security interest is more likely to fall within the 90-day preference period, and indeed on these facts now does. The transfer therefore appears to satisfy the prima facie case for avoidance under § 547(b) and can be saved only if it is still a contemporaneous exchange for new value.

Section 547(c)(1), which protects substantially contemporaneous exchanges, probably does not provide relief in this situation. Some courts believe that the 30-day grace period in § 547(e)(2) effectively places a statutory limit on contemporaneousness for the purposes of § 547(c)(1).[33] In other words, a security interest perfected more than 30 days after it attached cannot be substantially contemporaneous. As a result, while § 547(e)(2) may effectively eliminate the evils of the secret lien, it also ensnares some secured creditors who do not perfect within the 30-day time limit. Although other courts do not regard the 30-day grace period under § 547(e)(2) as a statutory limit on contemporaneousness, they are nevertheless unlikely to treat a lien deemed transferred more than 30 days after the loan was made as substantially contemporaneous with the loan.[34]

---

[33] *See, e.g.*, *In re Arnett*, 731 F.2d 358 (6th Cir. 1984) (so ruling when the § 547(e)(2) grace period was only 10 days).

[34] *See In re Proctor*, 2010 WL 3944694 (Bankr. D. Neb. 2010) (recording deed of trust 54 days after loan was made was not substantially contemporaneous). *But cf. In re McCaskill*, 434 B.R. 875 (Bankr. W.D. Mo. 2010) (security interest in an automobile that attached when the creditor contemporaneously released its lien on a different motor vehicle and which was perfected 34 days later was nevertheless

This does not render § 547(c)(1) meaningless, however. Consider the following problem.

Problem 6-7

Digger is a gardener with a number of residential clients. While insolvent and less than three months before filing for Chapter 7 bankruptcy protection, Digger sold a front loader for $8,000, its fair market value. Digger had purchased the front loader two years earlier from Supplier, who retained a perfected security interest in it to secure the unpaid portion of the purchase price. At the time Digger sold the front loader, Supplier had been pressuring Digger for payment of the $10,000 remaining due and threatening to repossess the machine. Digger obtained Supplier's permission to sell the front loader free of Supplier's lien and received $8,000 from the buyer. Under Article 9, Supplier's security interest attached to and was perfected in the $8,000 as proceeds of the front loader. U.C.C. § 9-315(a)(2), (c), (d). Twelve days after the sale, Digger gave Supplier the $8,000 received from the buyer. Does this transaction involve an avoidable preference? In answering this question, be sure to identify each transfer and the date on which it is deemed to have occurred.

When § 547(c)(1) does not apply, there may be one faint hope for lienholders who delayed recording their mortgage or perfecting their security interest: the earmarking doctrine, discussed briefly beginning on page 94. Consider the following problem.

When interest rates started to fall, Dryden decided to refinance the $95,000 mortgage on his home. On July 1, Dryden closed on the refinancing transaction by executing a note and mortgage in favor of Refinance Company. On the same date, Refinance Company disbursed the loan proceeds to Original Mortgagee. Because of a clerical error in Refinance Company's office, the new mortgage (and the release of the original mortgage) were not recorded

---

substantially contemporaneous, in part because the creditor believed its lien release was valid when filed rather than when executed); *In re Kerst*, 347 B.R. 418 (Bankr. D. Colo. 2006) (47-day delay in perfection did not prevent transfer from being substantially contemporaneous because the delay was largely attributable to a third party over whom neither the debtor nor the preference defendant had any control).

until August 15. Dryden filed for Chapter 7 bankruptcy protection on October 20. May the trustee avoid Refinance Company's mortgage?

Recall that the earmarking doctrine essentially treats the proceeds of a refinancing loan as never having been an asset of the debtor. It applies when: (1) there was an agreement between the new lender and the debtor that the funds would be used to pay a specified existing creditor; (2) that agreement was performed according to its terms; and (3) the transaction as a whole does not diminish the estate. In the hypothetical here, all that is arguably true. Indeed, Dryden never had possession or control of the funds; as is typical in refinancing transactions, they were transmitted directly by the new lender to the original lender.

However, the trustee seeks not to avoid the payment in this situation but the transfer of the lien. Even courts that recognize the earmarking doctrine restrict it to payments, not to transfers of liens.[35] To apply the earmarking doctrine to delayed pefection would, they conclude, ignore the language of § 547. Moreover, the theory underlying the earmarking doctrine is that the property transferred came from the new lender and thus was not ever property of the debtor. Whatever conceptual appeal that position has with respect to the funds would not seem to apply with respect to the creation of a lien on the collateral because the collateral is undeniably the debtor's property. Query whether there would be a preference due to change in the identity of the lienholder, if in the example above, Refinance Company became an assignee of the Original Mortgagee's mortgage and no new mortgage was created. In that situation, there is no transfer of an interest of the debtor in property, merely a transfer of Original Mortgagee's interest in the mortgaged property to Refinance Company.

(ii) PMSI Protection – § 547(c)(3)

Constructive preferences also arise – probably even more frequently – when a lender takes a PMSI. This is because, for preference purposes, the transfer of the lien cannot occur until the debtor acquires rights in the collateral, § 547(e)(3), and the debtor typically does not obtain such rights until after the loan is made. For these constructive preferences, § 547(c)(3) provides a bit more protection. It too has a 30-day time limit regarding perfection, but that limit – like the 20-day grace period in U.C.C. § 9-317(e) –

[35] *See In re Lee*, 530 F.3d 458 (6th Cir. 2008); *In re Lazarus*, 478 F.3d 12 (1st Cir. 2007).

begins not when the loan is made, but when the debtor receives possession of the property, which is usually some time later.

Problem 6-8

On April 1, Bank loaned $30,000 to Doctor by crediting that amount to Doctor's checking account. The loan agreement signed on that day provided that certain described equipment already owned by Doctor would secure the debt. Thus, under U.C.C. § 9-203, the security interest attached to the equipment on April 1.

A. Doctor filed a Chapter 7 bankruptcy petition on June 1. When is the security interest deemed to have been transferred and is that transfer avoidable if:
   1. To perfect its security interest under Article 9, Bank filed a financing statement covering the equipment on April 16;
   2. To perfect its security interest under Article 9, Bank filed a financing statement covering the equipment on May 5;
   3. Bank never filed a financing statement nor took any other action to perfect its security interest? *See* § 547(b), (c)(1), (e)(2).

B. How, if at all, would the analysis in Part A change if the transaction on April 1 created a PMSI: that is, both parties intended that Doctor would use the loaned funds to buy equipment that would serve as collateral for the loan, Doctor did so use the funds, and Doctor received the new equipment on April 10? *See* § 547(c)(1), (3), (e)(2), (3).

(iii) Improvement of Position Test – § 547(c)(5)

Some types of collateral – accounts receivable and inventory, in particular – normally turn over within a relatively short period of time. As the debtor operates its business, old accounts are collected and inventory is sold, while new accounts are generated and new inventory is acquired. Creditors who provide accounts or inventory financing do not want to restrict themselves merely to accounts and inventory on hand when the loan is made and the security agreement is signed. Such assets are likely not to be around by the time the debtor defaults. Instead, they typically want a "floating lien," one that extends to the new accounts and inventory as soon as the debtor acquires them. Article 9 of the Uniform Commercial Code expressly authorizes such floating liens by allowing a security interest to attach to after-acquired property. *See* U.C.C. § 9-204(a). Thus, most creditors who take a security interest in accounts and inventory provide in the security agreement that the security interest will attach to existing accounts and inventory and will automatically attach to any accounts and inventory that the debtor acquires in the future.

For debtors who seek bankruptcy protection, it is of course likely that some of the accounts and inventory on hand on the date of the petition will have been acquired within the preference period. Because a security interest in this new collateral is, by virtue of § 547(e)(3), deemed to have been transferred to the secured party when the debtor acquired it, that transfer might be an avoidable preference under § 547(b) if the debtor was insolvent at the time. Remember, there is a rebuttable presumption that the debtor is insolvent during the 90 days preceding bankruptcy. § 547(f).

Section 547(c)(5) provides a limited exemption to such preference avoidance, in recognition of the fact that the secured creditor is not preferred to the extent the new collateral replaces old collateral. A typical case to which § 547(c)(5) applies is as follows:

Scenario One

The obligation to Secured Party is secured by accounts, no matter when acquired, of Debtor, who at all relevant times is insolvent. The amount of the debt and the value of the accounts are as follows on the beginning of the preference period and on the day of the bankruptcy filing:

	90th Day Before Petition	**Petition Day**
Debt	$100,000	$100,000
Value of Collateral	$60,000	$60,000
Insufficiency	$40,000	$40,000

Despite the seeming constancy of these numbers, assume that, as is likely, some portion of the collateral – say $10,000 in accounts – on hand on the date of the petition was acquired within the preference period. Let's stop for a moment. How can it be that the debtor acquired collateral worth $10,000 during the preference period but the overall value of the collateral did not change? The most likely explanation is that the debtor also collected on other accounts worth $10,000 during the period. So, assume: (i) the debtor generated $10,000 in new accounts on the 50th day before the petition; and (ii) subsequently, but still before the filing of the petition, collected $10,000 on older accounts and used the proceeds of that collection to pay employees. Thus, the chart can be revised as follows:

		90th Day Before Petition	50th Day Before Petition	Petition Day
Debt		$100,000	$100,000	$100,000
Value of Collateral	**New**		$10,000	
	Total	$60,000	$70,000	$60,000
Insufficiency		$40,000	$30,000	$40,000

Technically, there are two transfers of the debtor's interest in property to the secured party during the 90-day preference period: (i) the attachment of the security interest to the newly acquired accounts and (ii) the attachment of the security interest to the proceeds of the collected accounts. However, the latter transfer is protected from avoidance by § 547(c)(1),[36] and thus, for our purposes, here we will ignore it. The point is that you must begin the preference analysis by identifying the potentially avoidable transfers within the preference period. The transfer that remains of concern – the transfer of the security interest in the newly generated accounts – is reflected as the $10,000 amount on the second line of the chart. Let's now return to the analysis.

Although § 547(e)(3) would deem the security interest in the new accounts to have been acquired during the preference period and therefore potentially avoidable under § 547(b), paragraph (c)(5) provides a preference defense. Because Secured Party's net position has not been improved by the additional collateral (the creditor was undersecured by $40,000 at both the start and the end of the preference period), the transfer of that security interest in the new accounts is not avoidable.

---

[36] The secured party received a security interest in the proceeds but lost the security interest in the collected accounts because those accounts ceased to exist to the extent paid. Thus, there was a contemporaneous exchange for new value. In short, collection results in a transmutation of collateral, not in an increase in collateral.

Under § 547(c)(5), a secured creditor's position is deemed to be improved – thereby giving rise to an avoidable preference – not if the amount of its secured claim is increased, but only if the amount of its unsecured claim is reduced. Consider this variation:

Scenario Two

		90th Day Before Petition	50th Day Before Petition	Petition Day
Debt		$100,000	$105,000	$110,000
Value of Collateral	**New**		$20,000	
	Total	$60,000	$80,000	$70,000
Insufficiency		$40,000	$25,000	$40,000

This time, although the total value of the collateral increased by only $10,000, assume that $20,000 of the collateral on hand on the date of the petition was acquired within the preference period. Assume that the increase in the debt is attributable to interest that has accrued on the secured obligation and the decreased value of the collateral by the petition date is due to the fact that some accounts were paid and the proceeds used to pay other bills.

Under § 547(b) there is a potential $20,000 preference. Nevertheless, § 547(c)(5) protects all of it. Secured Party was $40,000 undersecured on the 90th day before the petition and it was also $40,000 undersecured on the petition date. Secured Party's position has not improved and thus there is no avoidable preference.

Of course, even with § 547(c)(5), creation of the security interest in some of the new collateral may be avoidable. Consider this version of the facts:

Scenario Three

		90th Day Before Petition	50th Day Before Petition	Petition Day
Debt		$100,000	$105,000	$110,000
Value of Collateral	**New**		$25,000	
	Total	$60,000	$60,000	$75,000
Insufficiency		$40,000	$20,000	$35,000

Although the total value of the collateral increased by only $15,000, assume that $25,000 of the collateral on hand on the date of the petition was acquired within the preference period. As in Scenario Two, the increase in the debt is attributable to interest that has accrued on the secured obligation and the decrease in the value of the collateral is due to depreciation or collections that have since been spent.

Under § 547(b), there is a potential $25,000 preference. This time § 547(c)(5) protects only part of it. Secured Party was $40,000 undersecured on the 90th day before the petition but is only $35,000 undersecured on the petition date. Secured Party's position has improved by $5,000 and thus the § 547(c)(5) defense is unavailable to protect that $5,000 in improvement.

Now consider this wrinkle:

Scenario Four

		90th Day Before Petition	50th Day Before Petition	Petition Day
Debt		$100,000	$90,000	$90,000
Value of Collateral	**New**		$20,000	
	Total	$60,000	$80,000	$70,000
Insufficiency		$40,000	$10,000	$20,000

Assume that $20,000 of the collateral was acquired in the preference period, and the value of the collateral on the petition day is due to depreciation or collections that have since been spent. The reduction in the debt was the result of a $10,000 prebankruptcy payment on the secured obligation.

Note, there are two potentially preferential transfers here: (1) the $10,000 prepetition payment and (2) attachment of the security interest to the $20,000 of new collateral. Thus, the Secured Party's preference exposure is $30,000.

Whether the payment is in fact avoidable will probably depend on whether it was made in the ordinary course of business. *See* § 547(c)(2). However, the ordinary course of business defense has no applicability to the creation of the security interest in the new collateral. It applies only to payments.

In contrast, the § 547(c)(5) defense does not apply – at least not directly – to the payment. According to its language, it applies only to the creation of a security interest. The transfer of the security interest in the new collateral will be protected, if at all, by § 547(c)(5). Here, Secured Party went from being $40,000 undersecured to only $20,000 undersecured. Secured Party's position was therefore improved by $20,000. As a result, the transfer of the security interest in the $20,000 of new collateral is avoidable; § 547(c)(5) provides no help.

Problem 6-9

Does this result of Scenario Four make sense? In answering this question, consider what would have happened if there had been no prepetition $10,000 payment and the debt had remained at $100,000. How much of the security interest in the new $20,000 of collateral would have been avoidable?

As confusing as § 547(c)(5) may seem, this rule is reasonably workable when applied to accounts receivable. To calculate the reduction of the deficiency (or, in other words, the improvement of position), it is necessary to value the collateral. Because accounts are simply claims against third parties, they are normally valued at face value, *i.e.*, the amount owed by the account debtors, perhaps reduced by some statistically determined amount that reflects the fact that some accounts will turn out to be uncollectible or will entail collection costs.

The valuation problem created by § 547(c)(5) is far more complex with respect to inventory. If the unit value of inventory is constant and the number of units of inventory on hand on the date of bankruptcy is greater than the number of units on hand at the beginning of the preference period, § 547(c)(5) can properly be applied to make voidable as a preference the improvement in position represented by the increased number of units. However, in some cases the value of a secured party's collateral may increase during the preference period without the increase being preferential. To take a case not covered by § 547(c)(5), suppose Secured Party has a security interest in Airline's inventory of fuel and the price of oil – and hence the value of fuel – simply increased during the preference period. No preference results from the improvement in Secured Party's position because the appreciation was not the result of any transfer of an interest in the debtor's property under § 547(b).

This analysis is consistent with the core concept of what a security interest is. Under the Uniform Commercial Code, a security interest attaches to *property* of the debtor, not to the *value* represented by such property. Thus it is clear that if an undersecured secured party has a security interest in a unit of oil that doubles in value because of a change in world oil prices, the secured party is entitled to the benefit of the increase in value (limited to recovery of the amount of the secured obligation). As is the case generally with owners of property interests, an undersecured secured party takes the risk, and gets the benefit, of changes in value of its interest.

Sometimes, however, changes in value result both from appreciation and from additions to the collateral. Because § 547(b) does not purport to deal with the former but does cover the latter, sorting through the changes can be quite problematic. Moreover, an increase in value of inventory often is partly the result of an investment of labor. The best example is a security interest in inventory consisting of finished goods, such as furniture. As labor is used to convert the inventory of wood, glue, and fasteners into desks, credenzas, and tables, the resulting increase in value is not attributable to a transfer of property.

When analyzing a § 547(c)(5) problem, the place to start is by identifying the transfers and determining which, if any, satisfy the § 547(b) test for an avoidable preference. That places an outside limit on the preference recovery. Then move to § 547(c)(5) to determine if all or any portion of those transfers are not avoidable. If the secured party's position was improved by more than the amount of the avoidable transfer, § 547(c)(5) will not increase the secured party's liability, it will merely fail to reduce that liability.

(iv) Trilateral Preferences

Recall the discussion of the *Levit* case beginning on page 110. Consider the following example.

> Secured Party made a loan to Debtor and obtained a guarantee for that debt from Insider. Subsequently, within one year but more than 90 days before

Debtor filed its bankruptcy petition, Secured Party obtained and perfected a security interest in Debtor's property to secure the debt. The transfer of the security interest would have been an avoidable preference as to Secured Party if it had been made within 90 days prior to bankruptcy, but because it was made before the 90-day preference period, it would normally not be avoidable as a preference. However, a transfer to *or for the benefit of* an insider creditor is avoidable as a preference if the transfer is made within the one year before the petition. Under the common law of suretyship, Insider has a right of reimbursement from Debtor and thus qualifies as a creditor of Debtor. Moreover, the transfer of the security interest to Secured Party benefits Insider because, under that same law of suretyship, if Insider pays Secured Party, Insider would be subrogated to Secured Party's security interest (*i.e.*, the security interest would secure Insider's right to reimbursement from Debtor). Thus, under § 547(b), the grant of the security interest is a preference because it benefits an insider creditor, and thus the one-year period for preference avoidance applies.

Section 550(a) provides generally that an avoidable transfer can be recovered from the initial transferee. Thus, if no other rule intervened, Secured Party would have liability for the transfer even though the transfer was avoidable as a preference because of the benefit it provided to Insider, not because of the benefit it provided to Secured Party. However, two other provisions do intervene. Section 550(c) insulates noninsiders from liability for avoidable preferences made more than 90 days before the petition. Because there was some question about whether that provision applies to preferential transfers of property (rather than to payments), Congress also enacted § 547(i). That provision protects Secured Party in this hypothetical by providing that the transfer is not deemed avoided as to Secured Party. Combined, these two provisions allow Secured Party to retain and enforce its security interest but leaves Insider liable for the preferential transfer. Thus, the estate will be depleted by the transfer of the security interest, but Insider will have liability to replenish the estate for the value of that transfer.

(v) Statutory Liens – § 547(c)(6)

Statutory liens, even those arising during the preference period, are immune from preference avoidance. § 547(c)(6). The rationale for this is probably related to the fact that the timing of their creation is not readily subject to the control of either the debtor or the creditor. It may also have to do with the fact that statutory liens necessarily protect creditors whom the law wishes to favor. However, such liens are subject to their own special avoidance rules in § 545. *See infra* pages 250–251.

3. *Liens Impairing Exemptions – § 522(f)*

(a) Consensual Liens

Section 9-204(b)(1) is one of the few consumer protection rules incorporated into Article 9 of the Uniform Commercial Code. It prohibits a security interest from attaching to most after-acquired consumer goods unless the debtor acquires rights in the collateral within 10 days after the secured party gives value. The theory underlying it is that consumer debtors might not comprehend the significance of an after-acquired property clause in a written security agreement and thus might unintentionally encumber their property if the law allowed them to do so.

Nevertheless, creditors can still acquire a security interest in consumer goods. Typically this occurs when the creditor obtains a PMSI by providing the funds the debtor uses to purchase the collateral. However, it can arise in other circumstances as well. Article 9 allows a creditor to take a security interest in whatever consumer goods the debtor already owns, although other consumer protection statutes may provide restrictions on that ability.[37]

When the creditor perfects a non-PMSI through possession – a transaction commonly referred to as a pledge – the debtor likely understands the significance of parting with the goods: fail to pay and the goods will be sold. For example, if a debtor leaves goods in a pawn shop to secure repayment of a loan from the pawn shop, the debtor probably knows that the pawn shop may sell the goods if the debtor does not pay. However, if the creditor perfects by filing a financing statement, a consumer debtor may not appreciate the significance of the security agreement that the debtor signed and that granted a security interest in the goods. This is particularly troublesome if the property involved is something the debtor could otherwise exempt. Such property – *e.g.*, clothes and household furnishings – is generally far more valuable to the debtor than to any

---

[37] The FTC makes it an unfair credit practice for a creditor to take a nonpossessory, non-PMSI in certain listed household goods. *See* 16 C.F.R. §§ 444.1, 444.2.

creditor because the debtor's cost to replace it will likely exceed whatever amount a creditor could realize through a forced sale.

This is where § 522(f)(1) comes in. It allows a debtor in bankruptcy to avoid a nonpossessory, non-PMSI in certain categories of consumer goods, items used in the debtor's trade, and professionally prescribed health aids to the extent that the lien impairs an exemption to which the debtor would otherwise be entitled. In essence, it provides a level of consumer protection that Article 9 does not provide.

It is important to recognize, however, five limitations on the scope of this provision. First, it applies only if the security interest is "nonpossessory." If the secured party takes possession at the outset of the transaction with the debtor, the provision does not apply. Although the Code is silent about what happens if the secured party takes possession later, such as after default, most courts do not treat that as a possessory security interest.

Second, the provision applies only if the security interest is not a PMSI. This limitation probably exists for two reasons: (1) even consumer debtors probably expect that if they buy goods on credit but do not pay, they will lose the goods; and (2) without this limitation, consumers would find it extremely difficult to obtain credit for many needed purchases.

The Bankruptcy Code does not define or identify when a security interest is a PMSI.[38] As a result, courts have generally looked to state law to determine whether a security interest qualifies as a PMSI. Article 9 of the Uniform Commercial Code, as revised in 1998, provides that neither refinancing a purchase-money obligation (*i.e.*, substituting a new debt for the original debt) nor providing additional collateral for the secured obligation (referred to as "cross-collateralization") undermines PMSI status. U.C.C. § 9-103(f). However, these rules are expressly made inapplicable to consumer-goods transactions, *see* U.C.C. §§ 9-102(a)(24), 9-103(h), and thus pre-revision case law on the effect of such actions remains relevant.[39] Some of that case law held that these actions destroyed PMSI status.

Although there are few decisions dealing with how cross-collateralization affects § 522(f) of the Bankruptcy Code, several courts ruled that refinancing a purchase-money obligation destroys the purchase-money nature of the security interest for the purposes

---

[38] *But cf.* § 547(c)(3)(A) (effectively defining the types of security interests that qualify for the PMSI preference defense).

[39] In addition, even if Congress implicitly adopted the state-law meaning of a PMSI when it enacted the Bankruptcy Code in 1978, it is not clear that the meaning of the term does or should change when state law changes.

of § 522(f). Others have ruled to the contrary and treated refinancing as irrelevant. Still others, dissatisfied with either position, have taken a case-by-case approach:

> The courts in this Circuit which have discussed this issue have not adopted the Transformation Rule * * *. The courts view a strict application of the Transformation Rule as working "unintended and inequitable results" including the result of discouraging creditors from refinancing consumer loans. The problem with the dual status rule is the difficulty of determining when any one item is paid off and released from the security agreement. Thus, the courts have taken a case by case approach which examines whether the refinancing agreement can be characterized as merely a renewal of the original obligation or as a novation. A renewal allows the purchase-money character of the security to survive. A novation, on the other hand, extinguishes the purchase-money character of the loan.
>
> The * * * test for delineating between a novation and a renewal is the "degree to which the original obligation of the debtor has changed and, to some extent, on any additional consideration which was conveyed by the debtor to the creditor." The greater degree of change in obligation or increase in obligation, the more likely a novation will be found. The Court believes this middle-of-the-road approach is the proper test.
>
> In applying the test * * * to the facts in the present case, this Court finds that the purchase-money character of the security interest * * * did not survive the refinancing. The entire character of the Debtor's obligation to the Creditor was changed by the loan agreement entered into on May 25, 2001. Not only was additional money loaned, but the repayment period was extended from one year to 31 months and the interest rate was increased from a "one year, same as cash" arrangement to the rate of 21% per annum. Finally, the items of furniture which were originally security only for the $1,250 loan became collateral for both loans; and, on this basis, the Court finds that the refinancing agreement at bar must be characterized as a novation, rather than merely a renewal of the original obligation.[40]

The third limitation is that § 522(f)(1)(B) covers only that property that would otherwise be exempt. If the debtor lives in a jurisdiction that offers very limited exemptions to debtors, then § 522(f)(1)(B) will be of limited help.

---

[40] *In re Snyder*, 2001 WL 34059294 (Bankr. C.D. Ill. 2001).

Fourth, the provision covers only specified – albeit in broad terms – types of property. Read § 522(f)(4).

Problem 6-10

Several months before filing for bankruptcy, Disconnected granted Lender a nonpossessory, non-PMSI in the following items:

Item	Value
Diamond Ring	$900
DVR	$100
Laptop Computer	$300
High-Definition TV	$700
Skiing Equipment	$400
Smart Phone	$200

The security agreement does not cover either of the other two televisions that Disconnected owns. Disconnected filed bankruptcy and selected the exemptions in § 522(d). On which of these items, if any, may Disconnected use § 522(f)(1)(B) to avoid the lien? *See* § 522(f)(4).

The final limitation on the scope of § 522(f)(1)(B) is in § 522(f)(3), which places a dollar limit on the debtor's ability to avoid liens that impair an exemption in specified types of items used in the debtor's trade. Congress deemed this necessary because some states provide an unlimited or very high exemption for these items. However, the provision does not reach debtors in each of those states. The restriction is limited to states that either: (i) offer an unlimited exemption in the specified types of items used in the debtor's trade or (ii) prohibit avoidance of consensual liens on otherwise exempt property.[41] Some states with high exemptions for these types of items do neither. As a result, § 522(f)(3) has a limited scope.

---

[41] For a very thorough and thoughtful analysis of the rather cumbersome and confusing language of § 522(f)(3), see *In re Duvall*, 218 B.R. 1008 (Bankr. W.D. Tex. 1998).

(b) Judicial Liens

Whereas § 522(f)(1)(B) allows the debtor to avoid certain specified consensual liens on certain specified exempt property, § 522(f)(1)(A) allows the debtor to avoid judicial liens – other than those securing a domestic support obligation – on any exempt property. The brevity of § 522(f)(1)(A) does not, alas, imply simplicity. Courts have had to wrestle with several interpretive problems posed by its language and two of these have generated decisions by the Supreme Court.

In *Farrey v. Sanderfoot*,[42] the Court was faced with a common situation. Husband and Wife divorced. Pursuant to the property settlement, Husband got the marital home but was obligated to pay Wife over a period of time for her share of the house's value. To secure this obligation, Wife got a lien on the property. While it is common for such a lien to be created consensually, as part of a settlement agreement, in *Farrey* there was no consensual lien; instead the divorce court granted Wife a lien on Husband's property in its decree. A few months later, Husband filed for bankruptcy, claimed the property as exempt, and moved to avoid Wife's judicial lien under the provision that is now designated as § 522(f)(1)(A).

The equities of the situation strongly favored Wife, and the Court came to her rescue. It ruled:

> The statute does not say that the debtor may undo a lien on an interest in property. Rather, the statute expressly states that the debtor may avoid "the fixing" of a lien on the debtor's interest in property. The gerund "fixing" refers to a temporal event. That event – the fastening of liability – presupposes an object onto which the liability can fasten. . . . Therefore, unless the debtor had the property interest to which the lien attached at some point *before* the lien attached to that interest, he or she cannot avoid the fixing of the lien under the terms of [§ 522(f)(1)(A)].[43]

Husband countered that he had owned the residence with Wife before the judicial lien was created. However, looking to local property law, the Court concluded that the Husband's prior ownership of the property was terminated by the divorce decree. His current interest in the property came into being as a result of that decree, but did so at the same moment the judicial lien in Wife's favor attached. Because he had not owned

---

[42] 500 U.S. 291 (1991).

[43] *Id.* at 296.

his current interest before the lien attached, he could not use § 522(f)(1) to avoid Wife's lien.

The Bankruptcy Reform Act of 1994 responded to the Supreme Court's decision in *Farrey* by amending § 522(f)(1) to make judicial liens for support obligations unavoidable. This amendment, though, does not apply to property settlement obligations, the type of obligation at issue in *Farrey*. Moreover, the amendment does not address the Court's analysis of when a lien attaches to property, but leaves that issue to the vagaries of state property law. Accordingly, depending both on state law and on how a divorce decree or settlement is structured, a debtor may in rare instances be able to use § 522(f) to avoid a lien designed to enforce a divorce decree's division of property.

Farrey also continues to have some relevance outside of the context of a marital estate. In some jurisdictions, a judicial lien can extend to after-acquired property, particularly real property. When that occurs, the lien and the debtor's interest arise simultaneously. Under *Farrey*'s analysis, such a lien cannot be avoided.[44]

Many of the remaining interpretive issues concerning § 522(f)(1)(A) arise from the phrase "to the extent such lien impairs an exemption." When does a lien impair an exemption? In some states, for example, exemptions are defined in reference to the debtor's equity in the property. Thus, there can be no exemption to the extent that the property is encumbered. Do judicial liens in such states impair exemptions? If not, then states could effectively "opt out" of § 522(f)(1)(A) by the way they draft their exemption statutes. The Supreme Court rejected this on the same day it decided *Farrey*. Put simply, it ruled that to determine whether § 522(f) applies, "ask not whether the lien impairs an exemption to which the debtor is in fact entitled, but whether it impairs an exemption to which he *would have been* entitled but for the lien itself.[45]

Another recurring problem in determining whether a judicial lien impairs an exemption arises when there are other, consensual liens on the property. Consider the case of a debtor who has real property worth $58,000 that is subject to the following liens (listed in order of priority):

---

[44] *See In re Scarpino*, 113 F.3d 338 (2d Cir. 1997); *In re Pederson*, 230 B.R. 158 (9th Cir. BAP 1999).

[45] *Owen v. Owen*, 500 U.S. 305, 310–11 (1991).

Lien	Amount
First Mortgage	$25,000
Judgment Lien	$14,000
Second Mortgage	$41,000
Total:	**$80,000**

Obviously, if none of the liens is avoided, no equity in the property remains for the debtor. Accordingly, the first mortgagee would extract $25,000 in value from the property, the judgment lienor would get $14,000, and the second mortgagee would get the remaining $19,000 (retaining an unsecured claim for the balance remaining due).

If, however, the property subject to these liens qualifies as a homestead (and is therefore otherwise exemptible up to some statutory limit, say $20,000), the question becomes whether the judgment lien impairs the debtor's exemption and thus whether the judgment lien is avoidable under § 522(f)(1)(A). If the judgment lien is avoidable, a related question arises: does the freed-up value go to the debtor or to the second mortgagee? These were the issues presented in *In re Simonson*.[46]

The bankruptcy court concluded that the judgment lien was avoidable, but that the freed-up value went to the second mortgagee. Thus, in the above illustration, the first mortgagee gets $25,000 in value and the second mortgagee gets the remaining $33,000 in value. Arguably, this provides a windfall to the second mortgagee, who, absent avoidance, would receive only $19,000. In other words, the second mortgagee is permitted to reap the only benefit of a provision of the Code designed to benefit debtors. More to the point, because a second mortgagee will normally take subject to a judgment lien only if the judgment lien is recorded before the second mortgage, the second mortgagee should expect to take the property subject to that judgment lien, and it need not get the freed-up value to obtain the benefit of its bargain.

A divided Third Circuit reversed. The majority concluded that the judgment lien did not impair the debtor's exemption of "an interest of the debtor in property" because the second mortgage wiped out the debtor's equity and, therefore, destroyed the debtor's "interest." Accordingly, it left all of the liens in place. This result arguably created a windfall to the judgment lienor, whose lien is fortuitously protected from avoidance only because of the existence of a subsequent second mortgage. It is also arguably inconsistent with the Supreme Court's analysis in *Whiting Pools*, where there was an

46 758 F.2d 103 (3d Cir. 1985).

"interest[] of the debtor in property" within the meaning of § 541(a)(1), despite the debtor's lack of equity and even the lack of possession.

Judge Becker, in dissent, argued that the lien should be avoided and then preserved for the benefit of the debtor under § 522(i).[47] The following table illustrates the difference in approaches.

Bankruptcy Court		***Circuit Court***		***Judge Becker***	
Property Value	$58,000	Property Value	$58,000	Property Value	$58,000
First Mortgage	– $25,000	First Mortgage	– $25,000	First Mortgage	– $25,000
	$33,000		$33,000		$33,000
Second Mortgage ($41,000)	– $33,000	Judgment Lien	– $14,000	Debtor	– $14,000
	$0		$19,000		$19,000
		Second Mortgage ($41,000)	– $19,000	Second Mortgage ($41,000)	– $19,000
			$0		$0

The Bankruptcy Reform Act of 1994 adopted Judge Becker's position. It added § 522(f)(2) to the Code. Under the formulaic rule of that provision, the judgment lien described above is avoidable. Section 522(i) then allows the debtor to preserve the avoided lien for the debtor's benefit.

Another issue that continues to arise is the extent to which an avoidable judicial lien should be avoided. Consider the following case.

IN RE SILVEIRA
141 F.3d 34 (1st Cir. 1998)

Stahl, Circuit Judge.

This bankruptcy appeal requires us to decide the extent to which a Chapter 7 debtor may, pursuant to § 522(f)(1) & (f)(2)(A), avoid the fixing of a judicial lien on the debtor's property, when the market value of the property exceeds the sum of (1) all consensual (non-judicial) liens on the property and (2) the amount of the debtor's exempt interest under § 522(d). We hold that, in such a situation, section 522(f)(1) permits the avoidance of the targeted judicial lien only in part, not in its entirety. Because the district court concluded otherwise, we vacate the judgment and remand for further proceedings.

---

[47] This result is generally favored by most commentators. *See* NAT'L BANKR. CONFERENCE, REFORMING THE BANKRUPTCY CODE – FINAL REPORT 110–12 (May 1, 1994).

I

The debtor and appellee in this action, Thomas J. Silveira, owns, as his primary residence, a property that has been stipulated for purposes of this appeal to have a fair market value of $157,000. The property is subject to a mortgage of $117,680. The appellant, East Cambridge Savings Bank ("the Bank"), holds a $209,500 judicial lien on the property.

On May 9, 1995, Silveira filed a voluntary petition under Chapter 7 of the Bankruptcy Code. He claimed an exemption of $15,000 in the property pursuant to § 522(d)(1). Silveira then filed a motion to avoid the Bank's $209,500 judicial lien pursuant to § 522(f)(1) and (f)(2)(A). The bankruptcy court ruled that those provisions permitted the debtor to avoid the Bank's lien in its entirety and thus granted Silveira's motion. The Bank appealed to the district court, arguing that on the facts of this case, § 522(f)(1) & (f)(2)(A) permitted only a partial avoidance of its judicial lien. The district court disagreed and entered an order affirming the bankruptcy court's determination. This appeal followed.

II

* * * In this case, it is undisputed that the sum of the targeted judicial lien ($209,500), all other liens ($117,680) and the amount of the debtor's exemption ($15,000) exceeds the (stipulated) value of the debtor's property ($157,000), by $185,180. Thus, the Bank's judicial lien clearly does "impair" an exemption of the debtor within the meaning of § 522(f)(2)(A). The question here concerns the extent of the debtor's power under § 522(f)(1) to alleviate this "impairment."

The district court concluded that once a debtor's power of avoidance is triggered by the fact of an impairment of whatever size, that power permits the debtor to avoid the judicial lien causing the impairment in its entirety. The court thus held that Silveira was entitled to avoid the entire amount of the Bank's $209,500 lien. The Bank now argues that the district court misapplied § 522(f)(1)(A), and that Silveira is in fact entitled to avoid only so much of the Bank's lien as necessary to prevent impairment of the debtor's exemption within the meaning of § 522(f)(2)(A). We agree.

As an initial matter, we find unpersuasive Silveira's argument that the "plain language" of the statute supports the district court's view. On the contrary, the language of the relevant provisions seems to us to support the Bank's position. Section 522(f)(1) permits a debtor to "avoid the fixing of a lien on an interest of the debtor in property *to the extent that* such lien impairs an exemption [of the debtor]." § 522(f)(1) (emphasis added). Section 522(f)(2)(A), similarly, provides that a judicial lien "impair[s] an exemption *to the extent that*" the targeted lien, in combination with other liens and the value of the debtor's exemption, exceeds the value of the debtor's property.

§ 522(f)(2)(A) (emphasis added). If Congress intended for avoidance of judicial liens to be an "all-or-nothing" matter, one might wonder why the provisions' drafters chose to use the connective phrase "to the extent that," in lieu of the word "if," which obviously would have been a simpler construction. The statutory directive that a debtor may avoid a judicial lien "to the extent that" the lien impairs an exemption favors – or is at least readily amenable to – reading the definition of "impairment" in § 522(f)(2)(A) not only as a *condition* of avoidability, but also as a *proportional measure* of the scope of the debtor's avoidance power.

But even if the statute's language does not settle the issue, the debtor's proposed interpretation is unacceptable in view of the statute's intended purposes. Consider the following two hypothetical scenarios:

> *Hypothetical A*: The debtor owns a primary residence with a market value of $100,000, subject to an outstanding mortgage balance of $55,000, a judicial lien of $30,000 (not securing a debt), and no other liens. The debtor is entitled, under § 522(d)(1), to claim an exemption of $15,000 with respect to the property.
>
> *Hypothetical B*: Same as Hypothetical A, except that the debtor's property is subject to a judicial lien of $30,001 instead of $30,000.

In Hypothetical A, we can see that the sum of the judicial lien ($30,000), other liens ($55,000) and the debtor's exemption ($15,000) does *not* exceed the value of the debtor's property ($100,000). Thus the judicial lien in Hypothetical A does *not* impair the debtor's exemption within the meaning of § 522(f)(2)(A), and the debtor is *not* entitled to avoid any portion of that lien under § 522(f)(1).

In Hypothetical B, however, the sum of the judicial lien ($30,001), other liens ($55,000) and the debtor's exemption ($15,000) *does* exceed the property's value (by $1), and so the targeted judicial lien is deemed under § 522(f)(2)(A) to impair the debtor's exemption. Under Silveira's proposed interpretation, the fact of this impairment requires that the debtor in Hypothetical B be permitted to avoid the $30,001 judicial lien *in its entirety*. Thus, as Silveira would have it, a $1 *increase* in the amount of the (unavoidable) judicial lien in Hypothetical A would result in the debtor's acquiring the power to avoid the lien in full.[48]

We find it difficult to conceive of any reason that would counsel in favor of interpreting § 522(f)(1)(A) & (f)(2)(A) to produce such a result. * * *

---

[48] The debtor in Hypothetical A would also acquire full avoidance power (according to Silveira's approach) if the value of the debtor's property were reduced, or the amount of consensual liens were increased, by $1.

Here, the sum of the debtor's exemption ($15,000) and all consensual liens on his property ($117,680) is $24,320 *less* than the value of the property ($157,000); in other words, there is $24,320 of excess equity available. This means that if the Bank's judicial lien here had been for $24,320 or less, that lien would have been absolutely unavoidable under § 522(f)(1), because there would have been no "impairment" within the meaning of § 522(f)(2)(A).[49] The fact that the Bank's actual lien is for more than $24,320 surely provides no reason to place the Bank in a position worse than it would have been had its lien originally been limited to that amount. Fairness requires, therefore, that the Bank be permitted to pursue the fixing of its $209,500 judicial lien *up to* the amount of $24,320.

In more intuitive terms, it is obvious that the value of the debtor's property in this case is sufficient to cover the entire amount of the debtor's mortgage ($117,680) plus his claimed exemption ($15,000), with $24,320 of equity to spare. Nothing in § 522(f)(1) or § 522(f)(2) can be read to require that this excess equity be preserved either for the debtor or the bankruptcy estate, rather than being made available for the partial satisfaction of a judicial lien. And, as shown above, the fixing of a judicial lien in an amount equal to this excess equity would not create any impairment of the debtor's $15,000 exemption. It follows that no legitimate purpose underlying the statute would be served by permitting Silveira to avoid so much of the Bank's lien – $24,320 – as could be covered by the excess equity available in the property.

In summary, we apply § 522(f)(1)(A) and § 522(f)(2)(A) to the facts of this case as follows. First, pursuant to § 522(f)(2)(A), we determine that the sum of (i) the targeted judicial lien ($209,500), (ii) all other liens ($117,680), and (iii) the amount of the debtor's exemption ($15,000) – which sum equals $342,180 – exceeds the value that the debtor's property would have in an unencumbered state ($157,000), and exceeds that value by $185,180. Thus, the Bank's judicial lien impairs the debtor's exemption to the extent of $185,180. Because Silveira is entitled to avoid the Bank's lien to the extent of any impairment, Silveira is entitled to avoidance in the amount of $185,180. *See* § 522(f)(1)(A). The remainder of the Bank's judicial lien, in the amount of $24,320 ($209,500 minus $185,180), is not subject to avoidance by the debtor under § 522(f)(1)(A). * * *

---

[49] That is, the sum of (i) the judicial lien ($24,320), (ii) other liens ($117,680), and (iii) the debtor's exemption ($15,000) would not have exceeded the value of the debtor's property ($157,000).

QUESTION

The court concluded that the judicial lien should not be avoided in full because that would lead to an absurd result. Assuming that is correct, was the court right in avoiding the lien to the extent of $185,180 or should it have avoided the lien only to the extent of $15,000 (the debtor's exemption limit)? Why does this matter?

When the debtor is not the sole owner of the property, computing the extent to which the lien impairs the exemption also requires ascertaining the value of the debtor's share of the property and then deducting the amount of prior liens from that figure. *See* § 522(f)(2). This makes sense when the debtor is the sole obligor of the debt secured by the prior liens, but seems questionable when all of the co-owners are jointly obligated on the prior lien debts. In such instances, it would seem to make more sense to deduct the lien amounts from the total value of the property, not merely the debtor's share. Consider the following illustration:

Debtor and Spouse own realty as tenants in common (each with a 50% share). The property is valued at $100,000 and is subject to a mortgage debt, on which both of them are liable, of $45,000. There is a judicial lien against the property for $4,000 (arising from some debt of Debtor) and Debtor is entitled to an exemption of $20,000. The different computations can be illustrated as follows:

Value of Property	$100,000	Value of Property	$100,000
Debtor's ½ Share	$50,000	Mortgage Lien	($45,000)
Mortgage Lien	($45,000)		$55,000
	$5,000	Debtor's ½ Share	$27,500
Exemption	($20,000)	Exemption	($20,000)
Net Equity	$0	Net Equity	$7,500

Under the approach on the left, which subtracts the entire senior lien amount from Debtor's share, the judicial lien impairs the exemption and may be avoided. However, doing so would effectively leave Debtor with property worth $27,500 (one-half of the couple's net equity), which is more than the exemption amount. Under the approach on the right, which subtracts the senior lien from the total value of the property before computing Debtor's proportionate share, the $4,000 judicial lien does not impair the exemption and cannot be avoided. Even so, Debtor is still able to enjoy the full value of the exemption.

Courts are divided. A few follow a literalist (left) approach and deduct the lien amount from the value of the debtor's share.[50] Most follow an approach (right) more in keeping with the purpose of the provision and deduct the amount of such lien from the full value of the property.[51]

One final issue concerning § 522(f)(1)(A) is whether the debtor can use it to avoid a lien on property that is not properly exemptible if no objection to the debtor's claimed exemption was filed. Recall that the Supreme Court has held that if no objection is timely filed, the exemption is valid even if there is no reasonable basis for claiming it.[52] Nevertheless, several courts have ruled, based on varying rationales, that the judicial lienor may defend the avoidance action by arguing that the property is not exemptible.[53]

(c) Claiming Exemptions After Using the Trustee's Avoiding Powers

We have just seen that § 522(f) authorizes the debtor to avoid certain liens that impair exemptions. In addition, the debtor may benefit from the trustee's avoiding powers. This can occur in either of two ways. First, if the trustee uses the strong-arm powers to avoid a lien or successfully brings a preference claim to recover property or

---

50 *E.g.*, *In re Cozad*, 208 B.R. 495 (10th Cir. BAP 1997).

51 *E.g.*, *In re Miller*, 299 F.3d 183 (3d Cir. 2002); *In re Lehman*, 205 F.3d 1255 (11th Cir. 2000); *Nelson v. Scala*, 192 F.3d 32 (1st Cir. 1999); *In re Meyer*, 373 B.R. 84 (9th Cir. BAP 2007). When the property concerned is held in a tenancy by the entirety, the problem is even more difficult because the interests of the husband and wife may not readily be severable. For an interesting discussion and resolution of this issue, see *In re Snyder*, 249 B.R. 40 (1st Cir. BAP 2000), *aff'd*, 2 F. App'x 46 (1st Cir. 2001).

52 *Taylor v. Freeland & Kronz*, 503 U.S. 638 (1992) (excerpted *supra* beginning on page 140).

53 *See, e.g.*, *In re Schoonover*, 331 F.3d 575 (7th Cir. 2003) (the clock for lienholders begins running when the § 522(f) avoidance motion is served, not when the meeting of unsecured creditors is held); *In re Morgan*, 149 B.R. 147 (9th Cir. BAP 1993) (§ 522(f) empowers the debtor to avoid a lien impairing an exemption only if the debtor "would have been entitled" to the exemption at the time the petition was filed, but because the debtor becomes entitled to a baseless exemption under *Taylor* only later, upon the running of the objection period, avoidance is not permitted; also due process requires that the lien creditor receive notice that the encumbered property is claimed as exempt before the lienholder is barred from objecting).

avoid a lien, the debtor may be able to claim an exemption in the property concerned. *See* § 522(g). Second, if the trustee declines to bring such an action, the debtor may be able to use the trustee's powers to avoid a lien or recover property. *See* § 522(h).

Each of these provisions has its limitations. In particular, if the avoidable transfer was a voluntary one on the debtor's part, the debtor will not be able to claim an exemption in the otherwise recoverable property.[54]

Problem 6-11

Demobilized owns a car worth $8,000. State law affords debtors a $5,000 exemption for a motor vehicle. Last year, Demobilized granted Chiropractor a security interest in the car to secure Demobilized's obligation to pay for $6,000 of professional services from Chiropractor. Chiropractor never perfected the security interest. This week, Demobilized filed for bankruptcy protection.

A. May the trustee avoid Chiropractor's lien? *See* § 544(a).

B. If the trustee does, to what extent may Demobilized claim the car as exempt? *See* § 522(g); *In re Hicks*, 342 B.R. 596 (Bankr. W.D. Mo. 2006).

C. If the trustee does not, may Demobilized avoid the lien? *See* § 522(h).

D. Assume that Demobilized never granted Chiropractor a security interest but that two months ago Chiropractor obtained a $6,000 judgment against Demobilized and last week, prior to Demobilized's bankruptcy filing, Chiropractor had the sheriff levy on the car. This gave Chiropractor a judicial lien on the car. How, if at all, would the analysis of each of the questions above change?

4. Statutory Liens – § 545

Section 545 governs the validity of statutory liens. "Statutory lien" is defined in § 101(53) as a "lien arising solely by force of a statute on specified circumstances or conditions." It is distinguished from a "security interest," which includes any type of consensual lien created by agreement, § 101(50), and from a "judicial lien," which is one

[54] *See also* § 522(j), (k) (imposing additional limitations on the debtor's ability to benefit from the trustee's avoiding powers).

obtained by a legal or equitable proceeding or process, § 101(36). It also does not encompass most common-law liens that courts have created to protect certain creditors.

Section 545(2) avoids any statutory lien (other than a tax lien) that would be ineffective against a bona fide purchaser of the property. This test is similar to the rule in § 544(a)(3) (applicable only to real estate) and is different from the one in § 544(a)(1) (applicable to all property). In this sense, statutory liens are disfavored in bankruptcy relative to consensual and judicial liens.

One of the most important modern statutory liens is the mechanic's or materialman's lien, through which the unpaid suppliers of labor or material used in the improvement of real property are given a lien on the property improved to secure payment of their claims. Creation or enforcement of the lien often requires the filing of a notice of lien in the appropriate public office. Normally, filing must be made within a specified period after the labor has been performed or the materials supplied. Failure to file such a notice will normally make the lien junior to the rights of a bona fide purchaser and thus subject the lien to avoidance under § 545(2).[55] In this sense, failure to file has much the same effect as failing to perfect a security interest, which subjects the secured party to the trustee's strong-arm powers.

5. *Liens Securing Fines and Penalties – § 724(a)*

In Chapter 7, fines, penalties, and awards for multiple or punitive damages are subordinated to other claims. § 726(a)(4). Congress decided that, as a matter of equity, creditors should not recover on these noncompensatory claims until other creditors have been compensated for their actual losses. In particular, there was concern that penalty claims, especially for taxes, would swallow up too much of the estate, to the detriment of general, unsecured claimants.

To effectuate this policy with respect to secured claims, § 724(a) authorizes the Chapter 7 trustee to avoid the lien securing such a claim. Thus, a lien supporting a claim for a fine, penalty, or award of multiple or punitive damages will be avoided in a Chapter 7 case. The claimholder then shares in the estate assets only if there is enough to pay all nonpriority, unsecured claims in full.

---

[55] Failure to file may also subject the lien to avoidance under § 544(a)(3).

F. SETOFF

As a general rule, bankruptcy does not enhance creditors' rights; it selectively recognizes some, delays enforcement of others, and eliminates many. One of the few exceptions to this is setoff. Setoff rights are not treated as a lien under nonbankruptcy law. Rather, setoff is simply a method by which two entities, each of whom owes a debt to the other, may settle up with each other on a net basis.[56] However, the Bankruptcy Code elevates the creditor with setoff rights to the status of a secured claimant. § 506(a); *see also* §§ 542(b), 553(a). The effect of this is to ensure that creditors with setoff rights will obtain the benefit of those rights in bankruptcy.

There are at least three important limitations on this generality, however. First, the Bankruptcy Code does not explain when setoff rights exist. For that, recourse must be made to state law, which is remarkably nonuniform and occasionally quite confusing on this subject.

Second, setoff rights are not recognized in bankruptcy if they are created in a preferential manner. This rule is codified in § 553(a)(2) and (3). Note, however, that the rule regarding setoff rights is different from the rules regarding preference transfers. For example, a security interest or judicial lien created within the 90 days preceding bankruptcy that collateralizes a pre-existing debt meets the prima facie case of an avoidable preference. *See* § 547(b). In contrast, setoff rights created within the 90 days before bankruptcy are, by and large, invalidated only if the creditor's obligation to the debtor was created "for the purpose of obtaining a right of setoff against the debtor." § 553(a)(3)(C). In essence, avoidance of setoff rights under this rule requires a sort of intent to be preferred, a requirement that does not exist under § 547(b).[57]

Problem 6-12

Dutiful wanted to start a new business, but because of a poor credit history had great difficulty obtaining the needed financing until Dutiful went to

---

[56] Because setoff rights do not qualify as a lien, the setoff claimant often loses setoff rights when a third party has a lien on the claimant's obligation to pay. *See* Stephen L. Sepinuck, *The Problems with Setoff: A Proposed Legislative Solution*, 51 WM. & MARY L. REV. 51 (1988). *But see* U.C.C. § 9-340.

[57] On the other hand, the § 547(c)(2) preference defense for transfers in the ordinary course severely limits the transfers that are avoidable. While it does not on its face impose a requirement of an intent to prefer or to be preferred, it may have a somewhat similar effect.

> Savings & Loan ("S&L"). Dutiful's cousin is a loan executive at S&L and personally approved a $45,000 unsecured loan to Dutiful. For the next year, Dutiful was careful always to make the monthly payments to S&L on time, even when other bills went unpaid for weeks or months. When it became clear that the business would fail, Dutiful wanted to do everything possible to make sure that S&L got paid, so that Dutiful's cousin would not get in trouble. Dutiful knew that paying S&L in full or making any unusually large payment on the eve of bankruptcy would be an avoidable preference. So, Dutiful simply deposited all spare cash in a checking account at S&L the day before filing for bankruptcy. Will this action have the preferential effect that Dutiful seeks: benefitting S&L so that Dutiful's cousin does not get in trouble? *See* § 553(a), (b).

Third, § 553(b) places limits on the efficacy of setoff rights exercised prepetition. These limits are known as the "improvement in position test," and they are similar to the rule in § 547(c)(5). Unfortunately, the provision is notoriously difficult to understand and apply, probably because it is so poorly written. Read § 553(b) and then consider the following hypothetical.

> On January 2, 90 days before Debtor's bankruptcy, Debtor owed Bank $10,000 on an unsecured demand note. On that date, Debtor's checking account at Bank had a $1,000 balance. On March 20, Debtor deposited a check for $15,000 into the checking account. The deposit was made in the ordinary course of business and with the expectation that the proceeds of the check would be available for withdrawal when the check was collected. The check was collected on March 25 and, as a result, Debtor's credit balance was $16,000. Checks of Debtor were paid by Bank after that date. On March 29, Bank learned that Debtor was in serious financial difficulty. Bank immediately demanded payment of the note. Debtor could not pay and, on March 30, Bank exercised its state-law setoff rights by debiting Debtor's checking account $10,300, the amount then due under the note. After the setoff, Debtor's account was reduced to $2,000. The following chart depicts these transactions.

Date	Debt	Deposit Balance
January 2	$10,000	$11,000
March 25	$10,300	$16,000
March 30	$10,300	$12,300
April 1	$0	$2,000

On April 2, Debtor filed a Chapter 7 bankruptcy petition. On March 29 and at all times thereafter, Debtor was insolvent. Is the trustee in bankruptcy entitled, under § 553(b), to recover from Bank any part of the setoff?

Under § 553(b)(1), Bank's secured position must be calculated at two points: (1) on the date setoff is exercised; and (2) the earliest date, beginning on the 90th day before the petition, when there was an "insufficiency" in Bank's position. An insufficiency exists when the creditor is unsecured under § 506(a).

In this case, the 90th day before the petition was January 2. That was also the first date on which there was an insufficiency because, on that date, Bank was owed $10,000 and held $1,000 on deposit for Debtor. It thus had a secured claim for $1,000 and an unsecured claim – an "insufficiency" – for $9,000. By March 30, the day it exercised setoff, Bank's claim had risen to $10,300 but was fully secured. Thus, there was no insufficiency on the date the setoff was made. Accordingly, from the beginning of the 90-day period to the date setoff was made, Bank's secured position improved by $9,000. As a result, § 553(b)(1) deprives Bank of this benefit; the trustee may recover this amount from Bank.

There are two things to note about this rule. First, § 553(b)(1) requires a comparison of the insufficiency on only two dates. It does not take into account any intermediate increases or decreases in the insufficiency. Second, if Bank had not effected setoff before bankruptcy, it would have been able to assert setoff rights in bankruptcy to the full extent of its claim. Section 553(a) recognizes the right of setoff "except as otherwise provided in this section." Section 553(b) is a limitation on § 553(a), but it applies only to a setoff made "on or within 90 days before the date of the filing of the petition." Thus, a *postpetition* setoff is not affected by § 553(b) (although it would likely be enjoined by the automatic stay, as we will see in the next chapter). In this sense, the rule of § 553(b) is distinguishable from the improvement of position test in § 547(c)(5), which applies even when the secured party refrains from enforcing its security interest prepetition.

The rule of § 553(b) has what some regard as a drafting glitch, leading to absurd results. Consider the following problem.

Problem 6-13

At all relevant times until Bank exercised its setoff rights, Distressed owed Bank $25,000 on an outstanding loan. The amounts that Distressed had on deposit with Bank were as follows:

	Account Balance	**Debt to Bank**	**Insufficiency**
90th day	$25,000	$25,000	$0
89th day	$8,000	$25,000	$17,000
15th day*	$26,000	$27,000	$1,000
14th day	$0	$1,000	$1,000

* (day of setoff)

On the 15th day before the bankruptcy petition was filed, Bank set off the $26,000 in Distressed's account.

A. How much, if anything, may the trustee recover from Bank?

B. How, if at all, would the analysis of Part A change if on the 90th day before the petition was filed the deposit account had a balance of $24,999?

Prior to July 2001, when revised Article 9 of the Uniform Commercial Code went into effect, it was possible to obtain a security interest in a deposit account as original collateral, but Article 9 did not apply to such a transaction.[58] As a result, there was no guidance on how to perfect such a security interest and few attempted to obtain one. Revised Article 9 governs most security interests in deposit accounts[59] and virtually all

---

[58] A few states, including California, had a nonuniform version of Article 9 that governed such security interests. In all states, Article 9 applied to a security interest in a deposit account to the extent it contained proceeds of other collateral.

[59] *See* U.C.C. § 9-109(d)(11) (excluding from the coverage of Article 9 a security interest in a deposit

deposit account agreements expressly grant the depositary bank a security interest in the deposits to secure whatever obligations the depositor may owe or come to owe to the bank. Such security interests are automatically perfected. *See* U.C.C. §§ 9-104(a)(1), 9-314(a). As a result, whereas most depositary institutions had to rely on their common-law setoff rights (often augmented by a contractual provision granting the bank setoff rights) when the Bankruptcy Code was adopted, most now supplement those rights with an Article 9 security interest.[74]

Problem 6-14

The facts are the same as in Problem 6-13 but Bank has at all times had a perfected security interest in Distressed's deposit account. May the trustee recover anything from Bank? *See* U.C.C. § 9-340 cmt. 3 ("a bank may hold both a right of setoff against, and an Article 9 security interest in, the same deposit account").

---

account in a consumer transaction unless the deposit account is proceeds of other collateral); *see also* U.C.C. § 9-102(a)(26) (defining "consumer transaction").

[74] A depositary bank that obtains an Article 9 security interest in its customer's deposit accounts held at that bank does not give up its setoff rights. U.C.C. § 9-340 cmt. 3.

CHAPTER SEVEN
THE AUTOMATIC STAY AND OTHER DEBTOR PROTECTIONS

Several provisions of the Bankruptcy Code kick in immediately upon the filing of a bankruptcy petition to enjoin a wide variety of behavior by entities other than the debtor. These provisions include:

- § 362, which prohibits most creditor collection activity against the debtor, against property of the debtor, or against property of the estate.
- § 525, which prohibits certain discrimination merely because the debtor has filed a bankruptcy petition or received a discharge.
- § 366, which prohibits utilities from withholding service (*e.g.*, electricity, gas, water, telephone) from a debtor merely because of the petition or the debtor's failure to pay a prepetition bill. Utilities are permitted, however, to require a reasonable deposit to cover future service.
- § 108, which tolls certain statutes of limitations, as well as time periods in both the rules of court procedure and certain private agreements.

Another injunction, imposed by § 524, prohibits acts to collect discharged debts. A discharge of debts does not take place until later in the case. That provision will be discussed in chapter ten.

A. THE AUTOMATIC STAY

Without doubt, the most important and far-reaching of these provisions is § 362, which creates what is known as the automatic stay. It is one of the most litigated aspects of the Bankruptcy Code. As its legislative history indicates:

> The automatic stay is one of the fundamental debtor protections provided by the bankruptcy laws. It gives the debtor a breathing spell from his creditors. It stops all collection efforts, all harassment, and all foreclosure actions. It permits the debtor to attempt a repayment or reorganization plan, or simply to be relieved of the financial pressures that drove him into bankruptcy.

> The automatic stay also provides creditor protection. Without it, certain creditors would be able to pursue their own remedies against the debtor's property. Those who acted first would obtain payment of the claims in preference to and to the detriment of other creditors. Bankruptcy is designed to provide an orderly liquidation procedure under which all creditors are treated equally. A race of diligence by creditors for the debtor's assets prevents that.[1]

In short, the automatic stay is an almost necessary corollary to bankruptcy. It is doubtful that any effective, centralized, and deliberate bankruptcy process could be created without an injunction against creditor collection activity while the case is pending.

1. Scope of the Stay

The stay is quite broad. Any postpetition act to collect a *prepetition* claim is enjoined, whether the act is directed against the debtor, property of the debtor, or property of the estate. *See* § 362(a)(1)–(7). In addition, all efforts to collect a *postpetition* claim that are directed against property of the estate are also stayed. § 362(a)(3), (4). The combined effect of these rules is that almost all creditor activity must come to an immediate halt once the bankruptcy petition is filed. Still, some events escape the stay's broad scope. Read § 362(a). What constitutes the proscribed actions? Consider the following scenario:

> On March 1, Defunct Airlines filed a chapter 11 bankruptcy petition. Until that date, Defunct had maintained four arrival and departure slots (gates) at Airport. These slots had been allocated to it by the FAA two years before pursuant to the applicable federal regulations. On the date of the petition, Defunct ceased operations and stopped using the slots. FAA regulations permit the holders of slots to sell or lease the slots to others, but provide that, after a two-month grace period following bankruptcy, "any slot not utilized 65 percent of the time over a two-month period shall be recalled by the FAA."[2] On July 15, the FAA notified Defunct that its four slots had been withdrawn for nonuse and that they would be reallocated to another carrier in ten days. Has the FAA violated the stay?

---

1 H.R. REP. NO. 95-595, at 340.

2 14 C.F.R. § 93.227(a).

The answer is no. Because the FAA lacks discretion in this matter, recall of the slots is deemed to have occurred automatically, by operation of law. Thus, the FAA did not take any action postpetition that affected property of the estate. Put another way, § 362(a) does not stay the automatic expiration of property rights, only actions and efforts to transfer property rights.[3]

To apply § 362 properly, one must be clear about what is property of the estate and what is property of the debtor as discussed previously in chapter three.

Problem 7-1

Which of the following actions, if taken by a creditor postpetition, would violate the automatic stay as provided in § 362(a)? For each action that does violate the stay, identify which paragraph or paragraphs of subsection (a) apply.

A. Sending the debtor a bill for a prepetition debt.
B. Sending the debtor a bill for a postpetition debt.
C. Bringing suit against the debtor for a prepetition debt.
D. Filing a motion to dismiss for failure to state a claim in a state-court action brought by the debtor prepetition.
E. Recording a prepetition judgment against the debtor.
F. Receiving wire transfers from the debtor's employer pursuant to a prepetition order garnishing the debtor's wages. Does the answer depend on whether the creditor received notice of the bankruptcy?
G. Refusing to sell the debtor goods or services unless the debtor pays a prepetition debt.
H. Refusing to sell the debtor goods or services unless the debtor pays for them in advance.
I. Demanding payment of a prepetition debt from a guarantor of debtor.
J. Bringing an action against debtor's liability insurer for a prepetition claim.
K. Bringing an action to foreclose on collateral owned by someone other than a debtor when the collateral secures an obligation guaranteed by the debtor.

---

[3] *But cf.* § 108, discussed at the end of this chapter, which tolls the automatic expiration of some rights.

In analyzing stay issues, it is important to remember that one of the main purposes of the stay is to preserve the status quo. With respect to actions against the debtor, the automatic stay can provide a needed respite from the financial stress that precipitated the bankruptcy filing. With respect to actions against estate assets, this is even more important. It prevents dissipation of the estate in a manner inconsistent with the policies and rules of the bankruptcy process. Of course, although the Code itself does not expressly so provide, it is generally understood that filing a proof of claim with the bankruptcy court does not violate the stay. If it did, the bankruptcy system obviously could not function.

Sometimes, however, the concerns about protecting the debtor and preserving the estate can be in conflict. Consider the next problem. In doing so, begin by identifying the property that is at issue and who owns it. Then consider the subsequent problem and how it differs from the first.

Problem 7-2

Depositor had $1,000 in a savings account at Local Bank when Depositor filed for Chapter 7 bankruptcy protection. Depositor claimed the entire savings account as exempt. One week after the filing, Depositor sought to withdraw funds to pay rent. Local Bank refused to honor the withdrawal order, causing Depositor's landlord to threaten eviction.

A. Does Depositor have a cause of action against Local Bank for violation of the stay? Should Depositor have such a cause of action? *See* § 542(a), (b); Rule 4003(b); *see also In re Zavala*, 444 B.R. 181 (Bankr. E.D. Cal. 2011).
B. If you were counsel to Local Bank, how would you have advised it to respond to Depositor's withdrawal request?

Problem 7-3

Depositor borrowed $50,000 from Security Bank to help finance a new business venture. Unfortunately, the business venture has serious cash flow problems, and Depositor recently filed for bankruptcy protection while still owing Security Bank about $47,000. At the time of the bankruptcy filing, Depositor had $4,000 on deposit in a checking account at Security Bank. After the filing, Security Bank placed an administrative "freeze" on the checking account and refused to honor checks drawn on it. Has Security Bank violated the automatic stay? *See* §§ 362(a)(3), (4), (7), 363(e), 542(b); *see also* §§ 506(a), 553(a).

For many debtors, the automatic stay is one of the most desired features of bankruptcy. They file, in large measure, to stop a particular creditor from taking a particular action, such as foreclosing on the debtor's home. For such debtors, timing is critical. The debtor needs to file before that action is taken. If the debtor waits too long, such as until after the foreclosure sale is completed, the stay will provide no assistance.

In some cases, however, the debtor times the bankruptcy petition more with an eye on the past than to the future. For example, occasionally the debtor voluntarily pays a favored creditor and wants to ensure that the trustee will not be able to avoid the payment as a preferential transfer. In such a case, the debtor may wish to file only after the 90-day preference period has expired. Of course, this is one of the reasons that the preference period for insiders is one year. These are the persons the debtor is most likely to favor and it is far more difficult for a debtor who needs bankruptcy protection to delay filing for a year than for only 90 days.

Other timing considerations may apply. Consider the following problem.

Problem 7-4

Disabled was injured in a one-car automobile accident and incurred significant medical expenses that insurance would not cover. Eventually, Hospital obtained a judgment against Disabled and began garnishing her wages. Under the garnishment order, Disabled's employer pays $110 to Hospital every two weeks. Disabled comes to see you after this has gone on for two months. She very much wants to stop the garnishment because without that money she simply cannot pay her other living expenses. You conclude that, in a bankruptcy liquidation, creditors would receive nothing and, in fact, Disabled would have substantial, unused exemptions that she could use to protect additional property of any kind, including cash. Do you advise Disabled to file immediately? Why or why not? Consider §§ 522(g), (h), and 547(c)(8).

2. *Exceptions to the Stay*

Because the automatic stay is so wide-sweeping, virtually every revision to the Bankruptcy Code has added one or more exceptions to it. *See* § 362(b). For the most part, these exceptions fall into four general categories. One category includes the exceptions that are directed at specific creditors. Chief among these are:

- § 362(b)(2), which allows for collection of postpetition spousal and child support against non-estate property;
- § 362(b)(3), which authorizes the filing of a U.C.C. Article 9 continuation statement to maintain perfection of a security interest in property of the estate and authorizes the filing of an initial financing statement to perfect such a security interest in limited circumstances; and
- § 362(b)(10) and (22), which authorize a lessor of nonresidential property to obtain possession of the property if the lease expired before the bankruptcy petition or the lessor obtained a judgment for possession prepetition.[4]

We will now explore each of these provisions in a bit more depth. Begin by reading § 362(b)(2) and then attempting the two problems that follow.

Problem 7-5

Duke and Duchess have been married for fourteen years but are now separated. Duchess had filed for divorce and the case was still pending when Duke filed for bankruptcy protection. What aspects of the case, if any, may Duchess pursue and may the family court deal with prior to the bankruptcy court granting relief from the stay? Specifically:

A. May the divorce decree itself be entered?
B. May the court enter an order dividing the marital estate?
C. May the court enter an order assigning custody of the children and visitation rights for the noncustodial parent?
D. May the court set the amount of spousal or child support?
E. May the court enjoin Duke from contacting Duchess?

---

[4] *See also* § 362(b)(23) (excepting from the stay an eviction action based on the debtor's endangerment of the property or use of controlled substances on the premises); (b)(19) (permitting postpetition deductions from the debtor's wages to repay a loan from an employer-sponsored, ERISA-qualified plan).

Problem 7-6

Nine months ago, Duke and Duchess were divorced. The divorce decree ordered Duke to pay Duchess $2,000/month for three years but Duke has made no payments to Duchess and last week filed for Chapter 7 bankruptcy protection.

A. To collect the prepetition arrearages, may Duchess levy on Duke's car?
B. May Duchess garnish Duke's postpetition wages?
C. How, if at all, would the analysis to Parts A and B change if Duke had filed under Chapter 13? *See* § 1306.

Now read § 362(b)(3). It creates an exception to the automatic stay to permit a secured party – in two circumstances – to file postpetition an initial financing statement to perfect a security interest. First, by referring to § 546(b), § 362(b)(3) covers the situation described in § 546(b)(1)(A): when other law permits perfection to be effective against someone who acquired rights in the collateral before the secured party perfected. Several provisions in Article 9 do that, most notably U.C.C. § 9-317(e) and § 9-324(a), both dealing with PMSIs perfected within 20 days of when the debtor receives possession. The combined effect of these rules is that a secured party with a PMSI may, without violating the stay, perfect within 20 days of when the debtor receives possession. Some other laws, such as the law governing mechanics' liens, also allow for retroactive effect and would be covered by the rule of § 362(b)(3).

The second situation, which arises by virtue of the reference to § 547(e)(2)(A), is any time the secured party seeks to perfect within 30 days of when the security interest attached. Thus, a secured party may, without violating the stay, perfect any security interest that attached within the 30 days preceding its effort to perfect. Note, however, that the trustee's avoidance powers are not subject to this. Thus, even though the secured party may perfect, perfection is unlikely to help much against the trustee for reasons we saw in chapter six.

By referencing § 546(b), § 362(b)(3) also creates an exception to the automatic stay to permit a secured party to file postpetition a continuation statement. *See* § 546(b)(1)(B). Pursuant to U.C.C. Article 9, a filed financing statement is generally effective only for five years; after that period, the effectiveness of the financing statement lapses. U.C.C. § 9-515(a). For the security interest perfected by filing to remain perfected beyond that five-year period, the secured party must file a continuation statement within the six months prior to lapse. U.C.C. § 9-515(c)–(e).

Problem 7-7

Why is it necessary for a secured party to maintain perfection after the debtor files for bankruptcy protection? Put another way, how, if at all, would a postpetition lapse in perfection affect the secured party? *See* U.C.C. §§ 9-317(a), 9-322(a), 9-515 cmt. 3, ex. 2.

Now read § 362(b)(10) and (22), and subsection (*l*). These subsections except from the stay a lessor's actions to obtain the leased property in two specified situations, generally where the debtor's rights as lessee have been terminated prepetition and the lessor has to take action to evict the debtor, or, in the case of nonresidential real property, where the lease expires during the bankruptcy case and the lessor needs to take action to obtain the property.

But what if the debtor's rights as lessee have not been terminated prepetition or, in the case of nonresidential real property, the lease has not expired? Review the discussion of executory contracts and unexpired leases in chapter five. Many debtors with rented property – either residential or commercial – default on their rental obligations prior to filing for bankruptcy protection. Others are current on all lease payments and do not default prepetition. In either situation, particularly when residential property is involved, the lease is unlikely to have value to the estate in a Chapter 7 case.[5] Accordingly, the trustee will reject the lease. Unfortunately, "[t]he effect of rejection is one of the great mysteries of bankruptcy law."[6] There are several interrelated issues.

Technically, rejection constitutes a prepetition breach, § 365(g)(1), thus giving rise to a prepetition claim by the lessor against the estate.[7] Although the amount of the lessor's claim may be limited by § 502(b)(6), treating the lessor as having a prepetition claim makes sense if the debtor is already in default or plans to default. After all, the lease is a prepetition contract and the only way the lessor can share in estate assets to cover whatever losses arise is if the lessor has a prepetition claim. If, however, the debtor is current on all lease payments and plans to remain current, treating rejection as

---

[5] The lease might have value to the estate if the rent due under the lease were lower than the rent charged for leasing similar property.

[6] *In re Henderson*, 245 B.R. 449 (Bankr. S.D.N.Y. 2000).

[7] Accordingly, the claim will be generally dischargeable, even with respect to payments that were due postpetition.

a breach by the debtor (as opposed to a breach by the estate) is more problematic, at least if such treatment will precipitate an eviction. Because of this possibility, some courts have refused to treat the mere rejection of a residential lease as a breach for any purpose other than claim allowance.

Related to all this is whether and how the stay applies to property subject to a rejected lease. Generally, at least with respect to personal property and residential realty, rejection gives rise to a prepetition breach but it neither terminates the lease nor constitutes an abandonment of the leased property from the estate.[8] The upshot of this is clear: a landlord whose debtor has defaulted on lease payments – either prepetition or postpetition – and who is not able to rely on § 362(b)(10) or (22) must, prior to abandonment of the lease, obtain relief from the stay to evict the debtor and obtain control of the premises. Bringing an eviction action in such circumstances without first obtaining relief from the stay would violate § 362(a)(3). Relief should be reasonably easy to get after a postpetition default in payment, but may be difficult to obtain if the only default is prepetition.

Problem 7-8

> Nine months ago, Donatello entered into a one-year lease of a residential apartment from Landlord. Four months ago, Donatello filed a Chapter 7 bankruptcy petition. Up to that point, Donatello had made all rental payments on time. Three months ago, the Chapter 7 trustee abandoned the lease. For the last two months, Donatello has not paid the rent due under the lease.
>
> A. May Landlord, without first obtaining relief from the stay, bring an action to evict Donatello?
>
> B. May Landlord, without first obtaining relief from the stay, threaten to bring an eviction action if Donatello does not immediately pay the past due postpetition rent?

A second category of exceptions to the stay are those designed to prevent the stay from undermining certain commercial markets or corrupting certain financial products. *See* § 362(b)(6), (7), (11), (17), (27). The transactions noted in these sections are

---

[8] A slightly different rule applies when nonresidential real property is involved. If the trustee constructively rejects the lease by failing to assume it, the trustee must immediately surrender the property to the lessor. § 365(d)(4). In such a case, rejection is tantamount to termination of the debtor's right to occupy the property.

complex and the fear is that if a counterparty to one of these financial arrangements were to file for bankruptcy and the automatic stay prevented the consummation of the deal, the effect on the broader markets would be catastrophic.

A third category of actions excepted from the stay is designed to deal with debtors who file a bankruptcy petition after having a previous bankruptcy case dismissed or the stay lifted in the previous case. *See* § 362(b)(20), (21), (c)(3) & (4), (n); § 109(g). The use of serial bankruptcy petitions to repeatedly stop creditor collection activity has been widely derided as an abuse of the bankruptcy process.

By far the most common – and unsurprising – exceptions are those in the fourth category, which deals with governmental actions. For example, criminal proceedings against the debtor are not stayed. § 362(b)(1). Were the law otherwise, bankruptcy would become the haven of every culprit seeking to avoid or delay punishment for criminal conduct. Even if the prosecutor is bringing the criminal charges primarily in an effort to aid a creditor – as might be true if the victim were a relative of the prosecutor – most courts treat the exception for criminal prosecutions as applicable.[9] A contrary rule – one that based the exception to the stay on the prosecutor's motive – would require a federal judge to question the motivation of an executive official imbued with substantial discretion.

How far a criminal prosecution may go is a bit less clear. A court undoubtedly may convict. It may incarcerate the debtor/defendant, impose a fine, and may even order restitution as part of its sentence. Enforcement of a restitution order, on the other hand, may be subject to the stay.[10] There is similar disagreement about what creditors may do regarding criminal charges. Most allow them to file a criminal complaint – treating that as a necessary corollary to the prosecutor's discretion – but some courts have cautioned that creditors may not "utilize a criminal prosecution as a means of avoiding the automatic . . . stay . . . in an effort to continue to collect on a claim."[11]

---

[9] *See, e.g., In re Simonini*, 69 F. App'x 169 (4th Cir. 2003); *In re Gruntz*, 202 F.3d 1074 (9th Cir. 2000); *In re Williams*, 438 B.R. 679 (10th Cir. BAP 2010); *In re Bartel*, 404 B.R. 584 (1st Cir. BAP 2009).

[10] *Compare In re Barboza*, 211 B.R. 450, 452–53 (Bankr. D.R.I. 1997), *with United States v. Colasuonno*, 697 F.3d 164 (2d Cir. 2012); *In re Williams*, 438 B.R. 679 (10th Cir. BAP 2010).

[11] *In re Williamson-Blackmon*, 145 B.R. 18, 21 (Bankr. N.D. Ohio 1992); *see also In re Fidler*, 442 B.R. 763 (Bankr. D. Nev. 2010) (while prosecution could not be enjoined for violating the discharge injunction, jurisdiction would be retained to consider possible sanctions against complaining witness, including disgorgement of any restitution that might result from the conviction).

Of course, criminal proceedings represent only a small fraction of what states and the federal government do to enforce laws and regulations. Just as bankruptcy should not be a haven for the criminal, it should not be a sanctuary for those who, for example, pollute the environment, practice medicine without a license, maintain unsafe working conditions, or issue unregistered securities. Not surprisingly, therefore, governmental agencies are generally permitted to continue exercising their police, regulatory, and taxing authority, as are accrediting bodies, licensing boards, and stock exchanges. *See* § 362(b)(4), (8), (9), (12)–(16), (18), (25), (26), (28).

The most important of these provisions is § 362(b)(4), which broadly excepts from the stay a governmental unit's actions to enforce its police and regulatory power. Under this provision, the licensing authority may suspend the debtor from practicing law as a sanction for unprofessional conduct, a department of motor vehicles may suspend the debtor's driver's license for driving while intoxicated, the Equal Employment Opportunity Commission may order the debtor to rehire an illegally terminated employee, and the Environmental Protection Agency may order the debtor to stop polluting. Not only may government units issue such orders postpetition, they may also enforce the orders.

However, there are limits on the government's immunity from the stay. In particular, while § 362(b)(4) allows governmental units to enforce their police and regulatory powers and to *obtain* money judgments, they are not permitted to *enforce* money judgments. The idea behind this is fairly simple: the government is not subject to the stay when it acts as a *regulator*, but it is bound by the stay when it acts as a *creditor* or as an agent of private creditors. Unfortunately, this seemingly simple distinction is not always easy to apply. Consider the following case.

IN RE FIRST ALLIANCE MORTGAGE CO.
263 B.R. 99 (9th Cir. BAP 2001)

Marlar, Bankruptcy Judge.

INTRODUCTION

The bankruptcy court ruled that monetary claims asserted in a state court consumer protection action against the debtor were not exempt from the automatic stay, under the exception for an action to enforce a governmental unit's police or regulatory power. The Commonwealth of Massachusetts ("Commonwealth") appealed, and we reverse that portion of the order.[12]

---

[12] The bankruptcy court ordered that the injunctive relief count of the Commonwealth's action was

FACTS AND PROCEDURAL HISTORY

First Alliance Mortgage Co. ("FAMCO" or "debtor") is a financial services company and one of the affiliate debtors in jointly administered chapter 11 cases. FAMCO did business in several states, including Massachusetts.

Prepetition, the Commonwealth obtained a preliminary injunction against FAMCO, which prohibited it from engaging in the loan origination business. The preliminary injunction ensued from the Commonwealth's lawsuit, filed under the Massachusetts Consumer Protection Act, on October 30, 1998. The Commonwealth asserted claims for injunctive relief, civil penalties, attorneys' fees and costs, and restitution on behalf of 299 Massachusetts consumers who had borrowed money from FAMCO. Litigation was pending in that action when FAMCO filed for bankruptcy protection on March 23, 2000.

The Stay Relief Proceedings

On May 9, 2000, the Commonwealth filed a motion entitled "Commonwealth's Motion for Determination that the Automatic Stay Provision of the Bankruptcy Code Does Not Prevent the Commonwealth from Continuing its Superior Court Enforcement Action." It sought to continue to prosecute the state court action to a money judgment, but not to enforce such judgment. The Commonwealth alleged that the complaint was filed pursuant to the Massachusetts Consumer Protection Act, Mass. Gen. Laws ch. 93A § 4, which authorizes the Attorney General to commence an enforcement action against any person who is alleged to be engaging in unfair or deceptive acts or practices in violation of § 2(a) of the Act. The Commonwealth argued that the action was exempt from the automatic stay, under § 362(b)(4), which provides an exception to the automatic stay for "the commencement or continuation of an action or proceeding by a governmental unit . . . to enforce such governmental unit's . . . police and regulatory power." In the alternative, the Commonwealth sought relief from the automatic stay.

* * * The Commonwealth alleged in its motion that the debtor had been charging excessive points for mortgage loans, and had engaged in deceptive sales and training techniques designed to conceal and mislead borrowers regarding the true measure of points charged by FAMCO.

FAMCO filed its opposition, and the attached declaration of its executive vice president and CEO Jeffrey W. Smith. * * * In paragraph 10, Smith acknowledged the pending state court action, and stated: "I am informed and therefore believe that the Commonwealth . . . is seeking restitution and damages for 299 of its citizens that were

---

not subject to the automatic stay and could proceed. That portion of the order has not been appealed and shall stand.

among the over 35,000 borrowers on loans issued by Debtor nationwide." FAMCO also acknowledged, in its opposition, that the Commonwealth was seeking, in the state court action, the remedies of permanent injunction, restitution, civil penalties, and attorneys' fees and costs. Believing the injunctive relief to be moot because its operations had ceased, FAMCO also argued, in its brief, that the Commonwealth had "conced[ed] that the State Court Action was commenced 'to enjoin [the Debtor] from charging excessive points in its mortgage loans to Massachusetts borrowers . . . and from otherwise engaging in conduct that is unfair or deceptive.'" * * *

The Creditors' Committee joined in the opposition, and based its objection on the litigation costs to the estate, which could deplete the assets needed for the debtor's liquidation plan.

At the hearing, the bankruptcy court * * * discussed the merits of the stay exception as applied to the Commonwealth's claims. The court discussed the existence of about 35,000 potential claims against the debtor, all of which were similar to the 299 monetary claims asserted by the Commonwealth, and stated that all such claims should be liquidated in the bankruptcy case in order to treat similarly situated creditors fairly, and not deplete the liquidating estate.

The court then * * * accepted the undisputed facts, and determined that only the injunctive relief was exempt from the automatic stay. The court stated:

> * * * [I] believe that it is appropriate to let the Commonwealth proceed with respect to any injunctive relief, and to show to the people of * * * the Commonwealth, that it is attempting to exercise its police powers on their behalf * * *. But other than that, this Court will not grant relief from stay, to allow the Commonwealth to proceed with respect to determining any damages, or any restitution, or any award, or any civil penalties amounts at this time.

* * *

ISSUE

The sole issue is whether the Commonwealth's consumer protection action for civil penalties, attorneys' fees, and restitution for borrowers is exempt from the automatic stay under § 362(b)(4).

* * *

DISCUSSION

A. Scope of § 362(b)(4)

The filing of a bankruptcy petition operates as a stay, applicable to all entities, of "the commencement or continuation . . . of a judicial, administrative, or other action or proceeding against the debtor." § 362(a)(1). The general policy behind the automatic stay is to grant complete and immediate, albeit temporary, relief to the debtor from creditors, and to prevent dissipation of the debtor's assets before orderly distribution to all creditors can be effected. A main purpose of the stay is to protect the priority of payments to creditors.

The Code provides certain exceptions to the automatic stay, which are read narrowly. Section 362(b)(4) provides an exception for certain governmental police and regulatory actions. Section 362(b)(4) provides that the filing of a petition does not stay

> the commencement or continuation of an action or proceeding by a governmental unit . . . to enforce such governmental unit's . . . police and regulatory power, including the enforcement of a judgment other than a money judgment, obtained in an action or proceeding by the governmental unit to enforce such governmental unit's . . . police or regulatory power.

This provision permits a governmental unit to "commence or continue any police or regulatory action, including one seeking a money judgment, but it may enforce only those judgments and orders that do not require payment or authorize the government to exercise control over property of the estate." 3 Collier on Bankruptcy, § 362.05[5][b] at 362-59 to 362-60 (15th ed. 2001).

The legislative history of this section indicates that when a debtor is sued by a governmental unit in order "to prevent or stop violation of fraud, environmental protection, *consumer protection*, safety, or similar police or regulatory laws, *or attempting to fix damages for violation* of such a law, the action or proceeding is not stayed under the automatic stay." H.R. Rep. No. 595, 95th Cong., 1st Sess. 343 (1977) (emphasis added). By allowing such actions to proceed, this exemption prevents the bankruptcy court from becoming a "haven for wrongdoers." *In re Berg*, 230 F.3d 1165, 1167 (9th Cir. 2000).

Not every police or regulatory action is automatically exempt, however. Enforcement of laws that affect health, welfare, morals, and safety will not be stayed, but regulatory laws that directly conflict with the control of the *res* or property by the bankruptcy court will be stayed. *See In re Universal Life Church, Inc.*, 128 F.3d 1294, 1297 (9th Cir. 1997). The Ninth Circuit applies two tests for determining whether a state's actions fall within the scope of § 362(b)(4): the "pecuniary purpose" test and the "public policy" test. *Id.*

Under the "pecuniary purpose" test, the court must determine "whether the government action relates primarily to the protection of the government's pecuniary interest in the debtor's property or to matters of public safety and welfare." *Id.* at 1297. The relevant inquiry is whether the action is being pursued "*solely* to advance a pecuniary interest of the governmental unit," in which case the stay will be imposed. *Id.* Such actions have been described as those that would "result in an economic advantage to the government or its citizens over third parties in relation to the debtor's estate." *In re Charter First Mortg., Inc.*, 42 B.R. 380, 382 (Bankr. D. Or. 1984).

* * *

Courts also apply the "public policy" test in order to "distinguish between government actions that effectuate public policy and those that adjudicate private rights." *Universal Life Church*, 128 F.3d at 1297. Under this test, the court considers whether the government is exercising its legislative, executive, or judicial functions. *In re Poule*, 91 B.R. 83, 86 (9th Cir. BAP 1988). "Where the agency's action concerns only the parties who are immediately affected the debtor is entitled to the same protection it would receive under the automatic stay if the proceeding were instead in a judicial forum." *Charter First*, 42 B.R. at 384.

In the instant case, the bankruptcy court allowed the Commonwealth's action for injunctive relief to proceed, but held that the claims for civil penalties, attorneys' fees and restitution were stayed, because those actions did not meet the "pecuniary purpose" or "public policy" tests.

B. Civil Penalties and Attorneys' Fees

The Commonwealth initiated a lawsuit against FAMCO under the provisions of its consumer protection act. The purpose of that law is "to improve the commercial relationship between consumers and business persons and to encourage more equitable behavior in the marketplace." *Poznik v. Mass. Medical Prof'l Ins. Ass'n*, 628 N.E.2d 1, 4 (Mass. 1994). It "proscribes unfair or deceptive acts or practices in conduct of trade or commerce." *Veranda Beach Club Ltd. P'ship v. Western Sur. Co.*, 936 F.2d 1364, 1385 (1st Cir. 1991). As a deterrence measure, it also "imposes liability on persons seeking to profit from unfair practices." *Id.*; Mass. Gen. Laws ch. 93A § 2.

From legislative history and case law, it is well-established that consumer protection is a valid exercise of the police and regulatory power for purposes of § 362(b)(4). Here, the Commonwealth sought to impose civil penalties against FAMCO for its alleged unfair and deceptive loan practices. This action falls squarely within its public policy of protecting consumers and deterring violators.

Where the debtor is being prosecuted for engaging in fraudulent conduct, the automatic stay should not allow the debtor to be shielded from the government's attempt to protect its citizens and uphold its laws related to the health and welfare of its citizens. The Ninth Circuit recognized in *Universal Life Church* that the "[d]etection of fraud ha[s] been sustained as a valid basis for invoking the exception even when there is an additional pecuniary interest at stake." 128 F.3d at 1298. It further opined that "[i]ndeed, most government actions which fall under this exemption have some pecuniary component, particularly those associated with fraud detection." *Id.* at 1299.

Even courts that would treat restitution as outside the scope of § 362(b)(4) treat civil penalties and attorneys' fees as being within the scope of the exception.

The bankruptcy court in the case at bar expressed concern about the potential for multiple prosecutions in the various states where FAMCO did business, and the financial effect of such litigation on the bankruptcy estate. However, to hold that a governmental action does not come within § 362(b)(4) for such reason would run counter to the fundamental policy behind the exception, which is to prevent the bankruptcy court from becoming a haven for wrongdoers. *Berg*, 230 F.3d at 1167. The bankruptcy court has other avenues to prevent general harm to the estate, *i.e.*, its powers under § 105(a) to "issue any order, process, or judgment that is necessary or appropriate to carry out the provisions of this title."

FAMCO also contends that these causes of action are unnecessary since it has already ceased its loan origination business. However, civil penalties may be assessed for violations of the statute. Mass. Gen. Laws ch. 93A § 4. The penalties imposed for consumer fraud meet both the pecuniary purpose test and the public policy test. * * *

Therefore, we hold that § 362(b)(4) exempts the Commonwealth's prosecution to judgment of its claims for civil penalties and attorneys' fees from the automatic stay.

C. Restitution Claims

The Commonwealth is also seeking to recover restitution, in the form of money damages, on behalf of 299 Massachusetts borrowers, who are also creditors of the estate. The Commonwealth contends that the restitution claims are not "solely pecuniary" because they further the state's consumer protection policies, and the Commonwealth will not seek to enforce the judgment outside of the bankruptcy case. The Commonwealth further contends that *it* is the plaintiff, not such private third parties; therefore, continuing with the claims liquidation process in state court would promote public policy. FAMCO contends, on the other hand, that the restitution action is solely pecuniary and for the benefit of private parties.

Under the "pecuniary purpose" test, the inquiry is whether the action "relates *primarily* to the protection of the government's pecuniary interest in the debtor's property, or to matters of public policy." *Berg*, 230 F.3d at 1167 (emphasis added). Traditionally, courts have looked at what effect the action will have on the bankruptcy estate, and the supremacy of federal laws. Here, the bankruptcy court determined that the 35,000 similar, unliquidated claims against the estate could be more equitably adjudicated in the bankruptcy claims process.

We believe that a trilogy of Ninth Circuit cases supports the Commonwealth's position and requires us to reverse the bankruptcy court's decision.

The power to determine a debtor's liability or to liquidate a damages claim may legitimately be part of an exempt police or regulatory action. The Ninth Circuit Court of Appeals has held:

> Indeed, most government actions which fall under this exemption have some pecuniary component. . . . This does not abrogate their police power function. Only if the action is pursued "*solely* to advance a pecuniary interest of the governmental unit" will the automatic stay bar it.

Universal Life Church, 128 F.3d at 1299.

In *Universal Life Church*, the Ninth Circuit Court of Appeals held that the IRS issuance of a letter revoking the debtor's tax exempt status was exempt from the stay, even though the IRS also required the Church to file tax returns * * * which * * * estimated the outstanding tax to be more than $6 million. The appellate court rejected the debtor's position "that the IRS must have *no* pecuniary motive at all to fall within section 362(b)(4)," and held that the revocation letter was exempt from the stay because it served a "public policy purpose." 128 F.3d at 1298–99 (emphasis added).

In *Berg*, the Ninth Circuit Court of Appeals held that the purpose of pursuing litigation sanctions was to effectuate public policy, even though the monetary penalty would enure to the benefit of a private party. 230 F.3d at 1168. The court agreed with the reasoning that "although private parties may benefit financially from sanctions, the deterrent effect of monetary penalties can be essential for the government to protect its regulatory interests." *Id.*[13]

The third Ninth Circuit opinion in the trilogy convincing us that the Commonwealth's restitution claims are exempt from the automatic stay is *NLRB v. Continental Hagen Corp.*, 932 F.2d 828 (9th Cir. 1991). There, the National Labor Relations Board had filed an unfair labor practices complaint against the debtor, and

---

[13] We note that *Berg* involves sanctions rather than restitution, but the powerful policy considerations that the Ninth Circuit has articulated apply with equal force.

sought damages consisting of back wages for unionized employees and truck drivers. The Court of Appeals made the important distinction that the NLRB was not seeking to enforce a judgment, but only to obtain a money judgment and liquidate its claim. Therefore, the back pay provision would not jeopardize nor interfere with the pending bankruptcy proceeding. *Id.* at 834–35. The action also passed the public policy test, the court held, because the NLRB was not providing a forum for private parties, but was acting in its own name in furtherance of the policies of the federal labor laws. *Id.* at 834.

* * *

We * * * find a similarity between the cases which exempt actions for back pay, and the present action for restitution to citizens of Massachusetts for the debtor's violation of the consumer protection laws, so long as the Commonwealth seeks only the entry, and not the enforcement, of the money judgment.

These cases provide authority for the Commonwealth's argument that its money claims, which are part of the totality of its consumer protection remedies, are for a public purpose, and not solely for the pecuniary gain to the Commonwealth or its individual citizens. Nor does the entry of a monetary judgment reduce the estate or interfere with the bankruptcy. Such a judgment only serves to liquidate the Commonwealth's claim against the estate. FAMCO will be entitled to all of its defenses to the Commonwealth's action in the Massachusetts state court action. Furthermore, these cases support the conclusion that the Commonwealth was not seeking to adjudicate private rights, but was primarily pursuing remedies for alleged violations of its consumer protection laws.

A few courts in the Ninth Circuit, including a BAP panel, have held that a restitution judgment would create an unfair advantage for those victims over other creditors of the estate by interfering with the bankruptcy court's exclusive jurisdiction to adjudicate claims in bankruptcy. Those cases are * * * distinguishable * * *.

In *Poule*, the BAP held that the State Registrar of Contractors' assessment of an order of corrections, which required the debtor to reimburse a customer, resulted from the adjudication of purely private rights and thus did not fall under the § 362(b)(4) exception. 91 B.R. at 87. The assessment of civil penalties, on the other hand, served the public policy of punishing the debtor for fraudulent conduct, and therefore that portion of the action was not stayed. *Id.* at 86.

In *In re Dunbar*, 235 B.R. 465 (9th Cir. BAP 1999), *aff'd*, 245 F.3d 1058 (9th Cir. 2001), * * * the California Contractors' State License Board had issued an order of correction, following an administrative hearing, which required the debtor to pay $27,000 in restitution for the debtor's violations of the Business and Professions Code. The debtor argued that the government action should be enjoined because it violated the automatic stay. The BAP remanded the matter with instructions that the bankruptcy court should determine if the action violated the automatic stay. The BAP examined § 362(b)(4) and held that, to the extent the state agency had instituted proceedings to seek restitution based on a determination of the debtor's personal liability, such action was not excepted from the automatic stay. *Id.* at 474–75.

Poule and *Dunbar* are distinguishable on their facts. First, they involved violations of legislation enacted to protect individual consumers, who are injured by the acts of building contractors on specific jobs. The remedy typically sought is the assessment of restitution and damages for repair of shoddy workmanship. Thus, the debtor's noncompliance with an order of correction could lead to license revocation proceedings against the debtor. In such instances, almost always initiated by private citizens acting in their individual interests, the restitution action is an action to enforce private rights rather than to protect public interests.

In contrast, in this case, the state attorney general commenced a consumer protection action on behalf of 299 persons who were victimized by the debtor's violation of laws enacted to protect consumers. Thus, viewed in its entirety, the Commonwealth's efforts are not intended "solely" to advance a pecuniary interest or primarily to adjudicate private rights. Rather, the focus of the Commonwealth's action is to enjoin illegal conduct and achieve penalties and restitution as a deterrent to future unlawful activity.

* * *

The Commonwealth argues that the trend in the law is to look at restitution as just one arrow in the entire consumer protection quiver. For example, in *In re Luskin's, Inc.*, 213 B.R. 107 (D. Md. 1997), the Maryland Attorney General's Consumer Protection Division prosecuted an action against the debtor for advertising tactics that were in violation of the Consumer Protection Act. The state sought to obtain restitution for consumers who had relied on the advertisements. The debtor argued that the state was pursuing a pecuniary interest in his property by attempting to adjudicate the private rights of consumers adversely affected by the advertisements. The district court reversed the stay that had been imposed by the bankruptcy court, and determined that the consumer protection action, which included injunctive relief and restitution, was "a legitimate use of . . . police power and/or regulatory power even though it seeks to reduce a monetary claim to judgment." The state, it found, was attempting to halt unfair trade practices by implementing the statutory purpose of its consumer protection law, *i.e.*, to protect the public interest. *Id.* at 110.

The facts in our case are similar to those in *Luskin's.* The Massachusetts Consumer Protection Act was designed to impose liability on persons seeking to profit from unfair or deceptive acts or practices. The restitution count is only one component of an action that is concerned with the overall protection of the public. Moreover, the restitution judgment would simply liquidate all or part of the Commonwealth's unsecured claim against the debtor. It would not give priority of the estate's assets to the Commonwealth or elevate its citizens' rights over the rights of other claimants. We reject the view that merely because the police or regulatory action will determine the debtor's liability for a potpourri of money damages – including damages inuring to the benefit of third parties – that such portion must be severed from the entire action, and stayed.

* * *

Therefore, we hold that the bankruptcy court erred by determining that the Commonwealth's restitution claims were not exempt from the automatic stay pursuant to § 362(b)(4).

Problem 7-9

Applying the "public policy" and "pecuniary purpose" tests described in *First Alliance Mortgage*, determine which of the following actions may be taken postpetition without violating the automatic stay.

A. The Department of Motor Vehicles suspends the debtor's driver's license for failing to pay a prepetition speeding ticket.

B. The Equal Employment Opportunity Commission orders the debtor to pay an illegally terminated employee's wages for the period the employee was out of work.

C. The Environmental Protection Agency orders the debtor to clean up a site on which the debtor had dumped toxic chemicals.

D. The Pension Benefit Guaranty Corporation brings an action against the debtor for not adequately funding its employee pension fund.

3. *Duration of and Relief from the Stay*

The duration of the stay is governed by § 362(c). With regard to actions against property of the estate, the stay expires when the property ceases to be property of the estate.[14] For all other acts, the stay expires when the bankruptcy case is closed or dismissed or the debtor is either granted or denied a discharge, whichever occurs first.

What if a debt is nondischargeable? For example, if the bankruptcy court has ruled that a particular debt is nondischargeable – but has not yet granted or denied the debtor a discharge under § 727, § 1328, or § 1141, as the case may be – may the creditor take actions to collect that debt from non-estate assets? Courts do not agree. Some interpret the reference in § 362(c)(2) to "the time a discharge is granted or denied" to refer to a court's ruling on dischargeability.[15] Others interpret that language to cover any debt that is nondischargeable, regardless of whether the court has ruled on that issue.[16] Still other courts have rejected both of these interpretations and concluded that the stay applies even to nondischargeable debts until the court rules on the debtor's discharge.[17]

Problem 7-10

> Degree has an outstanding student loan debt to College. The bankruptcy court has ruled that this debt is nondischargeable under § 523(a)(8) but has not yet granted or denied Degree a discharge. Is there any reason why the stay should enjoin College from attempting to collect the debt from non-estate assets? In answering this question, consider what might happen – and who might benefit – if College collects the debt prior to completion of the bankruptcy case during which claimants will receive partial payment of their claims. *See* § 502(j); Rule 3008.

In some situations, the bankruptcy court may lift the stay before it would otherwise terminate to permit certain actions to occur. § 362(d). A party seeking such relief must file a motion, *see* Rules 4001, 9014, and bankruptcy courts normally deal with those motions on a fairly expeditious basis. Indeed, unless the court rules otherwise, the stay will normally terminate automatically 30 or 60 days after the motion is filed. § 362(e).

---

14 As noted above, the stay might expire earlier – or not come into existence at all – if the debtor had one or more bankruptcy proceedings pending during the year preceding the petition in the current case. *See* § 362(c)(3), (4).

15 *See, e.g.*, *In re Embry*, 10 F.3d 401 (6th Cir. 1993); *In re Gustafson*, 111 B.R. 282 (9th Cir. BAP 1990), *rev'd on other grounds*, 934 F.2d 216 (9th Cir. 1991).

16 *See, e.g.*, *In re Najafi*, 154 B.R. 185 (Bankr. E.D. Pa. 1993).

17 *See, e.g.*, *In re Neilsen*, 443 B.R. 718 (Bankr. W.D. Va. 2011); *In re Mu'min*, 374 B.R. 149 (Bankr. E.D. Pa. 2007); *In re Parker*, 334 B.R. 529 (Bankr. D. Mass. 2005).

The main bases for granting relief from the stay are: (i) for cause, including lack of adequate protection of an interest in property; and (ii) with respect to particular property, when the debtor lacks equity in it and the property is not necessary for a successful reorganization. § 362(d)(1), (2). Both of these grounds are primarily relevant only to creditors with secured claims. Let's consider the latter ground first.

Suppose the debtor owes a creditor $10,000 and the debt is secured by an automobile worth $8,000. Clearly, the debtor has no equity in the collateral; the car is not worth more than the debt it secures. If, in addition, the car is not necessary to a successful reorganization, then the creditor is entitled to relief from the stay. Once that relief is granted, the creditor may then pursue whatever rights the creditor has under nonbankruptcy law, most probably the right to repossess the car and foreclose its lien. Note, if the debtor is undergoing liquidation in Chapter 7, then by definition there will be no reorganization and the second prong of this test is satisfied. The only issue will be whether the collateral is worth more than the amount of the debt. If it is, then the estate (or the debtor, if the property is exempt) has equity and the stay will not be lifted under § 362(d)(2). In other words, if the property is worth something to the estate, relief from the stay will be denied to permit the trustee to try to extract value from the property for the benefit of claimants. If the property is worth something to the debtor, then relief from the stay will be denied so as to give the debtor time to find a way to preserve that value, before the creditor is permitted to use its nonbankruptcy rights to foreclose.

Now let's consider § 362(d)(1), which authorizes relief from the stay for cause, including lack of adequate protection of an interest in property. Lack of adequate protection most commonly exists when the secured creditor has little equity cushion and the collateral is depreciating or threatening to depreciate faster than the debtor is paying off the debt.

For example, suppose the debtor owes a creditor $10,000 secured by an automobile worth $10,500. If the debtor is continuing to use the car, the car will almost assuredly fall in value (it would be highly unusual for a car's value to rise with use). If the debtor has ceased making monthly payments on the car loan, the creditor is in jeopardy of not having its fully secured claim paid. In a situation such as this, the creditor is likely to move for relief from the stay. The court will then either grant such relief or issue an order conditioning such relief on the debtor's failure to make periodic – probably monthly – payments to the creditor to protect it from the likely diminution in value of the collateral. The debtor and the creditor may, of course, agree what would constitute adequate protection – *e.g.*, how much the monthly payments should be – but even if they do the court must evaluate whether what was agreed to is appropriate. Other parties may object to the agreed-upon adequate protection payments as not in the best interest of the estate.

Problem 7-11

Depleted recently filed for Chapter 7 bankruptcy protection. Depleted owns real property worth $300,000. Bank One has a first mortgage on the property to secure a $250,000 debt. Bank Two has a second mortgage on the property to secure a $100,000 debt.

A. Which of the banks, if any, is entitled to relief from the stay? What evidence must the bank seeking relief from the stay present to show that it is entitled to such relief? *See* § 362(g).

B. If one of the banks is entitled to relief from the stay, would the other bank have objections to that relief being granted?

C. If the property is worth $400,000, what additional facts might constitute a lack of adequate protection and entitle either or both of the banks to relief from the stay?

Although most of the § 362(d)(1) litigation focuses on lack of adequate protection, the provision is not so limited; it authorizes relief from the automatic stay whenever there is "cause." In rare situations, even unsecured creditors can get relief from the stay for cause. For example, suppose that a creditor were three weeks into a four-week trial against the debtor on a complex and hotly disputed antitrust claim when the debtor seeks bankruptcy protection. The bankruptcy court might well conclude that legal fees on both sides would be saved – and thus it would be in the best interest of the debtor and the creditors alike – if the trial were allowed to continue, rather than to start it anew in bankruptcy as part of the process of adjudicating claims. In general, courts have identified three factors that should be considered in deciding whether to lift the stay for such reasons:

> (1) whether the issues in the pending litigation involve only state law, so the expertise of the bankruptcy court is unnecessary; (2) whether modifying the stay will promote judicial economy and whether there would be greater interference with the bankruptcy case if the stay were not lifted because matters would have to be litigated in bankruptcy court; and (3) whether the estate can be protected properly by a requirement that creditors seek enforcement of any judgment through the bankruptcy court.[18]

---

[18] *In re Robbins*, 964 F.2d 342, 345 (4th Cir. 1992).

4. *Violations of the Stay*

Most bankruptcy courts zealously enforce the stay, which is considered a court injunction. Violations are punishable as civil contempt and compensatory damages are readily available. In this respect, it is important to note that no intent to violate is required. Indeed, the violator need not even be aware that a bankruptcy petition has been filed. However, an unknowing violation of the stay is unlikely to result in a finding of contempt.

In 1984, Congress amended § 362 by adding what is now paragraph (k)(1). That paragraph provides that an "individual" injured by a willful violation of the stay may recover actual damages, attorney's fees, and, in appropriate circumstances, punitive damages. In essence, this amendment gave debtors a private cause of action for willful violations of the stay, thus allowing them to avoid what may be a stricter standard under the civil contempt procedure.

The willfulness requirement does not mean that the creditor must intend to cause harm or even intend to violate the stay. It merely means that the creditor was informed of the stay and acted deliberately. Thus, a creditor willfully violates the stay simply by not stopping its computer from sending bills to the debtor after the creditor has received notice of the bankruptcy filing.[19]

What constitutes "actual damages" for the purposes of § 362(k)(1) is a matter of some dispute. Certainly any type of economic injury qualifies. There is also a growing consensus that damages for emotional distress are available, although some courts disagree and some limit such damages to cases where they accompany a demonstrable financial loss.[20]

An award of punitive damages must normally be predicated on some maliciousness or bad faith. Even so, the availability of punitive damages remains a hotly litigated issue; Congress's use of the term "individual" in § 362(k)(1) has created a difficult – though interesting – problem of statutory construction. The Code does not define the term and courts have struggled with whether it encompasses corporate and partnership

---

[19] *See, e.g.*, *In re Rijos*, 263 B.R. 382, 392 (1st Cir. BAP 2001) (expressly rejecting "the computer did it" defense).

[20] *Compare In re Dawson*, 390 F.3d 1139 (9th Cir. 2004), *cert. denied*, 546 U.S. 927 (2005) (ruling that damages for emotional distress are available), *with Aiello v. Providian Fin. Corp.*, 239 F.3d 876 (7th Cir. 2001) (no recovery in bankruptcy for emotional distress unless there is also some financial loss, but tort action may exist for emotional distress if creditor engaged in oppressive debt collection tactics or creditor's behavior was extortionate).

debtors. There is probably no good policy reason why punitive damages should be available only to human beings; however, every other Code reference to "individuals" is limited to human beings. *See* §§ 101(18)(A), 101(30), 101(41), 522(b)(1), 523(a), 727(a)(1), 1141(d)(2). Moreover, the 1984 Amendments that added § 362(k)(1) to the Code dealt almost exclusively with consumer bankruptcies. Perhaps not surprisingly, courts have split on this issue.[21]

Despite the ambiguity as to which debtors may benefit from § 362(k)(1), it is clear that some of those debtors who are so entitled relish the opportunity to pursue a claim for punitive damages for what is largely a minor stay violation. Because of this, courts have begun to express concern that some debtors and their counsel use § 362(k)(1) more as a sword than as a shield and that rewarding debtors too lavishly will create a cottage industry of precipitous § 362(k)(1) litigation.[22]

One of the other issues that arises periodically with respect to the stay is whether actions taken in violation of the stay are void or merely voidable. The distinction can matter because actions that are void have no legal effect and neither the debtor nor the trustee needs to do anything to undo the action taken. In contrast, if violations of the stay render the actions taken merely voidable, then the trustee or debtor must expend effort and resources to invalidate the action.

Because of this, a majority of courts treat actions in violation of the stay as void, not voidable.[23] However, bankruptcy courts have the power to annul an automatic stay retroactively for cause in order to rehabilitate stay violations. This comes up most commonly when the bankruptcy case is dismissed shortly after the petition was filed. The factors to consider are:

> (1) if the creditor had actual or constructive knowledge of the bankruptcy filing and, therefore, of the stay, (2) if the debtor has acted in bad faith, (3) if there was equity in the property of the estate, (4) if the property was necessary for an effective

---

[21] *See In re Rafter Seven Ranches L.P.*, 414 B.R. 722, 732–33 (10th Cir. BAP 2009) (discussing the split in authority).

It is worth noting that § 362(k) does not on its face make damages available only to the debtor. Accordingly, if an individual creditor suffered damage as a result of a stay violation – damage not merely to the estate, but to the creditor directly – then the creditor may be entitled to an award. *See St. Paul Fire & Marine Ins. Co. v. Labuzan*, 579 F.3d 533 (5th Cir. 2009).

[22] *See, e.g., In re Roman*, 283 B.R. 1 (9th Cir. BAP 2002).

[23] *In re Soares*, 107 F.3d 969, 976 (1st Cir. 1997); *In re Schwartz*, 954 F.2d 569, 572–73 (9th Cir. 1992). *But see Bronson v. United States*, 46 F.3d 1573 (Fed. Cir. 1995); *Picco v. Global Marine Drilling Co.*, 900 F.2d 846, 850 (5th Cir. 1990).

reorganization, (5) if grounds for relief from the stay existed and a motion, if filed, would likely have been granted prior to the automatic stay violation, (6) if failure to grant retroactive relief would cause unnecessary expense to the creditor, and (7) if the creditor has detrimentally changed its position on the basis of the action taken.[24]

Of these factors, the most important is the first. Hence the court in *Stancil* refused to annul the stay to validate a foreclosure sale held an hour after the petition was filed. The bankruptcy case, a joint petition of a mother and her son, was dismissed in short order because the mother was ineligible to file (which the foreclosing creditor knew), a joint petition between mother and son is improper, and the son knowingly failed to have the required credit counseling. Nevertheless, the creditor had been informed of the filing and held the foreclosure sale anyway.

B. ACTIONS AGAINST NONDEBTORS

Section 362(a) applies to actions and other proceedings against the debtor or the bankruptcy estate. It does not apply to actions against a third party. Although § 1301(a) extends the stay in Chapter 13 cases to individual co-obligors, the absence of such a provision in Chapters 7 and 11 suggests that Congress intended no protection for anyone other than the debtor in cases filed under those Chapters.

However, § 105 gives bankruptcy courts authority to issue orders necessary to protect the bankruptcy process. May a court use § 105 to provide relief to someone other than the debtor? Not if the only purpose of such an order would be to protect the third party. However, courts have stayed actions against nondebtors in a number of Chapter 11 cases after concluding that successful reorganization of the debtor would be jeopardized by continued action against a third party.

For example, some have enjoined actions against an insider/guarantor of the debtor's obligations because the guarantor's assets were needed to provide capital to the debtor in possession. However, such decisions have been sharply criticized,[25] in part because they fail to explain why the creditor who bargained for the guaranty should be made to wait and perhaps never be paid merely so that the guarantor may make a risky

---

24 *In re Stancil*, 487 B.R. 331, 339 (Bankr. D. Colo. 2013).

25 *See* Howard C. Buschman & Sean P. Madden, *The Power and Propriety of Bankruptcy Court Intervention in Actions Between Nondebtors*, 47 BUS. LAW. 913 (1992).

investment in a bankrupt business. Accordingly, some courts have expressly rejected use of § 105 in such circumstances.

Somewhat less controversial, but also less common, is when courts use § 105 to enjoin action against an officer or manager of the debtor if continuing the action would imperil the officer's or manager's ability to perform his or her duties in the Chapter 11 proceeding, such as running the debtor's business.

If the bankruptcy court does not intervene to enjoin a creditor's action against a nondebtor, then discovery relating to that action is, of course, not stayed. This is apparently true even with respect to discovery aimed at the debtor, so long as it relates to the claim against the nondebtor. *Cf.* § 362(a)(1) (staying "employment of process" against the debtor). In other words, the creditor is entitled to discovery against the debtor – and, if necessary, to an order compelling the debtor to comply – despite the presence of the automatic stay and even if the information sought could eventually adversely affect the debtor. However, prudence dictates that the party seeking discovery from the debtor first obtain relief from the stay.

C. PROHIBITIONS ON DISCRIMINATION

Insolvent debtors seeking a fresh start would have their hopes and plans seriously undermined if they could lose their jobs because of their financial difficulties. Yet outside of bankruptcy, there is little protection for debtors in this regard. For example, the Consumer Credit Protection Act prohibits employers from firing employees whose earnings have been subjected to garnishment,[26] but the narrowness of this rule is staggering. First, it applies only to debt collection through garnishment; it does nothing to protect debtors who have been subjected to other types of collection efforts or who are simply insolvent. Second, it does not protect debtors whose earnings have been garnished for two different debts, no matter how far apart the two garnishments were. Third, it does not prohibit a prospective employer from refusing to hire a job applicant merely because the applicant once had earnings garnished. Finally, although violations of this provision are punishable by fine or imprisonment, *see* 15 U.S.C. § 1674(b), they apparently do not give rise to a private cause of action.[27]

---

[26] 15 U.S.C. § 1674(a).

[27] *E.g.*, *LeVick v. Scaggs Cos.*, 701 F.2d 777 (9th Cir. 1983).

Debtors who file for bankruptcy protection fare somewhat better. The Bankruptcy Code prohibits public entities from denying licenses to, denying employment to, or terminating the employment of, a bankruptcy debtor *solely* because the debtor is insolvent, has filed for bankruptcy protection, or has not paid a dischargeable debt. § 525(a). Even private employers are prohibited from discharging an employee who filed for bankruptcy *solely* because of the filing, the employee's insolvency, or failure to pay a dischargeable debt. § 525(b).

Yet these protections too are remarkably limited. For example, they apply only when the action was taken "solely" because of one of the prohibited reasons.[28] Private employers, while prohibited from firing employees because of their pending bankruptcy, may nevertheless refuse to hire someone who is or has been in bankruptcy. *Compare* § 525(a), *with* (b).[29] They may also fire an employee who *intends* to file for bankruptcy protection because § 525(b), by its very nature, offers no protection prior to the actual filing.[30]

One additional protection for bankruptcy is worthy of note. Section 525(c) was added to the Code to prevent banks from discriminating in the making of student loans against prospective borrowers who have a bankruptcy filing on their record.[31] The quality of legislative drafting being what it is, however, the provision on its face does something entirely different and much more broad: instead of preventing discrimination against bankruptcy debtors when making federally guaranteed student loans (after all, why should the bank care about the borrower's bankruptcy filing if the loan is federally guaranteed?), it prohibits all banks that make student loans from discriminating against bankruptcy debtors when deciding to make *any* loan. The jury is still out on whether bankruptcy courts will restrict the provision to its intended meaning.

---

28 For this purpose, one of these reasons is the *sole* basis of a decision if it is the proximate cause, regardless of what may have motivated the agency or employer to base its action on that reason. *See FCC v. NextWave Personal Commc'ns, Inc.*, 537 U.S. 293 (2003).

29 *See also Myers v. TooJay's Mgmt. Corp.*, 640 F.3d 1278 (11th Cir. 2011); *In re Burnett*, 635 F.3d 169 (5th Cir. 2011); *Rea v. Fed. Investors*, 627 F.3d 937 (3d Cir. 2010).

30 *See In re Majewski*, 310 F.3d 653 (9th Cir. 2002).

31 *But cf. In re Taylor*, 263 B.R. 139 (N.D. Ala. 2001) (provision does not prohibit prospective lender from *considering* a past bankruptcy, merely from making a past bankruptcy the sole basis of denying a loan; provision also does not create a private right of action for its violation).

Another limit on discrimination is found in § 366, which applies to providers of utility services, such as gas, water, and electricity.[32] If, postpetition, a utility provider threatened to cut off service unless the debtor or trustee paid off any debt remaining for prepetition services, that threat would violate the automatic stay. *See* § 362(a)(1). However, no part of the stay would prevent a utility provider from demanding payment in advance or an excessively large deposit to cover postpetition services. This is where § 366 comes in. It prohibits a utility provider from refusing or discontinuing service merely because the customer is in bankruptcy or owes a prepetition debt to the provider. It does, however, allow the utility provider to demand adequate assurance of payment – in the form of a deposit or other security – for postpetition services. The bankruptcy court has authority to review and modify the demand for reasonableness.

There are few cases about the amount of a deposit that may be demanded from a consumer debtor. One such decision, which is probably representative, required a deposit equal to the combined total on the two highest monthly bills in the last 12 months.[33] The reason why there are so few cases on this issue in the consumer context is that consumer cases are not the ones that the utilities care most about. Not only is the dollar amount at risk in a consumer case fairly minimal, but the debtor still has great incentive to pay for postpetition service: pay or service will be discontinued.[34] The cases that matter to the utility are the business reorganization cases, particularly for debtors that operate manufacturing facilities that consume large amounts of water or electricity and have monthly bills in the five- or six-figure range. Not only is the dollar amount in such cases much more, but the risk of nonpayment is higher. Most consumer debtors will continue to consume utility services and therefore will pay the monthly bill to avoid having the service cut off. Business debtors might cease operations and not care about a cessation of utility service. Consequently, utility lawyers have indicated that they want a history of reasonable requests in consumer cases, so that when they appear

---

[32] Cable television is apparently not a utility service within the meaning of this rule. *See, e.g.*, *In re Darby*, 470 F.3d 573 (5th Cir. 2006).

[33] *In re Spencer*, 218 B.R. 290 (Bankr. W.D.N.Y. 1998) (relying in part on maximum deposit required under state law). *But cf. In re Cannon*, 2008 WL 2553475 (Bankr. E.D. Wis. 2008) (refusing to require a deposit for a debtor whose income was less that 170% of the Poverty Threshold set by state law and thus the utility would not be permitted to require a deposit under state law); *In re Steinebach*, 303 B.R. 634 (Bankr. D. Ariz. 2004) (utilities are not entitled to a deposit from consumers who have timely paid their bills).

[34] The stay does not prevent a utility provider from cutting off service because of the debtor's failure to pay for *postpetition* services. *See, e.g.*, *In re Jones*, 369 B.R. 745 (1st Cir. BAP 2007).

in front of the same judge later in business reorganization cases, their requests are more likely to be honored.

D. TOLLING RULES

When a Chapter 7 bankruptcy petition is filed and the trustee assumes responsibility for all of the debtor's assets, or at least the nonexempt assets, the trustee may understandably need some time to ascertain where they are, determine how valuable they are, and decide what to do with them. This task can be particularly difficult and time consuming with respect to those rights consisting of claims by the debtor against some other entity. Yet such claims may be subject to strict time limits of one sort or another. For example, a statute of limitations may be about to expire or a deadline for filing a pleading may be only a day or two away. Creditors can face a similar problem. For example, claims against the debtor are generally subject to the stay even though they are not dischargeable. If the bankruptcy petition were filed a few days or weeks before the applicable statute of limitations were to expire, the creditor could find itself barred from bringing an action until after the limitations period had run out.

Section 108 deals with all of these problems by imposing various tolling periods that delay expiration of some legal and contractual time periods. Each of its three subsections tolls a different type of time period:

§ 108(a)	§ 108(b)	§ 108(c)
Tolls statutes of limitation for actions that could be brought by the debtor.	Tolls time for trustee to file pleadings and do other similar things.	Tolls statutes of limitation for actions against the debtor.

Read § 108 and then attempt the following problems.

Problem 7-12

On June 1, Bank conducted a proper foreclosure sale of Dispossessed's home. Under state law, Dispossessed has six months to redeem the property from the foreclosure sale buyer by paying the foreclosure sale price (which is often significantly less than fair market value). On November 15th, two weeks before Dispossessed's statutory right of redemption was to expire, Dispossessed filed for Chapter 7 bankruptcy protection.

A. Does the stay prevent the right of redemption from expiring?

B. Does § 108(b) toll the period of redemption? *See In re Canney*, 284 F.3d 362 (2d Cir. 2002).

Problem 7-13

On June 1, Dealer purchased for $25,000 an option to buy a parcel of real property for $300,000 any time before December 1. On November 1, without having exercised the option, Dealer filed a Chapter 7 bankruptcy petition. Does the trustee have any right to exercise the option after December 1? *See* § 108(b).

PART III

LIQUIDATION IN CHAPTER 7

CHAPTER EIGHT
ADMINISTERING ESTATE PROPERTY

A. DEALING WITH ESTATE ASSETS GENERALLY

For each asset included in the estate, only a limited number of interested parties are likely to seek control over the asset or claim the right to extract value from it. Chief among these is, of course, the trustee. The others may include: the debtor, if all or part of the asset is exempt; any creditor with a lien on the asset; and anyone else with a property right in the asset.

Initially, of course, the debtor must assign a valuation to each asset listed in the schedules that the debtor must file either with the petition or shortly thereafter. The trustee and others may choose to accept that valuation or to conduct an independent investigation or appraisal. For example, with respect to real estate, the trustee may hire an appraiser, review any existing appraisals of the property that the debtor may have, or simply drive by the property and examine it. For intangible assets, such as a pending tort claim, the trustee may speak with the attorney handling the case, if there is one, in an effort to discern the likelihood of success and the probable amount of any recovery.

Regardless of how the trustee determines an asset's value, in most cases the trustee will decide fairly quickly whether the asset is likely to be worth anything to the estate. In other words, the trustee will decide whether the estate's interest in the asset is worth more than: (i) any exemption amount to which the debtor is entitled in the asset and (ii) the amount of all claims secured by unavoidable liens on the property. When valuing the estate's interest, the trustee will take into consideration whether anyone else has a property right in the asset. Thus, the trustee's calculus might look something like this:

Total Value of Asset
– Portion of Value Allocable to Other Person with a Property Interest
– Amount of Unavoidable Liens on the Asset
– Amount of Exemption to Which Debtor Is Entitled in Asset
= Value of Estate's Interest

If the asset has minimal or no value to the estate, the trustee will abandon the asset and, indeed, can be compelled to do so by anyone who does have an interest in it.[1] *See* § 554(a), (b). To abandon an asset, the trustee files a motion to do so and sends a copy of it to the U.S. Trustee and to all creditors. *See* Rule 6007(a). If no one objects, the court will likely issue an order authorizing the abandonment. Such an order divests the estate of any ownership rights in the asset and, in most cases, revests those rights in the debtor.[2] If a party in interest does object, the court will conduct a hearing to determine whether abandonment is in the best interest of the estate.

If, on the other hand, the trustee's computation suggests that the asset is worth more to the estate than the cost of administering it, the Chapter 7 trustee will take control over the asset and, in all likelihood, sell it. Section 363 is the provision that authorizes the trustee to use, sell, and lease property of the estate. When selling assets, the trustee need not follow the procedures required of lien creditors or mortgagees under state law. *See* Rule 6004(f). In other words, there are no specified advertising requirements and the sale need not be conducted as an auction. The trustee often simply finds a willing buyer and negotiates a price. Exactly how the trustee does this depends on the type of asset involved and on how owners of such assets normally locate interested buyers. Regardless of the method used, however, the trustee must, at least 21 days in advance of the sale, send to the parties listed in Rule 2002 a notice explaining the proposed transaction.[3] § 363(b). If no one objects by the applicable deadline (usually seven days before the sale),[4] the trustee will consummate the transaction. If someone does object, the court will conduct a hearing to determine whether to permit the trustee to sell the asset as proposed.

If the debtor's estate includes business assets, the court may authorize the trustee to operate the business for a limited period of time, if that is likely to be in the estate's best interest. § 721. In other words, the business assets may be worth more if sold as part of a going concern, so the court may allow the trustee to continue the debtor's business operations pending a sale of the business. In such cases, the trustee may sell

---

1 *See also* § 725 (requiring the trustee, before final distribution, to dispose of property in which an entity other than the debtor has an interest).

2 In some cases, the court may order abandonment directly to someone other than the debtor, usually to someone who already has an ownership interest in the property.

3 *See* § 363(b); Rule 2002(g), (i), (k). Note, because orders authorizing the sale are normally automatically stayed for 14 days to facilitate a possible appeal, *see* Rule 6004(h), notification of the sale probably needs to be given at least 35 days in advance.

4 *See* Rule 6004(b).

assets in the ordinary course of business even without notice and a hearing. § 363(c)(1). The trustee may also incur unsecured debt in the ordinary course of business. § 364(a).

In some cases the estate may share ownership of an asset with another person.[5] For example, the debtor may own a tract of land as tenants in common with siblings or as tenants by the entirety with a spouse. In such cases, the trustee has three options for dealing with the property. First, the trustee may seek to partition the property, using whatever rights a co-owner has under nonbankruptcy law to achieve such a division. Thus, if the applicable real estate law permits each tenant in common to bring an action to divide the property physically among the co-owners, the trustee may invoke that law. This will not always be practical, however. For example, one or more of the divided portions might be too small under the governing zoning laws to permit development or the whole property may have a single use – such as a ski slope – that would make splitting it up undesirable for all concerned.

Second, the trustee may simply try to sell the estate's interest. However, this will often be difficult and unwise. Few people are likely to be interested in buying the estate's undivided interest, given that any buyer of that interest would have to share ownership with the nondebtor co-owner, someone the buyer probably does not know and who may not be particularly gracious about the prospect of sharing the property with a stranger. In short, even though the property as a whole may be worth a great deal, the presence of a co-owner may significantly undermine the market for the estate's undivided share.

Third, if the trustee is unlikely to realize the full value of the estate's interest using either of the prior two options, the trustee may sell the entire property. In other words, the trustee may sell the interests of both the estate and the co-owner, provided that a proportionate share of the sale proceeds is distributed to the co-owner. *See* § 363(f)(2), (5), (h).

As you may remember from chapter five, the estate may contain one or more executory contracts or unexpired leases that the debtor entered into prepetition. Because such contracts and leases still require performance by both sides, they represent both potential assets and potential liabilities of the estate. The trustee will therefore evaluate each contract and lease to determine if it is of net value to the estate. The trustee will likely assume those with such value and reject those without it. § 365(a). In connection with this choice, the trustee may decide to assume an executory contract or unexpired lease solely for the purpose of assigning it to another party (*i.e.*, selling it). § 363(f).

---

[5] Another person may have nonpossessory property rights in the asset, such as an easement, which may affect the value of the asset or the ability of the trustee to deal with the property.

B. WHAT HAPPENS TO COLLATERAL

Almost everything written in the last few pages also applies to estate assets subject to one or more unavoidable liens. However, there are often competing interests at stake with respect to such property: (i) the trustee wants to extract whatever value the asset may have for the estate; (ii) the secured claimant certainly wants to preserve the asset's function as security and may want to liquidate the collateral promptly so as to realize upon its value; and (iii) the debtor may want to preserve the value of any exemption rights in the asset and, regardless of whether any portion of the asset's value is exempt, may want to retain possession and use of the asset. After all, the asset may be something the debtor needs – such as a house or motor vehicle – and the debtor may have little or no ability to obtain a replacement for it.

How these competing interests are treated in bankruptcy is a major aspect of many bankruptcy cases. It is also often a major factor in the debtor's decision about whether to file for bankruptcy protection at all and, if so, whether to do so under Chapter 7, 11, 12, or 13. We will explore the treatment of collateral under Chapters 11 and 13 in later chapters of this book. At present, we focus on what happens in Chapter 7 cases. In that context, the most significant factor in determining the fate of collateral is whether the collateral is worth more or less than the total of the claims it secures and any exemption amount to which the debtor is entitled. If it is worth more, then the collateral is of value to the estate and the trustee is the one with the incentive to maximize the price at which it will be sold. Accordingly, the trustee will conduct the sale.

1. *Sale by the Trustee*

In general, when the trustee sells property of the estate, the trustee does so subject to whatever liens exist on the property. When this occurs, the buyer typically pays the lienholder – either immediately or over time – to redeem the property from the lien. If the buyer fails to do this, the lienholder may use whatever nonbankruptcy rights are available to enforce the lien.[6]

---

[6] Nothing in § 362(a) would stay the creditor's efforts to foreclose on property sold by the trustee to someone other than the debtor, unless the debtor still retained an interest in the property due to an exemption. This rarely happens, as the proceeds from the sale would generally be used to give the debtor the value of the exemption.

However, the trustee is authorized to sell property free and clear of a lien, *see* § 363(f), provided the trustee adequately protects the interest of the lienholder, *see* § 363(e). As a practical matter, this means the lienholder is paid from the proceeds of the sale the amount of the debt secured by the lien. In some cases, the lienholder may want the trustee to use this approach, perhaps to avoid the hassle of conducting the sale itself. Sometimes, though, it is for more significant reasons. For example, the collateral may be personal property for which there is no customary market and the creditor may be unsure how to comply with the requirement of conducting a commercially reasonable sale.[7] Alternatively, the collateral may be real estate, as in the following problem.

Problem 8-1

Security Bank has for several years provided financing for Developer, who recently filed for Chapter 7 bankruptcy relief. Security Bank holds a properly recorded mortgage on all of Developer's real estate, which is spread over eight different Midwestern states. For each parcel, Developer owes Security Bank more than the property is worth. Several of these states do not permit nonjudicial foreclosure and, as a result, the foreclosure procedures are slow. Because time is money (at least with respect to interest that will accrue but not be paid), Security Bank would like to avoid the nonbankruptcy foreclosure process by having the trustee sell the real estate under § 363(f). Is that permissible? Should it be?

Section 506(c) permits the trustee to recover from the collateral the costs of preserving and disposing of it, to the extent the disposition benefits the lienholder. This rule is easy to state but less easy to apply because there is some disagreement about what sort of "benefit" is necessary. Consider a case in which the trustee sells the creditor's collateral. The creditor is saved the expenses associated with conducting such a sale – appraisal fees, advertising costs, storage expenses, *etc.* – and thus, the argument goes, can be called upon to reimburse the estate. Otherwise, the lienholder is benefitted by the trustee's action and gets a resulting windfall. However, this argument makes sense only insofar as the costs are ones that the lienholder would have incurred if it were conducting the sale outside of bankruptcy. If the creditor is oversecured and if such costs can be charged to the collateral under nonbankruptcy law (which is usually the case under the security agreement or mortgage and applicable law), then arguably the

---

7 *See* U.C.C. § 9-610(b).

creditor would never incur those costs; the costs would always be charged to and come out of the collateral, still leaving enough value for the creditor to be paid in full. In short, if the creditor is oversecured, the trustee's expenses in caring for and selling the collateral should normally come out of the estate's equity in the collateral. If the creditor is undersecured, then the trustee should abandon the collateral, thereby leaving the costs of dealing with the collateral to the creditor.[8] Thus, perhaps the only import of § 506(c) is to make clear that if the trustee incurs costs that the secured creditor would normally incur in dealing with the collateral, the trustee can recover those costs from the collateral and need not use other estate assets.

2. *The Four Rs*

Whenever the collateral is worth less than the combined total of the debts it secures and any exemption amount to which the debtor is entitled, the trustee will probably abandon the property under § 554(a) and can be compelled to abandon it under § 554(b). Abandonment takes the collateral out of the estate, which means that the trustee will not sell it, but does not affect the rights of the secured creditor or indicate what will happen to the collateral. The fate of the collateral will be left to the competing rights and interests of the debtor and the secured party, and one of four things is likely to occur: reaffirmation; redemption; repossession; or, perhaps, retention.

(a) Reaffirmation

In some cases, particularly when the debtor has built up a substantial amount of exempt equity in the collateral, the debtor may wish to reaffirm the debt that the collateral secures. Reaffirmation of the debt is in essence a waiver of the right to assert that the debt is discharged.[9] *See* § 524(c). If the debtor reaffirms the debt, the creditor

---

[8] If the trustee sells all of the debtor's assets as a going concern but the secured party has a security interest in only some of them, the secured party may be undersecured while the trustee nevertheless has the incentive to conduct the sale. Nevertheless, some evidence of how and to what extent the secured party benefitted from the sale is needed before costs of the sale can be charged to the secured party. *See In re Adam Aircraft*, 2013 WL 773044 (D. Colo. 2013).

[9] Remember, as discussed in chapter six, the discharge operates only on the debtor's personal obligation to pay the debt; it does not eliminate the debt itself or affect any liens on the collateral.

is often willing to allow the debtor to keep the collateral while making periodic payments to the secured creditor. If, despite reaffirming the debt, the debtor defaults after bankruptcy, the secured creditor may then exercise all of its nonbankruptcy remedies with regard to the collateral, including repossession and foreclosure. In addition, the creditor may attempt to collect the secured obligation – or a deficiency remaining after sale of the collateral – from the debtor, because the debtor will remain obligated on that debt due to the debtor's reaffirmation of the debt.

Reaffirmation is often the only feasible means for a Chapter 7 debtor to retain possession of desired collateral. Yet it has its drawbacks. First, reaffirmation requires the consent of the creditor. Some lenders prefer to cut their losses and terminate their relationships with bankrupt borrowers. Reaffirmation cannot be imposed on them. Second, the creditor will almost certainly require the debtor to reaffirm the entire obligation. For example, if a debt for $8,000 were secured by a lien on a car worth only $6,000, the debtor would likely have to promise to pay the entire $8,000 debt, perhaps with interest, costs, and the creditor's attorney's fees added on. It is for this reason that reaffirmation is normally used only with respect to property in which the debtor has equity. Third, reaffirmation agreements cannot impose an undue hardship on the debtor or the debtor's dependents. To ensure this, reaffirmation agreements are subject to a certification process. They must be filed with the court and either: (i) accompanied by a representation of no undue hardship by the debtor's attorney or (ii) approved by the court after a hearing on the matter. Court approval requires a finding that the agreement does not impose an undue hardship on the debtor and that it is in the best interest of the debtor. Read § 524(c), (k)–(m). As a debtor's attorney, what would you think about when deciding whether to make the required representation to the court? Does making a representation of no undue hardship place your ethical obligation to the client in conflict with your ethical obligation to the court?[10] Consider the following case that explores the meaning of the undue hardship requirement.

---

§ 524(a).

[10] For more on the attorney's ethical responsibilities with regard to reaffirmation agreements, see Gregory M. Duhl, *Divided Loyalties: The Attorney's Role in Bankruptcy Reaffirmations*, 84 AM. BANKR. L.J. 361 (2010).

IN RE RIGGS
2006 WL 2990218 (Bankr. W.D. Mo. 2006)

Federman, Bankruptcy Judge.

Debtor Rebecca Ann Riggs owns a 1993 Ford Explorer which is subject to a lien held by Super Cars, Inc. The Debtor filed a Statement of Intention with her Petition, stating she intended to reaffirm the debt to Super Cars. She then signed and filed a Reaffirmation Agreement for a debt of $4,822.69 with an annual percentage rate of 18.9% and requests that I approve the Agreement. Her attorney did not sign Part C of such Agreement. For the reasons that follow, the request to approve the reaffirmation agreement is denied.

DISCUSSION

* * *

Requirements and Enforceability of Reaffirmation Agreements

* * * [I]n order for a signed reaffirmation agreement to be enforceable by the creditor, a number of conditions must be met. First, it must be signed, filed, and approved before the debtor's discharge is entered. Second, the agreement must contain the many disclosures described in § 524(k). Most of the current standard reaffirmation forms filed in this district contain the necessary disclosures. Third, the debtor must not have rescinded the agreement prior to discharge. And fourth, either (i) the debtor must have been represented by an attorney during the course of negotiating the reaffirmation agreement or (ii) the court, after notice and hearing, must approve the agreement as not imposing an undue hardship on, and being in the best interest of, the debtor.

This fourth requirement presents the most difficulty. Part C of the standard reaffirmation agreement allows the attorney to attest that the debtor was fully informed and advised of the consequences of reaffirming the debt, that the debtor voluntarily entered into the agreement, and that the agreement does not impose an undue hardship on the debtor or a dependent of the debtor. If the attorney does not sign Part C of the reaffirmation agreement, the Court has no way to know whether the debtor was "represented by an attorney during the course of negotiating the reaffirmation agreement." Therefore, in order to approve a reaffirmation agreement that is not signed by an attorney, the court must conduct a hearing and determine that the reaffirmation agreement does not impose an undue hardship and is in the debtor's best interest.

In determining whether the agreement imposes an undue hardship on the debtor, the court starts with § 524(m), which was added by BAPCPA. * * * Unless the creditor is a credit union, if * * * the debtor does not have enough income after expenses (including other debts to be reaffirmed) to make the payment on the submitted reaffirmation agreement, there is a presumption that reaffirming the debt will impose an undue hardship on the debtor. In order to rebut that presumption, the debtor must demonstrate, in writing, to the satisfaction of the court, how he or she will come up with the money each month to make the payment. Examples of this might be cutting costs in other categories of expenses or earning additional income through overtime or the like. If the court is not satisfied with the explanation, and there is a presumption that the payment imposes an undue hardship on the debtor, then the court cannot approve the agreement, regardless of whether the attorney signed off on it.

Assuming the § 524(m) presumption does not apply, the agreement is only enforceable if the attorney signs it, or if the Court approves it. In either situation, the issue is whether the agreement imposes an undue hardship and is in the best interests of the debtor. Thus, as to reaffirmation agreements (other than those involving a consumer debt secured by real property), the statute places attorneys in the uncomfortable position of deciding whether such reaffirmation imposes an undue hardship and whether it is in the client's best interests. Oftentimes, their clients desperately want to keep their cars, and to continue making regular payments. But in signing the reaffirmation agreement, attorneys expose their clients to a potential deficiency judgment, which would be avoided if the reaffirmation agreement were held not to be enforceable.

In determining whether to sign off on a reaffirmation agreement, attorneys should be aware of the types of agreements which I have concluded should be subject to the closest scrutiny. First, I look at whether Part D shows an ability to make payments presently. If it does show that the debtor has the ability to make the payments, then the question is: In the event that circumstances in the future leave the debtor unable to make the payments, how devastating will a deficiency judgment be? This is primarily a function of two factors, the interest rate and the amount being reaffirmed. Here, the debt to be reaffirmed carries an interest rate of 18.9%. As a consequence, it will take more than two years for the debtor to repay the loan on a 1993 model car. If the car stops running at any time during that period, and the reaffirmation is enforceable, the debtor will then be obligated to Super Cars for the unpaid balance, and will need to be paying on another car as well. And, she will not be able to obtain a Chapter 7 discharge of the debt due to Super Cars until eight years after this case was filed. For those reasons, I will not approve the Reaffirmation Agreement. As a rule of thumb, if a creditor on a personal property loan requires an interest rate over 10%, or if the amount to be reaffirmed is in excess of $20,000, attorneys should not be reluctant to leave it up to the Court to determine whether the agreement is in the debtor's best interests.

* * *

The request for approval of the reaffirmation agreement between debtor and Super Cars, Inc., is denied.

Problem 8-2

The court in *Riggs* identified several factors bearing on whether a reaffirmation agreement imposes an undue hardship on and is in the best interest of the debtor. Among these were the debtor's ability to pay, the interest rate on the debt, and the possibility that old collateral might cease to operate while the debt remained unsatisfied. What other facts should judges consider when deciding whether to approve a reaffirmation agreement?

Nothing in the Code explains how the stay operates with respect to negotiations over reaffirmation agreements. One could argue that contacting the debtor or negotiating over a reaffirmation violates § 362(a)(6). Nevertheless, just as courts have had no difficulty concluding that filing a proof of claim does not violate the stay, they have not hesitated to conclude that a creditor may solicit a reaffirmation agreement.[11] Indeed, for the most part they may, without violating the stay, play hardball during reaffirmation negotiations, such as by conditioning agreement to reaffirm a secured debt on reaffirmation of unrelated unsecured debts.[12]

(b) Redemption

The second option some debtors have is to redeem the property under § 722. To redeem, the debtor must pay the lienor the amount of the "allowed secured claim." As discussed at the beginning of chapter six, that amount is limited by the value of the collateral. Thus, using the example above of an $8,000 debt secured by a lien on a $6,000 car, the debtor could redeem the car by paying the secured creditor $6,000 in cash. The debtor need not pay the $2,000 difference; that is treated as an unsecured

---

11 *E.g.*, *In re Duke*, 79 F.3d 43 (7th Cir. 1996); *Morgan Guar. Trust Co. v. Am. Sav. & Loan*, 804 F.2d 1487 (9th Cir. 1986).

12 *See In re Jamo*, 283 F.3d 392 (1st Cir. 2002).

claim in the bankruptcy case and will usually be discharged following whatever distributions the trustee makes.

Redemption is far from a panacea for debtors, however, because it suffers from three significant drawbacks. First, the debtor must come up with the necessary cash. Most courts do not permit the debtor to redeem by paying the required amount in installments.[13] Of course, most bankrupt debtors do not have a ready supply of cash. To get it, they must normally either borrow it or convert some of their exempt property into a liquid form. Borrowing may be impossible – because bankruptcy debtors typically have great difficulty finding willing lenders – and liquidating exempt assets may be undesirable.

Second, the value of the property to be redeemed – and therefore the redemption price – is measured by the property's replacement value, without reduction for the costs of sale or marketing. *See* § 506(a)(2). This will normally mean the price a retail merchant would charge for such property, given its age and condition.[14] § 506(a)(2). As a result, the debtor is likely to have to pay more for the property than the debtor could turn around and sell it for.

Third, redemption is available in only limited circumstances. It applies only to individual debtors and covers only tangible personal property that is intended primarily for personal, family, or household purposes. It is unavailable to corporate debtors and cannot be used either for real property or for property used in a business. Moreover, the property must be exempted under § 522 or have been abandoned by the trustee. For the most part, redemption is a paper right that is rarely exercised.

---

[13] *See, e.g., In re Bell*, 700 F.2d 1053 (6th Cir. 1983), *cited approvingly for this point by In re Taylor*, 3 F.3d 1512, 1515 (11th Cir. 1993); *In re Belanger*, 962 F.2d 345, 347 (4th Cir. 1992); *In re Edwards*, 901 F.2d 1383, 1386 (7th Cir. 1990).

[14] This measure applies whenever the property was "acquired for personal, family, or household purposes." Because redemption is limited to property "intended primarily for personal, family, or household use," § 722, this standard will typically apply to any proffered redemption. However, in unusual cases the property may not have been originally acquired for personal, family, or household purposes even though the debtor now intends to use it for such. In those cases, redemption is permissible but the Code does not necessarily measure value as the price a retail merchant would charge.

On the different approaches courts use to determine retail value, see *In re Clark*, 2007 WL 671346 (Bankr. N.D. Ohio 2007).

(c) Repossession

By far the most common thing that happens to collateral is repossession. Lienholders do not relish the idea of waiting a long time before getting paid, and thus they are often eager to enforce their liens, using whatever nonbankruptcy rights they have. Most debtors in bankruptcy have already defaulted on their obligations and have no ability or desire to try to cure those defaults. A note of caution for the creditor is in order, however. Even though secured claimants in a Chapter 7 case are not paid by the trustee, or indeed out of the bankruptcy estate at all, they are subject to the automatic stay, as discussed in chapter seven. They may therefore take no action to collect the debts due to them. *See* § 362(a)(6).

The Code does not merely prohibit collection activity, however; it also expressly enjoins acts against the collateral. Specifically, it prohibits creditors from doing any act to enforce a lien against property of the estate or to obtain possession of property of the estate. § 362(a)(3), (4). This gives the trustee time to determine if there is any basis for challenging the validity of a creditor's lien. The stay also bars acts against property of the debtor to the extent that the lien secures a prepetition claim. § 362(a)(5). Because of this latter rule, the stay remains in effect even after the trustee has abandoned the property[15] and protects the debtor who has exempt equity in the property.

Collectively, and perhaps individually, these provisions prohibit secured creditors from either repossessing their collateral or conducting a foreclosure sale after a bankruptcy petition has been filed. Indeed, many bankruptcy petitions are filed primarily to get this benefit: to stop the repossession or sale of the debtor's property, particularly a home.

---

[15] Generally, abandoned property revests in the debtor upon leaving the estate. When that occurs, there is no doubt that the stay still applies. *See* § 362(a)(5). Occasionally, however, courts order that property be abandoned to the secured creditor directly. The legislative history apparently supports this practice, stating that "[a]bandonment may be to any party with a possessory interest in the property abandoned." S. REP. NO. 989, at 92 (1978), *reprinted in* 1978 U.S.C.C.A.N. 5787, 5878; H. REP. NO. 595, at 377 (1977), *reprinted in* 1978 U.S.C.C.A.N. 5963, 6333. This practice may take the property outside the scope of the stay, obviating the need for the creditor to seek relief under § 362(d). *See* S. REP. NO. 989, at 52, *reprinted in* 1978 U.S.C.C.A.N. at 5838; H. REP. NO. 595, at 343, *reprinted in* 1978 U.S.C.C.A.N. at 6299 (both indicating that abandonment does not terminate the stay against property of the debtor "if the property leaves the estate and goes to the debtor"). Whether a creditor has a "possessory interest" in the property, however, probably depends upon the state of the foreclosure process that has taken place prior to the bankruptcy. The mere existence of a lien does not give a creditor a possessory interest in the property.

Application of the stay to secured claims has raised two recurring questions. First, does a creditor who repossessed collateral *before the bankruptcy petition was filed* violate the stay simply by refusing to return it postpetition upon the trustee's or debtor's demand?[16] Although the creditor has a right to adequate protection, *see* §§ 361, 362(d), and may be legitimately concerned about the collateral if, for example, the debtor has failed to procure or retain contractually required insurance on the collateral, most courts have ruled that the creditor's refusal to release the collateral does violate the stay.[17] Thus, there is some risk to a creditor here, *see* § 362(k)(1), and the better course of action is to respond to the turnover demand with a request for adequate protection of the lien interest or a motion for relief from the stay to get the dispute in front of the bankruptcy court as soon as possible.

Second, under what circumstances may the creditor obtain relief from the stay to foreclose on the collateral while the bankruptcy case is still pending? This is by far the more important question because it is common for lienholders to move for relief from the stay immediately after receiving notice of the debtor's bankruptcy filing.

As discussed in chapter seven, a creditor's right to such relief is governed by § 362(d), which requires that the stay be lifted either: (1) for cause, including the lack of adequate protection of the secured creditor's interest in the property; or (2) if the debtor has no equity in the property and the property is not necessary to a successful reorganization. In Chapter 7 cases, "cause" and lack of adequate protection are an issue only if the creditor is oversecured, and that is not typical in a Chapter 7 case. Secured creditors in Chapter 7 liquidation cases thus generally seek relief under § 362(d)(2) because the property is by definition not needed for a successful reorganization. Relief from the stay therefore depends on whether the property is worth more than the debt. In many cases it is not, and the secured party obtains quick relief from the stay,[18] repossesses the property using its nonbankruptcy rights, and then forecloses its lien by

---

[16] There is no question that collateral remains property of the estate and must be returned in response to a turnover order under § 542. *See United States v. Whiting Pools, Inc.*, 462 U.S. 198 (1983) (excerpted on pages 58–63).

[17] *See, e.g.*, *In re Weber*, 2013 WL 1891371 (2d Cir. 2013); *Thompson v. Gen. Motors Acceptance Corp.*, 566 F.3d 699 (7th Cir. 2009); *In re Johnson*, 501 F.3d 1163 (10th Cir. 2007). The result may be different if the secured party has a possessory lien that would be lost by releasing the collateral to the debtor. *See, e.g.*, *In re Vega*, 2013 WL 3157516 (Bankr. E.D. Mich. 2013) (relying on s 362(b)(3)).

[18] In general, the stay expires with respect to the property 30 days after the motion for relief is filed unless, before that period expires, the bankruptcy court orders otherwise. *See* § 362(e)(1).

selling the property under whatever nonbankruptcy rules are applicable.[19] Even if relief from the stay is not available, perhaps because the debtor has exempt equity in the property, as soon as the stay expires under § 362(c), the secured claimant may take whatever steps are allowed under nonbankruptcy law to enforce its lien.

(d) Retention

There may be one other option for the debtor: to retain the collateral while continuing to make the contractual payments on the secured obligation without reaffirming the obligation to pay the debt. This option is sometimes referred to as "ride-through" option. However, there are several potential impediments to this option.

The first impediment is § 521(a)(2). It requires the debtor to:

> file with the clerk a statement of his intention with respect to the retention or surrender of such property and, if applicable, specifying that such property is claimed as exempt, that the debtor intends to redeem such property, or that the debtor intends to reaffirm debts secured by such property.

It then further requires the debtor to perform the stated intention within 30 days of the date first set for the meeting of creditors, or a longer time as set by the court, and failure to do so results in the consequences stated in § 362(h). Some courts have interpreted this clause as requiring the debtor to choose between surrendering the collateral or retaining the collateral in connection with a redemption or reaffirmation, with others stating that the "ride through" option is not precluded by this clause.[20]

The second impediment is § 521(a)(6), which was added to the Code in 2005. It requires the debtor to reaffirm the debt or redeem the collateral – not merely to file a statement of intention, but to complete one of these tasks – within 45 days of the § 341

---

[19] There is one trap for the unwary here. Under Bankruptcy Rule 4001(a)(3), an order granting relief from the stay is itself stayed for ten days, unless the court orders otherwise. This is designed to give the debtor time to request a stay pending appeal of the order granting relief. If a creditor goes forward with collection activities within the ten-day period, the creditor risks contempt and sanctions for violating the stay.

[20] *See, e.g.*, *In re Dumont*, 581 F.3d 1104 (9th Cir. 2009) (detailing the arguments on both sides of the issue).

meeting. If the debtor fails to do so, the stay will expire as to the collateral.[21] *See* § 362(h).

However, there are several limitations on the reach and effect of § 521(a)(2) and (6). First, the debtor will apparently have complied with their mandates if the debtor enters into a reaffirmation agreement that the bankruptcy court refuses to approve.[22] In short, the debtor need not enter into an *enforceable* reaffirmation agreement. Consequently, a debtor could file a statement declaring an intention to reaffirm a debt and enter into a reaffirmation agreement, even if the debtor expects that the reaffirmation agreement will not be approved and the debt not reaffirmed, in order to protect the collateral from repossession by the creditor.

Second, § 521(a)(6) applies only if the creditor has a purchase-money security interest ("PMSI") in personal property collateral. It therefore does not apply to real estate collateral or to non-PMSI security interests in personalty. In addition, § 521(a)(6) applies only if the creditor has an *allowed* claim. If the creditor does not file a proof of claim – and in no-asset cases, no creditor does – the creditor will not have an allowed claim and arguably § 521(a)(6) does apply.[23]

Finally, and perhaps most significantly, § 521(a)(2) and (6) relegate the secured creditor to whatever rights it may have under nonbankruptcy law. If the debtor is not in default, the secured party will have no immediate right to repossess or foreclose on the collateral, even if the stay is no longer in effect. On the issue of default, § 521(d), also added in 2005, provides that the Bankruptcy Code does not invalidate a default-on-bankruptcy clause. However, if the agreement lacks such a clause or the clause is not

---

[21] Arguably, the 45-day period in § 521(a)(6) for the debtor to surrender, redeem, or reaffirm will always be trumped by the 30-day period in both § 521(a)(2)(B) and § 362(h), which commences on the date first set for the § 341 meeting, rather than the date of the actual meeting.

Although the debtor's failure to complete the stated intention within 45 days means that the stay has terminated with respect to the collateral and the collateral is no longer property of the estate, the debtor still retains the right to redeem the collateral after that time because nothing in § 521 alters the debtor's redemption rights under either § 722 or state law. *See, e.g.*, *In re Collins*, 2013 WL 752480 (Bankr. E.D. Ky. 2013); *In re Alvarez*, 2012 WL 441257 (Bankr. N.D. Ill. 2012); U.C.C. § 9-623.

If the debtor fails to file all of the required schedules within 45 days of the petition, the entire case must be dismissed. *See* § 521(i). Courts have no discretion not to dismiss if the debtor fails to file the statement or a request for an extension before the 45-day period expires. *See, e.g.*, *In re Ott*, 343 B.R. 264 (Bankr. D. Colo. 2006); *In re Fawson*, 338 B.R. 505 (Bankr. D. Utah 2006). *But cf. In re Parker*, 351 B.R. 790 (Bankr. N.D. Ga. 2006).

[22] *In re Wilson*, 2012 WL 2411918 (Bankr. N.D. W. Va. 2012).

[23] *See, e.g.*, *Coastal Fed. Credit Union v. Hardiman*, 398 B.R. 161 (E.D.N.C. 2008).

enforceable under applicable nonbankruptcy law,[24] and the debtor is not otherwise in default, retention may still be permitted. In addition, even if the stay expires (which is the effect of the application of § 521(a)(2) and (6)), any secured creditor can decide not to exercise its rights under nonbankruptcy law to enforce its lien on the collateral and decide to take the debtor's payments. *See* § 524(f).

Whenever the debtor has complied with § 521(a)(2) or (6) or the provisions do not apply, the stay remains in effect. As always, creditors in such situations must be careful about what they do. A bankruptcy court summed up what is permissible:

> Debtors' Intentions
>
> * * * Where an individual debtor files a chapter 7 case and the schedules include a consumer debt secured by property of the debtor, § 521(2) gives the debtor 30 days to file "a statement of his intention with respect to the retention or surrender of such property . . . ." * * *
>
> Where a debtor files the statement of intention within the statutory period, there is no need for the secured creditor to contact the debtor to determine what the debtor's intentions are with respect to the property. This is especially true where, as in this case, the statement is filed with the bankruptcy petition itself. The creditor can determine the debtor's intentions from the papers filed with the court, and has no need to contact the debtor whatsoever on this subject. In this manner the creditor can avoid a violation of the automatic stay.

---

24 *In re Henderson*, 2013 WL 2255170 (Bankr. D. Nev. 2013) (default-on-bankruptcy clause in retail installment contract for automobile is unenforceable under recently enacted Nevada statute); *In re Visnicky*, 401 B.R. 61 (Bankr. D.R.I. 2009) (indicating that Rhode Island's recent enactment of the Uniform Consumer Credit Code makes a default-on-filing clause unenforceable); *In re Rowe*, 342 B.R. 341 (Bankr. D. Kan. 2006) (ruling that a default-on-bankruptcy clause was unenforceable under the Kansas version of the Uniform Consumer Credit Code and that the 2005 revisions to § 521 merely relegated secured creditor to nonbankruptcy rights); *see also In re Steinhaus*, 349 B.R. 694 (Bankr. D. Idaho 2006) (suggesting that a default-on-filing clause is unenforceable under Idaho law); *In re Riggs*, 2006 WL 2990218 (Bankr. W.D. Mo. 2006) (suggesting that a default-on-filing clause may not be enforceable under Missouri law). *But see In re Jones*, 591 F.3d 308 (4th Cir. 2010) (default-on-filing clause is enforceable under West Virginia law and state statute requiring creditor to give notice of the right to cure before repossessing collateral was inapplicable because the default – filing for bankruptcy protection – could not be cured). *Compare In re Anderson*, 384 B.R. 652 (Bankr. D. Del. 2006) (ruling that a default on bankruptcy clause is valid in Delaware), *with In re Baker*, 390 B.R. 524 (Bankr. D. Del. 2008) (disagreeing with *Anderson*), *aff'd*, 400 B.R. 136 (D. Del. 2009).

Connecticut's statute regulating retail installment sales provides that filing a Chapter 7 petition or being a debtor in bankruptcy cannot be the basis for a default that gives rise to a right to repossess the collateral. *See* CONN. GEN. STAT. § 36a-785(a).

* * *

5. Creditor Contacts Where Debtor Intends to Make Payments

A secured creditor should be encouraged to send out payment coupons, envelopes and periodic statements if a debtor has filed a statement that the debtor plans to keep property subject to secured debt and to make payments. Debtors frequently complain to the court that they want to make their payments, but their creditors do not cooperate by providing payment coupons. Secured creditors hesitate to provide such cooperation for fear of violating the automatic stay or the discharge injunction.

* * * [However, it is proper] for the secured creditor to send monthly statements to the debtor after the bankruptcy filing, and payment coupons or other means to facilitate the making of monthly postpetition payments by the debtor. If the promissory note has an adjustable interest rate (as it did in this case), the creditor may properly give notice of changes in the interest rate.

If the debtor defaults in making postpetition payments, the creditor may properly give notice thereof, and any other notices that are appropriate and customary in connection with lien enforcement action based on the postpetition default. Further, if there are arrearages in payments at the time of filing, the creditor may properly contact the debtor to arrange for the payment or refinancing of the arrearages. However, the creditor may not use a monthly statement to collect anything more than current payments. In contrast, such conduct would violate the automatic stay for any unsecured debts, or any secured debts as to which the debtor does not indicate in the Statement of Intention that the debtor intends to keep the property.

Proper communications in this context initiated by a creditor are limited to written communications. One benefit of a written communication is that it creates a record which permits the evaluation of whether the communication was proper, and did not stray into improper collection activities.

Throughout this process, the creditor may properly respond to any inquiries initiated by the debtor. Any communication that is initiated by the debtor is not a violation of the automatic stay or the discharge injunction, insofar as the creditor responds to the inquiry. If a debtor calls, the creditor is both entitled to take the call, and to call back if necessary to provide the information requested. However, the creditor should not use such a call as an occasion for collection activities.[25]

Problem 8-3

Driver filed for Chapter 7 bankruptcy protection in a state with a $2,500 motor vehicle exemption. Driver owns a car subject to a perfected security interest in favor of Lender and has made all of the required monthly payments on time. For each of the situations below, determine: (i) what, if anything, Driver could do to keep the car; (ii) if redemption is available, what it would cost Driver to redeem the car; (iii) what Driver's best option is; and (iv) what Lender's best course of action is.

A. Driver uses the car for family and household purposes.
   1. The car is worth $8,000, the secured debt is $10,000, and the secured obligation represents the remainder due on the purchase price of the car.
   2. The car is worth $8,000, the secured debt is $10,000, and the secured obligation consists of a loan for home repair.
   3. The car is worth $12,000, the secured debt is $10,000, and the secured obligation represents the remainder due on the purchase price of the car.
   4. The car is worth $12,000, the secured debt is $10,000, and the secured obligation consists of a loan for home repair.

B. How, if at all, would the analysis in Part A change if Driver uses the car primarily for business purposes?

---

[25] *In re Henry*, 266 B.R. 457, 471–73 (Bankr. C.D. Cal. 2001); *see also Arruda v. Sears, Roebuck & Co.*, 310 F.3d 13 (1st Cir. 2002) (creditor may seek and enter into "redemption agreement" without violating § 524); *In re Garske*, 287 B.R. 537 (9th Cir. BAP 2002) (secured creditor does not violate § 524 by contacting the debtor – telephonically or in writing – to ascertain the debtor's plans after missing payments as long as the creditor does not seek to collect the debt as a personal liability of the debtor); *In re Ramirez*, 280 B.R. 252 (C.D. Cal. 2002) (secured creditor does not violate § 524 by sending the debtor monthly statements listing the debtor's voluntary payments and describing the future payments that the debtor must make to avoid repossession).

Chapter Nine
Priorities and Distribution

In a Chapter 7 proceeding, the trustee is authorized – and can be compelled – to abandon any property that is burdensome or of inconsequential value to the estate. § 554(a), (b). With respect to other property, presumably property that has some value to the estate, the trustee is required to "collect and reduce to money the property of the estate . . . and close such estate as expeditiously as is compatible with the best interests of parties in interest." § 704(a)(1). Basically, this means that the trustee must liquidate the valuable property of the estate as quickly as possible. The court may, if it is in the best interest of the estate, authorize the trustee to operate the debtor's business for a limited time. *See* § 721. This may occur to allow the trustee to sell existing inventory in the ordinary course of business, and thus realize greater proceeds than a liquidation in bulk would, or when the business is to be sold as a going concern. More rarely, authorization to operate the debtor's business will be granted when the business is actually generating a profit. In most cases, however, the trustee simply sells all of the property in the estate expeditiously and does not operate the debtor's business.

Section 363 sets forth the rules under which the trustee will liquidate the estate. It authorizes a trustee (who has received permission to operate the debtor's business) to use, sell, or lease most property in the ordinary course of business without further court permission. § 363(c)(1). It authorizes a trustee to use, sell, or lease property outside the ordinary course of business – and to use, sell, or lease cash collateral – only with court approval after notice and a hearing. § 363(b)(1), (c)(2). The trustee is even permitted to sell property in which some entity other than the estate has an interest, and on occasion the trustee can be given authority to sell such property free of the other party's interest. *See* § 363(f).

Just as under U.C.C. Article 9, sales under § 363 may be conducted by public auction or through a privately negotiated transaction. Rule 6004(f)(1). Because private sales are generally thought to yield higher prices than public auctions, they are more common. To facilitate such sales, the trustee may, with court approval, hire an appraiser or broker. § 327(a).

Of course, liquidating the estate is only part of the trustee's job. The trustee is also required to distribute money to claimants "as promptly as practical." Rule 3009. No court approval is needed for the trustee to distribute estate assets to creditors, but if there is any dispute about how the assets should be divided, the trustee is likely to seek a court order resolving the issue. Moreover, the United States Trustee is charged with supervising both the trustee appointed in each case and the disbursements the trustee makes. 28 U.S.C. § 586. On occasion, particularly when there are significant liquid assets on hand but recovery or liquidation of other assets is expected to take some time, the trustee may make preliminary distributions, followed by a final distribution at a later date. More commonly, the trustee makes either no distribution or only one distribution.

When distributing the estate to claimants, the trustee must follow the Code's priority and distribution scheme, which is depicted in the chart on the next page. The bulk of the scheme is laid out in § 726(a). It in turn references § 507, which references § 503, which references § 330(a). As you review the chart, review the relevant Code sections.

Pursuant to this scheme, bankruptcy claimants seeking a distribution from the vat comprising the bankruptcy estate present their tin cup at the spigot on the right. In doing so, however, the claimants must first queue up in the order of their statutory priority and then wait their turn.

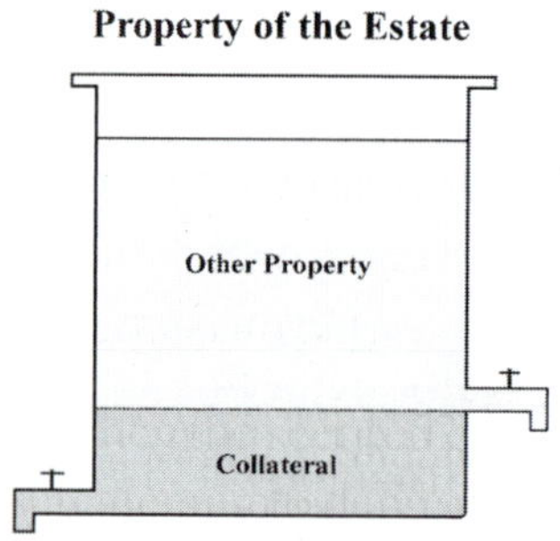

Claims within each ranking are to be paid in full before claims of a lower ranking are entitled to any payment at all. If there are insufficient assets to pay all of the claims within a single ranking, those claims share on a pro rata basis. § 726(b).

Even a cursory reading of these provisions should reveal two things. First, no single bankruptcy estate is likely to have claims from every rung in the distribution ladder. This is in part because several of the priorities are highly particularized and, consequently, rather rare. *See* § 507(a)(3), (6), (9). It is also because some priorities apply only to individual debtors, *see* § 507(a)(1)(A), (1)(B), (10), while several others apply only to businesses, and indeed to different types of businesses, *see* § 507(a)(4), (5), (6), (7), (9).

DISTRIBUTION OF THE ESTATE UNDER § 726(a)

1a	Trustee expenses incurred in administering the estate to pay support obligations	**Priorities § 507(a)**
1b	Spousal & child support claims	
2	Administrative expenses, including: • Costs & expenses of preserving the estate; taxes incurred by the estate • Compensation to professionals • Reimbursement of certain creditor expenses & compensation for certain creditor services • Certain amounts arising out of assumed and then rejected nonresidential real estate leases • Value of goods sold to debtor in ordinary course of debtor's business within 20 days prior to the filing of the bankruptcy petition	
3	Certain expenses arising from involuntary filings	
4	Certain employee wage claims (up to $12,475 per employee)	
5	Certain employee benefit claims (up to $12,475 per employee)	
6	Certain agricultural and aquicultural bailment claims (up to $6,150)	
7	Certain consumer deposits (up to $2,775)	
8	Certain unsecured tax claims	
9	Claims owed by depositary institutions to maintain capital levels	
10	Personal injury claims resulting from drunk driving	
11	Timely filed unsecured claims	
12	Untimely filed unsecured claims	
13	Prepetition claims for certain fines & penalties	
14	Interest on any of the claims listed above	
15	To debtor	

Second, the entire distribution scheme has a glaring omission: secured claims. That is because the trustee in a Chapter 7 case does not pay secured claims. Instead, as we saw in chapter six, the creditor will be paid in one of several alternative ways. If the estate has no interest in the collateral (either because the creditor is undersecured or all of the equity is exempt), the creditor may obtain relief from the stay (or wait for the stay to expire) and use its nonbankruptcy rights to foreclose on the collateral. Alternatively, the trustee may abandon the collateral to the debtor, who may then choose to stave off foreclosure by voluntarily paying the secured creditor. Such payments may occur either during the bankruptcy process (through redemption) or after the bankruptcy process (pursuant to a reaffirmation agreement or the creditor's tacit willingness to allow the debtor to retain the collateral if current on payments). If the estate does have an interest in the collateral, § 725 directs the trustee to sell the property prior to completing the distribution process detailed in § 726. That sale will either be subject to the lien, in which case the secured creditor will seek payment from the buyer, or free of the lien, in which case the trustee will pay the creditor the amount of the secured claim. *See* § 363(f). In either case, the trustee will put the remainder of the sale proceeds in the "vat" for distribution to creditors pursuant to the priorities stated in § 726.

Third, although all of the various priorities are designed to benefit the creditor holding the priority claim, they do so for different reasons. For some, such as an employee with a wage claim against an employer in bankruptcy, Congress has made the judgment that the creditor is likely to be particularly needy. In other words, that nonpayment by the estate may cause the creditor severe hardship and possibly even impel the creditor to seek bankruptcy protection. Congress enacted some of the other priority rules, such as the priority for taxes, simply to protect the public fisc. Finally, at least one of the priorities – the priority for administrative expenses – is based on a process concern: without payment of those expenses, the bankruptcy system itself might not be able to function. As you study these materials and the related statutory provisions, determine the underlying rationale for each priority rule discussed.

Being accorded priority status is extremely important.[1] In most Chapter 7 cases, little or nothing is paid to the nonpriority, unsecured claimants. While such creditors often fare a bit better in Chapter 11, 12, or 13 proceedings, they nevertheless remain at a distinct disadvantage.

---

[1] While the distribution scheme of § 726(a) applies only in Chapter 7 cases, the priorities listed in § 507(a) are also recognized in Chapter 11, 12, and 13 cases. *See* §§ 1129, 1222, 1225, 1322, 1325.

A. PRIORITIES

1. Support Claims

When Congress wrestled with bankruptcy reform in the 1990s and 2000s, many drafts of the legislation increased the types of debts that were nondischargeable. Although support claims already enjoyed exception from the discharge, *see* § 523(a)(5), critics of the reform proposals claimed that support claimants – ex-spouses and minor children – would be hurt by the proposals because they would have to compete for the debtor's postpetition assets against more creditors. Beyond that, some of their new competitors would be entities with experience in and resources devoted to debt collection.

To counter this concern, when Congress enacted bankruptcy reform in 2005, it raised spousal and child support claims from fifth priority to first priority. However, it is important to understand that nondischargeability and priority are two entirely different – and unrelated – concepts. When a claim is nondischargeable, the claimant remains free, after the stay expires or is lifted, to go after the debtor's nonexempt assets. Typically this means trying to get at the debtor's postpetition income. Priority, in contrast, deals with distributions of the bankruptcy estate. In short, priority is about what the claimant collects in the bankruptcy process, while nondischargeability is about the claimant's ability to collect outside of the bankruptcy process. Thus, the elevation in priority of support claims did nothing to address the point raised about increased competition outside of bankruptcy. Beyond that, the vast majority of individuals in Chapter 7 have no unencumbered, nonexempt assets and thus the trustee makes no distribution. The level of a claim's priority is therefore often irrelevant.

Another point worth noting about the first-tier priority for support claims is their interaction with administrative expenses. One of the arguments against elevating support claims was that placing them ahead of administrative expenses would be unworkable. Trustees would still have the duty to administer the estate, *see* § 704, but might never be paid for the work involved if the estate were exhausted by paying support claims. To deal with this, some of the trustee's expenses in "administer[ing] assets that would otherwise be available for the payment of [support] claims" come ahead of the support claims. *See* § 507(a)(1)(C) (referencing expenses incurred under § 503(b)(1)(A), (2), and (6)).

The priority treatment of support claims is one of several provisions in the Bankruptcy Code designed to protect support obligations. We have already seen that such claims have immunity from both preference liability and the debtor's exemptions,

nondischrg vs priority

§§ 547(c)(7), 522(c)(1), partial immunity from the stay, § 362(b)(2)(B), and protection from certain lien avoidance actions, § 522(f)(1)(A). As we will see in upcoming chapters, such claims are also protected from the discharge. *See* §§ 523(a)(5), 1328(a)(2). Collectively, these provisions make support claims the most favored type of claim in the bankruptcy process. However, such favor is qualified by some rather bizarre language in § 101(14A)(B). That language defines a "domestic support obligation," a term used in § 507(a)(1) and directly or indirectly used in all of the other provisions favoring support, as one "in the nature of alimony, maintenance, or support . . . without regard to whether such debt is expressly so designated."

What does this language mean? Consider a married couple in the process of getting divorced. They have the following assets:

Cash	$25,000
Home Equity	$75,000
Family Business	$300,000
Total:	$400,000

Although both spouses work, only one works in the family business. They agree – or the family court decides – to divide the marital assets equally. That means each should get $200,000 in assets (½ of $400,000). They also agree that the spouse who works in the family business should retain sole ownership of the business.[2] However, even if the other spouse gets the house and all of the cash, the total marital assets will not be divided equally. To remedy this, the parties agree – or the court orders – that the spouse who retains the business interest pay the other spouse $100,000. Because he or she does not have the cash to do that up front, the arrangement further provides for payments of $2,025 per month for five years. This is the equivalent of $100,000 at approximately 8% interest.

This monthly payment – which in reality is part of the equitable distribution of marital assets – resembles support. In short, periodic payments to be made incident to divorce might be support or might be a division of property over time. There is no easy way to tell the difference. Moreover, any label the court or the parties put on the

---

[2] Note that in some instances this may be required. For example, if the business were a law firm, the lawyer would not be permitted under Model Rule of Professional Conduct 5.4 to allow the former spouse to have an ownership interest in the firm.

payment obligation cannot be determinative because there are a variety of factors and incentives that go into choosing that label.[3]

Section 507(a)(1), through its implicit incorporation of § 101(14A)(B), requires courts to analyze each payment obligation to determine if it is truly support, in which case it is a priority claim, or if it is something else, in which case it is not a priority claim. Over the years, this issue has been heavily litigated, although more commonly in the context of a challenge to the dischargeability of the claim rather than to its priority.[4] When resolving such controversies, courts have been extremely protective of the creditor spouse and have engaged in some analytical gymnastics to interpret debts to a former spouse as support obligations.

For example, in *Shaver v. Shaver*,[5] a bankruptcy court, district court, and circuit court all ruled that a $190,000 debt to a former spouse was for support – largely because the debt terminated on the creditor spouse's death and she had no other means of support – even though (i) the family court decree described it as in exchange for property rights; (ii) the amended decree described it as in exchange for marital and dower rights; and (iii) the state court had no authority to award alimony in the case. In another case, *In re Brody*,[6] the separation agreement provided for payment of: (i) $1 million over four years, in satisfaction of the wife's right to equitable distribution of the marital estate; and (ii) $3,250/month for support for 36 months, terminable on her death, remarriage, or cohabitation. The wife had even asserted in state court that the first obligation was a property settlement. Nevertheless, a bankruptcy court, district court, and circuit court

---

3 Most notably, spousal support payments (not child support payments) are deductible to the payor and income to the recipient, whereas a division of property generates neither a deduction nor income. *See* 26 U.S.C. § 71. If the spouses are likely to be in different tax brackets, there will be a tax incentive to label the payments either as support or as a property division, and that incentive may have no relationship to why the obligation was created.

4 *See* § 523(a)(5). In 1994, Congress added § 523(a)(15) to the Code to make property settlement claims incident to divorce also nondischargeable, albeit subject to a balancing of equities. In 2005, Congress removed that balancing limitation, making all support and property settlement obligations to a former spouse nondischargeable. As a result, future litigation seeking to distinguish a support obligation from a property settlement debt is unlikely to arise in the context of dischargeability determinations.

5 736 F.2d 1314 (9th Cir. 1984).

6 3 F.3d 35 (2d Cir. 1993); *see also In re Werthen*, 329 F.3d 269 (1st Cir. 2003) ($833,000 state court property division award treated as additional support because alimony award was inadequate to meet the needs of the creditor spouse and children).

all treated both obligations as support claims. Similarly, in *Cummings v. Cummings*,[7] a divorce decree ordered Mr. Cummings to pay his ex-wife: (i) $5,150 per month in child support; (ii) 15 months of rehabilitative alimony; and (iii) $6.3 million as an equitable distribution of the marital estate, in three payments of $2.1 million. The bankruptcy court ruled that the entire $6.3 obligation was not support and the district court affirmed. The circuit court reversed, with instructions to determine what portion of the equitable distribution was support, based largely on statements by the divorce court that the ex-wife would depend on a portion of the equitable distribution to support herself and the children.

According to these and other courts, subjective intent and the substance of the obligation are the relevant inquiries, and neither state court treatment nor settlement labeling is to be regarded as conclusive.[8] One of the most critical factors is the duration of the payments. Specifically, if payments are to continue even after the creditor spouse dies or remarries, they are unlikely to qualify as support.[9] On the other hand, if the amount or duration of payments is subject to change if the creditor spouse's circumstances change, then the payment is likely to be support, because a property settlement would not normally be affected by a change in circumstances.[10]

2. *Administrative Expenses*

After support claims, administrative expenses have the highest priority. *See* § 507(a)(2). These include the costs of preserving and liquidating the estate. § 503(b)(1). This means that the costs of insuring estate assets, preparing them for sale,

---

[7] 244 F.3d 1263 (11th Cir. 2001).

[8] Some courts have ruled that the debtor's tax treatment of the payment obligations may collaterally estop *the debtor* from asserting the obligation is dischargeable. *See In re Robb*, 23 F.3d 895, 898–99 (4th Cir. 1994); *In re Davidson*, 947 F.2d 1294, 1297 (5th Cir. 1991). Other courts have disagreed. *E.g.*, *In re Sampson*, 997 F.2d 717, 724–25 (10th Cir. 1993); *In re Kritt*, 190 B.R. 382, 388–89 (9th Cir. BAP 1995). Because nondischargeability is based on priority status, these cases presumably apply to priority status as well.

[9] *Compare* 26 U.S.C. § 71(b)(1)(D) (limiting alimony for federal income tax purposes to obligations that terminate with the death of the payee). Note, however, that the converse is not necessarily true: even if the payments are to cease on the creditor spouse's death, they may still be a property settlement rather than a support obligation.

[10] *See Shaver*, 736 F.2d at 1316.

and the like are all a top priority.[11] Read § 503(b). Notice that, in order to be paid, administrative expenses must be approved by the court after notice and a hearing.

As broad as the administrative expenses priority is, it is not limitless, as the following case demonstrates.

IN RE RESOURCE TECHNOLOGY CORP.
662 F.3d 472 (7th Cir. 2011)

POSNER, Circuit Judge.

This appeal presents a novel issue: the priority of a claim against the debtor's estate in a Chapter 7 bankruptcy for damages arising from a tort committed by the debtor during the interval between the appointment of the trustee in bankruptcy and the liquidation a few months later of the bankrupt's assets that had been the source of the tort.

The *dramatis personae* (besides the Chapter 7 trustee) are Roti, the claimant; Resource Technology Corporation, the bankrupt (which the parties call "RTC"); and Congress Development Company ("CDC"), like Roti a creditor of the bankrupt estate.

Roti owned a Holiday Inn in a Chicago suburb. The hotel was adjacent to a landfill owned and operated by CDC. Back in 1996 CDC had hired RTC to build a system for preventing the methane, carbon dioxide, hydrogen sulfide, and other gases generated in the landfill from leaking; the system would also extract energy from the gas, which RTC would sell, paying CDC a royalty. So: a gas collection and control system.

In 1999 RTC was forced into bankruptcy under Chapter 11 (reorganization). Roti bought the Holiday Inn three years later, and in 2005 it followed RTC into Chapter 11, though for unrelated reasons. RTC's Chapter 11 bankruptcy was converted to a Chapter 7 bankruptcy (liquidation) in September 2005. A trustee was appointed on September 21 and six days later was authorized by the bankruptcy judge to operate the debtor's business for a period of just under three months, but the period could be extended and presumably would be until the liquidation was complete. RTC operated gas collection and control systems at other landfills, but the record is silent on how the liquidation of those assets proceeded.

---

[11] In reorganization cases, which may last many months or even years, the administrative expenses are frequently quite substantial and eat up the entire estate. This is because the administrative expenses might include all of the costs of running the debtor's business – including employees' wages, postpetition taxes, utilities, supplies, and even tort damages arising out of the normal operation of the business – and the business may well be earning less money than it takes to run.

Four days after the trustee was given operational control of RTC's business en route to liquidation, RTC's gas collection and control system at CDC's landfill failed; it had been malfunctioning for years and RTC had lacked the financial wherewithal to fix it. The system's failure released foul odors that, traveling underground, wafted into the hotel through electrical outlets and floor cracks. The odors sickened guests and employees, resulting (according to Roti) in a disastrous fall off in the hotel's business.

Illinois's environmental protection agency issued notices of violation of the Illinois Environmental Protection Act and other environmental regulations to both RTC and CDC. RTC's trustee responded that the bankrupt estate had no money to repair the gas collection and control system. On January 13 CDC was permitted to, and did, terminate its contract with RTC, and by February 7 the trustee had abandoned all of RTC's assets at CDC's landfill.

RTC was required by state and federal law to comply with environmental regulations, and "a trustee may not abandon property in contravention of a state statute or regulation that is reasonably designed to protect the public health or safety from identified hazards." *Midlantic National Bank v. New Jersey Dep't of Environmental Protection*, 474 U.S. 494, 507 (1986). There is no suggestion that the trustee abandoned RTC's assets at CDC's landfill either prematurely or belatedly.

In September 2006 Roti sold the Holiday Inn for $5 million. He claims that had it not been for the odors, he could have sold it for almost five times as much; his claim against RTC in the bankruptcy court is for the difference. * * *

The bankrupt estate has other creditors besides Roti. But he contends that his claim is an administrative claim that trumps the claims of the other creditors (with at least one exception, as we're about to note). Administrative expenses, which consist of the "actual, necessary costs and expenses of preserving the [bankrupt] estate," receive priority in the distribution of the estate's assets to creditors. 11 U.S.C. §§ 503(b)(1)(A), 507(a)(2).

The bankruptcy judge, seconded by the district judge, rejected Roti's administrative claim, and Roti has appealed to us. CDC also filed an administrative claim against the bankrupt estate, seeking reimbursement of expenses that it had incurred to rebuild RTC's system before it terminated its contract with RTC. That claim was allowed, in the amount of $1.5 million – adding to Roti's indignation at the rejection of his administrative claim.

The emission of foul odors as the result of negligent maintenance of the gas collection and control system, which interfered with Roti's use and enjoyment of his property and caused economic loss and property damage, was a nuisance, and thus a tort. And a tort for which RTC was responsible, though perhaps jointly with CDC, the owner of the landfill. Although RTC didn't own the landfill, its poor maintenance of its gas collection and control system was a cause and quite possibly the major cause of the leak of gas from the landfill into the Holiday Inn.

It is unusual for nuisance to be alleged against someone other than the owner or lessee of the property that emits the fumes or noise or dust or other harmful emanations that give rise to the nuisance claim. But the key to liability is not ownership; it's control. By virtue of its control of the gas collection and control system embedded in the landfill, RTC was the author of the nuisance, or at least a joint tortfeasor with CDC.

The trustee had been operating RTC's system for only four days before the failure occurred. The failure resulted from the many years of RTC's neglect, and there is no evidence that the trustee was aware of that neglect, did anything to exacerbate it, could have done anything to prevent the failure triggered by that neglect within the few days in which he was in nominal control of the system before it failed, or could have done anything to mitigate the damage afterward.

* * * [Nevertheless,] Roti does have a claim against the bankrupt estate, and that makes him a creditor, yet he is not asking, as an alternative to the recognition of his administrative claim, that he be dumped in with the general creditors; for him it is administrative claim or nothing, which is doubtless why the district court stopped with ruling that he has no administrative claim.

The reason administrative claims are given priority is that they are claims for reimbursement by the bankrupt estate of expenses incurred after the declaration of bankruptcy, in order to preserve and if possible enhance the value of the bankrupt estate for the benefit of its creditors. Such expenses are particularly important in a Chapter 11 case, in which the bankrupt business continues in operation with hopes (granted, they are usually dashed, as in the case of RTC) of survival as a going concern, albeit with an altered capital structure, such as the substitution of the creditors for the pre-bankruptcy shareholders as owners of the business. Unless those who extended credit to a bankrupt business were given a priority claim, it would be very hard for such businesses to obtain credit, as they would be competing for a diminished pool of assets with the pre-petition creditors.

A tort victim (Roti) is a creditor, but not a creditor whose actions benefit his debtor, the tortfeasor. Yet in *Reading v. Brown*, 391 U.S. 471 (1968), the Supreme Court held that at least in a Chapter 11 bankruptcy, tort claims arising from the continued operation of the bankrupt business should be treated as administrative claims, like other post-petition expenses. Tort liability is an expense of doing business, like labor or material costs, and should be treated the same way. Businesses operating in bankruptcy that were excused from tort liability would have an inefficient competitive advantage over their solvent competitors – and deficient incentives to use due care in the operation of the business. It could indeed be argued that in the interest of safety, insolvent firms, not being deterrable by threat of tort suits, should not be allowed to operate at all. *Reading* strikes a compromise between the safety interest and the interest in saving bankrupts from premature liquidation: the bankrupt that continues to operate (normally under Chapter 11) must give its tort victims priority access to such assets as the bankrupt estate retains.

RTC was in Chapter 7 bankruptcy when the tort occurred; can the principle of *Reading* be extended to Chapter 7, given that the goal of such a bankruptcy is liquidation of the bankrupt's assets at the highest possible price rather than the continuation of the bankrupt's business? Sometimes yes; for the dichotomy between operation and liquidation is too stark. There is an interval between the appointment of the trustee and the liquidation of the bankrupt's assets under his supervision, and during that interval he may have operating responsibilities. The policy that supports the *Reading* doctrine – the policy against permitting bankrupt firms to externalize the costs of their torts – depends on whether the bankrupt firm is operating, not which part of the Bankruptcy Code (that is, whether Chapter 7 or Chapter 11) it is operating under.

But at least as far as the gas collection and control system in CDC's landfill was concerned, the bankrupt in this case was not operating in any meaningful sense during the brief period in which the trustee was in charge. It had some minute revenue from energy sales – less than 10 percent of its normal revenue from such sales – but it is doubtful that this revenue covered its costs, or that the continued operation of the system in its diminished state can be attributed to anything other than the bankrupt's legal duty, noted in the Supreme Court's *Midlantic* decision, to minimize further contamination.

RTC had no money that the trustee could have spent on stemming the gas leak. Apart from the meager energy sales that we just mentioned, he did sell some gas engines for an amount not disclosed in the record (all we know is that it could not have exceeded $6 million). But the agreement of sale was made after CDC had terminated RTC's contract at the landfill, thus evicting RTC, so the trustee could not have used the proceeds of the engine sales to fix the leak. It's not as if he had embarked on a project to increase the value of RTC's assets and the workers on the project had committed a tort.

We thus are far from *Reading*, where the Chapter 11 receiver (equivalent to a trustee) was managing a building that was the debtor's principal asset, when the building burned down and in the process caused damage to adjacent buildings, triggering tort claims against the bankrupt estate. The receiver was either collecting rents or otherwise obtaining or attempting to obtain income for the estate from the building, and by doing so he was unavoidably running a risk of fire. In this case, in contrast, the trustee took over a bankrupt company at the point of collapse, and the collapse was unrelated to his control of the assets. He had neither the mandate nor the resources to do anything with them except liquidate them as quickly as possible, which he proceeded to do. He could and did do nothing with the assets that might (with however low a probability) have enhanced their value for the creditors, in which event they would have had to take the bad with the good – the risk of tort liability along with the prospects for successful management of the assets. The trustee operated a losing venture under legal compulsion. There is no basis for applying the doctrine of *Reading* to such a casc.

Affirmed.

Notes

1. In *Pennsylvania Department of Environmental Resources v. Tri-State Clinical Laboratories, Inc.*, 178 F.3d 685 (3d Cir. 1999), *cert. denied*, 528 U.S. 1075 (2000), the court ruled that a criminal fine imposed on a debtor in possession for postpetition violations of Pennsylvania's Solid Waste Management Act was not an administrative expense under § 503(b). The court ruled that while expenditures necessary to the operation of the business in a Chapter 11 case do qualify as administrative expenses, criminal fines are not a necessary part of any business. The court recognized that, if the fine were not treated as an administrative expense, the debtor might not have sufficient assets to pay the fine once the debtor's assets were liquidated, but saw "nothing in the statutes that [the debtor in possession] has violated, nor anything endemic to the process of bankruptcy, that would justify us in removing the Commonwealth's hand from the empty pockets of the criminal, and placing it in the pockets of creditors merely because those pockets are deeper."

2. Two related issues that arise somewhat frequently are: (i) whether an employer who terminates employees shortly after filing for bankruptcy protection incurs liability to the employees under the WARN Act, 29 U.S.C. § 2102, for failing to provide the required 60-days' notification of the termination; and (ii) if so, whether that liability is treated as an administrative expense. *See Torres v. United States*, 200 F.3d 179 (3d Cir. 1999) (an

employer in bankruptcy succeeds to the WARN Act obligations of the prepetition debtor only if the debtor has, leading up to and during the bankruptcy proceedings, continued in an "employer" capacity, operating the business as an ongoing concern); *In re Century City Doctors Hosp., LLC*, 2010 WL 6452903 (9th Cir. BAP 2010) (similar).

3. Even in Chapter 7 cases, the administrative expenses can be significant. This is often because the cost of paying many of the professionals involved in the bankruptcy case will be borne by the estate.

(a) The Trustee's Compensation

In Chapter 7 cases, the trustee receives $45 for each case filed. § 330(b). This amount comes out of the filing fee. In addition, the trustee is entitled to reasonable compensation for services but such compensation is capped at a percentage of the distributions to the claimants.[12] *See* §§ 326(a), 330(a). Because this compensation is fairly minimal, trustees usually look for other ways to enhance their income. As a majority of trustees are lawyers, most also seek employment as professionals under § 327 in those cases in which employing a professional is necessary and appropriate. This typically occurs when there will be litigation to recover a preference or fraudulent transfer. In essence, the trustees hire themselves as lawyers (subject to court approval), *see* § 327(d), and compensation for such professional services is not capped by a percentage of the distributions in the case. § 330(a). In the few districts that do not routinely permit a trustee to serve as his or her own lawyer, the trustees typically hire each other or their law firms, again subject to court approval. § 327(a).

---

[12] Technically, § 326(a) fixes a maximum fee. However, in many districts the trustee is permitted to take the maximum without having to provide any specific justification for it. For some reason, the $45 fee is not thought to be extra compensation that would take the trustee beyond the maximum permitted by § 326(a).

(b) Compensation for Employed Professionals

Generally speaking, the debtor's attorney in a Chapter 7 case is not compensated out of the estate. This is because the debtor's interests are typically adverse to those of the creditors, for whose benefit the estate is administered.[13] Accordingly, most Chapter 7 debtor's attorneys get their fees up front before the bankruptcy petition is filed. Failure to do this will subject the unpaid fee obligation to the debtor's discharge.

Even though the Chapter 7 debtor's attorney is seldom paid out of estate assets, and may well be paid through a prepetition retainer, the Bankruptcy Court has the authority and the duty to review the reasonableness of those fees and to order that any unreasonable amount either not be collected or be disgorged if already paid. *See* § 329(b). To permit the court to perform this review, the debtor's attorney must disclose all payments and fee arrangements. *See* § 329(a); Rule 2016(b). Many courts do not hesitate to reduce the fee charged by the debtor's attorney. The following case illustrates the procedural and substantive hurdles that debtor's counsel faces in obtaining payment for bankruptcy legal services. It also involves a rather unusual solution to the problem.

In re Leitner
221 B.R. 502 (Bankr. D. Neb. 1998)

Minahan, Jr., Bankruptcy Judge.

A myriad of issues are raised in this Chapter 7 case because, before filing this bankruptcy case, debtors' counsel obtained a promissory note and mortgage from debtors to assure payment for bankruptcy related legal services. I conclude that these extraordinary pre-bankruptcy transactions with counsel are legal and appropriate, provided that the multiple requirements of the Bankruptcy Code and Rules are met.

At the time the debtors sought legal advice from attorney Mr. Bert Blackwell, they agreed to pay Mr. Blackwell $1,100.00, and the bankruptcy filing fee in installments of

---

[13] The debtor's attorney's fees in a Chapter 7 case generally do not qualify for administrative expense treatment under § 503(b)(1) because they are typically not incurred to "preserve the estate." In addition, they do not qualify under § 503(b)(2), which references compensation authorized under § 330(a), because § 330(a) in turn references professionals employed under § 327 and the debtor's attorney is not normally hired under § 327. This latter point was actually the subject of some confusion because of a poorly drafted 1994 amendment to § 330(a), but the Supreme Court has now made it clear that the debtor's attorney does not qualify for payment from the estate except in the rare instance when the attorney is hired under § 327. *Lamie v. U.S. Trustee*, 540 U.S. 526 (2004).

$100.00 per month. He agreed to represent them in a Chapter 7 bankruptcy case and to advance the $175.00 filing fee. The debtors granted Mr. Blackwell a mortgage in their residence to secure the $1,275.00 debt. The mortgage was duly recorded prior to filing this bankruptcy case. Debtors' residence is valued at $11,800.00, and is encumbered only by Mr. Blackwell's mortgage. The debtors claim the remaining equity in the real estate as an exempt homestead under § 40-101 of the Nebraska Revised Statutes.

The debtors filed a reaffirmation agreement with the Clerk of the Bankruptcy Court seeking leave of the court to affirm their $1,275.00 obligation to Mr. Blackwell. The United States Trustee objected to approval of the reaffirmation agreement, asserting that the monthly installment payments of $100.00 may impose an undue hardship on the debtors. When the debtors sought leave to withdraw the reaffirmation agreement, I scheduled a hearing to examine the debtors' transactions with Mr. Blackwell.

The fee agreement between Mr. Blackwell and debtors represents a good faith attempt to deal with a difficult problem faced by bankruptcy practitioners whose clients cannot afford to pay Chapter 7 legal expenses in advance. However, the fee agreement and mortgage present a number of legal issues which I will address with the objective of providing counsel guidelines for structuring agreements with clients for the payment of Chapter 7 legal expenses on a deferred basis.

Bankruptcy practitioners are faced with a difficult situation when a financially troubled debtor wants to file a Chapter 7 bankruptcy case and cannot afford to pay attorney fees in advance. Prudent counsel will not agree to pay the bankruptcy filing fees and to file the bankruptcy case without a retainer because the debtor's obligations to pay for pre-bankruptcy legal services will be discharged in the bankruptcy case. One alternative is for counsel to suggest that the client file a Chapter 13 bankruptcy case so that the attorney fees can be paid on a deferred basis as an allowed administrative expense. However, the selection of the appropriate bankruptcy chapter should not be influenced by the need to pay attorney fees. Chapter 13 is most appropriate for debtors who want to retain non-exempt assets and make payments to creditors. If a debtor has few non-exempt assets and no debts excepted from discharge under § 523, Chapter 7 may be the most appropriate chapter for the insolvent debtor who has no desire or ability to make payments to creditors.

What course of action should bankruptcy counsel recommend to a debtor who has no ability to pay for legal services in advance, but whose circumstances strongly suggest that Chapter 7 liquidation is the most suitable bankruptcy alternative? Mr. Blackwell addressed this problem by obtaining a promissory note and mortgage and filing a Chapter 7 case. His clients are thus in the appropriate bankruptcy Chapter, but the transaction between counsel and his clients raises several specific issues:

1. Is debtors' counsel disqualified from representing the bankruptcy debtors because counsel is a prepetition creditor, holding a lien in property of the bankruptcy estate?

2. Are the debtors or counsel required to disclose the prepetition mortgage transaction and fee agreement to the court and to creditors?

3. Must the debtors' counsel file a fee application in the Chapter 7 case seeking allowance of his fees and approval of the fee agreement and mortgage?

4. Absent reaffirmation, will the Chapter 7 discharge order extinguish the debtors' personal obligation to pay for the legal services?

5. If a reaffirmation agreement is not approved, does the lien securing the obligation to pay attorney fees pass through the bankruptcy case unimpaired, thus permitting counsel to enforce the mortgage after the bankruptcy discharge is entered and the bankruptcy case is closed?

1. *Disqualification of Counsel*

The Eighth Circuit Court of Appeals has held that an attorney who is a prepetition creditor holding a mortgage on the debtor's real estate for prepetition and postpetition services related to a bankruptcy case is not a "disinterested person," and thus does not qualify for employment under § 327(a) in a Chapter 11 bankruptcy case. *See In re Pierce*, 809 F.2d 1356 (8th Cir. 1987). However, the "disinterested" requirements of §§ 327 and 328 do not apply to an attorney representing the debtor in a Chapter 7 case. The "disinterested" requirements of §§ 327 and 328 of the Bankruptcy Code apply to professionals who provide services to or for the benefit of the bankruptcy estate such as counsel for the standing trustee. These professionals must be retained with court approval and are generally compensated from property of the bankruptcy estate. Debtor's counsel does not represent the bankruptcy estate in a Chapter 7 case, except by special order of the court. Mr. Blackwell is not disqualified from representing the Chapter 7 debtors simply because he is a secured creditor of the debtors respecting unpaid fees for bankruptcy related legal services.

Attorney and clients are almost always in a debtor-creditor relationship respecting the provision of legal services. The fact that a client is indebted to counsel for undisputed charges for services rendered within the scope of the current representation does not provide an ethical or statutory basis for disqualification of counsel.

2. *Disclosure of Fee Arrangement and Mortgage*

Counsel's § 329 and Rule 2016 Statement must disclose the fee agreement. The debtors' bankruptcy schedules and statement of financial affairs must disclose the mortgage securing the fee agreement.

Section 329, in relevant part, requires that:

> (a) Any attorney representing a debtor in a case under this title, or in connection with such a case, whether or not such attorney applies for compensation under this title, shall file with the court a statement of the compensation paid or agreed to be paid, if such payment or agreement was made after one year before the date of the filing of the petition, for services rendered or to be rendered in contemplation of or in connection with the case by such attorney, and the source of such compensation.

Bankruptcy Rule 2016 further elaborates the disclosure requirements. However, Bankruptcy Rule 2016(b) and § 329(a) make no explicit requirement that liens be disclosed.

The existence of the encumbrance to secure the obligation to pay is an integral part of the fee agreement and it is highly relevant to the bankruptcy proceedings. Certainly, each and every term and provision of a fee agreement need not be disclosed, but in the context of a bankruptcy case, the existence of an encumbrance to secure payment of attorney fees is arguably an essential term of the bargain. I construe Rule 2016(b) to require disclosure of any lien that secures payment of counsel's fees. The Rule explicitly requires disclosure of "the source of such compensation." I hold that a mortgage securing a fee agreement is a potential "source of compensation" which must be disclosed in the Rule 2016(b) statement.

It is clear that the debtor must also disclose the mortgage. A bankruptcy debtor is required to list the name and address of all entities holding claims secured by property of the debtor as of the date of filing of the petition. *See* Schedule D, Creditors Holding Secured Claims. The bankruptcy schedules in this case list Mr. Blackwell as a secured creditor holding a mortgage on the debtors' real estate to secure a $1,275.00 debt. The statement of financial affairs also requires disclosure of the mortgage. The debtor must list all payments made or property transferred by or on behalf of the debtor to any person for consultation concerning debt consolidation, relief under the Bankruptcy Code, or preparation of a petition in bankruptcy within one year immediately preceding the commencement of the case. *See* Question Number 9, Statement of Financial Affairs.

In summary, an agreement between debtor and counsel for the payment of bankruptcy legal fees secured by a mortgage on debtors' property must be disclosed (i) by counsel in the § 329 and Rule 2016(b) statement, and (ii) by debtor in the bankruptcy schedules and statement of financial affairs.

3. *Fee Application Requirement*

Bankruptcy Rule 2016(a) requires any entity seeking compensation or reimbursement of expenses from the bankruptcy estate to file a fee application. A Chapter 7 debtor's counsel is not a professional retained to represent the bankruptcy estate, and debtor's counsel is not paid from the property of the estate. Debtors' counsel, Mr. Blackwell, does not seek compensation from the bankruptcy estate and he is not required to file a fee application.

However, the court may examine the fee agreement. Under Bankruptcy Rule 2017, the court has broad authority to determine whether the payment of money or transfer of property to an attorney for services is excessive. Bankruptcy Rule 2017 provides a procedural mechanism for the court to examine the reasonableness of a prepetition fee agreement. In appropriate circumstances the fees could be reduced, and the mortgage limited or avoided.

4. *Discharge of Debtors' Personal Liability*

The Chapter 7 debtor's personal obligation to pay for prepetition legal services will be discharged by the Chapter 7 discharge order, unless the debtor reaffirms the debt under § 524 of the Bankruptcy Code. A reaffirmation agreement between debtor and counsel will not be enforceable unless it is filed with the court. Counsel, as a party to the fee agreement, may not represent the debtor in regard to the reaffirmation agreement. Since the debtors are not represented by counsel in connection with the reaffirmation agreement, and there is no counsel to file the affidavit or declaration required by § 524(c)(3), the reaffirmation agreement is not enforceable unless approved by the court after a hearing attended by the debtors.

If the obligation to pay attorney fees is discharged, § 524(a)(2) enjoins counsel from any attempt to collect the debt as a personal obligation of the debtor.

5. *Mortgage Passes Through Bankruptcy*

Even though the Chapter 7 debtors' personal obligation to pay prepetition attorney fees will be discharged absent a valid reaffirmation of the debt, the mortgage will pass through the bankruptcy proceeding unimpaired. On the facts of this case, there is no suggestion that the mortgage is avoidable as a preference or fraudulent conveyance. None of the trustee's avoiding powers seem applicable. Section 522(f), which can be used to avoid certain non-purchase money security interests, is not applicable to security interests in real property, such as Mr. Blackwell's mortgage. However, § 522(f) could be used to avoid liens in the types of exempt personal property listed in that subsection of the Bankruptcy Code. In effect, § 522(f) will limit the ability of counsel to structure secured deferred financing.

Under § 506(a), Mr. Blackwell's prepetition claim is an allowed secured claim to the extent of equity in collateral. On the facts of this case the mortgage is fully secured. Thus, even if counsel fails to file a proof of claim, the mortgage will not be avoided under § 506(d). The discharge order entered in this case will discharge debtors' personal obligation, but the mortgage will survive and may be enforced. After the discharge order is entered in this case, the debtors will no longer be personally liable to Mr. Blackwell, however, Mr. Blackwell will be free to enforce the mortgage.

Finally, it should be noted that to the extent services are provided by the Chapter 7 debtor's attorney postpetition, many of the above issues become moot. In that instance, although the fee agreement must still be disclosed, the attorney is a postpetition creditor, the postpetition debt for attorney fees is not dischargeable, and a reaffirmation agreement is not necessary as to postpetition services.

Conclusion

Counsel is not disqualified from representing the Chapter 7 debtors by virtue of his holding a secured claim for undisputed prepetition legal services. The prepetition agreement between debtors and counsel concerning the payment of legal fees in installments and the granting of the mortgage must be disclosed (i) by counsel in the § 329 and Bankruptcy Rule 2016(b) statement, and (ii) by debtors in the bankruptcy schedules and statement of financial affairs. Counsel is not required to file a fee application or obtain bankruptcy court approval of the fee agreement, but the court may examine the fee agreement under Rule 2017. Unless the debtors[] reaffirm their obligation to pay counsel, the prepetition debt will be discharged by the Chapter 7 discharge order. Counsel may enforce his prepetition mortgage against the debtors' property under applicable non-bankruptcy law after the automatic stay of § 362 terminates.

Mr. Blackwell may continue to represent the debtors in this case. The motion to withdraw the reaffirmation agreement is sustained.

Question

Was the Leitners' arrangement with their attorney, Mr. Blackwell, designed solely to ensure payment of his legal services or did it also serve some additional objective? If so, what was that objective?

In those situations where the efforts of the debtor's attorney do benefit the estate, compensation from the estate will be possible. This is quite rare in Chapter 7 cases.[14]

The trustee's attorney and accountant are normally paid out of the estate. However, there are several protections built into the process to make sure that estate assets are not wasted in the process of employing and paying these professionals. First, the court must approve the employment in advance. Second, the professional to be hired must be "disinterested."[15] *See* §§ 327(a), 330(a). Because anyone who holds a prepetition claim cannot be disinterested, § 101(14)(A), an attorney or accountant whose bill for prepetition services remains even partly unpaid cannot be employed postpetition by the trustee, at least not unless the professional waives the right to payment for such services.[16] Moreover, paying the professional in full shortly before bankruptcy will likely not solve the problem. Because such a payment may well constitute an avoidable preference, the professional would have an interest adverse to the estate, and thus still not qualify as disinterested.[17]

---

[14] In Chapter 11, where the debtor is functioning as debtor in possession, retains control over the estate, and has many of the trustee's powers, § 1107(a), the debtor's attorney is usually compensated from the estate as are the professionals hired by the debtor in possession. §§ 330, 327. In Chapter 12 and 13 cases, the debtor's attorney's fees may qualify for payment as an administrative expense under § 330(a)(4)(B).

[15] There are some exceptions to the requirement that the professional be disinterested but these are mostly relevant to Chapter 11 cases and hence are discussed in chapter twelve of this book. In addition, slightly different rules apply to a professional hired to represent a creditors' committee in a Chapter 11, which is also compensated out of the estate. §§ 330, 327, 1107, 1103(a), (b). These too will be discussed in chapter twelve.

[16] As one court noted, when Congress enacted § 327(a) it "made a conscious choice that efficiency would be sacrificed for the appearance of propriety." *In re Siliconix, Inc.*, 135 B.R. 378, 380 (N.D. Cal. 1991) (quoting *In re Gray*, 64 B.R. 505, 508 (Bankr. E.D. Mich. 1986)).

[17] *See In re Pillowtex, Inc.*, 304 F.3d 246 (3d Cir. 2002) (so ruling even though no determination had been made that the payment was preferential and the professional agreed to return the funds and waive any revived claim for payment if the payment was determined to be a preference); *In re Triple Star Welding, Inc.*, 324 B.R. 778 (9th Cir. BAP 2005) (agreeing with *Pillowtex* but suggesting that the

The final and most significant method for ensuring that estate assets are not wasted through the employment of professionals is through substantial judicial oversight of the fees awarded. Such oversight can occur in either of two ways.

First, the bankruptcy court may determine and approve the terms of the professional's compensation in the appointment order. If the court does this, such as by setting an hourly rate or a contingent fee, the court may later reduce that compensation only if "the terms and conditions prove to have been improvident in light of developments not capable of being anticipated at the time" they were set. § 328(a).

Second, and more commonly, the court evaluates the reasonableness of the fee by examining the services with the benefit of hindsight. In doing so, the court is expressly charged with considering the nature and value of the services and the amount and reasonableness of the time spent. § 330(a)(3). Beyond this, courts routinely examine other factors, such as "the novelty and difficulty of the task, the requisite skill level, whether the case precluded other employment, the contingent nature of the fee, time limitations, thc amount of moncy involved and results obtained, and the experience, reputation, and ability of the [professional]."[18] As a result, courts may – and frequently do – refuse to compensate the professional at the rate and hours requested for the work performed, and instead they approve a fee request only in part.

Problem 9-1

Which of the following can qualify as administrative expenses in a Chapter 7 case?

A. Fees of the trustee's attorney incurred in challenging the discharge. *See* §§ 704(a), 503(b)(2), 330(a), 327(a).

B. Fees of the trustee's attorney incurred in seeking to avoid a preferential transfer.

C. Fees of the debtor's attorney incurred in defending the debtor against a challenge to the discharge. *See Lamie v. U.S. Trustee*, 540 U.S. 526 (2004).

D. Fees of a creditor's attorney incurred in challenging the discharge.

---

conflict would be removed if the professional returned the payment). *But cf. In re Enron*, 2003 WL 223455 (S.D.N.Y. 2003) (if the professional agrees to waive the right to litigate the preference issue and be bound by an examiner's determination, the conflict is removed and the professional is disinterested).

[18] *In re Commercial Fin. Servs., Inc.*, 427 F.3d 804, 811 (10th Cir. 2005).

(c) Allocation Problems

While virtually all allowable claims arise prepetition, administrative expenses are expenses that necessarily arise postpetition. Occasionally, determining whether a bill for payment represents a prepetition claim (with little or no priority) or a postpetition administrative expense (with a high priority) is difficult. The issue, which is not unlike some of the allocation problems relating to claims discussed in chapter four, can arise in a Chapter 7 case, particularly if the trustee is temporarily operating the debtor's business in the hope of selling it as a going concern. *See* § 721. More commonly, however, allocation problems come up in Chapter 11 cases in which the debtor is seeking to maintain and reorganize an ongoing business. Accordingly, we consider this issue in depth in chapter twelve.

3. *Wage and Benefit Claims*

The Bankruptcy Code assigns priority status to the claims of the debtor's employees for up to $12,475 in both pay and benefits earned during the 180 days immediately preceding the filing of the petition.[19] § 507(a)(4), (5). Even putting aside the fairly low dollar limitation, query whether these rules are adequate to protect the debtor's employees. Consider the following problem.

Problem 9-2

Diabolical Corp. engaged in unfair and discriminatory labor practices, resulting in the February 1 discharge of Emma, a senior management employee. Emma sued and, on October 31, received a reinstatement order and an award of back pay for the nine months she was out of work. Diabolical filed a bankruptcy petition the next day. How much, if any, of the back pay award qualifies for priority treatment under § 507(a)(4)? In answering this, think about the policies that may underlie § 507(a)(4).

---

[19] This amount is periodically adjusted. § 104.

The priority rule of § 507(a)(4) presents few problems with respect to wages, salary, or commissions.[20] With respect to vacation pay or sick leave pay, however, significant allocation problems can exist. Consider a situation in which the debtor's employees' right to vacation pay vests on a particular date each year, say on August 1. Is the vacation pay "earned" within the meaning of § 507(a)(4) on the date of vesting, or ratably over the year? The answer to this can be significant. If it is all "earned" on August 1, the debtor may be able to time its petition so that none of its employees' vacation pay will be earned within 180 days before the petition is filed and thus none of it will be accorded priority status.

In *In re Northwest Engineering Co.*,[21] Judge Easterbrook faced this issue and ruled that benefits such as vacation pay should be deemed to be "earned" ratably over the year, regardless of when vesting occurs. Vesting is still a necessary condition to having a valid claim – not merely to having priority, but to having a claim allowable under § 502 – but as long as the employees' right to the benefits have vested, they will be deemed to have been earned on a *per diem* basis over the year.

Severance pay apparently requires a different analysis than vacation pay. While wages, salaries, commissions, and even vacation pay are "earned" by the performance of services, severance pay due employees terminated prepetition is "earned" on the date the employee becomes entitled to receive such compensation, which is usually the date of termination, even if the amount of the pay is based on length of service.[22]

---

[20] In contrast, circuit courts were split on whether § 507(a)(5)'s priority for contributions to an employee benefit plan extends to an employer's obligation to pay workers' compensation insurance premiums, until the Supreme Court ruled that it does not. *See Howard Delivery Serv., Inc. v. Zurich Am. Ins. Co.*, 547 U.S. 651 (2006).

[21] 863 F.2d 1313 (7th Cir. 1988).

[22] *See Matson v. Alarcon*, 651 F.3d 404 (4th Cir. 2011). As the bankruptcy court in that case wrote,

> severance pay is not accrued as an alternative form of compensation in any meaningful fashion. If an employee chooses to quit of his or her own volition, he or she would not have "earned" and certainly would not be entitled to any severance pay. Rather, severance pay is "earned" on the day that an employee shows up to work and is terminated by the company without cause.

In re Land Am. Fin. Grp., Inc., 435 B.R. 343, 351 (Bankr. E.D. Va. 2010).

For employees terminated postpetition, most courts regard their claims for severance pay to be an administrative expense in full under § 503(b)(1) if the severance pay is *in lieu of notice*. However, because administrative expense treatment is based on service to the *estate*, not to *the debtor*, they may allocate the claim to pre- and postbankruptcy periods if the severance pay is based on length of employment. *See, e.g., In re Roth Am., Inc.*, 975 F.2d 949 (3d Cir. 1992). Moreover, if the employee is an insider, treatment as an administrative expense may be disallowed under § 503(c)(2).

4. Taxes

One of the most common priority claims is for unpaid taxes. Not all unpaid taxes are granted priority status, however. For the most part, only recent taxes are accorded priority. Read § 507(a)(8). The time limitations on the tax debts that qualify for priority under § 507(a)(8) are intended to impel the IRS to collect quickly. If the IRS allows a debtor's tax liability to languish, the resulting claim will not be a priority.[23] Now apply § 507(a)(8) to the following problem.

Problem 9-3

Duchovney, an individual, filed a Chapter 7 bankruptcy petition on February 12, 2013. At that time, Duchovney owed the IRS $21,000 in federal income taxes: $13,000 for calendar year 2008, $5,000 for 2009, and $3,000 for 2012. To what extent, if any, is Duchovney's tax obligation a priority claim?

Of course, many debtors with tax liability also owe interest and penalties on those tax debts. Prepetition interest on a tax claim is accorded the same priority as the underlying tax obligation.[24] Postpetition interest and penalties are not. They are not accorded priority status and in fact are subordinated to all nonpriority claims. *See* § 726(a)(4), (5).

The discussion so far of the priority accorded to tax claims applies only to *unsecured* tax claims. Secured tax claims are subject to a variety of special rules. *See, e.g.*, §§ 724, 726(a)(4).

---

[23] In connection with this, however, it is important to note that the taxpayer may have been the debtor in a previous bankruptcy case. If so, even though the debtor's unpaid tax liability was not discharged, § 523(a)(1), the automatic stay in that earlier case may have greatly reduced the time available to the IRS to assess and collect the taxes due. Although § 108(c) and the Internal Revenue Code toll some periods, 26 U.S.C. § 6503(h), the time for priority treatment is not one of them. However, the last clause of § 507(a)(8), added by the 2005 Amendments to the Bankruptcy Code, now provides that the clock on priority status is indeed suspended for however much time a prior automatic stay enjoined the IRS from collecting, plus 90 days.

[24] *See, e.g., In re Garcia*, 955 F.2d 16 (5th Cir. 1992).

Problem 9-4

A. In addition to the tax liabilities described in Problem 9-3, Duchovney owes the IRS $2,000 in interest on the 2009 taxes and $1,000 in penalties associated with those taxes. Another $500 in interest has accrued on those taxes postpetition. One month before the petition was filed, the IRS filed a notice of federal tax lien against Duchovney, perfecting the IRS's statutory lien on property Duchovney owns and which is worth $30,000. How will the debt to the IRS be treated in bankruptcy? *See* §§ 545, 547(c)(6), 724(a), 726(a)(4), (5).

B. Down & Out's estate includes a piece of real property worth $10,000 subject to three encumbrances in the following order of priority: (i) a $2,000 first mortgage, (ii) a tax lien securing a debt of $4,000, and (iii) a $3,000 second mortgage. None of the liens is avoidable under either § 544, § 545, § 547, or § 724(a). There are $2,500 in administrative expense claims for which there are no other assets of the estate to pay those claims. If the property is sold for $10,000 free and clear of all liens, how should the proceeds be disbursed? *See* § 724(b).

5. Other Priorities

Two other priorities worthy of note for a typical Chapter 7 case are contained in § 507(a)(7)[25] and (10). The former protects consumers who have paid a deposit in connection with the purchase or lease of goods or the purchase of services, if the seller or service provider seeks bankruptcy protection and never performs. The latter gives priority status to claims against the debtor for personal injury arising from driving while intoxicated, which claims may also be nondischargeable under § 523(a)(9).

Now try this review problem on priorities:

Problem 9-5

Duchovney, from Problems 9-3 and 9-4, filed a Chapter 7 bankruptcy petition on February 12, 2013. The trustee amassed and sold Duchovney's

---

[25] The amount is periodically adjusted under § 104.

nonexempt assets for $29,000, obtained and collected a $6,000 preference judgment, and thus has $35,000 for distribution. The claims filed in the bankruptcy case are for the following obligations:

1. $21,000 in federal income taxes: $13,000 for 2008, $5,000 for 2009, and $3,000 for 2012.
2. $500 for postpetition gas and electricity service at Duchovney's home.
3. $2,000 to Duchovney's lawyer for work performed in preparing the bankruptcy filing.
4. $15,000 to Duchovney's former wife pursuant to their divorce decree.
5. $10,000 in other general unsecured claims.

In addition, the bankruptcy trustee sought permission to pay the following expenses out of the estate:

6. $5,000 to the trustee for administering the assets of the estate.
7. $2,000 to the trustee for legal services in bringing the preference action.
8. $250 for insurance on the nonexempt assets prior to their sale.
9. $500 for the costs associated with selling (including advertising) the nonexempt assets.

Determine how much each creditor will receive from the bankruptcy estate. If there is a priority that is uncertain, determine which parties have the greatest incentive to litigate the issue.

B. DEALING WITH JOINTLY HELD AND COMMUNITY PROPERTY

The way the Bankruptcy Code deals with jointly held property – including property held in common and property held by the entireties – is not particularly complicated. First and foremost, the debtor's undivided interest is initially included in the bankruptcy estate. *See* § 541(a)(1). Second, the debtor may exempt his or her interest *to the extent* that it would be exempt from process under applicable nonbankruptcy law. § 522(b)(3)(A). If the debtor is using state exemptions, this *may* depend on whether there are creditors with claims against both the debtor and the debtor's spouse.[26]

---

[26] *See In re Williams*, 104 F.3d 688 (4th Cir. 1997) (indicating that exemption applies only to creditors of the debtor, not to joint creditors); *see also In re Bunker*, 312 F.3d 145 (4th Cir. 2002) (noting the same for the Virginia exemption for property held by the entireties and ruling that, because there were no joint creditors, such property was wholly exempt even though the spouses filed a joint

However, in some states even such joint creditors may not be able to attach entireties property, and thus the debtor should be able to exempt it.[27]

If some portion of jointly held property remains in the estate, the trustee is empowered to administer it for the benefit of the estate. This means that the trustee will either sever the debtor's interest from that of the nondebtor spouse and liquidate only the debtor's interest, or the trustee will sell the entire property and give the nondebtor spouse one-half the proceeds. *See* § 363(f), (h), (j). Of course, if the two spouses have filed jointly, the trustee would not have to release any of the sale proceeds.

The way the Bankruptcy Code deals with community property, on the other hand, is unfortunately – but necessarily – complicated. For spouses who live in a community property state,[28] community property consists of each spouse's earnings during the marriage, as well as anything acquired with the proceeds of those earnings. The underlying rationale is that each spouse contributes equally to the success of the marriage and thus each should own an equal share of property acquired during the marriage through the efforts of either of them. However, this does not mean that all of the couple's assets are community property. Assets that each spouse owned prior to and brought into the marriage – as well as any gift, bequest, or inheritance that one of them received during the marriage – is not community property; it is instead regarded as the separate property of that spouse. Income generated during the marriage from separate property may also be separate property, although some states treat it as community property. Moreover, the couple may, by agreement, alter these rules and transform separate property into community property or community property into separate property.

In most community property states, creditors can go after community property to satisfy community debts – that is debts incurred by one or both spouses while married – but cannot go after community property to satisfy debts incurred by one of the spouses before marriage. However, the rules on this vary from state to state and that presents a

---

petition).

[27] *See In re Hunter*, 970 F.2d 299 (7th Cir. 1992).

[28] Ten states have community property systems: Alaska, Arizona, California, Idaho, Louisiana, Nevada, New Mexico, Texas, Washington, and Wisconsin. Alaska's system is elective: spouses there may agree to hold their assets as community property. Wisconsin uses the term "marital property," rather than community property, but the concepts are largely the same.

Most common-law property states will recognize and treat as community property any community property owned by a couple that relocates there. Accordingly, the bankruptcy rules on community property are potentially relevant in almost every jurisdiction.

challenge for bankruptcy law in dealing with community property. After all, bankruptcy law is built on the edifice of state property law.

Hence, to deal with community property in bankruptcy, several issues needed to be resolved. They include:

(1) What property is initially included in the estate?
(2) What property may then be exempted?
(3) What property may the trustee administer (to the extent this somehow differs from the resolution of the two previous issues)?
(4) Should community property be distributed differently from other property?
(5) Should community claims be treated differently from other claims?
(6) How will the discharge operate on community claims?

As if this were not enough, the resolution of several of these issues might be affected by whether the spouses file for bankruptcy protection jointly or serially, or whether only one of the spouses files.

The Bankruptcy Code takes two main steps to deal with these questions. First, the property interests of both the debtor and the debtor's spouse in community property are, for the most part, included in the estate. *See* § 541(a)(2). Second, community property is segregated from the rest of the estate and used solely to pay community creditors. *See* § 726(c).

The special distribution rules for community claims are themselves a bit complicated. They involve the creation of four "sub-estates," each of which is available only for specified classes of claims and each of which must be distributed in the proper order. One court explained the rules as follows:

> Sub-estates are created in Section 726(c), consisting only of section 541(a)(2) property (*i.e.*, community property subject to community claims). Community claims – even community claims that would otherwise fit within the rubric of section 507 as priority claims – must look solely to the sub-estates (and distribution scheme) set up by section 726(c). § 726(c)(2). There are four sub-estates set up under section 726(c)(2), but community claims assertable against the non-debtor are restricted to recoveries out of the first and last sub-estates only. The last estate, being residual, might well be empty because the other sub-estates may (and usually will) be exhausted by satisfying other claims.
>
> The first sub-estate pays all community claims – including community claims assertable against the non-debtor spouse. The sub-estate consists only

of Section 541(a)(2) property excluding property that is solely liable for debts of the debtor. § 726(c)(2)(A). The second sub-estate pays only community claims assertable against the debtor, to the extent not already satisfied out of the first sub-estate. The second sub-estate contains the section 541(a)(2) property that was excluded from the first sub-estate, *i.e.*, section 541(a)(2) property that is solely liable for debts of the debtor. § 726(c)(2)(B). If the community claim is assertable against the non-debtor, it does not get to participate in this second tranche of property. The third sub-estate pays community claims assertable against only the debtor (and not the nondebtor spouse), to the extent not already paid from the first two sub-estates. This third sub-estate consists solely of non-community property. § 726(c)(2)(C). Finally, the residual sub-estate permits community claims assertable against the nondebtor spouse to re-enter the distribution, permitting recovery out of the general assets of the estate, if there are any left. Thus, only after exhausting community property in the estate may community claimholders then look to all remaining property of the estate. Community claimholders whose claims are assertable against the non-filing spouse must, after sharing with everyone else from the first sub-estate, then wait patiently on the sidelines while everyone else's claims are paid from the other two sub-estates, hoping that, at the end of the day, there will be something left. Usually there is not. And the community claimholders whose claims are assertable against the non-filing spouse are relegated to this position even if they would be classified as priority under section 507.[29]

The distribution scheme is also depicted in the following chart:

[29] *In re Whitus*, 240 B.R. 705, 709–10 (Bankr. W.D. Tex. 1999) [hyphens added for clarity – eds.].

	Sub-estate	Claims Distributed To
1	Community Property (other than property liable solely for the debts of the debtor)	All community claims
2	Community Property (only that liable solely for the debts of the debtor)	Community claims against the debtor
3	All other property	All claims against the debtor (using normal priority rules)
4	Remaining Property (*i.e.*, sub-estate # 2)	Community claims

Now consider the following scenario, which was something that could have occurred under the old Bankruptcy Act:

> Debtor, who is married and resides in a community property state, files for bankruptcy protection and receives a discharge. Debtor acquires a car after the discharge. The car is community property and not exempt property under applicable state law. A prepetition creditor of Debtor, whose claim *against Debtor* was discharged, then relies on its rights against Debtor's spouse to go after the car. The end result: the discharge is effectively circumvented.

Under the Code, unlike the Act, the discharge bars community creditors with unpaid prepetition claims from going *after community property acquired after the petition.* Such creditors may proceed in the future only against the separate property of the nonbankruptcy spouse. *See* § 524(a)(3), (b). The cumulative effect of the rules in § 541, § 726(c), and § 524(a)(3) is to give the debtor in a community property state a meaningful discharge.

CHAPTER TEN
DISCHARGE AND DISMISSAL

In Chapter 7 cases, the debtor makes all nonexempt assets available for distribution to creditors. In exchange, the debtor is generally entitled to a discharge of personal liability on prepetition debts to the extent they are unpaid in the bankruptcy process. Of course, in a large percentage of consumer bankruptcy cases there are no nonexempt assets for distribution to claimants. Even in these cases, § 727(a) provides the general rule that the court shall grant the debtor a discharge.

The scope of the discharge is broad. For the most part, it covers all prepetition debts, as well as some postpetition obligations treated as prepetition under § 502.[1] § 727(b). It even covers obligations for which the creditor has not filed a proof of claim. This is because a contrary rule would essentially allow creditors to opt in or out of the bankruptcy case, and that option would undermine the bankruptcy process.

As should not be surprising, because bankruptcy is an equitable proceeding, there are numerous exceptions to both the availability and the scope of the discharge. Some debtors are denied a discharge entirely. Read § 727(a). Others, even though granted a discharge, remain obligated on some specified debts; put another way, some prepetition debts are nondischargeable. Read §§ 727(b), 523(a).

A. DENIAL OF DISCHARGE

The grounds for denying a discharge of all of the debtor's debts in a Chapter 7 case are laid out in § 727(a). One of the most important is found in § 727(a)(8). That provision denies a discharge if the debtor has previously received a Chapter 7 or Chapter 11 discharge in a case commenced less than eight years before the petition date in the current case. A similar rule denies a discharge to a debtor who received a discharge in a Chapter 12 or Chapter 13 case commenced less than six years before the current case in certain circumstances. *See* § 727(a)(9). However, if in that earlier Chapter 12 or Chapter 13 case the creditors were paid in full or the debtor used his or her best efforts

---

[1] For example, as we have already seen, if a creditor repays a preference to the bankruptcy trustee, the debt is revived and treated as prepetition. § 502(h). That claim is then subject to the discharge.

and paid the creditors 70% of their claims, this limitation on a new discharge in a subsequent Chapter 7 case does not apply.

The principal rationales for these rules denying a second discharge are: (1) that they prevent the habitual or professional bankrupt, a person who makes it his or her business to run up debt and then take advantage of the Bankruptcy Code; and (2) a slightly more subtle notion that, regardless of any specific fraudulent intent, seeking a frequent discharge is itself a form of misconduct.

These policies are also evident in Chapter 13, which contains similar limitations on the availability of multiple discharges.[2] We will study those limitations in chapter eleven. For now, though, the following chart contains a brief comparison of the different limitations.

<table>
<tr><td colspan="2"></td><td colspan="2">Current Case</td></tr>
<tr><td colspan="2"></td><td>Chapter 7
§ 727(a)(8), (9)</td><td>Chapter 13
§ 1328(f)</td></tr>
<tr><td rowspan="4">Prior Discharge</td><td>Chapter 7</td><td rowspan="2">No new discharge if prior case was commenced within 8 years of new case</td><td rowspan="3">No new discharge if prior case was commenced within 4 years of new case[3]</td></tr>
<tr><td>Chapter 11</td></tr>
<tr><td>Chapter 12</td><td rowspan="2">No new discharge if prior case was commenced within 6 years of new case, unless exception applies</td></tr>
<tr><td>Chapter 13</td><td>No new discharge if prior case was commenced within 2 years of new case[3]</td></tr>
</table>

Perhaps the next most significant basis for denying a discharge is in § 727(a)(1). That provision limits a Chapter 7 discharge to individual debtors. The reason for this is that other entities, such as corporations and partnerships, do not need a discharge following their liquidation. An individual debtor needs a discharge to protect future earnings from prepetition creditors.[4] A liquidated corporation or partnership is little

[2] *See* § 1328(f). There are no similar restrictions on a discharge in Chapter 11 or Chapter 12. *See* §§ 1141, 1228.

[3] Section 1328(f) is ambiguous as to whether the petition in the prior case must have been filed or the prior discharge must have been granted within the applicable time period.

[4] Recall that an individual debtor's postpetition earnings from personal services are not part of the

more than a paper entity. The only reason it would need a discharge is if it somehow retained or received assets after closure of the bankruptcy case, which it should not be doing after a liquidation proceeding if the bankruptcy process works as intended. Such entities can get a discharge in Chapter 11 but they need none in Chapter 7.

The remaining grounds for denying a discharge all involve the debtor's misconduct:

1. making a fraudulent transfer or destroying property	§ 727(a)(2)
2. failing to maintain adequate financial records	§ 727(a)(3)
3. lying to the bankruptcy court or engaging in bribery	§ 727(a)(4)
4. failing to explain any loss of assets	§ 727(a)(5)
5. disobeying an order of the bankruptcy court	§ 727(a)(6)

Although few discharges are denied under these provisions,[5] when a creditor objects to the discharge, it is not uncommon for the creditor to raise several or all of these grounds simultaneously. For example, consider a debtor who, prior to bankruptcy, gave the objecting creditor a signed financial statement listing the debtor's assets. The creditor, before making a loan or otherwise extending credit, verified the existence and value of those assets. Then, in the bankruptcy case, some or all of those assets are not included on the debtor's schedules. This discrepancy may be the result of a fraudulent transfer, § 727(a)(2), or due to the fact that the debtor has concealed assets from the court, § 727(a)(4). Even if neither of these is true, the debtor will need to come forward with some explanation for the discrepancy or face a loss of the discharge under either § 727(a)(3) or (a)(5).

We have already seen that a fraudulent transfer may occur in the context of converting nonexempt assets into exempt assets. Of course, fraudulent transfers are not so limited. They may involve moving assets to places or jurisdictions where creditors cannot readily locate or access them. Alternatively, they may involve putting assets into the name of someone else to hide the identity of the true owner.

Making a false statement to the bankruptcy court can occur during a hearing on a contested matter or at the § 341 meeting. More commonly, it occurs on the debtor's

---

bankruptcy estate in a Chapter 7 proceeding. § 541(a)(6).

5 One reason for this is that debtors who anticipate a problem often file under Chapter 13, where these grounds for denying a discharge do not apply. *Cf.* § 1328. *But cf.* § 1325(a)(3) (requiring that to be confirmed a plan of reorganization must be proposed in good faith).

Although § 727 is not directly applicable in Chapter 11, § 1141(d)(3) denies a discharge to debtors who would be ineligible for a discharge under § 727 if the plan provides for liquidation of the debtor's assets and the debtor will not be engaged in business after confirmation.

schedules of assets and liabilities, which are filed with or shortly after the petition. Courts are fairly lenient about mistakes on the schedules because it is difficult for anyone to make an exhaustive and fully accurate list of all his or her assets, liabilities, and recent transfers. Moreover, the discharge is to be denied only for false statements made "knowingly and fraudulently." § 727(a)(4). Nevertheless, courts will protect the integrity of the process and even a failure to disclose exempt assets can be the basis for denying the discharge.[6] Consider the following cases.

IN RE MITCHELL
102 F. App'x 860 (5th Cir. 2004)

Per Curiam:

The bankruptcy court awarded Appellants James Richard Mitchell and Jackie Anice Mitchell a discharge of their Chapter 7 bankruptcy over the objection of their creditor, Appellee Cadle Company. The district court reversed the bankruptcy court on appeal, because it found that the Mitchells made several false oaths in their bankruptcy petition. We conclude that the Mitchells' bankruptcy petition demonstrates a reckless indifference to the truth sufficient to constitute a false oath. Agreeing with the district court, we affirm its reversal of the bankruptcy court.

* * *

A debtor may be denied discharge if he "knowingly and fraudulently, in or in connection with the case . . . [makes] a false oath or account." § 727(a)(4)(A). The party objecting to discharge must prove by a preponderance of the evidence that (1) the statement was made under oath, (2) the statement was false, (3) the debtor knew the statement was false, (4) the debtor made the statement with fraudulent intent, and (5) the statement related materially to the bankruptcy case.[7]

The Mitchells made the following errors and omissions in their bankruptcy filings: (1) they provided only half a month's income in response to a question that demanded

---

[6] *See Mertz v. Rott*, 955 F.2d 596 (8th Cir. 1992); *In re Song*, 2011 WL 6934462 (9th Cir. BAP 2011). After all, exempt assets begin in the estate and become exempt only through a process that begins with disclosure and provides the trustee and creditors with an opportunity to challenge the claimed exemption.

[7] The statements were made under oath, because they were included in the Mitchells' sworn bankruptcy petition. *See* Rule 1008. Omissions and incorrect valuations qualify as false statements. The complaining party need not prove that the debtor consciously chose to omit or misstate information, only that the debtor knew the truth when the omission or misstatement was made.

a full month's income; (2) they initially listed a life insurance policy as having no cash value and a face value of $15,000, though it actually had a cash value of approximately $3,500 and a face value of $100,000; (3) they omitted multiple payments made to creditors within 90 days of bankruptcy; (4) in their initial filing, they did not list a counterclaim against Cadle as an asset even though they listed Cadle's claim against them as a liability; (5) they failed to list Mr. Mitchell's substantial vintage-car refurbishing tools in their initial schedules, and their final amended schedules did not include all of the tools and undervalued the remainder; and (6) they omitted a set of Wedgewood china. In their amended petition they corrected items (2) and (4).

The bankruptcy court held that the Mitchells did not have fraudulent intent because their mistakes were honestly made, minor in importance, and relatively few in number. We disagree. Fraudulent intent may be proved by showing either actual intent to deceive or a reckless indifference for the truth. *In re Sholdra*, 249 F.3d at 382. We conclude that the Mitchells demonstrated a reckless disregard for the truth, as evidenced by their repeated insistence that their errors were due to carelessness, not bad intent. In *In re Beaubouef*, we discussed the impact of honest mistakes:

> The bankruptcy court correctly noted that a discharge cannot be denied when items are omitted from the schedules by honest mistake. However, the bankruptcy court found that the existence of more than one falsehood, together with [the debtor's] failure to take advantage of the opportunity to clear up all inconsistencies and omissions when he filed his amended schedules, constituted reckless indifference to the truth and, therefore, the requisite intent to deceive. These findings are . . . not clearly erroneous.

966 F.2d at 178. The Mitchells had numerous errors and omissions in their original schedules; they did not amend their schedules to correct several of those errors and omissions; and their only excuse was that they filled out the forms in great haste and did not bother going over forms prepared by their attorney to make sure they were accurate. That is the essence of a reckless disregard for the truth.

We do not agree with the bankruptcy court's holding that the availability of correct information elsewhere in the bankruptcy petition "cured" the Mitchells' undervaluation of their monthly income and the omission of their counterclaim. Debtors have a duty to answer each question truthfully, so a false answer to one question cannot be cured by providing true information in response to another question.

The Mitchells made numerous material false statements in their original and amended bankruptcy petitions. Their careless approach to the completion of their schedules demonstrates a reckless indifference to the truth, and their errors amounted to false oaths. We therefore affirm the district court's reversal of the bankruptcy court's judgment awarding a discharge, and we remand to the district court for further remand to the bankruptcy court with instructions that it enter an order denying discharge.

IN RE BALDRIDGE
256 B.R. 284 (Bankr. E.D. Ark. 2000)

Scott, Bankruptcy Judge.

This cause came before the Court upon the trial of the adversary proceeding objecting to the debtor's discharge pursuant to sections 727(a)(2), (a)(4)(A). Trial was held on September 7, 2000, after which the parties submitted written post trial argument whereupon the matter was under submission.

I. FACTUAL BACKGROUND

Baldridge's Inheritance

Danny Baldridge's father died sometime in the early 1990's and his step mother died several years after that. When the estate was finally settled, it was discovered that Danny Baldridge had somehow obtained more than his fair share of the estate. Accordingly, he was compelled to execute promissory notes to each of his four sisters in the amount of $18,452. When he did not pay on the notes, his sisters instituted a civil action in state court, sometime in 1999. These notes, listed on the schedules, constitute eighty percent of Baldridge's total debt.

Acquisition of Real Property

In September 1998, Baldridge's uncle was undergoing treatment for cancer and thought he was dying. In an effort to help his nephew, he decided to deed some rental property he owned to Baldridge. The uncle established the price of $30,000 for the property, which he believed had a value of $157,000, and executed and delivered a deed in favor of Baldridge who had prepared the deed for his uncle. Baldridge, unable to obtain any credit on his own, obtained the funds through his wife, with his mother-in-law providing the collateral for a loan. The next day, Baldridge approached his uncle with a substitute deed, this one granting the property solely to Kimberly Baldridge, Baldridge's wife. The uncle signed the substitute deed because Baldridge requested it. He had little interest in assisting Kimberly because, "I didn't hardly know Kimberly." As a condition of selling the property, the uncle also requested that Baldridge begin making payments to his sisters on the money he owed them. Baldridge made a couple of $100 payments, then ceased when his wife mortgaged the property and thereby incurred a new monthly household debt. The property was mortgaged in order to pay off Baldridge's substantial federal tax debt. The real property is not listed on the schedules although the debtor lists a $1,548 monthly mortgage payment as a household debt. The debtor also claims to own no real property, but he lists real estate taxes as an expense on his schedules.

Kimberly's Business

Kimberly Baldridge operates a medical care business known as DanAnne, Inc. which employs both Baldridge and Kimberly. Although Baldridge works a substantial number of hours at the business and, in the past, was paid for those hours, he now collects only $50 per week for his employment. This was done, he testified, because he had tax problems. That is, he did not want to pay taxes on the income he earned from his wife's business and therefore took a smaller sum as wages than in the past. Although he is entitled to between $400 and $600 per week for the work he performs, he reports only $50 in income from this work.

Instead of wages, the Baldridges arranged for substitute remuneration to be given to Baldridge. For example, debtor transferred the vehicle titled in his name to his wife's corporation which then purchased a new truck for his use. The business makes all of the loan and insurance payments on the vehicle which Baldridge uses for personal, rather than business, use. In fact, when his wife is required to travel for her business, she uses a car titled in her name and charges the corporation for the mileage.

Neither the sale of debtor's vehicle nor any ownership interest in any vehicle is listed on the schedules. In addition, although the debtor admits that the use of the truck constitutes income, that use is not reported on his federal tax returns.

Bank Accounts

Prior to filing his chapter 7 case, the debtor was either an owner of several bank accounts or authorized to sign on the accounts. Most, but not all, of the accounts were closed prior to the filing of the chapter 13 case because his accountant advised him that the IRS would soon levy on the accounts to collect on his federal tax obligations. Specifically, the debtor admitted to having at least three accounts, two with the Bank of the Ozarks and one at Metropolitan Bank. The accounts were either closed within the year prior to the filing of this case or soon thereafter. Maintenance of his own accounts are unnecessary because Baldridge has full access to his wife's bank accounts. He signs checks on his spouse's accounts as well as on her corporate account. These accounts are not listed on the petition.

II. CONCLUSIONS

A. False Oath: Section 727(a)(4)

Section 727(a)(4) provides the penalty for a debtor who fails to truthfully list all assets and fully answer the questions in the petition under oath. This section ensures that debtors will accurately report their interests in property in order that adequate information is available to anyone interested in the debtor's financial affairs. This serves the policy of permitting parties in interest to rely upon the information in the schedules without examination or investigation. In light of this requirement, the debtor has a "paramount duty" to ensure that the answers are made truthfully and completely. *In re Craig*, 252 B.R. 822, 828–29 (Bankr. S.D. Fla. 2000).

In order to demonstrate discharge should be denied under this paragraph, a plaintiff must prove by a preponderance of the evidence that:

(1) the debtor made a statement under oath;

(2) the statement was false;

(3) the statement related materially to the bankruptcy case;

(4) the debtor knew the statement was false; and

(5) the debtor made the statement with fraudulent intent.

False statements as well as omissions from the schedules may qualify as false oaths if they are made knowingly and with fraudulent intent. Of course, the omissions must relate to a material matter and may be material even if they do not cause financial prejudice. An omission is material if it relates to the discovery of assets. The materiality of an omission is not lessened by the fact that an omitted asset is exempt or otherwise unavailable for distribution to the creditors. * * *

1. Failure to List Bank Accounts on the Schedules. There is no dispute that the debtor failed to list at least three bank accounts on his schedules. Indeed, he freely admits to the existence of those accounts, merely shrugging that he forgot about them. Since one of the accounts at Bank of the Ozarks appears to have been utilized by both he and his wife for many personal and family expenses, this statement is not credible. The queries on the form schedules would have twice prompted Baldridge to recall that he owned or had access to several accounts. Moreover, the fact that he and his wife went through so many financial machinations, including closing accounts by removing his name, to avoid payment of his federal taxes, makes his statement that he didn't think of the accounts a clear falsehood.

Rather than contesting the omissions, Baldridge asserts that since there was little or no value in the accounts at the time they were closed, the omissions were not sufficiently material to permit denial of discharge. This argument ignores the purpose of the statute and improperly diminishes his obligations under the Bankruptcy Code.

The value of property which is not disclosed on the petition, particularly as it relates to bank accounts, may have little relevance to the concept of materiality. Few, if any, assets are more material to a consumer debtor's financial affairs than a bank account, for it is from that kind of asset that the creditors can discern not only an overall picture of the debtor's financial affairs, but also the details of the debtor's finances. Accordingly, the omission of any and all bank accounts to which the debtor had access constituted a false statement that related materially to the case.

2. *Failure to Disclose Transfer of Real Property.* In September 1998, less than one year prior to the filing of the chapter 13 petition, Baldridge acquired title to real property. Since he did not disclose either the acquisition or the subsequent transfer to his wife, he made a false oath within the meaning of section 727(a)(4).

Under Arkansas law, a deed, signed and delivered passes title to the grantee. Delivery, a substantive and specific act, occurs if the grantor intends to deliver title and the grantee evidences an intent to accept the deed. Delivery occurs even if the deed is later returned to the grantor for some other act or alteration to be made.

The uncontroverted testimony of Baldridge, as well as that of his uncle, indicates the uncle's intent to deliver the deed to Baldridge. Baldridge's uncle thought he was dying, and he desired to help his nephew. Accordingly, he directed that a deed be prepared, signed it, and handed it over to Baldridge. Baldridge accepted the deed. Indeed, as his wife testified, "Danny desperately wanted to purchase the property." At that moment, title passed to Baldridge, whether or not Baldridge delivered the agreed consideration, and despite the fact that the deed was returned the next day, unrecorded. Thus, under Arkansas law, in September 1999, Baldridge acquired title to real property with a value of well over $100,000. The next day, he caused the property to be transferred to his wife. Both of these transactions occurred within one year of the filing of the chapter 13 petition. Thus, when he stated on his petition that he had made no transfers of property, that statement, made under oath, was false.

3. *Failure to Disclose Transfer of Vehicle.* In or around December 1998, within one year of the filing of the chapter 13 petition, Baldridge transferred his interest in his 1990 Chevrolet S-10 to his wife's corporation. The corporation then purchased a 1999 Sierra for Baldridge to use as his personal vehicle. Neither the transfer nor the interest in the vehicle is disclosed on the schedules filed in the case. The failure to disclose the transfer of this vehicle on his schedules is an omission constituting a knowingly false statement which is materially related to his bankruptcy case.

4. *Fraudulent Intent.* Not only did the debtor know his statements and omissions were false, as discussed above, he made the false statements with the requisite fraudulent intent. It is well settled that fraudulent intent may be inferred from circumstantial

evidence or from a course of conduct. Moreover, statements made with reckless indifference to the truth are regarded as intentionally false. Baldridge and his wife freely admit to various financial schemes, including fraud on his federal income tax returns and transferring virtually all of his assets to his wife or his wife's corporation to ensure that his creditors not reach his assets.

Second, although specific questions on the bankruptcy schedule forms prompted disclosure of his bank accounts and other assets, he claims to have forgotten each and every bank account he held or had access to within a year. While a debtor may plausibly forget one of many accounts which may have been closed in the year prior to a bankruptcy filing, Baldridge's claim that he forgot that he held any accounts is so clearly false that the Court can infer a fraudulent intent.

In addition to the absurdity of forgetting all bank accounts, there are simply too many omissions of material matters for the Court to accept Baldridge's assertion that they were "inadvertent." Not only does Baldridge fail to disclose his true income, he fails to disclose each and every asset or transfer of asset of any value. Finally, the debtor's demeanor at trial, including the palpable rancor in his voice when discussing his sisters and their attempts to obtain their inheritance, are indicative of the debtor's motives behind secreting his property from the reach of all his creditors, not merely the IRS. While it is true that the immediate threat of seizure of property by the IRS may have been an impetus for some of the transactions, he clearly intended that no creditors, including his sisters, should be able to reach his assets. Therefore, with fraudulent intent, he omitted information that would have revealed his assets and financial transactions.

B. Transfer of Property: Section 727(a)(2)

The Court also finds that the plaintiff sustained her burden with regard to section 727(a)(2)(A). In order to meet this burden, a plaintiff must show by a preponderance of the evidence that:

(1) a transfer or concealment of property occurred;

(2) the property was property of the debtor;

(3) the transfer occurred within one year of the filing of the petition; and

(4) the debtor had, at the time of the transfer, intent to hinder, delay or defraud a creditor.

In addition to the transfers themselves, omitting information from the schedules may be construed as a concealment occurring both before and after the filing of the case for purposes of this section. Moreover, maintaining bank accounts in someone else's name may also constitute a concealment.

The Court has already determined that transfers of property of the debtor occurred within one year before the filing of the petition. The debtor transferred his interest in real property and a vehicle to his wife and his wife's corporation prior to the filing of the bankruptcy case.

Section 727(a)(2) also requires the Court to find an intent to deceive and this element involves a two-part inquiry. First, the debtor's actual intent must be found as a matter of fact from the evidence presented. The second prong of the inquiry involves a determination, as a matter of law, as to whether the demonstrated intent constitutes the intent proscribed by the statute. The question is whether the intent is sufficiently abusive to merit denial of discharge. * * *

In addition to the facts discussed above, in determining whether fraudulent intent existed, the Court has also considered the demeanor and testimony of the debtor which indicated to the Court a lack of truthfulness. While the Court believes the debtor's admissions that he made the transfers with the intent to remove them from the reach of his creditors, the Court further infers from all of the facts and circumstances that he had the requisite fraudulent intent in so doing. The Court does not believe the minimal explanations of neglect, lack of knowledge and mere inadvertence. There are simply too many omissions and transfers of assets to accept these explanations. The failure to come forward with credible explanations for the transactions, the lack of candor with the Court, the transfers to his wife, combined with the fact that the debtor continues to live off the income secreted or derived from the property he transferred to his wife, lead inescapably to the conclusion that Baldridge's transfers were fraudulently intended to shield assets from his creditors, including his sisters. Accordingly, it is hereby ordered that judgment will be entered in favor of the plaintiff and the debtor will be denied his discharge pursuant to § 727(a)(2), (a)(4).

Cases involving inadequate records are fairly rare. When they do arise, they occasionally involve documents that the debtor claims were stored in boxes that have mysteriously vanished. More often, such claims involve the debtor's failure to create records at all. Almost always, this arises in the context of a business. Debtors who had no business and whose income is derived from their personal services rarely lose a discharge under § 727(a)(3).

When a debtor has failed to maintain adequate records, the issue becomes whether that failure is justified. Courts have been somewhat lenient in this regard.[8] The applicable standard was articulated in *Meridian Bank v. Alton*:

> The Bankruptcy Code does not specify what constitutes justification for maintaining inadequate records; instead it requires the trier of fact to make a determination based on all the circumstances of the case. The issue of justification depends largely on what a normal, reasonable person would do under similar circumstances. The inquiry should include the education, experience, and sophistication of the debtor; the volume of the debtor's business; the complexity of the debtor's business; the amount of credit extended to debtor in his business; and any other circumstances that should be considered in the interest of justice.[9]

Of course, even in this setting, judicial tolerance has its limits. One debtor who produced no records of the two businesses he owned and operated, not even the checkbook registers he admittedly possessed, was denied a discharge on summary judgment.[10]

Problem 10-1

Desperate has been in serious financial trouble for several months. Two weeks ago, he sought the advice of a friend who works as a financial consultant. On that friend's advice, Desperate conveyed his only significant asset, a vacation home, to his daughter as a gift. Desperate has now come to you for assistance in obtaining bankruptcy relief.

A. If Desperate files a Chapter 7 bankruptcy petition, will Desperate have difficulty obtaining a discharge? *See* § 727(a)(2).

B. How, if at all, would the answer to Part A change if, before filing the bankruptcy petition, Desperate gets his daughter to transfer the vacation home back?

---

[8] *See, e.g., In re Sendecky*, 283 B.R. 760, 764 (8th Cir. BAP 2002) (debtor who operated concrete business and who had produced income tax returns, deposit account statements, and some credit reports was justified in not maintaining more detailed records because he was poorly educated, had no sophistication, had little business experience, and still lived with his parents).

[9] 958 F.2d 1226, 1231 (3d Cir. 1992).

[10] *In re Strbac*, 235 B.R. 880 (6th Cir. BAP 1999).

Problem 10-2

For the last four years Derek has been employed as a waiter at an upscale restaurant. Much of his income is in the form of tips. He has maintained no written records of his tip income. He and his co-workers have all declared exactly the same amount in tip income – three times their base salary – on their federal income tax returns, knowing that this was substantially less than what they actually received. At the § 341 meeting, Derek acknowledged that he probably earned more tip income than he declared for tax purposes. Should the court deny Derek's discharge under § 727(a)(3)? Why or why not?

Problem 10-3

For the last several years, Darius earned a good living as a stockbroker. Nevertheless, he has run up rather large debts on his credit cards and recently lost his job when the brokerage decided to downsize. In reviewing the debtor's schedules and financial records, including his periodic cash withdrawals from his checking account for the two-year period preceding the bankruptcy petition, the Chapter 7 trustee cannot determine what happened to: (i) a Rolex watch and some diamond cufflinks, which Darius purchased for about $3,000; or (ii) $20,000 in cash. How should the court rule on a § 727(a)(5) complaint if Darius testifies that: (i) the watch and cufflinks were stolen about a year ago, although Darius never reported the theft to the police or filed an insurance claim; and (ii) he lost the cash gambling at casinos in Atlantic City? Does it matter if the court believes the testimony? What questions should the attorney for the trustee ask Darius at the hearing?

B. NONDISCHARGEABLE CLAIMS

For numerous public policy reasons, Congress has chosen to make a growing variety of claims nondischargeable. That is, even if the debtor is granted a discharge, claims of these types will survive the bankruptcy process and the creditor will be able to engage in efforts to collect these claims once the stay is lifted or expires.

That said, it is important to remember one thing: even if a claim is nondischargeable, the claimant is still entitled to share in distributions from the bankruptcy estate. Nothing in § 726 excludes nondischargeable claims from the distribution scheme or subordinates them to dischargeable claims. If this seems counterintuitive, remember that some debtors may have no real prospect of earning money after bankruptcy. Thus, the bankruptcy process may well be the only place where the holder of a nondischargeable claim has any hope of receiving payment. Since the congressional decision to classify a claim as nondischargeable is based on the favored status of the claim, and is intended to enhance the prospect of repayment, such claims should not be and are not excluded from the distribution scheme.

Returning to our visual metaphor, unsecured bankruptcy claimants queue up – in order of their priority – for a distribution from the right-hand spigot of the estate vat. For those few who are paid in full, there is nothing left for them to do or to be concerned about. Most, however, are likely to receive little or nothing from the estate. If the debtor receives a discharge, most of those unpaid claimants are ineligible to go after assets in the debtor's vat. However, the unpaid claimants with nondischargeable claims are permitted to drain nonexempt assets from the debtor's vat (to the extent those assets are not or do not remain subject to liens). There will be no orderly, bankruptcy process for syphoning off such assets; the trustee will not be involved and bankruptcy priorities will be meaningless. Instead, the claimants with nondischargeable claims will be relegated to their nonbankruptcy creditor rights, which benefits them largely on a first-come, first-served basis (subject to rights of creditors with a lien on those assets).

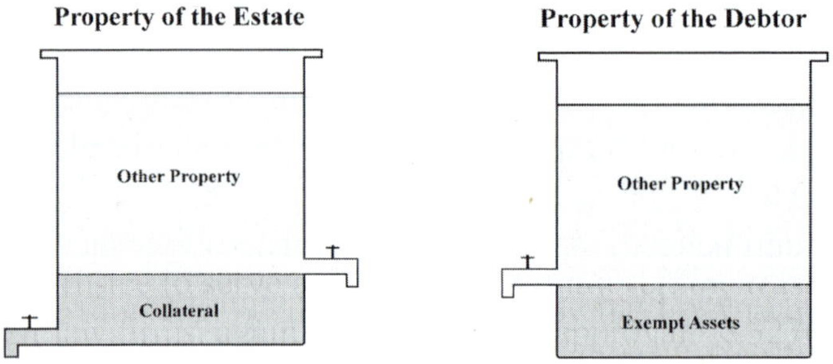

1. *Unscheduled Debts*

From the creditor's perspective, the *quid pro quo* for having the debtor's obligation discharged is being able to participate in the bankruptcy proceeding and being entitled to share in any distributions from the estate. If the debtor fails to list a creditor on the debtor's schedule of debts, the court will not notify the creditor of the bankruptcy filing. If the creditor does not otherwise learn of the bankruptcy, the creditor is denied the right to participate. When this occurs, the creditor's claim is generally excepted from the discharge.[11] § 523(a)(3).

In "no asset" Chapter 7 cases, however, there is an exception to this exception. In a "no asset" case, the failure to list a claim on the schedule of debts is largely immaterial because there would have been no distribution to the creditor anyway. As long as the creditor is still able to challenge the dischargeability of the debt on other grounds, the failure to list the claim caused no injury and should not render the claim nondischargeable.

While this makes perfect sense from a policy standpoint, courts have struggled with the text of the Code to reach this result. The particular controversy has centered on whether the debtor needs to reopen the case and amend the schedules in order to discharge the creditor's claim. Courts disagree.[12]

Problem 10-4

Dependable is contemplating filing for Chapter 7 bankruptcy relief and has brought you a list of creditors, debts, and assets. The list of debts includes $700 remaining due to Employer on a loan made some time ago to enable Dependable to buy needed medication. Dependable does not want Employer to know of the bankruptcy and intends to pay back the debt in full as soon as possible. Thus, Dependable does not want to list the debt to Employer on the schedules. What do you advise? In answering this, consider what might happen if the schedules filed with the bankruptcy court omit the debt to Employer.

2. *Certain Priority Claims*

Review the list of claims treated as priorities in § 507(a). Some of these claims – not all, merely some – are also nondischargeable. It may be surprising that priority status and nondischargeability do not go fully hand-in-hand. If you think about it

---

[11] In short, the *creditor*'s failure to file a proof of claim prevents the creditor from sharing in estate assets but does not affect the discharge. In contrast, the *debtor*'s failure to schedule a debt to a creditor potentially prevents the creditor from sharing in the estate and makes the creditor's claim nondischargeable.

[12] *See Colonial Sur. Co. v. Weizman*, 564 F.3d 526 (1st Cir. 2009) (discussing cases).

though, this makes perfect sense. Priority status is about favored treatment in bankruptcy; specifically, priority claims are the first unsecured claims to be paid out of the bankruptcy estate (after allocating the value of any collateral to the payment of secured claims and removing exemptible property). Nondischargeability provides favored treatment outside of bankruptcy, enabling the creditor to recover from whatever nonexempt assets the debtor is later able to acquire. In general, claims are accorded priority status because of the perceived need of the creditor. In contrast, claims are generally made nondischargeable to prevent the debtor from escaping responsibility for them. There is some overlap between these two concerns, but not much. Thus, for example, employee wages are accorded priority status. They are, however, dischargeable. Conversely, certain tort claims are, as we will see, nondischargeable, even though they are not entitled to any priority.

Three types of claims, though, get both priority treatment and nondischargeability: taxes, obligations incident to divorce, and claims for personal injury or death resulting from the debtor's operation of a vehicle or vessel while intoxicated. Yet, with respect to the first two of these, the symmetry between the scope of the priority rule and the scope of the nondischargeability rule is not exact.

(a) Taxes

In chapter nine we saw the priority accorded to tax claims. Recall that generally there is a three-year look back regarding income taxes: taxes accruing in the three years prior to the bankruptcy filing are generally nondischargeable. *See* § 523(a)(1)(A). However, the nondischargeability of tax debts is a bit broader in two ways. First, it also covers taxes for which the debtor never filed a return or filed a fraudulent return. § 523(a)(1)(B), (C). Second, it covers debts incurred to pay the taxes. *See* § 523(a)(14), (14A). Thus, if a debtor obtains a loan or a cash advance on a credit card and uses the money to pay nondischargeable taxes, the resulting debt to the creditor is also nondischargeable. There is no similar rule for debts incurred to pay other nondischargeable claims.

Applying the rules of § 523(a)(14) and (14A) can be difficult. Consider the following illustration.

> In April, when Taxpayer prepared her income tax return, she calculated that she owed $2,000 in back taxes. To avoid penalties on that liability, Taxpayer got a $2,000 cash advance on her Visa card and used the funds to pay her taxes. This raised the outstanding balance on her Visa card to $3,000.

Over the next several months, Taxpayer charged an additional $4,000 on her Visa card and made $2,500 in payments to the Visa card bank. What portion, if any, of her Visa bill is nondischargeable?

In short, how are payments to be allocated if some portion – but not all – of the debt is nondischargeable under § 523(a)(14) or (14A). The Code gives no guidance on this question.

In general, creditors with nondischargeable claims cannot go after the debtor's exempt assets. In other words, the exemptions apply not only during the bankruptcy process, but after it as well. *See* § 522(c). There are, however, a few exceptions, most notably, for nondischargeable tax debts and nondischargeable support claims. *See* § 522(c)(1). Thus, creditors with these claims may seek recompense from three different spigots in the illustrations below: the right-hand spigot from the estate (queuing up in order of priority) and both spigots on the debtor's vat of assets.

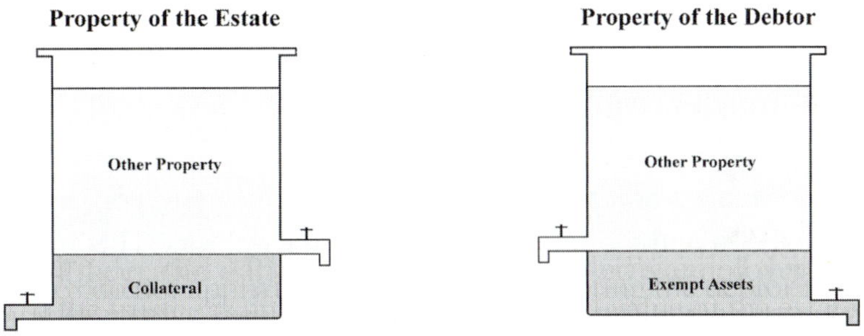

Problem 10-5

Explain the interaction and relationship of §§ 507(a)(8), 522(c), 523(a)(1), 523(a)(7), 724(a), and 726(a)(4) with respect to a claim for a tax penalty secured by a lien on the debtor's assets. In doing so, it may be useful to complete the right-hand column of the following table:

Attribute	Circle Correct Treatment		
Lien	survives		avoided
Priority	priority	normal	subordinated
Dischargeability	nondischargeable		dischargeable
Immune from Exemptions	yes		no

(b) Claims Incident to Divorce

Section 523(a)(5) makes creditor claims for domestic support obligations nondischargeable.[13] Review § 101(14A) and the discussion in chapter nine regarding how to distinguish spousal support from a property settlement obligation. Fortunately, for nondischargeability purposes, this distinction no longer matters in Chapter 7 cases. That is because while § 523(a)(5) is limited to support, § 523(a)(15) also makes nondischargeable property settlement obligations incident to divorce. Property settlement obligations do not, however, receive the other favored treatments the Code bestows on true support claims: priority status, partial immunity from the stay, immunity from exemptions, immunity from preference liability, and protection from certain lien avoidance actions.[14] *See* §§ 362(b)(2)(B), 522(c)(1), 547(c)(7), 522(f)(1)(A).

3. *Misconduct Claims*

(a) Willful and Malicious Injuries

Section 523(a)(6) makes nondischargeable debts for injury to persons or property resulting from the "willful and malicious" conduct of the debtor. This means that the bully who batters a neighbor or the arsonist who burns down a building cannot escape civil liability for those acts in Chapter 7. Perhaps more to the point, an insolvent person who plans to file for bankruptcy in a few days would not be able to do such acts with the intention of evading tort liability for them.

Of course, not all tortious acts involve the same degree of moral culpability that battery and arson do. The Code distinguishes those that give rise to dischargeable claims from those that create nondischargeable ones through use of the terms "willful" and "malicious." Those terms are somewhat vague, however, and the amount of litigation on what they cover is extensive.

One of the first issues to arise in interpreting the "willful and malicious" standard is whether it requires an act done with intent to harm or merely an intentional act that

---

[13] You may remember from chapter five that § 502(b)(5) disallows claims for unmatured support. Thus, only matured claims for support (*i.e.*, due or past due support obligations) get to share in distributions from the estate. However, under § 523(a)(5) all support claims – whether allowable or not – are nondischargeable.

[14] Moreover, only true support obligations are nondischargeable in Chapter 13. *See* § 1328(a)(2).

results in injury.[15] The Supreme Court purported to answer that question in *Kawaauhau v. Geiger* – a medical malpractice case based on negligence – by stating that willfulness requires an intent to injure. In other words, it is the injury – not the act– that must be willful. Most lower courts have interpreted the Court's decision to mean that the willfulness requirement of § 523(a)(6) is satisfied if either the debtor desires the injurious consequences or believes that such consequences are substantially certain to result from the debtor's actions.[16] Note, this is not an objective test. It is not sufficient that the debtor should have known of the likely injurious consequences. Nor, at least in theory, is it sufficient to show that the injurious consequences were substantially certain to occur. The debtor must have subjectively believed that the debtor's volitional act was substantially certain to produce the injury. That said, subjective intent is typically inferred from objective evidence, so that a volitional act that is almost certain to cause harm will often be sufficient to satisfy the willfulness requirement.

Maliciousness has also been the source of some controversy, but the consensus seems to be that it does not require a showing of personal hatred, ill-will, or spite. Instead, an act is malicious if it is "wrongful and without just cause or excuse."[17]

The upshot of all this is that a great deal of conduct is treated as nondischargeable under § 523(a)(6):

- Willful and deliberate copyright infringement[18] or trademark infringement.[19]
- Unauthorized reception and descrambling of cable TV service.[20]
- Illegally recording a conversation.[21]

---

[15] A similar issue arises under § 362(k)(1). See the discussion in chapter seven.

[16] *See In re Thoms*, 505 F. App'x 603 (8th Cir. 2013).

[17] *E.g.*, *Ball v. A.O. Smith Corp.*, 451 F.3d 66, 69 (2d Cir. 2006).

[18] *E.g.*, *In re Albarran*, 347 B.R. 369 (9th Cir. BAP 2006).

[19] *E.g.*, *Partners for Health and Home, L.P. v. Yang*, 488 B.R. 109 (C.D. Cal. 2012).

[20] *In re Feiner*, 254 B.R. 266 (Bankr. D. Kan. 2000); *cf. In re Figler*, 407 B.R. 181 (Bankr. W.D. Pa. 2009) (prepetition judgment for misappropriation of satellite television service not excepted from discharge under § 523(a)(2) but is excepted under § 523(a)(4) as larceny).

[21] *Mazurczyk v. O'Neil*, 268 B.R. 1 (Bankr. D. Mass. 2001).

- Deliberate breach of a covenant not to compete,[22] intentional interference with a business relationship,[23] or misappropriation of trade secrets,[24] but not necessarily every intentional breach of contract.[25]

- Willful inactivity by the executor of an estate – evidenced by a failure for three years to file tax returns on behalf of an estate or to take steps necessary to close the estate.[26]

- Sexual harassment,[27] sexual relations with a patient,[28] or transmission of a sexual disease.[29]

---

[22] *See, e.g.*, *In re Sarff*, 242 B.R. 620 (6th Cir. BAP 2000) (also involving misappropriation of trade secrets and intentional interference with business relations); *In re Duy*, 484 B.R. 742 (Bankr. D. Minn. 2012).

[23] *Piccicuto v. Dwyer*, 39 F.3d 37 (1st Cir. 1994); *Nat'l Sign & Signal v. Livingston*, 422 B.R. 645 (W.D. Mich. 2009).

[24] *In re McCoy*, 189 B.R. 129 (Bankr. N.D. Ohio 1995).

[25] *See Lockerby v. Sierra*, 535 F.3d 1038 (9th Cir. 2008) (intentional breach of contract is not a willful and malicious injury unless it constitutes an independent tort; under Arizona law, an intentional refusal to pay pursuant to settlement agreement was not an independent tort); *In re Williams*, 337 F.3d 504 (5th Cir. 2003) (employer's intentional violation of collective bargaining agreement by hiring nonunion workers did not give rise to a nondischargeable claim because employer was motivated by a desire to compete with other business, not to injure union); *In re Jercich*, 238 F.3d 1202 (9th Cir.) (intentional breach of contract will give rise to nondischargeable claim only if accompanied by tortious conduct, although it is not necessary that the conduct be actionable if no contract existed; breach of duty to pay an employee his wages was nondischargeable), *cert. denied*, 533 U.S. 930 (2001).

[26] *In re DiGiovanni*, 446 B.R. 709 (Bankr. E.D. Pa. 2011).

[27] *E.g.*, *In re Jones*, 300 B.R. 133 (1st Cir. BAP 2003).

[28] *In re Fors*, 259 B.R. 131 (8th Cir. BAP 2001) (debt of chiropractor for harm caused by sexual relations with employee/patient was nondischargeable). *But see In re Strybel*, 105 B.R. 22 (9th Cir. BAP 1989) (holding dischargeable debt of doctor who had housed woman when she feared violence from her husband and had terminated professional relationship before sexual relationship began).

[29] *E.g.*, *In re Moffitt*, 252 B.R. 916 (6th Cir. BAP 2000) (debt to ex-wife for intentional infliction of emotional distress, arising from transmission to her of sexually transmitted disease contracted through extra-marital affairs, was nondischargeable).

- Malicious prosecution,[30] filing a baseless lawsuit,[31] or otherwise engaging in vexatious litigation.[32]

- Even "slovenly living habits" that result in damage to a leased residence.[33]

In contrast, the failure to purchase insurance, even if required by law, may not generate a willful and malicious injury.[34]

Two additional points about § 523(a)(6) are worth noting. First, it does not distinguish between compensatory and punitive damages; both are nondischargeable.[35] Even attorney's fees incurred prepetition in an effort to recover for such injuries may be nondischargeable.[36] Second, claims for injuries or damage attributable to drunk driving, which are typically predicated on negligence, do not meet the "willful and malicious" standard for nondischargeability under § 523(a)(6). Because of that, in 1994 Congress added § 523(a)(9) to the Code. However, § 523(a)(9) makes nondischargeable only claims for personal injury; it does not cover debts for property damage.

---

30 *In re Abbo*, 168 F.3d 930 (6th Cir. 1999).

31 *In re Amaranto*, 252 B.R. 595 (Bankr. D. Conn. 2000); *see also Ball v. A.O. Smith Corp.*, 451 F.3d 66 (2d Cir. 2006) (attorney's debt to opposing party for Rule 11 sanctions was nondischargeable). *But cf. In re Searcy*, 463 B.R. 888 (9th Cir. BAP 2012) (attorney's fee award in favor of prosecutor's office and against inmate for pursuing frivolous claims was a nondischargeable fine or penalty under § 523(a)(7)).

32 *In re Keaty*, 397 F.3d 264 (5th Cir. 2005).

33 *In re Hatton*, 204 B.R. 470 (Bankr. E.D. Va. 1996); *see also In re Sintobin*, 253 B.R. 826 (Bankr. N.D. Ohio 2000) (debt for damage to rented property by the debtors' undisciplined children and the children's friends was nondischargeable). *But cf. In re Hansen*, 473 B.R. 240 (Bankr. E.D. Tenn. 2012) (debt to mortgagee was not a result of willful and malicious injury even though the property lost 80% of its value due to methamphetamine contamination caused by daughter's boyfriend, whom the debtors allowed to live in the basement); *In re McGuckin*, 418 B.R. 251 (Bankr. N.D. Ohio 2009) (judgment debt arising out of debtor's failure for years to clean bathroom or kitchen of leased residence could not be excepted from discharge as a "willful and malicious injury").

34 *See In re Walker*, 48 F.3d 1161 (7th Cir. 1995) (employer's failure to acquire workers' compensation insurance); *In re Shahrokhi*, 266 B.R. 702 (8th Cir. BAP 2001) (failure of taxi owner to purchase auto insurance). However, failure to purchase medical insurance for employees with funds withheld from their paychecks for that purpose does produce a willful and malicious injury, since that is effectively a defalcation. *In re Wright*, 209 B.R. 276 (E.D.N.Y. 1997).

35 *E.g., Jendusa-Nicolai v. Larsen*, 677 F.3d 320, 322 (7th Cir. 2012).

36 *E.g., In re Koch*, 2012 WL 4090179 (D. Minn. 2012).

(b) Fraudulently Incurred Obligations

Debts incurred through fraud or under false pretenses, like those for willful and malicious injury, are nondischargeable. Read § 523(a)(2). The underlying principle is much the same. Debtors who engage in tortious – sometimes even criminal – conduct should not be able to evade civil liability for their conduct through bankruptcy. There may, of course, be some overlap between paragraphs (2) and (6) of § 523(a) – in other words, some fraudulent conduct may cause a willful and malicious injury. Nevertheless, the two provisions have largely different scopes. Paragraph (a)(2) covers bad conduct that occurs in the creation of the debt – procurement of the debt through fraud or false pretenses – whereas paragraph (a)(6) deals with bad conduct that produces an injury for which the debtor is liable.

The first two subparagraphs of § 523(a)(2) cover different types of misrepresentations. Subparagraph (B) deals with written misrepresentations about the "financial condition" of the debtor or an insider of the debtor. Most courts interpret this phrase as covering only statements about the debtor's or insider's *overall* financial health, while others interpret it also to include any statement that conveys significant information about the debtor's or insider's finances.[37] In either case, the creditor must also prove: (i) the misrepresentation was materially false, (ii) the debtor intended to deceive, and (iii) the creditor reasonably relied on the facts misrepresented. Typically, all of this occurs in connection with a loan application. The debtor submits a financial statement with major errors or omissions and the creditor later seeks to have the debt deemed nondischargeable when the debtor defaults and files for bankruptcy protection. The major hurdle for the creditor is often the reasonable reliance requirement. If the creditor neglected to take fairly simple steps to verify the debtor's statements or took but failed to perfect a security interest, the claim will be dischargeable.[38]

Subparagraph (A), in contrast, deals with misrepresentations – whether written or oral – about something other than the financial condition of the debtor or an insider. Most commonly this concerns the intent – or lack of intent – to repay the debt. The

---

[37] *Stelmokas v. Kodzius*, 460 F. App'x 600 (7th Cir. 2012) (identifying both approaches).

[38] *See, e.g., In re Cribbs*, 2006 WL 1875366 (10th Cir. 2006) (bank did not rely on the promissory note that the debtor claimed in his financial statement to own and even, if it had, such reliance would not have been reasonable because the bank never asked to see the note); *In re Flaherty*, 335 B.R. 481 (Bankr. D. Mass. 2005) (bank unreasonably failed to investigate the ownership of the offered collateral – it did not request bills of sale or other documentation).

creditor asserts that the debtor expressly or implicitly misrepresented that the debtor intended to repay the debt.

One significant interpretative problem concerning subparagraph (A) arose from the fact that, whereas subparagraph (B) expressly requires reasonable reliance by the creditor, subparagraph (A) makes no mention of reliance. Courts nevertheless generally impute a reliance requirement into the provision in order to satisfy the element of causation inherent in the phrase "obtained by," and most had required that such reliance be objectively reasonable. However, in *Field v. Mans*,[39] the Supreme Court concluded that *justifiable* reliance, not *reasonable* reliance, was needed. This standard, drawn from the common law, is apparently an easier standard for the creditor to meet. It not only takes into account the creditor's experience and sophistication, but requires no investigation into the facts. All the creditor need do is examine the information and material provided to it.

Even before the Court's decision in *Field v. Mans*, credit card issuers made extensive use of § 523(a)(2)(A) in efforts to have the debts due them declared nondischargeable. Since the decision, they have used the provision even more. They argue, often successfully, that every time the cardholder uses a credit card to purchase goods or services or to obtain a cash advance, the cardholder impliedly represents to the issuer the ability and intent to pay. If facts show that the cardholder did not intend to pay, the debt will be nondischargeable. Consider the following case.

IN RE HASHEMI
104 F.3d 1122 (9th Cir.), *cert. denied*, 520 U.S. 1230 (1997)

Kozinski, Circuit Judge.

Appellant didn't leave home without his American Express cards. In fact, he and his family traveled to Europe in style, and charged it all. On his return, appellant owed American Express more than $60,000, the bulk of which represented charges made during the six-week trip. He promptly filed for bankruptcy, and American Express petitioned to have his debt declared nondischargeable under § 523(a)(2)(A), which precludes discharge of debts obtained through "actual fraud." The bankruptcy court denied appellant's request for a jury trial, ruled the debt nondischargeable and ordered appellant to pay American Express $69,793.67 plus interest. The district court affirmed the bankruptcy court's judgment and Dr. Hashemi appeals again. We must decide whether * * * American Express adduced sufficient proof of "actual fraud." * * *

---

[39] 516 U.S. 59 (1995).

[A]ppellant claims the bankruptcy court erred in finding that he defrauded American Express. Section 523(a)(2)(A) precludes discharge of any debt obtained by "false pretenses, a false representation, or actual fraud." In order to establish a debt's nondischargeability under this section, the creditor must show:

(1) the debtor made . . . representations;
(2) that at the time he knew they were false;
(3) that he made them with the intention and purpose of deceiving the creditor;
(4) that the creditor relied on such representations; [and]
(5) that the creditor sustained the alleged loss and damage as the proximate result of the misrepresentations having been made.

In re Britton, 950 F.2d 602, 604 (9th Cir. 1991). These requirements mirror the elements of common law fraud, and the creditor is required to prove each by a preponderance of the evidence. Appellant contends that American Express failed to establish his intent to defraud, that he made no false representations to American Express, and that if any such representations were made, American Express did not justifiably rely on them.

a. Fraudulent Intent. "[A] court may infer the existence of the debtor's intent not to pay if the facts and circumstances of a particular case present a picture of deceptive conduct by the debtor." *In re Eashai*, 87 F.3d 1082, 1087 (9th Cir. 1996). In *In re Dougherty*, 84 B.R. 653 (9th Cir. BAP 1988), our Bankruptcy Appellate Panel enumerated twelve factors relevant to determining a debtor's intent.[40] These factors are nonexclusive; none is dispositive, nor must a debtor's conduct satisfy a minimum number in order to prove fraudulent intent. So long as, on balance, the evidence supports a finding of fraudulent intent, the creditor has satisfied this element. We adopted *Dougherty*'s twelve-factor test as the law of the circuit in *Eashai*.

Applying the test set out in *Dougherty* and *Eashai*, as did the bankruptcy court, there is ample evidence to support the finding that appellant intended to defraud American Express. Appellant made nearly 170 charges totaling more than $60,000 during a six-week trip with his family to France. These charges exceeded appellant's annual income and, even before the trip, appellant already owed more than $300,000 in

---

[40] The factors are: (1) the length of time between the charges and the bankruptcy filing; (2) whether or not an attorney had been consulted concerning the filing of bankruptcy before the charges were made; (3) the number of charges made; (4) the amount of the charges; (5) the financial condition of the debtor at the time the charges were made; (6) whether the charges were above the credit limit of the account; (7) whether the debtor made multiple charges on the same day; (8) whether or not the debtor was employed; (9) the debtor's prospects for employment; (10) the financial sophistication of the debtor; (11) whether there was a sudden change in the debtor's buying habits; and (12) whether the purchases made were luxuries or necessities.

unsecured credit card debt. Appellant did have one major asset when he made the charges – a one-half ownership interest in an eight-unit condominium project. He claims the purpose of his trip was to borrow money from his mother-in-law to support this real estate venture. This does not explain why appellant stayed in France for six weeks, took his wife and two children with him, took a side-trip to the French Riviera, purchased cosmetics, expensive meals and other luxury items, and ultimately charged almost as much on his credit cards as he claims he planned to borrow. Moreover, while appellant was away, the holder of the second mortgage on his condominium project initiated foreclosure proceedings. This should have alerted appellant that he would not be able to repay his debt by selling his interest in the property. Given these facts, the bankruptcy court could reasonably infer that appellant tried to have a last hurrah at American Express's expense.

b. False Representations. Appellant also complains that he never made any fraudulent misrepresentations to American Express because American Express extended him an unlimited line of credit. We rejected the identical argument in *In re Anastas*, 94 F.3d 1280 (9th Cir. 1996). Each time a "card holder uses his credit card, he makes a representation that he intends to repay the debt. . . . When the card holder uses the card without an intent to repay, he has made a fraudulent representation to the card issuer." *Id.* at 1285. Because the bankruptcy court found that appellant had no intention of repaying his debt, each time he used his cards he made a fraudulent representation to American Express.

c. Justifiable Reliance. "[T]he credit card issuer justifiably relies on a representation of intent to repay as long as the account is not in default and any initial investigations into a credit report do not raise red flags that would make reliance unjustifiable." *Id.* at 1286. At the time appellant began his spending spree, his account was not in default. In fact, he owed American Express only $227. Moreover, appellant himself testified that he had repaid American Express balances of up to $60,000 "numerous times" before. American Express therefore had no reason to question the good faith of appellant's promise to repay. Because American Express provided ample evidence of each element of common law fraud, the bankruptcy court was fully justified in declaring appellant's debt nondischargeable.

Although this decision has proven to be persuasive with some courts, not all courts agree that a cardholder impliedly represents the ability and intent to repay by using a credit card or charge card. Some have followed an "assumption of the risk" theory, by which credit card issuers are deemed to have assumed the risk that the cardholder will use the card until it is revoked. Under this theory, fraud arises only when the cardholder has made charges after receiving notice that the card has been revoked.[41] Issuers governed by the assumption of the risk rule will generally find the obligations due them to be dischargeable.

Even if a court employs the implied representation theory, the credit card issuer may still encounter a problem proving justifiable reliance. For example, *In re Ellingsworth*[42] involved debtors who for years had depended on their credit cards to make ends meet. Based on their credit score, a bank then offered one of them another, pre-approved card with a $4,000 limit. The debtors verified by telephone their income and employment, but the bank sought no information about the value of their assets, the amount of their accumulated liabilities, or their monthly expenses. A full credit report would have listed their obligations in detail and implied their insolvency.

The debtors did not use the card for almost a year. Then, after one of them was demoted at work and they had exhausted their other sources of credit, they used the card until they reached the credit limit. The bulk of such use was to obtain cash advances. Then, without making a single payment on the card, they filed for bankruptcy. Because their monthly expenses left them with only about one half of what they needed to make even the minimum payments on their $70,000 in aggregate credit card debt, the court concluded that the debtors must have known that they could not repay the $4,000 debt on the new card and thus misrepresented their intent to repay. However, the court also concluded that if the debtors had applied to a bank for a $4,000 loan, and had revealed their true financial position on their credit application, the bank could not have justifiably relied on their promise to repay. It then questioned why credit cards should be treated differently and ruled that the bank's reliance was not reasonable.

The *Ellingsworth* decision can be criticized for focusing the justifiable reliance inquiry too much on ability to pay, rather than on intent to pay. One might also question the court's analogy to a request for a loan in which a financial statement is presented. After all, the debtors had provided no such statement and the Supreme Court's decision in *Field v. Mans* strongly suggests that justifiable reliance differs from reasonable reliance in that there is no duty to investigate. Still, the decision reveals the deep disagreement about whether consumers or credit card issuers are more at fault for the abuses of consumer credit.

---

[41] *See In re Morrow*, 488 B.R. 471 (Bankr. N.D. Ga. 2012); *see also In re Kukuk*, 225 B.R. 778 (10th Cir. BAP 1998) (debtor makes representation of intent, but not ability, to repay).

[42] 212 B.R. 326 (W.D. Mo. 1997).

The National Bankruptcy Review Commission described the law governing dischargeability of credit card debt as confusing, problematic, and "fraught with doctrinal difficulty."[43] With increasing frequency, credit card issuers were challenging the dischargeability of the debts due them, even in the absence of actual fraud. Impoverished debtors often lack the resources to litigate the issue. The result was a large group of inconsistent decisions and a great deal of what the Commission regarded as unnecessary litigation.

Congress addressed this issue by adding § 523(a)(2)(C) in 1984 and revising it in 2005. It provides a presumption for the purposes of subparagraph (A) – not subparagraph (B) – that a credit card debt totaling more than $650 for the purchase of luxury goods within the 90 days preceding bankruptcy was obtained under false pretenses, as are cash advances obtained in the 70 days before the petition totaling more than $925.[44]

Problem 10-6

> In the two months preceding Davidson's bankruptcy petition, Davidson obtained $500 in cash advances on a Visa card and $600 on a MasterCard. Davidson, who was unemployed at the time, used the money to buy food and to pay rent. Davidson hoped to land a new job, but so far has yet to obtain one. Are the debts for the cash advances dischargeable?

As noted above, courts widely agree that punitive damages resulting from a willful and malicious injury are covered by § 523(a)(6) and are nondischargeable. In contrast, the language of § 523(a)(2)(A), by making nondischargeable "any debt for money, property, [or] services . . . obtained by false pretenses," arguably does not encompasses punitive damages. Nevertheless, the Supreme Court has ruled that a treble damages award is wholly nondischargeable under § 523(a)(2),[45] and lower courts have interpreted this to mean that § 523(a)(2) covers punitive damages arising from the debtor's fraud, misrepresentation, or false pretenses.[46]

---

[43] NAT'L BANKR. REVIEW COMM'N, BANKRUPTCY: THE NEXT TWENTY YEARS 181 (Oct. 20, 1997).

[44] These amounts are subject to adjustment under § 104.

[45] *Cohen v. de la Cruz*, 523 U.S. 213 (1998).

[46] *See, e.g., In re Smith*, 407 B.R. 442 (6th Cir. 2008).

Another interesting question arises when the debtor and creditor enter into a settlement agreement regarding a tort or contract obligation that would have been nondischargeable under § 523(a)(2), (4), or (6). Is the debtor's obligation under the settlement agreement imbued with the nondischargeable status of the original debt? The Supreme Court ruled in 2003 that even if a settlement agreement released all the tort claims and left the creditor with only a contractual obligation, that obligation could still be nondischargeable:

> We agree with the Court of Appeals . . . that "[t]he settlement agreement and promissory note here, coupled with the broad language of the release, completely addressed and released each and every underlying state law claim." That agreement left only one relevant debt: a debt for money promised in the settlement agreement itself. To recognize that fact, however, does not end our inquiry. We must decide whether that same debt can *also* amount to a debt for *money obtained by fraud*, within the terms of the nondischargeability statute. Given this Court's precedent, we believe that it can.[47]

However, while agreeing that a novation does not necessarily change the character of the debt, the Court remanded for lower court consideration the debtor's argument that the particular settlement agreement not only worked a novation but also included an implicit promise not to challenge the dischargeability of the debt for fraud.

Problem 10-7

When buying a small business two years ago, Despicable gave Bank false and misleading financial statements upon which Bank reasonably relied when deciding to make a loan to Despicable. The parties are preparing now to enter into a settlement agreement that will significantly increase the interest rate on the loan. You represent Bank and are preparing to draft the agreement. You are comforted by the Supreme Court's decision quoted above but you are unsure how broadly lower courts will read and apply that decision. How would you draft the settlement agreement to avoid jeopardizing the nondischargeability of Despicable's obligation?

---

[47] *Archer v. Warner*, 538 U.S. 314, 318–19 (2003).

(c) Embezzlement, Larceny & Fraud in Connection with a Fiduciary Duty

Section 523(a)(4) also makes nondischargeable debts derived from fraud in a fiduciary capacity, embezzlement, and larceny. There is much less litigation under § 523(a)(4) than under § 523(a)(2), in part because courts have been somewhat reluctant to imply fiduciary obligations in normal commercial transactions. However, one U.S. Court of Appeals for the Fourth Circuit case may be a harbinger for increased use of § 523(a)(4). In that case, *In re Ellison*,[48] the debtors owned and managed a corporation that operated a travel agency. The business failed to remit money it had collected from customers to the clearing house established by several airlines for the tickets purchased on those carriers. The debtors were personally liable for this debt under a guaranty agreement. While such liability would not normally give rise to a § 523(a)(4) debt, the court ruled that the confluence of the following four facts resulted in the debtors' obligation to the clearinghouse falling under § 523(a)(4) as a debt for defalcation in a fiduciary capacity:

(1) the guarantees;
(2) the fact that the corporation's debt resulted from its breach of a fiduciary duty to the clearinghouse (pursuant to a written trust agreement);
(3) the fact that such debt was brought about by the debtors' personal conduct; and
(4) the fact that the debtors, as officers and directors of the corporation, breached a fiduciary duty to the corporation.

In a sense, this can be viewed as something like the mathematical concept of transition (if A=B and B=C, then A=C): if A breaches a fiduciary duty to B (the debtors breached a fiduciary duty to the corporation), causing B to breach a fiduciary duty to C (the corporation breached a fiduciary duty to the clearinghouse), then A (the debtors) have breached a fiduciary duty to C (the clearinghouse).

Subsequently, the U.S. Court of Appeals for the Fourth Circuit took *Ellison* a step further. In *In re Strack*,[49] the debtor was the CEO and majority shareholder of a corporation that had borrowed money on a secured basis. The security agreement required the corporation to segregate proceeds of collateral and "hold them in trust" for the secured party, but the debtor failed to comply, an act sometimes referred to as a "sale

---

[48] 296 F.3d 266 (4th Cir. 2002).

[49] 524 F.3d 493 (4th Cir. 2008).

out of trust." Reversing lower court rulings, the Court of Appeals held that the debtor had breached a fiduciary obligation to the secured party, thereby making his obligation on a guaranty nondischargeable under § 523(a)(4) as a defalcation while acting in a fiduciary capacity.

The case is particularly interesting for two reasons. First, most nondischargeability complaints dealing with sales out of trust are brought under § 523(a)(6), but the court expressly declined to reach the issue under that section, choosing instead to base its analysis on § 523(a)(4). Second, the court emphasized the language in the security agreement and the fact that it was the failure to remit the proceeds, not the unauthorized sale of the collateral, that constituted the breach of a fiduciary duty. Accordingly, secured parties may wish to make sure their security agreements have similar language. That said, query whether parties truly can or should be able to make their relationship a "fiduciary" one merely by including "trust" language in the documents for ordinary commercial transactions. Moreover, it is notable that these cases were decided by the U.S. Court of Appeals for the Fourth Circuit, which has interpreted the term "defalcation" in § 523(a)(4) as including even an innocent act by a fiduciary.[50] Although some circuit courts agree, other circuit courts require recklessness or extreme recklessness, at a minimum.[51]

Now it is time to do a major exercise on the scope of the dischargeability rules relating to misconduct. Answer the following problem.

Problem 10-8

Defoe is the sole owner and manager of Downtown Motors, LLC, which is a licensed Ford dealership that sells new Ford trucks and cars. Throughout its many years of operation, Downtown has purchased Ford vehicles with credit provided by Ford Motor Credit Company ("FMCC"), which has had a perfected security interest in all of Downtown's inventory of vehicles. Defoe guaranteed Downtown's debt to FMCC. Pursuant to the security agreement, whenever Downtown sells a Ford vehicle, it must, within seven days, report the sale to FMCC and remit to FMCC the financed portion of the purchase price of the car. In other words, if Downtown purchased a truck with $20,000 in credit from FMCC and later sold the truck for $27,000, it must pay FMCC the $20,000 plus interest within seven days of the sale.

---

[50] *In re Uwimana*, 274 F.3d 806 (4th Cir. 2001).

[51] *See In re Bullock*, 670 F.3d 1160 (11th Cir. 2012) (discussing the split in authority).

Throughout their relationship, FMCC has monitored Downtown's compliance with the security agreement by having its representatives visit the dealership, determine which vehicles are not on the lot, and compare that with its own records of the vehicles for which financing remains outstanding. On a few occasions, the FMCC inspector discovered that Downtown had not timely reported a sale or remitted the sale proceeds, but Downtown always promptly rectified the situation.

About a year ago, Downtown started to experience severe financial problems. Last month, FMCC has discovered that 23 vehicles that it had financed are not on Downtown's lot. When confronted about this, Defoe first claimed that a few vehicles were sold the day before and the remainder were being test driven by prospective purchasers. Later, Defoe admitted that Downtown had sold the vehicles but that, under his direction and in the hope of keeping the business afloat, Downtown used the funds for other purposes: to pay taxes, utilities, and employees.

Last week, Downtown and Defoe both filed for Chapter 7 bankruptcy protection. You are an associate at the law firm that represents FMCC. FMCC plans to file a complaint challenging the dischargeability of Defoe's debt to FMCC under both § 523(a)(4) and (6). After researching the applicable law, prepare a written analysis of the likelihood of success. Assume that Defoe and the bankruptcy court are both located in the district where your law school is located. Assume further that the security agreement between Downtown and FMCC, which Defoe authenticated on behalf of Downtown, provides that "Downtown shall hold all proceeds of vehicle sales in trust for FMCC."

4. *Educational Loans*

Section 523(a)(8), as originally enacted, made educational loan debts to a governmental unit or nonprofit institution of higher learning nondischargeable if it became due less than five years before the petition was filed. Since then, in a series of amendments, Congress has expanded the nondischargeability rule by lengthening and then removing the time restriction, expanding the types of entities to whom the debt may be owed, and by expanding the types of indebtedness covered. As a result, the rule is now quite broad.

For example, most courts regard it as applicable even when the debtor is not the student, but is a relative or friend who borrowed money or guaranteed a debt to help finance the student's education.[52]

Similarly, the provision generally covers former students who, after graduation, consolidate their student loans in order to alter the repayment schedule or get the benefit of a general decline in interest rates. While the proceeds of such a consolidated loan are, technically, not used to pay educational expenses, most courts had little difficulty concluding that the debtor's obligation on such a loan is to be treated under what is now subparagraph (A) in the same manner as the obligations it replaced.[53] Moreover, refinanced student loan debt now generally falls within the scope of subparagraph (B). Borrowing from a relative or employer to repay student loans may, however, produce a different result.[54]

Third, the provision probably now covers extensions of credit in kind. Such credit is fairly common; it arises when a school allows a student to attend without prepaying tuition (*i.e.*, provides instruction for which the student promises to pay later) or provides room, board, or books on credit. Although some courts ruled that such extensions of credit are not "loans" and thus are not covered by what is now subparagraph (A),[55] subparagraph (B), which covers "indebtedness incurred by the taxpayer solely to pay

---

[52] *See, e.g.*, *Pelkowski v. Ohio Student Loan Comm'n*, 990 F.2d 737 (3d Cir. 1993); *see also* § 523(a)(8)(B) (making nondischargeable a "qualified education loan," as defined in 26 U.S.C. § 221(d)(1), which covers debts incurred to finance the education of a spouse or dependent).

While the educational loan debt owed by the parent of the student can be nondischargeable, a parent claim against the student for reimbursement is apparently not covered by § 523(a)(8) and is therefore dischargeable. *See In re Posner*, 434 B.R. 800 (Bankr. E.D. Mich. 2010).

[53] *See, e.g.*, *Sheer v. Educ. Credit Mgmt. Corp.*, 245 B.R. 236 (D. Md. 1999); *In re Flint*, 238 B.R. 676 (E.D. Mich. 1999).

[54] *See, e.g.*, *In re Nies*, 334 B.R. 495 (Bankr. D. Mass. 2005) (loan made by hospital pursuant to its physician recruitment program to enable the debtor to repay student loans was not a consolidated loan and served no educational purpose); 26 U.S.C. § 221(d)(1) (excluding debts owed to a "related" person and loans incurred under any qualified employer plan).

[55] *See, e.g.*, *In re Mehta*, 310 F.3d 308 (3d Cir. 2002) (attending classes is neither an educational benefit overpayment nor a loan, at least if not evidenced by a promissory note, and is not part of a funded program); *In re Renshaw*, 222 F.3d 84 (2d Cir. 2000) (providing tuition, room, and board on credit is not a loan and is not part of a funded "program," but rejecting notion that money need actually change hands). *Cf. McKay v. Ingleson*, 558 F.3d 888 (9th Cir. 2009) (allowing student to attend classes without prepayment was an advance that qualifies as a "loan").

qualified higher education expenses,"[56] apparently brings within the scope of the provision virtually all credit associated with schooling, regardless of whether it was in the form of a loan and regardless of whether it was made, insured, or guaranteed by a governmental unit or nonprofit organization.

Still, § 523(a)(8) does not make all educational loan debt nondischargeable. Nondischargeability is expressly subject to one major limitation: that the debt not impose an "undue hardship" on the debtor and the debtor's dependents. The phrase "undue hardship" is not defined but is explored in the following case.

IN RE GERHARDT
348 F.3d 89 (5th Cir. 2003)

Jones, Circuit Judge:

Over a period of years, Jonathon Gerhardt obtained over $77,000 in government-insured student loans to finance his education at the University of Southern California, the Eastman School of Music, the University of Rochester, and the New England Conservatory of Music. Gerhardt is a professional cellist. He subsequently defaulted on each loan owed to the United States Government.

In 1999, Gerhardt filed for Chapter 7 bankruptcy and thereafter filed an adversary proceeding seeking discharge of his student loans pursuant to § 523(a)(8). The bankruptcy court discharged Gerhardt's student loans as causing undue hardship. On appeal, the district court reversed, holding that it would not be an undue hardship for Gerhardt to repay his student loans. Finding no error, we affirm the district court's judgment.

I. STANDARD OF REVIEW

* * * Generally, a bankruptcy court's findings of fact are reviewed for clear error and conclusions of law are reviewed de novo.

Whether courts review the "undue hardship" determination de novo is a matter of first impression in this circuit. A number of our sister circuits have confronted this precise issue, determining that the dischargeability decision is a question of law subject to de novo review. Similarly, this court has held that determining dischargeability of a debt arising from a willful and malicious injury under § 523(a)(6) is a question of law subject to de novo review. The decision to discharge Gerhardt's debts represents a

---

[56] *See* 26 U.S.C. § 221(d)(1).

conclusion regarding the legal effect of the bankruptcy court's factual findings as to his circumstances. Thus, the district court correctly applied de novo review to the bankruptcy court's dischargeability holding, and this court applies the same standard on appeal.

II. UNDUE HARDSHIP TEST

This circuit has not explicitly articulated the appropriate test with which to evaluate the undue hardship determination. The Second Circuit in *Brunner* crafted the most widely-adopted test. *See In re Cox*, 338 F.3d 1238, 1241 (11th Cir. 2003); *In re Ekenasi*, 325 F.3d 541, 546 (4th Cir. 2003); *Rifino*, 245 F.3d at 1087–88; *Brightful*, 267 F.3d at 327–28; *Roberson*, 999 F.2d at 1135–36. To justify discharging the debtor's student loans, the *Brunner* test requires a three-part showing:

> (1) that the debtor cannot maintain, based on current income and expenses, a "minimal" standard of living for [himself] and [his] dependents if forced to repay the loans; (2) that additional circumstances exist indicating that this state of affairs is likely to persist for a significant portion of the repayment period of the student loans; and (3) that the debtor has made good faith efforts to repay the loans. *Brunner*, 831 F.2d at 396.

Because the Second Circuit presented a workable approach to evaluating the "undue hardship" determination, this court expressly adopts the *Brunner* test for purposes of evaluating a Section 523(a)(8) decision.

A. Minimal Standard of Living

Under the first prong of the *Brunner* test, the bankruptcy court determined that Gerhardt could not maintain a minimal standard of living if forced to repay his student loans. Evidence was produced at trial that Gerhardt earned $1,680.47 per month as the principal cellist for the Louisiana Philharmonic Orchestra ("LPO"), including a small amount of supplemental income earned as a cello teacher for Tulane University. His monthly expenses, which included a health club membership and internet access, averaged $1,829.39. The bankruptcy court's factual findings are not clearly erroneous. Consequently, we agree with the bankruptcy court's conclusion of law, which we review de novo, that flows from these factual findings. Given that Gerhardt's monthly expenses exceed his monthly income, he has no ability at the present time to maintain a minimal standard of living if forced to repay his loans.

B. Persisting State of Affairs

The second prong of the *Brunner* test asks if "additional circumstances exist indicating that this state of affairs is likely to persist [for a significant period of time]." *Brunner*, 831 F.2d at 396. "Additional circumstances" encompass "circumstances that impacted on the debtor's future earning potential but which [were] either not present when the debtor [ ] applied for the loans or [have] since been exacerbated." *In re Roach*, 288 B.R. 437, 445 (Bankr. E.D. La. 2003). This second aspect of the test is meant to be "a demanding requirement." *Brightful*, 267 F.3d at 328. Thus, proving that the debtor is "currently in financial straits" is not enough. *Id.* Instead, the debtor must specifically prove "a total incapacity . . . in the future to pay [his] debts for reasons not within [his] control."[57] *In re Faish*, 72 F.3d 298, 307 (3d Cir. 1995) (quoting *In re Rappaport*, 16 B.R. 615, 617 (Bankr. D.N.J. 1981)).

Under the second prong of the test, the district court correctly concluded that Gerhardt has not established persistent undue hardship entitling him to discharge his student loans. Gerhardt holds a masters degree in music from the New England Conservatory of Music. He is about 43 years old, healthy, well-educated, and has no dependents, yet has repaid only $755 of his over $77,000 debt. During the LPO's off-seasons, Gerhardt has collected unemployment, but he has somehow managed to attend the Colorado Music Festival. Although trial testimony tended to show that Gerhardt would likely not obtain a position at a higher-paying orchestra, he could obtain additional steady employment in a number of different arenas. For instance, he could attempt to teach full-time, obtain night-school teaching jobs, or even work as a music store clerk. Thus, no reasons out of Gerhardt's control exist that perpetuate his inability to repay his student loans.

In addition, nothing in the Bankruptcy Code suggests that a debtor may choose to work only in the field in which he was trained, obtain a low-paying job, and then claim that it would be an undue hardship to repay his student loans. Under the facts presented by Gerhardt, it is difficult to imagine a professional orchestra musician who would not qualify for an undue hardship discharge. Accordingly, Gerhardt "has failed to demonstrate the type of exceptional circumstances that are necessary in order to meet [his] burden under the second prong" of *Brunner*. *Brightful*, 267 F.3d at 330. Finding no error, the judgment of the district court is affirmed.

---

[57] Some examples of "additional circumstances" include "psychiatric problems, lack of usable job skills, and severely limited education." *Roach*, 288 B.R. at 445.

NOTES

1. Although most courts apply the *Brunner* test,[58] a few have adopted a "totality of the circumstances" test.[59] Unlike the *Brunner* test, the totality of the circumstances test considers whether the debtor has made, but does not require the debtor to have made, a good faith effort to repay the educational loans.[60]

2. The *Brunner* test can be difficult to satisfy. This is perhaps best illustrated by *In re Elpel*,[61] a case involving two Gonzaga Law School graduates. The bankruptcy court ruled that the couple's combined $194,000 educational loan indebtedness was a hardship, but not an undue one, even though neither was able to find permanent work as an attorney. Both passed the Washington State bar exam, but after efforts to obtain permanent employment in Washington proved unsuccessful, they moved to Arizona and began work for a title company. Because their combined monthly take-home pay was $3,615 and their monthly living expenses were $2,175, the court concluded they could make monthly payments of $1,413 on their educational loans without incurring an undue burden. The court noted that the debtors had "not yet obtained a middle class lifestyle" and acknowledged the emotional burdens this debt created, but it nevertheless declined to discharge any of their student loan debt.[62]

---

58 As noted in *Gerhardt*, the *Brunner* test has been adopted by the Second, Third, Fourth, Fifth, Seventh, Ninth, and Eleventh Circuits. More recently, it has also been adopted by the Sixth and Tenth Circuits. *See In re Olyer*, 397 F.3d 382 (6th Cir. 2005); *Educ. Credit Mgmt. Corp. v. Polleys*, 356 F.3d 1302, 1309 (10th Cir. 2004).

59 *In re Long*, 322 F.3d 549, 553 (8th Cir. 2003); *In re Kelly*, 312 B.R. 200 (1st Cir. BAP 2004).

60 For certain health education assistance loans, a completely different standard and statute apply. *See* 42 U.S.C. § 292f(g).

61 No. 97-04740-WIR (Bankr. W.D. Wash. Sept. 1, 1998).

62 For a thoughtful and interesting decision going the other way, see *In re Speer*, 272 B.R. 186 (Bankr. W.D. Tex. 2001) (involving a technical school "supposedly" providing instruction in aircraft mechanics and repair that in reality "failed to educate the [debtor] properly, if at all").

Another good example of the difficulty of satisfying the *Brunner* test is illustrated by *In re Olyer*.[63] The debtor in the case was a 48-year-old married pastor with three children. Before founding his church, the debtor earned a master's degree, worked as a salesman and audio engineer, and once owned his own business. More recently, his family's annual income for the preceding two years was less than $10,000, well below poverty level for a family of five. The church congregation provided the family with an apartment and a monthly salary based on contributions that averaged about $1,200. The family had no health insurance and the debtor repeatedly experienced detached retinas as a result of a persistent medical condition. His only debts were $40,000 worth of student loans. Although the bankruptcy court and Bankruptcy Appellate Panel both held that the debtor qualified for a hardship discharge of his student loans, the U.S. Court of Appeals for the Sixth Circuit concluded that the debtor failed to satisfy the second prong of the *Brunner* test and reversed. It ruled that the debtor's "choice to work as a pastor of a small start-up church cannot excuse his failure to supplement his income so that he can meet knowingly and voluntarily incurred financial obligations. By education and experience he qualifies for higher-paying work and is obliged to seek work that would allow debt repayment before he can claim undue hardship."[64]

3. In *In re Roberson*,[65] the U.S. Court of Appeals for the Seventh Circuit affirmed the bankruptcy court's conclusion that the debtor's educational loans were nondischargeable but nevertheless also affirmed its decision to allow the debtor a two-year deferment before he had to start paying the debt. Although there is no clear authority for this, several courts have done it.

A few courts have also held that even if the debtor fails to demonstrate undue hardship, a discharge of a portion of the student loan debt may be in

---

63 397 F.3d 382 (6th Cir. 2005).

64 *Id.* at 386. *But cf. Hedlund v. Educ. Res. Inst., Inc.*, 2013 WL 2232325 (9th Cir. 2013) (bankruptcy court was not clearly erroneous in concluding that debtor who had twice failed the bar examination and had made only minimal voluntary payments on his student loans but had allowed a wage garnishment to remain in place for 16 months had acted in good faith and that his student loans presented an undue hardship).

65 999 F.2d 1132 (7th Cir. 1993).

order under the court's § 105 powers, so that the debtor will be able to pay.[66] The bulk of authority is to the contrary, however. Absent a finding of undue hardship, there can be no discharge of student loans at all. If undue hardship is present, courts may use their § 105 powers to discharge only the portion of the student loan debt posing the hardship.[67] Most courts using this last approach refuse to bifurcate any single loan into dischargeable and nondischargeable portions but will apply the undue hardship analysis to each loan separately and discharge some but not others.

4. Recall the discussion of the Religious Liberty and Charitable Donation Protection Act of 1998 on pages 125–126 of the book. That legislation insulated from avoidance most prepetition contributions to religious organizations. The legislation did not, however, amend § 523(a)(8). Courts have responded to this silence in at least three ways. Some have ruled that a debtor's practice of tithing within the Act's 15% safe harbor is protected activity and thus is not relevant to whether student loan debt creates an undue hardship. Some have ruled that religious contribution are per se non-necessary expenses and thus the contributed amount must be included in the debtor's income when assessing undue hardship. A third line of cases analyzes the issue on a case-by-case basis.[68]

Now that we've covered most of debts that are nondischargeable, try your hand at the following problem.

---

66 *See, e.g.*, *In re Hornsby*, 144 F.3d 433 (6th Cir. 1998).

67 *See, e.g.*, *In re Aldrete*, 412 F.3d 1200, 1207 (10th Cir. 2005); *In re Miller*, 377 F.3d 616, 621–23 (6th Cir. 2004) (interpreting *Hornsby* as requiring undue hardship for whatever portion is discharged); *In re Cox*, 338 F.3d 1238, 1243 (11th Cir. 2003), *cert. denied*, 541 U.S. 991 (2004); *In re Saxman*, 325 F.3d 1168, 1174–75 (9th Cir. 2003).

68 *See In re Larson*, 426 B.R. 782, 790–91 (Bankr. N.D. Ill. 2010) (discussing the three approaches, rejecting the per se approach, and declining to decide which of the other approaches should apply after determining that under either approach the debtors' contribution of less than 5% of their income was "reasonable and necessary to their standard of living"); *see also Educ. Credit Mgmt. Corp. v. Rhodes*, 464 B.R. 918 (W.D. Wash. 2012) (declining to adopt the per se approach but indicating significant hostility toward allowing voluntary contributions while treating the student loan debt as an undue hardship).

Problem 10-9

Destitute, who has consulted with a local attorney about filing for bankruptcy, has the following assets and liabilities:

Assets	**Value**
Car *(subject to lien)*	*$10,000*
Exempt assets (clothes & household goods)	$5,000
Nonexempt Assets (cash & mutual fund account)	$5,000
Total:	**$20,000**

Liabilities	**Amount**
Educational Loans	$20,000
Spousal Support	$20,000
Credit Cards	$10,000
Car Loan (secured)	*$10,000*
Total:	**$60,000**

Although employed, Destitute sees no end in sight to debt and is contemplating filing for Chapter 7 bankruptcy relief. Assume that Destitute has not yet defaulted on any payment obligations and, largely for that reason, still has $20,000 of unused credit on various major credit cards. What prebankruptcy transactions might Destitute engage in to enhance assets or reduce liabilities postbankruptcy? Which of these transactions will have the desired effect? Consider §§ 507(a), 522(c), (g), 523(a), 547(b), (c), and 727(a).

5. *Litigating Nondischargeability Issues*

There are four points to note about how disputes concerning the dischargeability of a specific claim are resolved. First, most nondischargeable claims are automatically excluded from the discharge; the discharge order will simply exclude debts covered under most of the paragraphs of § 523(a) without expressly identifying them. As a result, disputes about whether a specific claim is or is not dischargeable need not be resolved by the bankruptcy court. Certainly, either party may ask the bankruptcy court for a declaratory order on the issue.[69] Rule 4007(a). Indeed, parties may do so at any time during the bankruptcy case and may even petition the court to reopen the case if the issue arises after the case has been closed. Rule 4007(b). However, they also may litigate the issue in a nonbankruptcy forum. Typically this occurs when the creditor pursues the debtor to recover payment after the stay is lifted or expires and the debtor defends on the basis of the discharge. Thus, any state or federal court can resolve disputes about the scope and meaning of many of the nondischargeability provisions. That option is risky for the creditor, however. If the creditor is wrong about the nondischargeability of the debt, any effort to collect it postdischarge will violate the discharge injunction of § 524 and subject the creditor to damages (*i.e.*, the debtor's attorney's fees).

Claims covered by § 523(a)(2), (4), and (6) are treated differently. They will be discharged unless the creditor specifically asks the bankruptcy court to declare them nondischargeable. § 523(c)(1). In other words, the bankruptcy court has exclusive jurisdiction to determine the dischargeability of a claim under these provisions. When the court sends creditors notice of the bankruptcy filing and of the first meeting of creditors, it will also fix a deadline for filing an objection to the discharge under § 727 and for filing complaints to determine the dischargeability of a debt under § 523(c). *See* Rule 2002(f). Normally this deadline is 60 days after the § 341 meeting. *See* Rule 4007(c).

Second, many claims allegedly covered by § 523(a)(2), (4), or (6) – all of which involve debtor misconduct – are based on a prebankruptcy judgment. When that is the case, the creditor will often try to collaterally estop the debtor from challenging the nondischargeability complaint. In other words, if the debtor had previously been held liable for fraud, theft, or the like, the creditor will seek to prevent the debtor from relitigating in the nondischargeability dispute the facts that formed the basis for that conclusion.

Before giving preclusive effect to a prebankruptcy judgment, bankruptcy courts are cautious to make sure that all the elements inherent in the § 523(a)(2), (4), or (6) exception were actually adjudicated. If the elements truly were adjudicated, however,

---

[69] And the creditor may have incentive to do so, because litigating this issue in bankruptcy court may be less expensive than litigating it elsewhere.

and if they were decided under the same or greater burden of proof,[70] collateral estoppel will apply. In this respect, a state court default judgment apparently can qualify as adjudication on the merits, and thus be accorded preclusive effect, if that is how the state would regard it. Similarly, a consent judgment can also be the basis for collateral estoppel.

Third, the losing party in nondischargeability litigation may be liable for attorney's fees. The debtor gets them if the court determines that the creditor's position was not "substantially justified" and the award would not otherwise be unjust. § 523(d). The creditor may be entitled to them by contract, statute, or other rule of law.[71] As one court put it:

> (1) If allegations are tried and adjudicated [in bankruptcy court], for the first time, in a § 523 action, attorneys fees must be awarded if a statute, a contract, or a black letter principle of law . . . so commands. And such fees *might* be awarded if a statute, contract, or black letter principle of law permits, but does not require, such an award.
>
> (2) If the underlying claim was tried and adjudicated before bankruptcy and was found to warrant an award of fees because of statute, contract, or black letter principle of law, then the debtor must ask herself whether what she is going to ask the bankruptcy court to decide (by defending the action) is the same thing that was decided before, albeit under § 523 rather than under non-bankruptcy law. She defends at her own peril because if the court concludes that there is no distinction, she will not be permitted to have foisted on her opponents the cost of demonstrating a second time in a second forum what the substance and nature of the claim and injury actually were.[72]

That said, much may depend on the wording of the agreement. Consider the following:

---

[70] This is now rarely an issue after the Supreme Court's decision in *Grogan v. Garner*, 498 U.S. 279 (1991), which held that a "preponderance of the evidence" standard applies for all discharge exceptions under § 523(a).

[71] *Travelers Cas. & Sur. Co. v. Pac. Gas & Elec. Co.*, 549 U.S. 443 (2007).

[72] *In re Behn*, 245 B.R. 444, 448 (Bankr. W.D.N.Y. 2000) (said in reference to litigation under § 523(a)(2), (4), or (6); it is unclear whether its analysis applies to litigation under other provisions of § 523(a)).

If there is an attorney's fees provision in an agreement between the parties, we look to the language of the agreement to determine whether an award of attorney's fees is warranted in a tort action.

* * * Here, the Agreement allowed attorney's fees to the prevailing party in "any action at law or in equity" if it was "to enforce or to interpret" the terms of the Agreement. * * * [T]he Complaint involved a § 523(a)(2)(A) action for fraud. Redwood's theory was that Debtor misrepresented that he was the sole buyer of the Theater when in fact he intended to transfer an interest to Mr. Knopf. Redwood did not allege any breach of the Agreement or seek to enforce any rights under the Agreement. Redwood also did not allege that the Agreement included any term requiring the identification of any prospective assignee of an interest in the Theater. To the contrary, the Agreement specifically permitted an assignment of Debtor's rights in the Theater. Therefore, in finding no fraud by Debtor, the bankruptcy court was not enforcing or interpreting the terms of the Agreement. Accordingly, * * * Debtor was not entitled to attorney's fees under the Agreement even though he was the prevailing party.[73]

The fourth point about litigating nondischargeability is a tactical one. Should a creditor who has the choice of bringing a complaint under § 523(a) or § 727(a) bring both or only one? How should courts deal with such situations? Consider the following problem.

Problem 10-10

Desperate has been in serious financial condition for several months. During this time, Desperate has been "kiting credit": borrowing from new lenders to pay off existing creditors in order to forestall collection efforts. In one such transaction, Desperate borrowed $25,000 from Savings & Loan after providing the loan officer with a personal financial statement that overstated assets and understated liabilities. More recently, as it became apparent that the whole scheme would come crashing down, Desperate conveyed a valuable painting that had been in the family for generations to Daughter as a gift. A few days later, Desperate filed for bankruptcy relief.

---

[73] *In re Davison*, 289 B.R. 716, 724–25 (9th Cir. BAP 2003).

A If Savings & Loan has an option, would it be better off challenging the discharge under § 727, the dischargeability of its claim under § 523(a), or both?

B. If Savings & Loan and Desperate work out a deal under which Savings & Loan will dismiss its § 727 action and, in exchange, Desperate will consent to a judgment that the debt is nondischargeable, how should the court rule?

C. DISMISSAL FOR ABUSE OR CAUSE

As an alternative or in addition to challenging the discharge or the dischargeability of a debt owed to it, a creditor may seek to have the entire bankruptcy case dismissed. One basis for dismissing the case of an individual consumer is if granting bankruptcy relief would be an abuse of the Chapter 7 process. *See* § 707(b). This includes failure to satisfy the means test, which was covered in chapter two. However, other factors are relevant to whether relief would be an abuse of the Chapter 7 bankruptcy process so as to warrant dismissal of the case. For example, a debtor who misrepresented his or her financial condition,[74] "kited" credit prior to filing,[75] or used nonexempt assets to acquire luxuries shortly before filing for Chapter 7 bankruptcy protection[76] would be abusing the bankruptcy process. Similarly, a debtor who has the ability to pay his or her debts but nevertheless passes the means test under § 707(b)(2) might still be abusing the bankruptcy process.[77] However, if the debtor's income falls below the state median, only the judge or U.S. Trustee may file a motion to dismiss for abuse of this kind. *See* § 707(b)(6), (7).

The bankruptcy court may also dismiss a case for cause. Section 707(a) lists three, nonexclusive examples of cause: (1) unreasonable delay by the debtor that is prejudicial

---

[74] *See, e.g.*, *In re Bryant*, 47 B.R. 21 (Bankr. W.D.N.C. 1984).

[75] *See In re Wilson*, 125 B.R. 742, 745–46 (W.D. Mich. 1990) (debtor made minimal payments on credit cards with advances from other credit cards).

[76] *See, e.g.*, *In re Mitchell*, 357 B.R. 142 (Bankr. C.D. Cal. 2006) (in sixteen months prior to filing, unemployed debtor spent $29,000 on dining out, women's fashions and accessories, electronics, and beauty treatments); *In re Lenartz*, 263 B.R. 331 (Bankr. D. Idaho 2001) (debtors spent a $12,000 tax refund to acquire unnecessary, exempt goods within the month prior to bankruptcy).

[77] *See, e.g.*, *In re Witcher*, 702 F.3d 619 (11th Cir. 2012).

to creditors, (2) nonpayment of the filing fee, and (3) failure to file timely a statement about what the debtor plans to do with property constituting collateral for a debt. Note, these specific examples and the provision generally apply to all types of debtors – individuals and corporations – without regard to how their debts arose.

D. EFFECT OF THE DISCHARGE

Once a debt is discharged, the creditor is permanently enjoined from trying to collect it. § 524(a)(2). A creditor who, with knowledge of this injunction, willfully violates it, will be in civil contempt and sanctioned accordingly.[78] However, most courts have held that there is no private right of action for violations. In other words, the debtor has no claim for damages arising from violations of the discharge injunction.[79]

Despite the injunction on creditor efforts to collect a discharged debt, nothing stops the debtor from voluntarily paying such an obligation. *See* § 524(f). This raises some interesting issues. For example, what if a creditor refuses to do further business with the debtor unless the discharged debt is paid? Does the communication of such a policy constitute an effort to collect the debt and thus violate § 524(a)(2)? Consider the following case.

---

[78] It is unclear whether bankruptcy courts may award punitive damages for a willful violation of the discharge injunction. Some courts have ruled that they cannot because punitive damages can be awarded only for *criminal* contempt, not civil contempt, and bankruptcy courts lack criminal contempt powers. *See, e.g.*, *In re Holley*, 473 B.R. 212 (Bankr. E.D. Mich. 2012), *aff'd*, 2013 WL 791549 (E.D. Mich. 2013). Other courts have ruled to the contrary. *See, e.g.*, *In re Nicholas*, 457 B.R. 202 (Bankr. E.D.N.Y. 2012).

[79] *See, e.g.*, *Walls v. Wells Fargo Bank*, 276 F.3d 502 (9th Cir. 2002); *Cox v. Zale Delaware, Inc.*, 239 F.3d 910 (7th Cir. 2001); *Pertuso v. Ford Motor Credit Co.*, 233 F.3d 417 (6th Cir. 2000) (all ruling that no private cause of action exists for violations of the discharge injunction). *But cf. Bessette v. AVCO Fin. Servs., Inc.*, 230 F.3d 439 (1st Cir. 2000), *cert. denied*, 532 U.S. 1048 (2001) (agreeing that there is no private right of action but noting that the bankruptcy court may use § 105 to enforce the discharge injunction by awarding damages for its violation).

IN RE VOGT
257 B.R. 65 (Bankr. D. Colo. 2000)

Matheson, Bankruptcy Judge.

The Plaintiffs filed this adversary proceeding alleging that the Defendant extracted payment of a debt that had been discharged in the Plaintiffs' earlier bankruptcy proceeding by promising to withdraw or amend a credit report that showed the debt to still be owing. * * *

As is often the case in consumer bankruptcy proceedings, matters that appear on their face to be simple and straightforward turn out to be inordinately complex. Such is the case with the instant proceeding.

* * *

As to the * * * allegations that the acts of the Defendant violated the injunctive provisions of section 524(a)(2) of the Code, the initial question is whether any remedy is available for a violation of those provisions. None is explicitly provided for by the statute.

* * * This factor might not be particularly troublesome, but for the fact that the parallel stay provision of section 362 does contain an explicit remedy for a violation of the 362(a) stay. But, that remedy is limited to cases involving an "individual" debtor who is injured by a willful violation of the stay. [§ 362(k)(1).] Because of this limiting factor, some courts have held that there is no remedy available for a corporate debtor that has suffered injury because of a stay violation. *In re Chateaugay Corp.*, 920 F.2d 183 (2d Cir. 1990). If that case, and others like it, are correct, then it is difficult to extrapolate a remedy for a violation of the statutory stay under section 524.

Notwithstanding the limiting language of section [362(k)(1)], other courts have fashioned an implied remedy under section 105 of the Code. *In re Skinner*, 917 F.2d 444 (10th Cir. 1990); *In re Atlantic Business & Community Corp.*, 901 F.2d 325 (3d Cir. 1990). This Court believes that this is clearly the better view and that the same reasoning applies when section 524(a) has been violated. The Court adopts the reasoning of the court in *Molloy v. Primus Automotive Financial Services*, 247 B.R. 804, 816–20 (C.D. Cal. 2000), finding that section 524 carries with it an "implied private right of action." The question, then, is whether the Plaintiffs have established a claim that may give rise to a remedy.

The allegations of the complaint, supplemented by counsel's representations at the hearing, show that at the time the Plaintiffs filed bankruptcy they had a debt outstanding to Dallas Leasing, aka Illinois Capitol Group ("Dallas"). Dallas was timely scheduled as a creditor and given notice of the bankruptcy proceeding. At some point, believed to be after the filing of the bankruptcy, Dallas assigned its claim to the Defendant.

In the spring of 1999, some five years after filing bankruptcy, the Plaintiffs applied for a home mortgage loan. They were then informed that the Defendant still asserted that the Dallas debt was due and owing and that the same had been assigned to the Defendant for collection. The existence of this outstanding debt disqualified the Plaintiffs from receiving the loan they sought.

The Plaintiffs contacted the Defendant "in an effort to clarify the error" and to explain that the debt had been discharged in the earlier bankruptcy. At that point the Defendant agreed to correct "the erroneous information" only if the Plaintiffs paid the debt in the amount of $2,582. The Plaintiffs paid this amount because they feared they would lose their home loan if they did not do so.

The Plaintiffs ultimately got a home loan. However, they allege "on information and belief" that the Defendant had failed to modify the "negative" credit information even after having been paid the $2,582. The result was that Plaintiffs incurred additional closing costs and fees and had to pay a higher interest rate to obtain their loan.

The Court must initially observe that the Plaintiffs' complaint evidences some misconceptions about the effect of an order of discharge. Section 727 of the Code specifies that a discharge "discharges the debtor from all debts that arose before the date of the order for relief under this chapter, and any liability on a claim that is determined under section 502." Section 524(a), then, specifies the effect on the creditors of the discharge. In particular, section 524(a)(2) provides that a discharge:

> Operates as an injunction against the commencement or continuation of an action, the employment of process, or an act, to collect, recover or offset any such debt as a personal liability of the debtor.

It is apparent from the complaint in this case that the Plaintiffs believe that the effect of the order of discharge is to wipe away the debt. But that clearly is not the case. For example, pursuant to section 524(a)(3), it is clear that a creditor that holds security for the discharged debt can still foreclose on the collateral to collect that debt. And, the debtor's discharge does not affect the ability of a creditor to seek repayment of the debt from a third party surety or guarantor. § 524(e). Thus, the discharge does not wipe away the debt. It only serves to eliminate the debtor's personal responsibility to pay the debt.

The distinction is important, because the initial suggestion here is that the Defendant was somehow in error, or, perhaps, in violation of some provision of the Bankruptcy Code, when it continued to report that, in its records, the Dallas debt was still due and owing, notwithstanding the order of discharge in the Plaintiffs' bankruptcy case. But the Court cannot fault the Defendant for taking this position. At least, it cannot be said that the Defendant's position in this regard, standing alone, was in any way "an act" to effect collection of the debt. Nor can the Defendant be faulted, under section 524, for refusing to correct this report. If there is a violation of section 524(a)(2), that violation must be found in the alleged position taken by the Defendant that the information would be corrected only if the Plaintiffs paid the debt.

There are many cases that consider what constitutes "an act" to force collection of a debt. The efforts of the courts to parse this phrase require the wisdom of Solomon to interpret, or at least the interpretive skill of a Florida ballot counter. It is largely a matter of the court knowing it when it smells it. Some examples may be instructive.

In *In re Olson*, 38 B.R. 515 (Bankr. N.D. Iowa 1984), a doctor's office sent a letter to a debtor. It advised the debtor that, in view of the bankruptcy, the doctor could provide no further medical services unless "you wish to pay your account voluntarily." The doctor was found to have violated section 524(a)(2).

Olson leaves many questions. For example, what would have been the result had the doctor merely written and said "no more medical services will be provided," in response to which the debtor, sorely in need of the doctor's services, then went to the doctor and tendered payment? Clearly, no violation of section 524 would have occurred. Would the result change if, after receiving the letter, the debtor called the doctor to inquire what might be done to enable the debtor to continue to be treated, and the doctor responded, "pay your bill"? In reality, the doctor's actions are equally coercive in each instance. It is hard to see the logic of the court's position.

In *In re Esposito*, 119 B.R. 305 (Bankr. M.D. Fla. 1990), the creditor, much like the doctor in *Olson*, advised the debtor that their previous business relationship could be continued postdischarge, and the creditor would ship new merchandise to the debtor, provided the debtor paid $8,000 on the discharged debt. The debtor paid the money but, despite repeated promises and misrepresentations, no merchandise was ever delivered. The court there found that the action of the creditor was "nothing more than a subterfuge and an underhanded act to collect" and violated section 524.

Esposito poses the same kinds of questions as did *Olson.* The *Esposito* court may well be correct that the creditor engaged in an underhanded subterfuge, and should perhaps be held liable for breach of an agreement to send new merchandise (which gave the court the necessary aroma to discern a violation of section 524). But, what would have been the result had the creditor performed his promise and shipped new merchandise?

In *Van Meter v. American State Bank*, 89 B.R. 32 (W.D. Ark. 1988), a bank required a customer to pay an earlier loan that had been discharged in bankruptcy before the bank would extend new credit to the debtors. The court there found that the loan repayment was not "voluntary" and that the creditor's action violated 524(a)(2).

It is interesting that none of the cases consider the provisions of section 525 of the Code. That section deals with discriminatory acts by a governmental unit. It specifies that a governmental unit may not discriminate against a debtor who has not paid a dischargeable debt by refusing to renew a franchise, charter or permit, or by conditioning such a renewal on payment. Thus, pursuant to 525(a), the government could not, for example, condition the grant of a new agricultural loan on a debtor's repayment of a discharged debt. Similarly, section 525 prohibits a student loan lender from denying new credit to a debtor, or conditioning the extension of new credit on the repayment of a discharged debt.

The provisions of section 525 become meaningless if the courts in the cases discussed above are correct. If section 524(a)(2) bars a lender from conditioning the making of a new student loan on the repayment of a discharged loan, as the court concludes in *Van Meter*, then it adds nothing for Congress to add section 525 to the Code. *See, Brown v. Pennsylvania State Employees Credit Union,* 851 F.2d 81 (3d Cir. 1988) (recogniz[ing] that the Code must be read to give effect to both 524 and 525, and [ruling] that it was not a violation of 524 for a credit union to send a letter to a debtor saying, in effect, "if you pay your debt we will extend continued services").

In all of these cases the courts have split hairs into microscopic fragments. Clearly, section 524(a)(2) is implicated if the creditor, after the debtor's discharge, writes a letter to the debtor saying: "Your discharge be damned – pay your debt!" This is exactly the kind of hectoring, dunning demand that Congress intended to stop. But what of the following:

1. A creditor writes saying: "I won't provide future services unless you pay."
2. The creditor writes saying: "I would be pleased to do business with you in the future, but only if you pay what is owed."
3. The debtor says: "If I pay you my past debt, will you reinstate my credit line?"
4. The debtor says: "I very much want to do business with you again. Is there anything I can do to reinstate our business relationship?" And the lender replies: "Yes. Pay your account in full."

It is difficult to conclude that, in all of these cases, the creditor has crossed over the line.

In the instant case it is the Debtors who approached the creditor. The creditor was under no obligation under the Bankruptcy Code to change the way it reported the status of the loan. False reporting, if not done to extract payment of the debt, is simply not an act proscribed by the Code. There is absolutely no showing in this case that the

Defendant had manufactured a false report in order to extract payment. To the contrary, here, nearly five years had elapsed since the order of discharge had entered and the Defendant had apparently never made an effort to contact the Plaintiffs or to otherwise seek to collect the discharged debt. Under these circumstances, the Court does not consider the demand of the creditor for payment, as a condition to changing its credit report, as "an act" to extract payment.

It appears that the real complaint here is less that the creditor demanded payment, and more with the allegation that the Defendant, having received payment, failed to perform. But that allegation is made "on information and belief." No evidence has been proffered to the Court to show whether the Defendant failed to perform, or whether the credit reporting agencies failed to correct their credit reports.

This case must be contrasted with *Esposito*. There the creditor told the debtor that new merchandise was available and would be released upon payment of the discharged debt. It is not clear from the decision whether the initial contact was made by the debtor or the creditor. After the debtor made the payment he was repeatedly told that merchandise was on its way, and relied on those representations in expending money to start a new business. It is small wonder that the court took exception to the creditor's actions.

This case is simply not the same as any of those discussed. The facts here may present a claim by the Plaintiffs for breach of contract, or perhaps even for fraud, if evidence can be generated to show that the Defendant did indeed take the money and failed to perform. Those are not claims over which this Court has jurisdiction. * * * And, as to the 524 claim set forth in the Second Claim for Relief, the Court concludes that a claim has not been established. Accordingly, the case is dismissed, without prejudice.

Problem 10-11

Before filing for bankruptcy protection, Davis defaulted in paying rent to Landlord on a residential apartment. The trustee, as is typical, did not assume the lease. Thus, the lease was deemed rejected, and the default gave rise to a prepetition claim. No distributions were made to any creditors and Davis never paid the rental arrearages. After the bankruptcy court entered an order granting Davis a discharge, Landlord brought a state-court action to evict Davis. Does that proceeding violate the discharge injunction? Does it matter whether Landlord is also attempting to collect the back rent? Review the material in chapter 5 on rejection of executory contracts and unexpired leases. *See, e.g.*, *In re Stephens,* 53 F. App'x 392 (8th Cir. 2002); *In re Dabrowski*, 257 B.R. 394 (Bankr. S.D.N.Y. 2001).

As the court explained in *Vogt*, bankruptcy discharge operates on the debtor's personal liability; it does not eliminate the debt itself. Thus, for example, a guarantor will remain liable despite the debtor's discharge and, absent lien avoidance, any collateral will retain *in rem* liability. Much the same principle applies to the terms of contracts that the debtor entered into prepetition. The debtor will have no remaining payment obligation but the contract itself survives. This can be important if other aspects of the contract fall into dispute.

For example, if a mortgage loan contract provides for arbitration, and the debtor wishes to bring a claim against the lender postdischarge, the arbitration provision remains enforceable. The debtor's agreement to arbitrate has not been discharged.[80] Similarly, a clause in a prepetition contract entitling a lender to attorney's fees can be enforced with respect to the fees arising during postdischarge litigation; the attorney's fees provision "may have fallen dormant, but it was reviviscible."[81]

Because liens are generally not affected by the discharge, the creditor retains the right to enforce the lien but not the right to pursue the debtor for a deficiency or any other portion of the discharged obligation. This dichotomy is easy to state but occasionally difficult to apply. For example, in one case the creditor got into trouble after it continued to pursue a detinue action – an action to recover for the wrongful taking of personal property – after the debtor received a Chapter 7 discharge. The court ruled that the creditor did not violate the discharge injunction by bringing the detinue action or even by seeking a contempt citation for the debtor's failure to comply with a court order to turn over the collateral, but that it did violate the discharge injunction by accepting payments to allow the debtor to avoid contempt after learning that the debtor no longer had the collateral.[82]

---

80 *Green Tree Servicing, LLC v. Brough*, 930 N.E.2d 1238 (Ind. Ct. App. 2010); *In re Wells Fargo Bank*, 300 S.W.3d 818 (Tex. Ct. App. 2009).

81 *Siegel v. Fed. Home Loan Mortg. Corp.*, 143 F.3d 525, 531 (9th Cir. 1998).

82 *In re Butler*, 2011 WL 806078 (Bankr. C.D. Ill. 2011).

E. TAX IMPLICATIONS OF THE DISCHARGE

In general, a discharge of indebtedness creates taxable income to the debtor. 26 U.S.C. § 61(a)(12). Although this may not intuitively seem correct, it really does makes sense. Consider a borrower who borrows $100 from a friend. This transaction does not have tax consequences. While the borrower now has $100 in cash that the borrower did not have before, the borrower also has an obligation to repay an equal amount. Taking the loan and the obligation to repay it together, there has been no change to the net worth of the borrower (or of the lender). If the lender forgives the debt, however, the borrower's net worth will change. In essence, the borrower would have received cash and have no duty to repay it. That change is treated as gross income.

If this general rule were applied in bankruptcy cases, the debtor who is struggling to overcome crippling financial problems would potentially be burdened with a large tax liability by virtue of the bankruptcy discharge. To avoid this, the Internal Revenue Code excludes from gross income any discharge of indebtedness that occurs in a case under Title 11. 26 U.S.C. § 108(a)(1)(A). It also excludes from gross income a discharge of indebtedness that occurs outside of bankruptcy when the debtor/taxpayer is insolvent. 26 U.S.C. § 108(a)(1)(B).

This exclusion is not an unqualified boon for bankruptcy debtors, however. To the extent discharge of indebtedness income is excluded from gross income under this rule, the debtor's "tax attributes" are reduced. 26 U.S.C. § 108(b). This means that if the debtor has a net operating loss, that loss – which can be used to offset future income for tax purposes – will be reduced. If the debtor has no net operating loss, the debtor's basis in property can be reduced, creating a larger taxable gain if it is ever sold. *See* 26 U.S.C. § 108(b)(2).

F. BANKRUPTCY CRIMES

A variety of conduct that might lead to a denial of discharge under § 727 is also criminal. For example, a debtor who conceals assets or knowingly files false schedules can be fined and imprisoned for up to five years. 18 U.S.C. § 152. A creditor who files a fraudulent claim or a trustee who embezzles from the estate is also guilty of a crime and is subject to the same penalty. 18 U.S.C. §§ 152, 153.

In 1994, Congress created the new crime of "bankruptcy fraud." It covers any person who, as part of a scheme to defraud, files a bankruptcy petition or files a document in a bankruptcy proceeding. 18 U.S.C. § 157. This crime too is punishable by up to five years in prison.

The definition of bankruptcy fraud is extremely broad. It may cover the "credit card spree" case, in which a debtor enjoys a luxurious vacation, made possible by charging as much as possible on credit cards, with the intention of filing bankruptcy upon returning home. It remains to be seen whether this provision will be interpreted so expansively and invoked as frequently as this type of abuse occurs. At present, bankruptcy lawyers should advise clients to be very cautious, particularly during that period between the time they decide to file for bankruptcy and the time they actually do.

PART IV

REORGANIZATION

CHAPTER ELEVEN
INDIVIDUAL DEBT ADJUSTMENT IN CHAPTER 13

A. IN GENERAL

In Chapter 7 liquidations, the debtor's assets and liabilities are essentially frozen as of the moment of the bankruptcy filing. The case then generally proceeds as follows. The debtor's assets – to the extent not exempt – go into the bankruptcy estate. The debtor keeps the exempt assets while the trustee liquidates the nonexempt assets of the estate and distributes the proceeds to prepetition creditors. The debtor is then relieved of the duty to pay most prepetition debts and all of the debtor's subsequent earnings are free from the reach of creditors to collect on discharged claims. Property subject to a valid security interest is either relinquished to the creditor or a mutually acceptable payment schedule is worked out.

There are several drawbacks to this procedure. The most notable from the debtor's standpoint is that, if the debtor has equity in a home in excess of the exemption amount, the debtor will likely lose the home. The main problem from the creditors' standpoint is that many of them receive little or no payment of their claims, even from debtors with the potential to earn substantial income.

Chapter 13 is intended to address these drawbacks. It focuses largely on future income rather than on accumulated assets. In essence, the debtor agrees to turn over a portion of future income to pay prepetition claims. In exchange, the debtor will keep most assets, regardless of whether their value exceeds any exemption amount to which the debtor is entitled. In short, the debtor generally keeps all prepetition assets – both exempt and nonexempt – and pays creditors out of future income. Payments are actually made periodically to a trustee, who applies them first to administrative expenses and then distributes the remainder to creditors pursuant to a court-approved plan. When the debtor has fully complied with the plan – that is, when the debtor has made all required payments – the debtor's prepetition obligations are discharged to the extent they remain unpaid.

Thus, many debtors facing bankruptcy must make a fundamental choice: to give up nonexempt assets and seek an immediate discharge under Chapter 7 or to try paying creditors over time under Chapter 13. Several rules and incentives in the Bankruptcy Code have great impact on this choice. Among them are:

dismissed outright or converted to Chapter 7.[3] Consider the following excerpt from the report of the National Bankruptcy Review Commission.

> While the concept of a repayment plan is valuable . . . [t]he high non-completion rate of Chapter 13 plans is cause for substantial concern. For more than a decade, two-thirds of all Chapter 13 plans have failed before the debtor completes payments, and sometimes before unsecured creditors have received anything at all. While some of the debtors convert to Chapter 7 when plan payments become infeasible, about half of all debtors who initially file for Chapter 13 are dismissed with no resolution of their financial problems and no discharge.
>
> Noncompletion may have a number of causes. Some commentators suggest that debtors frequently encounter repeated financial difficulties or face new crises, such as the loss of a job or a health emergency. Bankruptcy does not insulate against subsequent disaster. The same kinds of spotty employment or medical problems that caused debtors' initial financial problems may reemerge, or new problems might appear. Subsequent difficulties, coupled with the higher "catch-up" payments on secured debt, can foil well-intentioned repayment efforts. Others suggest that debtors propose unrealistic plans that are doomed from the inception, sometimes due in part to inadequate advice. In an effort to meet the requirements of the Bankruptcy Code in the treatment of certain creditors or to meet the informal payment requirements of some judges or trustees, debtors may commit to payment plans that would consume or exceed every dollar of discretionary income, and make optimistic assumptions about their income, expected over-time pay, and so on, but do not

---

[3] One study of all Chapter 13 cases closed within a six-month period in one federal district indicated that in only 32.4% of cases did the debtor complete the plan and receive a discharge. *See* Ed Flynn, *A Small New Window on Outcomes in Chapter 13*, AM. BANKR. INST. J., Mar. 2000, at 22 (summarizing Scott F. Norberg, *Consumer Bankruptcy's New Clothes: An Empirical Study of Discharge and Debt Collection in Chapter 13*, 7 ABI L. REV. 415 (1999)). In 49.3% of cases, the case was dismissed after confirmation of a plan; the remaining 18.3% were dismissed before a plan was confirmed. Interestingly, there was no statistically significant relationship between completion of the plan and debtor income, percentage payback, or plan duration. However, debtors with higher secured debt were more likely to complete their plan, as were debtors who had filed an earlier Chapter 13 petition.

Another study indicated that 60% of Chapter 13 cases are dismissed and another 12% are converted to Chapter 7. *See* Lars Lefgren & Frank L. McIntyre, *Explaining the Puzzle of Cross-state Differences in Bankruptcy Rates*, 52 J.L. & ECON. 367, 371 (2009).

CHAPTER ELEVEN
INDIVIDUAL DEBT ADJUSTMENT IN CHAPTER 13

A. IN GENERAL

In Chapter 7 liquidations, the debtor's assets and liabilities are essentially frozen as of the moment of the bankruptcy filing. The case then generally proceeds as follows. The debtor's assets – to the extent not exempt – go into the bankruptcy estate. The debtor keeps the exempt assets while the trustee liquidates the nonexempt assets of the estate and distributes the proceeds to prepetition creditors. The debtor is then relieved of the duty to pay most prepetition debts and all of the debtor's subsequent earnings are free from the reach of creditors to collect on discharged claims. Property subject to a valid security interest is either relinquished to the creditor or a mutually acceptable payment schedule is worked out.

There are several drawbacks to this procedure. The most notable from the debtor's standpoint is that, if the debtor has equity in a home in excess of the exemption amount, the debtor will likely lose the home. The main problem from the creditors' standpoint is that many of them receive little or no payment of their claims, even from debtors with the potential to earn substantial income.

Chapter 13 is intended to address these drawbacks. It focuses largely on future income rather than on accumulated assets. In essence, the debtor agrees to turn over a portion of future income to pay prepetition claims. In exchange, the debtor will keep most assets, regardless of whether their value exceeds any exemption amount to which the debtor is entitled. In short, the debtor generally keeps all prepetition assets – both exempt and nonexempt – and pays creditors out of future income. Payments are actually made periodically to a trustee, who applies them first to administrative expenses and then distributes the remainder to creditors pursuant to a court-approved plan. When the debtor has fully complied with the plan – that is, when the debtor has made all required payments – the debtor's prepetition obligations are discharged to the extent they remain unpaid.

Thus, many debtors facing bankruptcy must make a fundamental choice: to give up nonexempt assets and seek an immediate discharge under Chapter 7 or to try paying creditors over time under Chapter 13. Several rules and incentives in the Bankruptcy Code have great impact on this choice. Among them are:

Incentives Against Chapter 13

1. Only individual debtors (*i.e.*, human beings) with a regular source of income and fairly modest levels of debt are eligible for Chapter 13. § 109(e).

2. The Chapter 13 plan must provide for creditors to be paid at least what they would receive in Chapter 7, § 1325(a)(4), and must provide for the payments to be made within five years, and often within three, § 1322(d).

3. The plan must provide for full payment of all priority claims, unless the holder agrees to something less. § 1322(a)(2). This can be particularly problematic (*i.e.*, make it impossible to draft a confirmable plan) if the debtor owes a large amount for priority taxes, support arrearages, or for a personal injury resulting from drunk driving.

4. If all creditors are not to be paid in full, the debtor must for at least three years, and possibly for as long as five, turn over all "disposable income" (*i.e.*, income over reasonable and necessary living expenses) to the trustee for payment to creditors. § 1325(b).

5. The administrative expenses generated by a Chapter 13 case – comprised largely of the trustee's fees – must be paid first, *see* § 1322(a)(2), and can substantially increase the cost of completing a Chapter 13 plan.

Incentives Against Chapter 7

1. Debtors with high income may fail the means test, thus making it likely that a Chapter 7 petition would be dismissed as an abuse of the bankruptcy process. § 707(b).

2. Debtors who received a bankruptcy discharge in the last several years and thus are ineligible for a Chapter 7 discharge, § 727(a)(9), may be able to get a new discharge in Chapter 13. § 1328(f).

3. Debtors receive a sightly broader discharge in Chapter 13 than in Chapter 7 (in other words, some debts that are nondischargeable in Chapter 7 can be discharged in Chapter 13). § 1328(a).

4. Because civil fines are dischargeable in a Chapter 13, a Chapter 13 debtor whose driver's license has been suspended *solely* for failure to pay traffic tickets is entitled to have the license restored. § 525(a).

5. Debtors in Chapter 13 can cure defaults on secured obligations, "de-accelerate" the debts, and strip down some secured claims (except most home mortgages and purchase-money loans). § 1322(b)(2), (b)(5), (c).

Whether a Chapter 7 or a Chapter 13 is the right choice for an individual debtor requires a full analysis of both the debtor's financial circumstances and the application of the Code to those circumstances.

The trouble with Chapter 13 is that it does not address the sources of the debtor's financial problems. Put another way, both Chapters 7 and 13 treat the debtor's accumulated debt *as* the problem. This works fairly well in Chapter 7 because bankruptcy freezes everything as of the petition date and does not try to deal directly with the debtor's financial future. Chapter 13, on the other hand, is a lengthy process that seeks to "rehabilitate" the debtor by putting the debtor on a tight budget requiring regular payments to creditors for several years.[1] However, Chapter 13 does little to deal with or even identify whatever created the debtor's financial distress, although a Chapter 13 discharge is conditioned on the debtor's completion of a course on personal financial management.[2] § 1328(g). This may help debtors whose problems are in fact attributable to poor financial management but is unlikely to assist those whose financial distress arose from a job loss, divorce, medical condition, or other event beyond their control. Moreover, by providing for all disposable income to be paid to creditors for the next several years, Chapter 13 presumes that the causes of the debtor's financial distress will not continue or recur. As a result of these often erroneous assumptions, Chapter 13 does not typically result in success, at least if success is measured by the completion of a plan and the granting of a discharge. In fact, most Chapter 13 debtors fail to make all of the scheduled payments and never get a discharge in Chapter 13; their cases are either

---

[1] Note, however, that because of differing priorities and other reasons, the plan may provide for paying some creditors before others.

[2] This is to be distinguished from and is apparently more significant than the credit counseling that is an eligibility requirement for bankruptcy relief. *See* § 109(h).

dismissed outright or converted to Chapter 7.[3] Consider the following excerpt from the report of the National Bankruptcy Review Commission.

> While the concept of a repayment plan is valuable . . . [t]he high non-completion rate of Chapter 13 plans is cause for substantial concern. For more than a decade, two-thirds of all Chapter 13 plans have failed before the debtor completes payments, and sometimes before unsecured creditors have received anything at all. While some of the debtors convert to Chapter 7 when plan payments become infeasible, about half of all debtors who initially file for Chapter 13 are dismissed with no resolution of their financial problems and no discharge.
>
> Noncompletion may have a number of causes. Some commentators suggest that debtors frequently encounter repeated financial difficulties or face new crises, such as the loss of a job or a health emergency. Bankruptcy does not insulate against subsequent disaster. The same kinds of spotty employment or medical problems that caused debtors' initial financial problems may reemerge, or new problems might appear. Subsequent difficulties, coupled with the higher "catch-up" payments on secured debt, can foil well-intentioned repayment efforts. Others suggest that debtors propose unrealistic plans that are doomed from the inception, sometimes due in part to inadequate advice. In an effort to meet the requirements of the Bankruptcy Code in the treatment of certain creditors or to meet the informal payment requirements of some judges or trustees, debtors may commit to payment plans that would consume or exceed every dollar of discretionary income, and make optimistic assumptions about their income, expected over-time pay, and so on, but do not

---

[3] One study of all Chapter 13 cases closed within a six-month period in one federal district indicated that in only 32.4% of cases did the debtor complete the plan and receive a discharge. *See* Ed Flynn, *A Small New Window on Outcomes in Chapter 13*, AM. BANKR. INST. J., Mar. 2000, at 22 (summarizing Scott F. Norberg, *Consumer Bankruptcy's New Clothes: An Empirical Study of Discharge and Debt Collection in Chapter 13*, 7 ABI L. REV. 415 (1999)). In 49.3% of cases, the case was dismissed after confirmation of a plan; the remaining 18.3% were dismissed before a plan was confirmed. Interestingly, there was no statistically significant relationship between completion of the plan and debtor income, percentage payback, or plan duration. However, debtors with higher secured debt were more likely to complete their plan, as were debtors who had filed an earlier Chapter 13 petition.

Another study indicated that 60% of Chapter 13 cases are dismissed and another 12% are converted to Chapter 7. *See* Lars Lefgren & Frank L. McIntyre, *Explaining the Puzzle of Cross-state Differences in Bankruptcy Rates*, 52 J.L. & ECON. 367, 371 (2009).

E. Dubois pledged some corporate stock worth $200,000 as security for a loan to Child. Dubois has no personal liability on the loan. *See In re Glance*, 487 F.3d 317 (6th Cir. 2007).

F. Darren owes $40,000 to Bank for student loans. Darren has $15,000 on deposit at Bank in a checking account. *See* § 506(a).

G. Delilah hit Pedestrian with her car. Pedestrian has a pending lawsuit against Delilah for $10,000 in medical expenses incurred and $200,000 in pain and suffering. Delilah denies liability and claims the amount sought for pain and suffering is grossly excessive. The case is in the discovery phase. *Cf. In re Mazzeo*, 131 F.3d 295 (2d Cir. 1997); *In re Verdunn*, 89 F.3d 799 (11th Cir. 1996); *In re Knight*, 55 F.3d 231 (7th Cir. 1995).

2. *The Mechanics of Chapter 13*

As is true for proceedings under other Chapters, a Chapter 13 debtor must file with the bankruptcy petition or shortly thereafter a variety of schedules giving information about the debtor's employment, income, expenses, debts, and property, as well as estimates of future monthly income and expenses. Rule 1007(c). The debtor must file a plan with the petition or within 14 days thereafter unless an extension is granted. Rule 3015(b). Some districts use a standardized, model plan that the debtor or the debtor's attorney simply fills in.[7]

The debtor must begin making payments to the trustee within 30 days after the plan is filed, even if the plan is not yet confirmed. § 1326(a)(1). Any payment received by the trustee before confirmation is to be held by the trustee until the plan is either confirmed or not confirmed. If the plan is not confirmed, the trustee gives the money back to the debtor. If the plan is confirmed, the trustee distributes the money pursuant to the plan. § 1326(a)(2).

A Chapter 13 trustee does not have the same duties as a Chapter 7 trustee. A Chapter 13 trustee does not, for example, collect, preserve, or sell property of the estate. § 1302(b)(1). Nonetheless, the Chapter 13 trustee does have important functions, including objecting to improper creditor claims and, when appropriate, objecting to the debtor's discharge. § 1302(b)(1). The trustee's main duties, though, relate to the plan.

---

[7] The latest version of the Chapter 13 Plan Form for the Western District of Washington can be obtained at www.wawb.uscourts.gov.

The trustee is expected to recommend approval or disapproval of the plan, § 1302(b)(2)(B), ensure that the debtor commences making payments within 30 days, § 1302(b)(5), and make payments to creditors under the plan. § 1326(c). If the debtor falls behind in making payments, it is the trustee who monitors the debtor's performance, urges compliance, and, if necessary, brings the matter to the court's attention, typically through a motion to dismiss the case. If the debtor fails to commence payments on time, the court "may" convert the case to Chapter 7[8] or dismiss it. § 1307(c)(4). Courts have been known to dismiss a case merely because the debtor is late on the first payment.

Within 21 to 50 days after the petition, the U.S. Trustee must call a meeting of creditors pursuant to § 341(a). Rule 2003(a). Proofs of claim are to be filed within 90 days after the first date set for the meeting of creditors. Rule 3002(c). The Chapter 13 plan is typically filed with the petition, and if not filed with the petition, must be filed within 14 days thereafter. Thus, the plan will be available at the first meeting of creditors. Rule 3015(b). Although the U.S. Trustee or a designee presides at the meeting of creditors, Rule 2003(b), and the court ultimately decides whether to confirm the debtor's plan, the true gatekeeper in the Chapter 13 confirmation process is usually the Chapter 13 trustee. The trustee's staff examines the debtor's plan before the creditors' meeting and the trustee uses that meeting to raise with the debtor's counsel any deficiencies in the plan. Further information may be sought from the debtor who must be present at the meeting. § 343. If these problems can be worked out at the meeting, the trustee may place the debtor's case on what amounts to a consent calendar and, unless there are valid creditor objections, confirmation will follow. In some districts, confirmation may occur immediately after the creditors' meeting. *See* § 1324; Rule 3015. Creditors have no right to vote on the plan, although they can object to confirmation. § 1324. The court's decision on confirmation is based solely on whether the plan complies with the Code's requirements. § 1325(a), (b). Money may be paid to the trustee directly by the debtor or, pursuant to court order, by the debtor's employer or other source of the debtor's income. § 1325(c). After confirmation, the trustee will

---

[8] It is not entirely clear whether the court may convert the case to Chapter 7 for nonpayment if the debtor prefers a dismissal. Several courts have interpreted § 1307(b) as giving a Chapter 13 debtor the absolute right to dismiss the case. *See, e.g., In re Barbieri*, 199 F.3d 616 (2d Cir. 1999). However, following the Supreme Court's decision in *Marrama v. Citizens Bank of Mass.*, 549 U.S. 365 (2007), which dealt with conversion from Chapter 7 to Chapter 13, a growing number have ruled that a bankruptcy court may, due to the debtor's bad faith, refuse to dismiss and instead convert the case from Chapter 13 to Chapter 7. *See In re Jacobsen*, 609 F.3d 647 (5th Cir. 2010); *In re Rosson*, 545 F.3d 764 (9th Cir. 2008). *But cf. In re Procel*, 467 B.R. 297 (S.D.N.Y. 2012) (treating *Barbieri* as still binding).

disburse the money to creditors under the plan. § 1326(c). When, and if, all payments under the plan have been completed, the debtor is discharged. § 1328(a).

3. *The Stay*

In all types of bankruptcy proceedings, the debtor's creditors are enjoined from making any effort to collect a prepetition claim from the debtor. *See* § 362(a)(6). While nothing in the language of § 362 purports to alter the scope of the stay in Chapter 13 cases, other provisions of the Code impact the reach of the stay in Chapter 13. Consider the following problem.

Problem 11-2

Dominick, who filed for Chapter 13 relief three weeks ago, owes several thousand dollars in past due, prepetition child support to his ex-wife, Carlotta. He is also failing to pay postpetition support. May Carlotta use the state's support enforcement mechanisms – including garnishment and contempt – to enforce either or both of these obligations? *See* §§ 362(b)(2)(B), 541(a)(6), 1306(a); *see also In re Steenstra*, 280 B.R. 560 (Bankr. D. Mass. 2002).

4. *The Co-Debtor Stay*

As a general rule, the automatic stay does not protect co-debtors: people other than the debtor who are also liable on one or more of the debtor's obligations. Thus, in most bankruptcy cases, creditors are free to pursue co-debtors while the debtor's bankruptcy case is pending. Such co-debtors are often friends or family members, many of whom may not have fully appreciated the consequences of co-signing or guaranteeing the debtor's obligation. Creditors often use the threat of collecting against co-debtors to coerce debtors into paying or reaffirming their debts. In short, after a debtor defaults and files bankruptcy, the creditor in effect says "pay me or grandma pays." Faced with this pressure, the debtor may capitulate.

To prevent such tactics, and perhaps to entice debtors into Chapter 13, Congress included the co-debtor stay in Chapter 13, § 1301(a). It prevents creditors from attempting to collect a consumer debt from an individual co-debtor during the pendency of the bankruptcy case. Because Chapter 13 plans typically call for payments over several years, the co-debtor gets substantial protection from this rule. More important, the Chapter 13 bankruptcy debtor, now relieved of the pressure to protect co-debtors, can deal with the creditor on the same basis as other creditors and obtain a more complete fresh start.

The co-debtor stay is not absolute. Congress included several significant limitations. First, it covers only individual (*i.e.*, human being) co-debtors. Second, it applies only to consumer debts. These are defined as debts incurred for personal, family, or household purposes. § 101(8). It thus covers the home mortgage loan, but apparently not tax liability.[9] Third, relief from the stay is available if the co-debtor actually received the consideration giving rise to the debt (*i.e.*, if the bankruptcy debtor is a guarantor of the debt, rather than the other way around). § 1301(c)(1). Fourth, relief from the stay is available to the extent the plan does not provide for full payment to the creditor. § 1301(c)(2). Thus, if the debtor owes $1,000 and the plan proposes to pay $700, the creditor can get relief to collect the remaining $300, plus any interest, fees, and other charges to which the creditor is otherwise entitled. Similarly, if the plan does not provide for paying postpetition interest, the creditor may get relief from the stay to recover that from the co-debtor. Finally, if the creditor's interests would be "irreparably harmed," such as if the co-debtor's financial situation were deteriorating or the co-debtor was about to flee the jurisdiction, the stay may be lifted. § 1301(c)(3).

B. THE PLAN

1. *General Requirements*

Three main provisions govern the contents of Chapter 13 plans. The first, § 1322(a), identifies a few, very general requirements. The most notable of these is that priority claimants must be paid in full. The second, § 1322(b), identifies a few additional things a plan *may* do. These too are phrased very generally and, with some exception, permit the debtor to do most anything. For example, the debtor may pay all or any part of a claim. § 1322(b)(6), (8). To do this, the plan may group claims into different classes, provided it does not "discriminate unfairly" among classes of claims and provided it treats all claims within a class alike. § 1322(a)(3), (b)(1). The plan may also modify most secured claims and cure defaults, § 1322(b)(2), (3), (5).

The third main provision governing plans is § 1325, which provides the rules on confirmation. Although some of its requirements are also fairly general – even vague –

---

9 *See, e.g., In re Westberry*, 215 F.3d 589 (6th Cir. 2000).

others provide a lot more detail. Of particular note are the rules in § 1325(a)(3)–(6), (b). They require that the plan be proposed in good faith, that each claimant receive the liquidation value of its claim, that secured and priority claimants be paid in full (or agree to some other treatment), and that nonpriority, unsecured creditors either be paid in full or that the debtor allocate all disposable income for the "applicable commitment period" to the payment of creditors. The applicable commitment period depends on income but is usually either three or five years. § 1325(b)(4).

The materials that follow explore each of these requirements in some detail. In order to see the whole picture, however, it is useful to keep all of them in mind as each is studied individually. Toward this end, the chart on the following page should help compare some of Chapter 13's requirements to the distribution scheme of Chapter 7 (it also depicts the rules applicable under Chapter 11).

Although this chart is relatively simple, it is worth thinking about the implications of the rules it depicts. For example, because a Chapter 13 plan must pay priority claims in full (unless, as is unlikely, the creditor agrees to accept less), the debtor must have sufficient income to pay spousal and child support arrearages and accrued unsecured tax liability in order to consummate a Chapter 13 plan and receive a Chapter 13 discharge. The chief benefit to Chapter 13 with respect to such claims is that the claims may be paid over a three- or five-year period, and they may be paid without interest.[10] Thus, for example, a debtor who owed $10,000 in priority income taxes would have to pay that amount over the multi-year life of the plan, even though the present value of such payments would be substantially less than $10,000.[11]

---

[10] Although this is certainly true for taxes and technically true for support, because support claims are nondischargeable in Chapter 13 (whereas tax debts are dischargeable), postpetition interest on support claims, if not paid under the plan, will remain and will not be discharged. *In re Pitt*, 240 B.R. 908 (Bankr. N.D. Cal. 1999); *see also In re Pardee*, 218 B.R. 916 (9th Cir. BAP 1998), *aff'd on other grounds*, 193 F.3d 1083 (9th Cir. 1999).

Of course, even when interest is not required, the plan must pay creditors, *in present value terms*, what they would get in a Chapter 7 liquidation. § 1325(a)(4). Thus, if – but only if – there would be enough to pay these priority claims in full in a liquidation, then interest is effectively required in Chapter 13.

[11] If paid in 36 equal monthly installments of $277.78, the present value of the entire stream of payments would be approximately $8,864, using an 8% discount rate. If the payment were made in one lump sum at the end of a three-year plan, the present value would be approximately $7,938, again using an 8% discount rate.

TREATMENT OF CLAIMS AGAINST THE ESTATE

<table>
<tr><th></th><th>Distribution in Chapter 7</th><th>Chapter 11</th><th>Chapter 13</th></tr>
<tr><td>1a</td><td>Trustee expenses in administering the estate to pay support claims</td><td rowspan="2">See rows 3–7 below</td><td rowspan="3">Unless creditor agrees otherwise, must be paid in full (without interest) over life of plan

§ 1322(a)(2)</td></tr>
<tr><td>1b</td><td>Spousal & child support claims</td></tr>
<tr><td>2</td><td>Administrative expenses, including:
• Costs & expenses of preserving the estate; taxes incurred by estate
• Compensation to professionals
• Reimbursement of specified creditor expenses</td><td>Unless creditor agrees otherwise, must be paid in full on the effective date of the plan

§ 1129(a)(9)(A)</td></tr>
<tr><td>3</td><td>Certain expenses arising from involuntary filings</td><td rowspan="5">Must be paid in full on the effective date of the plan, unless creditor agrees otherwise or class agrees to be paid in full (with interest) over life of plan

§ 1129(a)(9)(B)</td><td>n/a</td></tr>
<tr><td>4</td><td>Certain employee wage claims (up to $12,475)</td><td rowspan="4">Unlikely to exist; if it does, unless creditor agrees otherwise, must be paid in full (without interest) over life of plan

§ 1322(a)(2)</td></tr>
<tr><td>5</td><td>Certain employee benefit claims (up to $12,475 per employee)</td></tr>
<tr><td>6</td><td>Certain agricultural and aquicultural bailment claims (up to $6,150)</td></tr>
<tr><td>7</td><td>Certain consumer deposits (up to $2,775)</td></tr>
<tr><td>8</td><td>Certain tax claims</td><td>Must be paid in full within five years
§ 1129(a)(9)(C)</td><td>See rows 1–2 above</td></tr>
<tr><td>9</td><td>Claims owed by depositary institutions to maintain capital levels</td><td rowspan="5">Classified by and treated under plan, subject to rules on confirmation

§§ 1123, 1129</td><td>n/a</td></tr>
<tr><td>10</td><td>Personal injury claims resulting from drunk driving</td><td>See rows 1–2 above</td></tr>
<tr><td>11</td><td>Timely unsecured claims</td><td rowspan="3">Classified by and treated under plan, subject to rules on confirmation

§§ 1322, 1325</td></tr>
<tr><td>12</td><td>Untimely unsecured claims</td></tr>
<tr><td>13</td><td>Prepetition claims for fines & penalties</td></tr>
<tr><td>14</td><td>Postpetition interest on the claims listed above</td><td>Plan may provide for</td><td>Paid on nondischargeable debts if claims are fully paid</td></tr>
<tr><td>15</td><td>To debtor</td><td>To the extent the plan provides</td><td>Unless otherwise provided</td></tr>
</table>

2. *Disposable Income*

In exchange for allowing debtors to keep their property and discharge their debts, Chapter 13 contemplates that the debtor will make some payment to creditors out of future earnings. This is accomplished primarily through § 1325(b)(1)(B), which requires that the debtor's plan either pay creditors in full or allocate all of the debtor's "projected disposable income" to the plan for the applicable commitment period.[12] "Disposable income" is defined generally to mean "current monthly income" less amounts reasonably necessary to be expended for the maintenance or support of the debtor or a dependent of the debtor. *See* § 1325(b)(2)(A).

The 2005 Amendments defined "current monthly income" so as to resolve some of the interpretive problems that had previously divided courts. The term now includes income from tax exempt sources, such as pension and workers' compensation benefits (but not social security),[13] even though creditors would not normally be able to reach income from such sources.[14] *See* § 101(10A)(A). In addition, the income of a nondebtor spouse must be counted to the extent it reduces the amount of the debtor's income that is "reasonably necessary" for the maintenance and support of the debtor's household. § 101(10A)(B).

The 2005 Amendments also resolved some of the interpretive problems on the expense side of the equation. If the debtor's income exceeds the median for a household of the same size, reasonable expenses are to be computed using the formula in the means

---

[12] The "applicable commitment period" is defined in reference to the debtor's "current monthly income," not the debtor's "disposable income." While § 1325(b)(2)(B) allows self-employed debtors to deduct "expenditures necessary for the continuation, preservation, and operation" of the business when computing *disposable income*, they apparently do not get to deduct such expenditures when computing "current monthly income." As a result, the gross income – not the net revenue – of the debtor's business is used to determine the "applicable commitment period." *See In re Harkins*, 491 B.R. 518 (Bankr. S.D. Ohio 2013).

[13] *See* § 101(10A)(B).

[14] Incoming child support is not included in the debtor's "current monthly income" for this purpose. *See* § 1325(b)(2).

Courts disagree about whether a debtor's voluntary contributions to an employer's qualified retirement plan are excluded from "current monthly income." Some conclude that they are excluded, some conclude that they are excluded only to the extent that the debtor was making such contributions prepetition, and some conclude that they are included. *See, e.g.*, *In re Seafort*, 669 F.3d 662 (6th Cir. 2012); *In re Parks*, 475 B.R. 703 (9th Cir. BAP 2012) (both ruling they are included); *In re Drapeau*, 485 B.R. 29 (Bankr. D. Mass. 2013) (ruling they are excluded).

test. § 1325(b)(3). While this calculation would seem straightforward, there can still be complications. For example, the computation is based in part on the size of the debtor's "household." Given the plethora of today's living arrangements – *e.g.*, children or stepchildren of a debtor who reside partly with the debtor and partly with their other parent; a niece who lives with the debtor while her parents are temporarily abroad on active military duty – it is not always clear what the size of the debtor's household is.[15]

Far more difficult problems arise if the debtor's income does not exceed the state median. In such cases, the court must determine whether each of the debtor's listed expenses – for telephone, cable television, schooling, as well as for food, clothing, shelter, and transportation – is necessary. This is a thankless and somewhat distasteful job for bankruptcy judges. Some judges have responded by not scrutinizing all expenses and instead focusing on luxury items and obvious indulgences. Others conduct a more full inquiry to determine which expenses are unnecessary for a reasonable (*i.e.*, Spartan) lifestyle.[16] Not surprisingly, the different standards, compounded by different judicial notions of what is reasonable, have led to very inconsistent results, particularly with respect to such items as clothing, recreation, and education expenses.

Some courts do not seem to be particularly bothered by the general lack of consistency about what constitutes disposable income. Consider the following excerpt:

> Since § 1325(b)(2)(A) speaks in terms of expenditures that are "reasonably necessary," it is safe to assume that the judicial distinction between disposable and nondisposable income must be made by an objective, reasonable-person standard. The more difficult question concerns how one defines this standard.
>
> There are expenditures that a chapter 13 debtor might make which all reasonable people would agree are excessive – such as for a yacht or personal jet. At the other end of the spectrum, there are expenditures nobody could reasonably challenge – such as for food and shelter. The problem lies in the vast gray area between these extremes – *i.e.*, those expenditures with respect to which reasonable people could disagree on the question of whether they are appropriate under the circumstances.

---

[15] *See Johnson v. Zimmer*, 686 F.3d 224 (4th Cir. 2012) (upholding the bankruptcy court's decision to treat part-time residents of the debtor's household as fractional members).

[16] *See In re McGovern*, 278 B.R. 888 (Bankr. S.D. Fla. 2002), *vacated on other grounds*, 297 B.R. 650 (S.D. Fla. 2003).

One approach a court could take in deciding this question would be to hold a particular expenditure to be "reasonably necessary" if it concludes that reasonable persons could disagree as to whether the expenditure is reasonably necessary. Because this in effect means that an expenditure would be allowed even if only a small minority of reasonable people would view the expenditure as appropriate, it is too lenient.

Conversely, a court might hold an expenditure to be excessive if *any* reasonable person could view it as such. This standard swings too far in the opposite direction, making it virtually impossible for the debtor to justify other than the most vital of expenditures.

A third approach would follow the simple majority. If the court concludes that most (reasonable) people would view the expenditure as excessive, then the expenditure will be so treated. There is much to recommend this approach: it is more moderate than either of the other two approaches mentioned and, because it yields to the perceived consensus, it could promote consistency and uniformity among the courts regarding this issue.

In most cases, however, this approach is unworkable because there is little or no evidence upon which the judge can rely in determining whether "most people" would regard a particular expenditure as reasonable. And while it is always appropriate to refer to whatever case law is on point, the infinite variety of factual contexts in which these cases are decided, as amply demonstrated by a review of the reported decisions in this field, along with what is likely to be a relatively small number of pertinent decisions, do not make this source a particularly reliable means for eliciting a consensus.

Given these limitations, the decision of whether a particular expense is reasonable is and ought to be based on the judge's own opinion, for the judge is, in § 1325(b)(2) decision-making, the hypothetical reasonable person.[17]

The last sentence about the bankruptcy judge may be correct as a statement of law but is highly questionable as a matter of fact. How many bankruptcy judges do the shopping for their households and are familiar with the current costs of living and of raising young children?

Picking up on this, several courts have adopted a sort of amalgam approach for dealing with the issue of what expenses are reasonably necessary. Consider the following excerpt:

---

[17] *In re Gonzales*, 157 B.R. 604, 607–08 (Bankr. E.D. Mich. 1993).

Whether income is "reasonably necessary" for the debtors' maintenance and support is open to interpretation. The Code requires a meaningful and realistic budget, accompanied by the devotion of most of the debtor's surplus income to repay creditors. Chapter 13 debtors are not required to adopt a totally spartan existence; neither are they permitted to continue an extravagant lifestyle at the expense of creditors. Courts apply § 1325(b) to allow debtors to maintain a reasonable lifestyle while simultaneously insuring they make a serious effort to pay creditors by eliminating unnecessary and unreasonable expenses. This section contemplates some sacrifices or alteration in prepetition consumption levels by Chapter 13 debtors, while allowing them to sustain basic needs not related to their former lifestyles.

Some expenditures are clearly essential, or nondiscretionary, such as reasonable amounts budgeted for food, clothing and shelter. The Code, however, recognizes that debtors "cannot live by bread alone." *In re Gonzales*, 157 B.R. 604, 608 (Bankr. E.D. Mich. 1993). Chapter 13 debtors are allowed some latitude regarding discretionary spending for items such as recreation, clubs, entertainment, newspapers, charitable contributions and other expenses in their budget. Excessive amounts allocated to nondiscretionary expenses also constitute discretionary spending. The Court has the duty to examine the entire budget in Chapter 13 cases to determine whether all listed expenses are reasonable and necessary under § 1325(b).

> No matter where the "fat" is hidden, such discretionary expenditures typically have more to do with enhancing one's quality of life, acquiring spiritual fulfillment, or just simply relaxing and enjoying oneself, than with subsistence. Since no two people have the same tastes, interests or philosophical dispositions, these discretionary costs can run the gamut from making charitable donations to buying a ticket for a tractor-pull event.[ ] By lumping all discretionary expenses together, whether they derive from categories more commonly thought of in subsistence terms or from categories commonly thought of as clearly discretionary in nature, the bankruptcy specific expenditures, that is to say, micromanage the details of a debtor's life. * * *
>
> The proper methodology is to aggregate all expenses projected by the debtor which are somewhat more discretionary in nature, and any excessive amounts in the relatively nondiscretionary line items

> such as food, utilities, housing, and health expenses, to quantify a sum which, for lack of a better term, will be called "discretionary spending." *Id.* at 609. * * *
>
> Discretionary expenses identified by courts include charitable contributions, gifts, recreation, private school tuition, payments for boats, campers and other luxuries, health club and country club dues, and newspapers and magazines. Courts also scrutinize cable TV services, veterinary expenses, cell phones, unspecified home repairs, and deductions for voluntary retirement funds.[18]

While this approach of aggregating all of the expenses and looking for the collective fat may seem reasonable, it can allow the court to essentially obscure what it truly finds objectionable. Indeed, in the excerpted case, the court went on to identify the monthly expenses for school activities, recreation, gifts, food, home maintenance, and medical expenses – totaling $1,350 – as all involving some discretionary spending. It then calculated the discretionary amount as $550–$650 per month, but gave no indication where the excess came from. Query how debtors and their counsel are to devise Chapter 13 plans without more guidance.

Added to this is one more complication: a big one. The discussion above dealt with the meaning of the term "disposable income" in § 1325(b)(2) and (3). In other words, it concerned the debtor's income and expenses as of the date the petition was filed. But what the debtor must commit to the plan is "projected disposable income": the amount of projected income minus projected expenses for the length of the applicable commitment period. § 1325(b)(1).

Consider how these two things might differ. For above-median-income debtors, the means test formula used to compute disposable income does not represent "current" income at all; instead, it represents the average monthly income received in the six months preceding the filing of the petition. A debtor who was unemployed for a substantial portion of that period but who now has a well-paying job is very likely to have significantly more disposable income than the mandatory calculation would suggest.[19] The reverse can also occur: a debtor who has recently lost a high-paying job

---

[18] *In re Gleason*, 267 B.R. 630, 633–34 (Bankr. N.D. Iowa 2001).

[19] The same may be true even if the debtor does not have a job but has the ability to get one. *See In re Jobe*, 197 B.R. 823 (Bankr. W.D. Tex. 1996) (the debtor, an able-bodied man in his early 50s with a pension from the U.S. Army, must find work to meet the "best interests" test; failure to do so, combined with a few misrepresentations, constitutes bad faith).

or who received unusual payments in the six-month period before the chapter 13 filing may show disposable income that is far beyond the debtor's projected disposable income.

In 2010, the Supreme Court ruled that bankruptcy courts must consider such factors in computing "projected disposable income."[20] That may be easy to do when the discrepancy is attributable to the backward-looking approach mandated for above-median-income debtors and recent events have already occurred to make it clear that the debtor's future income or expenses will be markedly different from what they were in the recent past. Thus, for example, in computing protected disposable income, the debtor should be denied a deduction for a home mortgage or car loan expense if the debtor has indicated an intention to surrender the property.[21]

In other respects, however, calculating projected disposable income remains quite difficult. It requires – or at least seems to require – courts to prognosticate about what the debtor's income and expenses will be for the next several years. Predicting the state of the overall economy for a three- or five-year period is notoriously difficult; predicting the future financial circumstances of a specific individual debtor is virtually impossible. Perhaps the debtor is likely to be promoted during that period and receive a raise.[22] Perhaps the debtor will be laid off due to poor performance, illness, financial problems peculiar to the debtor's employer, or a slowdown in the employer's industry. There is little a court can do to assess the probability of these events. As a result, courts tend to ignore such possibilities and rely on the power granted in § 1329 to modify plans when conditions change. This may be the most practical solution.

One final point is in order. In computing disposable income, the debtor may subtract charitable contributions – up to 15% of the debtor's gross income for the year in which the contributions are made – from the debtor's current monthly income. § 1325(b)(2)(A). There is no requirement that the debtor have a prior practice of making charitable contributions, as would normally be true for debtors who tithe. Apparently,

---

[20] *Hamilton v. Lanning*, 130 S. Ct. 2464, 2475–76 (2010).

[21] *In re Quigley*, 673 F.3d 269 (4th Cir. 2012); *In re Darrohn*, 615 F.3d 470 (6th Cir. 2010); *see also In re Liehr*, 439 B.R. 179 (10th Cir. BAP 2010).

[22] A debtor who expects a pay increase – beyond the amount necessary to cover projected increases in the cost of living – may have little incentive to disclose that expectation. Only if that additional income is needed to satisfy other requirements for confirmation, *e.g.*, §§ 1322(a)(2), 1325(a)(4), (5), is the debtor likely to include the additional income in the debtor's proposed plan. However, if the debtor receives a pay increase before the plan is confirmed, failure to disclose that fact may result in revocation of the confirmation. § 1330.

therefore, Chapter 13 debtors may make annual gifts – under the 15% ceiling – to a qualified charity at the expense of the debtor's creditors.[23]

Problem 11-3

You represent Dauphin, the manager of several upscale coffee shops. Dauphin's annual income is slightly over $90,000. Dauphin lives as if it were even higher. Dauphin, who is single and has no dependents, has a $600,000 home subject to a $500,000 mortgage. The monthly mortgage payment is $3,675. Dauphin also owns a $45,000 Mercedes subject to a $40,000 security interest. Dauphin's monthly car payments are $975.

A. If Dauphin seeks Chapter 13 relief, to what extent will the mortgage and car payments affect Dauphin's disposable income?

B. How, if at all, would the result be different if, instead of owning the car, Dauphin had leased it for four years for $975/month?

3. Treatment of Secured Claims

(a) In General

The main rules applicable to secured claims are in §§ 1322(b)(2), (5), and 1325(a)(5). Read those provisions. To understand their collective meaning, we start with § 1325(a)(5). It provides the debtor with three options with respect to secured claims:

(i) anything to which the claimant consents, § 1325(a)(5)(A);

(ii) surrender of the collateral to the claimant, § 1325(a)(5)(C); or

(iii) retain the collateral subject to the lien and pay the creditor the present value of the secured claim amount, § 1325(a)(5)(B).

The second option is useful when the debtor has no need for the collateral or lacks sufficient income to pay for it. In such cases, the debtor may propose a plan that provides for surrender of the collateral to the secured party. This can present a bit of a

---

23 *See In re Cavanagh*, 250 B.R. 107 (9th Cir. BAP 2000) (so ruling with regard to measuring disposable income, but noting that the debtor's reason for commencing or increasing donations in the plan may be relevant to good faith); *In re Kirschner*, 259 B.R. 416 (Bankr. M.D. Fla. 2001) (same, but also imposing monitoring conditions to ensure contributions are made).

procedural problem for the creditor if it is undersecured. Rule 3002 imposes a deadline for filing a proof of claim. If the debtor proposes to surrender collateral to the secured creditor, who will then foreclose its lien, the resulting deficiency may not be known until after the filing deadline for the proof of claim. What should the potentially undersecured creditor do? One court answered the question this way:

> An undersecured creditor should file, within the bar date for unsecured claims, a proof of claim. The claim may be filed as fully secured or, alternatively, the amount of the unsecured component may be estimated or may simply be shown as undetermined. When the collateral is subsequently liquidated and the deficiency determined, the creditor may file an amended claim for the then-quantified unsecured amount. The amended claim relates back to the timely filed claim and will not be objectionable on the basis of timeliness. Even creditors who believe themselves to be safely oversecured may file a cautionary claim for a potential deficiency, thus protecting themselves against that eventuality. If it turns out that no deficiency is realized, the cautionary claim may be withdrawn.[24]

The third option, which is probably the most commonly used, must be understood in reference to § 1322(b)(2). That section permits a debtor's Chapter 13 plan to modify a secured claim other than a claim secured solely by a principal residence. This is a staggering grant of authority. It means, among other things, that the debtor may use a Chapter 13 plan to cure a default, modify the payment terms (*i.e.*, the amount of periodic payments and the length of the payment period), and alter the interest rate, all while retaining the collateral.

Despite this broad grant of power, it is important to understand how the rules of § 1325(a)(5)(B) circumscribe that power. First, if the claim is secured by personal property, the debtor must adequately protect the creditor's interest in the collateral during the plan period. §§ 361, 1325(a)(5)(B)(iii)(II). This means, among other things, that if the debtor is going to retain the collateral, the debtor must protect the secured claimant from depreciation of the collateral, typically by making periodic payments on the secured obligation at a rate at least equal to the depreciation. If the claimant holds a purchase-money security interest in personal property, this obligation to provide adequate protection begins no later than 30 days after the petition, even if the plan has not yet been confirmed, § 1326(a)(1)(C).

---

[24] *In re Brooks*, 370 B.R. 194, 200 (Bankr. C.D. Ill. 2007).

Second, the debtor must pay a secured claimant, in present value terms, the amount of its secured claim.[25] To compute this, we need to know two things: (i) the amount of the secured claim and (ii) the present value of the property to be distributed to the claimant.

The amount of a secured claim is something we discussed at the beginning of chapter six. According to § 506(a), a creditor's "secured claim" is limited by the value of the collateral. Thus, a creditor owed $10,000 who has the only lien on property worth $8,000 has a secured claim for $8,000 and an unsecured claim for $2,000. Because the creditor need retain its lien only with respect to its secured claim, the debtor's right to modify claims not secured by a principal residence permits the debtor to bifurcate a secured creditor's claim into its secured and unsecured portions and to treat the two claims differently. In short, a Chapter 13 debtor may strip down a lien, something the Supreme Court ruled that the debtor cannot do in Chapter 7.[26] As a result, if the property appreciates postpetition, the debtor will reap that benefit.

Determining the value of collateral is often a difficult task. When a dispute arises, each of the parties involved may submit the opinion of one or more expert witnesses, and those opinions may well differ widely. Compounding that is the problem of ascertaining what the proper valuation standard is.[27] Should value be based on what the creditor could get if the debtor surrendered the collateral: liquidation value? Or should it be based on the benefit to the debtor from retaining the collateral: replacement value?

In *Associates Commercial Corp. v. Rash*,[28] the Supreme Court ruled that the latter standard applied. At the time, § 506(a) mandated simply that value "be determined in light of the . . . proposed disposition or use" of the collateral. The Court concluded that the "disposition or use" of the collateral turns on the alternative the debtor chooses: surrender or retention. If the plan provides for the debtor to retain the collateral, the

---

[25] Some courts do not permit the debtor to use both § 1325(a)(5)(B) and (C) with respect to the same loan, such as by surrendering some of the collateral and paying off the secured claim on the remainder. *See In re Williams*, 168 F.3d 845 (5th Cir. 1999); *In re Snyder*, 2012 WL 1110119 (Bankr. N.D.N.Y. 2012). Other courts permit the debtor to do this. *See, e.g., United States v. White*, 340 B.R. 761 (E.D.N.C. 2006); *In re McCommons*, 288 B.R. 594 (Bankr. M.D. Ga. 2002).

[26] *See Dewsnup v. Timm*, 502 U.S. 410 (1992) (discussed in chapter six, part C).

[27] This problem was already discussed with respect to determining insolvency for preference purposes (chapter three, part G.1(a)(iv)), the process of claiming exemptions (chapter four, part D.2), and the improvement of position test in § 547(c)(5) (chapter six, part F.3(b)(iii)).

[28] 520 U.S. 953 (1997).

valuation must be based on such "disposition or use." Applying a liquidation-value standard when the retention option is invoked attributes no significance to that decision. A replacement-value standard, on the other hand, distinguishes retention from surrender.

Of course, merely settling on a replacement-value standard does not solve all valuation questions. The Court recognized this in a notorious footnote:

> Whether replacement value is the equivalent of retail value, wholesale value, or some other value will depend on the type of debtor and the nature of the property. We note, however, that replacement value, in this context, should not include certain items. For example, where the proper measure of the replacement value of a vehicle is its retail value, an adjustment to that value may be necessary: A creditor should not receive portions of the retail price, if any, that reflect the value of items the debtor does not receive when he retains his vehicle, items such as warranties, inventory storage, and reconditioning. Nor should the creditor gain from modifications to the property – *e.g.*, the addition of accessories to a vehicle – to which a creditor's lien would not extend under state law.[29]

Perhaps in response to this, Congress amended § 506(a) by adding paragraph (2), which sets retail value, considering the age and condition of the property, as the applicable standard.

Regardless of what the applicable standard is, the parties and the bankruptcy courts cannot undertake costly, fact-intensive litigation in every case. Prior to *Rash*, some courts commonly started with the average of the NADA retail and wholesale amounts and then made adjustments if special circumstances dictated.[30] Although *Rash* appears to reject such an approach, some post-*Rash* opinions have held that it is not inconsistent with *Rash*, provided the parties are permitted to show reasons for increasing or decreasing that amount.[31]

Once the value of the collateral is established, that value must be compared to the present value of property to be distributed under the plan to the secured party. How is present value calculated? Let's return to our example of a creditor with a $10,000 claim secured by property valued at $8,000, and who thus has an $8,000 secured claim. The

---

[29] *Id.* at 965 n.6.

[30] *E.g.*, *In re Valenti*, 105 F.3d 55 (2d Cir. 1997).

[31] *E.g.*, *In re De Anda-Ramirez*, 359 B.R. 794 (10th Cir. BAP 2007); *In re Getz*, 242 B.R. 916 (6th Cir. BAP 2000).

plan could provide for payment of the full $8,000 on the date of confirmation. That is unlikely, however. More commonly, it would provide for monthly payments until the secured claim is paid off. If the plan provided for 20 monthly payments of $400, the total amount paid would be $8,000. However, even though that stream of 20 monthly payments of $400 *totals* $8,000, it is not *worth* $8,000. Think about it, would you rather have $8,000 now or that stream of 20 payments? If you had the cash up front, you could use it or invest it (*e.g.*, earn interest on it). In short, the present value of that stream of 20 payments is less than the sum of the payment amounts. Determining how much less depends largely on what prevailing interest rates are; valuing the stream of payments requires that we discount each payment by the interest that could have been earned if the payment had been made immediately.

The Code offers no specific guidance on the interest rate to be used in discounting future payments to arrive at the present value of a secured claim. Some courts favored the contract rate, in part because it was easy to determine. However, in *Till v. SCS Credit Corp.*,[32] the Supreme Court ruled that bankruptcy courts should use a "formula approach," which begins by looking to the national prime rate – what commercial banks charge creditworthy commercial borrowers to compensate for the opportunity costs of the loan, the risk of inflation, and the relatively slight risk of default – and then, because bankrupt debtors pose a greater risk of nonpayment than solvent commercial borrowers, adjust the prime rate upward accordingly. The appropriate size of that risk adjustment "depends on such factors as the circumstances of the estate, the nature of the security, and the duration and feasibility of the reorganization plan."[33]

So, where does this leave us? Consider the following scenario:

> Eighteen months ago, Debtor purchased a $4,000 high-definition television from Creditor. Debtor paid nothing down but agreed to pay $140 each month for three years. This payment stream amortizes the debt at 15% interest. Creditor retained a security interest in the television. Debtor stopped making payments after twelve months and, because the agreement imposes interest at a higher rate upon default, currently owes $3,200. The television is now worth $1,500.
>
> Creditor has a secured claim of $1,500 and an unsecured claim of $1,700. Debtor may retain the television and modify the claims as long as the plan calls

---

32 541 U.S. 465 (2004).

33 *Id.* at 479.

for Creditor to retain its lien on the secured claim and payments with a present value of $1,500 (plus whatever distribution is appropriate on Creditor's unsecured claim). If we were to compute present value using the pre-default contract rate of interest, monthly payments would be approximately $50 if the plan called for payment over three years. If payment were to be made over a shorter period, payments would be higher; if payments were to be made over a longer period, they would be lower. Because the contract rate of interest is so much higher than prevailing market interest rates, the court might permit the debtor to compute present value using a lower interest rate, thereby reducing the amount of the required monthly payment.[34]

The final restriction on the debtor's distribution of property to a secured claimant is that, if the plan provides for the claim to be paid through periodic payments, those payments must be made on a monthly basis and must not vary in amount. § 1325(a)(5)(B)(iii)(I).

Problem 11-4

Why do you think Congress enacted the requirement that periodic payments be in equal amounts? What abuse or impropriety did Congress seek to prevent? How might the requirement also present a challenge to Doctor, who filed a Chapter 13 petition while completing a surgical residency, or Dory, who filed between three-month tours as a deckhand on a fishing boat?

Some debtors and courts are finding it difficult to harmonize the requirement that payments be made in equal monthly amounts, the rule that requires administrative expenses to be paid in full, with priority over other claims,[35] and the rules that require adequate protection payments to begin within 30 days of the petition and to continue after confirmation.[36] Some courts interpret the first of these rules, § 1326(b)(1), as requiring not merely that administrative expenses be accorded priority but that they actually be paid *before* other claims, even secured claims. If a debtor is in fact required

---

[34] Pursuant to § 1325(a)(5)(B)(iii)(II), an amount adequate to protect the secured claimant against depreciation would have to be included in the monthly payment. Whether a higher interest rate can provide that adequate protection is unclear.

[35] § 1326(b)(1).

[36] §§ 1326(a)(1)(C), 1325(a)(5)(B)(iii)(II).

to pay administrative priority claims first, the debtor might have insufficient funds remaining to pay a secured claimant a stable amount each month that will both adequately protect the secured claimant and pay off the secured claim during the life of the plan. To deal with this, these debtors seek to make adequate protection payments to a secured claimant in one amount followed later, after the administrative expenses are paid off, with payments on the secured claim in a different, usually higher, amount. Although this would appear to violate the requirement of § 1325(a)(5)(B)(iii)(I) that payments be in equal monthly amounts, several courts have allowed it on the theory that the requirement of equal monthly payments does not kick in until the payments on the secured claim begin, and that adequate protection payments do not qualify as payments on the claim.[37] Other courts disagree and prohibit the debtor from making adequate protection payments in one amount followed by payments on the claim in a higher amount.[38] Fortunately, these courts do not regard § 1326(b)(1) as requiring that administrative expenses be paid before secured claims, merely concurrently with them. This allows the debtor to create a plan that provides for simultaneous payment, in equal monthly installments, on both secured claims and administrative expenses.[39]

(b) Limitations on Modification of Secured Claims

There are two limitations on modification of secured claims in Chapter 13. First, § 1322(b)(2) does not permit the debtor to modify a claim secured solely by the debtor's principal residence. Thus, the debtor cannot alter the interest rate or payment period on such debts.[40] The debtor is not powerless over such mortgage debts, however. In

---

[37] *See, e.g.*, *In re Butler*, 403 B.R. 5 (Bankr. W.D. Ark. 2009); *In re Marks*, 394 B.R. 198 (Bankr. N.D. Ill. 2008); *In re DiSardi*, 340 B.R. 790 (Bankr. S.D. Tex. 2006).

[38] *See, e.g.*, *In re Kirk,* 465 B.R. 300 (Bankr. N.D. Ala. 2012); *In re Willis*, 460 B.R. 784 (Bankr. D. Kan. 2011); *In re Sanchez*, 384 B.R. 574 (Bankr. D. Or. 2008); *In re Denton*, 370 B.R. 441 (Bankr. S.D. Ga. 2007).

[39] The requirement in § 1325(a)(5)(iii)(I) of *equal* monthly payments does not appear in the Chapter 11 rules on cramdown. *Cf.* § 1129(a)(9)(C). This might give some debtors an incentive to file under Chapter 11 rather than under Chapter 13.

[40] For examples of other things that would constitute an impermissible modification, see *In re Collins*, 2007 WL 2116416 (Bankr. E.D. Tenn. 2007). Note, the debtor may be able to modify a home-mortgage claim with the creditor's consent. *See In re Wilcox*, 438 B.R. 428 (Bankr. D. Colo. 2010).

particular, the debtor may cure a prepetition default any time prior to the sale of the property. *See* § 1322(b)(5), (c)(1). Thus, a debtor who has defaulted on a home mortgage loan and whose debt has been accelerated may propose a plan providing for payment of the amount of the arrearage over the 3–5 year life of the plan while paying the current installments as they come due under the mortgage.[41] If the debtor has the resources to carry out such a plan, the mortgage debt is effectively de-accelerated – *i.e.*, the original payment schedule is effectively reinstated – and the loss of the home that might have occurred in Chapter 7 is avoided.

Although some debtors argued that this anti-modification rule applies only to the secured portion of an undersecured claim, thus still permitting bifurcation of a claim into its secured and unsecured portions and modification of the unsecured portion, the Supreme Court rejected that argument in *Nobelman v. American Savings Bank*.[42] As a result, claims secured solely by the debtor's home cannot be modified, although most courts permit modification if the claim is wholly unsecured, as in the case of a second mortgage when the first mortgage debt exceeds the value of the property.[43] In effect, they allow a completely underwater second mortgage to be stripped off whereas a partially underwater second mortgage cannot be stripped down.[44] For this reason, valuation of the property can be critically important. For this purpose, most courts

---

[41] *See* § 1322(b)(5) (suggesting that installments may then continue after the plan is completed); § 1328(a)(1) (indicating that the discharge does not extend to long-term obligations treated under § 1322(b)(5)).

[42] 508 U.S. 324 (1993).

[43] *See, e.g., In re Zimmer*, 313 F.3d 1220 (9th Cir. 2002); *In re Lane*, 280 F.3d 663 (6th Cir. 2002); *In re Pond*, 252 F.3d 122 (2d Cir. 2001); *In re Tanner*, 217 F.3d 1357 (11th Cir. 2000); *In re Bartee*, 212 F.3d 277 (5th Cir. 2000); *In re McDonald*, 205 F.3d 606 (3d Cir.), *cert. denied*, 531 U.S. 822 (2000); *In re Griffey*, 335 B.R. 166 (10th Cir. BAP 2005); *In re Mann*, 249 B.R. 831 (1st Cir. BAP 2000). *But cf. In re Dickerson*, 222 F.3d 924 (11th Cir. 2000), *cert. denied*, 532 U.S. 972 (2001) (treating *Tanner* as binding but expressing disagreement with it).

Courts disagree about whether the debtor may strip off a wholly underwater lien on a residence if the debtor is not entitled to a Chapter 13 discharge. *See, e.g., In re Davis*, 716 F.3d 331 (4th Cir. 2013); *In re Fisette*, 455 B.R. 177 (8th Cir. BAP 2011) (and cases cited therein).

[44] It is important to understand that this lien stripping is possible in Chapter 13 because § 1322 authorizes the debtor to modify claims; the lien stripping is not accomplished under § 506. Thus, if the debtor disclaims reliance on § 1322 and asserts a right to strip off a lien under § 506, the debtor will likely lose. *See In re Woolsey*, 696 F.3d 1266 (10th Cir. 2012).

compare the value of the home to the amount of the mortgage debt as of the petition date, not as of the date of confirmation.[45]

It is worth noting that an underwater second mortgage can apparently be stripped off even if the first and second mortgage were created simultaneously in favor of the same lender.[46] Accordingly, mortgage lenders should reconsider their willingness to make two loans, each with its own mortgage, instead of one. Whatever reasons impel them to follow this practice may not justify the concomitant Chapter 13 risk.

It is also important to note that the limitation on modifying home mortgage claims does not apply if collateral in addition to the debtor's home secures the debt. Thus, for example, if the debt is secured by a multi-unit dwelling and the debtor resides in only one unit, the debtor may modify the mortgage loan.[47] Another potential problem for lenders is if the debtor's use changes after the loan transaction is entered into. Although courts disagree about whether the anti-modification rule of § 1322(b)(2) requires that the debtor use the property as a principal residence on the date of the bankruptcy petition or merely when the mortgage loan was made, a majority of those addressing the issue have ruled that the relevant time is the petition date.[48]

Despite the general prohibition on modifying home mortgage claims, if final payment on the debt falls due during the life of the plan, modification – and hence bifurcation of the claim into its secured and unsecured portions – is permitted under

---

[45] *See, e.g.*, *In re Sarno*, 463 B.R. 163 (Bankr. D. Mass. 2011); *cf. In re Abdelgadir*, 455 B.R. 896 (9th Cir. BAP 2011) (determination of whether the debtor used the home as a principal residence should be based on how the debtor used the property on the petition date).

[46] *In re Horner*, 2012 WL 2603541 (Bankr. D. Haw. 2012).

[47] *See In re Scarborough*, 461 F.3d 406 (3d Cir. 2006); *see also In re Reyes*, 2009 WL 4825200 (Bankr. W.D. Wash. 2009) (debtor who rented rooms in her residence to boarders and who informed lender of that fact at the time the mortgage loan was made could modify the lender's claim).

Prior to the 2005 Amendments, some boilerplate clauses in the mortgage often triggered a similar result. For example, several courts held that the debtor could modify a home mortgage loan because the mortgage included appliances, machinery, furniture, and equipment on the premises. *See, e.g.*, *In re Johns*, 37 F.3d 1021 (3d Cir. 1994). Some courts also ruled that escrows for taxes and insurance meant that more than the principal residence secured the loan. The 2005 Amendments broadened the scope of the anti-modification rule by adding a definition of "debtor's principal residence" and a related definition of "incidental property." *See* § 101(13A), (27B). Now, the use of such escrows will not make a mortgage loan modifiable in Chapter 13.

[48] *See, e.g.*, *In re Benafel*, 461 B.R. 581 (9th Cir. BAP 2011).

§ 1322(c)(2).[49] What if final payment became due before the petition? Consider the following problem.

Problem 11-5

Dirigible gave Creditor a note for $100,000 providing for 36 monthly interest payments and a final "balloon" payment of the $100,000 principal on the third anniversary of the note. The note was secured by a mortgage on Dirigible's residence. Dirigible made all of the interest payments on time but failed to pay the principal. Dirigible then filed a petition under Chapter 13. Dirigible's plan proposed to pay the $100,000 principal, together with interest, in sixty equal monthly installments.

A. Should confirmation be denied on the ground that the plan is a modification of the rights of Creditor under § 1322(b)(2)? *See* § 1322(c)(2).

B. How, if at all, would the analysis change if Dirigible's mortgage had required equal monthly payments over 30 years but Dirigible defaulted and the mortgagee accelerated the debt and obtained a foreclosure judgment for the full, accelerated amount prepetition?

One further point must be made about curing a default on a home mortgage loan. The requirement in § 1325(a)(5) that the present value of property "distributed under the plan" equal or exceed the amount of the secured claim arguably presents a significant problem for a debtor with a home mortgage. If the amounts distributed *under the plan* means amounts paid *during the plan*, then a debtor who wishes to keep the home must pay off the mortgage debt during the 3–5 year life of the plan. Such an interpretation would seem to conflict with the debtor's right under § 1322(b)(5) to cure a home mortgage default and then continue to make the contractually required monthly payments on the mortgage loan.[50] The case law on this issue is surprisingly sparse but it seems highly doubtful that Congress expected debtors to pay off their home mortgages in 3–5 years. Indeed, the ability to keep one's home is one of the main enticements of Chapter 13. Perhaps for this reason, most courts to have ruled on this issue have

---

49 *See In re Paschen*, 296 F.3d 1203 (11th Cir. 2003); *In re Eubanks*, 219 B.R. 468 (6th Cir. BAP 1998). *But see In re Witt*, 113 F.3d 508 (4th Cir. 1997).

50 *See In re Gordon*, 217 B.R. 973 (Bankr. M.D. Ga. 1997) (rejecting, for these reasons, the argument that all payments on secured claims must be made during the life of the plan).

concluded that the requirement to pay the secured claim in full during the plan applies only if the debtor modifies the claim. In other words, the debtor may choose one of two options: (i) to cure a default and continue to make payments according to the original terms of the note; or (ii) to modify the terms of the note and complete payments of the secured portion of the claim within the life of the plan – but the debtor may not both modify a secured claim and make payments beyond the life of the plan.[51]

The second limitation on modification of secured claims in a Chapter 13 plan is the final – so-called "hanging" – paragraph of § 1325(a), which is difficult to cite because it is not incorporated into a numbered paragraph. The paragraph is also difficult to understand because it suffers from multiple syntactic ambiguities. Condensed and slightly reformatted to highlight those ambiguities, the clause reads as follows:

> section 506 shall not apply to a claim . . . if
> ① the creditor has a purchase-money security interest securing the debt . . . ,
> ② the debt was incurred within [910 days preceding the petition], and
> ③ the collateral . . . consists of
> (a) a motor vehicle
> (b) acquired for the personal use of the debtor, or
> ④ if the collateral consists of any other thing of value, the debt was incurred within [one year before the petition].

Before examining the ambiguities, let us make sure we understand what the clause does. Consider the following illustration:

> Fifteen months before filing a Chapter 13 petition, Detroit purchased a new car on credit from Car Dealer, who retained and perfected a security interest in the car to secure the purchase price. Detroit uses the car to travel to and from work, for personal errands, and to shuttle family members. On the petition date, the car was worth $23,000 and the amount remaining due on the secured loan was $29,000.

Because clauses ①, ②, and ③ of the hanging paragraph have all been satisfied, the operative provision – the opening clause – applies. Thus, § 506 does not apply to Car Dealer's claim. What this means is that the claim is not bifurcated into a $23,000 secured claim and a $6,000 unsecured claim. Instead, Car Dealer's entire claim is treated as a secured claim.

---

[51] *See, e.g.*, *JPMorgan Chase Bank v. Galaske*, 476 B.R. 405, 410–12 (D. Vt. 2012).

The importance of this relates back to § 1325(a)(5). Detroit has three options with respect to Car Dealer's secured claim: (i) propose something Car Dealer accepts; (ii) surrender the car to Car Dealer; or (iii) provide for Car Dealer to retain the lien and for payments that have a present value at least equal to the allowed amount of the secured claim.[52] Because the secured claim is the full $29,000 debt, not the $23,000 value of the car, the present value of the payments under the plan must equal or exceed $29,000. In short, when the hanging paragraph applies, the debtor may not strip down the lien.

Let us now return to the ambiguities. Clause ④ is an alternative to clauses ② and ③(a). In other words, a one-year limitation applies, rather than a 910-day limitation, if the collateral consists of something other than a motor vehicle. What is unclear is whether clause ④ is an exception to clause ①. In other words, if the collateral is not a motor vehicle, must the creditor have a purchase-money security interest? Most courts have ruled that clause ④ is not an exception to clause ① and that the creditor must have a PMSI for the hanging paragraph to apply.[53]

Similarly unclear is whether clause ④ is an exception to clause ③(b). If the collateral is a motor vehicle not acquired for the personal use of the debtor – *i.e.*, a motor vehicle acquired for business use or for the use of a dependent of the debtor – does the clause apply, or is clause ④ limited to claims secured by things other than motor vehicles? Courts are divided.[54]

Perhaps the greatest controversy generated by enactment of the hanging paragraph was what happens if the debtor surrenders the collateral. Debtors argued that by treating the entire claim as secured, the hanging paragraph left the claimant without an unsecured claim. So, the debtors argued, they could surrender the collateral and owe nothing more, even if the collateral was worth less than the debt, thereby using a provision designed to benefit secured parties to their detriment. Numerous bankruptcy courts accepted this argument but several circuit courts have soundly rejected it and held that the secured party still has an unsecured claim for the deficiency owing after foreclosure.[55]

---

[52] In addition, Detroit would have to provide adequate protection under § 1325(a)(5)(B)(iii)(II). Query what this means when the secured claim is deemed to be greater than the value of the collateral pursuant to the hanging paragraph.

[53] *See, e.g.*, *In re Thompson*, 2009 WL 1758757 (Bankr. N.D. Ohio 2009).

[54] *Compare In re Tanguay*, 427 B.R. 663 (Bankr. E.D. Tenn. 2010) (clause applies), *with In re Cabell*, 2011 WL 6018277 (Bankr. N.D. Ind. 2011) (clause does not apply).

[55] *See In re Barrett*, 543 F.3d 1239 (11th Cir. 2008); *Tidewater Fin. Co. v. Kenney*, 531 F.3d 312

Problem 11-6

Eighteen months ago, Dwyer purchased furniture on credit from Seller and gave Seller a security interest in the furniture to secure the $5,000 purchase price. The sales agreement called for payment of $150/month for three years – in essence, a 5% interest rate. When Dwyer filed for Chapter 13 bankruptcy protection, Dwyer was current on all payments. The furniture is now worth $1,800. Dwyer still owes $2,600 in principal. The applicable commitment period for Dwyer's plan is three years. Dwyer wishes to retain the furniture.

A. 1. What is the minimum amount that must be distributed to Seller under the plan for the plan to be confirmed without Seller's consent?

   2. What is the maximum period of time that such distributions can be made for the plan to be confirmed without Seller's consent?

B. How, if at all, would the analysis to Part A change if Dwyer had purchased the furniture nine months ago, the furniture was now worth $2,000, and the amount remaining due was $3,800?

C. Seller has recently been offering to sell customers furniture under Seller's "4-4 Plan," which involves 100% financing at a 4% annual interest rate over a four-year period. Under such a deal, a customer buying furniture priced at $10,000 would be required to make 48 payments of $225. The debt would be secured by the furniture sold. To increase sales, Seller is considering offering a lower interest rate (but raising the price) or offering a lower price (but raising the interest rate). For example, Seller is trying to choose between offering that same furniture at a price of $10,800 with 0% interest or at a price $9,215 with 8% interest. Each of these alternative arrangements would require payments of $225 for 48 months.

   1. Which option would be better for Seller if the buyer filed for relief under Chapter 7 and wanted to keep the furniture?

   2. Which option would be better for Seller if the buyer filed for relief under Chapter 13 and wanted to keep the furniture? *See In re Taranto*, 365 B.R. 85 (6th Cir. BAP 2007).

(4th Cir. 2008); *In re Ballard*, 526 F.3d 634 (10th Cir. 2008); *In re Long*, 519 F.3d 288 (6th Cir. 2008); *Capital One Auto Fin. v. Osborn*, 515 F.3d 817 (8th Cir. 2008); *In re Wright*, 492 F.3d 829 (7th Cir. 2007); *see also In re Rodriguez*, 375 B.R. 535 (9th Cir. BAP 2007).

(c) Payments "Outside the Plan"

One of the main drawbacks to Chapter 13 is its expense. The trustee receives a percentage – as much as 10% but usually around 5% – of all disbursements to creditors made under the plan. With respect to unsecured creditors, unless the plan provides for payment to them in full, the trustee's fees effectively reduce the amount the creditors receive. With respect to secured claims, the burden of the trustees' fees falls initially on the debtor. If the debtor wants to retain the collateral, the debtor must pay the secured claim in full. § 1325(a)(5)(B). The trustee's fees therefore cannot reduce the secured creditor's take. In other words, to keep the collateral, the debtor will have to pay an additional amount just for the privilege of having the trustee make the payments to the secured creditor. For example, if the plan calls for a secured creditor to receive $100 per month and the trustee to receive a 5% commission on disbursements, the plan will have to allocate $105 to the payment of the secured creditor so that, after the trustee's commission is taken out, the creditor will receive the required $100. Because the debtor is usually devoting all disposable income to the plan and has no more to contribute, the trustee's fees reduce that finite fund of disposable income and, as a result, reduce the recovery of the unsecured claimants. It is therefore the unsecured claimants who pay to have the trustee make disbursements to secured claimants.

It is easy to appreciate why the trustee should act as the disbursing agent generally. If the debtor were allowed to pay creditors directly, the trustee would not learn whether payments were being made unless creditors complained; the situation could become chaotic and difficult to administer. With respect to secured claims, however, this rationale is less powerful. In many instances, particularly in the case of a residential mortgage, the debtor will owe the same payments after confirmation as before. Moreover, these payments may well continue long after the plan is completed because debtors are not discharged from debts dealt with under § 1322(b)(5). § 1328(a)(1). Thus, it makes some sense for the debtor to pay these claims directly.

The clear implications from § 1326(c) are that the court may approve a plan allowing the debtor to act as disbursing agent and that the trustee is not entitled to a commission on payments made directly by the debtor. *See* 28 U.S.C. § 586(e)(2). The savings generated by direct payments to creditors can be substantial, and they can make the difference between a confirmable plan and a nonconfirmable one.[56]

---

[56] *See, e.g.*, *In re Slaughter*, 188 B.R. 29 (Bankr. D.N.D. 1995) (savings of $1,700 annually, without which the plan would be infeasible).

Nevertheless, courts have not reached total agreement about when it is appropriate to permit the debtor to pay claims directly. Most treat a residential mortgage debt as one the debtor may pay directly,[57] although many require that amounts to cure an arrearage be paid through the trustee.[58] Debtors are sometimes allowed to be disbursing agents on other secured claim cases as well.[59] The willingness of courts to allow this practice – which if taken to an extreme could leave the trustee system seriously underfunded – apparently varies significantly from district to district and often depends on a variety of factors, including whether the plan modifies the obligation and whether the debtor is in default. Some courts have a local rule on the issue.

4. *Treatment of Unsecured Claims*

Assuming the plan allocates all of the debtor's disposable income to the plan for the applicable commitment period, the debtor has *almost* unfettered discretion with respect to the treatment of unsecured claims. The debtor may alter the contractual payment schedule, pay only a small portion of the claim, or treat the claim differently from other unsecured claims, and yet still discharge the unpaid portion upon completion of the plan. There are, however, three important limitations on this freedom.

First, each priority claim – with the exception of support claims assigned to a governmental unit for a purpose other than collection – must be paid in full unless the claimant agrees to accept something less. § 1322(a)(2), (4). Second, unsecured creditors must receive at least the liquidation value of their claims. *See* § 1325(a)(4).

Problem 11-7

Diver received a college degree two years ago and accepted a job as an oceanographer trainee for $21,000 per year. Thrilled with being out of school and earning income, Diver went a little wild with consumption. Diver has settled down now. Indeed, Diver recently married and has two stepchildren to

---

57 *See, e.g., In re Aberegg*, 961 F.2d 1307 (7th Cir. 1992).

58 *E.g., In re Lopez*, 372 B.R. 40 (9th Cir. BAP 2007), *aff'd*, 550 F.3d 1202 (9th Cir. 2008).

59 *E.g., In re Bradley*, 705 F.2d 1409 (5th Cir. 1983) (auto loan); *In re Giesbrecht*, 429 B.R. 682 (9th Cir. BAP 2010) (bankruptcy court abused its discretion in not permitting debtors to pay car loan directly).

support. Unfortunately, Diver is unable to pay off the large credit card bills generated in those wilder days and those bills are continuing to accrue interest. As a result, Diver has decided to file under Chapter 13. After reviewing Diver's assets, you determine that there would be $3,600 in nonexempt assets in a Chapter 7 case. The cost of liquidating those assets would be $200. Diver proposes a three-year plan calling for payments of $100/month, which is a fair estimate of Diver's disposable income. The Chapter 13 trustee's commission would be 5% of amounts disbursed under the plan. The appropriate discount rate for determining the present value of future payments is 4%. Does Diver's proposed plan comply with § 1325(a)(4)?

Third, disparate treatment of different unsecured claims – which is expressly authorized, *see* § 1322(b)(1) – is circumscribed in three ways:

(1) the debtor may group claims into different "classes," but all of the claims within a single class must be substantially similar, *see* § 1122(a);
(2) all claims within a single class must be treated alike, § 1322(a)(3); and
(3) the plan must not unfairly discriminate among the different classes of claims, § 1322(b)(1).

In Chapter 11 cases, creditors vote on a debtor's reorganization plan by class, and thus classification may play an important role in the debtor's strategy for gaining acceptance of the plan. In Chapter 13, debtors do not need creditors to approve the plan; the court will confirm the plan if it meets the requirements of § 1325. Thus, the sole reason for a Chapter 13 debtor to separate nonpriority, unsecured claims into different classes is to prefer one class over another in the percentage or timing of payment.

The Code's prohibition on "unfair discrimination" – a term left undefined – implies that the debtor may discriminate to some extent. In other words, by prohibiting only "unfair" discrimination, the Code permits discrimination that is fair. On the other hand, the prohibition presumably has some relevance beyond the other statutory requirements for confirmation of a Chapter 13 plan. Thus, presumably it means more than merely ensuring that claimants receive the liquidation value of their claims, *see* § 1325(a)(4), or that debtors not paying creditors in full allocate all disposable income to the plan for the applicable commitment period, *see* § 1325(b).

There are innumerable bankruptcy court cases on the meaning of "discriminate unfairly," and they differ widely in their interpretation of the term. Some general themes are discernable, however.

Discrimination is permissible if it is necessary to have a successful plan that benefits all creditors. For example, a debtor who has a subsidized low-income lease that is in default may need to pay the arrearage in full in order to cure the default and assume the lease. Otherwise, the debtor will lose the subsidized housing, thus increasing monthly expenses. A plan that discriminates in order to cure the default on such a lease – even to the extent of paying 100% of the lease arrearage and only 10% of other unsecured claims – is not unfair.[60]

When the proposed discrimination serves some other purpose, it is more questionable. Several of the early cases on unfair discrimination involved claims on which there was a co-debtor, typically a family member or friend of the debtor. Often, the debtor would propose to classify separately such claims and pay the holder of the claims a greater percentage than that allocated to holders of other unsecured claims. Courts did not agree on how to handle such proposals and Congress responded in 1984 by adding the "however" clause to § 1322(b)(1). Unfortunately, this clause speaks only to different treatment, not to "unfair discrimination," leaving the precise meaning of the clause unclear. Some courts have interpreted the amendment as permitting disparate treatment in favor of co-debtor claims, but still subject to the unfair discrimination standard, and thus decline to confirm a plan that discriminates excessively.[61] Other courts regard favored treatment of co-debtor claims as either wholly exempt from unfair discrimination analysis,[62] or as permissible provided the plan satisfies the other requirements for confirmation, most notably the requirement that it be proposed in good faith.[63]

Much of the litigation on unfair discrimination has involved plans that prefer the holders of nondischargeable claims over other claimants. Although Chapter 13 offers debtors a slightly expanded discharge over a Chapter 7 discharge, several debts remain nondischargeable even after successful completion of a Chapter 13 plan. These include student loans, debts arising from drunk driving accidents, and restitution or fines

---

60 *In re Davis*, 209 B.R. 893 (Bankr. N.D. Ill. 1997).

61 *See, e.g.*, *In re Ramirez*, 204 F.3d 595 (5th Cir. 2000) (interpreting some rather contradictory statements in *In re Chacon*, 202 F.3d 725 (5th Cir. 1999)).

62 *See, e.g.*, *In re Monroe*, 281 B.R. 398 (Bankr. N.D. Ga. 2002).

63 *See, e.g.*, *In re Rivera*, 490 B.R. 130 (1st Cir. BAP 2013); *In re Renteria*, 470 B.R. 838 (9th Cir. BAP 2012).

stemming from criminal convictions.[64] *See* § 1328(a). Chapter 13 becomes enticing to debtors if they can hold on to their homes and automobiles, use their disposable income to pay off only their nondischargeable debts, pay their other unsecured creditors with little or nothing, and walk away with a fresh start. The issue arises frequently with respect to student loans. Consider the following hypothetical and the brief discussion that follows.

> Donald and Debra financed part of their college education through student loans. They live in an apartment; their possessions, including an automobile, are entirely exempt under state law. They owe $50,000 in student loans and, because of their excessive use of credit cards in the early years of their marriage, $25,000 to a variety of other creditors. They are behind on some of their payments and are being pressed by their creditors. They have consulted a financial counselor and have decided to turn over a new leaf and clear up their financial problems so that in the future they can consider buying a house and having a family. They do not wish to have a Chapter 7 discharge on their credit record because they believe it would inhibit their ability to obtain a home loan later on. They file under Chapter 13 and propose a five-year plan that classifies their student loan debts separately from their other unsecured obligations. The portion of their annual income that qualifies as "disposable" is $13,000. The plan calls for $12,000 per year to be devoted to paying their student loans and $1,000 per year to be paid on the debts owed to their "other creditors." By the end of the plan, the debtors will have paid off all of their student loans – including postpetition interest – but only 20% of the debts owing to their other creditors. Should the court deny confirmation on the ground that the plan unfairly discriminates against the other creditors under § 1322(b)(1)?

Minority View: In order to be fair under § 1322(b)(1), the classification must rationally further a legitimate interest of the debtor and not be inconsistent with a policy explicit or implicit in the Code. This approach is appropriate because the right to classify preferentially is one of the incentives placed in Chapter 13 by Congress to induce debtors to choose Chapter 13 over Chapter 7, under which nonpriority creditors must be paid pro rata. If Donald and Debra were to exercise their right to convert to

---

[64] Support obligations are also nondischargeable, *see* § 1328(a)(2), but they are also priority claims. *See* § 507(a)(1). They therefore *must* be classified separately – recall that only similar claims may be classified together, § 1322(b)(1) – and they must be paid in full. *See* § 1322(a)(2).

Chapter 7, the other creditors would get nothing and the debtors would have their postpetition income to pay off their nondischargeable student loans. With respect to student loan claims, even though they are not accorded priority status, Congress has favored them with nondischargeability to help ensure that they are paid. Favored treatment in a Chapter 13 plan does not frustrate that policy, it furthers it.[65]

Majority View: Section 1322(b)(1)'s reference to unfair discrimination means unfair *to the creditors*; it is a creditor protection device. While § 1322(b) implicitly allows debtors to discriminate in a reasonable manner in classifying claims, the discrimination in the hypothetical unfairly imposes on the other creditors the burden of paying the debtors' student loans. In 1990, when Congress made student loans nondischargeable in Chapter 13, it could have provided a special classification for student loans, as it did in 1984 for co-signed consumer debts, *see* § 1322(b)(1), or it could have made payment of student loans a priority in Chapter 13. It did neither. Hence, there is no reason to believe that Congress intended to favor student loans in Chapter 13 by, in effect, subordinating the claims of other creditors.[66]

Possible Alternatives: One possible alternative, if the applicable commitment period is only three years, is to lengthen the plan and discriminate only after the third year. If, under § 1325(b), debtors must allocate all disposable income to the plan for three years, general unsecured creditors simply have no right to expect income for a longer period of time. Any amount the debtors pay after this three-year period represents a voluntary effort. Even if general unsecured creditors do not benefit from this extra effort, arguably nothing has truly been taken away from them. Thus, while the debtors may not discriminate during the applicable commitment period, they may allocate payments after that time solely to the nondischargeable claims.[67]

A slightly similar approach applies to debtors whose income is above the state median and who must therefore follow the rules of the means test in calculating disposable income. This creates the possibility that the debtor's actual discretionary income might exceed the debtor's projected disposable income that must be allocated to the plan. If so, several courts allow the debtor to allocate that excess to the student

---

[65] *See* Stephen L. Sepinuck, *Rethinking Unfair Discrimination in Chapter13*, 74 AM. BANKR. L.J. 341 (2000).

[66] *E.g.*, *In re Groves*, 39 F.3d 212 (8th Cir. 1994).

[67] *See, e.g.*, *In re Simmons*, 288 B.R. 737 (Bankr. N.D. Tex. 2003); *In re Thibodeau*, 248 B.R. 699, 706 (Bankr. D. Mass. 2000).

loan creditors because the other creditors have no right to those funds and thus such discrimination is not "unfair."[68]

Yet another approach taken or suggested by some courts is to permit the debtor to deal with nondischargeable debt under § 1322(b)(5).[69] This provision allows the debtor to cure a default and remain current on a debt for which the contractual payments would continue beyond the duration of the plan. Under this approach, the debtor may make payments on long-term student loan debt at the contractual rate even if paying general unsecured claims at a much lower rate. Moreover, if there has been no prepetition default, the debtor may be permitted to make these payments directly, rather than through the trustee, thereby avoiding the trustee's fees on these disbursements. However, the bulk of the case law prohibits even this modicum of favored treatment of nondischargeable student loans.[70]

5. *Good Faith*

There are two requirements of good faith in Chapter 13: (i) the petition must be filed in good faith, § 1325(a)(7); and (ii) the plan must be proposed in good faith, § 1325(a)(3). Collectively, these rules require the bankruptcy court to examine both the debtor's prepetition conduct and the debtor's proposed treatment of creditors. These two things are not reviewed in isolation from each other. Quite the contrary: the plan must be viewed in relation to the debtor's prepetition conduct. Thus, for example, while neither filing the petition after incurring debt nor proposing to modify a secured claim is, by itself, strong evidence of bad faith, doing both can be.[71]

---

[68] *E.g.*, *In re Stull*, 489 B.R. 217 (Bankr. D. Kan. 2013); *In re King*, 460 B.R. 708 (Bankr. N.D. Tex. 2011); *In re Abaunza*, 452 B.R. 866 (Bankr. S.D. Fla. 2011); *In re Sharp*, 415 B.R. 803 (Bankr. D. Colo. 2009).

[69] *See, e.g.*, *In re Groves*, 39 F.3d at 215 (quoting and expressing agreement with the bankruptcy court's statements on this issue); *see also In re Johnson*, 446 B.R. 921 (Bankr. E.D. Wis. 2011); *In re Truss*, 404 B.R. 329 (Bankr. E.D. Wis. 2009).

[70] *See, e.g.*, *In re Kubeczko*, 2012 WL 2685115 (Bankr. D. Colo. 2012); *In re Edmonds*, 444 B.R. 898 (Bankr. E.D. Wis. 2010); *In re Martellaro*, 404 B.R. 548 (Bankr. D. Mont. 2008).

[71] *Compare In re Blackmon*, 459 B.R. 144 (Bankr. S.D. Fla. 2011) (debtors who purchased vehicles in contemplation of filing for bankruptcy and then proposed plans that modified the claims by lowering the contractual interest rate did not propose their plans in good faith), *with In re Powell*, 2013 WL 1829837 (Bankr. D. Kan. 2013) (Chapter 13 plan that proposed to lower from 10.99% to 4.75% the

It is impossible to catalogue all of the factors that are potentially relevant to good faith. Nevertheless, there are two factors that frequently arise: (i) proposing to pay little or nothing to unsecured claimants and (ii) seeking repeated discharges.

(a) Minimal Payment Plans

One of the principal benefits to the debtor of the Chapter 13 process is the ability to save nonexempt assets that would go to creditors in Chapter 7. The price the debtor pays for this benefit is that the debtor must allocate to the plan all of the debtor's projected disposable income for three years. § 1325(b)(1)(B).

What if the debtor has no disposable income? Consider the following hypothetical.

> Debtor owns a house and an automobile that are subject to security interests that secure debts greater than the value of the collateral. Debtor is in default on these debts and, even under Chapter 7, would probably have to surrender the assets to the secured creditors. Debtor also has a large amount of unsecured debt, but unsecured creditors will receive nothing in Chapter 7 because Debtor has no unencumbered, nonexempt property. Debtor files for Chapter 13 bankruptcy protection and proposes to devote all projected disposable income for three years to the plan. However, all of this income will be paid to satisfy the claims of the home mortgagee and auto lender. Thus, the effect of the plan is to save Debtor's house and automobiles but nothing is paid to other creditors with unsecured claims. Is this a proper use of Chapter 13?

In the early years of the Code, courts had difficulty with "zero payment" or nominal payment plans like this one. Some courts construed the "good faith" requirement of § 1325(a)(3) as barring zero payment plans. Most simply treated the debtor's proposed level of debt repayment as one of the most important factors – in a long list of factors – for courts to consider in evaluating good faith.[72]

By enacting § 1325(b)(1)(B) in 1984 – which requires that the debtor use all disposable income to pay creditors – Congress addressed the issue, but only obliquely.

---

interest rate on the car loan taken out 48 days before the debtor filed the petition was in good faith in part because there was no evidence that the debtor was contemplating bankruptcy at the time of the transaction).

[72] *See, e.g.*, *In re Estus*, 695 F.2d 311 (8th Cir. 1982) (identifying eleven criteria for courts to use).

It did not specifically bar zero payment plans and, of course, some debtors with *regular* income have no *disposable* income. Indeed, the legislative history strongly suggests that Congress did not wish to limit Chapter 13 to those debtors willing and able to pay a certain percentage of their debts. Thus, plans calling for no or only minimal payments to unsecured creditors do not present a significant good faith problem. As the Tenth Circuit observed:

> The policy of allowing a fresh start does not license debtors to lightly rid themselves of the burden of their indebtedness without an honest attempt at repayment. Yet neither does that policy compel debtors, in Dickensian fashion, to labor for the rest of their lives under the crushing weight of gigantic debt; under our law the world is not to be made a debtor's prison by a lifelong sentence of penury.[73]

When minimal payment is combined with heinous prefiling conduct, however, the situation is very different. Until recently, Chapter 13 offered debtors a substantially enhanced discharge. Certain obligations – including those for willful and malicious injuries – which could not be discharged in Chapter 7 were dischargeable in Chapter 13. The rationale for giving a broader discharge in Chapter 13 was premised on the assumption that the Chapter 13 debtor was actually paying creditors, whereas the typical consumer in Chapter 7 paid little or nothing to unsecured claimants.[74] If a substantial portion of the debtor's obligations were for claims that would be nondischargeable in Chapter 7 and the debtor proposed to pay those claims little or nothing in Chapter 13, courts generally balked.

The Sixth Circuit summed the matter up this way:

> The bankruptcy court made much of the point that an attempt to discharge a debt under Chapter 13 which is not dischargeable under Chapter 7 is not conclusive evidence that the Chapter 13 plan was not made in good faith. We

---

[73] *In re Young*, 237 F.3d 1168, 1178 (10th Cir. 2001).

[74] This premise is implicit in the scope of Chapter 13's more limited hardship discharge. A Chapter 13 debtor who, due to circumstances for which the debtor should not justly be held accountable, is unable to complete a plan can nevertheless receive a discharge if the unsecured creditors have received as much as they would have received in a Chapter 7 liquidation and modification of the plan to accommodate the debtor's new circumstances is not practicable. § 1328(b). However, such a hardship discharge does not rid the debtor of those debts that would have been nondischargeable in Chapter 7. § 1328(c).

agree. It is not conclusively bad faith for a debtor to seek to discharge a debt incurred through his own criminal or tortious conduct, but that factor may be considered. Although we consider as a factor what [the debtor] did to incur the judgment, it is what he has done since the judgment to avoid paying it that is most important. Our decision rests on much more than the fact that this debt is not dischargeable under Chapter 7; it rests on [the debtor's] unrelenting efforts to reduce the assets available to his creditors, to make only minimal payments and over the shortest possible time, and to make even those only when threatened with garnishment. The plan before us was not tendered in good faith, but was one more effort to avoid paying the judgment creditors.[75]

Problem 11-8

Review the facts of Problem 11-3. If Dauphin proposes to retain the home and Mercedes and files a plan that calls for continuation of the regularly monthly payments on both the mortgage loan and car loan, may the court refuse to confirm the plan under § 1325(b)(3)? *See In re Walsh*, 711 F.3d 1120 (9th Cir. 2013); *Baud v. Carroll*, 634 F.3d 327 (6th Cir. 2012).

(b) Repeated Filings

Section 727(a)(8) prevents a discharge in a Chapter 7 case if the debtor received a discharge in a previous case commenced less than eight years prior. This rule reflects a policy against recidivism in bankruptcy. Congress apparently believes that one fresh start is okay, but a debtor who needs frequent fresh starts is abusing the bankruptcy process.

---

[75] *In re Caldwell*, 895 F.2d 1123, 1127–28 (6th Cir. 1990).

On the other hand, if debtors have made substantial payments on their tort liabilities before filing for Chapter 13 relief and propose to make significant payments under the plan, they may pass over the hurdle of good faith even if the main reason for seeking such relief is to discharge debts that would be nondischargeable in Chapter 7. *See, e.g.*, *In re Francis*, 273 B.R. 87 (6th Cir. BAP 2002), *aff'd*, 69 F. App'x 766 (6th Cir. 2003) (confirming a plan that paid only 2–3% on general claims because it allocated all disposable income to the plan for five years, the debtor had already paid $43,000 of a $229,000 debt for fraud, the debtor had waited several years after the state court judgment before filing, and the debtor's relatives were adding $15,000 to the pot).

Until recently, there was no bar against successive discharges in Chapter 13. The reason for this was to encourage the use of Chapter 13. Because Chapter 13 was seen as a way for debtors to pay their debts, rather than escape them, it followed that debtors should be able to use Chapter 13 as often as they wished.

In reality, of course, Chapter 13 debtors do not normally pay their creditors in full and often pay them only a small fraction of their claims. Beyond that, debtors besieged by creditors sometimes file under Chapter 13 solely to obtain the protection of the automatic stay, with no intent to complete a repayment plan. Thus, the debtor may simply be buying time until creditors are able to have the case dismissed, perhaps with the intent of filing again and again, thereby delaying creditors almost indefinitely.

In 1984, Congress added § 109(g) to address this problem. It prohibits refiling for 180 days after a dismissal resulting from the debtor's willful failure to obey a court order or failure to prosecute the case, or after voluntary dismissal following a creditor's motion for relief from the automatic stay. As with any effort to create a general rule to deal with highly individualizcd circumstanccs, this onc is probably both underinclusive and overinclusive. For example, because of the different nature of Chapter 13, creditors of a Chapter 13 debtor do not regularly move for relief from the stay. Thus, a debtor may choose to file under Chapter 13 to stave off foreclosure or eviction, then voluntarily dismiss, only to file again when the mortgagee or landlord brings another action. Section 109(g) does not prohibit such behavior. On the other hand, debtors sometimes miss deadlines, such as those for the § 341 examination or for the filing of schedules or statements, because they lack adequate legal advice and are not aware of them. If the court dismisses for such errors, § 109(g) may delay the debtor from receiving much needed bankruptcy relief.

Another type of repeated filing involves what is euphemistically known as a "Chapter 20": a Chapter 13 petition filed shortly after receiving a Chapter 7 discharge. Congress probably envisioned Chapters 7 and 13 as offering alternative forms of relief for debtors. If a debtor is willing to turn over nonexempt property to a trustee for distribution to creditors, the debtor can receive a Chapter 7 discharge without using future income to pay creditors. Three drawbacks to this are that the debtor may be left with certain nondischargeable debts, must deal with secured creditors without much help from the bankruptcy court, and will not be able to get another discharge for six years. On the other hand, if a debtor is willing to use all disposable income for three years to pay creditors under Chapter 13, the debtor may retain possession of exempt and encumbered property and may strip down liens, other than home mortgages and some purchase-money security interests.

Some debtors have sought the best of both bankruptcy worlds by first getting rid of ordinary debts in Chapter 7 and then filing in Chapter 13 to deal with nondischargeable debts and security interests. This effectively allows them to target their postpetition disposable income toward payment of the debts that they cannot or do not wish to discharge. In essence, a Chapter 20 plan, if permitted, would allow the debtor to discriminate among creditors in a way that § 1322(b)(1) would not permit if the debtor had filed under Chapter 13 initially. Not surprisingly, courts have reacted with some hostility toward such Chapter 20 plans. Some courts even treated them as bad faith *per se* but the Supreme Court rejected that view largely because of the absence of a statutory bar to successive filings or discharges in Chapter 13.[76]

Indeed, there apparently are some justifications for filing under Chapter 13 shortly after receiving a Chapter 7 discharge, such as if the debtor has too much debt to be eligible for Chapter 13 relief or insufficient income to fund a feasible plan without first discharging some debt. Nevertheless, § 1328(f), enacted in 2005, has significantly cut back on Chapter 20 cases. While it does not stop a debtor from *filing* a Chapter 13 petition shortly after receiving a discharge, it significantly restricts a debtor's ability to obtain a Chapter 13 discharge shortly after receiving a Chapter 7 discharge. Read that provision and then tackle the following problem.

Problem 11-9

Delaney filed a Chapter 7 bankruptcy petition on May 1, 2009, and received a discharge in that case on November 1, 2009. If Delaney files for Chapter 13 bankruptcy protection on August 1, 2013, and completes the plan on September 15, 2018, will Delaney be entitled to a discharge? *See* § 1328(f). If Delaney is entitled to a discharge in the Chapter 13 case, should confirmation of the plan be denied as not in good faith under § 1325(a)(3)?

6. *Avoidance Powers*

In Chapter 7, the trustee uses a variety of powers to avoid certain prepetition and postpetition transfers. *See* §§ 544, 545, 547, 548, 549, 553. These powers are a necessary aspect of the trustee's principal function of collecting and liquidating the property of the estate. § 704(a)(1). The Chapter 13 trustee, however, acts primarily as

---

[76] *Johnson v. Home State Bank*, 501 U.S. 78, 87 (1991).

a disbursing agent and may choose not to exercise those powers. Indeed, the method of compensating trustees gives the Chapter 7 trustee an incentive to maximize the size of the bankruptcy estate through the use of avoiding powers, whereas a Chapter 13 trustee may not have such an incentive.

What if, however, the trustee or the debtor wishes to avoid a transfer? For example, suppose a creditor levied on substantial assets shortly before the bankruptcy petition were filed. In a Chapter 7 case, that preferential transfer, once avoided, might significantly enhance the recovery of general creditors. However, if the debtor files under Chapter 13, which requires that creditors receive at least what they would get in Chapter 7 – a calculation that necessarily factors in the impact of the trustee's avoiding powers – but is unable to avoid the preferential transfer, the debtor may not be able to fund a confirmable plan.

Chapter 5 of the Bankruptcy Code, which includes the avoiding powers, is expressly made applicable in Chapter 13 cases. § 103(a). However, in enumerating the powers of the Chapter 13 trustee, § 1302(b) makes no reference to the avoiding powers. Moreover, while a Chapter 11 debtor in possession is expressly granted the avoiding powers of a trustee, § 1107(a), there is no such grant of authority to a Chapter 13 debtor. Is there any way, then, to avoid preferences, fraudulent transfers, and the like in a Chapter 13 case? Several courts have ruled that there is not.[77]

---

[77] *See, e.g., In re Knapper,* 407 F.3d 573 (3d Cir. 2005) (Chapter 13 debtor could not invoke trustee's strong-arm powers); *In re Stangel*, 219 F.3d 498 (5th Cir. 2000) (debtor lacked standing to bring § 545 action); *In re Hanson*, 332 B.R. 8 (10th Cir. BAP 2005). *Contra In re Dickson*, 427 B.R. 399 (6th Cir. BAP 2010) (debtor has derivative standing to pursue avoidance claims under § 544 and § 547 when the trustee declines to do so); *In re Cohen*, 305 B.R. 886 (9th Cir. BAP 2004) (debtor has standing to use trustee's § 544 strong-arm powers).

Even if the debtor cannot use the trustee's powers to avoid an unperfected lien, the debtor may be able to claims-objection process to the same end. *See Sovereign Bank v. Strother*, 2013 WL 3243555 (N.D.N.Y. 2013); Rule 3001(d).

A similar issue arises with respect to § 108(a) and (b), which extend the time for the trustee to bring certain nonbankruptcy actions and perform some other acts. Most courts dealing with the issue have concluded that these rules do not apply to a Chapter 13 debtor. *See, e.g., Estate of Carr ex rel. Carr v. United States*, 482 F. Supp. 2d 842 (W.D. Tex. 2007); *Straub v. Richardson*, 92 So. 3d 548 (La. Ct. App. 2012). *But see In re Dawson*, 411 B.R. 1 (Bankr. D.D.C. 2008); *In re McConnell*, 390 B.R. 170 (Bankr. W.D. Pa. 2008); *Thomas v. GMAC Residential Funding Corp.*, 309 B.R. 453 (D. Md. 2004).

C. THE EFFECT OF CONFIRMATION

Confirmation of the plan is *not* the culmination of a Chapter 13 case. In particular, it does not terminate the stay or qualify the debtor for a discharge. The discharge is not granted until the debtor finishes making all payments under the plan, § 1328(a), or becomes entitled to a hardship discharge, § 1328(b). The stay remains generally in effect until the case is closed, dismissed, or the debtor is either granted or denied a discharge. § 362(c)(2). Because the discharge does not come until all payments are made, the stay generally remains until that time as well.

What confirmation does do is vest all property of the estate in the debtor.[78] § 1327(b). More important, confirmation binds the debtor and all creditors to the plan. § 1327(a).[79] The plan therefore becomes the blueprint for the parties' future relations. It is binding even on those creditors who are not provided for under it. In short, the plan is given *res judicata* effect as to all claims against the debtor.[80]

This effect engenders two recurring issues. First, what happens if the confirmed plan contains an improper or unauthorized provision? In general, a confirmed plan cannot be collaterally attacked. Thus, if a timely objection was not made and if the time for appealing the confirmation order has expired, the plan will normally be binding despite any impropriety in it. This allows the debtor to engage in what some have termed discharge by ambush: putting language in the plan discharging an otherwise nondischargeable debt, have the plan confirmed without following the procedures for litigating nondischargeability issues (which are supposed to be resolved through adversary proceedings rather than the confirmation process), and then give preclusive effect to the plan. Although bankruptcy courts have a duty not to confirm such a plan even if no creditor objects, a plan that is confirmed remains binding.[81] Of course, a

---

[78] This means that § 362(a)(3) and (4) no longer apply to such property. *See* § 362(c).

[79] Section 1327(c) provides that the property revested in the debtor is free of any claims "provided for by the plan," unless the plan provides otherwise. Thus, if a secured claim is not provided for in the plan, the lien survives. If the secured claim is provided for in the plan, the secured creditor should ensure that the plan provides for its lien to be retained on the collateral. *See In re Regional Bldg. Sys., Inc.*, 254 F.3d 528 (4th Cir. 2001).

[80] *See, e.g.*, *In re Layo*, 460 F.3d 289 (2d Cir. 2006) (confirmed plan that treats claimant as secured is res judicata and prevents subsequent lien avoidance action).

[81] *United Student Aid Funds, Inc. v. Espinosa*, 130 S. Ct. 1367 (2010) (creditor's receipt of the proposed plan satisfied due process).

debtor's attorney who circumvents proper procedures in this way has engaged in sanctionable conduct.[82]

Second, what happens if the debtor fails to perform under the plan? When that occurs, the debtor will not receive a discharge, the case will be converted to Chapter 7 or dismissed, and the claims of creditors will be restored to their original amount, less any payments actually received under the Chapter 13 plan. *See* § 1307. It will also usually be grounds for getting relief from the stay.

IN RE CARONA

254 B.R. 364 (Bankr. S.D. Tex. 2000)

Steen, Bankruptcy Judge.

Sterling Bank ("Sterling") seeks relief from the automatic stay to execute on its security interests in certain trucks and trailers because Richard Carona ("Debtor") has failed to make payments to the chapter 13 trustee in this case as required by the Debtor's confirmed chapter 13 plan. For reasons set forth below, relief from the stay is granted by separate order issued this date.

FACTS

The facts are undisputed.

August 27, 1999	Debtor filed this case under chapter 13 of the Bankruptcy Code.
March 23, 2000	Debtor's Chapter 13 plan was confirmed.
July 19, 2000	Sterling filed its motion for relief from the automatic stay, alleging principally that the Debtor had failed to make payments to the chapter 13 trustee as required by the Debtor's plan.

The Debtor's chapter 13 plan does not include any provision that would alter the post-confirmation vesting provisions of § 1327(b) of the Bankruptcy Code. There was no proceeding to avoid Sterling's security interests and the plan did not provide for vesting the trucks and trailers in the Debtor free and clear of Sterling's security interests. At the time of the hearing on Sterling's motion for relief from the stay, the Debtor was $8,700 delinquent in payments to the chapter 13 trustee.

---

[82] *See In re Patton*, 261 B.R. 44, 48 (E.D. Wash. 2001); *In re Lemons*, 285 B.R. 327 (Bankr. W.D. Okla. 2002); *In re Hensley*, 249 B.R. 318 (Bankr. W.D. Okla. 2000).

Although Debtor's counsel was present at the hearing on Sterling's motion for relief from the stay and although counsel argued enthusiastically for the Court to deny the motion, the Debtor did not appear at the hearing and the Debtor presented no evidence at that hearing to refute Sterling's evidence that the Debtor was $8,700 delinquent in plan payments. The Debtor has not filed a motion to modify the plan to cure the payment defaults.

CONTENTIONS OF THE PARTIES

Sterling contends that the Debtor's default is sufficient "cause" to justify relief from the automatic stay to allow Sterling to execute on its security interests, and to sell the collateral. The Debtor contends (i) that the confirmation of its chapter 13 plan revests the trucks and trailers in the Debtor, (ii) that the trucks and trailers are, therefore, no longer property of the estate, (iii) that the bankruptcy automatic stay no longer applies since the property is no longer property of the estate, (iv) that confirmation of the chapter 13 plan, in effect, rewrites the contract between the Debtor and Sterling and (v) therefore Sterling's appropriate remedy is to seek dismissal of the case and the concomitant revocation of the effects of the confirmation order.

Neither party has briefed the issues or cited authority for its contentions.

CONCLUSIONS OF LAW

Analysis of the Debtor's argument requires an interpretation of the definition of property of the estate and an interpretation of the reach and termination of the automatic stay in bankruptcy. It is helpful to view these concepts in broad generalities, first, and then to look at the finer points of the Debtor's arguments.

1. GENERAL CONCEPTS AS APPLICABLE TO THIS CASE

At the moment that a bankruptcy petition is filed, Bankruptcy Code § 541 creates an estate consisting of all property interests owned by the Debtor. Also at the beginning of the case, Bankruptcy Code § 362(a) creates an automatic stay that prohibits creditor action to collect pre-petition debt. For purposes of this discussion, it is important to note that the stay prohibits: (i) collection of pre-petition claims against the debtor, (ii) acts to foreclose on property of the estate, and (iii) acts to enforce pre-petition liens against property of the debtor. The automatic stay terminates (as to property of the estate) when the property ceases to be property of the estate. Otherwise, (as applicable to the current facts) the automatic stay terminates when the case is dismissed or the debtor is discharged.

Confirmation of a chapter 13 plan: (i) binds the debtor and each creditor to its terms; and (ii) vests property of the estate in the debtor (unless the plan provides otherwise), subject to liens and security interests (unless those liens and security interests are voided by appropriate proceedings).

2. DOES THE AUTOMATIC STAY APPLY, POST-CONFIRMATION, TO STERLING?

The Debtor correctly argues that, as of the date that the chapter 13 plan was confirmed, the trucks and trailers ceased to be property of the estate and became property of the debtor. Therefore, the stay effected by Bankruptcy Code § 362(a)(2), (3), and (4) was terminated. However, Bankruptcy Code § 362(a)(5) provides that:

> [Filing a bankruptcy] petition operates as a stay . . . of any act to create, perfect, or enforce against property of the debtor any lien to the extent that such lien secures a claim that arose before the commencement of the case.

There is no question that the trucks and trailers are now property of the debtor and there is no question that Sterling's security interests were liens to secure a pre-petition claim. The stay effected [by] § 362(a)(5) remains in effect. Therefore, the Debtor is incorrect in arguing that Sterling's motion should be denied as moot.

3. DOES A POSTPETITION DEFAULT IN PAYMENTS TO THE CHAPTER 13 TRUSTEE CONSTITUTE SUFFICIENT "CAUSE" TO GRANT RELIEF FROM THE AUTOMATIC STAY?

The Debtor argues that the confirmation order, in effect, rewrote the contract between the Debtor and Sterling and that Sterling is bound by that order. Therefore, the Debtor argues, relief from the stay is inappropriate until the case is dismissed or until the confirmation order is revoked. The Court disagrees.

The Debtor's argument ignores the fact that the Debtor is *also* bound by the confirmation order. The Debtor is obligated by the plan and by the confirmation order to make payments to the Trustee. Even assuming the Debtor's conceptual approach, (*i.e.* that the confirmation order creates a new contract between the Debtor and Sterling), there does not appear to be any reason why (and the Debtor has pointed out no reason why) a postpetition default by the Debtor does not justify the same results that would occur outside of bankruptcy, that is, foreclosure on a lien or security interest. That foreclosure may first require permission of the bankruptcy court (*i.e.* relief from the automatic stay of § 362(a)(5)), but the Debtor has pointed out no reason why the Debtor's default is not "cause" sufficient to justify the court to grant that relief.

The jurisprudence and the principal treatise on chapter 13 support the view that a postpetition default is sufficient cause to grant relief from the stay to allow foreclosure by a secured creditor. Judge Ellington, in *In re Lee*, 167 B.R. 417, 426–27 (Bankr. S.D. Miss. 1992), *aff'd*, 22 F.3d 1094 (5th Cir. 1994) expresses the rule as follows, and cites no fewer than 5 cases in support of the proposition:

Since a creditor's rights are redefined by the terms of the confirmed plan, where a debtor materially defaults under the terms of his confirmed plan the creditor may be entitled to relief from the automatic stay under Bankruptcy Code § 362.

In the leading treatise on chapter 13, Judge Lundin indicates that a post-confirmation default is sufficient cause to grant relief from the stay unless the Debtor timely modifies the plan to cure the default. The Court of Appeals for the Fifth Circuit has clearly held that the chapter 13 plan can be modified to cure post-confirmation defaults. *Matter of Mendoza*, 111 F.3d 1264 (5th Cir. 1997). Therefore, if a debtor wants to avoid the possibility that the Court will grant relief from the stay on account of the debtor's postpetition defaults under the plan, the debtor should assure timely plan modification to cure the default.

CONCLUSION

In summary, the Court concludes that the automatic stay of § 362(a)(5) survives plan confirmation with respect to pre-petition claims. The Court further concludes that a material default in payments to the chapter 13 trustee constitutes sufficient cause to grant relief from the stay when the Debtor has taken no steps to cure the deficiency promptly or to modify the plan to cure the default. Therefore, an order will be issued this date granting Sterling relief from the automatic stay.

In researching the law for this opinion, the Court examined and considered a number of cases that deal with the intricacies of the interplay between §§ 362, 1306, and 1327. Because this case involves a *pre*-petition claim secured by property of the debtor and a postpetition default under a confirmed plan, the Court does not need to consider whether a stay exists with respect to postpetition claims and with respect to execution of those claims against property of the debtor. Nor does the Court need to consider the extent to which property/earnings of the debtor post-confirmation constitute property of the estate. Nor does the Court need to consider the applicable consequences, if any, of a plan provision that abrogates § 1327(b) to allow property to remain in the estate rather than being vested in the debtor post-confirmation. Each of these distinctions might be significant in different circumstances and for different purposes. Although the Court finds the decision in *In re Fisher*, 203 B.R. 958 (N.D. Ill. 1997) to be persuasive, and although the Court finds Judge Lundin's discussion of that case in his chapter 13 treatise to be especially illuminating, any further discussion of those issues in this decision would be dicta.

NOTE

The last paragraph of the *Carona* decision identifies a number of things the court did not need to address. To understand what the court was getting at, consider this. While any effort to collect a prepetition debt remains stayed, *see* § 362(a)(6), efforts to collect a postpetition debt directed at nonexempt property now vested in the debtor would not be stayed. Yet while that rule is fairly clear, what remains unclear is how it applies to the debtor's future income. Is the portion of the income allocated to the plan immune from the reach of creditors? What about the remaining portion – the debtor's nondisposable income – which is by definition to be used to pay the debtor's necessary living expenses? The following case addresses this issue.

1. Paying Postpetition Obligations

IN RE LEAVELL
190 B.R. 536 (Bankr. E.D. Va. 1995)

St. John, Bankruptcy Judge.

This case is before the court on the motion of the debtor, Alfreda Epps Leavell, for a finding of contempt and imposition of sanctions against Littmans, Inc. ("Littmans") and its counsel, W. Wayne Tiffany ("Tiffany"). After reviewing the evidence and arguments of counsel, we make the following determinations.

FINDINGS OF FACT

The debtor filed the instant Chapter 13 case on December 8, 1994. Six days later, she purchased a ring and a video cassette recorder from Littmans. The debtor did not disclose her bankruptcy status when she purchased these items. After the debtor failed to pay for these items, Littmans, through Tiffany, obtained a judgment against her on July 19, 1995 and began to garnish her postpetition earnings. Upon learning of the garnishment, counsel for the debtor notified Tiffany of the pending Chapter 13 case but her request to dismiss the garnishment was refused. Thereafter, the debtor filed this motion for contempt and sanctions, requesting damages, attorney fees, and sanctions on the grounds that the garnishment action violated the automatic stay.[83]

---

[83] The debtor did not argue that the lawsuit and judgment obtained by Littmans violated the stay.

We note that the debtor's confirmed Chapter 13 plan required $75.00 per month for 36 months. According to her schedules, the debtor earns $1,550.00 per month. Under the terms of the plan, all property of the estate re-vested in the debtor upon confirmation. The Court entered an order confirming the Chapter 13 plan on February 6, 1995. Littmans did not file a proof of claim for the postpetition debts and the plan failed to provide for said debts.

ANALYSIS

The automatic stay operates to prohibit certain collection efforts upon the filing of the bankruptcy petition. It bars collection actions against the (1) debtor which actions could have been brought pre-petition; (2) property of the debtor in an effort to collect pre-petition debts; and (3) property of the estate regardless of whether the debt arose before or after the filing of the bankruptcy petition. In the case at bar, we are concerned only with the third prohibition since the debt was incurred postpetition. * * *

The case at bar poses two issues for the Court to consider. The threshold issue is whether there can be any property of the estate upon which the automatic stay can operate upon confirmation of a Chapter 13 plan. If the answer is negative, then Littmans and Tiffany did not violate the automatic stay since there was nothing upon which the stay can protect. If the answer is affirmative, then we must determine whether all postpetition earnings become property of the estate and thus protected by the automatic stay.

Littmans and Tiffany argued that property of the estate in the instant case ceased to exist upon the confirmation of the plan. Since the plan did not provide otherwise, they argue, the order of confirmation vested all property of the estate in the debtor. They conclude that they did not violate the stay because there was no property of the estate remaining upon which the stay can operate.

We first note that courts have disagreed on whether property of the estate exists after the Chapter 13 plan is confirmed. There are several lines of cases as to how to reconcile seemingly conflicting provisions of §§ 1306(a) and 1327(b). One line of cases has held that upon confirmation of the plan, property that is necessary to implement the Chapter 13 plan remains property of the estate upon which the stay operates to protect. In contrast, another line of cases has held that two things occur upon confirmation of the plan: (1) property of the estate is vested in the debtor unless provided for otherwise in the plan; and (2) there is no longer any property of the estate remaining upon which the

---

Therefore, we do not address this issue.

stay can operate. In another line of reasoning, [one court has] held that although confirmation of the plan vests property of the estate with the debtor, the debtor's ownership interest in such property is limited to the extent that it is required to implement the plan. In other words, the debtor gets ownership and possessory rights to the property but the debtor is not free for all purposes to do with it as he pleases.

After reviewing the * * * cases and the reasoning therein, the Court agrees with the first line of cases. Upon confirmation of the plan, the estate continues to exist. There are several reasons for this conclusion. First, there must be some property of the estate remaining after confirmation for the Chapter 13 Trustee to administer and upon which the Trustee makes a final report. If there never is any property of the estate after confirmation, then what is there for the Trustee to collect from the debtor and then disburse to and for the benefit of the creditors under the confirmed plan? If they do not receive and disburse property of the estate, why are they needed?

Second, to determine that § 1327(b) mean[s] that there is no property of the estate after confirmation would render § 1306(a) superfluous. This is necessarily so because Congress intended to protect earnings and property that are acquired by the debtor postpetition and necessary to implement the plan. Without § 1306(a), any property that the debtor acquires post-confirmation can be seized without regards to the Chapter 13 process. Congress did not say in § 1306(a) that earnings and properties acquired postpetition are property of the estate until the Chapter 13 plan is confirmed. Rather, it said that such property and earnings are property of the estate until the case is closed, dismissed, or converted.

Third, our decision would also give § 1306(b) full effect. Section 1306(b) provides:

> Except as provided in a confirmed plan or order confirming a plan, the debtor shall remain in possession of all property of the estate.

This section does not apply until confirmation. If at the time after confirmation there is no property of the estate, then there is no reason to grant the debtor possession.

Finally, the clear language of § 1306 demonstrates that confirmation of the plan is not relevant to determining whether property is or is not property of the estate. The relevant events in this determination are commencement of the case and either dismissal, closing or conversion of the case. If Congress had intended for confirmation to so drastically affect the expansive definition of property of the estate in § 1306, it knew how to draft such a provision.

We next address the effect of confirmation on the debtor's postpetition earnings. The debtor argues that all postpetition earnings are property of the estate under § 1306(a) and thus protected by the automatic stay from collection actions by post-confirmation creditors. Specifically, the debtor argues that not only postpetition earnings are property of the estate, but also that they remain so until the case is closed, dismissed or converted to a case under Chapter 7, 11, or 12.

The debtor also argues that policy considerations favored a judgment in her favor. She argues that allowing Littmans to garnish the portion of the earnings over $75.00 would result in great prejudice to her. Such a garnishment threatens her ability to complete her plan payments because it reduces the debtor's already limited resources. The garnishment may force the debtor to use the money allocated to pay the plan and thus frustrate her ability to complete the Chapter 13 plan and thus destroy her ability to receive a discharge. Furthermore, if the plan cannot be consummated, the unsecured creditors would also be prejudiced since they would not receive any payments. We decline to adopt these arguments.

Addressing the debtor's legal argument, we conclude that earnings acquired post-confirmation and necessary to implement the Chapter 13 plan remains property of the estate after the plan is confirmed unless the plan states otherwise. Only that portion that is necessary to make the plan payments becomes property of the estate and protected by the automatic stay. The balance of such post-confirmation earnings belongs to the debtor as her individual property and is not insulated from postpetition claims nor protected by the automatic stay. Applying these conclusions of law to the facts of the instant case, only $75.00 of the debtor's monthly earnings is protected by the automatic stay. This meant that Littmans could garnish up to $1,475.00 per month from the debtor's net monthly income of $1,550.00. Littmans garnished $417.59. Accordingly, Littmans (and Tiffany) did not violate the automatic stay when it garnished the debtor's income to satisfy the postpetition debts.

We note that [some] courts have reached even stronger conclusions. These courts held that pursuant to § 1327(b) all property of the estate vests in the debtor upon confirmation of the plan, without regard to whether or not such property is necessary to implement the plan. We disagree because this interpretation would allow the creditor to levy against all of the debtor's property, including that property in the hands of the Chapter 13 Trustee. The holding of these courts would require debtors to specifically delay re-vesting in the plan or to vest property of the estate in an entity other than the debtor. We do not believe that this was Congress' intent. Section 1327(b) is an efficient adaption of Bankruptcy Act Section 70(I). It implements a major theme of Chapter 13 by preserving to the debtor possession of all property, except as otherwise required to effectuate the confirmed plan.

Turning to the debtor's policy arguments, we find them equally unpersuasive. The primary concern proffered by the debtor is that the Court should protect the debtor from herself. She chose to purchase the ring and video cassette recorder when she possibly could not afford to pay for them. She was in bankruptcy and, according to her schedules, could barely pay her living expenses and make her plan payments. The prejudice the debtor raises was her own doing and the Court will not allow her to use the bankruptcy process as a sword against the unwary creditor who extended credit to her without knowledge of her bankruptcy.

Addressing the debtor's argument concerning the unsecured creditors, the Court finds that argument unpersuasive. Unsecured creditors have an interest in the debtor being able to perform under the plan to completion and without postpetition creditors being able to deprive the debtor of its ability to do so by seizing property or wages. If the case is dismissed, the unsecured creditors can pursue their claims through non-bankruptcy forums to obtain the benefit of their bargain. We do recognize that the unsecured creditors would receive 0% of their claims, according to the debtor's schedules, should the case be converted. However, the Code provides many provisions that favor postpetition creditors over pre-petition creditors. Therefore, we cannot conclude that the prejudice to the unsecured creditors is so severe to warrant another outcome.

Furthermore, we find the prejudice to Littmans more equitably compelling. First, it would have no remedy to enforce its claim until [the] case is closed, dismissed or converted. Second, Littmans could not share in the distribution of this plan. It would not qualify to file a postpetition claim under § 1305(a) and § 1305(c) because the items purchased by the debtor were not necessary for the debtor's performance under the plan. Third, Littmans does not have standing to modify the plan to include [its] claims under § 1329. Since it cannot file a proof of claim as contemplated in § 1305 and thus get an allowed claim, it necessarily does not have standing to modify the plan.

As a final note, our decision is limited to postpetition earnings as contemplated by § 1306(a)(2). We do not deal with property acquired postpetition as set forth in § 1306(a)(1). Postpetition earnings dedicated to the Chapter 13 Trustee are easily discernible for purposes of determining whether such funds are necessary to implement the plan. Property other than earnings are not so readily discernible and must be determined on a case-by-case basis. Therefore, we expressly limit this opinion to the post-confirmations earnings.

NOTE

Some other courts have rejected this approach and held that all of the debtor's postpetition earnings are estate property and therefore are protected by the stay.[84] As one of them explained:

> The chapter 13 plan payment is not the only payment necessary for the successful completion of a chapter 13 plan. Frequently, the confirmed plan requires the debtor make payments directly to a secured creditor, in this case the mortgage company, and in other cases, the car finance company. If the direct payments are not timely made, the secured creditor will seek relief from the automatic stay in order to repossess the vehicle or sell the home at foreclosure. If relief is granted, the chapter 13 case typically converts to a chapter 7 proceeding or is dismissed, both to the prejudice of the unsecured creditors provided for in the chapter 13 plan. Saving the family home or the family car is a key incentive to selecting chapter 13 over chapter 7 – a selection frequently more beneficial to unsecured creditors than chapter 7. Not only is the plan payment to the chapter 13 trustee necessary for the success of the plan, but the direct payments to the secured creditors are also necessary.
>
> * * * In addition to these plan payments, the debtor must also be able to pay his living expenses. Confirmation requires that the debtor devote his entire net disposable income to the chapter 13 plan. § 1325(b). Confirmation also requires the court to find that the plan be feasible. § 1325(a)(6). Successful plans require strict adherence to the debtor's budget. A garnishment necessarily reduces the income available to the debtor to make his plan payment to the trustee, the direct payments to his secured creditors, and the payment of his current living expenses. Since the debtor's entire net disposable income must be devoted to the chapter 13 plan, there is nothing left over for a creditor to seize that does not affect a debtor's ability to successfully complete the chapter 13 plan. All post-confirmation earnings – not just the amount of the plan payment

---

[84] *See, e.g.*, *In re Fisher*, 203 B.R. 958 (N.D. Ill. 1997); *In re Holden*, 236 B.R. 156 (Bankr. D. Vt. 1999), *aff'd*, 258 B.R. 323 (D. Vt. 2000); *In re Rangel*, 233 B.R. 191 (Bankr. D. Mass. 1999).

– are necessary for the success of a chapter 13 plan and must be property of the post-confirmation chapter 13 estate. They are protected by the automatic stay.[85]

2. *Modifying a Confirmed Plan*

During the multi-year duration of the plan, many things may affect the debtor's finances. On the negative side, the debtor may experience a job loss, an illness with associated medical expenses and loss of income, a divorce, an uninsured casualty to property, or simply unanticipated expenses, such as for necessary repairs to a home or car. On the positive side, the debtor may receive a raise, find a better paying job, get married to a person with substantial assets or high income, or even win the lottery. Accordingly, § 1329 allows for post-confirmation modification of a plan. Unfortunately, that authorization includes no guidance on when a court may or must modify the plan. In other words, it provides no standard for determining whether or when modification is appropriate, although it does require that a modified plan satisfy all requirements normally applicable to plan confirmation. This raises a difficult question: given the *res judicata* effect of confirmation, what has to change before a court must or should entertain motions to modify? Given the lack of guidance in the Code, it is not surprising that courts have come to differing conclusions on this question. Some require that the proponent of modification show that there has been an unanticipated, substantial change in the debtor's financial circumstances.[86] Others have found no such requirement in § 1329 and declined to imply one.[87] This latter approach appears to be the prevalent view.[88]

Probably the most common reason debtors seek to modify a confirmed plan is a reduction in income. If the court believes that the modification is proposed in good faith and the debtor will be able to make the payments under the modified plan, it is likely to

---

[85] *In re Reynard*, 250 B.R. 241, 248–49 (Bankr. E.D. Va. 2000).

[86] *See, e.g., In re Arnold*, 869 F.2d 240 (4th Cir. 1989).

[87] *See, e.g., In re Witkowski*, 16 F.3d 739 (7th Cir. 1994).

[88] *See Barbosa v. Solomon*, 235 F.3d 31 (1st Cir. 2000) (agreeing with *Witkowski* and leaving the decision on modification to the discretion of the bankruptcy judge, subject to review on an abuse-of-discretion standard); *In re Brown*, 219 B.R. 191 (6th Cir. BAP 1998); *In re Powers*, 202 B.R. 618 (9th Cir. BAP 1996).

approve the modification. Apparently, debtors may even use § 1329 to modify their plans in order to cure post-confirmation defaults on their home mortgage loans.[89]

Another reason debtors sometimes seek modification is if property serving as collateral suddenly depreciates and the debtor no longer views it as worthwhile to continue making the payments called for under the plan in order to retain the property. For example, in *In re Coffman*,[90] the debtors owed $6,775 on a car valued at $5,450. Their plan stripped the lien down, treating the creditor as secured to the extent of $5,450 and unsecured as to the remainder, and required the debtors to make monthly payments of $121.30 on the secured claim. Fifteen months into the plan, the car began to malfunction and repair efforts proved unsuccessful. The debtors then decided to surrender the car to the creditor and sought modification to avoid making the remaining $121.30 payments. The court refused to permit the modification, noting that debtors receive the benefit of any appreciation in property collateralizing a secured claim and thus it was only fair that they bear the risk of any depreciation. It then regarded the debtor's request as a motion to reconsider a claim under § 502(j), for which the requisite "cause" was lacking.

Occasionally, a creditor or the trustee seeks a modification. For example, in *In re Arnold*,[91] the debtor's income increased from a projected $80,000 at the inception of the plan to $200,000 two years later. The Fourth Circuit affirmed the bankruptcy court's decision to increase the monthly payments from $800 to $1500 and to extend the term of the plan to five years. A similar issue arises when assets that were part of the estate, but which confirmation re-vested in the debtor, appreciate postpetition. Consider the following problem.

Problem 11-10

Delighted's confirmed Chapter 13 plan called for Delighted to make direct payments on a home mortgage loan and payments of $1,200/month to the trustee for distribution to unsecured claimants. If those payments are made, and after deducting the trustee's fees, the resulting distributions will be sufficient to pay creditors approximately 24% of their claims. Eighteen months after confirmation, and after real estate values had appreciated

---

[89] *See In re Mendoza*, 111 F.3d 1264 (5th Cir. 1997); *In re Hoggle*, 12 F.3d 1008 (11th Cir. 1994).

[90] 271 B.R. 492 (Bankr. N.D. Tex. 2002).

[91] 869 F.2d 240 (4th Cir. 1989).

> substantially, Delighted sold the home for $137,000 more than the value listed in Delighted's schedules. Even after using some of the sales proceeds to pay off the mortgage loan, the remainder, if allocated to the plan, would be sufficient to pay off all creditors in full. What should the court do? *Compare In re Murphy*, 474 F.3d 143 (4th Cir. 2007), *and Barbosa v. Soloman*, 235 F.3d 31 (1st Cir. 2000), *with In re Burgie*, 239 B.R. 406 (9th Cir. BAP 1999).

Even when modification is available, debtors should be careful about requesting it. As one commentator noted:

> Should you let a sleeping dog lie? Chapter 13 plans, once confirmed, can be modified. However, modification triggers a re-examination of the debtor's affairs, including his or her income and assets. Absent a modification of a chapter 13 plan, usually only the debtors are aware of their financial status and prospects; they have, in effect, an information monopoly. Modifying a plan requires disclosing financial information by debtors and the break-up of that monopoly.[92]

One case put an interesting twist on this issue. In *Petro v. Mishler*,[93] the trustee was concerned that the debtors, because of their ages and work potential, might earn extra income not factored into their plan's payment schedules. At his request, the bankruptcy court required the debtors to provide the trustee with sworn statements of their income and check stubs every six months as a condition to approving the plan. The U.S. Court of Appeals for the Seventh Circuit reversed, concluding that this effectively and impermissibly added a confirmation requirement to § 1325(a). It did, however, note that the debtors had to submit their income tax returns to the trustee, who could then use these as a basis for seeking to modify the plan under § 1329.

---

[92] Joseph R. Prochaska, *Breaking the "Information Monopoly": The Perils to a Debtor of Modifying a Chapter 13 Plan*, AM. BANKR. INST. J., Mar. 2000, at 18.

[93] 276 F.3d 375 (7th Cir. 2002).

3. *The Scope of the Chapter 13 Discharge*

If the debtor does complete all of the required payments under the plan, then the debtor is entitled to a discharge of the unpaid portion of prepetition claims.[94] § 1328(a). The 2005 Amendments significantly cut back on the scope of the discharge in Chapter 13, bringing it much closer to that available in Chapter 7. *See* § 1328(a). Debts treated as nondischargeable in Chapter 7 pursuant to § 523(a)(1)(B), (1)(C), (2)–(5), (8), and (9) are also nondischargeable in Chapter 13. § 1328(a)(2). In addition, four other types of debts rendered nondischargeable under § 523 are subject to analogous rules in Chapter 13:

Provision	Nature of Debt	Analogous Chapter 13 Rule
§ 523(a)(1)	Most Priority Taxes	§ 1322(a)(2)
§ 523(a)(6)	Willful & Malicious Injury	§ 1328(a)(4)
§ 523(a)(7)	Fines	§ 1328(a)(3)
§ 523(a)(13)	Criminal Restitution	

The most significant debts that are treated as nondischargeable in Chapter 7 but as dischargeable in Chapter 13 are debts incurred to pay taxes and property settlement obligations. *See* § 523(a)(14), (14A), (15).

Problem 11-11

Compare each pair of nondischargeability rules identified below. Are they different and, if so, which is broader?

A. § 523(a)(6) and § 1328(a)(4).
B. § 523(a)(7) and § 1328(a)(3).
C § 523(a)(13) and § 1328(a)(3).

---

[94] The court must, prior to entering the discharge order, expressly find that there is no reason to believe that the debtor has engaged in specified bad acts. *See* § 1328(h).

Problem 11-12

Last year, Dastardly, then 19 years old, was indicted for assault and battery. Although the criminal case was dismissed, the victim has brought a civil action against Dastardly seeking $400,000 in compensatory damages and $1 million in punitive damages. Discovery has been completed and trial is scheduled to commence next week.

A. How, if at all, does the civil action affect Dastardly's eligibility for Chapter 13 relief? *See* § 109(e).
B. If Dastardly files for Chapter 13 relief today, the court confirms Dastardly's plan, and Dastardly completes the plan, will Dastardly's liability for damages arising from the assault and battery be discharged? *See* § 1328(a), (h).
C. How, if at all, would the analysis of each of the questions above change if Dastardly waits to file until after the trial and judgment is entered against him for $400,000?
D. If Dastardly files for Chapter 13 relief today and proposes a plan that pays unsecured claimants 5% of their claims over five years, should the plan be confirmed? *See* § 1325(a)(3).

Problem 11-13

Shortly before filing a petition under Chapter 13, Disabled, a construction worker, developed a hernia that, unless repaired, would prevent Disabled from continuing his current employment. Disabled consulted Surgeon, who was informed about the bankruptcy petition. Disabled's health insurance will not cover all of the cost of the operation. Surgeon has never encountered a Chapter 13 patient before and calls you for legal advice concerning how the bankruptcy affects Surgeon's ability to obtain payment. Surgeon's usual practice is to send a bill for professional services after the services are performed. How would you advise Surgeon? *See* §§ 1305(a)(2), (c), 1328(a), (d).

D. CONVERSION TO CHAPTER 7

If the plan proposed by the debtor fails to satisfy the criteria for confirmation, the bankruptcy court will typically give the debtor the opportunity to revise the plan so that it can be confirmed. If the debtor cannot devise a confirmable plan, the court may dismiss the case or convert it to Chapter 7. § 1307(c). Moreover, the debtor has a nonwaivable right to convert the case to one under Chapter 7 at any time. § 1307(a). Courts disagree about whether the means test applies upon conversion from Chapter 13 to Chapter 7.[95]

If conversion occurs before confirmation, there will typically be assets on hand – in particular, postpetition disposable income – that were part of the Chapter 13 estate but which would not have been part of a Chapter 7 estate if the case had been originally filed as a liquidation. *See* § 1326(a) (requiring the debtor to begin making payments within 30 days after a plan is filed but requiring the trustee to retain such payments until confirmation or denial of confirmation). Prior to 1994, it was unclear what happened to these assets in the Chapter 7 proceeding. Circuit courts were split on whether the money remained in the estate for the benefit of creditors or was returned to the debtor.[96] In fact, the U.S. Court of Appeals for the First Circuit described the issue as "excruciatingly close,"[97] and Judge Posner acknowledged that the arguments on both sides were "equally good alternative[s]."[98] Perhaps this was because of the strong policy supporting each side: failing to retain the income in the estate leaves open the possibility of "strategic conversions"; on the other hand, including it may discourage Chapter 13 filings.

The 1994 Amendments to the Code resolved the issue by providing expressly that assets earned postpetition in a Chapter 13 case, and which remain on hand, are not part of the estate if the debtor converts to a Chapter 7 liquidation.[99] *See* § 348(f). The assets

---

[95] *Compare In re Perfetto*, 361 B.R. 27 (Bankr. D.R.I. 2007) (test does not apply after conversion), *with In re Fox*, 370 B.R. 639 (Bankr. D.N.J. 2007) (test does apply).

[96] *Compare In re Calder*, 973 F.2d 862 (10th Cir. 1992); *In re Lybrook*, 951 F.2d 136 (7th Cir. 1991) (both holding that such income remained in the estate), *with In re Young*, 66 F.3d 376 (1st Cir. 1995); *In re Bobroff*, 766 F.2d 797 (3d Cir. 1985) (both holding that it does not).

[97] *Young*, 66 F.3d at 378.

[98] *Lybrook*, 951 F.2d at 137.

[99] *See also In re Stamm*, 222 F.3d 216 (5th Cir. 2000). There is an exception if the debtor converts the case in bad faith. *See* § 348(f)(2). In such instances, all property in the estate as of the date of

are returned to the debtor. This apparently holds true even if, prior to conversion, a plan was confirmed and that plan requires the trustee to distribute the funds to creditors.[100]

A more difficult problem arises if, during the Chapter 13 proceeding, the debtor used postpetition earnings to build up equity in a home or vehicle that served as collateral for a debt. The physical asset – the home or vehicle – is unquestionably property of the estate. Yet what about the portion of the equity attributable to the postpetition payments? Courts are divided.[101]

Problem 11-14

Delinquent is employed, is paid weekly, and earns $30,000/year. Delinquent has $26,000 in reasonable annual living expenses, including income taxes and including payments on Delinquent's secured obligations (*see* the home and car loans described below, each incurred to acquire the collateral securing it). Delinquent has the following assets and liabilities.

Assets		**Liabilities**		**Monthly Payment**
$100,000	House	$93,000	Home Mortgage	$750
$4,500	Car	$6,000	Car Loan	$250
$3,900	Furnishings	$6,000	Battery Judgment	
$100	Cash	$60,000	Student Loans	
$3,500	Household Goods	$3,000	Credit Cards & Utilities	
$112,000		$165,000		

---

the conversion remains property of the estate.

[100] *See In re Michael*, 699 F.3d 305 (3d Cir. 2012).

[101] *Compare In re Robinson*, 472 B.R. 854 (Bankr. M.D. Fla. 2012); *In re Pruneskip*, 343 B.R. 714 (Bankr. M.D. Fla. 2006) (both ruling that equity built up during Chapter 13 proceeding was not in the estate upon conversion to Chapter 7), *with In re Wegner*, 243 B.R. 731 (Bankr. D. Neb. 2000) (postpetition, pre-conversion appreciation is not, upon conversion, property of the estate but equity acquired by paying down loan is property of the estate unless exempted); *In re Peter*, 309 B.R. 792 (Bankr. D. Or. 2004) (Chapter 7 estate included equity in vehicle that debtor had created by paying down the vehicle loan while case was proceeding under Chapter 13).

Delinquent is current on the car loan payments but two months behind on the home mortgage payments. Delinquent incurred the car loan two years ago. That loan calls for 48 equal monthly installments. The home mortgage secures a 20-year note that Delinquent signed four years ago. Interest is accruing on the student loans at an annual rate of 9% and on the battery judgment at a rate of 12% per annum. Would Delinquent be better off filing for bankruptcy protection under Chapter 7 or Chapter 13? Why?

CHAPTER TWELVE
THE CHAPTER 11 PROCESS

A. STARTING A CHAPTER 11 CASE

1. Theory of Chapter 11

Chapter 11 proceedings are somewhat similar to those under Chapter 13. Under each, the debtor's future income is used to pay some portion of prepetition claims. In Chapter 13 proceedings, the future income is generated through the debtor's earnings. Hence, Chapter 13 proceedings are limited to debtors with regular income. § 109(e). In Chapter 11 cases, the future income is generated primarily by using the assets of a business, such as inventory, equipment, or accounts receivables. In Chapter 13, the future income used to pay prepetition claims is based on a budget that takes into account the debtor's anticipated living expenses. In Chapter 11, the future cash flow available to pay prepetition claims is calculated after taking into account the expenses necessary to generate that cash flow. In both types of cases, the debtor may also engage in a partial liquidation – that is, sell some assets – as part of the reorganization. In addition, both types of proceedings are based on the premise that a debtor's "going concern value" likely exceeds the debtor's liquidation value. In other words, a debtor who continues to generate income through gainful employment or operation of a business is worth more than a debtor who ceases all revenue-generating activity.

While there are similarities, there are also some notable differences. Chapter 13 is restricted to individual debtors, whereas Chapter 11 is geared toward business debtors. That said, the proceedings do have overlapping applicability. A sole proprietor of a business may use Chapter 13 to reorganize the business as long as the debtor is an individual with regular income and falls within the debt limits.[1] Alternatively, an individual debtor may file a Chapter 11 petition even if the debtor does not have a business. Indeed, an individual whose debts exceed the limits of eligibility for Chapter 13 and whose income would presumptively make filing under Chapter 7 an abuse of the bankruptcy process, *see* § 707(b), may have no recourse other than to file under Chapter 11.

---

1 *See* Robert M. Lawless & Elizabeth Warren, *The Myth of the Disappearing Business Bankruptcy*, 93 CAL. L. REV. 743 (2005).

Another difference between the two processes is that in a Chapter 13 case, the creditors may object to a reorganization plan as part of the confirmation process but they do not vote on the plan. § 1325. Chapter 11, on the other hand, is largely a consensual process. The creditors, once grouped into classes, vote on the proposed plan. The court will confirm the plan only if all classes of creditors accept the plan, § 1129(a)(8), or the plan meets the exacting requirements necessary to confirm it over the objection of one or more classes. § 1129(b). This process leads to much more negotiation in advance of the confirmation hearing than is typical in a Chapter 13 case. There are other important differences between the confirmation requirements for each type of case. In Chapter 13, the court may confirm a plan over the objection of an unsecured creditor only if the plan satisfies the disposable income test, which requires that all future disposable income for the applicable commitment period be used to pay prepetition claims. § 1325(b). In Chapter 11, confirmation over the objection of an impaired class of creditors requires compliance with the absolute priority rule. § 1129(b). This means that no class of creditors may receive anything of value unless the plan provides for full payment to all objecting classes with a higher priority. It also means that the debtor's interest holders (*e.g.*, stockholders) cannot retain any interest in the debtor unless all objecting classes of claims are paid in full.[2]

The bottom line is that many of the rules you will explore in this chapter of the book will be somewhat familiar to – but not precisely the same as – what we covered in the preceding chapter. The same is true for the policies underling the two types of reorganizations. Both are based on the fundamental belief in a second chance. A typical consumer debtor may have gotten in over his or her head because of job loss, medical crisis, divorce, excessive consumption, or poor financial management. Chapter 11 cases typically involve a business debtor that has encountered difficulty because of business-related problems. Perhaps the market for the debtor's product or services was not as robust as predicted. Perhaps the debtor was the victim of bad management decisions or failed to implement an otherwise viable business plan. Perhaps the debtor encountered an excessive amount of liability due to some malfunction or defect in its product. Perhaps the debtor experienced problems not of its own doing, such as a general economic downturn or an economic dislocation due to war, embargo, shortage of raw materials, or something else not under the debtor's control. Chapter 11, like Chapter 13, is about permitting the debtor to deal with the causes of its financial

---

[2] *See* Douglas G. Baird & Donald S. Bernstein, *Absolute Priority, Valuation Uncertainty, and the Reorganization Bargain*, 115 YALE L.J. 1930 (2006); *cf.* Anthony J. Casey, *The Creditors' Bargain and Option-Preservation Priority in Chapter 11*, 78 U. CHI. L. REV. 759 (2011).

difficulties and regroup for another try. In Chapter 13, this is thought good for society because it prevents individuals from becoming wards of the state and gives them a financial incentive to remain a productive member of the economy. In Chapter 11, this second chance may also benefit society given that businesses employ workers and presumably produce some product or service that is valued in the market.[3]

However, there is a counter-policy at work in Chapter 11 that may not apply in Chapter 13. Chapter 13 debtors – who are, after all, individuals – necessarily survive the bankruptcy process.[4] Whether given or denied bankruptcy relief, the individual will continue to exist, and thus bankruptcy policy must be cognizant of that. Businesses, on the other hand, need not survive. While it may be desirable that they do, their survival is not preordained. Nor is it clear that their survival is necessarily a good thing. Perhaps businesses that encounter financial distress should not be rehabilitated but liquidated, and the capital investment in the business put to a better use. In all likelihood, the better result will vary; some businesses should be liquidated and others reorganized. If that is true, the law must now confront a critical question: who should decide? Should the current managers and owners be in charge of this process or should the creditors of the business have control? What should be the role of the bankruptcy court in deciding these questions? These issues form the background for much of the debate regarding the viability of the Chapter 11 process itself.[5] As you study the Chapter 11 process, keep these questions in mind and ask yourself how they form the basis for the various rules we will encounter.

When considering these questions, also bear in mind that, by all accounts, successful reorganization in Chapter 11 may be rare. Many Chapter 11 cases produce no confirmed plan and are converted to Chapter 7 liquidations. In many others, the plan that is confirmed is essentially a liquidating plan: one that provides an orderly break up

---

[3] That being said, confirming a Chapter 11 plan is a difficult and expensive process. By some estimates, less than one-third of filed Chapter 11 cases result in a confirmed plan. A. Mechele Dickerson, *A Behavioral Approach to Analyzing Corporate Failures*, 38 WAKE FOREST L. REV. 1, 33 & n.118 (2003).

[4] A Chapter 13 debtor might, of course, die before completing the payment plan, but such an event would in all probability be unrelated to the bankruptcy proceeding itself.

[5] *See, e.g.*, Richard M. Hynes, *Reorganization as Redemption*, 6 VA. L. & BUS. REV. 183 (2011); Stephen J. Lubben, *The Types of Chapter 11 Cases*, 84 AM. BANKR. L.J. 233 (2010); Douglas G. Baird & Robert K. Rasmussen, Antibankruptcy, 119 Yale L.J. 648 (2010); Elizabeth Warren & Jay Lawrence Westbrook, *The Success of Chapter 11: A Challenge to the Critics*, 107 MICH. L. REV. 603 (2009); Robert K. Rasmussen, *Empirically Bankrupt*, 2007 COLUM. BUS. L. REV. 179 (2007).

and sale of the estate assets rather than the continued operation of the debtor's business. In many of those that do yield a confirmed plan of reorganization, the debtor defaults on the plan, which may then lead to a new bankruptcy proceeding, often under Chapter 7. Few Chapter 11 cases produce a confirmed plan of true reorganization that the debtor performs and from which the debtor emerges as a viable business. Perhaps this should not be surprising, given that bankruptcy deals with the symptoms of the debtor's problems – excessive debt – rather than the root causes (*e.g.*, economic recession, poor management, fierce competition, or labor disputes).

2. *Filing the Chapter 11 Case*

Section 109(d) provides that an entity eligible to seek relief under Chapter 7 – other than stockbrokers or commodity brokers – may file a Chapter 11 petition.[6] Individuals who file under Chapter 11 are subject to the same credit counseling provisions examined in chapter two of this book, § 109(h), and repeat filers are subject to the dismissal provisions in § 109(g), discussed in chapter eleven of this book.

A Chapter 11 case may be commenced as either a voluntary case or an involuntary case.[7] § 303. However, few involuntary petitions are filed under Chapter 11 because most petitioning creditors prefer the Chapter 7 process under the oversight of a trustee.

Filing the Chapter 11 petition creates the bankruptcy estate. The estate includes all rights of the debtor in property as of the commencement of the case as well as all proceeds, profits, or other products produced from property of the estate. § 541. Given that a fundamental assumption underlying reorganization is that the debtor will use postpetition income to pay prepetition claims, it makes sense that all assets generated from the use of estate property likewise become property of the estate. Thus, in a typical Chapter 11 case, a debtor will use its equipment, inventory , accounts receivable, and other assets to produce income to be used in the reorganization process. That future income is then also property of the estate.[8]

---

[6] Uninsured state banks and certain financial clearing organizations are also permitted to file a Chapter 11 proceeding, even though they may not be eligible to file a Chapter 7 proceeding. *Compare* § 109(d), *with* § 109(b).

[7] The rules relating to involuntary petitions were covered briefly in chapter two of this book.

[8] If an individual files a Chapter 11 petition, earnings from the individual's postpetition services, as well as all property the individual acquires after commencement of the case, are included in the bankruptcy estate. § 1115. This rule is virtually identical to the rule in Chapter 13. *See* § 1306.

In a Chapter 11 case, the debtor remains in possession of property of the estate and operates the business unless there is cause for the court to appoint a trustee to take over. §§ 1101(1), 1105(b), 1107. The circumstances that justify appointment of a trustee will be discussed later in this chapter. For the moment, consider the implications of the debtor in possession concept. When a business debtor files a Chapter 11 petition, the same management team that was in charge of the business before the petition is generally still in charge of the business after the petition. Filing the petition does not magically make that team any better at its job of running a successful and profitable business. The petition gives the existing management no additional wisdom, skills, or ability to make accurate economic predictions. On the other hand, consider the alternative. To have a chance at a successful reorganization, the business must continue to operate and often cannot afford the significant amount of time it may take for a new management team to get up to speed on what needs to be done. Thus, while the existing management may not be the best team to run the business in the long run, there may be no other viable options for the short run.

In part because of this, Chapter 11 requires – particularly at the beginning of the process but continuing throughout the case – that the debtor in possession provide information about the operation of the business to the creditors, the court, and the U.S. Trustee's office. This allows those entities to monitor what the debtor in possession is doing. For example, within 14 days of when the debtor files a Chapter 11 petition,[9] the debtor must also file: schedules of assets, liabilities, executory contracts, and claimed exemptions if the debtor is an individual (Official Form 6); a statement of financial affairs (Official Form 7); and a list of the 20 largest unsecured creditors (Official Form 4). Rule 1007. Those forms provide creditors with their first look at the debtor's financial situation. Sometime between the 20th and 40th day after the order for relief, the U.S. trustee will hold the first meeting of creditors. That meeting will enable creditors to ask the debtor questions concerning its assets, liabilities, and plans for the reorganization. § 341; Rule 2003. Unlike in Chapter 7, where few creditors are likely to attend the § 341 meeting, in Chapter 11 cases creditors often use that meeting to obtain the information they need to determine what actions to take to protect their interests.

---

[9] Of course, the debtor must also pay the filing fee and other fees as specified in 28 U.S.C. § 1930. In a Chapter 11 case, a quarterly fee to the U.S. Trustee's office is required, depending upon the amount of disbursements in that quarter.

3. *Immediate Considerations*

With or shortly after the petition, each of four provisions of the Bankruptcy Code may quickly come into play. First, as in Chapter 7 and 13 cases, filing the petition invokes the automatic stay. § 362. Thus, creditors with prepetition claims cannot seek to collect on those claims, absent relief from the stay. Similarly, creditors with liens on property of the estate cannot enforce those liens without first obtaining relief from the stay. Second, if the debtor is to continue to operate its business, it needs to be able to continue to sell its products, buy inventory and supplies, and collect its receivables. Section 363 gives the debtor in possession such authority, subject to various restrictions. The most stringent restrictions involve the use of cash collateral. Third, to finance its operations, the debtor may need continued access to credit. Such credit may be the intra-day credit extended by a bank when it allows a depositor to access newly deposited funds before they have cleared, the relatively short-term credit of suppliers who deliver without prepayment, or long-term capital financing. Section 364 gives the debtor in possession authority to incur such credit, again subject to a variety of limitations. Finally, the debtor in possession may need to decide quickly whether to assume or reject some of its unexpired leases or executory contracts. *See* § 365. The need for haste in this regard is sometimes attributable to the fact postpetition rent on an unexpired lease may qualify as an administrative expense, a prospect that could significantly burden the estate and make reorganization much more difficult.

Debtors who have planned well for bankruptcy know how they wish to deal with these issues when they file their petition. To the extent they need court approval under one or more of these provisions for any or all of what they want to do, the debtor's counsel usually prepares motions and proposed orders for the bankruptcy court to hear on an expedited basis. Such requests typically cover the debtor's proposed use of cash collateral to pay current operating expenses but may also deal with other matters, such as the sale of assets or incurring credit. Although local practice varies, these requests are often made and the orders entered on an *ex parte* basis. That is, the court reviews these requests on an emergency basis without the opportunity to conduct a full evidentiary hearing and without notice to all of the creditors who may have an interest in what is being proposed. *Cf.* Rules 9013, 4001(b)(2), (c)(2). As a result, they are often referred to as "first day orders." When that occurs, the orders are typically limited to a few days or weeks, during which time the debtor may file and serve on creditors a motion for more long-term authority. Nevertheless, in some cases, the decisions made on these early requests can dramatically affect all future reorganization efforts. Consider the following case, which concerns the efforts of a debtor in possession to stay in operation.

IN RE KMART CORP.
359 F.3d 866 (7th Cir.), *cert. denied*, 543 U.S. 986 (2004)

Easterbrook, Circuit Judge.

On the first day of its bankruptcy, Kmart sought permission to pay immediately, and in full, the pre-petition claims of all "critical vendors." (Technically there are 38 debtors: Kmart Corporation plus 37 of its affiliates and subsidiaries. We call them all Kmart.) The theory behind the request is that some suppliers may be unwilling to do business with a customer that is behind in payment, and, if it cannot obtain the merchandise that its own customers have come to expect, a firm such as Kmart may be unable to carry on, injuring all of its creditors. Full payment to critical vendors thus could in principle make even the disfavored creditors better off: they may not be paid in full, but they will receive a greater portion of their claims than they would if the critical vendors cut off supplies and the business shut down. Putting the proposition in this way implies, however, that the debtor must *prove*, and not just allege, two things: that, but for immediate full payment, vendors *would* cease dealing; and that the business will gain enough from continued transactions with the favored vendors to provide some residual benefit to the remaining, disfavored creditors, or at least leave them no worse off.

Bankruptcy Judge Sonderby entered a critical-vendors order just as Kmart proposed it, without notifying any disfavored creditors, without receiving any pertinent evidence (the record contains only some sketchy representations by counsel plus unhelpful testimony by Kmart's CEO, who could not speak for the vendors), and without making any finding of fact that the disfavored creditors would gain or come out even. The bankruptcy court's order declared that the relief Kmart requested – open-ended permission to pay any debt to any vendor it deemed "critical" in the exercise of unilateral discretion, provided that the vendor agreed to furnish goods on "customary trade terms" for the next two years – was "in the best interests of the Debtors, their estates and their creditors." The order did not explain why, nor did it contain any legal analysis, though it did cite § 105(a). * * *

Kmart used its authority to pay in full the pre-petition debts to 2,330 suppliers, which collectively received about $300 million. This came from the $2 billion in new credit (debtor-in-possession or DIP financing) that the bankruptcy judge authorized, granting the lenders super-priority in post-petition assets and revenues. Another 2,000 or so vendors were not deemed "critical" and were not paid. They and 43,000 additional unsecured creditors eventually received about 10¢ on the dollar, mostly in stock of the reorganized Kmart. Capital Factors, Inc. appealed the critical-vendors order immediately after its entry on January 25, 2002. A little more than 14 months later, after all of the critical vendors had been paid and as Kmart's plan of reorganization was on the verge of approval, District Judge Grady reversed the order authorizing payment. He concluded that neither § 105(a) nor a "doctrine of necessity" supports the orders.

Appellants insist that, by the time Judge Grady acted, it was too late. Money had changed hands and, we are told, cannot be refunded. But why not? Reversing preferential transfers is an ordinary feature of bankruptcy practice, often continuing under a confirmed plan of reorganization. If the orders in question are invalid, then the critical vendors have received preferences that Kmart is entitled to recoup for the benefit of all creditors. Confirmation of a plan does not stop the administration of the estate, except to the extent that the plan itself so provides. * * *

Now it is true that we have recognized the existence of a longstanding doctrine * * * that detrimental reliance comparable to the extension of new credit against a promise of security, or the purchase of assets in a foreclosure sale, may make it appropriate for judges to exercise such equitable discretion as they possess in order to protect those reliance interests. Thus once action has been taken to distribute assets under a confirmed plan of reorganization, it would take some extraordinary event to turn back the clock. These appeals, however, do not question any distribution under Kmart's plan; to the contrary, the plan (which was confirmed after the district court's decision) provides that adversary proceedings will be filed to recover the preferences that the critical vendors have received. No one filed an appeal, which means that it is appellants in this court that now wage a collateral attack on the plan of reorganization.

Appellants say that we should recognize their reliance interests: after the order, they continued selling goods and services to Kmart (doing this was a condition of payment for pre-petition debts). Continued business relations may or may not be a form of reliance (that depends on whether the vendors otherwise would have stopped selling), but they are not *detrimental* reliance. The vendors have been paid in full for post-petition goods and services. If Kmart had become administratively insolvent, and unable to compensate the vendors for post-petition transactions, then it might make sense to permit vendors to retain payments under the critical-vendors order, at least to the extent of the post-petition deficiency. Because Kmart emerged as an operating business, however, no such question arises. The vendors have not established that any reliance interest – let alone any language in the Code – blocks future attempts to recover preferential transfers on account of pre-petition debts.

* * * Section 105(a) allows a bankruptcy court to "issue any order, process, or judgment that is necessary or appropriate to carry out the provisions of" the Code. This does not create discretion to set aside the Code's rules about priority and distribution; the power conferred by § 105(a) is one to implement rather than override. Every circuit that has considered the question has held that this statute does not allow a bankruptcy judge to authorize full payment of any unsecured debt, unless all unsecured creditors in the class are paid in full. We agree with this view of § 105. "The fact that a [bankruptcy] proceeding is equitable does not give the judge a free-floating discretion to redistribute rights in accordance with his personal views of justice and fairness, however enlightened those views may be." *In re Chicago, Milwaukee, St. Paul & Pacific R.R.*, 791 F.2d 524, 528 (7th Cir. 1986).

* * * So does the Code contain any grant of authority for debtors to prefer some vendors over others? Many sections require equal treatment or specify the details of priority when assets are insufficient to satisfy all claims. *E.g.*, §§ 507, 1122(a), 1123(a)(4). Appellants rely on §§ 363(b), 364(b), and 503 as sources of authority for unequal treatment. Section 364(b) reads: "The court, after notice and a hearing, may authorize the trustee to obtain unsecured credit or to incur unsecured debt other than under subsection (a) of this section, allowable under section 503(b)(1) of this title as an administrative expense." This authorizes the debtor to obtain credit (as Kmart did) but has nothing to say about how the money will be disbursed or about priorities among creditors. * * * Section 503, which deals with administrative expenses, is likewise irrelevant. Pre-filing debts are not administrative expenses; they are the antithesis of administrative expenses. Filing a petition for bankruptcy effectively creates two firms: the debts of the pre-filing entity may be written down so that the post-filing entity may reorganize and continue in business if it has a positive cash flow. Treating pre-filing debts as "administrative" claims against the post-filing entity would impair the ability of bankruptcy law to prevent old debts from sinking a viable firm.

That leaves § 363(b)(1): "The trustee [or debtor in possession], after notice and a hearing, may use, sell, or lease, other than in the ordinary course of business, property of the estate." This is more promising, for satisfaction of a pre-petition debt in order to keep "critical" supplies flowing is a use of property other than in the ordinary course of administering an estate in bankruptcy. Capital Factors insists that § 363(b)(1) should be limited to the commencement of capital projects, such as building a new plant, rather than payment of old debts – as paying vendors would be "in the ordinary course" but for the intervening bankruptcy petition. To read § 363(b)(1) broadly, Capital Factors observes, would be to allow a judge to rearrange priorities among creditors (which is what a critical-vendors order effectively does), even though the Supreme Court has cautioned against such a step. *See United States v. Reorganized CF & I Fabricators of Utah, Inc.*, 518 U.S. 213 (1996). Yet what [this decision] principally [said] is that priorities do not change unless a statute supports that step; and if § 363(b)(1) is such a statute, then there is no insuperable problem. If the language is too open-ended, that is a problem for the legislature. Nonetheless, it is prudent to read, and use, § 363(b)(1) to do the least damage possible to priorities established by contract and by other parts of the Bankruptcy Code. We need not decide whether § 363(b)(1) could support payment of some pre-petition debts, because *this* order was unsound no matter how one reads § 363(b)(1).

The foundation of a critical-vendors order is the belief that vendors not paid for prior deliveries will refuse to make new ones. Without merchandise to sell, a retailer such as Kmart will fold. If paying the critical vendors would enable a successful reorganization and make even the disfavored creditors better off, then all creditors favor payment whether or not they are designated as "critical." This suggests a use of § 363(b)(1) similar to the theory underlying a plan crammed down the throats of an impaired class of creditors: if the impaired class does at least as well as it would have under a Chapter 7 liquidation, then it has no legitimate objection and cannot block the reorganization. For the premise to hold true, however, it is necessary to show not only that the disfavored creditors *will* be as well off with reorganization as with liquidation – a demonstration never attempted in this proceeding – but also that the supposedly critical vendors would have ceased deliveries if old debts were left unpaid while the litigation continued. If vendors will deliver against a promise of current payment, then a reorganization can be achieved, and all unsecured creditors will obtain its benefit, without preferring any of the unsecured creditors.

Some supposedly critical vendors will continue to do business with the debtor because they must. They may, for example, have long term contracts, and the automatic stay prevents these vendors from walking away as long as the debtor pays for new deliveries. *See* § 362. Fleming Companies, which received the largest critical-vendors payment because it sold Kmart between $70 million and $100 million of groceries and related goods weekly, was one of these. No matter how much Fleming would have liked to dump Kmart, it had no right to do so. It was unnecessary to compensate Fleming for continuing to make deliveries that it was legally required to make. Nor was Fleming likely to walk away even if it had a legal right to do so. Each new delivery produced a profit; as long as Kmart continued to pay for new product, why would any vendor drop the account? That would be a self-inflicted wound. To abjure new profits because of old debts would be to commit the sunk-cost fallacy; well-managed businesses are unlikely to do this. Firms that disdain current profits because of old losses are unlikely to stay in business. They might as well burn money or drop it into the ocean. Again Fleming illustrates the point. When Kmart stopped buying its products after the contract expired, Fleming collapsed (Kmart had accounted for more than 50% of its business) and filed its own bankruptcy petition. Fleming was hardly likely to have quit selling of its own volition, only to expire the sooner.

Doubtless many suppliers fear the prospect of throwing good money after bad. It therefore may be vital to assure them that a debtor will pay for new deliveries on a current basis. Providing that assurance need not, however, entail payment for pre-petition transactions. Kmart could have paid cash or its equivalent. (Kmart's CEO told the bankruptcy judge that COD arrangements were not part of Kmart's business plan, as if a litigant's druthers could override the rights of third parties.) Cash on the barrelhead was not the most convenient way, however. Kmart secured a $2 billion line of credit when it entered bankruptcy. Some of that credit could have been used to assure vendors that payment would be forthcoming for all post-petition transactions. The easiest way to do that would have been to put some of the $2 billion behind a standby letter of credit on which the bankruptcy judge could authorize unpaid vendors to draw. That would not have changed the terms on which Kmart and any of its vendors did business; it just would have demonstrated the certainty of payment. If lenders are unwilling to issue such a letter of credit (or if they insist on a letter's short duration), that would be a compelling market signal that reorganization is a poor prospect and that the debtor should be liquidated post haste.

Yet the bankruptcy court did not explore the possibility of using a letter of credit to assure vendors of payment. The court did not find that any firm would have ceased doing business with Kmart if not paid for pre-petition deliveries, and the scant record would not have supported such a finding had one been made. The court did not find that discrimination among unsecured creditors was the only way to facilitate a reorganization. It did not find that the disfavored creditors were at least as well off as they would have been had the critical-vendors order not been entered. * * * Even if [§ 363(b)(1)] allows critical-vendors orders in principle, preferential payments to a class of creditors are proper only if the record shows the prospect of benefit to the other creditors. This record does not, so the critical-vendors order cannot stand.

QUESTION

The request for a critical-vendors order is premised on the belief that each critical vendor will refuse to do business with the debtor in possession unless the debtor's prepetition debt to the vendor is or will be paid. If the debtor has evidence that this is how critical vendors are acting, must the debtor capitulate to that pressure, or is there some other way to respond?

NOTES

1. For a case approving payment of critical vendors, see *In re Tropical Sportswear International, Inc.*, 320 B.R. 15 (Bankr. M.D. Fla. 2005).

2. A motion to pay prepetition wage claims of critical employees may fare better than a request to pay critical vendors because employee wage claims are entitled, at least in part, to priority.[10]

3. The 2005 Amendments to the Bankruptcy Code added some protection to vendors, whether "critical" or not. Those that sold goods to the debtor in the ordinary course of business may reclaim them if the goods were delivered within 45 days before the petition,[11] § 546(c)(1), and failing that, are entitled to administrative expense treatment for the sale price if the goods were delivered within 20 days before the petition, § 503(b)(9). While this rule *permits* creditors to reclaim goods under the circumstances specified, it remains unclear whether the provision is an independent source of such a reclamation right or whether it merely allows the vendor to exercise such a right that exists under nonbankruptcy law.[12] The issue is important because the

---

[10] *See In re CEI Roofing, Inc.*, 315 B.R. 50 (Bankr. N.D. Tex. 2004); § 507(a)(4), (5).

[11] The reclamation right is rarely helpful to vendors because the goods sold typically become part of the debtor's inventory and are encumbered by a security interest in favor of one or more of the debtor's creditors. Reclamation rights are subordinate to the rights of an unavoidable lien. *See* U.C.C. § 2-702(3); *see, e.g., In re Advance Mktg. Sys.*, 360 B.R. 421 (Bankr. D. Del. 2007).

[12] *See, e.g., In re Momenta, Inc.*, 455 B.R. 353 (Bankr. D.N.H. 2011); *In re Circuit City Stores, Inc.*, 441 B.R. 496 (Bankr. E.D. Va. 2010); *In re Magwood*, 2008 WL 509635 (Bankr. M.D. Ala. 2008); *In re Dana Corp.*, 367 B.R. 409 (Bankr. S.D.N.Y. 2007).

most common nonbankruptcy source of a right to reclaim – U.C.C. § 2-702 – generally requires that the seller exercise the right within ten days, not 45 days.

The *Kmart* case sets up a basic operational issue at the beginning of every Chapter 11 case in which the debtor plans to reorganize rather than liquidate. Who must the debtor pay to stay in operation and where does the debtor get the funds to pay those critical performers? Although these matters may, by necessity, be dealt with in haste in connection with the "first day orders," they are often given very substantial attention as the case progresses. Again, decisions made in connection with them can significantly affect the prospect for successful reorganization. Accordingly, in the next section, we consider the relevant Bankruptcy Code requirements in some detail.

B. MANAGING A CHAPTER 11 CASE

1. *Using Assets of the Estate to Generate Income*

(a) Section 364: Obtaining Credit

Few bankruptcy debtors are flush with cash. Most are insolvent and the few who are not are usually suffering from significant cash flow problems. Beyond that, in either the normal course of their businesses or on the path to bankruptcy, debtors will likely have collateralized almost all of their assets, including deposit accounts and accounts receivable. Thus, as they enter bankruptcy, debtors are likely to have little unencumbered cash or other liquid assets that would normally be used to pay ongoing business expenses, such as rent, utilities, and wages.

Obviously, the debtor in possession must obtain funds to pay its operating expenses if its business is to survive. However, the debtor in possession cannot use cash collateral (defined in § 363(a)) without either the consent of the secured party or a court order. § 363(c). Each of those would almost assuredly require some form of adequate protection of the creditor's interest. Without much in the way of unencumbered assets to offer in exchange for the use of cash collateral, the debtor in possession will need some source of financing (often referred to as DIP financing) if it hopes to reorganize during the course of bankruptcy. Section 364 provides rules on how debtors in possession may obtain DIP financing and what they may provide in exchange for it. Read § 364.

As you can see, § 364 establishes a sort of hierarchy of preferred financing. It does so by placing more and higher hurdles in the path of financing the more unusual it is or the more the debtor in possession must provide to the lender in return for the financing. Its rules can be summarized as follows:

1. The debtor in possession may incur *unsecured* debt/credit in the ordinary course of business without court approval. § 364(a).
2. The debtor in possession may incur *unsecured* debt/credit outside the ordinary course of business only with court approval after notice and an opportunity for a hearing. § 364(b).
3. The debtor in possession may incur *unsecured* debt/credit with the highest administrative priority or junior secured debt/credit only with court approval after notice and an opportunity for a hearing and only if the types of financing discussed above are unavailable. § 364(c).
4. The debtor in possession may incur *secured* debt/credit with priority over existing liens only with court approval after notice and an opportunity for a hearing, only if the types of financing discussed above are unavailable, and only if the existing lienholder's interest is adequately protected. § 364(d).

Prior to filing the petition, the debtor will often have negotiated with its existing lenders for additional financing. If the existing lenders are unwilling to provide more financing (the court cannot order a lender to loan more money to the debtor), the debtor will usually try to obtain a new lender. Whoever the DIP financier is, whether an existing lender or a new lender, it will generally insist that the new debt be fully secured and superior in priority to all other debt obligations of the estate, including other claims secured by the same assets. Most lenders will not even consider lending on an unsecured basis, even though such loans would generally qualify for priority as administrative expenses. §§ 503, 507(a)(2); *see also* § 507(b). Lenders willing to provide postpetition financing are typically in a very strong negotiating position.

If you were representing a lender approached to provide DIP financing, what conditions would you insist on? If you were representing existing creditors of the debtor, what provisions would you object to? If you objected to the financing proposed and the bankruptcy court approved the financing, what are your options for obtaining a reversal of the court's decision? Consider the following case.

IN RE SAYBROOK MANUFACTURING CO.
963 F.2d 1490 (11th Cir. 1992)

Cox, Circuit Judge:

Seymour and Jeffrey Shapiro, unsecured creditors, objected to the bankruptcy court's authorization for the Chapter 11 debtors to "cross-collateralize" their pre-petition debt with unencumbered property from the bankruptcy estate. The bankruptcy court overruled the objection * * *. We conclude that * * * cross-collateralization is not authorized under the Bankruptcy Code. Accordingly, we reverse and remand.

I. Facts and Procedural History

Saybrook Manufacturing Co., Inc., and related companies (the "debtors"), initiated proceedings seeking relief under Chapter 11 of the Bankruptcy Code on December 22, 1988. On December 23, 1988, the debtors filed a motion for the use of cash collateral and for authorization to incur secured debt. The bankruptcy court entered an emergency financing order that same day. At the time the bankruptcy petition was filed, the debtors owed Manufacturers Hanover approximately $34 million. The value of the collateral for this debt, however, was less than $10 million. Pursuant to the order, Manufacturers Hanover agreed to lend the debtors an additional $3 million to facilitate their reorganization. In exchange, Manufacturers Hanover received a security interest in all of the debtors' property – both property owned prior to filing the bankruptcy petition and that which was acquired subsequently. This security interest not only protected the $3 million of post-petition credit but also secured Manufacturers Hanover's $34 million pre-petition debt.

This arrangement enhanced Manufacturers Hanover's position vis-a-vis other unsecured creditors, such as the Shapiros, in the event of liquidation. Because Manufacturers Hanover's pre-petition debt was undersecured by approximately $24 million, it originally would have shared in a pro rata distribution of the debtors' unencumbered assets along with the other unsecured creditors. Under the financing order, however, Manufacturers Hanover's pre-petition debt became fully secured by all of the debtors' assets. If the bankruptcy estate were liquidated, Manufacturers Hanover's entire debt – $34 million pre-petition and $3 million post-petition – would have to be paid in full before any funds could be distributed to the remaining unsecured creditors.

Securing pre-petition debt with pre- and post-petition collateral as part of a post-petition financing arrangement is known as cross-collateralization. The Second Circuit aptly defined cross-collateralization as follows:

> [I]n return for making new loans to a debtor in possession under Chapter XI, a financing institution obtains a security interest on all assets of the debtor, both those existing at the date of the order and those created in the course of the Chapter XI proceeding, not only for the new loans, the propriety of which is not contested, but [also] for existing indebtedness to it.

In re Texlon Corp., 596 F.2d 1092, 1094 (2d Cir. 1979).

Because the Second Circuit was the first appellate court to describe this practice in *In re Texlon*, it is sometimes referred to as *Texlon* -type cross-collateralization. Another form of cross-collateralization involves securing post-petition debt with pre-petition collateral. This form of non-*Texlon*-type cross-collateralization is not at issue in this appeal. The Shapiros challenge only the cross-collateralization of the lenders' pre-petition debt, not the propriety of collateralizing the post-petition debt. * * *

The Shapiros filed a number of objections to the bankruptcy court's order on January 13, 1989. After a hearing, the bankruptcy court overruled the objections. * * * The Shapiros then appealed to this court.

* * *

B. Cross-Collateralization and Section 364

Cross-collateralization is an extremely controversial form of Chapter 11 financing. Nevertheless, the practice has been approved by several bankruptcy courts. Even the courts that have allowed cross-collateralization, however, were generally reluctant to do so.

In *In re Vanguard*, 31 B.R. 364 (Bankr. E.D.N.Y. 1983), for example, the bankruptcy court noted that cross-collateralization is "a disfavored means of financing" that should only be used as a last resort. *Id.* at 366. In order to obtain a financing order including cross-collateralization, the court required the debtor to demonstrate (1) that its business operations would fail absent the proposed financing, (2) that it is unable to obtain alternative financing on acceptable terms, (3) that the proposed lender will not accept less preferential terms, and (4) that the proposed financing is in the general creditor body's best interest. *Id.* This four-part test has since been adopted by other bankruptcy courts which permit cross-collateralization.

The issue of whether the Bankruptcy Code authorizes cross-collateralization is a question of first impression in this court. Indeed, it is essentially a question of first impression before any court of appeals. Neither the lenders' brief nor our own research has produced a single appellate decision which either authorizes or prohibits the practice.

* * * We conclude that cross-collateralization is inconsistent with bankruptcy law for two reasons. First, cross-collateralization is not authorized as a method of post-petition financing under section 364. Second, cross-collateralization is beyond the scope of the bankruptcy court's inherent equitable power because it is directly contrary to the fundamental priority scheme of the Bankruptcy Code. *See generally* Charles J. Tabb, *A Critical Reappraisal of Cross-Collateralization in Bankruptcy*, 60 S. Cal. L. Rev. 109 (1986).

Section 364 authorizes Chapter 11 debtors to obtain secured credit and incur secured debt as part of their reorganization. * * * By their express terms, sections 364(c) & (d) apply only to future – *i.e.*, post-petition – extensions of credit. They do not authorize the granting of liens to secure pre-petition loans. * * *

Given that cross-collateralization is not authorized by section 364, we now turn to the lenders' argument that bankruptcy courts may permit the practice under their general equitable power. Bankruptcy courts are indeed courts of equity, *see* § 105(a), and they have the power to adjust claims to avoid injustice or unfairness. This equitable power, however, is not unlimited.

> [T]he bankruptcy court has the ability to deviate from the rules of priority and distribution set forth in the Code in the interest of justice and equity. The Court cannot use this flexibility, however, merely to establish a ranking of priorities within priorities. Furthermore, absent the existence of some type of inequitable conduct on the part of the claimant, which results in injury to the creditors of the bankrupt or an unfair advantage to the claimant, the court cannot subordinate a claim to claims within the same class.

In re FCX, Inc., 60 B.R. 405, 409 (E.D.N.C. 1986).

Section 507 of the Bankruptcy Code fixes the priority order of claims and expenses against the bankruptcy estate. Creditors within a given class are to be treated equally, and bankruptcy courts may not create their own rules of superpriority within a single class. Cross-collateralization, however, does exactly that. As a result of this practice, post-petition lenders' unsecured pre-petition claims are given priority over all other unsecured pre-petition claims. The Ninth Circuit recognized that "[t]here is no . . . applicable provision in the Bankruptcy Code authorizing the debtor to pay certain pre-petition unsecured claims in full while others remain unpaid. To do so would impermissibly violate the priority scheme of the Bankruptcy Code." *In re Sun Runner Marine, Inc.*, 945 F.2d 1089, 1094 (9th Cir. 1991).

The Second Circuit has noted that, if cross-collateralization were initiated by the bankrupt while insolvent and shortly before filing a petition, the arrangement "would have constituted a voidable preference." *In re Texlon*, 596 F.2d at 1097. The fundamental nature of this practice is not changed by the fact that it is sanctioned by the bankruptcy court. We disagree with the district court's conclusion that, while cross-collateralization may violate some policies of bankruptcy law, it is consistent with the general purpose of Chapter 11 to help businesses reorganize and become profitable. Rehabilitation is certainly the primary purpose of Chapter 11. This end, however, does not justify the use of any means. Cross-collateralization is directly inconsistent with the priority scheme of the Bankruptcy Code. Accordingly, the practice may not be approved by the bankruptcy court under its equitable authority.

Conclusion

Cross-collateralization is not authorized by section 364. Section 364(e), therefore, is not applicable and this appeal is not moot. Because *Texlon*-type cross-collateralization is not explicitly authorized by the Bankruptcy Code and is contrary to the basic priority structure of the Code, we hold that it is an impermissible means of obtaining post-petition financing. The judgment of the district court is reversed and the case is remanded for proceedings not inconsistent with this opinion.

QUESTION

Should other courts follow the *Saybrook* prohibition on cross-collateralization? *Cf. In re Cooper Commons, LLC*, 430 F.3d 1215 (9th Cir. 2005) (discussing scope of financing orders under § 364(e)), *cert. denied*, 546 U.S. 1174 (2006). See also the discussion of various DIP financing provisions in George W. Kuney, *Hijacking Chapter 11*, 21 EMORY BANKR. DEV. J. 19 (2004).

(b) Section 363: Using and Selling Assets

The estate of a typical Chapter 11 debtor includes inventory, equipment, deposit accounts, and accounts receivables. It also usually contains one or more interests in real estate, either in fee or as lessee, and a multitude of contracts on which performance is owed to the debtor. It may also include chattel paper, promissory notes, investment securities, and various types of intellectual property. In all likelihood, all or substantially all of these assets are encumbered by one or more liens. To determine whether and under what conditions the debtor in possession may use these assets to generate income, one must first look to § 363 and Bankruptcy Rule 4001. In general, these provisions are designed to strike a balance: allowing a business to continue its operations without excessive creditor interference or unnecessary court involvement while protecting creditors from dissipation of the estate's assets.

Section 363 contains a variety of rules concerning the ability of the debtor in possession to use property of the estate during the case.[13] These rules are separated into three different conceptual blocks, based on the type of asset and the kind of proposed use:

(i) assets that will be used, sold, or leased in the ordinary course of business – § 363(c)(1);

(ii) cash collateral – § 363(c)(2); and

(iii) assets that will be used, sold, or leased not in the ordinary course of business – § 363(b)(1).

Starting with first and the easiest category, the debtor in possession may use, sell or lease assets in the ordinary course of business without notice and hearing to creditors. § 363(c)(1). For example, if the debtor has a manufacturing business, the debtor in possession may use raw materials to manufacture its product and may sell its inventory, as long as it does so in the ordinary course of its business. What is "ordinary course of business"? We have seen that phrase in the § 547(c)(2) preference defense. Here, though, it has a slightly different and probably broader meaning. As the U.S. Court of Appeals for the Second Circuit Court of Appeals stated:

> The term "ordinary course of business" generally has been accepted to embrace the reasonable expectations of interested parties of the nature of transactions that the debtor would likely enter in the course of its normal, daily business. Although never specifically articulated by this Court, two tests have emerged to determine whether a transaction is "ordinary." These tests are (1) the "creditor's expectation test" also known as the "vertical test," and (2) the "industry-wide test" also called the "horizontal test." * * *
>
> Under the vertical test, the court views the disputed transaction from the vantage point of a hypothetical creditor and inquires whether the transaction subjects a creditor to economic risks of a nature different from those he accepted when he decided to enter into a contract with the debtor.

---

[13] Note, § 363 is phrased as a grant of authority to the trustee. However, it also operates as a grant of authority to the debtor in possession because the debtor in possession is entitled to exercise most of the trustee's powers. § 1107(a).

> The horizontal test involves an industry-wide perspective in which the debtor's business is compared to other like businesses. In this comparison, the test is whether the postpetition transaction is of a type that other similar businesses would engage in as ordinary business.[14]

Apparently, a proposed use of estate assets must satisfy both the vertical and horizontal tests to qualify as in the ordinary course of business.[15]

Of course, many of the estate's assets will be encumbered and the lienholder may not be happy about the debtor's proposed use of the assets. For example, a creditor with a security interest in the debtor's inventory will likely be very concerned if the debtor plans to sell the inventory postpetition. After all, buyers in the ordinary course will likely take free of the creditor's lien,[16] and, as we have seen, the creditor's interest in after-acquired inventory will likely be cut off by § 552(a) (assuming that any inventory acquired postpetition cannot be traced as proceeds of inventory or other collateral on hand as of the petition date). Thus, postpetition sale of the inventory may result in the rapid depletion of the creditor's collateral, particularly if the proceeds of that sale are used to pay employees, utilities, or other current expenses of the business. For this reason, a creditor with a security interest in assets that the debtor in possession wants to sell in the ordinary course often immediately moves for adequate protection of the value of its secured claim. *See* § 363(e). In fact, this is often part of the constellation of first day orders mentioned above. The creditor will move that the court adequately protect its secured claim in existing inventory, for example, by requesting a replacement lien in new inventory that the debtor in possession purchases subsequent to the petition.

The second category of assets covered by § 363 is "cash collateral," a term defined in § 363(a). To use cash collateral, the debtor in possession must first obtain either the approval of the court or the consent of any creditor with a lien on the cash collateral. § 363(c). This is true even if the proposed use would be in the ordinary course of the debtor's business. Why is cash collateral treated more restrictively than other types of assets in which a creditor may have an interest? Because cash – or at least a security interest in cash – can be ephemeral. When assets such as inventory are sold in the ordinary course of business, they generate proceeds. Any creditor with a security interest in the inventory will automatically have a security interest in all of the

---

14 *In re Lavigne*, 114 F.3d 379, 384–85 (2d Cir. 1997).

15 *See In re Roth Am., Inc.*, 975 F.2d 949, 952–54 (3d Cir. 1992).

16 *See* U.C.C. § 9-320(a).

identifiable proceeds.[17] While cash collateral too can generate proceeds – such as if used to buy other assets – it often does not. When cash is used to pay operating expenses – employees, taxes, or utilities – the value of the creditor's collateral simply dissipates. Because secured creditors are entitled to adequate protection of their secured claim, § 363(e), the Code requires creditor or court consent to the use of cash collateral. Predictably, therefore, an order regarding the debtor's use of cash collateral, and providing adequate protection of the creditors's lien, is one of the first day orders that enable the debtor in possession to operate the business.

The final category covered by § 363 is the use, sale, or lease property of the estate outside of the ordinary course of business. Any such action requires court approval after notice to creditors and the opportunity for a hearing. § 363(b)(1). Courts generally apply some version of the business judgment rule to these decisions: if there is a good business reason for allowing the proposed action, the court will approve the use, sale, or lease of property of the estate.[18]

If the debtor engages in unauthorized postpetition transactions – such as by using cash collateral without court or creditor permission or by selling assets outside of the ordinary course of business without prior court approval – any transfer of estate property in connection with that transaction can be avoided. *See* § 549. There is protection for a good faith transferee of real estate, § 549(c), but no protection for transferees of any other type of property. Moreover, the transferee has no defense for the value of what it provided in exchange. Thus, a person who postpetition buys the debtor's accounts in a transaction outside of the ordinary course of business and who fails to make sure that the bankruptcy court has authorized the sale, risks having to return the accounts without any setoff, recoupment, or defense for the amount it paid.[19] Similarly, a person who postpetition sells goods to the debtor and who is paid with cash collateral will have to return the payment if the debtor was not authorized to use the cash collateral for this purpose, even if the transaction was in the ordinary course of the debtor's business.[20] Because of this, parties who conduct business with bankruptcy debtors must be extremely careful.

---

[17] *See* § 552(b); U.C.C. § 9-315(a)(2).

[18] *E.g.*, *In re Iridium Operating LLC*, 478 F.3d 452, 466 (2d Cir. 2007).

[19] *In re Straightline Invs., Inc.*, 525 F.3d 870 (9th Cir. 2008).

[20] *In re Delco Oil, Inc.*, 599 F.3d 1255 (11th Cir. 2010).

Problem 12-1

Dash Manufacturing, Inc. is in the business of manufacturing plastic component parts for Hybrid Motor Corp., a major automobile manufacturer. When Hybrid needs components for a particular automobile, Hybrid and Dash engineers work on a design for the part, and Dash produces a mold for the plastic part. Once the engineers are satisfied that the part is correctly designed, Dash then manufactures the part from the specially designed molds.

Dash is financed by Intercontinental Bank. Intercontinental has a perfected security interest in Dash's equipment, inventory, and accounts. The current amount outstanding on that loan is $500,000. Intercontinental estimates that the total value of its collateral is $400,000 ($200,000 in equipment, $50,000 in inventory, and $150,000 in accounts). The bulk of those accounts ($120,000) are owed by Hybrid and more than half of Hybrid's obligation is more than 90 days past due. Hybrid's cars have not been selling well and there have been rumors in the popular press that Hybrid may file for bankruptcy. Intercontinental is considering accelerating the loan and foreclosing on its collateral pursuant to U.C.C. Article 9 because Dash has missed the last two months' payments of interest on the loan.

Yesterday, Dash informed Intercontinental that it would be filing a Chapter 11 petition by the end of the week. Dash told the loan officer that, after the filing, Dash will sell some trucks it no longer needs and will seek contracts to supply parts to another automobile manufacturer, Hotrod Cars, Inc. Dash also told the loan officer that Hybrid will be paying half the amount it owes to Dash so that Dash can fund its payroll at the end of the week. Dash has asked Intercontinental to enter into a stipulated agreement allowing Dash to use proceeds from the trucks and the Hybrid payment to pay employees their regular salaries and wages the week following the petition and to pay the monthly rent coming due on Dash's manufacturing facility. Dash has also asked Intercontinental to provide postpetition financing in the form of a $100,000 line of credit.

A. You represent Intercontinental. How do you advise it to respond to Dash's proposal? Should Intercontinental object to the sale of the trucks? If Intercontinental is willing to provide the line of credit so long as it does not end up in a worse position, what terms should it insist on including in the stipulation regarding such financing?

B. You represent Plastic Co., which sells Dash the ingredients Dash uses to make plastic auto parts. Dash owes Plastic Co. approximately $40,000 for past deliveries and Plastic Co. is scheduled to deliver $20,000 worth of product to Dash next week. Plastic Co. has received notice of Dash's Chapter 11 filing and a copy of a stipulated agreement between Intercontinental and Dash. The agreement provides that Intercontinental has a security interest in all inventory, equipment, accounts, and proceeds of that collateral the debtor has an interest in at the time of the petition or acquires an interest in after the filing of the petition to secure any and all obligations owed to Intercontinental, whether those obligations were incurred pre- or postpetition. Should Plastic Products object to the stipulation? Should Plastic Products make the scheduled delivery?

Several issues arise in connection with § 363 sales outside of the ordinary course of business. First, what happens if the assets to be sold are encumbered by one or more non-avoidable liens? Read § 363(e), (f), (k). Unless the order specifies otherwise, assets are sold subject to existing liens. Of course, most buyers want the assets they purchase to be unencumbered, so the court may order the assets to be sold free and clear of liens. In such cases, the lienholder is entitled to adequate protection, which typically is provided by granting the lienholder a lien on the sale proceeds or a replacement lien on some other assets of the estate. In the event that two or more lienholders are disputing who has priority, the court may either resolve that issue when authorizing the sale or simply order that they will retain their relative priorities – whatever they may be – in the sale proceeds, and then resolve the priority issue at a later date.

A second, less common, issue is whether asset sales under § 363 can make the buyer liable for claims against the debtor under principles of successor liability. Successor liability is a common-law doctrine aimed at preventing an entity from forming a new business entity, transferring substantially all of its assets to the new entity, and leaving the creditors against the old entity without recourse to those assets. The doctrine applies whenever: (i) the sale is a de facto consolidation or merger, (ii) the purchaser is a mere continuation of the seller, or (iii) the transfer of assets is for the fraudulent purpose of escaping liability. In analyzing whether a transaction is a de facto merger and whether the buyer is a mere continuation of the seller, courts look at such factors as whether the entities conduct the same business, whether the new entity operates from the same location as the old, whether the new entity has substantially the same employees, and whether the entity is controlled or managed by the same persons. Because the prospect of successor liability is likely to reduce the price buyers are willing to pay for the debtor's assets, it is a doctrine somewhat at odds with bankruptcy policy generally, which seeks to maximize the value of the estate for the benefit of the debtor's creditors. Accordingly, application of successor liability following § 363 sales is controversial, and courts sometimes expressly order the buyer to take free of such liability.[21]

A third issue is whether the debtor in possession may sell or lease substantially all of the assets of the estate prior to confirmation of a plan of reorganization. The debtor in possession may have important reasons for proposing such action. For example, it may have already negotiated a sale with a buyer who is unwilling to wait for months while a plan is negotiated and confirmed. On the other hand, a sale of substantially all of the estate assets will likely restrict the options available for reorganization and often lead to a liquidating plan. Moreover, to that extent that the sale order provides what will happen to the sale proceeds, it may effectively alter the priorities established by the Code and deprive creditors of both substantive and procedural rights inherent in the plan confirmation process. Even something more innocuous than a sale of most assets – such as a compromise of major prepetition litigation (which is a "use" of assets) – may significantly impact the confirmation process. How should courts respond to such motions? Consider the following case.

IN RE TORCH OFFSHORE, INC.
327 B.R. 254 (E.D. La. 2005)

Lemmon, District Judge.

A. Background.

On January 7, 2005, Torch Offshore, Inc., the owner and operator of an 11-vessel fleet in the Gulf of Mexico, filed a petition for bankruptcy protection under Chapter 11. Since entering bankruptcy protection Torch has repeatedly expressed its intention to sell off all or most of its assets due to its declining prospects for successfully reorganizing its business. On April 6, 2005, Torch filed a motion seeking bankruptcy court approval of the sale of the majority of its assets under § 363(b) to Cal Dive International, Inc. for $92 million. At a hearing on Torch's motion on April 27, 2005, Torch modified its proposal to reflect that (1) three vessels * * * that were subject to a lien in favor of General Electric Capital Corporation ("GECC") would be sold to GECC for $18.36 million, or to the highest bidder; and (2) six vessels * * * would be sold to Cal Dive for

---

[21] *See In re Trans World Airlines, Inc.*, 322 F.3d 283 (3d Cir. 2003); *see also* Michael H. Reed, *Successor Liability and Bankruptcy Sales Revisited – A New Paradigm*, 61 BUS. LAW. 179 (2005).

$80 million, or to the highest bidder. One other vessel, * * * estimated to bring in $2 million, would be auctioned separately. The effect of these sales would be to divest Torch of all of its operating assets.

On May 4, 2005, the bankruptcy court approved the sales procedures, and the auctions took place on June 2, 2005. An $18.36 million offer by GECC was the highest bid on the vessels subject to its lien. An $80.45 million offer by Cal Dive was the highest bid on the six vessels covered by its original proposal, and a $2.55 million offer by Cal Dive was the highest bid on the [remaining vessel]. Epic Divers was the highest bidder, at $2.8 million, on certain other equipment. The total amount of the proposed sale is $85.8 million.

On June 8, 2005, the bankruptcy court conducted a hearing on whether to approve the sales. The Official Committee of Unsecured Creditors (the "Committee") objected to the sales, arguing that they constituted a *sub rosa* plan of reorganization and violated the standards announced in *In re Braniff Airways, Inc.*, 700 F.2d 935 (5th Cir. 1983) and *In re Continental Air Lines, Inc.*, 780 F.2d 1223 (5th Cir. 1986). The bankruptcy court specifically instructed counsel for the Committee that under the theory of *Continental*, he had to "show specifically what protection is being denied to you by these sales under Section 363," and asked counsel several times to identify "what rights, what benefits are the unsecured creditors being deprived of by this sale rather than a sale through – rather than the benefits that would accrue to them under a plan of reorganization?" Although counsel for the Committee indicated that it wished the opportunity to file a reorganization plan, the court perceived that the unsecured creditors would receive no payments either under the sales or through a reorganization plan, and termed the Committee's objections to the asset sales to be "not specific enough to satisfy me or to satisfy the test from *Continental Air Lines*."

At the end of the hearing, the court orally approved the sales, and entered written orders of approval on June 15, 2005. The court rejected the Committee's argument that the sales violated the standards of *Continental* and *Braniff* * * *.

The Committee appeals the ruling of the bankruptcy court approving the sales, arguing that there is no business justification for the sales and that they constitute a *sub rosa* reorganization plan in violation of *Braniff*. * * *

B. Analysis.

* * *

2. The proposed asset sales.

[Section] 363(b) provides that "[t]he trustee, after notice and a hearing, may use, sell, or lease, other than in the ordinary course of business, property of the estate." In

In re Continental Air Lines, Inc., 780 F.2d 1223 (5th Cir. 1986), the debtor sought to enter into leases for new aircraft under § 363 after filing bankruptcy. Certain institutional creditors objected. The court held that when a proposed use, sale, or lease of assets is outside the ordinary course of business, the first step is for the debtor in possession to demonstrate that there are "business justifications" for the proposed transaction, necessitating an analysis of the factors enunciated in *In re Lionel Corp.*, 722 F.2d 1063 (2d Cir. 1983):

> the proportionate value of the asset to the estate as a whole, the amount of elapsed time since the filing, the likelihood that a plan of reorganization will be proposed and confirmed in the near future, the effect of the proposed disposition on future plans of reorganization, the proceeds to be obtained from the disposition vis-a-vis any appraisals of the property, which of the alternatives of use, sale or lease the proposal envisions and, most importantly perhaps, whether the asset is increasing or decreasing in value. This list is not intended to be exclusive, but merely to provide guidance to the bankruptcy judge.

Continental, 780 F.2d at 1226. Additionally, lower courts facing a proposal to use, sell, or lease assets outside the ordinary course of business must determine "whether the proposed transactions otherwise violate or are incompatible with the provisions of Chapter 11," including the requirement that the sales not be a *sub rosa* plan of reorganization prohibited by *In re Braniff Airways, Inc.*, 700 F.2d 935 (5th Cir. 1983).

(a) Are there business justifications for the proposed sales?

Consideration of the *Lionel* factors clearly reveals that there are business justifications for the asset sales. The fact that the sales encompass virtually all of the assets of the estate is not determinative, but one consideration in determining whether there is a business justification for the proposed sales. The auctions occurred approximately six months after the filing of the bankruptcy petition, and during these six months the debtor explored whether it could reorganize its business or had to liquidate its operating assets. No plan of reorganization has been proposed, and there is no indication that a sale of the debtor's assets pursuant to any such plan would result in a greater value to the estate than the proceeds realized by the auctions. The Committee points out that the assets were recently appraised at $228 million, but this is not an indication of market value because no firm was willing to offer this amount at the well advertised twelve-hour-long auctions, during which the debtor received almost 100 bids. Most importantly, the undisputed evidence before the bankruptcy court indicated that maintaining the vessels was costing the debtor an exorbitant amount of money, and the condition of the vessels was deteriorating over time. The court affirms the bankruptcy court's finding that there are sound business justifications for the asset sales.

(b) Do the asset sales exceed the scope of § 363(b)?

The Fifth Circuit examined the scope of § 363(b) in *In re Braniff Airways, Inc.*, 700 F.2d 935 (5th Cir. 1983). The *Braniff* debtor entered into an agreement to dispose of all of its assets to an entity known as PSA in exchange for travel scrip. Numerous creditor objections were filed. The court held that the PSA Agreement was invalid because the transaction was "much more than the 'use, sale or lease' of Braniff's property authorized by § 363(b)":

> Three examples will illustrate our rationale. The PSA Agreement provided that Braniff would pay $2.5 million to PSA in exchange for $7.5 million in scrip entitling the holder to travel on PSA. It further required that the scrip be used only in a future Braniff reorganization and that it be issued only to former Braniff employees or shareholders or, in a limited amount, to unsecured creditors. *This provision not only changed the composition of Braniff's assets, the contemplated result under § 363(b), it also had the practical effect of dictating some of the terms of a future reorganization plan.* The reorganization plan would have to allocate the scrip according to the terms of the PSA agreement or forfeit a valuable asset. *The debtor and the Bankruptcy Court should not be able to short circuit the requirements of Chapter 11 for confirmation of a reorganization plan by establishing the terms of the plan sub rosa in connection with a sale of assets.*
>
> Second, under the agreement between Braniff and its creditor, the secured creditors were required to vote a portion of their deficiency claim in favor of any future reorganization plan approved by a majority of the unsecured creditors' committee. Again, such an action is not comprised by the term "use, sell, or lease," and it thwarts the Code's carefully crafted scheme for creditor enfranchisement where plans of reorganization are concerned.
>
> Third, the PSA transaction also provided for the release of claims by all parties against Braniff, its secured creditors and its officers and directors. On its face, this requirement is not a "use, sale or lease" and is not authorized by § 363(b).

Id. at 940 (emphasis added). The court therefore determined that the PSA Agreement was not authorized under § 363(b) * * *. *Braniff* requires review of agreements that do more than constitute the simple "use, sale or lease" of assets to ensure that they do not exceed § 363(b) and constitute *sub rosa* plans of reorganization. *See Matter of The*

Babcock & Wilcox Co., 250 F.3d 955, 960 (5th Cir. 2001) ("*Braniff* stands merely for the proposition that the provisions of § 363 permitting a trustee to use, sell, or lease the assets do not allow a debtor to gut the bankruptcy estate before reorganization or to change the fundamental nature of the estate's assets in such a way that limits a future reorganization plan."); *see also* 3 *Collier on Bankruptcy* ¶ 363.02[4], at 363-20 (Lawrence P. King ed., 15th ed. 1996) ("Attempts to determine plan issues in connection with the sale [under § 363(b)] will be improper and should result in a denial of the relief requested.")[.]

In re Cajun Electric Power Cooperative, Inc., 119 F.3d 349 (5th Cir. 1997) illustrates the limits of *Braniff.* The *Cajun Electric* debtor entered into a settlement regarding its obligations connected with the River Bend nuclear reactor (paying some monies, giving up some claims, and being released from future obligations pertaining to the plant). The court approved the settlement, rejecting the arguments of the creditors of the debtor that it was prohibited by *Braniff:*

> The instant settlement is not a *sub rosa* reorganization of the type disapproved in *Braniff.* It does not dispose of all claims against Cajun, nor does it restrict creditors' rights to vote as they deem fit on a proposed reorganization plan. Finally, the settlement does not dispose of virtually all of Cajun's assets, leaving "little prospect or occasion for future reorganization."[22] Instead it disposes of one particular "asset," River Bend, which is not so much the crown jewel of Cajun's estate but its white elephant. The removal of River Bend from the estate will facilitate Cajun's reorganization, and will do so without denigrating the rights of the unsecured trade creditors.
>
> Undeniably, the settlement removes $107 million in cash and transmission lines worth $20 million from the debtor's estate; it also precludes Cajun from pursuing litigation – an uncertain prospect at best – against Gulf States and RUS. However, Cajun retains as much as $1.1 billion in non-River Bend

[22] The fact that the sale disposes of essentially all of the assets of the estate does not necessarily disqualify the sale as a *sub rosa* plan. Several courts have approved the sale of all of an estate's assets under certain circumstances. *See In re Cummins Utility, L.P.*, 279 B.R. 195, 198 (Bankr. N.D. Tex. 2002) (approving the sale of all of the debtor's assets because all parties supported it, and the court "was persuaded by the parties that the Debtor's business was rapidly deteriorating"); *In re Condere Corp.*, 228 B.R. 615, 627 (Bankr. S.D. Miss. 1998) (approving sale of all debtor's assets because debtor would otherwise run completely out of money in two to four weeks, and "the proposed sale in the instant case is a simple exchange of assets for cash. It is unlike the far reaching terms of the sale the Fifth Circuit objected to in *Braniff.*"). The current sales are only exchanges of assets for cash. They do not contain any provisions dictating the terms of any future reorganization plan, preordaining the way creditors will vote on such a plan, or attempting to vary the priorities of Torch's creditors.

> assets. In sum, the settlement does not "alter creditors' rights, dispose of assets, and release claims to the extent proposed in the wide-ranging transaction disapproved in" *Braniff.* The cases are entirely distinguishable, and the settlement at issue does not effect a *sub rosa* plan.

Id. at 355 (citations omitted).

Because "each hearing on a § 363(b) transaction cannot become a mini-hearing on plan confirmation," the *Continental* court held:

> that when an objector to a proposed transaction under § 363(b) claims that it is being denied certain protection because approval is sought pursuant to § 363(b) instead of as part of a reorganization plan, the objector must specify exactly what protection is being denied. If the court concludes that there has in actuality been such a denial, it may then consider fashioning appropriate protective measures modeled on those which would attend a reorganization plan.

Continental, 780 F.2d at 1228.

The Committee does not demonstrate how any specific protection will be lost because the vessel sales will take place pursuant to § 363(b) rather than as part of a reorganization plan, and its complaints are simply a list of virtually every procedural protection afforded by Chapter 11, without a specific explanation of how these protections are being denied.

The Committee presented general arguments that the assets sales will cause them to lose the ability to receive a disclosure statement, will result in the failure of administrative and tax claims to be paid, will divest them of plan voting rights, and will deprive them of the ability to file a competing reorganization plan. The Committee fails to provide any specific reason why a disclosure statement would be valuable, other than a cryptic reference to "denied discovery," which denial was not appealed. Additionally, although the Committee argues that the "plan process" would require that administrative, priority, and tax claims would have to be paid in full, it fails to explain why this process would be different from what will occur pursuant to the asset sales. The entire argument that the Committee's proposal for its plan of reorganization may afford protections not available in the § 363(b) sales depends on the validity of the assertion that the [vessels] "could then be operated at a profit." This bare assertion has no factual basis in the record.

* * * Accordingly, the bankruptcy court's orders approving the sales are affirmed.
* * *

(c) Section 365: Executory Contracts and Unexpired Leases

In chapter five of this book, we briefly examined § 365, which governs the bankruptcy treatment of the debtor's executory contracts and unexpired leases. A Chapter 11 debtor in possession must carefully examine its executory contracts and unexpired leases to determine whether to assume, assign, or reject them. In making that decision the inquiry is – or at least should be – what is best for the estate; which action will generate the greatest revenue or impose the least cost. Although certain unexpired leases will be automatically rejected if not assumed within a specified time period, *see* § 365(d)(4), for most executory contracts and unexpired leases, the debtor in possession need not make a decision until confirmation. *See* § 365(d)(1); Rule 6006. Indeed, if the debtor in possession intends to assume an executory contract or unexpired lease, the debtor will often include a provision to that effect in the reorganization plan itself. *See* § 1123(b)(2). This allows the debtor in possession to avoid binding itself before it knows whether the plan will be confirmed. If the debtor in possession chooses to assume or, more commonly, to reject before confirmation, it must file a motion to that effect. The court then reviews the debtor's decision somewhat deferentially; the court normally defers to the debtor's business judgment unless there is evidence that the debtor is exercising its judgment for illegitimate reasons.[23]

Generally, a debtor in possession will take some time – often many months – to decide whether to assume or reject each executory contract and unexpired lease. The uncertainty during this period can be very frustrating for the counterparty, who will likely have several significant concerns: (i) how much time will the court give the debtor in possession to make a decision; (ii) must the debtor in possession perform its obligations during the period before assumption or rejection; (iii) must the counterparty perform its obligations before the debtor in possession assumes or rejects the unexpired lease or executory contract; and (iv) how, if at all, does rejection affect any interests in property that the counterparty has already transferred to the debtor.

With respect to the first issue, read § 365(d)(2) and (d)(4). Subsection (d)(2) allows a party to ask the court to set a deadline for assumption or rejection. Obviously, in setting such deadlines, courts must balance a variety of competing considerations. These include: (i) the potential harm to each party and the likelihood of such harm; (ii) the possible benefit to the estate; (iii) the debtor's ability to satisfy its postpetition obligations; (iv) the contract's importance to the debtor's business and to a successful

---

[23] *See In re Pomona Valley Med. Grp., Inc.*, 476 F.3d 665, 670 (9th Cir. 2007).

reorganization; and (v) whether the debtor has had a sufficient time to appraise its financial situation and potential value of its assets in formulating a reorganization plan.[24]

As to the second issue, whether the debtor in possession must perform its postpetition obligations under the contract or lease before assumption or rejection, § 365 provides no comprehensive answer. For unexpired leases of nonresidential real property, § 365(d)(3) requires that the debtor in possession timely perform all postpetition obligations. For unexpired leases of personal property used for business purposes, § 365(d)(5) requires that the debtor in possession timely perform all obligations arising more than 60 days after the petition. Both of these provisions clearly apply when the debtor is the lessee, but it is less clear whether they also apply when the debtor is the lessor. The Ninth Circuit has ruled they do not.[25] Do you agree? Compare the language of § 365(d)(3) to the language of (d)(4).

Even when the provisions do apply, there is occasionally some dispute as to which contractual obligations "aris[e]" after the petition and before rejection. For example, if the debtor in possession rejects a lease and vacates the property in the middle of a month, must it nevertheless pay the entire monthly rental that became due at the beginning of the month?[26] If the lease requires the debtor to pay the real estate taxes, what happens if the taxes accrue prepetition but, pursuant to the lease, the lessor does not bill the debtor for them until after the petition?[27] This latter question should be reminiscent of the issues discussed in chapters three and five concerning which assets and liabilities of the debtor are allocable to the prepetition period and which to the postpetition period.

Aside from § 365(d)(3) and (d)(5), nothing in § 365 specifies whether the debtor in possession must perform postpetition obligations. Because those provisions apply only to leases, nothing in the section covers executory contracts at all. The only marginally helpful provision is § 363(e), which permits a counterparty to seek adequate protection of its interests.

---

24 *See In re Adelphia Commc'ns Corp.*, 291 B.R. 283, 292–93 (Bankr. S.D.N.Y. 2003).

25 *See In re BCE West, L.P.*, 319 F.3d 1166 (9th Cir. 2003) (dealing with § 365(d)(3)).

26 *Compare HA-LO Indus., Inc. v. CenterPoint Props. Trust*, 342 F.3d 794 (7th Cir. 2003); *In re Koenig Sporting Goods, Inc.*, 203 F.3d 986 (6th Cir. 2000), *with In re Ames Dept. Stores*, 306 B.R. 43 (Bankr. S.D.N.Y. 2004).

27 *Compare In re Montgomery Ward Holding Corp.*, 268 F.3d 205 (3d Cir. 2001), *with In re Handy Andy Home Improvement Ctrs.*, 144 F.3d 1125 (7th Cir. 1998).

As to the third issue, whether the counterparty must perform prior to assumption or rejection, the Code says very little. Presumably if the counterparty suspends performance, it risks being in breach and liable for any resulting damages. It may, however, be able to treat the debtor's bankruptcy as grounds for demanding adequate assurance of future performance.[28] In other words, it may be able to seek adequate protection. *See* § 363(e). It may also be able to get the court to force the debtor to make a prompt decision on whether to assume or reject. Failing either of those, it may be able to claim administrative expense priority for the value of its postpetition performance accepted by the debtor.

Of course, if the debtor assumes the executory contract or unexpired lease, the estate becomes bound and must perform all of the debtor's obligations under the contract or lease, including curing any defaults. § 365(b). If the assumed contract or lease is not assigned to a third party, then any obligation the debtor in possession fails to perform will qualify as an administrative expense. § 503. Thus, for anyone seeking to maximize the assets of the estate, the decision to assume an executory contract or unexpired lease is not a riskless proposition.

The last issue concerns the effect of a rejection of an executory contract or unexpired lease.[29] We already know that the counterparty will have a claim against the estate for breach of contract and that claim will be treated as a prepetition obligation. § 365(g). We also know that, to the extent any executory (*i.e.*, unperformed) obligations remain on either side of the transaction, those executory obligations need not be performed. But what about obligations already performed? That is, suppose the debtor in possession has already received property pursuant to a rejected contract. Must the debtor in possession return the property to the counterparty? Alternatively, assume the debtor has transferred property to the counterparty. Does rejection of the contract nullify the transfer such that the assets automatically revert to the estate?[30]

---

[28] *See* U.C.C. § 2-609; RESTATEMENT (SECOND) OF CONTRACTS § 251 (1981).

[29] Collective bargaining agreements, a special type of executory contract, are dealt with specifically in § 1113. To assume or reject a collective bargaining agreement, the Chapter 11 debtor must comply with this section. The debtor may use Chapter 11 as a mechanism to force renegotiation of collective bargaining agreements. *See, e.g.*, *In re Northwest Airlines Corp.*, 483 F.3d 160 (2d Cir. 2007). The intersections between bankruptcy law and labor law are complex and beyond the scope of an introductory course on bankruptcy, for which this book is designed.

[30] *Cf. Precision Indus., Inc. v. Qualitech Steel SBQ, LLC*, 327 F.3d 537 (7th Cir. 2003) (§ 363(f) sale of property the debtor had previously leased cut off the lessee's rights even though § 365(h)(1)(A) provides that rejection does not affect the lessee's rights).

The answers to these questions are complicated by the fact that § 365 contains numerous rules relevant to these questions, and many of the rules apply to only a narrow class of contracts or property. Beyond that, the rules are probably more attributable to lobbying by special interest groups than to fidelity to a consistent or coherent policy. Read § 365(h), (i), (n). Then consider the following case.

THOMPKINS v. LIL' JOE RECORDS, INC.
476 F.3d 1294 (11th Cir. 2007)

Tjoflat, Circuit Judge:

This appeal requires us to consider what happens when a debtor-in-possession in a Chapter 11 bankruptcy case, who negotiated the purchase of copyrights prior to the bankruptcy proceeding, later uses the bankruptcy code to reject those contracts that transferred ownership of the copyrights to the debtor. Our resolution of that question determines the outcome of much of this suit by a rap artist who created the works giving rise to the copyrights in question. The artist sold copyrights in his works to a music recording company in exchange for a recording contract that entitled the artist to future royalties. The recording company later went bankrupt, becoming the debtor-in-possession. In confirming the debtor's reorganization plan, the bankruptcy court ordered that all of the debtor's contracts with the artist be rejected under the bankruptcy code and the copyrights sold to a rival recording company and its owner, two of the defendants in the instant case.

Years later, the artist sued the defendants, alleging that they did not actually gain ownership of the copyrights through the bankruptcy, or if they did, they now owe him royalties. Based on that premise, the artist asserts numerous claims sounding in federal and state law. The district court granted summary judgment in favor of the defendants on all claims, and for the reasons set forth below, we affirm.

I.

* * *

A.

[In May 1989, Luther Campbell ("Campbell"), a member of 2 Live Crew, signed Jeffrey J. Thompkins ("Thompkins") to an Exclusive Recording Agreement (the "1989 Agreement" or "Agreement") with Campbell's recording company, Luke Records, Inc. ("Luke Records").

The Agreement covered a contract period of five years. Under its terms, Thompkins was required to record albums under the group name "Poison Clan" and deliver master recordings ("masters") for production and release by Luke Records. Luke Records was given "exclusive, unlimited and perpetual rights throughout the world" to the copyrights in the sound recordings and a license to exploit the musical compositions. In exchange, Luke Records agreed to pay Thompkins royalties according to specified rates.] The Agreement obligated Luke Records generally to "commercially release each LP [album] recorded and delivered" by Thompkins under certain conditions. * * *

From 1989 through 1994 (the year in which the 1989 Agreement expired by its terms), Thompkins recorded three albums as Poison Clan: *2 Low Life Muthas*, *Poisonous Mentality*, and *Rufftown Behavior*. Luke Records distributed each of these.

B.

On March 28, 1995, Luke Records became the subject of an involuntary Chapter 7 bankruptcy petition filed by its creditors in the U.S. Bankruptcy Court for the Southern District of Florida. That June, Campbell individually filed a voluntary Chapter 11 bankruptcy petition, and Luke Records moved to convert its Chapter 7 case into one under Chapter 11. The bankruptcy court granted Luke Records' motion on June 14, 1995 and jointly administered the Luke Records and Campbell bankruptcies (footnote omitted).

* * * [The bankruptcy cases continued throughout the following months, and on March 22, 1996, the bankruptcy court confirmed a plan of reorganization. The confirmation order expressly provided that "all executory contracts and unexpired leases of the Debtors are hereby rejected." Following confirmation, the bankruptcy court issued orders in both bankruptcy cases setting bar dates for claims arising from rejected executory contracts. Parties to the rejected contracts were allowed thirty days to file "any claims arising as a result of such rejection," and claims not timely filed were to be "deemed waived and will not be entitled to distribution under the confirmed Joint Plan." Thompkins did not file any proof of claim for rejection damages. As a final step in the reorganization process, the parties executed an assignment to Lil' Joe Records, Inc. of all of Luke Records' and Campbell's copyrights.]

C.

Nearly six years later, on March 5, 2002, Thompkins filed the instant suit against Lil' Joe Records, Inc., Lil' Joe Wein Music, Inc., and Weinberger (hereinafter collectively, "Lil' Joe") in the U.S. District Court for the Northern District of Georgia seeking damages, declaratory relief, and permanent injunctive relief for alleged violations of the Copyright Act. * * * On December 7, 2004, the district court * * * granted Lil' Joe's motion for summary judgment on the ground that the earlier bankruptcy Confirmation Order precluded Thompkins's claims, and denied Thompkins's motion for summary judgment. The district court entered final judgment for Lil' Joe on December 16, 2004. Thompkins now appeals, challenging the district court's order granting Lil' Joe's motion for summary judgment.

II

* * *

Thompkins first asserts a claim of infringement under the Copyright Act, alleging that Lil' Joe has illegally exploited copyrights owned by Thompkins in dozens of songs that he authored and performed on recordings [pursuant to the 1989 agreement ("the Poison Clan Songs"). * * *

With regard to the Poison Clan Songs, Thompkins argues that any copyrights he transferred to Luke Records under the 1989 Agreement reverted to his ownership when Luke Records rejected the Poison Clan contracts as executory under the bankruptcy Joint Plan. Thompkins further argues that, upon reversion of the copyrights, those assets ceased to constitute part of the bankruptcy estate and thus were not transferred to Lil' Joe under the Joint Plan, notwithstanding the language of the Plan and the various supporting documents and bankruptcy orders suggesting that the copyrights were meant to be transferred. Accordingly, Thompkins argues, Lil' Joe infringed his copyrights when it exploited them after the plan confirmation. Lil' Joe disputes Thompkins's interpretation of the effect of the Joint Plan confirmation, arguing instead that Luke Records' ownership of the copyrights was unaffected by its rejection of any contracts. Thus, Lil' Joe contends, those copyrights were transferred to Lil' Joe among other Luke Records assets disposed of by the terms of the Joint Plan.

The terms of the 1989 Agreement clearly transferred ownership of the disputed copyrights to Luke Records in the course of its business relationship with Thompkins, well before the bankruptcy. The parties now dispute the effect on copyright ownership caused by Luke Records' rejection of the 1989 Agreement in the bankruptcy as an executory contract pursuant to § 365.[31] Because post-bankruptcy ownership of the

---

[31] Under § 365(a), "the trustee, subject to the court's approval, may assume or reject any executory contract . . . of the debtor." This provision has spawned much litigation over the proper definition of an "executory contract," and courts have struggled to formulate a coherent approach to the issue. The parties in this case have likewise grappled with the definition of the contracts at issue between Thompkins and Luke Records. On appeal, the parties agree that the contracts were "executory" for the purposes of § 365 and that Luke Records rejected them. But this rare point of agreement between the parties is unique to the appeal in this case; in the district court, Thompkins maintained exactly the opposite position, asserting that the contracts were improperly treated as executory by the bankruptcy

copyrights determines Thompkins's ability to assert copyright claims on the Poison Clan Songs in this suit, we must decide whether Luke Records' rejection of the 1989 Agreement had any effect on Luke Records' – or, more precisely, its bankruptcy estate's – continued ownership of those copyrights in the bankruptcy.

We hold that the rejection of the 1989 Agreement did not cause ownership of the Poison Clan Song copyrights to revert to Thompkins; thus, the copyrights properly passed into Luke Records' bankruptcy estate and from there were legally assigned to Lil' Joe. In essence, Thompkins asks this court to deem an executory contract rejection under § 365 to be the functional equivalent of a rescission, rendering void the contract and requiring that the parties be put back in the positions they occupied before the contract was formed (footnote omitted). This is not the purpose of § 365, nor does Thompkins cite any authority to show otherwise.

In support of his argument, Thompkins relies on the proposition that a debtor cannot accept only the benefits of an executory contract while eschewing the burdens. He also correctly observes that § 365 of the bankruptcy code ordinarily deems rejection of an executory contract to be "a breach of such contract . . . immediately before the date of the filing of the [bankruptcy] petition." § 365(g). Thompkins apparently concludes that because Luke Records' rejection of the 1989 Agreement constituted a pre-petition breach of that contract, that event somehow reverses any transfer of asset ownership

---

court.

Fortunately, we need not descend into the morass and attempt to define "executory" in this case. The parties do not contest that issue on appeal, and even if they were so inclined, we might otherwise be precluded from reconsidering the "executoriness" of the contracts. That issue was already decided by various bankruptcy court orders deeming the relevant contracts to be executory and confirming their rejection. In addition to the Confirmation Order generally deeming any unassumed contracts to be rejected, the order setting the bar date for rejection claims in the Luke Records bankruptcy specifically designated the "exclusive recording contracts" with Poison Clan as rejected executory contracts.

Although we do not find it necessary to reexamine whether the 1989 Agreement was properly treated as "executory," we note that the bankruptcy court's approval of the rejection of the 1989 Agreement would be consistent with the "functional approach" to "executoriness" that we have tacitly approved in our precedent. That is, "[e]ven though there may be material obligations outstanding on the part of only one of the parties to the contract, it may nevertheless be deemed executory . . . if its assumption [ ][or] rejection would ultimately benefit the estate and its creditors." *In re Gen. Dev. Corp.*, 177 B.R. 1000, 1012 (S.D. Fla.1995), *aff'd*, 84 F.3d 1364, 1365, 1374 (11th Cir. 1996). The bankruptcy court presumably determined that rejection of the 1989 Agreement would benefit the Luke Records estate by maximizing the value of the copyrights. The enhanced value of the copyrights in turn increased the value of the estate and the amount available to be paid to all of Luke Records' creditors – including Thompkins, had he properly filed a claim in the bankruptcy.

previously carried out by the rejected contract. In other words, Luke Records' rejection of the "burdens" of the 1989 Agreement prevents Luke Records from keeping the "benefits," which, in Thompkins's view, are the copyrights Luke Records received.

It is true that a debtor must either assume an executory contract in its entirety or completely reject it, but Thompkins misunderstands the implications of rejection under § 365. Thompkins's argument basically calls for an interpretation of rejection as an outright dissolution of the contract. But rejection "does not embody the contract-vaporizing properties so commonly ascribed to it. . . . Rejection merely frees the estate from the obligation to perform; it does not make the contract disappear." *In re Drexel Burnham Lambert Group, Inc.*, 138 B.R. 687, 703 (Bankr. S.D.N.Y. 1992). More specifically, "[r]ejection has absolutely no effect upon the contract's continued existence; the contract is not cancelled, repudiated, rescinded, or in any other fashion terminated." *Id.* at 703.

The *Drexel Burnham Lambert Group* case, cited by Thompkins himself, presents a useful illustration of what a § 365 rejection does and does not affect. The corporate debtor, in an attempt to avoid its prospective obligations to compensate its former general counsel under the terms of an employment agreement, sought to reject the agreement as executory under § 365. Among the compensation provided for in the agreement were various monetary payments, plus three stock portfolios purchased by the former general counsel from the debtor upon execution of the agreement and held in escrow for future disbursement. The debtor claimed that by rejecting the employment contract – the means by which the stock portfolios were purchased and escrowed by the general counsel – the debtor "pull[ed] the plug" on the general counsel's rights to the escrowed portfolios. *Id.* at 695.

The bankruptcy court granted the debtor's motion to reject the contract, resulting in a prepetition breach under the terms of § 365(g) and converting the monetary balance owed to the general counsel into "a general unsecured claim that can be paid in 'tiny Bankruptcy Dollars.'" *Id.* at 711. As to the stock portfolios, however, the court "repudiate[d] Debtor's contention that rejection vaporizes or otherwise avoids [the general counsel's] interest in the escrowed funds." *Id.* The terms of the agreement gave the general counsel "both legal title and the equitable interest" in the escrowed stock, and the only right the debtor company retained in the stock upon execution of the agreement was a contingent interest subject to a condition subsequent, which ultimately never materialized. *Id.* at 710. When the condition subsequent became moot, the general counsel "became entitled to immediate possession" of the stocks, and that possession was unaffected by the rejection of the contract. *Id.*

Like the debtor in *Drexel Burnham Lambert Group*, Thompkins argues that Luke Records "pulled the plug" on its own claim of ownership over the copyrights when it rejected the contract; thus, he contends, the copyrights could not have been assigned to Lil' Joe out of Luke Records' estate. But like the bankruptcy court in *Drexel Burnham Lambert Group*, other courts have observed that rejection differently affects the unperformed portions of an executory agreement and those provisions of the agreement that, by their nature, are fully executed. The rejection of a pre-petition executory contract pursuant to which the debtor acquired property does not obligate the debtor to return the property.

There is no debate that Thompkins's transfer of his copyrights to Luke Records under the 1989 Agreement was an executed sale of property. The terms of the Agreement leave Thompkins not even so much as a contingent interest in the copyrights. Nor did Thompkins negotiate any specific requirements for the sale or promotion of his records; Luke Records needed only to "commercially release" each record, which it undisputedly did, and all matters of business judgment in such efforts were reserved to Luke Records and binding on Thompkins. To the extent the 1989 Agreement was "executory," in the sense of not being fully executed, it was only insofar as Luke Records was required to pay Thompkins royalties based on any future sales of his records. The transfer of the copyrights was fully executed, however, and Luke Records held full legal and equitable title under the terms of the Agreement.

Thus, when the bankruptcy court approved the rejection of the Agreement, it freed Luke Records from the obligation, or "burden," to pay royalties under the contractual terms and gave Thompkins a pre-petition claim for damages resulting from the breach. It also would have released Thompkins from any outstanding obligation to perform under the Agreement – *i.e.*, to convey any as-yet unrealized "benefit" to Luke Records. But the bankruptcy court's Confirmation Order did not effectively rescind the 1989 Agreement and reverse the executed transfer of the Poison Clan Song copyrights to Luke Records. The rejection had no effect on Luke Records' ownership of the copyrights, and they passed from the estate to Lil' Joe under the terms of the Joint Plan and Confirmation Order (and the later documents executing the agreed upon and confirmed terms of the reorganization). Accordingly, Thompkins cannot support a claim of copyright infringement against Lil' Joe as to the Poison Clan Songs, and we affirm the grant of summary judgment on that claim in favor of Lil' Joe. * * *

NOTE

In *Thompkins*, the debtor was the transferee of intellectual property. A similar issue arises when the debtor is a transferor. For example, assume the debtor is a licensor of a trademark. Does rejection of the license under § 365 prohibit the licensee from continuing to use the trademark? Subsection (n) generally allows a licensee of intellectual property from the debtor to retain its rights. However, "intellectual property" does not include a trademark. *See* § 101(35A). Nevertheless, the Seventh Circuit has ruled that the omission of trademarks from the definition of "intellectual property" simply means that § 365(n) does not affect trademarks one way or the other. More to the point, the court ruled that rejection of the license constitutes a breach of the license agreement but does not terminate the licensee's right to use the trademark. *See Sunbeam Prods., Inc. v. Chicago Mfg., LLC*, 686 F.3d 372 (7th Cir. 2012).

Problem 12-2

Darling Home Services, Inc. provides repair services to homeowners. It has leased office space in a strip mall. Monthly lease payments are $1,000. The lease is in the second year of a four-year term. Darling also leases a high-speed copier and three computers from Computing Supply, Inc. This lease is for 12 months and was executed two months ago. It obligates Darling to pay $300 per month and obligates Computer Supply to provide up to 10 hours of network support services each month for no additional charge (if Computing Supply provides more than 10 hours of such services in a month, it is entitled to be paid $50 per hour for any portion of an hour spent above the 10 hours in the month for network support services). Darling also recently entered into a contract with a condominium association to provide home repair services to the homeowners in the association for $35 per hour up to 50 hours per month. Darling filed a Chapter 11 petition last week.

A. What are Darling's options and obligations regarding each of the two leases and the services contract while Darling is in the process of formulating its reorganization plan?
B. What would you advise the landlord, Computing Supply, and the condominium association to do in terms of their respective relationships with Darling?

(d) Lien and Transfer Avoidance

In chapters two and six of this book, we explored the bankruptcy code provisions on recovering prepetition payments as avoidable preferences. In chapter six we also covered the various provisions that empower the trustee to avoid liens, including § 544 (the strong-arm power), § 545 (statutory liens), and § 547 (preferences). Added to them is § 549, which allows the trustee to avoid any postpetition transfer of estate property that is not authorized by the Code or approved by the court. In Chapter 11 cases, all of these avoidance powers may be exercised by the debtor in possession. § 1107.

The power of the debtor in possession to avoid these types of transfers influences the bankruptcy process. It can affect the terms of a plan of reorganization, the plan confirmation process and, more preliminarily, the negotiations over the debtor's authorization to continue operations and use estate property. To illustrate this dynamic, consider the following situation.

> First Bank has been providing operating financing for DEF, Inc., a debtor that has filed a Chapter 11 bankruptcy. First Bank has a properly perfected security interest in DEF's inventory and accounts but is undersecured. That is, the value of the inventory and accounts on the day the bankruptcy was filed was less than the amount owed to First Bank. Prior to the bankruptcy filing, First Bank received several payments on its debt that are preferential given the undersecured nature of its claim (and that are not protected from avoidance under § 547(c)). DEF has filed a cash collateral motion to use the proceeds of inventory sales and account collections to pay employees. First Bank has objected to the debtor's motion and has requested adequate protection of its security interest in the inventory and accounts. If the debtor filed a preference action and won, First Bank would have to return the preference payments. This would have the effect of increasing the amount of First Bank's unsecured claim in the debtor's bankruptcy but also increasing the amount of cash in the bankruptcy estate. In the negotiations between First Bank and the debtor, the debtor and First Bank might agree that the debtor will not pursue its preference action against First Bank in return for First Bank dropping its objection to the debtor's use of cash collateral and agreeing to a lesser standard of adequate protection for the use of that cash collateral. Similarly, if there is some issue regarding whether First Bank's security interest is perfected, the debtor will use that fact in negotiating with First Bank regarding use of cash collateral. Obviously, if the security interest is in fact unperfected, First Bank's security

interest in the proceeds of the collateral does not have to be adequately protected.

These simple examples illustrate that the transfer avoidance issues play out differently in a Chapter 11 proceeding. They form the backdrop of considerations that the creditor and debtor take into account in negotiating how that creditor will be treated during the process of the case and ultimately the plan proposal.

Problem 12-3

Revisit the facts of Problem 12-1. What clauses, if any, does the discussion above of lien and transfer avoidance suggest that Intercontinental Bank should seek to include in the postpetition financing stipulation and order?

2. The Costs of Administering the Estate

(a) Distinguishing Prepetition Claims from Administrative Expenses

As mentioned in chapter nine, while almost all allowable claims arise prepetition, administrative expenses necessarily arise postpetition. Occasionally, determining whether a particular obligation represents a prepetition claim or a postpetition administrative expense is difficult. Consider the following case.

IN RE LUCRE, INC.
434 B.R. 807 (Bankr. W.D. Mich. 2010)

Jeffrey R. Hughes, Bankruptcy Judge.

FACTUAL BACKGROUND

[Lucre provides telecommunications services to its Verizon customers. AT&T, one of Lucre's competitors, was required by the Telecommunications Act of 1996 to provide Lucre – and did provide Lucre – with access to its facilities to rout calls through a separate, dedicated circuit referred to by the parties as the "Verizon DEOT." Their relationship was acrimonious, however, with repeated accusations of sabotage, dilatory conduct, and improper motives.]

Lucre commenced its case in October 2005. AT&T had been charging Lucre $3,185.78 per month for the Verizon DEOT service prepetition and it immediately began billing the same amount to the newly created Chapter 11 estate. However, AT&T's invoices did not include this monthly charge after May 2006. Lucre contends that the billing stopped because Lucre had legitimately terminated the service at that time. AT&T, though, points out that Lucre continued to use the Verizon DEOT for years thereafter and, as a consequence, AT&T contends that it is entitled to continued monthly reimbursement. Indeed, AT&T insists that at some point in time the regulated rate it could charge increased to $17,947.80 per month. [AT&T filed an administrative expense request for approximately $1.1 million. Lucre objected to the request, claiming: (i) that its obligation to AT&T is a prepetition claim, not an administrative expense; and (ii) the amount sought was grossly excessive because Lucre received little or no benefit from its postpetition use of the Verizon DEOT.] * * *

DISCUSSION

Licenses, Leases, and Executory Contracts.

This court begins by examining the contractual relationship that gives rise to AT&T's administrative claim. Lucre, in a sense, is like the medieval German merchant who had to transport his goods down the Rhine in order to get them to market. AT&T, in turn, is the baron whose castle stood in between. The merchant would have presumably solved his predicament by paying a toll each time he required safe passage and indeed Lucre has solved its own predicament in a similar fashion, albeit the arrangement here was for unlimited usage over some period of time. But either way, the accommodations reached by the merchant and Lucre both resulted in a license being granted, for a license is nothing more than the permission by competent authority to do an act which, without such permission, would be illegal, a trespass, a tort, or otherwise not allowable.

The court further observes that a license is conceptually the same as a lease. Lucre wanted to connect calls from Verizon but Lucre, at least in 2001, did not believe that it could do so without routing those calls through AT&T's "property" – that is, through its system. Therefore, Lucre needed AT&T's permission to use its system and, in fact, AT&T not only gave that permission but actually added to that system by providing the dedicated line needed to route the Verizon calls directly to Lucre. Granted, AT&T and Lucre do not agree as to the fee Lucre was to pay for AT&T's permission or the duration of the permission given. However, there is no disagreement that AT&T could again deny Lucre access to its system if Lucre materially breached its agreement to pay just as a landlord would be entitled to repossess the demised premises if the tenant failed to pay the rent he had agreed upon as it came due. Indeed, it would seem that the only thing that distinguishes a lease from a license, at least when land is involved, is possession. That is, a lease involves the landlord's actual relinquishment of the property's possession to the tenant whereas the licensor is able to retain possession, albeit the possession retained is then limited by whatever rights the licensee is also entitled to enjoy under the terms of the license.

The court makes this comparison between a license and a lease because of its decision in *In re Sturgis Iron & Metal Co.*, 420 B.R. 716 (Bankr. W.D. Mich. 2009). That case involved the commercial lease of a large piece of equipment to the debtor and the subsequent rejection of that lease by the Chapter 11 estate. The question in *Sturgis* was whether the lessor was entitled to the actual rent due on the lease during the two postpetition months that preceded rejection or whether the lessor was entitled to only some reasonable amount for that interval based upon the benefit realized by the estate, which, at least according to the debtor, was almost none at all.

This court concluded that the lessor in *Sturgis* was entitled to the actual rent. It employed the following logic:

- The commencement of a bankruptcy case creates an estate comprised of all of the debtor's interests in property, including whatever the debtor might hold as a tenant under a lease.
- However, none of the interests acquired by the estate can be any greater than what the debtor had previously held unless the Bankruptcy Code itself creates a greater right.
- Therefore, the estate must pay the actual rent due for its continued possession of the leased property since the Bankruptcy Code includes no provision that permits the estate to alter what is in effect the *sine qua non* of the estate's continued right to possession under a lease – the payment of an agreed upon rent.

But if, as this court has now concluded, a license functions much like a lease, the reasoning in *Sturgis* should apply equally in the instant case. That is, the Chapter 11 estate created when Lucre filed its bankruptcy petition unquestionably acquired Lucre's prepetition rights under the Verizon DEOT contract to have continued access to the dedicated line that routed Verizon customers to Lucre. However, the estate's enjoyment of that access also depended unequivocally upon Lucre continuing to pay the same fee that Lucre had agreed upon prepetition to gain that access and that fee, according to AT&T, was $3,185.75 per month for the original five years and $17,974.80 per month thereafter until the license was either terminated or rejected.

However, the analogy to leases that *Sturgis* provides is not perfect, for this court, in deciding *Sturgis*, made a point of distinguishing between unexpired leases and executory contracts, and licenses, it seems, can also have attributes of an executory contract. Take again, as an example, the German merchant. If all that is involved is the exchange of a toll for passage, then the arrangement resembles a lease. But, if the baron also promised to service the barge and feed the crew as part of an overall package, then the arrangement would more resemble an executory contract. Indeed, in the instant case, the court would not be surprised if the Verizon DEOT contract also included a promise by AT&T to maintain the hardware and software used in order to ensure static free and uninterrupted connections. Therefore, the inevitable question arises as to whether the addition of such executory elements to a license makes a difference in determining what should be awarded the licensor as an administrative expense if the estate ultimately elects to reject the license.

This court submits that there is no distinction. The issue in each instance is simply whether an administrative claim should be allowed or not and the resolution of that issue is dictated by Section 503(b)(1), not Section 365. As for Section 503(b)(1), it focuses only upon whether the cost or expense, however incurred, was (1) actual and (2) necessary for preserving the estate.

In other words, it should be irrelevant whether AT&T had made executory promises to Lucre under the Verizon DEOT contract as well. Granted, these additional executory promises, if made and then breached, would have justified Lucre's withholding payment of the agreed upon licensing fee and likely would have warranted a setoff for damages incurred. But those additional promises would not alter the underlying fact that (1) AT&T had nonetheless given Lucre a license to use a dedicated line in its system for an agreed upon fee, and (2) utilization of that line (*i.e.*, the Verizon DEOT) was necessary for Lucre to route Verizon customer traffic until the alternate line agreed upon in the settlement could be installed. Therefore, the analysis under Section 503(b)(1) should remain the same – that is, the Chapter 11 estate created when Lucre filed its petition could no more enjoy the continued use of AT&T's system under the license previously granted than could Lucre have enjoyed the continued possession of demised premises under a lease previously given without, in each case, the estate also paying as an administrative expense the agreed upon fee or rent in return.

Lucre certainly argues that it should pay AT&T something much less than what was agreed as its administrative expense because it never benefited from the license granted. As Lucre puts it, * * * "[the Verizon DEOT has] been nothing but trouble for Lucre from the beginning." That may be. But Lucre's clear desire throughout the Chapter 11 administrative period was to maintain Verizon as a revenue source. Moreover, there is no question that the Verizon traffic had to be routed through some third party system before Lucre could earn that revenue. Therefore, this court is hard-pressed to understand how AT&T's license to Lucre to use its system, as troublesome as it might have been, was not a necessary expense of preserving the estate unless and until Lucre was able to find an alternative route for its Verizon customer traffic through another system.

In fact, whether the Verizon DEOT was even used postpetition is of no consequence, for it is enough that the license that Lucre had been given prepetition provided the ensuing bankruptcy estate an interest in AT&T's system that it would have otherwise not had. Rights arising under a license, though, cannot exist without the licensee also paying the promised fee. Fees associated with the license, then, by their very nature are an expense associated with the license's preservation. Granted, the estate's accumulation of fees on account of an unwanted license can prove expensive; however, the same can be said about utilities and other carrying costs that accumulate whenever the estate remains in possession of a marginal building. If such costs are burdensome, the appropriate relief is to reject the license or to abandon the building. However, until that rejection or abandonment occurs, the plain language of Section 503(b)(1)(A) recognizes these accruals as necessary expenses entitled to priority without adjustment of any kind.

Administrative Claims and Postpetition Inducement – Mammoth Mart, Jartran, and White Motor.

Although Section 503(b)(1) as in fact written seems to allow as AT&T's administrative expense the actual fee associated with the Verizon DEOT license, Lucre relies upon case law interpreting Section 503(b)(1) to assert that AT&T must meet other tests as well. [Lucre argues that three cases (*Mammoth Mart, Jartran,* and *White Motor* require a postpetition inducement by the estate for the creditor to provide the property or services in order for the expense to qualify for administrative expense priority.] In particular, Lucre cites *In re White Motor Corp.*, 831 F.2d 106 (6th Cir. 1987). *White Motor* involved a contract between Employee Transfer Corporation ("ETC") and the debtor. The contract required ETC to provide relocation services for the debtor's employees. These services included managing and maintaining homes purchased by ETC from debtor's relocated employees until ETC resold the homes to third parties. As of debtor's petition date, ETC owned eleven homes which had not yet been sold. ETC continued to manage these homes postpetition by making mortgage payments, paying taxes and insurance premiums, and generally maintaining the property. At issue in *White Motor* was whether ETC could recover those amounts as an administrative expense.

The Sixth Circuit denied the request. It said:

> The test for whether a claim qualifies for payment as an administrative expense is set forth in *In re Mammoth Mart, Inc.*, 536 F.2d 950 (1st Cir. 1976). In *Mammoth Mart* the court stated that a claimant must prove that the debt (1) arose from a transaction with the debtor-in-possession as opposed to the proceeding entity (or, alternatively, that the claimant gave consideration to the debtor-in-possession); and (2) directly and substantially benefitted the estate.

White Motor, 831 F.2d at 110. The court also offered this further explanation concerning the first prong of this test:

> A creditor provides consideration to the bankrupt estate only when the debtor-in-possession induces the creditor's performance and performance is then rendered to the estate. If the inducement came from a pre-petition debtor, then consideration was given to that entity rather than to the debtor-in-possession. *In re Jartran, Inc.*, 732 F.2d 584 (7th Cir. 1984). However, if the inducement came from the debtor-in-possession, then the claims of the creditor are given priority.

Id.

What Lucre contends is that it never induced AT&T to continue providing postpetition access to its system for the Verizon traffic. * * *

"Inducement," though, is not as important in this instance as Lucre would make it. Granted, *White Motor*, as well as many other courts, have cited the Bankruptcy Act case of *In re Mammoth Mart, Inc.* as establishing a general test for allowing requests for administrative expenses. *See, e.g., In re Jartran, Inc.*, 732 F.2d 584, 586–87 (7th Cir. 1984). However, *Mammoth Mart* actually addressed only a very narrow issue – whether employees whose jobs were terminated shortly after the commencement of the debtor's case could recover as an administrative expense all of the severance pay to which they were contractually entitled even though that pay was attributable to service provided prepetition. * * *

In re Jartran, Inc., which is the other case relied upon in *White Motor*, involved the same narrow issue. In that instance, the debtor had an arrangement with some agencies to place Yellow Page advertising on its behalf. Ads had been ordered prepetition and the opportunity to cancel had by that time already passed with respect to many of those orders. Nonetheless, the agencies maintained that they should be paid as administrative claimants for the fees associated with this advertising because the debtor's obligation to reimburse them did not in fact arise until after the case had commenced. *Jartran*, not surprisingly, rejected this argument.

> In the case before us, no inducement by the debtor-in-possession was required because the liability for the costs of the ads was irrevocably incurred before the petition was filed.
>
> * * *
>
> It is clear, . . . that appellants' claim here arises out of commitments made before the debtor-in-possession came into existence.

Id. at 588.

And, in fact, *White Motor* also follows suit, for the focus in that instance was only upon the eleven properties that ETC had already purchased and had been maintaining under ad hoc contracts entered into between ETC and the debtor prepetition. The Sixth Circuit certainly recognized that ETC had continued postpetition to incur expenses associated with these properties' maintenance and that the estate had benefited from the services ETC had rendered. Nonetheless, the Sixth Circuit concluded that the ongoing expenses were associated with commitments that ETC had already made beforehand with the debtor concerning these eleven properties and, as such, administrative priority was not warranted.

> Although we feel that the services provided post-petition were beneficial to WMC as debtor-in-possession, *we find that ETC's claims arise from commitments made before the debtor-in-possession came into existence.*

White Motor, 831 F.2d at 110 (emphasis added). * * *

The concern, then, in *Mammoth Mart*, *Jartran*, and *White Motor* was a limited one that arose only because the claim in question seemed to straddle the petition date. As such, the issue in each instance was whether the particular claim should be treated as having arisen pre- or postpetition. In turn, each court's response was based upon its recognition that the whole purpose of permitting administrative priority to a claimant was to induce otherwise reluctant entities to continue providing whatever the bankruptcy estate needed for its preservation, maintenance, and rehabilitation.

* * *

Mammoth Mart then went on to explain how a court was to address claims arising from a contract that had been entered prepetition.

> For a claim in its entirety to be entitled to first priority under § 64(a)(1) [now § 503(b)(1)(A)], the debt must arise from a transaction with the debtor-in-possession. When the claim is based upon a contract between the debtor and the claimant, the case law teaches that a creditor's right to payment will be afforded first priority only to the extent that the consideration supporting the claimant's right to payment was both supplied to and beneficial to the debtor-in-possession in the operation of the business.

Id.

Finally, *Mammoth Mart* offered examples of when such "straddling" contract claims are to be treated as postpetition administrative expenses and when they are to be left to fend with the rest of the creditors holding prepetition claims.

> When third parties are induced to supply goods or services to the debtor-in-possession pursuant to a contract that has not been rejected, the purposes of § 64(a)(1) plainly require that their claims be afforded priority. It is equally clear that a claimant who fully performs under a contract prior to the filing of the petition will not be entitled to first priority even though his services may have resulted in a direct benefit to the bankrupt estate after the filing.

Id.

However, what cannot be lost in *Mammoth Mart* and its effort to address such straddling claims is that court's unequivocal affirmation of the Supreme Court's much more general ruling in *Reading Co. v. Brown*, 391 U.S. 471 (1968), concerning the allowance of administrative expenses. This is what *Mammoth Mart* said:

> Since the debtor-in-possession is a separate legal entity that is carrying on the business principally for the benefit of the pre-filing creditors, *the Court has reasoned that fairness requires that any claims incident to the debtor-in-possession's operation of the business be paid before those of creditors for whose benefit the continued operation of the business was allowed.* ***

536 F.2d at 954 (emphasis added).

* * *

In sum, then, the inducement language used in *White Motor* and *Jartran* must be read in the broader context of Section 503(b)(1) and its effort to include within its scope all "actual and necessary costs . . . ordinarily incident to operation of a business." *Reading*, 391 U.S. at 483. Inducement, as *White Motor, Jartran*, and *Mammoth Mart* all illustrate, is important only when a court is called upon to determine whether a claim arising from a prepetition contract with the debtor is (1) in fact deserving of administrative priority because its incursion was actually incidental to the estate's continued operation or (2) simply residue of a prepetition transaction that is no more deserving of priority than any other prepetition claim.

The Sixth Circuit has said in *In re Sunarhauserman*, 126 F.3d 811, 817 (6th Cir. 1997): "*Reading* does not eliminate the requirement that a debt arise post-petition in order to be accorded administrative expense priority." But the converse is equally true – that if it is clear that a debt did arise postpetition, then *Reading* requires that it be treated as an administrative expense so long as the expense is "ordinarily incident" to the operation of the postpetition business. Indeed, *Jartran* well illustrates this point.

Again, the agencies in *Jartran* were denied administrative priority for the advertising that had been irrevocably placed by them on the debtor's behalf prepetition. It made no difference that the debtor's contract with them did not permit billing for that advertising until after the case had begun. What has been overlooked, though, is that these same agencies, under the same prepetition contract, had also placed advertising on behalf of the debtor before the bankruptcy's commencement that the debtor, now as debtor-in-possession, could still revoke postpetition. As for costs associated with this advertising, both the court and the debtor agreed that these bills should be paid as administrative expenses even though the estate was no more involved in the inducement of this advertising than it was involved in the inducement of the advertising for which no priority had been awarded. The distinguishing factor, according to the court, was simply whether the debtor-in-possession could later change its mind. In other words, so long as the estate had had that option but had not exercised it, the court in *Jartran* was not going to deny the agencies' administrative priority for something that otherwise fell clearly within the parameters that *Reading* had previously set.

AT&T is not an eleemosynary society nor is the estate created when Lucre filed for Chapter 11 relief a charity case. Rather, what is before this court is a matter of commerce and the question posed by these two businesses is simply this: Should the estate, as opposed to the prepetition debtor, be treated as AT&T's customer for what all agree was Lucre's unimpaired ability to continue having the desirable Verizon telephone traffic routed through AT&T's system for some three-and-one-half years after Lucre had become the estate's debtor-in-possession? For Lucre, then, to insist that its utilization of AT&T's system for this extended period falls outside of what *Reading* would regard as "ordinarily incident" to the estate's success is disingenuous. The Verizon DEOT that AT&T provided may have been both expensive and bothersome. However, until Lucre actually replaced it with some alternative system, AT&T was how Lucre, as debtor-in-possession, accomplished the estate's business objectives. As such, AT&T has a basis for asserting the administrative claim that it makes.

* * *

Administrative Claims and Benefit to the Estate – Mammoth Mart, American Anthracite, and United Cigar.

Lucre's remaining argument against the allowance of AT&T's claim as filed is that it exceeds the actual benefit Lucre realized from its use of the Verizon DEOT and, as such, its claim should be reduced accordingly. In fact, if the court accepts Lucre's contention that what AT&T did provide postpetition was more trouble then it was worth, then this argument becomes just a variant of what Lucre has already argued concerning inducement – that AT&T should receive nothing as an administrative expense with respect to the Verizon DEOT.

In taking this position, Lucre again points to the test *White Motor* adopted for evaluating administrative claims. However, this time Lucre focuses on the second prong of that test, which is that the claimant must also "prove that the debt . . . directly and substantially benefitted the estate." *White Motor*, 831 F.2d at 110. Lucre, though, fails to appreciate how the courts were referring to benefit as they made their decisions in these cases. For example, it arose in *Mammoth Mart* in this fashion:

> For a claim in its entirety to be entitled to first priority under § 64(a)(1), the debt must arise from a transaction with the debtor-in-possession. When the claim is based upon a contract between the debtor and the claimant, the case law teaches that a creditor's right to payment will be afforded first priority only to the extent that the consideration supporting the claimant's right to payment was both supplied to and beneficial to the debtor-in-possession in the operation of the business.

536 F.2d at 954. * * *

Of course, when properly read in context, what these courts said is nothing more than common sense. After all, the very purpose of administrative priority is to encourage third parties to provide goods and services needed by the estate for its preservation and, hopefully, rehabilitation. However, that purpose is complicated whenever the administrative claim arises in connection with a contract already made between the debtor and the claimant. Again, as *Mammoth Mart* itself explained:

> When third parties are induced to supply goods or services to the debtor-in-possession pursuant to a contract that has not been rejected, the purposes of § 64(a)(1) plainly require that their claims be afforded priority. It is equally clear that a claimant who fully performs under a contract prior to the filing of the petition will not be entitled to first priority even though his services may have resulted in a direct benefit to the bankrupt estate after the filing. Similarly, even when there has technically been performance by the contract creditor during the reorganization period, he will not be entitled to § 64(a)(1) priority if the bankrupt estate was not benefitted in fact therefrom.

536 F.2d at 954.

In sum, then, *Mammoth Mart*, *Jartran*, and *White Motor* state what should be self-evident – that whenever a pre-existing contract is involved, it is not enough that the estate benefited from whatever the other party had provided under its terms. The estate must also have been involved in some way regarding the provision of the same. Likewise, the converse should be equally apparent – that the estate must in all cases have benefited in some way from whatever activity it induced, although, as *Reading* teaches, "benefit" must be read broadly enough to include torts and other claims of a similar nature.

Unfortunately, subsequent courts have gone beyond what *Mammoth Mart*, *Jartran*, and *White Motor* actually held to impose a much stricter limitation upon what is to be allowed administrative priority whenever the claim in question arises from a prepetition lease or contract that the estate later rejects. What these subsequent courts have held is that priority is to be given only to the extent the estate in fact benefited from the rejected lease or contract. "Benefit," though, does not appear in Section 503(b)(1). Nor is it easy to add a beneficial component to Section 503(b)(1)'s "actual" and "necessary" language and still reconcile *Reading*'s inclusion within the scope of that section, a decidedly non-beneficial claim like the tort involved there.

* * * For these reasons, then, this court is not persuaded * * * that administrative claims are to be allowed "only to the extent the estate was benefited."

Problem 12-4

Office Station provides and delivers office supplies to large businesses in several major metropolitan areas. One of its regular customers is Daylight Software, which places orders every other week. On March 15, Daylight faxed a purchase order for some $8,000 in office supplies to Office Station. On March 17, Daylight filed for Chapter 7 bankruptcy protection and the following day the court authorized the trustee to operate Daylight's business. On March 20, Office Station delivered the supplies and the trustee accepted them. Is Office Station's bill entitled to administrative expense treatment? *See* § 503(b). If not, what could Office Station do to protect itself better? *See* § 546.

Problem 12-5

Down & Out Corp., which has a fiscal and taxable year beginning on July 1, filed a bankruptcy reorganization petition on April 10, 2013. Since that time, Down & Out has operated and continues to operate its business as debtor-in-possession. What priority are Down & Out's federal income tax obligations for the taxable years ending on June 30, 2013 and June 30, 2014? *See* 26 U.S.C. § 1398(d)(2)(D).

(b) Employment of Professionals in Chapter 11

In previous chapters, most notably chapter nine, we discussed the employment of professionals in a bankruptcy case, including the treatment of the fees of such professionals as administrative expenses. While creditors often complain about the cost of the Chapter 11 process, and in particular about the amount of professional fees, there is little empirical data that demonstrates those costs are excessive.[32] Moreover, there are several protections in the system to prevent excessive fees. First, the bankruptcy court must approve the attorney that the debtor in possession wishes to hire and that attorney must be disinterested. § 327. Second, that attorney must disclose all compensation received from the debtor in the year prior to the petition date. § 329. Finally, to be paid from the estate, the attorney must submit fee applications and those applications must be approved by the court. §§ 330, 328. Section 330 sets forth the criteria that the bankruptcy court takes into account in determining the amount of the reasonable compensation for the attorney for the debtor in possession. These provisions also apply to other professional persons employed by the debtor in possession, including accountants, appraisers, and consultants. Review the discussion in chapter nine on compensation for employed professionals.

3. *Creditors' Involvement in the Chapter 11 Case*

(a) Individual Creditors

Creditors in Chapter 11 cases may need to file a proof of claim. § 501. Bankruptcy Rule 3003 provides that if the creditor's claim is not included in the debtor's schedules or is scheduled as "disputed, contingent, or unliquidated," the creditor must file a proof of claim to be dealt with in the plan. Thus, it is important for a creditor in a Chapter 11 case to consult the schedules to determine how its claim is treated. Even if the creditor agrees with the designation of the claim on the schedules, the creditor may still file a proof of claim. The debtor in possession will examine the proofs of claim and object to those it thinks should be disallowed. *See* § 502; Rule 3007.

---

[32] *See, e.g.*, Stephen J. Lubben, *What We "Know" About Chapter 11 Cost Is Wrong*, 17 FORDHAM J. CORP. & FIN. L. 141 (2012); Nancy B. Rapoport, *Rethinking Professional Fees in Chapter 11 Cases*, 5 J. BUS. & TECH. L. 263 (2010); Stephen P. Ferris & Robert M. Lawless, *The Expenses of Financial Distress: The Direct Costs of Chapter 11*, 61 U. PITT. L. REV. 629 (2000).

Aside from filing a proof of claim, an unsecured creditor may have little involvement in the proceeding. If the creditor's claim is small or the distribution on the claim is likely to be minimal, it may not be worth the creditor's time to be involved. Unsecured creditors with substantial claims, however, may deem it prudent to review carefully and potentially object to any of a variety of actions that might reduce their recovery. The actions they are likely to be particularly concerned with include: the terms of any proposed DIP financing; the terms of a proposed sale of assets outside the ordinary course of business (*i.e.*, whether the estate is to get full or fair value); the decision to assume or reject executory contracts and unexpired leases; and requests to pay administrative expenses, in particular the salaries of the debtor's executives and the fees of the debtor's counsel. In addition, creditors with large unsecured claims may actively participate in negotiating the plan of reorganization.

Secured creditors are more likely to be actively involved in the case. While unsecured claimants are typically concerned with the estate as a whole, secured claimants are concerned with protecting their interest in the collateral. Anything that might jeopardize that interest is a cause for concern. Thus, they carefully consider and may object to efforts by the debtor to sell or lease their collateral, whether inside or outside of the ordinary course of business. They take great interest in the terms of any DIP financing and, in particular, whether that financing might impair their priority. And, of course, they defend lien avoidance actions.

In addition to all of this, secured claimants often demand adequate protection of their liens or seek relief from the automatic stay under § 362(d). Review the material in chapter seven on relief from the stay. This is a particularly fertile area for litigation in Chapter 11 because it often takes many months before a plan is confirmed (if indeed one ever is confirmed). During that time, the collateral may be depreciating in value. In addition, while oversecured creditors are entitled to postpetition interest on their claims (up to the value of their interest in the collateral), § 506(b), undersecured creditors do not accrue interest on either the secured or unsecured portion of their claims. Accordingly, undersecured creditors often evaluate whether the debtor will be able to confirm a feasible reorganization plan within a reasonable time. If it appears that the debtor will not be able to do so, the creditor is likely to move for relief from the stay under § 362(d)(2), which as you may recall has two elements: that the debtor lacks equity in property and the property is not necessary to an effective reorganization. The creditor has the burden of proof to show the debtor's lack of equity in the property, but the debtor has the burden to show the property is necessary for an effective reorganization. § 362(g). The debtor's burden can be difficult to satisfy. As the Supreme Court stated:

> What this requires is not merely a showing that if there is conceivably to be an effective reorganization, this property will be needed for it; but that the property is essential for an effective reorganization *that is in prospect.* This means, as many lower courts, including the en banc court in this case, have properly said, that there must be "a reasonable possibility of a successful reorganization within a reasonable time" (citation omitted). The cases are numerous in which § 362(d)(2) relief has been provided within less than a year from the filing of the bankruptcy petition. And while the bankruptcy courts demand less detailed showings during the four months in which the debtor is given the exclusive right to put together a plan, *see* § 1121(b), (c)(2), even within that period lack of any realistic prospect of effective reorganization will require § 362(d)(2) relief.[33]

Obviously, as part of any motion for relief from the automatic stay under § 362(d) or for adequate protection under § 363(e), a creditor will have to prove the validity of its secured claim. If the debtor in possession has a possible ground for avoiding the creditor's lien or for recovering a preferential payment to that creditor, the creditor may hesitate to make such motions. In fact, such a creditor may seek to provide the DIP financing and, as part of the financing package, have the debtor in possession (and successors in interest, such as a trustee) waive all such claims as against that creditor.

The bottom line of such interaction is that not only must creditors in a Chapter 11 proceeding scrutinize the activities of the debtor in possession, they must also be vigilant regarding the actions of other creditors, who may be seeking to improve their relative position through their dealings with the debtor in possession.

(b) The Creditors' Committee

Another way in which unsecured creditors monitor what is happening in the debtor's Chapter 11 case is through the unsecured creditors' committee. The U.S. Trustee appoints an unsecured creditors' committee that consists of the creditors willing to serve who have the seven largest claims of similar types. § 1102(a), (b). Additional committees of creditors may be appointed to represent other types of claimants.

---

[33] *United Sav. Ass'n of Texas v. Timbers of Inwood Forest Assocs., Ltd.*, 484 U.S. 365, 375–76 (1988).

§ 1102(a). The purpose of the committee is to provide information to other creditors with similar types of claims, to provide comments to the debtor from those creditors, to investigate the debtor's financial condition, to consult with the debtor in possession regarding the case administration, and to participate in the formulation of a confirmable plan. §§ 1102(b)(3), 1103(c). In large cases involving thousands of creditors, where it is often impractical to send notice of every minor matter to every creditor, the court may order that some notices be sent only to the unsecured creditors' committee. Rule 2002(i). The committee may employ attorneys and other professionals to perform services for the committee. § 1103(a). The committee often uses these professionals to participate in actions that can significantly affect the estate, such as major preference litigation and objections to sizeable claims.[34] The professionals employed by the committee generally receive compensation from the estate pursuant to §§ 328 and 330, and their right to receive such compensation qualifies for administrative expense priority. § 503(b)(2). As with other professional persons paid from estate assets, the bankruptcy court must scrutinize their fee requests for reasonableness.[35]

(c) Appointment of a Trustee or Examiner

If creditors are dissatisfied with how the debtor in possession is managing the business or administering the estate, they have two additional tools at their disposal. First, they may seek to replace the debtor in possession with a trustee, who will administer the estate. Second, they may request appointment of an examiner to investigate the debtor's conduct. Read §§ 1104, 1106. Both of these are regarded as rather extreme measures. After all, the debtor in possession's existing management team often has an ownership interest in the debtor and hence a financial incentive to successfully reorganize. In addition, the existing management team usually has substantial familiarity with the debtor's business; it often has expertise in the production

---

[34] Recall from chapter four that claims owed to the debtor's interest holders are sometimes recharacterized as equity. *See supra* page 196.

[35] For a discussion of some of the issues that may arise in utilizing creditors' committees, see Michelle M. Harner, *An Empirical Analysis of the Role of Creditors' Committees in Business Reorganizations*, 64 VAND. L. REV. 749 (2011); Kurt F. Gwynne, *Intra-committee Conflicts, Multiple Creditors' Committees, Altering Committee Membership and Other Alternatives for Ensuring Adequate Representation under Section 1102 of the Bankruptcy Code*, 14 AM. BANKR. INST. L. REV. 109 (2006); Daniel J. Bussel, *Creditors' Committees as Estate Representatives in Bankruptcy Litigation*, 10 STAN. J.L. BUS. & FIN. 28 (2004).

of the debtor's products, a relationship with the debtor's suppliers and customers, and awareness of the strengths and limitations of the debtor's personnel. Shunting this experience aside in favor of a court-appointed guardian of the estate will often cause a major disruption of the business while that guardian tries to learn the ropes.

On the other hand, the existing management team may be the source of many of the debtor's financial problems. It may be incompetent. It may be receiving compensation far beyond the worth of the services it is providing. It may even be looting the estate. If the creditors can prove this, if they can prove that the debtor in possession is not moving toward proposing a plan of reorganization, is not dealing fairly with one or more creditors or classes of creditors, or is engaged in fraud or excessive mismanagement, the court may appoint a trustee or examiner.[36] Even acrimony between the debtor in possession and its creditors may be sufficient cause to appoint a trustee or examiner.[37] However, there is a presumption against granting such relief and the creditors will have to prove such an appointment is warranted by clear and convincing evidence.[38]

(d) Dismissal or Conversion of the Chapter 11 Case

A creditor, a creditors' committee, or the U.S. Trustee may also move to dismiss the Chapter 11 case or, provided the debtor is eligible to be in Chapter 7, to convert the case to a liquidation proceeding.[39] Read § 1112. In addition to the reasons listed in that section for dismissal or conversion of the Chapter 11 case, some courts grant such motions if the court finds the case has not been filed in good faith.[40] The usual reason for obtaining such a dismissal or conversion is the inability to formulate a confirmable plan of reorganization.[41]

---

[36] *See, e.g.*, Jonathan C. Lipson, *Understanding Failure: Examiners and the Bankruptcy Reorganization of Large Public Companies*, 84 AM. BANKR. L.J. 1 (2010); Clifford J. White, III & Walter W. Theus, Jr., *Chapter 11 Trustees and Examiners After BAPCPA*, 80 AM. BANKR. L.J. 289 (2006).

[37] *See In re Marvel Entm't Corp.*, 140 F.3d 463 (3d Cir. 1998).

[38] *See In re G-I Holdings, Inc.*, 385 F.3d 313 (3d Cir. 2004).

[39] The debtor may also seek to convert the case to Chapter 7 pursuant to § 1112(a).

[40] *See, e.g.*, *In re Integrated Telecom Express, Inc.*, 384 F.3d 108 (3d Cir. 2004).

[41] *See, e.g.*, *In re Wiersma*, 227 F. App'x 603 (9th Cir. 2007); *In re Hedquist*, 450 F.3d 801 (8th Cir.

In the event the case is converted to a Chapter 7 case, administrative expenses incurred in the Chapter 11 case are subordinated to the administrative expenses incurred in the Chapter 7 case. § 726(b).

QUESTION

How does the ever-present possibility that the case may be converted to Chapter 7, coupled with that subordination of preconversion administrative expenses to postconversion administrative expenses pursuant to § 726(b), affect the terms of DIP financing?

4. *Role of the U.S. Trustee*

The U.S. Trustee's office monitors all Chapter 11 cases. 28 U.S.C. § 586. It is particularly concerned with preventing fraud and abuse, reviewing professional fees for reasonableness, appointing and monitoring creditors' committees, ensuring that the estate is administered promptly and efficiently, and reviewing disclosure statements and financial reports.[42] In a Chapter 11 case, the debtor in possession must provide periodic financial reports to the court and the U.S. Trustee. *See* §§ 1107, 1106(a)(1); Rule 2015. These periodic reports of the financial activities of the debtor in possession provide valuable information regarding the estate's income and disbursements during the case.[43] Failure to file the required reports may result in dismissal or conversion of the Chapter 11 case pursuant to § 1112.

Problem 12-6

Revisit the facts of Problems 12-1 and 12-3. Dash has been in bankruptcy for six months and has not yet proposed a plan of reorganization. During that time, Dash has generated approximately $60,000 in income each month. Monthly operating expenses have averaged $58,000. Its inventory and accounts (all of which were acquired postpetition) are now worth only about

---

2006).

[42] See the U.S. Trustee's website at http://www.usdoj.gov/ust/eo/ust_org/about_ustp.htm.

[43] For an example of the monthly reporting forms, see http://www.usdoj.gov/ust/r18/k_mor1.pdf.

$60,000, in part because Dash has been much more successful in collecting its accounts. Intercontinental Bank estimates that the current value of Dash's equipment is about $150,000 due to depreciation. Intercontinental had provided a postpetition line of credit up to $75,000 secured by all assets of Dash, and Dash has drawn $70,000 on that line of credit. Dash has spent quite a bit on marketing pitches in an effort to get new business, but has been largely unsuccessful. Almost $35,000 in cash has been paid to Dash's lawyers pursuant to court approval. Hybrid is still Dash's major customer and Hybrid just filed a Chapter 11 bankruptcy petition. You represent Intercontinental. What actions do you recommend that Intercontinental take now?

C. CONFIRMING A CHAPTER 11 PLAN

1. *Overview of Confirmation Process*

While the debtor in possession is operating the business, it is also negotiating with creditors for purposes of proposing a plan of reorganization. The debtor in possession prepares two basic documents, a disclosure statement and a reorganization plan. The disclosure statement is designed to give information to all creditors regarding the financial condition of the debtor and its plans for the future operation of its business. The reorganization plan details how existing claims against the estate will be paid. After circulating the disclosure statement and reorganization plan, the creditors and equity holders entitled to vote on the plan will cast their ballots. After that, the bankruptcy court will hold a confirmation hearing. If all classes of creditors and equity holders have accepted the plan, and the plan complies with the statutory requirements, *see* § 1129(a), the court will confirm the reorganization plan. If any class of creditors or equity holders entitled to vote on the plan does not accept the plan, then the debtor may ask the court to confirm the plan anyway in a process known as a "cramdown." A reorganization plan confirmed through a cramdown must meet additional statutory requirements, *see* § 1129(b). A confirmed reorganization plan then governs the relationship between the debtor and the creditors as to all claims that arose before confirmation. § 1141. In other words, the debtor remains obligated on prepetition claims (and debts incurred during the bankruptcy case) only to the extent so provided in the plan.

As discussed more fully below, other parties in interest may seek to file their own plans of reorganization. Those other parties in interest, particularly creditors, often seek to file a liquidating plan of reorganization as they generally have less information and expertise in running the debtor's business. The U.S. Trustee is not authorized to file a plan of reorganization. § 307.

In the process of formulating a plan, the debtor in possession will negotiate for positive votes on the plan. As we study the requirements for plan confirmation and the process of plan confirmation, consider how the debtor's need to get positive votes may influence how certain types of creditors are treated. Also consider which types of creditors are likely to have the most negotiating leverage and are thus likely to be able to obtain (extort?) the best treatment in the reorganization plan.

2. *Exclusive Period for Filing a Plan*

To facilitate an orderly reorganization process and give the debtor a reasonable chance to solve its financial problems, § 1121(b) gives the debtor in possession the exclusive right to file a plan for the first 120 days after the order for relief. Other parties in interest (such as creditors) may not file a plan until after this period expires.[44] The court may extend or reduce the 120-day period for cause, but may not extend it beyond 18 months after the date of the order for relief. § 1121(d). The debtor's exclusivity period also will end even if the debtor has filed a plan if that plan has not been accepted by the creditors within 180 days after the order for relief. § 1121(c)(3). Extending the exclusivity period can affect the negotiations between the debtor in possession and the creditors over the plan's contents because it potentially delays a payout to claimants. Given that, what should a bankruptcy court consider when deciding whether to extend or reduce these time periods? One court has identified nine factors:

(1) the large size of the debtor and the consequent difficulty in formulating a plan of reorganization for a huge debtor with a complex financial structure;
(2) the need of the creditors' committee to negotiate with the debtor and the ability to prepare adequate information;
(3) the existence of good faith progress towards reorganization;
(4) the existence of an unresolved contingency;
(5) the fact that the debtor is paying bills as they become due;
(6) the length of previous extensions of exclusivity;

---

[44] This exclusivity ends immediately if a trustee is appointed and once a trustee is appointed, the trustee or any party in interest may file a plan, § 1121(c)(1), which is typically a plan for liquidation of the estate's assets.

(7) breakdowns in plan negotiations, such that the continuation of the debtor's exclusivity period would result in the debtor having an unfair bargaining position over creditors;
(8) the debtor's failure to resolve fundamental reorganization matters essential to its survival; and
(9) the gross mismanagement of the debtor.[45]

3. *Preparing a Disclosure Statement*

Section 1125 details the requirements of the disclosure statement. A disclosure statement must be distributed to all holders of claims or interests before or at the time that solicitations for acceptances of the plan of reorganization are made. The disclosure statement must also be approved by the bankruptcy court prior to such circulation. § 1125(b). The bankruptcy court holds a hearing on whether the disclosure statement satisfies the requirements of the Code and parties in interest are given a chance to object to it. Rule 3017. If the bankruptcy court approves the disclosure statement, the court will establish a timeline for the confirmation process and a deadline by which the votes on the plan must be cast. Rule 3017. A party circulating an approved disclosure statement in good faith is insulated from liability under other law for the content of the disclosure statement, most notably liability under securities laws. § 1125(e).

The key substantive requirement for a disclosure statement is that it provides "adequate information" so that the recipients are able to reach an informed decision on how to vote on the plan. Read § 1125(a). What is "adequate information"? One court has adopted the following list of 19 factors to consider:

1. The circumstances that gave rise to the filing of the bankruptcy petition;
2. A complete description of the available assets and their value;
3. The anticipated future of the debtor;
4. The source of the information provided in the disclosure statement;
5. A disclaimer, which typically indicates that no statements or information concerning the debtor or its assets or securities are authorized, other than those set forth in the disclosure statement;
6. The condition and performance of the debtor while in Chapter 11;
7. Information regarding claims against the estate;

---

45 *In re Hoffinger Indus., Inc.*, 292 B.R. 639, 643-44 (8th Cir. BAP 2003).

8. A liquidation analysis setting forth the estimated return that creditors would receive under Chapter 7;
9. The accounting and valuation methods used to produce the financial information in the disclosure statement;
10. Information regarding the future management of the debtor, including the amount of compensation to be paid to any insiders, directors, and/or officers of the debtor;
11. A summary of the plan of reorganization;
12. An estimate of all administrative expenses, including attorney's fees and accountant's fees;
13. The collectability of any accounts receivable;
14. Any financial information, valuations or *pro forma* projections that would be relevant to creditors' determinations of whether to accept or reject the plan;
15. Information relevant to the risks being taken by the creditors and interest holders;
16. The actual or projected value that can be obtained from avoidable transfers;
17. The existence, likelihood and possible success of non-bankruptcy litigation;
18. The tax consequences of the plan; and
19. The relationship of the debtor with affiliates.[46]

The court then cautioned

> that the list is but a yardstick against which the adequacy of disclosure may be measured; the precise information required will be governed by the facts and circumstances presented in each case. * * *
>
> Generally, a disclosure statement must contain all pertinent information bearing on the success or failure of the proposals in the plan of reorganization. A disclosure statement should likewise contain all material information relating to the risks posed to creditors and equity interest holders under the proposed plan of reorganization. The disclosure statement, on the other hand, should not be burdened with "overly technical and extremely numerous

46 *In re Cardinal Congregate I*, 121 B.R. 760, 765 (Bankr. S.D. Ohio 1990).

additions," where such information would serve only to diminish the understanding of a typical creditor or interest holder.[47]

4. Confirmation Requirements

As noted above, confirmation requires either the consent of all classes or, failing that, compliance with the requirements for cramdown. The court holds a confirmation hearing at which the votes are counted and any objections to the plan are considered. § 1128. If both the consensual and cramdown processes fail, the debtor in possession will not have a confirmed plan of reorganization. Inability to confirm a plan is grounds for dismissal or conversion of the Chapter 11 case. § 1112.

(a) Consensual Confirmation

(i) Claim Classification

A reorganization plan must classify claims and interests to facilitate the voting process prescribed in § 1126. *See* §§ 1129(a)(1), 1123(a)(1). A reorganization plan cannot be confirmed through a consensual process unless all classes of impaired claims or interests accept the plan. § 1129(a)(8). Creditors and equity holders vote on a plan of reorganization individually, but creditors' claims and equity holders' interests are grouped into classes of claims and interests for purposes of determining acceptance of the plan. § 1122.

All of the claims or interests within a class must be "substantially similar" to each other. Thus, claims are not classified with interests. Secured claims are not classified with unsecured claims. Priority claims are not classified with nonpriority claims. Beyond that, whether substantially similar claims must be classified together is a matter of some controversy.[48] Because voting is by class, the debtor may try to classify claims in such a way as to get the class to vote positively on the plan. Claims or interests that are not impaired are deemed to have accepted the plan. § 1126(f). At least one class of impaired claims must accept the plan, without counting votes of any insider, if there is at least one class of impaired claims. § 1129(a)(10).

---

[47] *Id.* at 765–66 (citations omitted).

[48] *See, e.g.*, *In re Vill. at Camp Bowie I, L.P.*, 710 F.3d 239 (5th Cir. 2013).

A claim or interest is impaired unless the creditor's or holder's rights are not altered by the plan, or the plan reinstates the claim or interest to its original terms with compensation for the damages caused by the debtor's default. § 1124. The plan must expressly designate which classes of claims and interests, if any, are not impaired. §§ 1129(a)(1), 1123(a)(2). The plan must also specify the treatment of all impaired class of claims or interests. §§ 1129(a)(1), 1123(a)(3). Unless a class member agrees to less favorable treatment as to its claim or interest, each claim or interest must be treated the same as others within its class. §§ 1129(a)(1), 1123(a)(4).

A class of impaired claims accepts the plan only if, of the class members voting, the positive votes are more than one-half in number and are held by claimants with at least two-thirds in dollar amount of the voted claims. § 1126(c). To illustrate, assume that a class of claims consists of ten claims that total $60,000. If all ten claimants vote, at least six must vote yes, and the amount of claims held by creditors voting yes must be at least $40,000. If only nine claimants vote and the total amount of their nine claims is $55,000, then the number of claimants voting yes must be at least five and the total dollar amount of the claims of the creditors voting yes must be $36,667 (two-thirds of $55,000). If any one claimant in this hypothetical class (ten claimants with $60,000 in total claims) has a claim for more than $20,000, it can control the voting in that class by voting no (regardless of how many other creditors in that class vote yes) because that will prevent two-thirds in amount of the claims in that class from accepting the plan.[49]

A class of impaired interests is deemed to accept if at least two-thirds in amount of interests voting in that class accept the plan. The voting requirement for impaired interests does not include the one-half in number requirement applicable to impaired claims. § 1126(d).

If a vote is not made in good faith, or if the vote is not solicited in good faith, a party may request the court to "designate" the vote. § 1126(e). The effect of such designation is that the vote is not counted in the numerical thresholds for acceptance by the class of claims or interests.

It is not always easy to know when a creditor's vote is made in bad faith. Perhaps the most common situation occurs when a competitor buys up the controlling portion of a class of claims in the hope of forcing the debtor to sell coveted assets or enter into a strategic joint venture. Consider the following decision.

---

[49] In any class consisting of two or more claims, one claimant, cannot dictate the outcome by voting yes. Even if a single claimant had 99% of the amount of the claims in a class, its vote alone does not satisfy the requirement that more than a majority of the claimants in the class vote yes.

IN RE DBSD NORTH AMERICA, INC.
634 F.3d 79 (2d Cir. 2011)

Gerald E. Lynch, Circuit Judge.

These consolidated appeals arise out of the bankruptcy of DBSD North America, Incorporated and its various subsidiaries (together, "DBSD"). The bankruptcy court confirmed a plan of reorganization for DBSD over the objections of the two appellants here, Sprint Nextel Corporation ("Sprint") and DISH Network Corporation ("DISH").

Before us, Sprint argues that the plan improperly gave shares and warrants to DBSD's owner – whose interest lies below Sprint's in priority – in violation of the absolute priority rule of § 1129(b)(2)(B). DISH, meanwhile, argues that the bankruptcy court erred when it found DISH did not vote "in good faith" under § 1126(e) and when, because of the § 1126(e) ruling, it disregarded DISH's class for the purposes of counting votes under § 1129(a)(8). * * *

On Sprint's appeal, we conclude * * * that the plan violated the absolute priority rule.[50] On DISH's appeal we find no error, and conclude (1) that the bankruptcy court did not err in designating DISH's vote, [and] (2) that, after designating DISH's vote, the bankruptcy court properly disregarded DISH's class for voting purposes * * *. We therefore affirm in part, reverse in part, and remand for further proceedings.

BACKGROUND

* * *

ICO Global Communications founded DBSD in 2004 to develop a mobile communications network that would use both satellites and land-based transmission towers. In its first five years, DBSD made progress toward this goal, successfully launching a satellite and obtaining certain spectrum licenses from the FCC, but it also accumulated a large amount of debt. Because its network remained in the developmental stage and had not become operational, DBSD had little if any revenue to offset its mounting obligations.

On May 15, 2009, DBSD (but not its parent ICO Global), filed a voluntary petition in the United States Bankruptcy Court for the Southern District of New York, listing liabilities of $813 million against assets with a book value of $627 million. Of the various claims against DBSD, three have particular relevance here:

---

[50] [This portion of the court's decision is excerpted later in this chapter – eds.].

The First Lien Debt: a $40 million revolving credit facility that DBSD obtained in early 2008 to support its operations, with a first-priority security interest in substantially all of DBSD's assets. It bore an initial interest rate of 12.5%.

The Second Lien Debt: $650 million in 7.5% convertible senior secured notes that DISH issued in August 2005, due August 2009. These notes hold a second-priority security interest in substantially all of DBSD's assets. At the time of filing, the Second Lien Debt had grown to approximately $740 million. It constitutes the bulk of DBSD's indebtedness.

Sprint's Claim: an unliquidated, unsecured claim based on a lawsuit against a DBSD subsidiary. Sprint had sued seeking reimbursement for DBSD's share of certain spectrum relocation expenses under an FCC order. At the time of DBSD's filing, that litigation was pending in the United States District Court for the Eastern District of Virginia and before the FCC. In the bankruptcy case, Sprint filed a claim against each of the DBSD entities jointly and severally, seeking $211 million. The bankruptcy court temporarily allowed Sprint's claim in the amount of $2 million for voting purposes.

After negotiations with various parties, DBSD proposed a plan of reorganization which, as amended, provided for "substantial de-leveraging," a renewed focus on "core operations," and a "continued path as a development-stage enterprise." The plan provided that the holders of the First Lien Debt would receive new obligations with a four-year maturity date and the same 12.5% interest rate, but with interest to be paid in kind ("PIK"), meaning that for the first four years the owners of the new obligations would receive as interest more debt from DBSD rather than cash. The holders of the Second Lien Debt would receive the bulk of the shares of the reorganized entity, which the bankruptcy court estimated would be worth between 51% and 73% of their original claims. The holders of unsecured claims, such as Sprint, would receive shares estimated as worth between 4% and 46% of their original claims. Finally, the existing shareholder (effectively just ICO Global, which owned 99.8% of DBSD) would receive shares and warrants in the reorganized entity.

Sprint objected to the plan, arguing among other things that the plan violates the absolute priority rule of § 1129(b)(2)(B). That rule requires that, if a class of senior claim-holders will not receive the full value of their claims under the plan and the class does not accept the plan, no junior claim- or interest-holder may receive "any property" "under the plan on account of such junior claim or interest." In making its objection, Sprint noted that the plan provided for the existing shareholder, whose interest is junior to Sprint's class of general unsecured claims, to receive substantial quantities of shares and warrants under the plan – in fact, much more than all the unsecured creditors

absolute priority

received together. Sprint argued that "[b]ecause the Plan fails to satisfy" the absolute priority rule, "it cannot be confirmed."

The bankruptcy court disagreed. It characterized the existing shareholder's receipt of shares and warrants as a "gift" from the holders of the Second Lien Debt, who are senior to Sprint in priority yet who were themselves not receiving the full value of their claims, and who may therefore "voluntarily offer a portion of their recovered property to junior stakeholders" without violating the absolute priority rule. It held that it would permit such gifting "at least where, as here, the gift comes from secured creditors, there is no doubt as to their secured creditor status, where there are understandable reasons for the gift, where there are no ulterior, improper ends . . . and where the complaining creditor would get no more if the gift had not been made."

Meanwhile, DISH, although not a creditor of DBSD before its filing, had purchased the claims of various creditors with an eye toward DBSD's spectrum rights. As a provider of satellite television, DISH has launched a number of its own satellites, and it also has a significant investment in TerreStar Corporation, a direct competitor of DSDB's in the developing field of hybrid satellite/terrestrial mobile communications. DISH desired to "reach some sort of transaction with [DBSD] in the future if [DBSD's] spectrum could be useful in our business."

Shortly after DBSD filed its plan disclosure, DISH purchased all of the First Lien Debt at its full face value of $40 million, with an agreement that the sellers would make objections to the plan that DISH could adopt after the sale. As DISH admitted, it bought the First Lien Debt not just to acquire a "market piece of paper" but also to "be in a position to take advantage of [its claim] if things didn't go well in a restructuring."

Internal DISH communications also promoted an "opportunity to obtain a blocking position in the [Second Lien Debt] and control the bankruptcy process for this potentially strategic asset." In the end, DISH (through a subsidiary) purchased only $111 million of the Second Lien Debt – not nearly enough to control that class – with the small size of its stake due in part to DISH's unwillingness to buy any claims whose prior owners had already entered into an agreement to support the plan.

In addition to voting its claims against confirmation, * * * DISH proposed to enter into a strategic transaction with DBSD, and requested permission to propose its own competing plan (a request it later withdrew).

DBSD responded by moving for the court to designate that DISH's "rejection of [the] plan was not in good faith." § 1126(e). The bankruptcy court agreed, finding that DISH, a competitor to DBSD, was voting against the plan "not as a traditional creditor seeking to maximize its return on the debt it holds, but . . . 'to establish control over this strategic asset.'" *DBSD II* (quoting DISH's own internal presentation slides). The bankruptcy court therefore designated DISH's vote and disregarded DISH's wholly-owned class of First Lien Debt for the purposes of determining plan acceptance under § 1129(a)(8). * * *

After designating DISH's vote and rejecting all objections, the bankruptcy court confirmed the plan. The district court affirmed, and DISH and Sprint appealed to this Court. * * *

DISCUSSION

II. *DISH's Appeal*

A. The Treatment of DISH's Vote

1. *Designating DISH's Vote as "Not in Good Faith*"

To confirm a plan of reorganization, Chapter 11 generally requires a vote of all holders of claims or interests impaired by that plan. *See* §§ 1126, 1129(a)(8). This voting requirement has exceptions, however, including one that allows a bankruptcy court to designate (in effect, to disregard) the votes of "any entity whose acceptance or rejection of such plan was not in good faith." § 1126(e).

The Code provides no guidance about what constitutes a bad faith vote to accept or reject a plan. Rather, § 1126(e)'s "good faith" test effectively delegates to the courts the task of deciding when a party steps over the boundary. Case by case, courts have taken up this responsibility. No circuit court has ever dealt with a case like this one, however, and neither we nor the Supreme Court have many precedents on the "good faith" voting requirement in any context; the most recent cases from both courts are now more than 65 years old and address § 1126(e)'s predecessor, § 203 of the Bankruptcy Act. Nevertheless, these cases, cases from other jurisdictions, legislative history, and the purposes of the good-faith requirement give us confidence in affirming the bankruptcy court's decision to designate DISH's vote in this case.

We start with general principles that neither side disputes. Bankruptcy courts should employ § 1126(e) designation sparingly, as "the exception, not the rule." *In re Adelphia Commc'ns Corp.*, 359 B.R. 54, 61 (Bankr. S.D.N.Y. 2006). For this reason, a party seeking to designate another's vote bears the burden of proving that it was not cast in good faith. Merely purchasing claims in bankruptcy "for the purpose of securing the approval or rejection of a plan does not of itself amount to 'bad faith.'" *In re P-R Holding*, 147 F.2d at 897. Nor will selfishness alone defeat a creditor's good faith; the Code assumes that parties will act in their own self interest and allows them to do so.

Section 1126(e) comes into play when voters venture beyond mere self-interested promotion of their claims. "[T]he section was intended to apply to those who were not attempting to protect their own proper interests, but who were, instead, attempting to obtain some benefit to which they were not entitled." *In re Figter*, 118 F.3d at 638. A bankruptcy court may, therefore, designate the vote of a party who votes "in the hope that someone would pay them more than the ratable equivalent of their proportionate part of the bankrupt assets," *Young*, 324 U.S. at 211, or one who votes with an "ulterior motive," that is, with "an interest other than an interest as a creditor," *In re P-R Holding*, 147 F.2d at 897.

Here, the debate centers on what sort of "ulterior motives" may trigger designation under § 1126(e), and whether DISH voted with such an impermissible motive. The first question is a question of law that we review *de novo*, and the second a question of fact that we review for clear error, *see In re Baker*, 604 F.3d at 729, recognizing that "a decision that someone did or did not act in good faith" hinges on "an essentially factual inquiry and is driven by the data of practical human experience," *In re Figter*, 118 F.3d at 638 (quotation marks omitted).

Clearly, not just any ulterior motive constitutes the sort of improper motive that will support a finding of bad faith. After all, most creditors have interests beyond their claim against a particular debtor, and those other interests will inevitably affect how they vote the claim. For instance, trade creditors who do regular business with a debtor may vote in the way most likely to allow them to continue to do business with the debtor after reorganization. And, as interest rates change, a fully secured creditor may seek liquidation to allow money once invested at unfavorable rates to be invested more favorably elsewhere. We do not purport to decide here the propriety of either of these motives, but they at least demonstrate that allowing the disqualification of votes on account of *any* ulterior motive could have far-reaching consequences and might leave few votes upheld.

The sort of ulterior motive that § 1126(e) targets is illustrated by the case that motivated the creation of the "good faith" rule in the first place, *Texas Hotel Securities Corp. v. Waco Development Co.*, 87 F.2d 395 (5th Cir. 1936). In that case, Conrad Hilton purchased claims of a debtor to block a plan of reorganization that would have given a lease on the debtor's property – once held by Hilton's company, later cancelled – to a third party. Hilton and his partners sought, by buying and voting the claims, to "force [a plan] that would give them again the operation of the hotel or otherwise reestablish an interest that they felt they justly had in the property." *Id.* at 398. The district court refused to count Hilton's vote, but the court of appeals reversed, seeing no authority in the Bankruptcy Act for looking into the motives of creditors voting against a plan.

That case spurred Congress to require good faith in voting claims. As the Supreme Court has noted, the legislative history of the predecessor to § 1126(e) "make[s] clear the purpose of the [House] Committee [on the Judiciary] to pass legislation which would bar creditors from a vote who were prompted by such a purpose" as Hilton's. *Young*, 324 U.S. at 211 n.10. As then-SEC Commissioner Douglas explained to the House Committee:

> We envisage that "good faith" clause to enable the courts to affirm a plan over the opposition of a minority attempting to block the adoption of a plan merely for selfish purposes. The *Waco* case . . . was such a situation. If my memory does not serve me wrong it was a case where a minority group of security holders refused to vote in favor of the plan unless that group were given some particular preferential treatment, such as the management of the company. That is, there were ulterior reasons for their actions.

1937 Hearing, *supra*, at 181–82. One year after Commissioner Douglas's testimony, and two years after the *Waco* case, Congress enacted the proposed good faith clause as part of the Chandler Act of 1938. The Bankruptcy Code of 1978 preserved this good faith requirement, with some rewording, as § 1126(e).

Modern cases have found "ulterior motives" in a variety of situations. In perhaps the most famous case, and one on which the bankruptcy court in our case relied heavily, a court found bad faith because a party bought a blocking position in several classes after the debtor proposed a plan of reorganization, and then sought to defeat that plan and to promote its own plan that would have given it control over the debtor. In another case, the court designated the votes of parties affiliated with a competitor who bought their claims in an attempt to obstruct the debtor's reorganization and thereby to further the interests of their own business. In a third case, the court found bad faith where an affiliate of the debtor purchased claims not for the purpose of collecting on those claims but to prevent confirmation of a competing plan.

Although we express no view on the correctness of the specific findings of bad faith of the parties in those specific cases, we think that this case fits in the general constellation they form. As the bankruptcy court found, DISH, as an indirect competitor of DBSD and part-owner of a direct competitor, bought a blocking position in (and in fact the entirety of) a class of claims, after a plan had been proposed, with the intention not to maximize its return on the debt but to enter a strategic transaction with DBSD and "to use status as a creditor to provide advantages over proposing a plan as an outsider, or making a traditional bid for the company or its assets." In effect, DISH purchased the claims as votes it could use as levers to bend the bankruptcy process toward its own strategic objective of acquiring DBSD's spectrum rights, not toward protecting its claim.

We conclude that the bankruptcy court permissibly designated DISH's vote based on the facts above. This case echoes the *Waco* case that motivated Congress to impose the good faith requirement in the first place. In that case, a competitor bought claims with the intent of voting against any plan that did not give it a lease in or management of the debtor's property. In this case, a competitor bought claims with the intent of voting against any plan that did not give it a strategic interest in the reorganized company. The purchasing party in both cases was less interested in maximizing the return on its claim than in diverting the progress of the proceedings to achieve an outside benefit. In 1936, no authority allowed disregarding votes in such a situation, but Congress created that authority two years later with cases like *Waco* in mind. We therefore hold that a court may designate a creditor's vote in these circumstances.

We also find that, just as the law supports the bankruptcy court's legal conclusion, so the evidence supports its relevant factual findings. DISH's motive – the most controversial finding – is evinced by DISH's own admissions in court, by its position as a competitor to DBSD, by its willingness to overpay for the claims it bought,[51] by its attempt to propose its own plan, and especially by its internal communications, which, although addressing the Second Lien Debt rather than the First Lien Debt at issue here, nevertheless showed a desire to "to obtain a blocking position" and "control the bankruptcy process for this potentially strategic asset."

The Loan Syndications and Trading Association (LSTA), as *amicus curiae*, argues that courts should encourage acquisitions and other strategic transactions because such transactions can benefit all parties in bankruptcy. We agree. But our holding does not "shut[ ] the door to strategic transactions," as the LSTA suggests. Rather, it simply limits the methods by which parties may pursue them. DISH had every right to propose for consideration whatever strategic transaction it wanted – a right it took advantage of here – and DISH still retained this right even after it purchased its claims. All that the bankruptcy court stopped DISH from doing here was using the votes it had bought to secure an advantage in pursuing that strategic transaction.

DISH argues that, if we uphold the decision below, "future creditors looking for potential strategic transactions with chapter 11 debtors will be deterred from exploring

[51] The fact that DISH bought the First Lien Debt at par is circumstantial evidence of its intent, though we do not put as much weight on the price as the bankruptcy court did. It is certainly true, as the Loan Syndications and Trading Association points out in an amicus brief, that purchasers may have many good business reasons for buying debt at par, especially when, as in this case, the debt is well secured and interest rates dropped between the original issuance of the debt and its purchase. Buying claims at or above par therefore could not provide the sole basis for designating a creditor's vote. Nevertheless, a willingness to pay high prices may tend to show that the purchaser is interested in more than the claim for its own sake. The weight to be given to such evidence is primarily an issue for the finder of fact, and we see no clear error in the bankruptcy court's reliance on the factor in this case.

such deals for fear of forfeiting their rights as creditors." But our ruling today should deter only attempts to "*obtain* a blocking position" and thereby "control the bankruptcy process for [a] potentially strategic asset" (as DISH's own internal documents stated). We leave for another day the situation in which a *preexisting* creditor votes with strategic intentions. We emphasize, moreover, that our opinion imposes no categorical prohibition on purchasing claims with acquisitive or other strategic intentions. On other facts, such purchases may be appropriate. Whether a vote has been properly designated is a fact-intensive question that must be based on the totality of the circumstances, according considerable deference to the expertise of bankruptcy judges. Having reviewed the careful and fact-specific decision of the bankruptcy court here, we find no error in its decision to designate DISH's vote as not having been cast in good faith.

(ii) Feasibility

To confirm the plan, the court must find that the plan is feasible. This means that the plan must provide adequate means for the debtor to implement it. §§ 1129(a)(1), 1123(a)(5). It also means that confirmation is not likely to be followed by liquidation or further reorganization, unless those actions are contemplated by the plan itself. § 1129(a)(11). In short, if the plan provides for the debtor's business to continue, it must provide for whatever financing the business needs and not leave the business overburdened with debt. The plan must also identify principals who will be involved in running the debtor after confirmation. §§ 1129(a)(1), (5), 1123(a)(6), (7). This provision allows the creditors and interest holders to determine whether the persons so identified are capable of running the debtor after confirmation of the plan. In assessing feasibility, the information in the disclosure statement will often be critical. The disclosure statement should contain fairly detailed information about the past and projected business operations of the debtor.

If the reorganization plan is for an individual debtor, the debtor's future income sufficient to consummate the plan must be devoted to the plan. § 1123(a)(8).

(iii) Compliance with Bankruptcy Code and Other Law

The proponent of the plan must also comply with the applicable provisions of the Bankruptcy Code. § 1129(a)(2). If the debtor is the proponent, this means that the debtor must have operated the business postpetition in accordance with all of the Code requirements, including circulating the requisite financial reports, and complied with all court orders. The proponent of the plan must also propose the plan in good faith and not by any means forbidden by law. § 1129(a)(3). This term is generally interpreted to mean that there exists "a reasonable likelihood that the plan will achieve a result consistent with the objectives and purposes of the Bankruptcy Code."[52] All transfers of property for which the plan provides must comply with applicable law outside of the Bankruptcy Code. § 1129(a)(16). If the debtor is subject to rate regulation, the debtor must obtain approval of the regulatory body for any proposed rate changes. § 1129(a)(6).

(iv) Required Payments of Claims and Expenses

Payments made pursuant to the plan to a person who rendered services to the debtor in possession or who has paid expenses chargeable to the estate must be approved by the court as reasonable. § 1129(a)(4). This requirement operates in addition to the payments to professional persons approved pursuant to § 330 and § 328. In addition, all required bankruptcy-related fees must be paid no later than the effective date of the plan. § 1129(a)(12).

Payment to priority claimants depends upon the type of priority claim involved. Administrative expenses must be paid in full in cash equal to the allowed amount of the claim no later than the effective date of the plan, unless the administrative expense claimant has agreed to a different treatment. § 1129(a)(9)(A).

Each holder of most other priority claims must receive – if its class has accepted the plan – deferred cash payments that have a present value as of the effective date of at least the allowed amount of the claim. § 1129(a)(9)(B)(i). In other words, such priority claimants must be paid in full over time, but with postconfirmation interest. If such claimant's class has rejected the plan, the claimant must be paid in full in cash on the effective date of the plan. § 1129(a)(9)(B)(ii). Of course, any individual claimant may agree to less favorable treatment.

Unsecured priority tax claims are entitled to cash payments in regular installments with a present value at least equal to the amount of the claim. The distributions on such claims must be made within five years of the order for relief and on at least as favorable

---

52 *In re Madison Hotel Assocs.*, 749 F.2d 410, 425 (7th Cir. 1984).

of terms as the most favored nonpriority unsecured claimants. § 1129(a)(9)(C). The tax claimant may agree to less favorable treatment. Secured tax claims that would qualify for § 507(a)(8) priority but for their secured status are entitled to the same treatment. § 1129(a)(9)(D).

Claimants with impaired nonpriority claims who have not accepted the plan are entitled to receive the present value of the liquidation value of their claim. § 1129(a)(7). This rule is known as the "best interests of creditors test" but could probably be described more accurately as the "liquidation value test." To apply this rule, the court must estimate the liquidation value of the estate – as of the date of confirmation – and what each creditor would get under a hypothetical distribution pursuant to § 726. That in effect means that a secured claim gets the value of its collateral. As we have repeatedly encountered, valuation issues are a critical part of bankruptcy. Because this is a hypothetical distribution, a dissenting secured creditor will try to prove that the value of its collateral is higher than the value that the debtor in possession has allocated to that creditor. Similarly, dissenting unsecured creditors will try to demonstrate that the debtor in possession has not allocated enough value to paying its unsecured claims based upon this hypothetical liquidation based distribution.

A creditor whose claim is partially secured (so that the creditor has both a secured claim and an unsecured claim) has a choice to elect to treat its entire claim as a secured claim, in effect waiving its unsecured claim, and receive the present value of its collateral value in a payment stream that equals the dollar amount of its entire claim. §§ 1129(a)(7)(B), 1111(b)(2). Thus, if the creditor has a $10,000 total claim, secured by $4,000 in collateral value (in essence a $4,000 secured claim and a $6,000 unsecured claim), a creditor making the § 1111(b)(2) election must receive a total stream of payment totaling $10,000 with a present value of at least $4,000. Few creditors make this election. Those that do usually anticipate that the collateral will appreciate postconfirmation and that the debtor will nevertheless default. If so, the creditor will then have a lien on the full, appreciated value of the collateral to secure the total amount the creditor is owed.

In addition, holders of unsecured claims who have objected to confirmation of an individual debtor's Chapter 11 plan must either receive full payment of the amount of the claim or the debtor's entire disposable income for five years (or for the plan period if longer) must be devoted to payments under the plan. § 1129(a)(15). This provision is comparable to the provision found in § 1325(b).

Finally, retiree benefits are given special protection by virtue of § 1114. *See* § 1129(a)(13).

(b) Cramdown

If not all classes of impaired claims and interests vote yes on the plan, the debtor in possession (or other plan proponent) may attempt to obtain confirmation through the cramdown process of § 1129(b). Cramdown requires compliance with all rules discussed for consensual confirmation, except for the requirement that all impaired classes must accept the plan. It also requires compliance with three other rules designed to protect creditors. Note, however, that cramdown protections apply only if one or more impaired *classes* of creditors vote against the plan; they do not apply if *individual creditors* vote against the plan but are outvoted by the other members of their class.

The first additional requirement for cramdown is that at least one class of impaired claims (if there are any such classes) must accept the plan. § 1129(a)(10), (b). The second cramdown requirement is that the plan must not discriminate unfairly against any class of impaired claims. This is similar to the requirement in § 1322(b)(1), explored in chapter eleven. In general, it does not prohibit all disparate treatment of classes but does require that:

> (i) there is a reasonable basis for discriminating, (ii) the debtor cannot consummate the plan without discrimination, (iii) the discrimination is proposed in good faith, and (iv) the degree of discrimination is in direct proportion to its rationale."[53]

Third, the plan must be fair and equitable as to all dissenting classes of claims and interests. § 1129(b). "Fair and equitable" is defined differently for secured claims, unsecured claims, and interests. For secured claims, there are three alternative methods for satisfying the fair and equitable test: (i) allow the secured claimant to retain its lien (to the extent of the amount of the secured claim)[54] and provide for cash payments with a present value of the secured claim; (ii) sell the collateral and give the secured claimant the proceeds of the sale; or (iii) provide the secured claimant with the "indubitable equivalent" of the claim. The first option involves selecting the appropriate interest rate to compute the present value of the planned payments. Although the Supreme Court's decision in *Till*, discussed in chapter eleven, technically applies only in Chapter 13

---

53 *Mercury Capital Corp. v. Milford Conn. Assocs., L.P.*, 354 B.R. 1, 10 (D. Conn. 2006).

54 This requirement may influence an undersecured creditor to elect to treat its entire claim as a secured claim under § 1111(b) because it would retain the lien for the entire amount of its claim, not just the current value of the collateral.

cases, most courts follow its approach in Chapter 11 as well and begin with the prime interest rate and then make adjustment for risk, even if this produces a rate that would be below market for the type of credit involved.[55]

The third option typically means providing some appropriate alternative collateral. However, as the U.S. Court of Appeals for the Ninth Circuit has indicated, the substitute

> "must both compensate for present value and insure the safety of the principal. To the extent a debtor seeks to alter the collateral securing a creditor's loan, providing the 'indubitable equivalent' requires that the substitute collateral not increase the creditor's risk exposure."[56]

As to unsecured claims classes, the fair and equitable requirement means that either the dissenting class of unsecured claimants will receive property with a present value equal to the full amount of their claims or all classes of claims and interests that are junior in priority to the dissenting class will not "receive or retain" any property under the plan "on account of such junior claim or interest." § 1129(b)(2)(B). This is known as the "absolute priority rule." The rule for dissenting classes of interests is similar. *See* § 1129(b)(2)(C).

The rules on confirmation generally – and the absolute priority rule, in particular – have a significant impact on the negotiations over the content of the reorganization plan. The absolute priority rule implies that, unless all classes of creditors accept the plan or are paid, in present value, the full amount of their claims, the equity holders will not be permitted to retain any interest in the reorganized debtor. The only hope those owners have of recovering anything on their investment is if the debtor in possession – whose representatives are really bargaining on behalf of the debtor's equitable owners – can get the creditors to accept the plan. The creditors, however, cannot force the debtor in possession to pay them anything. Thus, the dynamic[57] often ends up something like this:

Illustration

> The debtor in possession offers creditors plan payments equal to some (small) percentage of their claims. The creditors insist on more, and they threaten to vote against the plan unless the debtor in possession agrees. This

---

[55] *See, e.g., In re Texas Grand Prairie Hotel Realty, LLC*, 710 F.3d 324 (5th Cir. 2013).

[56] *In re Wiersma*, 227 F. App'x 603 (9th Cir. 2007) (citations and internal quotations omitted).

[57] *See* Michelle M. Harner & Jamie Marincic, *Behind Closed Doors: The Influence of Creditors in Business Reorganizations*, 34 SEATTLE U. L. REV. 1155 (2011).

would invoke the absolute priority rule and leave the owners with nothing. The debtor in possession responds by threatening to convert the case to Chapter 7, in which case the business will be liquidated for presumably less than its value as a going concern. This may deprive creditors of their best source of recovery. It is as if the parties were seated around a pot of money and none of them has the ability to grab it. All they can do is thwart each other's attempts. Superimposed on this is the frequent reality that the debtor in possession is losing money. Often its operating costs – when combined with the administrative expenses (*e.g.*, legal fees) of the bankruptcy proceeding – exceed its incoming revenue. It is like a bunch of hungry people bargaining over a dish of ice cream . . . in a very hot room.

One wrinkle in all of this is the fact that often the debtor needs an infusion of capital to have a feasible reorganization. The debtor's equitable owners are the logical source for that new capital because they were the ones who initially had faith in the debtor's business and are the ones most likely to want an ownership interest in the reorganized debtor once the plan is confirmed. In recognition of this, and to facilitate reorganizations, many courts have allowed one or more of the existing owners to contribute new capital and then retain some or all of the ownership of the reorganized debtor, even though some dissenting classes of creditors are not paid in full. The existence and operation of this "new value exception" to the absolute priority rule is hotly debated. The first time the Supreme Court dealt with the issue, it ruled that even if the "new value" exception exists, contribution of labor and expertise by the prior owner (so called "sweat equity") is not sufficient "new value."[58] Now consider the Supreme Court's slightly more recent discussion of the new value exception.

BANK OF AMERICA NATIONAL TRUST & SAVINGS ASS'N V. 203 NORTH LASALLE STREET PARTNERSHIP
526 U.S. 434 (1999)

Justice Souter delivered the opinion of the Court.

The issue in this Chapter 11 reorganization case is whether a debtor's prebankruptcy equity holders may, over the objection of a senior class of impaired creditors, contribute new capital and receive ownership interests in the reorganized entity, when that opportunity is given exclusively to the old equity holders under a plan

---

58 *Norwest Bank Worthington v. Ahlers*, 485 U.S. 197 (1988).

adopted without consideration of alternatives. We hold that old equity holders are disqualified from participating in such a "new value" transaction by the terms of § 1129(b)(2)(B)(ii), which in such circumstances bars a junior interest holder's receipt of any property on account of his prior interest.

I

Petitioner, Bank of America National Trust and Savings Association (Bank), is the major creditor of respondent, 203 North LaSalle Street Partnership (Debtor or Partnership), an Illinois real estate limited partnership. The Bank lent the Debtor some $93 million, secured by a nonrecourse first mortgage on the Debtor's principal asset, 15 floors of an office building in downtown Chicago. In January 1995, the Debtor defaulted, and the Bank began foreclosure in a state court.

In March, the Debtor responded with a voluntary petition for relief under Chapter 11 of the Bankruptcy Code, which automatically stayed the foreclosure proceedings. The Debtor's principal objective was to ensure that its partners retained title to the property so as to avoid roughly $20 million in personal tax liabilities, which would fall due if the Bank foreclosed. The Debtor proceeded to propose a reorganization plan during the 120-day period when it alone had the right to do so, *see* § 1121(b). The Bankruptcy Court rejected the Bank's motion to terminate the period of exclusivity to make way for a plan of its own to liquidate the property, and instead extended the exclusivity period for cause shown, under § 1121(d).

The value of the mortgaged property was less than the balance due the Bank * * *. Under the plan, the Debtor separately classified the Bank's secured claim, its unsecured deficiency claim, and unsecured trade debt owed to other creditors. *See* § 1122(a). The Bankruptcy Court found that the Debtor's available assets were prepetition rents in a cash account of $3.1 million and the 15 floors of rental property worth $54.5 million. The secured claim was valued at the latter figure, leaving the Bank with an unsecured deficiency of $38.5 million.

So far as we need be concerned here, the Debtor's plan had these further features:

(1) The Bank's $54.5 million secured claim would be paid in full between 7 and 10 years after the original 1995 repayment date.

(2) The Bank's $38.5 million unsecured deficiency claim would be discharged for an estimated 16% of its present value.

(3) The remaining unsecured claims of $90,000, held by the outside trade creditors, would be paid in full, without interest, on the effective date of the plan.

(4) Certain former partners of the Debtor would contribute $6.125 million in new capital over the course of five years (the contribution being worth some $4.1

million in present value), in exchange for the Partnership's entire ownership of the reorganized debtor.

The last condition was an exclusive eligibility provision: the old equity holders were the only ones who could contribute new capital.[59]

The Bank objected and, being the sole member of an impaired class of creditors, thereby blocked confirmation of the plan on a consensual basis. *See* § 1129(a)(8). The Debtor, however, took the alternate route to confirmation of a reorganization plan, forthrightly known as the judicial "cramdown" process for imposing a plan on a dissenting class. § 1129(b).

There are two conditions for a cramdown. First, all requirements of § 1129(a) must be met (save for the plan's acceptance by each impaired class of claims or interests, see § 1129(a)(8)). Critical among them are the conditions that the plan be accepted by at least one class of impaired creditors, *see* § 1129(a)(10), and satisfy the "best-interest-of-creditors" test, *see* § 1129(a)(7). Here, the class of trade creditors with impaired unsecured claims voted for the plan, and there was no issue of best interest. Second, the objection of an impaired creditor class may be overridden only if "the plan does not discriminate unfairly, and is fair and equitable, with respect to each class of claims or interests that is impaired under, and has not accepted, the plan." § 1129(b)(1). As to a dissenting class of impaired unsecured creditors, such a plan may be found to be "fair and equitable" only if the allowed value of the claim is to be paid in full, § 1129(b)(2)(B)(i), or, in the alternative, if "the holder of any claim or interest that is junior to the claims of such [impaired unsecured] class will not receive or retain under the plan on account of such junior claim or interest any property," § 1129(b)(2)(B)(ii). That latter condition is the core of what is known as the "absolute priority rule."

The absolute priority rule was the basis for the Bank's position that the plan could not be confirmed as a cramdown. As the Bank read the rule, the plan was open to objection simply because certain old equity holders in the Debtor Partnership would receive property even though the Bank's unsecured deficiency claim would not be paid in full. The Bankruptcy Court approved the plan nonetheless, and accordingly denied the Bank's pending motion to convert the case to Chapter 7 liquidation, or to dismiss the case. The District Court affirmed, as did the Court of Appeals.

The majority of the Seventh Circuit's divided panel found ambiguity in the language of the statutory absolute priority rule, and looked beyond the text to interpret

---

[59] The plan eliminated the interests of noncontributing partners. More than 60% of the Partnership interests would change hands on confirmation of the plan. The new Partnership, however, would consist solely of former partners, a feature critical to the preservation of the Partnership's tax shelter.

the phrase "on account of" as permitting recognition of a "new value corollary" to the rule. According to the panel, the corollary, as stated by this Court in *Case v. Los Angeles Lumber Products Co.*, 308 U.S. 106 (1939), provides that the objection of an impaired senior class does not bar junior claim holders from receiving or retaining property interests in the debtor after reorganization, if they contribute new capital in money or money's worth, reasonably equivalent to the property's value, and necessary for successful reorganization of the restructured enterprise. The panel majority held that

> "when an old equity holder retains an equity interest in the reorganized debtor by meeting the requirements of the new value corollary, he is not receiving or retaining that interest 'on account of' his prior equitable ownership of the debtor. Rather, he is allowed to participate in the reorganized entity 'on account of' a new, substantial, necessary and fair infusion of capital."

In the dissent's contrary view, there is nothing ambiguous about the text: the "plain language of the absolute priority rule . . . does not include a new value exception." (opinion of Kanne, J.). Since "[t]he Plan in this case gives [the Debtor's] partners the exclusive right to retain their ownership interest in the indebted property *because of* their status as . . . prior interest holder[s]," *id.*, the dissent would have reversed confirmation of the plan.

We granted certiorari to resolve a Circuit split on the issue. * * * We do not decide whether the statute includes a new value corollary or exception, but hold that on any reading respondent's proposed plan fails to satisfy the statute, and accordingly reverse.

II

The terms "absolute priority rule" and "new value corollary" (or "exception") are creatures of law antedating the current Bankruptcy Code, and to understand both those terms and the related but inexact language of the Code some history is helpful. The Bankruptcy Act preceding the Code contained no such provision as subsection (b)(2)(B)(ii), its subject having been addressed by two interpretive rules. The first was a specific gloss on the requirement of § 77B (and its successor, Chapter X) of the old Act, that any reorganization plan be "fair and equitable." The reason for such a limitation was the danger inherent in any reorganization plan proposed by a debtor, then and now, that the plan will simply turn out to be too good a deal for the debtor's owners. *See* H.R. Doc. No. 93-137, pt. I, p. 255 (1973) (discussing concern with "the ability of a few insiders, whether representatives of management or major creditors, to use the reorganization process to gain an unfair advantage"; "[I]t was believed that creditors, because of management's position of dominance, were not able to bargain effectively without a clear standard of fairness and judicial control"). Hence the pre-Code judicial response known as the absolute priority rule, that fairness and equity required that "the creditors . . . be paid before the stockholders could retain [equity interests] for any purpose whatever." *Northern Pacific R. Co. v. Boyd*, 228 U.S. 482, 508 (1913).

The second interpretive rule addressed the first. Its classic formulation occurred in *Case v. Los Angeles Lumber Products Co.*, in which the Court spoke through Justice Douglas in this dictum:

> "It is, of course, clear that there are circumstances under which stockholders may participate in a plan of reorganization of an insolvent debtor. . . . Where th[e] necessity [for new capital] exists and the old stockholders make a fresh contribution and receive in return a participation reasonably equivalent to their contribution, no objection can be made. . . .
>
> [W]e believe that to accord 'the creditor his full right of priority against the corporate assets' where the debtor is insolvent, the stockholder's participation must be based on a contribution in money or in money's worth, reasonably equivalent in view of all the circumstances to the participation of the stockholder." 308 U.S. at 121–22.

Although counsel for one of the parties here has described the *Case* observation as "black-letter' principle," it never rose above the technical level of dictum in any opinion of this Court, which last addressed it in *Norwest Bank Worthington v. Ahlers*, 485 U.S. 197 (1988), holding that a contribution of "labor, experience, and expertise" by a junior interest holder was not in the "money's worth" that the *Case* observation required. Nor, prior to the enactment of the current Bankruptcy Code, did any court rely on the *Case* dictum to approve a plan that gave old equity a property right after reorganization. Hence the controversy over how weighty the *Case* dictum had become, as reflected in the alternative labels for the new value notion: some writers and courts (including this one, see *Ahlers*, 385 U.S. at 203–04, n.3) have spoken of it as an exception to the absolute priority rule, while others have characterized it as a simple corollary to the rule.

Enactment of the Bankruptcy Code in place of the prior Act might have resolved the status of new value by a provision bearing its name or at least unmistakably couched in its terms, but the Congress chose not to avail itself of that opportunity. In 1973, Congress had considered proposals by the Bankruptcy Commission that included a recommendation to make the absolute priority rule more supple by allowing nonmonetary new value contributions. Although Congress took no action on any of the ensuing bills containing language that would have enacted such an expanded new value concept, each of them was reintroduced in the next congressional session. *See* H.R. 31,

94th Cong., 1st Sess., §§ 7-303(4),[60] 7-310(d)(2)(B) (1975).[61] After extensive hearings, a substantially revised House bill emerged, but without any provision for nonmonetary new value contributions. After a lengthy markup session, the House produced H.R. 8200, 95th Cong., 1st Sess. (1977), which would eventually become the law. It had no explicit new value language, expansive or otherwise, but did codify the absolute priority rule in nearly its present form. *See* § 1129(b)(2)(B)(iv) ("[T]he holders of claims or interests of any class of claims or interests, as the case may be, that is junior to such class will not receive or retain under the plan on account of such junior claims or interests any property").

For the purpose of plumbing the meaning of subsection (b)(2)(B)(ii) in search of a possible statutory new value exception, the lesson of this drafting history is equivocal. Although hornbook law has it that "Congress does not intend *sub silentio* to enact statutory language that it has earlier discarded," *INS v. Cardoza-Fonseca*, 480 U.S. 421, 442–43 (1987), the phrase "on account of" is not *silentium*, and the language passed by in this instance had never been in the bill finally enacted, but only in predecessors that died on the vine. None of these contained an explicit codification of the absolute priority rule, and even in these earlier bills the language in question stated an expansive new value concept, not the rule as limited in the *Case* dictum.

The equivocal note of this drafting history is amplified by another feature of the legislative advance toward the current law. Any argument from drafting history has to account for the fact that the Code does not codify any authoritative pre-Code version of the absolute priority rule. Compare § 1129(b)(2)(B)(ii) ("[T]he holder of any claim or interest that is junior to the claims of such [impaired unsecured] class will not receive or retain under the plan on account of such junior claim or interest any property") with *Boyd*, 228 U.S. at 508 ("[T]he creditors were entitled to be paid before the stockholders

---

[60] Section 7-303(4) read: "[W]hen the equity security holders retain an interest under the plan, the individual debtor, certain partners or equity security holders will make a contribution which is important to the operation of the reorganized debtor or the successor under the plan, for participation by the individual debtor, such partners, or such holders under the plan on a basis which reasonably approximates the value, if any, of their interests, and the additional estimated value of such contribution."

[61] Section 7-310(d)(2)(B) read: "Subject to the provisions of section 7-303(3) and (4) and the court's making any findings required thereby, there is a reasonable basis for the valuation on which the plan is based and the plan is fair and equitable in that there is a reasonable probability that the securities issued and other consideration distributed under the plan will fully compensate the respective classes of creditors and equity security holders of the debtor for their respective interests in the debtor or his property."

[and] could retain [a right of property] for any purpose whatever"), and *Case*, 308 U.S. at 116 ("[C]reditors are entitled to priority over stockholders against all the property of an insolvent corporation").

The upshot is that this history does nothing to disparage the possibility apparent in the statutory text, that the absolute priority rule now on the books as subsection (b)(2)(B)(ii) may carry a new value corollary. Although there is no literal reference to "new value" in the phrase "on account of such junior claim," the phrase could arguably carry such an implication in modifying the prohibition against receipt by junior claimants of any interest under a plan while a senior class of unconsenting creditors goes less than fully paid.

III

Three basic interpretations have been suggested for the "on account of" modifier. The first reading is proposed by the Partnership, that "on account of" harks back to accounting practice and means something like "in exchange for," or "in satisfaction of." On this view, a plan would not violate the absolute priority rule unless the old equity holders received or retained property in exchange for the prior interest, without any significant new contribution; if substantial money passed from them as part of the deal, the prohibition of subsection (b)(2)(B)(ii) would not stand in the way, and whatever issues of fairness and equity there might otherwise be would not implicate the "on account of" modifier.

This position is beset with troubles, the first one being textual. Subsection (b)(2)(B)(ii) forbids not only receipt of property on account of the prior interest but its retention as well. A common instance of the latter would be a debtor's retention of an interest in the insolvent business reorganized under the plan. Yet it would be exceedingly odd to speak of "retain[ing]" property in exchange for the same property interest, and the eccentricity of such a reading is underscored by the fact that elsewhere in the Code the drafters chose to use the very phrase "in exchange for," § 1123(a)(5)(J) (a plan shall provide adequate means for implementation, including "issuance of securities of the debtor . . . for cash, for property, for existing securities, or in exchange for claims or interests"). It is unlikely that the drafters of legislation so long and minutely contemplated as the 1978 Bankruptcy Code would have used two distinctly different forms of words for the same purpose. . . .

The second difficulty is practical: the unlikelihood that Congress meant to impose a condition as manipulable as subsection (b)(2)(B)(ii) would be if "on account of" meant to prohibit merely an exchange unaccompanied by a substantial infusion of new funds but permit one whenever substantial funds changed hands. "Substantial" or "significant" or "considerable" or like characterizations of a monetary contribution would measure it by the Lord Chancellor's foot, and an absolute priority rule so variable would not be much of an absolute. Of course it is true (as already noted) that, even if old equity holders could displace the rule by adding some significant amount of cash to the deal, it would not follow that their plan would be entitled to adoption; a contested plan would still need to satisfy the overriding condition of fairness and equity. But that general fairness and equity criterion would apply in any event, and one comes back to the question why Congress would have bothered to add a separate priority rule without a sharper edge.

Since the "in exchange for " reading merits rejection, the way is open to recognize the more common understanding of "on account of " to mean "because of." This is certainly the usage meant for the phrase at other places in the statute, *see* § 1111(b)(1)(A) (treating certain claims as if the holder of the claim "had recourse against the debtor on account of such claim"); § 522(d)(10)(E) (permitting debtors to exempt payments under certain benefit plans and contracts "on account of illness, disability, death, age, or length of service"); § 547(b)(2) (authorizing trustee to avoid a transfer of an interest of the debtor in property "for or on account of an antecedent debt owed by the debtor"); § 547(c)(4)(B) (barring trustee from avoiding a transfer when a creditor gives new value to the debtor "on account of which new value the debtor did not make an otherwise unavoidable transfer to . . . such creditor"). So, under the commonsense rule that a given phrase is meant to carry a given concept in a single statute, the better reading of subsection (b)(2)(B)(ii) recognizes that a causal relationship between holding the prior claim or interest and receiving or retaining property is what activates the absolute priority rule.

The degree of causation is the final bone of contention. We understand the Government, as *amicus curiae*, to take the starchy position not only that any degree of causation between earlier interests and retained property will activate the bar to a plan providing for later property, but also that whenever the holders of equity in the Debtor end up with some property there will be some causation; when old equity, and not someone on the street, gets property the reason is *res ipsa loquitur*. An old equity holder simply cannot take property under a plan if creditors are not paid in full.

There are, however, reasons counting against such a reading. If, as is likely, the drafters were treating junior claimants or interest holders as a class at this point,[62] then

---

[62] It is possible, on the contrary, to argue on the basis of the immediate text that the prohibition against receipt of an interest "on account of" a prior unsecured claim or interest was meant to indicate only that there is no *per se* bar to such receipt by a creditor holding both a senior secured claim and

the simple way to have prohibited the old interest holders from receiving anything over objection would have been to omit the "on account of" phrase entirely from subsection (b)(2)(B)(ii). On this assumption, reading the provision as a blanket prohibition would leave "on account of" as a redundancy, contrary to the interpretive obligation to try to give meaning to all the statutory language. One would also have to ask why Congress would have desired to exclude prior equity categorically from the class of potential owners following a cramdown. Although we have some doubt about the Court of Appeals's assumption that prior equity is often the only source of significant capital for reorganizations, old equity may well be in the best position to make a go of the reorganized enterprise and so may be the party most likely to work out an equity-for-value reorganization.

A less absolute statutory prohibition would follow from reading the "on account of" language as intended to reconcile the two recognized policies underlying Chapter 11, of preserving going concerns and maximizing property available to satisfy creditors. Causation between the old equity's holdings and subsequent property substantial enough to disqualify a plan would presumably occur on this view of things whenever old equity's later property would come at a price that failed to provide the greatest possible addition to the bankruptcy estate, and it would always come at a price too low when the equity holders obtained or preserved an ownership interest for less than someone else would have paid.[63] A truly full value transaction, on the other hand, would pose no threat to the bankruptcy estate not posed by any reorganization, provided of course that the contribution be in cash or be realizable money's worth, just as *Ahlers* required for application of *Case*'s new value rule.

---

a junior unsecured one, when the senior secured claim accounts for the subsequent interest. This reading would of course eliminate the phrase "on account of" as an express source of a new value exception, but would leave open the possibility of interpreting the absolute priority rule itself as stopping short of prohibiting a new value transaction.

[63] Even when old equity would pay its top dollar and that figure was as high as anyone else would pay, the price might still be too low unless the old equity holders paid more than anyone else would pay, on the theory that the "necessity" required to justify old equity's participation in a new value plan is a necessity for the participation of old equity as such. On this interpretation, disproof of a bargain would not satisfy old equity's burden; it would need to show that no one else would pay as much. No such issue is before us, and we emphasize that our holding here does not suggest an exhaustive list of the requirements of a proposed new value plan.

IV

Which of these positions is ultimately entitled to prevail is not to be decided here, however, for even on the latter view the Bank's objection would require rejection of the plan at issue in this case. It is doomed, we can say without necessarily exhausting its flaws, by its provision for vesting equity in the reorganized business in the Debtor's partners without extending an opportunity to anyone else either to compete for that equity or to propose a competing reorganization plan. Although the Debtor's exclusive opportunity to propose a plan under § 1121(b) is not itself "property" within the meaning of subsection (b)(2)(B)(ii), the respondent partnership in this case has taken advantage of this opportunity by proposing a plan under which the benefit of equity ownership may be obtained by no one but old equity partners. Upon the court's approval of that plan, the partners were in the same position that they would have enjoyed had they exercised an exclusive option under the plan to buy the equity in the reorganized entity, or contracted to purchase it from a seller who had first agreed to deal with no one else. It is quite true that the escrow of the partners' proposed investment eliminated any formal need to set out an express option or exclusive dealing provision in the plan itself, since the court's approval that created the opportunity and the partners' action to obtain its advantage were simultaneous. But before the Debtor's plan was accepted no one else could propose an alternative one, and after its acceptance no one else could obtain equity in the reorganized entity. At the moment of the plan's approval the Debtor's partners necessarily enjoyed an exclusive opportunity that was in no economic sense distinguishable from the advantage of the exclusively entitled offeror or option holder. This opportunity should, first of all, be treated as an item of property in its own right. While it may be argued that the opportunity has no market value, being significant only to old equity holders owing to their potential tax liability, such an argument avails the Debtor nothing, for several reasons. It is to avoid just such arguments that the law is settled that any otherwise cognizable property interest must be treated as sufficiently valuable to be recognized under the Bankruptcy Code. Even aside from that rule, the assumption that no one but the Debtor's partners might pay for such an opportunity would obviously support no inference that it is valueless, let alone that it should not be treated as property. And, finally, the source in the tax law of the opportunity's value to the partners implies in no way that it lacks value to others. It might, indeed, be valuable to another precisely as a way to keep the Debtor from implementing a plan that would avoid a Chapter 7 liquidation.

Given that the opportunity is property of some value, the question arises why old equity alone should obtain it, not to mention at no cost whatever. The closest thing to an answer favorable to the Debtor is that the old equity partners would be given the opportunity in the expectation that in taking advantage of it they would add the stated purchase price to the estate. But this just begs the question why the opportunity should be exclusive to the old equity holders. If the price to be paid for the equity interest is the best obtainable, old equity does not need the protection of exclusiveness (unless to trump an equal offer from someone else); if it is not the best, there is no apparent reason for giving old equity a bargain. There is no reason, that is, unless the very purpose of the whole transaction is, at least in part, to do old equity a favor. And that, of course, is to say that old equity would obtain its opportunity, and the resulting benefit, because of old equity's prior interest within the meaning of subsection (b)(2)(B)(ii). Hence it is that the exclusiveness of the opportunity, with its protection against the market's scrutiny of the purchase price by means of competing bids or even competing plan proposals, renders the partners' right a property interest extended "on account of" the old equity position and therefore subject to an unpaid senior creditor class's objection.

It is no answer to this to say that the exclusive opportunity should be treated merely as a detail of the broader transaction that would follow its exercise, and that in this wider perspective no favoritism may be inferred, since the old equity partners would pay something, whereas no one else would pay anything. If this argument were to carry the day, of course, old equity could obtain a new property interest for a dime without being seen to receive anything on account of its old position. But even if we assume that old equity's plan would not be confirmed without satisfying the judge that the purchase price was top dollar, there is a further reason here not to treat property consisting of an exclusive opportunity as subsumed within the total transaction proposed. On the interpretation assumed here, it would, of course, be a fatal flaw if old equity acquired or retained the property interest without paying full value. It would thus be necessary for old equity to demonstrate its payment of top dollar, but this it could not satisfactorily do when it would receive or retain its property under a plan giving it exclusive rights and in the absence of a competing plan of any sort (footnote omitted). Under a plan granting an exclusive right, making no provision for competing bids or competing plans, any determination that the price was top dollar would necessarily be made by a judge in bankruptcy court, whereas the best way to determine value is exposure to a market. This is a point of some significance, since it was, after all, one of the Code's innovations to narrow the occasions for courts to make valuation judgments, as shown by its preference for the supramajoritarian class creditor voting scheme in § 1126(c). In the interest of statutory coherence, a like disfavor for decisions untested by competitive choice ought to extend to valuations in administering subsection (b)(2)(B)(ii) when some form of market valuation may be available to test the adequacy of an old equity holder's proposed contribution.

Whether a market test would require an opportunity to offer competing plans or would be satisfied by a right to bid for the same interest sought by old equity is a question we do not decide here. It is enough to say, assuming a new value corollary, that plans providing junior interest holders with exclusive opportunities free from competition and without benefit of market valuation fall within the prohibition of § 1129(b)(2)(B)(ii).

The judgment of the Court of Appeals, accordingly, is reversed, and the case is remanded for further proceedings consistent with this opinion.

One way debtors have attempted to circumvent the absolute priority rule is through having a senior class of creditors gift some of its recovery to the interest holders, bypassing a junior class. Sometimes the senior class of creditors is willing to do this in order to retain the expertise of the interest holders. However, the practice is rather controversial. Consider the additional excerpt from the court's opinion in *In re DBSD North America, Inc.*

IN RE DBSD NORTH AMERICA, INC.
634 F.3d 79 (2d Cir. 2011)

* * *

DISCUSSION

I. *Sprint's Appeal*

Sprint raises only one issue on appeal: it asserts that the plan improperly gives property to DBSD's shareholder without fully satisfying Sprint's senior claim, in violation of the absolute priority rule. *See* § 1129(b)(2)(B). That rule provides that a reorganization plan may not give "property" to the holders of any junior claims or interests "on account of" those claims or interests, unless all classes of senior claims either receive the full value of their claims or give their consent. Because the existing shareholder received shares and warrants on account of its junior interest, Sprint argues, Sprint's class of general unsecured creditors had a right to receive "full satisfaction of their claims" or at least "an amount sufficient to obtain approval from the class." But the plan provided neither, and so Sprint asks us to vacate the order confirming it or to provide other relief that would satisfy Sprint's claim.

* * *

B. Gifting and the Absolute Priority Rule

Sprint argues that the plan violated the absolute priority rule by giving shares and warrants to a junior class (the existing shareholder) although a more senior class (Sprint's class) neither approved the plan nor received the full value of its claims. *See* § 1129(b)(2)(B). The appellees respond, and the courts below held, that the holders of the Second Lien Debt, who are senior to Sprint and whom the bankruptcy court found to be undersecured, were entitled to the full residual value of the debtor and were therefore free to "gift" some of that value to the existing shareholder if they chose to. We recently avoided deciding the viability of this "gifting doctrine" in a similar context, *see In re Iridium Operating LLC*, 478 F.3d 452, 460–61 (2d Cir. 2007), but we now face the question squarely. We look through the district court to the bankruptcy court's decision, and review its analysis of law *de novo.*

Long before anyone had imagined such a thing as Chapter 11 bankruptcy, it was already "well settled that stockholders are not entitled to any share of the capital stock nor to any dividend of the profits until all the debts of the corporation are paid." *Chi., Rock Island & Pac. R.R. v. Howard*, 74 U.S. (7 Wall) 392, 409–10 (1868). In the days of the railroad barons, however, parties observed this rule in the breach. Senior creditors and original shareholders often cooperated to control the reorganization of a failed company, sometimes to make the process go smoothly – to encourage the old shareholders to provide new capital for the reorganization or to keep them from engaging in costly and delaying litigation – or sometimes simply because the senior creditors and the old shareholders were the same parties. For their cooperation, the old owners would often receive or retain some stake in whatever entity arose from the reorganization. Junior creditors, however, often received little or nothing even though they technically stood above the old shareholders in priority.

In response to this practice, the Supreme Court developed a "fixed principle" for reorganizations: that all "creditors were entitled to be paid before the stockholders could retain [shares] for any purpose whatever." *N. Pac. Ry. Co. v. Boyd*, 228 U.S. 482, 507–08 (1913). "[A] plan of reorganization," the Court later stated, "would not be fair and equitable which . . . admitted the stockholders to participation, unless" at very least "the stockholders made a fresh contribution in money or in money's worth in return for 'a participation reasonably equivalent to their contribution.'" *Marine Harbor Props., Inc. v. Mfrs. Trust Co.*, 317 U.S. 78, 85 (1942). Courts came to call this the "absolute priority rule."

The Bankruptcy Code incorporates a form of the absolute priority rule in its provisions for confirming a Chapter 11 plan of reorganization. For a district court to confirm a plan over the vote of a dissenting class of claims, the Code demands that the plan be "fair and equitable, with respect to each class of claims . . . that is impaired under, and has not accepted, the plan." § 1129(b)(1). The Code does not define the full extent of "fair and equitable," but it includes a form of the absolute priority rule as a prerequisite. * * * § 1129(b)(2)(B).

Absent the consent of all impaired classes of unsecured claimants, therefore, a confirmable plan must ensure either (i) that the dissenting class receives the full value of its claim, or (ii) that no classes junior to that class receive any property under the plan on account of their junior claims or interests.

Under the plan in this case, Sprint does not receive "property of a value . . . equal to the allowed amount" of its claim. Rather, Sprint gets less than half the value of its claim. The plan may be confirmed, therefore, only if the existing shareholder, whose interest is junior to Sprint's, does "not receive or retain" "any property" "under the plan on account of such junior . . . interest." We hold that the existing shareholder did receive property under the plan on account of its interest, and that the bankruptcy court therefore should not have confirmed the plan.

First, under the challenged plan, the existing shareholder receives "property" in the form of shares and warrants in the reorganized entity. The term "property" in § 1129(b)(2)(B) is meant to be interpreted broadly. But even if it were not, there is no doubt that "any property" includes shares and warrants like these.

Second, the existing shareholder receives that property "under the plan." The disclosure statement for the second amended plan, under the heading "ARTICLE IV: THE JOINT PLAN," states:

> Class 9–Existing Stockholder Interests
>
> In full and final satisfaction, settlement, release, and discharge of each Existing Stockholder Interest, and on account of all valuable consideration provided by the Existing Stockholder, including, without limitation, certain consideration provided in the Support Agreement, . . . *the Holder of such Class 9 Existing Stockholder Interest shall receive the Existing Stockholder Shares and the Warrants.*

(emphasis added). We need not decide whether the Code would allow the existing shareholder and Senior Noteholders to agree to transfer shares outside of the plan, for, on the present record, the existing shareholder clearly receives these shares and warrants "under the plan."

Finally, the existing shareholder receives its shares and warrants "on account of" its junior interest. The Supreme Court has noted that "on account of" could take one of several interpretations. *See Bank of Am. Nat'l Trust & Sav. Ass'n v. 203 N. LaSalle St. Partnership*, 526 U.S. 434, 449 (1999). The interpretation most friendly to old equity

– which the Supreme Court rejected as "beset with troubles . . . exceedingly odd . . . [and] unlikely" – reads "on account of" as "in exchange for." Even under this generous test, the existing shareholder here receives property "on account of" its prior junior interest because it receives new shares and warrants at least partially "in exchange for" its old ones. The passage from the plan quoted above states as much: the existing shareholder receives shares and warrants "[i]n full and final satisfaction, settlement, release, and discharge of each Existing Stockholder Interest."

The gift here even more easily satisfies the two less restrictive tests the Supreme Court examined (and viewed more favorably) in *203 North LaSalle*, both of which read "on account of" to mean some form of "because of." The existing shareholder received its property "because of," and thus "on account of," its prior interest, for the same reasons set forth above.[64]

This conclusion is not undermined by the fact that the disclosure statement recites, and the district court found, additional reasons why the existing shareholder merited receiving the shares and warrants. First, a transfer partly on account of factors other than the prior interest is still partly "on account of" that interest. Upholding this principle in *203 North LaSalle*, the Supreme Court refused to characterize a benefit given to existing shareholders "merely as a detail of the broader transaction" in which those shareholders also contributed new capital. Instead, receipt of property partly on account of the existing interest was enough for the absolute priority rule to bar confirmation of the plan.

Second, the other reasons that the appellees assert drove the award of warrants and shares to old equity here are themselves "on account of" the existing shareholder's prior interest. The existing shareholder did not contribute additional capital to the reorganized entity; rather, as the bankruptcy court explained, the gift aimed to ensure the existing shareholder's "continued cooperation and assistance" in the reorganization. The "continued cooperation" of the existing shareholder was useful only because of the shareholder's position as equity holder * * *; an unrelated third party's cooperation would not have been useful. And "assistance" sounds like the sort of "future labor,

---

[64] We note that not all distributions of property to a junior class are necessarily "on account of" the junior claims or interests. For example, the Supreme Court has left open the possibility that old equity could take under a plan if it invests new value in the reorganized entity, at least as long as a "market valuation" tests the adequacy of its contribution. *203 North LaSalle*, 526 U.S. at 458. In such a situation, the party receiving the property may argue – though we do not now decide the correctness of such an argument – that it does not receive anything "on account of" its interest but only on account of its new investment. For another example, our decision does not stop a senior claim-holder from receiving property on account of its senior claim just because the claim-holder also happens to hold a junior claim on account of which it receives nothing. There may well be other examples.

management, or expertise" that the Supreme Court has held insufficient to avoid falling under the prohibition of the absolute priority rule. Thus, notwithstanding the various economic reasons that may have contributed to the decision to award property to old equity here, it is clear that the existing shareholder could not have gained its new position but for its prior equity position.

In sum, we conclude that the existing shareholder received "property," that it did so "under the plan," and that it did so "on account of" its prior, junior interest.

The Supreme Court's interpretations of § 1129(b)(2)(B) give us confidence in ours. Although that Court has not addressed the exact scenario presented here under the codified absolute priority rule, its two post-Code cases on the rule are instructive. In both cases, the prior owners tried to avoid the absolute priority rule by arguing that they received distributions not on account of their prior interests but rather on account of the new value that they would contribute to the entity. *See 203 N. LaSalle*, 526 U.S. at 437; *Ahlers*, 485 U.S. at 199. In both cases, the Supreme Court rejected those arguments. Although dictum in an earlier case had suggested that contributing new value could allow prior shareholders to participate in the reorganized entity, *see Case,* 308 U.S. at 121, the Court refused to decide whether § 1129(b)(2)(B) permitted such new-value exchanges. Instead, the Court held that neither "future labor, experience and expertise," *Ahlers*, 485 U.S. at 199, nor capital contributions "without benefit of market valuation," *203 N. LaSalle*, 526 U.S. at 458, could suffice to escape the absolute priority rule, even assuming the ongoing validity of the Case dictum.

203 North LaSalle and *Ahlers* indicate a preference for reading the rule strictly. Given that the Supreme Court has hesitated to allow old owners to receive new ownership interests even when contributing new value, it is doubtful the Court would allow old owners to receive new ownership without contributing any new value, as in this case. As the Court explained in Ahlers, "the statutory language and the legislative history of § 1129(b) clearly bar any expansion of any exception to the absolute priority rule beyond that recognized in our cases at the time Congress enacted the 1978 Bankruptcy Code." 485 U.S. at 206. The Supreme Court has never suggested any exception that would cover a case like this one.

The appellees, unsurprisingly, see the case in a different light. They contend that, under the "gifting doctrine," the shares and warrants rightfully belonged to the secured creditors, who were entitled to share them with the existing shareholder as they saw fit. Citing *In re SPM Manufacturing Corp.*, 984 F.2d 1305 (1st Cir. 1993), the appellees argue that, until the debts of the secured creditors "are paid in full, the Bankruptcy Code's distributional priority scheme, as embodied in the absolute priority rule, is not implicated." DBSD was not worth enough, according to the bankruptcy court's valuation, to cover even the secured lenders' claims, much less those of unsecured creditors like Sprint. Therefore, as the bankruptcy court stated in ruling for the appellees, "the 'Gifting' Doctrine – under which senior secured creditors voluntarily offer a portion of their recovered property to junior stakeholders (as the Senior Noteholders did here) – defeats Sprint's Absolute Priority Rule objection." We disagree.

Most fatally, this interpretation does not square with the text of the Bankruptcy Code. The Code extends the absolute priority rule to "any property," § 1129(b)(2)(B)(ii), not "any property not covered by a senior creditor's lien." The Code focuses entirely on who "receive[s]" or "retain[s]" the property "under the plan," not on who *would* receive it under a liquidation plan. And it applies the rule to any distribution "under the plan on account of" a junior interest, regardless of whether the distribution could have been made outside the plan, and regardless of whether other reasons might support the distribution in addition to the junior interest.

* * *

Even if the text of § 1129(b)(2)(B) left any room for the appellees' view of the case, we would hesitate to accept it in light of the Supreme Court's long history of rejecting such views. That history begins at least as early as 1868, in *Howard*, 74 U.S. (7 Wall) 392. In that case, the stockholders and mortgagees of a failing railroad agreed to foreclose on the railroad and convey its property to a new corporation, with the old stockholders receiving some of the new shares. The agreement gave nothing, however, to certain intermediate creditors, who sought a share of the distribution in the courts.

The stockholders defended their agreement with nearly the exact logic the appellees employ here:

> The road was mortgaged for near three times its value. . . . If, then, these stockholders have got anything, it must be because the bondholders have *surrendered* a part of *their* fund to them. If the fund belonged to the bondholders, they had a right so to surrender a part or a whole of it. And if the bondholders did so surrender their own property to the stockholders, it became the private property of these last; a gift, or, if you please, a transfer for consideration from the bondholders. . . . What right have these complainants to *such* property in the hands of the stockholders?

Even in 1868, however, the Supreme Court found that "[e]xtended discussion of that proposition is not necessary." "Holders of bonds secured by mortgages as in this case," the Court noted, "may exact the whole amount of the bonds, principal and interest, or they may, if they see fit, accept a percentage as a compromise in full discharge of their respective claims, but whenever their lien is legally discharged, the property embraced in the mortgage, or whatever remains of it, belongs to the corporation" for distribution to other creditors. Similarly, in this case, the secured creditors could have demanded a plan in which they received all of the reorganized corporation, but, having chosen not to, they may not "surrender" part of the value of the estate for distribution "to the stockholder[ ]," as "a gift." Whatever the secured creditors here did not take remains in the estate for the benefit of other claim-holders.

* * *

We recognize the policy arguments against the absolute priority rule. Gifting may be a "powerful tool in accelerating an efficient and non-adversarial . . . chapter 11 proceeding," Leah M. Eisenberg, *Gifting and Asset Reallocation in Chapter 11 Proceedings: A Synthesized Approach*, 29 AM. BANKR. INST. J. 50, 50 (2010), and no doubt the parties intended the gift to have such an effect here. As one witness testified below, "where . . . the equity sponsor is out of the money, . . . a tip is common to [e]nsure a consensual bankruptcy rather than a contested one." Enforcing the absolute priority rule, by contrast, "may encourage hold-out behavior by objecting creditors . . . even though the transfer has no direct effect on the value to be received by the objecting creditors." Harvey R. Miller & Ronit J. Berkovich, *The Implications of the Third Circuit's* Armstrong *Decision on Creative Corporate Restructuring: Will Strict Construction of the Absolute Priority Rule Make Chapter 11 Consensus Less Likely?*, 55 AM. U. L. REV. 1345, 1349 (2006).

It deserves noting, however, that there are substantial policy arguments in favor of the rule. Shareholders retain substantial control over the Chapter 11 process, and with that control comes significant opportunity for self-enrichment at the expense of creditors. This case provides a nice example. Although no one alleges any untoward conduct here, it is noticeable how much larger a distribution the existing shareholder will receive under this plan (4.99% of all equity in the reorganized entity) than the general unsecured creditors put together (0.15% of all equity), despite the latter's technical seniority. Indeed, based on the debtor's estimate that the reorganized entity would be worth approximately $572 million, the existing shareholder will receive approximately $28.5 million worth of equity under the plan while the unsecured creditors must share only $850,000. And if the parties here were less scrupulous or the bankruptcy court less vigilant, a weakened absolute priority rule could allow for serious mischief between senior creditors and existing shareholders.

Whatever the policy merits of the absolute priority rule, however, Congress was well aware of both its benefits and disadvantages when it codified the rule in the Bankruptcy Code. The policy objections to the rule are not new ones; the rule has attracted controversy from its early days. Four Justices dissented from the Supreme Court's 1913 holding in *Boyd*, and that decision "was received by the reorganization bar and bankers with something akin to horror," James N. Rosenberg, *Reorganization – The Next Step,* 22 COLUM. L. REV. 14, 14 (1922). The Commission charged with reviewing the bankruptcy laws in the lead-up to the enactment of the Bankruptcy Code suggested loosening the absolute priority rule to allow greater participation by equity owners. Yet, although Congress did soften the absolute priority rule in some ways, it did not create any exception for "gifts" like the one at issue here. We therefore hold that the bankruptcy court erred in confirming the plan of reorganization.

In the 2005 Amendments to the Bankruptcy Code, Congress did enact an exception to the absolute priority rule. If the Chapter 11 debtor is an individual, § 1115(a) adds to the estate the debtor's postpetition earnings from personal services and other property that the debtor acquires postpetition and another new provision, § 1129(a)(15), incorporates the requirement from Chapter 13 that the debtor allocate all disposable income to the payment of claimants. Section 1115(b) then authorizes the debtor to retain property of the estate. This rule is not limited to postpetition earnings and other assets acquired postpetition, however; it purports to cover property acquired by the individual prepetition. Thus arguably the 2005 Amendments opened a rather large hole in the absolute priority rule in the Chapter 11 case of an individual debtor.[65]

Problem 12-7

Joyce Duong operated a grocery store as a sole proprietor, Joyce's Foods. State Bank had a properly perfected security interest in the inventory to secure an operating loan. The security agreement provided for all proceeds of inventory to be applied to payment of the loan. State Bank then advanced monthly operating expenses as that money was required in the business. Monthly operating expenses were approximately $100,000 per month. Monthly proceeds of the inventory and accounts varied from $80,000 to $120,000 per month. Joyce's Foods has been in operation for over 5 years.

---

[65] *Compare In re Lively*, 717 F.3d 406 (5th Cir. 2013); *In re Stephens*, 704 F.3d 1279 (10th Cir. 2013); *In re Maharaj*, 681 F.3d 558 (4th Cir. 2012) (all ruling that the amendment should be construed narrowly to apply only to postpetition earnings and other postpetition property), *with In re Friedman*, 466 B.R. 471 (9th Cir. BAP 2012) (ruling that the absolute priority rule is now not applicable in a Chapter 11 case filed by individual debtors).

Last year, SuperFoods built a supermarket within one mile of Joyce's Foods. That supermarket opened six months ago. On the day the supermarket opened, the inventory of Joyce's Foods had a value of $100,000 if sold in the ordinary course of business. Since the supermarket opened, monthly proceeds of inventory dropped to $70,000 to $90,000 per month. During the six months, the amount of the outstanding loan balance grew from $100,000 to $250,000.

On July 1, Duong, d/b/a Joyce's Foods, filed a bankruptcy petition under Chapter 11 of the Bankruptcy Code. At the time of the filing, the loan had a principal balance of $250,000 and the inventory had a liquidation value of $50,000 and a value of $100,000 if sold in the ordinary course of business. At the time of the filing, Duong owed $5,000 to the IRS for personal income taxes from the prior year. The IRS has assessed the taxes but has not filed a notice of tax lien for those taxes. Also at the time of filing, Duong was in the second year of a five-year contract with Fresh Foods Supply in which Fresh Foods promised to supply specified groceries to Joyce for resale in the store with a minimum monthly purchase obligation of $10,000. At the time of filing, Duong owed Fresh Foods $50,000 for past deliveries.

During the first two months of Duong's Chapter 11 case, the inventory was sold and the money from the sale of inventory was used to buy new inventory and pay most of the ongoing business operating expenses. State Bank obtained a cash collateral order that granted it a security interest in the new inventory as a replacement lien for the loss of its lien in the prepetition inventory. State Bank has not advanced any additional funds during the pendency of this bankruptcy case. After the petition was filed, Duong did not purchase any groceries from Fresh Foods.

On the day that Duong filed her plan and disclosure statement for court approval, the inventory had a value of $80,000 if sold in the ordinary course of business. The entire $80,000 value was composed of inventory purchased after the commencement of the case. The plan provided as follows:

Class 1: $50,000 in expenses used to run the business during the bankruptcy case by incurring unsecured credit and attorney's fees will be paid over the course of one year with 5% interest ($4,280 per month).

Class 2: State Bank's secured claim of $50,000 will be paid with 6% interest over the course of 2 years ($2,216 per month).

Class 3: State Bank's unsecured claim of $200,000 will be paid $20,000 without interest over the course of 1 year ($1,667 per month).

Class 4: Fresh Foods' unsecured claim of $50,000 will be paid $25,000 without interest over the course of 5 years ($417 per month).

Class 5: Internal Revenue Service claim of $5,000 for unpaid income taxes will be paid in full without interest over the course of 1 year ($417 per month).

The plan also provided that all executory contracts that were not assumed were rejected. The plan provided that operating expenses were reduced to $70,000 per month and income had remained steady and was expected to remain steady at $80,000 per month. Duong will continue to own and operate the grocery store. The plan states that the liquidation value of the business is $60,000.

A. Your client is State Bank. Identify and explain all of the arguments State Bank might raise to keep this plan from being confirmed. Evaluate the merits and likelihood of success of each argument. How would you advise State Bank to vote on the plan and why?

B. Your client is Joyce Duong. Determine whether the plan can be confirmed in a cramdown. If not, restructure the plan so that a cramdown would be possible.

5. *Effect of Confirmation*

A confirmed reorganization plan binds all claimants and interest holders to its terms. § 1141(a). It also revests all estate property in the debtor. § 1141(b). Unless the debtor is an individual, a confirmed plan discharges all preconfirmation debts, except to the extent it provides otherwise. § 1141(d). However, this discharge does not apply to certain liquidating plans. *See* § 1141(d)(3). If the debtor is an individual, the discharge does not cover debts made nondischargeable by § 523(a) and, as in Chapter 13, receives no discharge at all unless the debtor makes all payments required by the plan. § 1141(d)(2), (5)(A). However, the court may under certain circumstances grant an individual debtor a sort of hardship discharge prior to completion of payments. § 1141(d)(5)(B), (C).

After confirmation, the debtor must carry out the plan and is subject to the court orders that help implement the plan. §§ 1142, 1143. Within 180 days after confirmation, a party in interest may request revocation of the confirmation if the confirmation was procured by fraud. § 1144.

6. *Modification of a Confirmed Plan*

After confirmation but before substantial completion of the plan, the non-individual reorganized debtor or plan proponent may seek to modify the confirmed plan. Any modification must be such that the plan, as modified, still complies with the requirements for confirmation. § 1127(b). If the debtor was an individual, § 1127(e) allows modification even if the plan has been substantially consummated and the debtor, any holder of an unsecured claim, a trustee, or the U.S. Trustee may make the request for modification. The modification of an individual's reorganization plan may not be required to satisfy the provisions of § 1129 as the new subsection (e) does not so state, in contrast to the explicit statements in subsection (b).

D. SPECIAL CASES

Congress enacted the Bankruptcy Code in 1978. On many occasions since then, as a result of changing economic circumstances and lobbying by specific industries, Congress has amended the Code to deal with evolving practices or concerns. While many of these concerns have been in the consumer context, Chapter 11 has not been immune from this periodic amendment process. The following three situations are examples of what has resulted. As you think about these situations and what you have learned about Chapter 11 so far, is there a need for further refinement of the Chapter 11 process?

1. *Prepackaged Chapter 11 Plans*

Given the time and expense in putting together a reorganization plan, some debtors file for Chapter 11 relief with the disclosure statement, plan of reorganization, and creditors' acceptances, all ready to go. These debtors file the case and want to go immediately to confirmation. This phenomena is known as a "prepackaged plan."[66] Section 1121 allows a debtor to file a plan at the same time as the petition for relief. Section 1125(g) allows pre-filing solicitations of votes on a plan as long as that

[66] *See* 4 WILLIAM L. NORTON, JR., NORTON BANKRUPTCY LAW & PRACTICE ch. 86 (2d ed. 2007).

solicitation complies with nonbankruptcy law. Section 1126(b) allows prepetition votes on the plan. *See also* Rule 3018(b).

2. *Single Asset Real Estate Cases*

Many of the cases raising difficult issues in Chapter 11 reorganizations have been so called "single asset" cases. The typical "single asset" case is a partnership or corporate debtor that owns an apartment building, hotel, or some other piece of income-generating real property.[67] Typically, the real property generates a cash flow that is not adequate to pay back both the mortgagee who helped finance the debtor's acquisition or remodeling of the property and the trade creditors who provide services and supplies to the property. The real property is also often worth less than the amount of the debt that the property secures. The debtor files bankruptcy to stop the inevitable foreclosure process and to strip the value of the mortgage down to the value of the property. With a stripped down mortgage, the property might have a neutral or positive cash flow (sufficient to pay the mortgage payments and trade creditors necessary to run the property). The current owners of the debtor also need to remain in ownership positions in order to avoid adverse tax consequences, as in the *LaSalle* case. The mortgage holder generally prefers to foreclose its interest rather than to be forced into a continuing relationship with the debtor. The mortgage lender also generally asserts the real property is worth much more than the value the debtor proposes to pay the mortgage holder.

This single asset case was common in the early 1990s, a time of extreme devaluation of real estate properties. In 1994, Congress added several Bankruptcy Code provisions to deal with the issues that frequently arise in such cases. Most of the amendments were designed to protect the mortgage lender. For example, the holder of a secured claim in a single asset case is now able to get relief from the automatic stay if the debtor has not filed a confirmable reorganization plan within 90 days after the order for relief or the debtor has not been paying the secured claimant at least interest on the secured claim. § 362(d)(3). The secured party is also protected against multiple bankruptcy filings. § 362(d)(4).

---

[67] *See* § 101(51B) (defining a "single asset real estate" case).

3. Small Business Cases

Because of the expense and time believed to be involved in Chapter 11 reorganizations, in 2005 Congress enacted several provisions designed to make the process more feasible for small business debtors. A small business debtor is defined in § 101(51D), (51C). That definition excludes real estate single asset debtors and is subject to a debt cap (adjustable periodically under § 104). A small business debtor has additional reporting requirements, § 308, and may be prevented in some circumstances from having the automatic stay apply, § 362(n). In a Chapter 11 small business case, the U.S. Trustee may decide not to appoint a creditors' committee. § 1102(a)(3). A small business debtor also has additional duties under § 1116. The small business debtor has a longer period of exclusivity for filing a plan of reorganization, § 1121(e), and may not have to file a disclosure statement if the reorganization plan contains adequate information, § 1125(f). The court may also speed up the plan confirmation process by conditionally approving a disclosure statement so that the debtor may solicit votes, and then hold a hearing where the disclosure statement and plan confirmation is considered all at once. § 1125(f); Rule 3017.1. The time for confirming a plan is thus presumed to be a shorter period of time. § 1129(e).